EARL BLACKWELL'S
ENTERTAINMENT CELEBRITY REGISTER

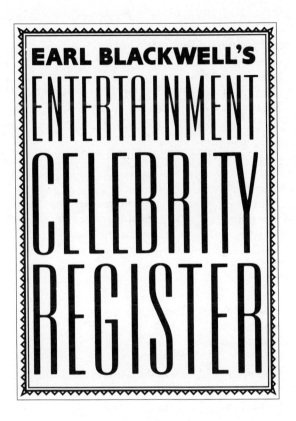

EARL BLACKWELL'S ENTERTAINMENT CELEBRITY REGISTER

Celebrity Service International, Inc.

NEW YORK   CHICAGO   DETROIT   LONDON

Entertainment Celebrity Register

Published by Visible Ink Press,
a division of Gale Research Inc.
835 Penobscot Building
Detroit, MI 48226-4094

Visible Ink Press is a trademark of Gale Research Inc.

ISBN 0-8103-9400-6

Cover Design: Cynthia Baldwin
Interior Design: Arthur Chartow, Bernadette M. Gornie

10 9 8 7 6 5 4 3 2 1

First Edition

A Tribute To Mr. Celebrity

In 1963, Cleveland Amory defined celebrity as "a name which, once made by news, now makes news by itself." Celebrating his 50th Anniversary in the celebrity business (as Founder and Chairman of Celebrity Service International), Earl Blackwell is not only a confidant to the industry, but a friend to the stars. With contributions from legendary performers in theatre and film, here is a toast to our Mr. Celebrity.

"Celebrities move around madly. Earl Blackwell has contributed to the peace and pleasantness of my life by putting me in touch with my famous friends who are never where one hopes them to be."

HELEN HAYES

"*The Celebrity Register* was an idea as necessary and obvious as the original *Who's Who,* but it took someone with imagination, energy, ability and knowledge of the needs of the media and the theatrical industry to bring it into being. Earl Blackwell was that special man."

DOUGLAS FAIRBANKS, JR.

"Earl's 'staying power' shows not only in his dedication to his work, but also in his friendship—after 35 years of being a happy recipient I know what I'm talking about!"

AUDREY HEPBURN

The Culture of Celebrity

"The pursuit of fame is part of the history of Western
culture's ideal of personal freedom and self-expression"
—Leo Braudy, author of *The Frenzy of Renown:
Fame and Its History*

Celebrities "ease the pain of doubt and hold at bay the fear of change," notes Lewis H. Lapham, editor of *Harper's Magazine*, who had at one time considered celebrities to be "frivolous and ornamental figures." But when he glanced at the newsstand he realized that "the celebrities posed on the covers of the magazines impart ... a sense of stability and calm to a world otherwise dissolved in chaos.... Indifferent to the turmoil of the news, [they bestow] on the confusion of events the smiles of infinite bliss ... the hope of immortality. Elvis lives, and so does anybody else who can transform the corruption of the private flesh into the incorruptiblity of a public image."

Certified Celebrities Found Within

In his article on celebrityhood for *Psychology Today*, Dan Hurley identified "the various levels of fame: There are gods, there are saints, there are heroes, there are stars, there are celebrities, there are celebutantes, there are the little people." The five hundred personalities from the world of stage, screen, and television profiled in this special entertainment edition of the now-legendary *Celebrity Register* are certified celebrities. But what is a celebrity, and how do the " little people" participate in the creation of fame?

Whence Fame?

Jib Fowles, professor of media studies at the University of Houston in Clear Lake told Hurley that "very little serious thinking or research has gone into [the] field [of celebrityhood]. Which is amazing, considering how important stars are to our society." Fowles thinks that celebrities are the key to a given society, because they are selected by the society to resolve common needs. "Fame sits at the crossroads of personal psychology, social context and historical tradition," according to *The Frenzy of Renown*. Fame is mandated when individual needs seeking fulfillment coalesce in one figure; as the executive editor of *Interview*, a publication devoted to celebrities, mused, "We all long for what we don't have—and maybe that's why we have famous people." Society provides the material with which those needs are expressed, measured, and met; fame thereby accrues to a gladiator championing a community that prizes victory in combat, to a poet who sings the greatness of a nation courting the immortality of words, or to a jester providing relief for those beset by woeful cares. The tradition of elevating certain individuals to the task of symbolically fulfilling these needs—by accepting the mantle of fame—is as old as history itself. In fact, according to *The Frenzy of Renown*, the history of fame can be traced back to Alexander the Great, Caesar, Cicero, and Virgil.

A New Era of Celebrity Dawns

Nonetheless, some, like the editors of *Spy* magazine, think that the "Age of Celebrity" dawned with the advent of *People* magazine, which began publication in 1974 and circulates to almost three and one-half million readers, not counting those untold millions reading in waiting rooms nationwide. Sandra Pesmen, writing in *Advertising Age*, notes that "we're a nation of voyeurs. Celebrities get and hold the public's attention whenever they're featured in any of the national press, from high-toned dailies such as *The New York Times*, *The Boston Globe* or the *Los Angeles Times* to the flashy, trashy grocery store tabloids." Celebrities form the main focus of publications such as *Interview*, established in 1969, *US*, first published in 1977, *Details*, which began publication in 1982, *Premiere*, established in 1987, and *Memories*, founded in 1988; *Entertainment Weekly* and *Egg* were both launched in 1990 as major celebrity-watchers.

Mainstream Coverage Branches Out, Meets Counter-Coverage

People has successfully moved its celebrity reporting to television, as has *Spy*, dubbed by one critic "the semi-intellectual hipster's answer to *People*, ... the magazine that treats celebrities tongue-in-cheek, but assumes you already know who they are from reading other trashy celebrity magazines." With its 1990 TV special "Spy Magazine Presents How To Be Famous," the writers and editors continued to poke irreverent fun at celebrities, while also reminding all of us that we are secret celebrity watchers, too. *Spy* was created, according to one of its editors, with the intention of providing a "fresh alternative to fawning American celebrity worship. We're one little dash of skepticism and critical sensibility in a world of *People* magazines and 'Entertainment Tonights.' There's plenty of Pollyanna positive stuff like *USA Today*. We serve a real function of being a smart, adversarial voice." In some ways *Spy* sees itself as a means of saving American culture from its celebrity worship, but in fact does as much to fuel it, because the success of its humor depends on that worship.

Oscars Go Global

And America is not alone in seeking continued celebrity access. In 1990 the Academy Awards ceremony, one of the great entertainment celebrity gatherings of the year, was not only broadcast to audiences around the world, but was actually broadcast from locations worldwide, including London, Moscow, and Sydney. Entertainment figures, in fact, seem to lose their national identity when they become citizens of the celebrity world. The work of such stars as **Sonia Braga, Daniel Day Lewis, Isabella Rossellini, Raul Julia,** and **Bob Hoskins**—who will no doubt be entered in the next *Celebrity Register*—easily transcends national boundaries.

New Lights on the Horizon

Other stars now glimmering in the firmament who seem likely to make the next Register include

> **Michelle Pfeiffer,** who began making films in 1980, gained attention with *Into the Night* (1985), *The Witches of Eastwick* (1987), *Tequila Sunrise* (1988), and *Dangerous Liaisons* (1989), and broke out bigtime with *The Fabulous*

Baker Boys (1989), but still thinks she looks like a duck

★ **Morgan Freeman,** who compiled a distinguished stage career before creating the role of the driver in *Driving Miss Daisy*—first on stage and then in the 1989 hit film—whose film credits also include *Brubaker* (1980), *Marie* (1985), *Street Smart,* (1987), *Clean and Sober* (1988), the critically acclaimed *Glory* (1989), and *Bonfire of the Vanities* (1990), and who spent the summer of 1990 playing opposite actress-comedienne Tracey Ullman in *The Taming of the Shrew* for Joseph Papp's Shakespeare in the Park

★ **Jerry Seinfeld,** who received a 1988 American Comedy Award as funniest male stand-up comic, hosted "Spy Magazine Presents How To Be Famous" in 1990, and later that year made TV history starring in a hit series that blends situation comedy with stand-up routines

★ **Ellen Barkin,** whose engaging style permeated *Diner* (1981) and *Tender Mercies* (1982), sizzled in *The Big Easy* (1987) and *Siesta* (1987) and made a tidal wave in *Sea of Love* (1989), but who considers herself a character actor despite her *femme fatale* leading roles opposite the likes of Dennis Quaid and Al Pacino

★ **Denzel Washington,** who initially worked in stage and film but first gained widespread public recognition as a featured character in the long-running TV series "St. Elsewhere," then successfully crossed back into films with *Cry Freedom* (1987), *The Mighty Quinn* (1989), an Oscar-winning performance in *Glory* (1989), and a leading part in filmmaker Spike Lee's 1990 release, *Mo' Better Blues*

★ **Laura Dern,** a second-generation celeb who grew up onscreen in such films as *Teachers* (1984), *Mask* (1985), and *Smooth Talk* (1985), teamed professionally with some of the film world's finest in director **David Lynch's** *Blue Velvet* (1986), teamed personally with director **Rennie Harlin**—whose first two films, *Die Harder: Die Hard II* and *The Adventures of Ford Fairlane* were released in 1990—and worked again with Lynch, opposite Nicholas Cage, in 1990's *Wild at Heart*

■ **Mickey Rourke,** who stole the show in *Body Heat* (1981), stole hearts in *Diner* (1982), stole fire in *Rumble Fish* (1983), rounded out the 80s with such controversial films as *9 1/2 Weeks* (1986), *Angel Heart* (1987), and *Barfly* (1987), ended the decade opposite **Ellen Barkin** and **Morgan Freeman** in *Johnny Handsome* (1989) and entered the 90s with what was rumored to be unfaked sex in *Wild Orchid*, followed boldly by the title role in *Francis of Assisi*, shown in Cannes 1990 while his *Homeboy* went directly to video

■ **Julia Roberts,** who first came to attention in the gentle film *Mystic Pizza* (1988), gained momentum in *Steel Magnolias* (1989), and soared in *Pretty Woman* (1990) before co-starring on- (*Flatliners*, 1990) and off-screen with certified celeb Keifer Sutherland and moving on to *Sleeping With the Enemy* (1991).

■ and filmmaker **David Lynch,** who's been called by the *New York Times* "Hollywood's most revered eccentric, sort of a psychopathic Norman Rockwell," whose credits include *Eraserhead* (1977), *Elephant Man* (1980), *Dune* (1984), and *Blue Velvet* (1986), who has produced and written lyrics for an album by the singer Julee Cruise, whose quirky TV series Twin Peaks was gaining an enthusiastic audience in 1990 even as his next controversial feature film—*Wild at Heart*, featuring Nicolas Cage, Laura Dern, Isabella Rossellini, Willem Dafoe, and **Harry Dean Stanton**—was accorded the 1990 Cannes Film Festival prize for best film, and who is considered by Mel Brooks to be "Jimmy Stewart from Mars"

So, as politician Gary Hart told Hurley, "People vicariously live out their lives through celebrities, and you can't do that unless you know more about them." Read on.

EARL BLACKWELL'S
ENTERTAINMENT CELEBRITY REGISTER

Eddie Albert

"Man has carbon monoxide in his brain, DDT and synthetic nitrate in his liver, asbestos in his lungs, mercury poisoning in his cells and strontium 90 in his bones. We have a serious problem about survival," says this veteran stage-screen-TV actor who, in recent seasons, has spent almost as much time sharing with audiences his concerns about poverty, pollution and other problems of the planet as he has in performance. He was welcomed back to Broadway in 1983 in the revival of Kaufman and Hart's 1938 Pulitzer Prize winning comedy *You Can't Take It With You*.

Albert made his debut into the world on 22 April 1908 in Rock Island, Illinois, billed originally as Edward Albert Heimberger. When radio announcers with whom he sang, danced and pattered after leaving the University of Minnesota habitually announced him as "Eddie Hamburger," he decided to simplify his name. Albert first earned critical acclaim on Broadway as the light-comedian lead of *Brother Rat* in 1936, a role he repeated in Hollywood co-starring with a young newcomer named Ronald Reagan. He's now made some 60 films, including *Roman Holiday* (for which he received his first Academy Award nomination in 1955), *Oklahoma!*, *The Teahouse of the August Moon*, *I'll Cry Tomorrow* and *The Heartbreak Kid* (for which he received a second Oscar bid in 1972). In between films were Broadway appearances in *The Boys from Syracuse*, *Miss Liberty*, *The Music Man*, *The Seven Year Itch* and others. He also had a seven-year run playing a city-slicker lawyer transplanted to the country in the TV sitcom "Green Acres" (1964-71), a three-year run playing a private eye on "Switch" (1975-78), a role as a "Falcon Crest" scoundrel (1987) and one as Breckinridge Long in the made-for-TV 30-hour miniseries "War and Remembrance" (1988).

After World War II and Navy duty in the Pacific, he married Mexican-American actress Margo (best remembered as the Shangri

La dweller who ages dramatically when she leaves her Himalayan paradise in *Lost Horizon*) in 1945. (She died in 1985.) They had an actor son, Edward Albert (who made his debut in the film *Butterflies Are Free*) and a daughter, Maria.

Alan Alda

After 15 years of relative obscurity as a stage and screen actor, he finally gained stardom as Capt. Benjamin Franklin "Hawkeye" Pierce on "M*A*S*H." The long-running TV comedy sensation began in 1972 and earned Alda several Emmy Awards for his role as the insubordinate and skirt-chasing, but skilled and dedicated, combat surgeon. At Alda's insistence, "M*A*S*H" creator Larry Gelbart agreed to insert into each episode at least one operating-room sequence. "I was worried the show would become a 30-minute commercial for the Army," says the actor. "On the other hand, the opportunity to make a humane statement was so great. . . . It's the only comedy show on TV that shows the results of war. It's humor with feeling."

The son of actor Robert Alda, Alan was born in N.Y.C. on 28 January 1936. The younger Alda occasionally teamed with his father to entertain soldiers at the Hollywood Canteen and in the early 50's they appeared together in a summer stock production of *3 Men on a Horse*. After graduating at 20 from Fordham U., Alda appeared again with his father onstage in Rome and on TV in Amsterdam. He served in the Army Reserve, studied acting at the Cleveland Playhouse on a 3-year Ford Foundation grant, performed Off-Broadway and did TV guest shots. *The Owl and the Pussycat* (1964) was his first Broadway success, followed two years later by the musical *The Apple Tree*, for which he received a Tony nomination. His pre-"M*A*S*H" films (except 1968's *Paper Lion*) were forgettable, but he starred in Truman Capote's memorable 1972 TV prison drama, "The Glass House."

Married since 1957 to classical clarinetist and photographer Arlene Weiss, Alda and his wife raised their three daughters in Leonia, N.J. (they currently live in Long Island). A non-materialist, he prefers "small-town living" and cherishes his privacy. Influenced by his spouse, he is an ardent feminist and member of Men for

ERA. "I never wanted to be famous," he says. "What I wanted was to be very, very good at what I do and though I realized that if I was, then I'd be famous, that always seemed a little absurd." A compulsive worker, he adds, "To me, work is love. Work is at the heart of health." Alda wrote and directed some "M*A*S*H" episodes before its '83 demise. He also starred in the films *The Seduction of Joe Tynan* ('79) and *The Four Seasons* ('81). He wrote both ("Since I was a little boy, I've wanted to be accepted as a writer") and directed the latter. In 1985 he produced, co-scripted, directed and acted in the film, *Sweet Liberty*. Alan wrote the screenplay, directed and appeared with co-star Ann-Margaret in *A New Life*, released in 1988. Other films: *Crimes and Misdemeanors* ('89) and *Betsy's Wedding* ('90).

Jane Alexander

Vitriolic theatre critic John Simon once described her with uncharacteristic warmth: "a strangulated charm and tragic sweetness, a slightly nasal melancholy and deep rooted womanliness." Of her own talents she has said: "I grew up thinking I was never very pretty and so I was attracted to parts that weren't physically glamorous; I could identify with them because they seemed to fit my own emotional past. I go at a part like an athlete. It's like working towards the Olympics. I gear myself to give my best and my most. . . . I'm not a person who sees life as a comedy. If you gave me a Rorschach, I'd probably see dark images."

Born Jane Quigley in Boston, Massachusetts, on 28 October 1939, she was encouraged from the age of 6 to become an actress by her father, a prominent Boston surgeon. As a 9-to-5 secretary by day and drama student of Mira Rostova by night, Alexander devised an innovative strategy for breaking into show business. On nighttime visits to the theatre district in New York she sought out the stage managers of hit plays and asked them to keep her in mind in case any actress suddenly departed, and so she was picked to be Sandy Dennis's stand-by in "A Thousand Clowns." She originated the role of the white mistress of the black heavyweight champion in *The Great White Hope* at Washington's Arena Stage, directed by her husband Edwin Sherin. Later, on Broadway, she won a Tony and was nominated for an Academy Award for her performance in the film version. She was nominated again for her part as the frightened bookkeeper entangled in the Watergate conspiracy in "All The President's Men," and a third nomination came for her part as the mother in the 1984 film about nuclear holocaust, "Testament." Alexander became known to television audiences as Eleanor Roosevelt in the 1976 adaptation of Joseph P. Lash's bestseller *Eleanor and Franklin,* and revived her critically acclaimed characterization in the show's sequel, "The White House Years." She won an Emmy for her work in the controversial TV drama "Playing for Time," about the tortures of a group of female musicians in a Nazi concentration camp. In 1985 Jane appeared in the CBS miniseries "Blood and Orchids." On the lighter side, she teamed with Elizabeth Taylor in the 1985 TV movie, "Malice in Wonderland," in which she portrayed acidulous Hollywood gossip Hedda Hopper to Taylor's Louella Parsons. As an actress she has a knack for finding classy parts. "Things come up suddenly these days, but that's all right because I work better under pressure." She dives into her parts "like a chameleon looking for food," becoming the outrageous "Calamity Jane," or Annie Sullivan in William Gibson's "Monday After the Miracle." Taking another creative turn, Jane was the co-executive producer and star of the 1986 film "Square Dance."

Steve Allen

Destined one day to bear the sobriquet "TV's Man for All Seasons" because he has "never been off television in 35 years for more than a few weeks at a time," the multi-talented Steve Allen told an interviewer in 1984 he considers the 24 one-hour PBS shows "Meeting of the Minds" his most significant television work, for "they'll certainly long outlast me. That series . . . is the only thing that has any lasting, social importance." Described by friend Andy Williams as "the only man I know who's listed in every one of the Yellow Pages," the actor-host-musician fits into many categories from A to Z—comedian-composer-clarinetist-columnist, pianist-playwright-poet-philosopher-publisher or satirist-singer-songwriter-scholar.

Certainly born with more talents "all natural to me" than first names, Stephen Valentine Patrick William Allen made his debut on 26 December 1921 in New York City into a family of vaudevillians and toured some 18 schools as class clown before landing his first job in radio. By 1950, with established credentials as an ad-lib comedian with a highly successful Los Angeles radio show described as having an "anything-goes structure," he switched to New York television. That year, he hosted the half-hour "Steve Allen Show" and made the guest circuit. "The Tonight Show" first aired in 1954, with Allen developing and using virtually all the elements now familiar to talk-show viewers. For a number of months in 1956, he was doing 90 minutes of "Tonight" (1954-1956), 60 minutes of "The Steve Allen Show" (1956-1959) on Sunday night opposite Ed Sullivan, and filming the title role in "The Benny Goodman Story" for Universal-International. Dropping out of the nightly position for other endeavors, he followed with: "The Steve Allen Playhouse" (1961-1964), "I've Got a Secret" (1964-1966), "Meeting of Minds" (1977-1978), "Comedy Zone" (CBS), "Life's Most Embarrassing Moments" (ABC) and music and comedy series for the Disney Channel. Known to work on dozens of different projects at the same time, he has written dozens of books, including two novels, two volumes of short stories and two of poetry, as well as humorous and political works. His 1989 bestseller, *Murder on the Glitter Box*, was followed by its sequel, *Murder in Manhattan*, in 1990. In 1986 his book *How To Be Funny*, written with Jane Wollman, was published. Another 1990 book is titled *Ripoff*. He's written over 4,000 songs, including "The Theme from Picnic," "This Could Be the Start of Something Big" and "Impossible," and made some 40 record albums. In addition to his current "works in motion" and an ongoing lecture tour, he appears as a pianist on the concert stage, in his own musical comedy revue "Seymour Glick is Alive But Sick," and as a performer in jazz clubs throughout the land.

Allens' first marriage, to Dorothy Goodman, ended after eight years in 1952 (three sons). In 1954, he married actress Jayne Meadows (one son), whose Broadway credits include "Kiss Them for Me." Meadows has also been active on the TV guest spot circuit and starred in a majority of the "Meeting of Minds" series. Allen believes that "the raw material of most jokes, funny plays, funny essays, or whatever, is bad news," so, as millions watched a $250,000 fire consume parts of his San Fernando Valley home in October, 1984, he gamely told an inane TV reporter that, although homes in the neighborhood do sell for upwards of a million dollars, "I don't think we'll be trying to sell ours this week."

In 1986, Mr. Allen was named to the TV Hall of Fame.

Woody Allen

He calls himself a "latent heterosexual" and says he has an intense desire to return to the womb—"anybody's." "I'm a compulsive worker. What I really like to do best is whatever I'm not doing at the moment," he claims. "When I'm writing jokes I wish I was directing movies. And when I'm writing a play, I wish I was performing in a nightclub." The versatile, philosophical comedian's understated wit has been dominating American humor since the mid '60s in print, on recordings, and on the stage and screen.

Born Allen Stewart Konigsberg ("When the other kids learned my name they'd beat me up. So I'd tell them my name was Frank, but they'd still beat me up") in Brooklyn, New York, 1 December 1935, he says he was "a fearful student. . . . I went to both NYU and CCNY but I was always a freshman, year after year, never even a sophomore. I was a motion picture major, I wanted to be a cowboy. But when I was in high school I used to mail jokes to columnists. They were terrible jokes." His special brand of cynical parody and devastating understatement was soon in demand on TV talk shows and in top nightclubs. He entered films in 1965 as both screenwriter and performer in *What's New, Pussycat?* He directed his first film, *Take the Money and Run*, in 1969, the year he divorced his second wife, Louise Lasser. (She subsequently appeared in two of his films.) He achieved a peak of success in the '70s, with a string of highly successful comedies, six starring his longtime lover (before Mia Farrow), Diane Keaton. Until *Annie Hall* (1977), his films were typically disjointed but contained a comic brilliance, highlighted by self-effacing parody, inside jokes, and spoofing of great filmmakers (Antonioni, Bergman, Eisenstein), authors and philosophers. *Annie Hall*, with its balanced structure and high seriousness underlying its humor, was his most acclaimed film—critically and commercially. It earned him two Oscars, as director and co-screenwriter. He didn't collect them in person, however, because the award ceremony conflicted with his firm Monday night date playing jazz clarinet at Michael's Pub in Manhattan.

For his next film he received another Academy Award nomination as director, but *Interiors* (1978) was a departure for him on two counts: it was a straight, gloomy, Bergmanesque drama, and Allen didn't appear in it. *Manhattan* (1979) was a brilliant comic romance, with a Gershwin soundtrack (it won him his second Best Director award from the N.Y. Film Critics, complementing the one he'd received for *Annie Hall*), but response to his early '80s films (*Zelig*, *Broadway Danny Rose*, etc.) was mixed. Then in 1985 he scored with *The Purple Rose of Cairo*, with *New York Times* film critic Vincent Canby going so far as to declare that the "sweet, lyrically funny, multi-layered work . . . again demonstrates that Woody Allen is our premier filmmaker who, standing something over five feet tall in his sneakers, towers above all others." His third full-length play, *The Floating Light Bulb*, which premiered at Lincoln Center in 1981, was less successful than its predecessors: *Don't Drink the Water* and *Play it Again, Sam*. *Getting Even, Without Feathers* and *Side Effects* are book collections of his *New Yorker* pieces.

Presently, Woody Allen appears active in all areas of life. His recent films include: *Radio Days* (1987), *September* (1987), *Another Woman* (1988), and *Crimes and Misdemeanors* (1989), which earned Oscar nominations for best film and best director. Allen also co-starred with Bette Midler in writer-director Paul Mazursky's *Scenes From a Mall*. Perhaps his dearest accomplishment arrived in December, 1987, when he and his longtime lady, Mia Farrow, announced the birth of their son, Satchel.

Robert Altman

"**W**hen I make films like *Nashville* and *Buffalo Bill and the Indians*," the iconoclastic director told an interviewer in the late '70s, "it's not to say we're the worst country in the world. I'm just saying we're at this point and it's sad." As Hollywood's preeminent "philosopher and commentator on social mores" in the 1970s, Altman was among the world's most honored filmmakers: his *M*A*S*H* (1970) had won the Grand Prize at the Cannes Film Festival and *Nashville* (1975) the Best Film and Best Director Awards of

both the New York Film Critics Circle and The National Board of Review. And in 1979, when 20 of the world's leading critics were asked to name the decade's best films, Robert Altman was the only director with two on the final list; *Nashville* and *McCabe and Mrs.*

Miller (the latter an exploration of the contributions prostitutes made toward the taming of the American West).

That same year, however, the director's career suddenly cooled with the failures of *A Wedding* ("irritatingly cynical," wrote the *Daily News*) and *Quintet,* which, to one critic, demonstrated that Altman "has developed a profound grasp of the obvious. He has really made a '50s Bergman movie." His *Popeye* (1980) was a commercial success, but the money men were now skittish about bankrolling this brilliant and strikingly original but unpredictable maverick. In 1981 he sold his Lion's Gate Films studio, saying "I feel my time has run out. Every studio wants *Raiders of the Lost Ark,*" and at 56 began, for the first time in his life, to direct plays. He staged, first in Los Angeles and then Off-Broadway, two one-act plays by novice playwright Frank South, and Ed Graczyk's *Come Back to the 5 & Dime, Jimmy Dean.* After this "sabbatical" Altman went back to making movies, including film versions of *Jimmy Dean* and David Rabe's play *Streamers* (Golden Lion Award for Best Acting—to Matthew Modine—at the 1983 Venice Film Festival), and *O.C. and Stiggs,* "an adult exploitation film." In 1985 he directed *Secret Honor* and *Fool For Love,* and in 1986 he wrote the screenplay for and directed *Beyond Therapy.* Touching television, Altman directed *The Caine Mutiny Court-Martial,* which aired in May, 1988, and in collaboration with cartoonist Garry Trudeau made an eleven-part television series about a fictional presidential candidate, *Tanner '88.* The same year, he also contributed to the opera anthology *Aria,* which featured films by European directors as well.

Born 20 February 1925 in Kansas City, Missouri, Robert Altman was a bomber pilot in the Pacific in World War II. Following three years at the University of Missouri he worked in industrial films and finally landed TV work with Alfred Hitchcock. After that he was hired and fired by a host of producers, eventually learning to "get comfortable in my own failure." As for his prospects with the major studios, he says he will continue to show them projects, but "they don't want to make the same pictures I do and I'm too old to change," which simply means that some of his future films will be independently financed, as *Nashville* was.

Loni Anderson

"I was thought of as being sexy, but I was never thought of as being a sex symbol until I became blond," says the not-so-dumb blonder-than-life star of TV's "WKRP in Cincinnati" (1978-82).

Born 5 August 1950 into a comfortable upper-middle class family in Minneapolis, Loni was married at 17 after a whirlwind courtship of exactly two weeks with the 26-year-old brother of a friend. She soon realized the marriage was doomed to fail and so she and her husband split after three months, when she discovered she was pregnant. Moving back home with her parents, Loni raised her daughter while attending college. By the time she auditioned for the part of "WKRP's" va-va-voom receptionist in 1977, she had behind her a  college degree plus "more than ten years of stage experience." Since her sitcom debut, she has appeared on screen in *Sizzle* (1981), *Stand On It* (1983), *Stroke R Ace* (1983) and *Fast Eddie* (1984), did a voice-over for the film *All Dogs Go To Heaven* (1989), and appeared in numerous made-for-TV movies, including *Stranded, Easy Street, Necessity* and *Too Good To Be True*. Co-starring with Lynda Carter in "Partners in Crime," an NBC series that aired fall, 1984 (presently in syndication), Anderson is far from relaxed about her success. Insecure about her looks, she says she wouldn't dream of setting foot outside the front door of her California abode without being thoroughly made up and ready to face her public.

She and second husband Ross Bickell divorced in 1981 and she married long-time boyfriend Burt Reynolds in Jupiter, Florida, on 29 April 1988. They have a son, Quinton Anderson Reynolds (August 1988). A collector of Snow White memorabilia, Loni lives with her happy new family in Holmby Hills, California.

Richard Dean Anderson

Since 1976 TV audiences have been gazing into the penetrating dark brown eyes of the tall (6'2"), dark and rugged Richard Dean Anderson. From his five years as Dr. Jeff Webber on ABC TV's popular daytime soap, "General Hospital" (1976-1981), the talented actor went on to star as the eldest brother in the TV series "Seven Brides for Seven Brothers" (1982) before doing two seasons in "Emerald Point, N.A.S." (1983-1984). Starring in the title role of ABC-TV's action-adventure series "MacGyver" since 1985, Anderson took time out to make his film debut in "Ordinary Heroes" (1986), a remake of "Pride of the Marines."

Born 23 January 1950 in Minneapolis, Minnesota, Anderson

was raised in a creative environment. His mother was an artist and his father, Stuart, was a jazz bassist. Anderson' first career goal was to become a professional hockey player. This goal soon changed when, playing on his high school varsity team, Anderson broke both arms in separate incidents on the ice. Seeking a less violent profession, he developed an interest in performing. He studied drama at St. Cloud State College and at Ohio State University before moving to Los Angeles to pursue a professional acting career. Anderson paid his dues while trying to break into the business, sometimes working as a street mime or juggler or as a jester singer at a Renaissance style cabaret. He even landed a job as a writer/director/performer of shows at Marineland. Getting closer to his chosen field, Anderson worked as a stage manager for the Improvisational Theatre Company. Finally, the determined actor got a break when he landed a role in "Superman of the Bones" at the Pilgrimmage Theatre in Los Angeles.

As a youth, Anderson crossed the country by hopping freight trains. A natural athlete who also completed a 5600 mile solo bicycle tour from Minnesota to Alaska and back, he no longer has the free time to pursue his favorite outdoor sports: sky-diving, scuba diving and snow skiing. Even with his busy schedule, Anderson tries to keep up with his first love by playing hockey on a regular basis.

Julie Andrews

"**D**oes Mary Poppins have an orgasm? Does she go to the bathroom? I assure you she does," declares the actress once pegged as the biggest goody-goody in Hollywood. "You're always remembered best for the things that are successful," she says, referring to her perky parts in *The Sound of Music* and *Mary Poppins*. (Actually her early attempts to squeeze out of her virginal mold like *Darling Lili* and *Star* were box office bombs.) "I think of part of myself as a very passionate person, but I don't think that comes across. I don't know where it comes from, that reserve or veneer of British niceness. But it doesn't bother me if people don't spot the passion. I know it's there," and she adds, smiling, "as long as Blake knows," referring to her movie-maker husband Blake Edwards whom she married in 1969. (She has one daughter from her first marriage to childhood sweetheart Tony Walton, the set and costume designer; she and Edwards have adopted two Vietnamese orphans.)

Two of Edwards's films helped change people's view of Julie Andrews. In *S.O.B.*, a sticky sweet American actress is forced by her director-husband to bare her breasts in one scene; in *Victor/Victoria* Andrews plays a woman impersonating a homosexual Polish count who, in turn, plays a celebrated Parisian female impersonator.

"Most people think I'm ten years older than I am because I've been around so long," says Andrews. Born Julia Elizabeth Wells in Walton-on-Thames, England, 1 October 1935, she began in show business when her divorced mother remarried and formed a vaudeville team with her new husband, who gave Julie vocal lessons. At the age of 12 she was singing arias at the London Hippodrome; at age 13 she gave a special command performance for the Queen of England and was her family's main source of financial support. While portraying Cinderella in 1953 she was signed to star in the New York production of *The Boyfriend*. Anticipating homesickness, she sailed for America and recalls, "I was green as grass. I was immensely impressed and I thought, 'My God, this is bigger than anything I'd expected. Better pull my socks up a bit.'" She became famous on opening night of *The Boyfriend*, which was also her 19th birthday. At 21 she played Eliza Doolittle in *My Fair Lady;* next she starred opposite Richard Burton in *Camelot*. Snubbed by the producers of the film version of *My Fair Lady* (Audrey Hepburn got the part) she won an Academy Award for her performance as P.L. Travers's steel-and-sugar British nanny Mary Poppins. Andrews has also appeared in such non-musical films as *Hawaii*, *The Americanization of Emily*, *"10,"* *The Tamarind Seed*, *Torn Curtain*, *Little Miss Marker*, *The Man Who Loved Women*, *That's Life*, and *Duet for One*. A veteran of television, Andrews' first series, "The Julie Andrews Hour" on ABC, won a total of eight Emmy Awards and her first Christmas special, "Julie Andrews . . . The Sound of Christmas" (aired December 1987), won 5 Emmys. Another ABC-TV special aired in the 1990-91 season. A recent one-woman concert tour was applauded by reviewers and a new record album "Love, Julie" was released in 1987 with a collection of standard and contemporary ballads. Her literary endeavors began with her first children's book, *Mandy*, published in 1971, followed by another book *The Last of the Really Great Whangdoodles*. (Her pen name is Julie Edwards.) The Andrews-Edwards family live year-round in Gstaad, Switzerland.

Years ago writer Helen Lawrenson wrote that she wasn't deceived by the "lie-die goo" of Andrews' Mary Poppins-on-the-cross image. She wrote: "When you've fought your way up the ladder as she has done, baby, you're *tough*."

Ann Margret

She worked with top veterans for her 1961 film debut, playing Bette Davis' sheltered daughter in Frank Capra's *Pocketful of Miracles.* Her second movie was the last remake of Rodgers and Hammerstein's *State Fair* and her third, *Bye Bye Birdie,* launched her to stardom. Throughout the sixties she was typecast, both in musicals and dramas, as a teen-market sex kitten, a sort of female counterpart to Elvis Presley (the co-star of her fourth film, *Viva Las Vegas!*). Except for *The Cincinnati Kid* and the *Stagecoach* remake (in which she played Claire Trevor's role), she made no noteworthy films until, in 1971, her poignant performance in Jules Feiffer and Mike Nichols' *Carnal Knowledge* surprised many and earned her a supporting Oscar nomination. She received another Academy Award nomination four years later, for her lead role as the mother in *Tommy.*

Born Ann-Margret Olsson in Valsjobyn, Sweden, on 28 April 1941, she came to the U.S. as a child and was raised in various Illinois towns. She first entered the TV spotlight at 16 on "Ted Mack's Amateur Hour," and sang with a band at Northwestern University, which she attended for a year. Her film career has been augmented by appearances on TV specials and in nightclubs. She wrote *Exercises for the Tired Businessman.*

In 1967 she married Roger Smith, who gave up his successful acting career to become her personal manager. While rehearsing her nightclub act in late summer of 1972, she fell 22 feet from a high scaffold. The accident almost ended her career, but after extensive reconstructive facial surgery she resumed work and solidified her superstar status.

The 1980's were very productive for Ann-Margret. In 1983 she played Blanche duBois in a TV version of *A Streetcar Named Desire* and in 1985 filmed *Twice in A Lifetime.* She starred in the telefilms

"Who Will Love My Children?" (1983), "The Two Mrs. Grenvilles" (1986-87) and several motion pictures, including, *The Return of The Soldier* (1983), *52-Pick-up* (1987), and *A New Life* (with Alan Alda in 1987). She also returned to the stage again, doing what she does extraordinarily well—dancing and singing up a storm at Caesar's Palace.

Anne Archer

For her role as the resilient wife and mother whose very existence is threatened in *Fatal Attraction*, Anne Archer again received widespread acclaim, with Golden Globe and Academy Award nominations for Best Supporting Actress. Since her film debut in *The All American Boy* (1970) opposite Jon Voight, the talented beauty has starred with a wide variety of Hollywood's dynamic and glamorous leading men, including Roger Moore (*The Naked Face*), Sylvester Stallone (*Paradise Alley*), Sam Elliott (*Lifeguard*), John Ritter (*Hero at Large*), and Ryan O'Neal (*Green Ice*). Even with that list of credits, Anne claims that her most demanding film experience was *Waltz Across Texas*, a 1982 film that she co-produced and in which she co-starred with her husband, Emmy-Award-winning sports producer/ director Terry Jastrow, under their own Aster Corporation banner. Fortunately, Anne has not limited herself to the big screen. National TV audiences had the opportunity to watch her opposite William Holden in the original telefilm "The Blue Knight," the miniseries "Seventh Avenue," and "The Pirate," with Franco Nero. Also drawn to the stage, in 1981 she made her New York debut as Maude Mix in the acclaimed Off-Broadway production of "A Coupla White Chicks Sitting Around Talking" and reprised the role in 1985 in Los Angeles. The 1988 season saw Anne star at Tourvel in the Williamstown production of "Les Liaisons Dangereuses." Recent movies include *Eminent Domain* (1990) and *Narrow Margin* (1991).

Born 25 of August 1947 in Los Angeles, Anne was surrounded by show business. Her mother, Marjorie Lord, played opposite Danny Thomas on the popular TV series "Make Room for Daddy." Her father, John Archer, was also an actor. In 1954 her parents divorced and four years later Anne and brother Gregg had another show business person in their lives, stepfather/producer Randolph

Hale. Always drawn to the business, Anne received a theatre arts degree from Claremont College.

When not busy with one of her many projects, Anne devotes her time to issues and concerns of Planned Parenthood Federation of America, which appointed her National Public Advocacy Chairperson. In recognition of her commitment, *Ms* magazine named Anne as one of 1988's six "Women of the Year." A mother of two, Anne resides with second husband Jastrow, son Thomas (son of first husband William Davis, born August, 1972) and son Jeffrey (born 18 October 1984), in her native Los Angeles.

Rosanna Arquette

"Creativity doesn't come from some stupid white powder, it comes from God," explains this reed-thin actress who has been described as a cross between Audrey Hepburn and Jane Fonda. A drug rehabilitation program has brought her sobriety and stardom in such films as John Sayles' *Baby It's You* and *Desperately Seeking Susan.*

Rosanna was born in 1960; her grandfather was Cliff Arquette (Charlie Weaver on the old Jack Paar Show) and her parents were both political activists. (Pop was a member of Chicago's innovative theatre group The Committee; her mother, Mardi, is a well-respected poet.) The eldest of five children, Rosanna spent her childhood swinging from one peace march to another. She lived for three years at the Virginia commune of a guru named Bapak. At age 14, with her boyfriend, she hitchhiked to San Francisco. Later, in Los Angeles, she became the platonic roommate of her idol, actor John Heard. By the time she was 18 she was a veteran of TV specials and several films.

In 1984 she was voted the Best Actress of the year by the pernickity Boston Society of Film Critics for her performance in *Baby, It's You.* (Her competition had been Meryl Streep, Shirley MacLaine and Debra Winger, certainly not a wayward lot.) In an utterly different role that same year she played Gary Gilmore's young girlfriend in the TV version of Norman Mailer's *The Executioner's Song.* She also was the bare-breasted hitchhiker in Blake Edward's *S.O.B.*, the valiant "Johnny Belinda" in a TV remake of that classic and her other credits include *Silverado*, *The Aviator*, *After*

Hours, Eight Million Ways to Die, Nobody's Fool, Amazon Women on the Moon, and *The Big Blue.* In 1988 she starred in the CBS-TV movie "Promised a Miracle."

"As an actress I suck," she sighed in a 1985 interview with Guy Flatley for the *New York Daily News.* "I have an awful lot to learn. . . . I have instinct, but now I need technique." If she sounds self-reproachful she isn't. She's a winner whose only regret is "dropping out of school in the eleventh grade. I feel stupid—even though I *can* balance my checkbook." So stay tuned, Rosanna fans, there's much more to come.

"By the time I'm 40 I want to raise money for incredible causes. I'm not doing movies just to have a Jacuzzi, you know."

Rosanna married James Newton Howard in September, 1986, but their relationship faltered and they separated in May, 1988.

Bea Arthur

Cast as a liberal foil to "All in the Family's" Archie Bunker during the 1971 television season, Bea Arthur displayed a formidable comic command in the two-part guest shot that caused such a rating sensation she was back the following season (and six more) as "Maude," TV's favorite "liberal, libertarian and libber." Through Maude, an upper-middle-class matron with a WASP background and a quartet of husbands, the show delved deftly into such provocative issues as abortion, alcoholism, cosmetic surgery (Arthur herself had a face-life during the course of the show), marijuana, pornography and pre-marital sex. Said Walter Kerr of Bea Arthur, "She has a very firm, haughty way of informing you that the next line—no matter what it says—is going to be funny." She returned to the tube in the fall of 1985 in the NBC series, "The Golden Girls." Sharing the set with a talented ensemble (Rue McClanahan, Betty White, Estelle Getty), her portrayal of the level-headed "Dorothy" earned Bea an Emmy (1988) for Best Leading Actress in Comedy.

Born Bernice Frankel, 13 May 1924 in New York City, she grew up and was educated in Cambridge, Maryland, before returning to New York and embarking on an acting career. Arthur was extremely active in the early heyday of Off Broadway (*Threepenny Opera*—

1954), and was cited for an "impressive portrayal of the dominating brothel madam, Bella" in *Ulysses in Nighttown* (1958). She was dubbed "the divine Beatrice" by Tallulah Bankhead when they worked together in the ill-fated *Ziegfeld Follies* (1956). Other notable roles include Yente, (*Fiddler on the Roof*, 1964) and Vera Charles, *Mame's* severest friend (1966—winning her a Tony). (Arthur recreated the role for the 1974 film and has appeared in a number of other movies.) For a change of pace, she played the romantic attraction to Richard Kiley in the ABC-TV film "One More Time" (1988).

Arthur married fellow New School actor (now director) Gene Saks in 1950. The couple raised two adopted sons before divorcing. Although she relaxes at her California home by gardening and cooking gourmet specialties, Bea has shed much of the Earth Mother image of "Maude" by streamlining her statuesque (5'9") figure. As she once told a reporter, "my training has been total; I've done everything except stag movies and rodeos."

Peggy Ashcroft

"**S**he can be enchantingly feminine," says Sir John Gielgud of Dame Peggy Ashcroft, whom he has both directed and played opposite in the theatre, "yet turn and play monstrous, villainous people, parts you wouldn't think her right for." Although she admits she loves performing "bitches," she explains her standards as an actress in a role: "you show people in all their weakness and beastliness, yes, but you have to put yourself in their position, too. I don't think artists should make judgments on the characters they play." Although the senior theatrical "dame" in the English theatre has had scores of personal theatrical triumphs in Britain for decades, she won a host of new ardent American admirers (awards, as well) with her magnificently moving performances in film and television in *Passage to India* and "The Jewel in the Crown," respectively. She played Agatha Christie in a 1986 mystery fantasy, "Murder by the Book." In 1988 she appeared with Shirley MacLaine in the movie *Madame Sousatzka* and could be heard via voice-over in *When The Wind Blows*.

Born Edith Margaret Emily Ashcroft 22 December 1907, she was educated at Woodford School, Croydon (the Ashcroft Theatre there was named in her honor in 1962) and the Central School of Dramatic Arts. Since her first appearance on stage in *Dear Brutus* (1926) she literally hasn't stopped trodding the boards, playing all the classics, all the works of major playwrights of yesterday and today. She has said the role of Winnie in Beckett's *Happy Days* is "the greatest part ever written—nearer to Everywoman than any other I can think of, and like climbing Everest to play." Although theatre is definitely her first and great love, she has commented on her recent film and television work. "I do think I'm very fortunate that just at the age when playing a stage role night after night is becoming difficult, I've had these opportunities. . . . Acting is the same whatever you do. But that long sustaining of energy is not demanded of you." Ashcroft is the mother of two children and has been thrice divorced.

Edward Asner

The burly actor was first embraced by audiences as the gruff, irascible newsman Lou Grant, boss of a Minneapolis television newsroom in "The Mary Tyler Moore Show" and then as City Editor of a Los Angeles newspaper in the gritty drama "Lou Grant." After assuming the presidency of the Screen Actors Guild following a crippling strike in 1981, his outspoken politics caused a bitter rift within SAG, but the union, and Asner, survived. "The entertainer is designed to please and as soon as he takes a political stand, he's immediately going to alienate a certain number of people. In my case, I still regard myself as a viable performer who is quite bankable," he has said. Yet Asner blamed the controversy over his politics for contributing to the demise of "Lou Grant." He entered the lists once again in 1985 with a new TV series, "Off the Rack."

Edward Asner was born on 15 November 1929 in Kansas City. In addition to theatre and occasional film appearances, his mainstay was episodic television until he won, by audition, his role on "The Mary Tyler Moore Show" in 1970. The ensemble sitcom remained a top rated program for seven years, earning Asner three Emmy awards and the chance to expand his character in an evolving storyline. A master of comic timing, he created a character who made perfect foils out of the star's peppy Mary Richards and the pompous Ted Baxter, played by the late Ted Knight. When Lou

Grant was transposed into a serious, hour-long format, Asner replaced that delightful sarcasm with depth and authenticity. The critically acclaimed drama about a hard-as-nails editor who shepherds a group of ambitious reporters earned mixed ratings and was cancelled by CBS in 1981, but was revived in reruns in 1984.

An active member of Common Cause, SANE, and other liberally oriented groups, Asner was swept into the union office after leading strike activities. But he soon found himself in hot water over his criticism of U.S. involvement in El Salvador. Also under heated debate was Asner's support of a SAG merger with two other performers' unions, a move opposed by a conservative SAG faction. Said Asner, "I want the Guild to be identified with the labor movement. The rollback in unionism in this country is a dangerous thing. It spells disaster for workers—and actors are definitely workers." He resigned as SAG president in 1985. But he still is active in causes such as homelessness and the American policy in Central America.

Full swing into his acting career, Asner starred in the brief NBC-TV series "Bronx Zoo" (1986-87), as the principal of an inner city high school. After touring the country in the play "Born Yesterday" he opened as Harry Brock on Broadway (with Madeline Kahn) in January 1989. The USA Network aired his 4-hour miniseries "Not a Penny More, Not a Penny Less" in 1990.

Asner is divorced from Nancy Lou Sykes, whom he married in 1959. They have three children.

Richard Attenborough

After seeing him at a London auction bidding for the bust of Prime Minister Nehru, a civil servant from India tried to interest this British actor-director in making a movie based on a book about the life of Mohandas Gandhi. "I took the book with me on a holiday to the south of France," says Richard Attenborough, "and before I was halfway through it, I knew I had to make the film." And although he also had to go to India more than 50 times, became ensnarled in red tape there, and was villified by the indigenous press and filmmakers for receiving government funds ("Can you imagine the British government giving [us] money to make a movie about

Winston Churchill?") he was rewarded for his 20 years of producing (and months of directing) with a film in which Ben Kingsley, who portrayed Gandhi, won an Oscar. "I wanted to tell the story of Gandhi the man," Attenborough said, "and all the connotations and premises and peripheral matters didn't matter to me." *Gandhi* also heralded a renewed interest in the world's most populous democracy, as demonstrated in such films as *A Passage to India*, *The Far Pavillions* and the 14-part television miniseries, *The Jewel in the Crown*.

During the 1940s, the future Sir Richard Attenborough (knighted in 1976) was one of the most saccharine "tennis anyone?" juveniles on the British screen. Sick of his image, he donned a false nose and was soon hamming it up as a competent character actor in many films including *Seance on a Wet Afternoon*, *Dr. Doolittle*, *A Severed Head*, and *The Great Escape*. A seasoned vet in all areas of the cinema, he also direct *Oh What a Lovely War*, *Young Winston*, and *A Bridge Too Far*, and produced *The L-Shaped Room*.

Born in Cambridge, England, 29 August 1923 (to an Anglo-Saxon scholar and educator; his naturalist brother, David, is well known to television viewers), Attenborough was determined at the age of 12 to become an actor after seeing a Charlie Chaplin film. While studying at London's Royal Academy of Dramatic Art, he met fellow student Sheila Sim, whom he married in 1945 (three children), and with whom he lives in West London. His first post-*Gandhi* film was a complete change of pace—*A Chorus Line* (1985). His most recent project is *Cry Freedom*, a film he directed and co-produced about South African anti-Apartheid martyr Steve Biko.

Dan Aykroyd

"I have friends who don't care what I do, who have never seen "Saturday Night Live" and with whom I associate on a totally different scale. The entertainment business is not the be-all and end-all for me," says the comic-actor-writer, whose friends must have been on Mars between 1975 and 1979, when he was an integral part of SNL's phenomenally successful early years. He received a 1977 Emmy Award for his memorable comedic contributions, both as one of SNL's seven original cast members and as one of its stable of writers. One of his recurring routines, performed with the flamboyant John Belushi, was the Blues Brothers, a dead-pan singing duo bedecked in dark suits, fedoras and sunglasses. Aykroyd calls his late partner "my wife. The only man I could ever dance with. . . . His loss is so tremendous." If he'd known of Belushi's drug habit, which caused the comedian's death, "I would have slapped all this stuff out of his hands."

A Canadian, born in Ottawa, Ontario, on 1 July 1952, Aykroyd was a rebellious youth who left Ottawa's Carlton College at 20 to join the Toronto branch of the Second City improvisational troupe, where he was spotted by SNL producer Lorne Michaels. Arriving in the U.S. in 1975, the year of the show's debut, he became popular with his Cone-head family skits and his varied impressions of Nixon, Carter, Tom Snyder, et al. His film debut was in 1979's *1941*, and the following year he wrote the film version of *The Blues Brothers*, in which he starred with Belushi. His other films include: *Neighbors* (1981, also with Belushi), *Twilight Zone—The Movie* (1983), *Trading Places* (1983) and—also as co-writer—*Ghostbusters* (1984). Aykroyd has co-starred with a variety of talented people including Chevy Chase in *Spies Like Us* (1985), Charles Grodin in *The Couch Trip* (1987), Tom Hanks in *Dragnet* (1987), Kim Basinger in *My Stepmother Is An Alien* (1988), Gene Hackman in *The Von Metz Incident* (1988), and he reunited with Bill Murray and Sigourney Weaver for *Ghostbusters II* (1989). The same year, he earned an Oscar nomination for best supporting actor for *Driving Miss Daisy*, which took best film honors.

His wife (married 29 April 1983) is actress Donna Dixon. He has three sons by an earlier marriage. He's part-owner of Crooks—a Toronto bar—and the popular Hard Rock Cafe. He claims, " I have this kind of mild nice-guy exterior, but inside, my heart is like a steel trap. I'm really quite robotic."

Lauren Bacall

O f her early film career, which spanned hardly a dozen years, she has said she arrived in Tinsel Town knowing "they would never have one goddam bit of respect for me as an actress, a talent, a potential, whatever, and of course, I was right. I was a commodity, a piece of meat." The cut was, of course, choice. "Baby" Bacall left behind a nascent Broadway career and a full-fledged modeling career at *Harper's Bazaar* under the tutelage of Diana Vreeland to make her film debut in *To Have and Have Not* (1944). Although she captured the eye of the movie-going public and the heart (and hand) of the legendary actor Humphrey Bogart all before the age of 21, the sloe-eyed beauty has confessed: "I was not a woman of the world. I'd lived with Mother all my life." Her sleek, sultry look and whiskey voice sustained her for the next five years. By then, she had *The Big Sleep, Dark Passage, Key Largo* and *Young Man With a Horn* under her cinch belt. "What I learned from Mr. Bogart, I learned from a master, and that, God knows, has stood me in very good stead." Indeed she was doing well in sophisticated comedy and her cutting delivery seemed more than natural in

such efforts as *How to Marry a Millionare* (1953), *Woman's World* (1954), *Written on the Wind* (1956) and *Designing Woman* (1957). To be sure, much of the cynicism must have come from the daily disparity of being mother of two (Stephen and Leslie) and chatelaine of a drunk tank affectionately known in Hollywood lore as the Holmby Hills Rat Pack which had her husband as the cheese. "I knew I couldn't last with that bunch if I didn't keep up."

Shortly after Bogey's death in 1957, she fled back to New York, where on 16 September 1924 she was born Betty (and to intimates remains) Joan Perske in Greenwich Village. A graduate of Julia Richman High School, she had also studied acting at the American Academy of Dramatic Arts. From the security of the famous Dakota apartments, she again essayed Broadway with *Goodbye Charlie* (1959), married actor Jason Robards, and had a second son, Sam. The Robards divorced eight years later. "Well, there is nothing to say about *that* except that it's over. *Period.*" Her first big success on Broadway was a two-year run in *Cactus Flower* (1966), but Broadway bitchery has proved to be her strong suit, although her own backstage behavior has not always been what becomes a legend most. She was awarded a Tony for her portrayal of Margo Channing in *Applause* (1970, the musical version of *All About Eve*), which ran for two years before a national tour, an appearance on London's West End and a televised adaptation. A second Tony followed for her characterization of Tess Harding in *Woman of the Year* (1981), which also ran for two years before a national tour. A mannequin for Blackglama advertisements, she also looks to commercials for a Long Island jeweler and a decaffeinated coffee miller as her "source" of television revenues.

Successful films from Bacall's mature career include *Murder on the Orient Express* (1974), Robert Altman's *Health* (1980) and *The Fan* (1981), based on the best-selling novel. She also appeared in *Mr.*

North (1987), *Appointment With Death* (1987) and touched television with the PBS special *Bacall on Bogart* (1988). Her autobiography *By Myself* (1978) was a bestseller in both hardcover and paperback editions. Casting her mind over the past, she once reflected, "The harshness you might feel is bound to be reflected in your face—and I have enough things coming out on my face."

Pearl Bailey

"**O**h! Life is so full and rich." Pearl Mae Bailey has unquestionably provided life with part of that richness, entertaining two generations with her records, her performances on Broadway, in night clubs and vaudeville (still her favorite form of show business), in films, on television, and in five popular books. "Papa was a preacher. Holy Roller, I suppose you'd call it. From him I got the wisdom, the philosophizing, the soul."

Bailey was born in Newport News, Virginia, 29 March 1918, and first sang at religious services led by her father. "In his church you've got to have a lot of rhythm," she says. "Folks sway, and sometimes they shout." Following her famous tap-dancing brother, Bill Bailey, she started singing in small clubs in Washington at 13, and starred with Count Basie and Cootie Williams. Johnny Mercer and Harold Arlen signed her for the Broadway production of *St. Louis Woman* in 1946 for which she received the Donaldson Award as best newcomer on Broadway. Her other Broadway shows include *Bless You All* (1950), *House of Flowers* (1954) and the all-black production of *Hello, Dolly!*, which in 1967 won her Entertainer of the Year award from *Cue* magazine. But Pearl Bailey is best known for her recordings—songs such as "Tired," "Legalize My Name," and "Takes Two to Tango," and albums like "The Bad Old Days" and "For Adult Listening." Her autobiography, *The Raw Pearl*, came out in 1968.

In 1975 and 1976, Bailey was appointed by President Gerald R. Ford as Special Advisor to the U.S. Mission to the United Nations. She traveled to the Middle East and Africa, including Jordan, Egypt, Kuwait, Liberia, Senegal and the United Arab Emirates. When she departed, U.S. Ambassador Jamil Baroody of Saudi Arabia thanked the U.S. for "having retained as a representative . . . a Pearl not cultured by Mimimoto, but cultured in the art of the theatre and in her genuine humanitarian attitude towards all those who know her."

Bailey and her husband, French jazz drummer Louis Bellson, were married in 1952 and have two children. She has been honored in the Middle East with such awards as King Hussein of Jordan's Ben-Ali Freedom Medal, and Egypt's First Order of Arts and Science of Egypt. In 1978, Bailey received an Honorary Degree from a Georgetown University and soon after enrolled as freshman. Earning a place on the Dean's List was one of her proudest achievements. Graduating in 1985 with a B.A. in Theology, she wrote a song to mark the happy occasion.

Pearl presented a wonderful Christmas gift to the public with her performance in the PBS television special "Miss Ruby's Southern Holiday Dinner," which aired in 1988.

Anne Bancroft

"Who would have thought that when I left California, I would wind up sleeping in Golda Meir's bed?" In preparation for *Golda* (1977-78), William Gibson's dramatization of Golda Meir's autobiography, *My Life,* Anne Bancroft did just that—travelling to Israel, accompanying Meir to religious, political and social events. "Golda was a legend to me. She was out of my realm," said Bancroft before meeting Meir. In search of a personal link to aid her in her portrayal, Bancroft jetted to Israel—as soon as they met that bond was established; "I was suddenly calm. My anxiety was gone. I looked into her eyes and I knew. I knew I would be OK. . . . When I work I have to find a personal image that is similar to the person I'm relating to in the play. If you don't lock into something extremely personal within yourself the play will have gone by without your having felt anything." An Oscar winner (*The Miracle Worker*—1962), Bancroft has been visible on the screen in *Garbo Talks,* in hubby Mel Brooks' mordant comedy *To Be or Not To Be, Agnes of God, 'night, mother,* and *84 Charing Cross Road.*

Born Anne Marie Italiano, 17 September 1931, in the Bronx, she breezed through a Hollywood screen test at age 18, was then becalmed for the next six years in a series of B and lower movies. "Everybody drank beer for breakfast," she recalls hazily of those years. "We had a ball." Hung over from the California merry-go-round and her four-year marriage to Texan Martin May, she returned to New York in 1955, lived with her parents, and enrolled in Herbert Berghof's acting classes. "It was the beginning of a whole new approach to acting, a deeper, more fulfilling and more thinking approach. I learned to think a little to set certain tasks for myself. My work became much more exciting." Bancroft first reached Broadway star status in 1958 opposite Henry Fonda in *Two for the Seesaw*. She stayed with the highly acclaimed show for a year and half, and recalls, "For the first time in my life I was a star, an honest-to-gosh star, in an important production. There was a tremendous sense of achievement in me and I really felt like an actress." The down-to-earth luminary received Oscar nominations for *The Pumpkin Eater* (1963), *The Graduate* (1968) and *The Turning Point* (1977). Other standout Bancroft appearances include Neil Simon's *Prisoner of Second Avenue*, *The Elephant Man* (1980) and *Torch Song Trilogy* (1988).

The hard-driving actress has mellowed considerably since her 1964 marriage to writer/director Mel Brooks (one son). "Oh, I still get deeply involved in the roles I take. Mel gets totally involved when he's writing, too, and I am shut out, alone. But life is not all work now. Work is just part of life."

Roseanne Barr

"Hi I'm a housewife, domestic goddess."

"We're all married to the same guy. . . . You may marry the man of your dreams, ladies, but 15 years later you are married to a reclining chair that burps."

"Mom, where's my English book?" "I sold it."

"The 'Terrible Twos' last until your kids move out of the house."

"Mom, I've got a knot in my shoe." "Wear loafers."

"It's OK to be fat. So you're fat. Just be fat and shut up about it."

Her one-liners have people doubled-up with laughter. Her television series "Roseanne" won the People's Choice Award (1989) as Favorite Comedy Show and she picked up two People's Choice Awards in 1990. Roseanne Barr is thrilled with her success. She jokes, "As long as I bitch and get paid for it, I'm the luckiest person in the world."

Born in Salt Lake City, Utah, circa 1953 to a working-class Jewish family, she told *USA Weekend*, "Mormon country was not the best place for Jews. I survived by never saying I was Jewish. I was very quiet. I'd sit in the back of the classroom and had very few friends." She had to drop out of high school at 18, when she was hit by a car. She admitted during a Barbara Walters interview that she was institutionalized as a teenager for her rebellious behavior (she recently visited the hospital to give the patients a Barr-boost talk.) After a slow recovery, Roseanne moved to Colorado Springs where she met her future husband, Bill Pentland (a mail sorter at a local post office). Without appropriate funds to live in "style", the newlyweds set up house in a 9-by-36-foot trailer. Three children later (Jessica, Jennifer, Jacob) the family moved into a "larger" 600-square-foot house in Denver. She claims, "It wasn't 'Dynasty,' but it was cool. We thought we were artsy folks." Discouraged from showing her standup routines in the 70's because of her down-to-earth, sometimes brash bits, Roseanne only performed at private parties, biker bars and punk clubs. It wasn't until she appeared on "The Tonight Show" that all hell broke loose. With her sitcom scoring high in the ratings, she's assured of theatrical longevity. Her Recovering Housewife Tour was launched in Las Vegas in June, 1990, giving fans more of her stand-up humor, which they can experience live or on cable television as an HBO special. Her autobiography *Stand Up: My Life As a Woman* (1989) is a frank tell-all of her struggles—a serious side to the funny lady. A cartoon show featuring Barr as a young girl, "Little Rosie," premiered on television in September, 1990.

With obstacles in the past and now a huge jump from her grassroot beginnings, Roseanne lives in California; she and Bill split in 1989 and she is now married to comedian/writer Tom Arnold. Roseanne has her life mapped out: "I went into standup so I could do television and movies. Right now, I'm in the seventh year of a 10-year plan. In year 10, I become Woody Allen. I write and direct $3-million films. I wear glasses. I move to New York."

Kim Basinger

In a very short period of time Kim Basinger has gone from a successful New York model/covergirl to one of Hollywood's leading ladies, starring opposite such leading men as Sean Connery, Burt Reynolds, Robert Redford, Sam Shepard and Dan Aykroyd. Her film role, as Domino in James Bond's *Never Say Never Again*, brought

her widespread attention and led to other roles, including the temptress opposite Robert Redford in *The Natural*, the nymphomaniac opposite Burt Reynolds in *The Man Who Loved Women*, the experimenting lover, Elizabeth, opposite Mickey Rourke in *9½ Weeks*, and the alien opposite Dan Aykroyd in *My Stepmother Is an Alien*.

Born 8 December 1953, one of five children, Kim grew up in Athens, Georgia. She inherited her father's love for music and became accomplished on the piano and guitar. Kim, dedicated to become a well-rounded talent, took ballet training for 15 years and practiced to perfect her singing voice. The next step was moving to New York, where Basinger's good looks, talent and winning personality helped to make her a sought-after model. After five years Kim left her career and drove cross-country to Los Angeles to become an actress. Success was hers when she landed the lead in the TV movie "Katie: Portrait of a Centerfold." Basinger made her feature film debut opposite Jan-Michael Vincent in *Hard Country*, followed by *Mother Lode* with Charlon Heston. In the midst of her screen successes, her 1980 marriage to Ron Britton fizzled, and they filed for divorce in December, 1988.

Basinger is enjoying her rise to stardom and the diversity of roles. Hoping to add to her comedy credits, she was chosen to appear in the darkly funny 1989 film *Batman* with Michael Keaton. She insists, "I love comedy and think it's the most powerful thing we have in the entertainment industry. I think people don't laugh enough and good humor is very seldom written. So I love it once I get something good. I love the ride along the way." Her next comedy is *The Marrying Man*, opposite Alec Baldwin, from an original script by Neil Simon.

Jason Bateman

He's the type of guy that any young girl would want to bring home. His innocent, friendly smile has brought him admirers of all ages—grandmothers, mothers, and daughters all adore jovial Jason. Handsome, clean-cut looks might have opened a few doors for him, but Bateman's acting gift is securing his standing in Hollywood.

Born in Rye, New York, 14 January 1969, Jason was destined for show biz. Jason's father, producer/theatrical manager Kent Bateman,

was already deeply involved in the industry, and it seemed only natural that
his offspring would follow in his footsteps. Jason began his career at ten
years old, when he accompanied a friend
to an audition for an educational film,
and instead he got the lead role. Bateman
became popular in television commercials and then landed a role at age 12 on
the Michael Landon series "Little House
on the Prairie." It's been a steady rise
ever since, with other roles rolling his
way, including guest appearances on
the Ricky Schroder series "Silver Spoons,"

a lead on the comedy series, "It's Your Move," a major motion
picture, *Teen Wolf* (1987—produced by his father), and a made-for-
television film "Moving Target" (1988). His claim to fame was a
continuation of the former "Valerie" (1985-88) show starring Valerie
Harper.

Rather than wasting time on sibling rivalry, Jason and his
actress/sister Justine are creatively intertwined. Along with their
father they formed a Hollywood repertory stage company and
produced a telefilm, "Can You Feel Me Dancing?" Brother and sister
also starred together in this family venture. Bateman can plan on
being busy for quite some time; his latest is a 1989 release, *Philly Boy*.
Always active, Jason likes sports (skiing, basketball, surfing) and is
an outstanding driver (won the 1987 Long Beach Grand Prix) on the
Celebrity circuit. At such a young age, his race has just begun.

Justine Bateman

N ominated for a Golden Globe Award in 1987 for Best
Supporting Actress in a TV series, miniseries, telefilm,
Justine Bateman was very close to fulfilling her motto: "Anything I
want to do, I will do." Beginning in 1982 Justine portrayed "Mallory
Keaton," the eldest daughter of the Keaton family on the prime-
time show "Family Ties." Playing opposite Michael J. Fox, she
acquired her own fans with her smooth acting ability. As the
straight-faced, zany sister of "Alex," "Mallory" flipped over clothes
sales, mall trips, dress shops and her "Hey Pops" boyfriend, Nick.

Justine Bateman was born in Rye, New York, on 19 February
1966 to a film producer father and a flight attendant mother. Along
with her younger brother, actor Jason Bateman, she began her
acting career at an early age. She performed in various theatrical

productions, including "Up the Down Staircase," "Barefoot in the Park," and "Midsummer's Night Dream." Her favorite role to date was a family production, as well as her professional stage debut. She starred as "Katherine," a suicidal young woman who is sent to a mental institution. The play was directed by her father, Kent Bateman; her mother assisted behind-the-scenes and Jason co-starred with his sister. She also worked with Jason in a made-for-TV-movie "Can You Feel Me Dancing?" (1986) in which she played the role of a blind girl fighting to overcome her handicap. On the big screen, Justine starred in a trite teen movie *Satisfaction* (1988).

Although 1989 proved the last season for "Family Ties," Justine is confident her career will move forward; she wants to direct and act in upcoming features for both film and television. The young actress remains single and lives in California. She enjoys writing poetry and experimenting with photography.

Alan Bates

Without any of the usual Hollywood hype, this Britisher has risen on Cupid's wings to become the "International Reluctant Heartthrob." The *New York Times'* Judy Klemesrud asked him what his secret was and he answered, "I haven't a clue," later adding, "I think I've played a lot of parts which in themselves are attractive, such as Birkin in *Women in Love* (he wrestled nude with Oliver Reed in front of a raging amber fire in the 1970 film), the tenant farmer in *The Go Between*, and Saul Kaplan, the Soho artist in *An Unmarried Woman*. They are all very different, but they somehow have a mysterious quality." To this list of rugged yet sensitive brooders and broad-shouldered teddy bears add *Whistle Down The Wind* playing a fugitive murderer mistaken for Jesus Christ, *King of Hearts* as the soldier crowned king in a French loony bin, the prisoner in *The Fixer*, the father in *Joe Egg*, Diaghilev in the movie about the life of

Nijinsky, and an amnesiac (1985) desired by Glenda Jackson, Ann-Margret and Julie Christie in the *The Return of the Soldier.*

The oldest of three brothers, Alan Bates was born 17 February 1934 and studied acting at London's Royal Academy of Dramatic Art on scholarship. A Royal Air Force veteran, he made his stage debut in 1955 at Coventry with the Midland Theatre Company in *You and Your Wife.* Soon afterward he joined the English Stage Company where his most notable role was as "the other man" in John Osborne's *Look Back in Anger* (which he encored in his Broadway debut in 1957). As one of the two eccentric brothers in Harold Pinter's *The Caretaker,* he repeated his London performance on Broadway in 1961, and did the same with *Poor Richard* and *Butley* for which he won a Tony in 1973. Clive Barnes exulted, "Bates gives one of the greatest performance I've ever seen." He has appeared in many BBC made-for-TV dramas, including John Mortimer's "Voyage Around My Father," with Sir Laurence Olivier. His other movie roles have included *Zorba the Greek, Georgy Girl, The Rose, Duet for One, A Prayer for the Dying,* and *We Think the World of You.*

The 5-foot-11 inch actor remained a bachelor until he was 36, and now lives happily in England with his wife ("she's British, but we met in New York") Victoria Ward, a former actress, and their twin sons Tristan and Benedick.

Meredith Baxter-Birney

One can't help but think of the word "family" when discussing this 5'7" blonde-haired blue-eyed actress. Three of her television series roles revolved around family—as a young Catholic in "Bridget Loves Bernie" (1972), where argumentative relatives played a key role in a mixed-religion marriage; as the eldest daughter of Kate and Doug Lawrence in the long-running "Family" (1976-1980); and as the radical 60's hippie, Elyse Keaton, mother of money-conscious, pro-republican, Alex, in the NBC hit "Family Ties" (1982-1989). Perhaps being raised in a theatrical household added to Meredith's choice to become involved in the industry, but through the years she has collected an impressive array of distinguished roles.

Born in Los Angeles, 21 June 1947, Meredith is the daughter of

Tom and Whitney (Blake) Baxter. Her mother, Whitney Blake, played "Dorothy Baxter," wife of "George" on the timeless "Hazel" show. Showing an interest in singing, Meredith started with lessons in her early teens. She expanded her artistic drive by performing in school while attending Hollywood High School. She then went on to continue her studies at Michigan's Interlochen Arts Academy. Taken a bit off course, Meredith had to put her plans on hold when she married in her teens and became a young mother before she was 20 (son, Ted). Her career stayed on hold until after the birth of her second child (daughter Eva) and an eventual divorce.

It didn't take long for Meredith to focus her energies in the right direction; her career zoomed. Motion pictures included *Ben* (1972), *Bittersweet Love* (1976) and *All The President's Men* (1976). Stints on stage include roles in "Vanities," "Butterflies Are Free," "Guys and Dolls," "Tally's Folly," and "The Diaries of Adam and Eve," which was also presented on PBS in 1988. In addition to her well-known television series, Meredith has starred in a variety of juicy made-for-TV movies, such as "The Night That Panicked America" (1975), "The Rape of Richard Beck" (1985), "The Long Journey Home" (1987), "Kate's Secret" (1987) and in the much-acclaimed uplifting story about an institutionalized woman who overcame her mental retardation, "Winnie" (1989).

Meredith married her co-star David Birney, of "Bridget Loves Bernie," in 1974. The couple have three children; Kate (1975) and twins Mollie and Peter (1984). The couple filed for divorce in February, 1989.

Warren Beatty

It's hard to talk about him without mentioning *something* about sex, unless, of course you're referring to him as Shirley MacLaine's brother. Joan Collins had the same problem when she wrote about him in her autobiography. "He loved the telephone," she said of her ex-amoroso. "He made twenty to thirty calls a day, often to the same people three or four times. . . . Telephoning, however, was secondary to his main passion, which was making love—and he was also able to accept phone calls at the same time."

Elia Kazan's *Splendor in the Grass* (1961) first shot him to fame in a starring role opposite amour-of-the-moment, Natalie Wood. A series of film flops (*Lilith, The Roman Spring of Mrs. Stone*) and headline-making "relationships" (with Jean Seberg, Leslie Caron, the earlier-mentioned Collins and Julie Christie) followed. ("I think a very short relationship where you tell the truth to somebody is in many ways more satisfying than a longer relationship when the truth becomes more painful. . . . And I've always been antagonized by the Freudian Victorian assumption that a hyperactive life with women was necessarily a manifestation of misogynistic feelings or latent homosexuality. I've always felt that was a stupid generalization, that sometimes it might be the case, but as often as not it isn't.")

Born in Richmond 30 March 1937 and raised in Arlington, Va., in what he describes as a "a very middle class atmosphere with all its rigidities," he was the high school football star, class president ("I was a cheerful hypocrite"), and American Legion Boys Stater. He was offered ten football scholarships from as many major colleges and universities, all of which he turned down because he decided to study acting at Northwestern University. He dropped out, moved to New York and studied acting with Stella Adler; there he support- ed himself by working as a bricklayer and as a sandhog on the third tube of the Lincoln Tunnel under the Hudson River. Beginning with small parts in television, he also worked in summer stock. Between jobs he supported himself by playing piano at night so he could audition by day. In a winter stock production of *Compulsion,* he was discovered by playwright William Inge and director Joshua Logan and shipped to Hollywood (after the critics went wild over his Broadway debut in Inge's *A Loss of Roses*). "This boy," said Logan, "is the sexiest thing around." The winner of the Hollywood press ladies' Sour Apple Award for the Most Uncooperative Actor in Movies when he made *Splendor in the Grass,* he returned from a two- year absence from acting to triumph both as an actor and producer, functioning in this dual role on such box office bonanzas as *Bonnie and Clyde, Shampoo, Heaven Can Wait* and *Reds,* the cinematic saga of John Reed, radical journalist of the World War I era. Beatty has also starred in *McCabe and Mrs. Miller, $, The Parallax View,* and *Ishtar.* He was the Executive Producer for the 1987 Molly Ringwald vehicle, *Pickup Artist,* and in 1990 he starred in and directed *Dick Tracy.*

"He plays so much on what the audience responds to in him— the all-American combination of innocence and earnestness," wrote one critic, "—that he's in danger of turning into Li'l Abner." Well, "Abner's" also an activist and a supporter of a variety of liberal causes. "Anyone who says an artist should stay out of politics is a *fool,*" he decrees. "I'm talking about an artist who is able to say what truth is. The real artist—the person who is able to perceive and clarify the truth—if that person is activated, then that artist is what

Solzhenitsyn says he is: 'An alternative government.' And you know he's right." Sharing his Hollywood experiences, he released an autobiography, *Warren Beatty and Desert Eyes: A Life and a Story*, in 1987.

Never married, but constantly dating, we weren't able to confirm if the song "You're So Vain"—by yet another ex, Carly Simon,—is really about him or not. Lately he's been romantically linked on-and-off with his *Dick Tracy* co-star, Madonna.

Harry Belafonte

This entertainment giant, like fellow contemporary folk singer Pete Seeger, has often used his stage as a forum for musical messages against injustice. "We gave birth to Joan Baez, and Bob Dylan and James Taylor and all those other great people," says Harry Belafonte, "and they began to write in the folk tradition of the day. . . . I fully believed in the civil rights movement. I had a personal commitment to it and I had my personal breakthroughs. I felt that if we could just turn the nation around, things would fall into place. And it actually happened."

That his own career fell into place is almost as amazing as the eventual firsts he was to engineer. Belafonte was born 1 March 1927 in Harlem. He moved with his parents to Jamaica when he was eight, but returned in time to go to high school in New York before joining the Navy in 1944. Later, as a Harlem janitor, he was given a pair of tickets that were to change his life: the passes enabled him to see the American Negro Theater, and he was hooked. Although he meant to be an actor, when he was heard singing in a sketch he was hired by a Greenwich Village nightclub. After buying into his own restaurant he discovered folk music, and in short order became The Calypso King. After turning out hit records, he returned to acting, both in films and on Broadway, and, true to his West Indian entrepreneurial spirit, was again in charge when he produced his own films starting with 1958's *The World, the Flesh and the Devil*. Carrying with him a commitment to more opportunities for blacks, he created an apprenticeship program to train black and Puerto Rican technicians for his 1970 film *The Angel Levine*. Then he joined forces (and dollars) with Sidney Poitier to make the *Uptown Saturday*

Night trilogy, as well as *Buck and the Preacher*. He landed the hip-hop culture in 1984's *Beat Street*. This singer of work and chain-gang songs won Emmys for his TV music specials, awards for his civil rights works with Dr. Martin Luther King (1982's MLK Nonviolent Peace Prize), and introduced South African singers Letta Mbulu and Miriam Makeba and Greece's Nana Mouskouri to the U.S. He is also committed to the struggle of black South Africans and has been active in Athletes & Artists Against Apartheid. Belafonte was also a major force behind the making of the record, "We Are the World," which garnered millions for African famine relief.

Mixing his music with his beliefs, he recorded "Paradise in Gazankulu" (1988), filled with beautiful, haunting poetry and songs of South Africa. Ironically, Belafonte was not allowed to go to South Africa and the musical tracks for the album were laid down in Johannesburg, then shipped back to Belafonte in the United States to complete. In February, 1988, he traveled to Harare, Zimbabwe, in his role as UNICEF Goodwill Ambassador and performed a concert that was recorded on video.

Belafonte is married to Julia Robinson, once the only white dancer in the Katherine Dunham Company. They have two children, Gina and David. He has two other children from his first marriage: Shari (actress/model) and Adrienne (the mother of his two grandchildren). In 1989 Belafonte was scheduled to produce a television mini-series for ABC-TV "The Mandelas—a South African Saga" with guest stars Sidney Poitier, Jane Fonda, and Marlon Brando. "In the future," says Belafonte, "I'll be doing exactly what I'm doing now and have been doing for 20 years, only better. And I'll still be trying to use my life wisely." Future projects include a film version of August Wilson's play *Joe Turner's Come and Gone*, with producing and perhaps acting credits involved.

Shari Belafonte

People are quick to point out that children of celebrities can ride on the crest of parental success and cash in on the strength of their names. Not the case with Shari Belafonte. Before her name became a household word, her face was the focus of attention. Shari's dark brown eyes, brown hair, and well-built 5'5" body saturated the television screens with the much-talked-about Calvin Klein commercials. It was not until Shari was a familiar model, making it on her own, that the public learned she was the daughter of legendary entertainer Harry Belafonte.

Born in New York City, 22 September 1954, Shari spent most of her young years with her mother, Frances. She later attended a

Massachusetts boarding school and then graduated from Buxton in Williamstown. She enrolled in Hampshire College and one year later transferred to Carnegie-Mellon University where she graduated with a Bachelor of Fine Arts degree in drama. At college, Belafonte met and fell in love with Robert Harper and the two were married in 1977. The couple moved to Washington, DC, followed by Los Angeles, where Shari landed a job as a publicist's assistant at Hanna-Barbera. Simultaneously, she was submitting photos and resumes around town to casting agents, and struck lucky when she was picked up by famous agent Nina Blanchard. Television commercials and print ads brought exposure; she made her acting debut in the feature film *If You Could See What I Hear* (1982). She says: "I'd been studying acting since grade school and been around the business ever since I can remember. . . . Consciously, I always said I would never get into show business but, subconsciously, I knew that entertaining was my life."

Shari's career has expanded to encompass various aspects of show biz. She had a continuing role as Julie Gillette in the ABC-TV series "Hotel," guest roles on such series as "Hart to Hart," "The Love Boat," "Trapper John M.D.," and "Code Red." She has reported on-air for "Good Morning America," hosted "AM Los Angeles," and filmed the 1989 feature film *Speed Zone*. She has appeared on over 300 magazine covers; sharing her beauty expertise, Shari released a home video, "Massage for Health" (1988), and developed a new line of cosmetics, "Montaj . . . For a World of Color."

Belafonte is now adjusting to the single life; she and Robert split in 1988.

Barbara Bel Geddes

The matriarch of the Ewing family in the top-rated television series "Dallas," Eleanor Southward Ewing ("Miss Ellie"), also known as Barbara Bel Geddes, returned to the series in the 1985 season and the family was mighty glad to see her back. And so were the hordes of fans who were devastated when "Miss Ellie" underwent bypass surgery in 1983 and was to leave the show permanently. The rate of her recovery plus the urgency of her many fans restored her health, courage, and determination, so she was back to holding the Ewings together. The series, which had its beginning in 1978 and for which Bel Geddes won an Emmy award, had opened a new frontier for her, after an earlier brilliant career of the Broadway stage in addition to a parcel of Hollywood movies and television specials.

Born in New York City 31 October 1922, the daughter of celebrated scenic designer Norman Bel Geddes, she was raised in a creative household. Her first stage role was in *School for Scandal* at the Clinton (Conn.) Playhouse in 1939. She made her Broadway debut in *Out of the Frying Pan* (1940), and appeared in *Little Darling* (1942), *Nine Girls* (1943), *Mrs. January and Mr. X* (1944). In 1945 she appeared in the controversial *Deep Are the Roots* for which she won the Clarence Derwent Award. She was the recipient of a Theatre World Award in 1946. A series of memorable stage appearances followed, including *The Moon Is Blue* (1952), *The Living Room* (1954), Tennessee Williams' *Cat on a Hot Tin Roof* (1955), *The Sleeping Prince* (1956), *Silent Night, Lonely Night* (1959), Jean Kerr's *Mary, Mary* (1961), *The Porcelain Years* (1965), *Everything in the Garden* (1967), *Finishing Touches* (1973) and *Ah, Wilderness,* (1975). Her movies, spanning a time period of 1946 through 1971, included *The Long Night, I Remember Mama, Blood on the Moon, Caught, Panic in the Streets, Fourteen Hours, The Five Pennies, Five Branded Women, By Love Possessed, The Todd Killings,* and *Summertree.* As an author and illustrator Bel Geddes has produced several books, among them *I Like To Be Me* (1963) and *So Do I* (1972); she has also designed greeting cards. Bel Geddes's first marriage was to Carl Schreuer in 1944 (one child, daughter Susan); it ended in divorce. Her second marriage was to the late Windsor Lewis in 1951 (a second daughter, Betsy).

Jean-Paul Belmondo

"New blood, new looks, new vitality new *fluidum*, new eroticism, new normality for that malady-ridden strain of today's neurotic actors"—from Marlene Dietrich's "ABC" under B for Belmondo. Called by film-maker Jean-Pierre Melville the most accomplished actor of his generation and considered France's coolest film sigh, he popped upon the scene in 1960 as the irresistible hoodlum in Jean-Luc Godard's New Wave *Breathless,* after he

fluttered many a heart throughout the world (from Bangor to Bangkok, femme college students plastered his broken-nosed image to their bedroom ceilings) in such films as *The Man from Rio, Up to His Ears* (opposite Ursula Andress, for whom he later left his wife Elodie, a son and two daughters; he left *her* in 1972), *The Thief of Paris, Borsalino, L'Incorrigible, Le Voleur* and *Stavisky*. Preferring to play sympathetic characters, Belmondo is also attached to—and has made a success of—the theme of "virile friendship" between men. Having worked with a stellar cast of French directors—Truffaut, Malle, Godard and de Broca among them—and international beauties—including Jean Seberg and Catherine Deneuve—Belmondo served as executive producer on many of his films, but with many of them dubbed, his films in later years often did not catch on overseas. Sticking primarily to French soil seems to suit his fancy; he refused the lure of Hollywood until 1986 when he starred in *Hold-Up*. For a change of scene, he spent most of 1988 filming in various locales (Africa, Singapore, San Francisco, Paris) for the 1989 film *L'Itineraire d'un Enfant Gaté*.

Born in Neuilly-sur-Seine, France, 9 April 1933, the son of sculptor Paul Belmondo (president of the Academie des Beaux-Arts) young Belmondo garnered boyhood achievements in sports. At 16 he was a "walking disaster, a school flunk-out and brawler." When he announced one day that he wanted to become an actor, his distinguished papa grudgingly arranged an audition with a friend from the Comedie Française, from whom he received the following verdict: "He has no talent, and no voice. Besides, he's ugly." This did not disturb our hero. Four years later, with an education at the Conservatoire d'Art Dramatique behind him, he once again called at the Comedie Française and much to everyone's surprise but his own, was accepted. After playing Molière with his hands in his pockets ("You imbecile," snapped a director. "Do you call yourself an actor?") his brief tenure with the illustrious company came to an end and he was soon playing the back rooms of Paris cafes ("where the boss grudgingly moves out the beer-stained tables and would rather watch television anyway"). After several months in France's chaotic drama wasteland ("I love a good scrap, but now I can't afford it any more"), he was caught up *in nouvelle vague*, some stage work and then made his sensational film debut as a leading man in *Breathless*. ("Hell, everyone knows that an ugly guy with a good line gets the chicks," he said at the time. There seems to be a style now for ugly men. Look at Lee Marvin. Look at Quinn. Mean guys.")

Noted for his pranks, he was booted out of a Spanish town for throwing furniture out of the window. In Hong Kong he and his sidekick rode up and down an elevator naked as trees in a March wind. Sports preoccupy him completely. He is an ex-welterweight, does his own film stunts, and is part owner of a soccer team, Les Polymuscles. "He's an animal," says director Daniel Boulander. "In a way, he's the image of the modern world. He represents ease, but a little bit lost. He's always a little mocking, there's always a little wink in his eye. He even walks with humor. Wrong or right, I suppose he represents France."

Richard Benjamin

Discriminating filmgoers will long remember his erotic grunts as Philip Roth's onanistic anti-hero in *Portnoy's Complaint* back in 1972. Prior to becoming a different Roth character in the earlier *Goodbye, Columbus* (1968), this New York City-born (22 May 1938) actor had been known best as "Paula Prentiss's husband." ("If you are married to an actress and your wife is getting all the calls . . . it is very hard on the ego. But Paula solidified things for me. I married this gorgeous long-legged girl who wasn't Jewish and became a man.") By the 1970s Richard Benjamin was getting the calls even more often than his wife and being cast in such big-screen offerings as the sardonic comedy classic *Catch-22* (1970), *Diary of a Mad Housewife (1970)*, and *The Last of Sheila* (1973). During a subsequent dry period, he bummed around (mostly playing tennis) with fellow actor George Segal ("When one of us would get a job, the other would say, 'Oh, no, what am I going to do now?'") but soon began turning up again in the likes of *The Sunshine Boys* with George Burns and Walter Matthau in 1975, with Matthau and Glenda Jackson in *House Calls* in 1977, and with George Hamilton in 1978 in another comedy classic, *Love At First Bite*.

Taking seriously some wifely advice ("Take [the chance] or shut up and stop complaining when other directors do something you don't like") he applied his proven comedic talents to directing Peter O'Toole in 1982's high-laugh-quotient exploration of early television, *My Favorite Year*. In 1984, he had another hit on his hands with *City Heat* in which he directed Burt Reynolds and Clint Eastwood. Leaving his director's hat on, Benjamin followed with *The Money Pit* (1986), *Little Nikita* (1987), and the Dan Aykroyd/Kim Basinger comedy *My Stepmother Is an Alien* (1988).

A joint production (with Paula Prentiss) away from the cameras was son Ross Thomas, born in 1974.

Tom Berenger

It's always interesting when a talented actor who has been around for some time is suddenly thrust into stardom with one role. Such is the case with Tom Berenger, who was first seen on the big screen in the 1975 film *Beyond the Door*, and twelve years later, after playing such characters as the psychotic killer in *Looking for Mr. Goodbar* (1977), a TV private eye in *The Big Chill* (1983), a piano player and writer in *Eddie and the Cruisers* (1983), and a cowboy hero in the comedy *Rustlers Rapsody* (1985), he finally reached stardom in the role of the ruthless Sargeant Barnes in the critically acclaimed 1987 film *Platoon*, which won Berenger a Golden Globe Award and an Academy Award nomination for Best Actor. Since that film's phenomenal success, Berenger has been more in demand, displaying his remarkable talents in a vivid range of roles such as a policeman in *Someone To Watch Over Me* (1987), an unfriendly mountain man in *Shoot To Kill* (1987), a farmer leading a double life in *Betrayed* (1988) and a priest in *Last Rites* (1988). The rugged actor's next film, *Major League*, was released in 1989.

Born 31 May 1950 in Chicago, Berenger had originally intended to go into journalism. After he enrolled in the University of Missouri, however, his interests changed to drama. In college Berenger starred in a production of *Who's Afraid of Virginia Woolf*. After moving to New York, Berenger studied acting at H.B. Studios in Manhattan and performed in a number of stage productions. His theatrical credits include the roles of Jocko in *End as a Man*, a Circle Repertory production, Orestes in *Electra,* Jack in *The Rose Tattoo*, a Long Wharf Theatre production, and Stanley Kowalski in *A Streetcar Named Desire*, which toured Japan after it was staged at home by the Milwaukee Repertory Company. Moving over to TV, Berenger acted in the daytime soap "One Life To Live" and made TV movies "Johnny We Hardly Knew Ye" (1977) and "Flesh and Blood" (1979) before acting in the CBS-TV seven-hour version of Sidney Sheldon's *If Tomorrow Comes* (1985).

With scripts to choose from, Berenger decided to take time off from the big screen to return to the stage in the Long Wharf Theatre's production of *National Anthems*, performed in New Haven, Connecticut, through the beginning of 1989. Berenger, father of two children (Allison, born in 1977, and Patrick, born in 1979) by his first marriage to Barbara, currently resides in South Carolina with his second wife, Lisa (married 29 July 1986) and their two daughters, Chelsea and Chloe.

Candice Bergen

"I t takes a long time to grow up. Longer than they tell you," she says. The beautiful blonde daughter of ventriloquist Edgar Bergen ("a complicated and original figure of a father") grew up in the shadow of her "big brother"—Bergen's glib, wisecracking, smartly-attired dummy, Charlie McCarthy. Only after her father's death, she feels, did she come into her own as actress, wife, person. "His death ('78) left a space for me. I was much more able to live according to my own expectations. I always felt my fame was ill-gotten, sort of borrowed from his, and that perhaps I tried to keep some kind of rein on it. Even when he was in retirement I felt I was poaching on his territory."

Born in Beverly Hills, 9 May 1946, she attended posh schools in Washington, D.C., and Switzerland. "My parents were smart. They let me go. They'd always been smarter than other parents, I guess. When other fathers gave their kids automobiles, mine gave me a horse, that kind of thing. But still there were those awful vacations back in Beverly Hills. I'd return from Switzerland after a vacation worn out by the ordeal." After dropping out of the University of Pennsylvania ("I was tired of sorority houses, tired of beer"), she became a model. ("I suppose it's 'in' to say modeling is boring. But I did find it completely dehumanizing. A model treats her face like a computer. You keep it oiled up and greased and use it like an instrument.") About that time—age 19—she landed her first movie role, in *The Group* ('66). ("They kept calling me. When I couldn't think of a good enough excuse, I saw them and got the part.") In Sidney Lumet's adaptation of Mary McCarthy's bestselling novel, she played an enigmatic Lesbian.

Except for the 1971 Mike Nicholas-Jules Feiffer *Carnal Knowledge,* her film career was, charitably speaking, lackluster for nearly a decade-and-a-half. But in *Starting Over* ('79) she revealed a hitherto untapped flair for comedy and her performance was nominated for a best supporting actress Academy Award. *Rich and Famous* ('81; George Cukor's last film) confirmed her talent for comedy. Her own sense of humor is often self-deprecating, especially when she talks of her glamorous image and her film career. "It's one of my few acknowledged strong suits—my sense of irony about myself and others." An accomplished photographer and a writer for leading national magazines and newspapers, she appropriately played photo-journalist Margaret Bourke-White in the celebrated 1982 film *Gandhi.*

The 1980's were particularly rewarding for her; an Oscar nomination in February, 1980; marriage later that year at age 34 to director Louis Malle; publication in 1984 of her acclaimed autobiography, *Knock Wood;* her Broadway debut under Nichols' direction as Sigourney Weaver's replacement in the hit play *Hurlyburly;* starring roles in made-for-television movies "Hollywood Wives" (1984) and "Mayflower Madam" (1987). A perfect match came along in 1988 when she was signed to play the title role in "Murphy Brown," a television hit that showcases her comedic talents. She impressed the critics, delighted her fans, and won the 1988 Golden Globe Award for Best Actress in a Comedy Series.

Candice shares her duplex apartment on Manhattan's Central Park South with husband Louis Malle and their daughter, Chloe (born 8 November 1985). They also spend time at his 18th-century chateau in southern France. She says, "My marriage is the keystone of my life. . . . I was really at the point where I had given up (on the idea of marrying). I had spent a lot of my life waiting for my prince, and I made some terrible mistakes in the process. It wasn't until I gave up that I found him."

Polly Bergen

"I 'm one of those people who always needs a mountain to climb. When I get as far up a mountain as I think I'm going to get, I try to find another mountain." So says this singer, actress, lecturer and businesswoman whose business venture in 1984 was designing shoes. She started in show business as a country singer, turned to pop music and movies, then branched out into TV, torching her way to an Emmy in "The Helen Morgan Story" (1957). In the late 1960s, she promoted her own cosmetic company and at one time also owned three dress shops and served on boards of corporations. Despite the demands of her business (Polly Bergen Shoes) she says she doesn't plan to give up any of her other careers, admitting

that she's something of a workaholic. "I'm not good at being idle. I suppose it comes from an early work ethic background where work is what you did." Since 1975, she's also been on the lecture circuit, talking about "The Psychology of Being a Woman" and promoting the ERA. In 1983 she made a TV dramatic "comeback" as a Navy wife on the high-rated miniseries, "Winds of War." She continued in the limelight, appearing in the film *Making Mr. Right* (1986), a TV-movie "Addicted to His Love" (1988) and then reprising her role as Pug's wife in "War & Rememberance" (1988). In 1990 she assumed the Olympia Dukakis role in the TV series version of Steel Magnolias.

Born Nellie Paulina Burgin, 14 July 1930, in Knoxville, Tenn., she was the daughter of a construction engineer and raised a Southern Baptist. She remembers growing up in "one-room apartments" and attending 45 schools in 28 states before she was 18 as the family moved around the country to road and bridge construction sites. "I was determined to be a singer," she says, and her father, who liked singing hillbilly songs almost as much as engineering, had no objections. She was a professional singer by age 13. Discovered singing hillbilly tunes in a Hollywood cafe, she was hired as the heart-shaped interest in some early Martin-Lewis films, and went on to make it big on records, in supper clubs, and on TV (her own show, plus "To Tell the Truth").

Starting in 1965, she and a partner marketed a line of turtle oil cosmetics, selling out eight years later to Faberge, and serving as a director for three years. She was the first woman appointed to the board by the Singer Company.

Her first marriage to actor Jerome Courtland ended in divorce in 1955. After marrying agent Freddie Fields in 1956, Polly retired briefly to raise their three children (his daughter by a previous marriage and two the couple adopted). They were divorced in 1975 and she married attorney Jeffrey Endervelt in 1982.

Ingmar Bergman

A poet of the joy and pain of human existence, this Swedish filmmaker has long been ranked as one of the foremost creative forces in world cinema. "His films are Munch paintings come to life," wrote one critic, "offering the highest happiness and the deepest misery. Offering all that being alive can bring." Others suggest he is "a poet with the camera," who has "a mesmeric ability to extract hidden resources from his cast." Because he has used film as a medium of personal expression, his body of work has a rare cohesiveness around one major theme—and a well-known one for any Bergman devotee: "mankind's search for love in a universe where God remains inexplicably silent." Some of his major films include *The Seventh Seal, The Magician, Wild Strawberries* (the film many consider his finest), *Through a Glass Darkly, Virgin Spring, Persona, The Silence, Hour of the Wolf, The Passion of Anna,* the multipart *Scenes from A Marriage, Cries and Whispers,* and *Fanny and Alexander,* which he has announced as his last film (and which won an Oscar as Best Foreign Language Film of 1983).

Born Ernst Ingmar Bergman 14 July 1918 in the Swedish University town of Uppsala, he endured an upbringing as the son of a clergyman that was characterized by rigid punishments of the cane and the closet. Early on he learned to escape through movies, and managed ways to see them. His childhood profoundly influenced his themes: "When you are born and brought up in a vicarage," he once said, "you are bound at an early stage to peep behind the scenes of life and death." Among his earliest toys were a magic lantern and a puppet theater, foreshadowing his present dual commitment to the screen and the stage. It was in 1937, when Bergman entered the University of Stockholm to study art history and literature, that he got his first chance to direct a play. He later dropped out of school to be a glorified errand boy at the Royal Opera House, where he began "to learn my craft." In 1940, he got a job as a scriptwriter, but his name never came to light until his first attempt at an original screenplay *Hets* (*Torment* in the American version) won eight "Charlies" (the Swedish equivalent of the Oscar), and the Grand Prix at the 1946 Cannes Film Festival. But it was not until his 1956 *Smiles of a Summer Night* that he began to gain substantial acclaim as author and director. Hollywood honored him in 1970 with the Irving Thalberg Award.

He has been credited for the development of a number of best-known Swedish stars, among them Ingrid Thulin, Liv Ullmann, Bibi Andersson, and Harriet Andersson, and is known for having wooed or married most of them. At least six marriages are known of, though his most famous relationship was with his mistress Liv Ullmann (the mother of his daughter) until in 1971 he married Ingrid von Rosen, his second wife. He has fathered nine children and is said to remain cordial with all of his ex-wives and ex-mistresses. He returned from exile (caused by tax troubles) to his homeland in 1977 to receive the Swedish academy of Letters Great Gold Medal, one of only seventeen persons to receive it in this century. In 1978 he resumed his directorship of Stockholm's Royal Dramatic Theatre, and in the same year, the Swedish Film Institute established a prize for excellence in filmmaking in his name. Letting the public share in some of his secrets and escapades, he released his autobiography *The Magic Lantern* in fall, 1988. His most recent work in film is the script about his parents' stormy marriage. This work, to be directed by Bille August, may see completion in 1990-91.

As one critic summed it up, "He has made forty-three films in forty years; he has had six wives and nine children; he has lived in exile, been sick unto death, fearful unto loathing, as well as having had the strength and charm to find life 'rich and entertaining.'" He is often found at his beloved retreat on the remote Baltic island of Faro.

Milton Berle

"**I**n my day, we did everything live. It was real; it was fun. You screwed up, tough; you had egg on your face. Now, it's all tape and retakes and canned laughter. That robs TV of its spontaneity." Such a fixture was he during the years 1948 to 1956 that Tuesdays, when his "Texaco Star Theatre" was telecast, became known as "Berlesday." Rubber-faced "Uncle Miltie" leaned heavily on props like false noses and frenetic costume changes, and in addition to usurping his own guests stars' spots he took an active

part in directing, producing, and overseeing the musicians, stagehands, and sound men on his weekly show, all with unshakable confidence. In his more recent incarnations on the tube he's been a bit more subdued and has on a number of occasions performed as a straight actor in serious dramas. But in the TV history books, the man with "the Bugs Bunny smile" will be remembered mainly as "The Thief of Badgags," "Public Energy No. 1," and the medium's first master of "brash and boisterous bombast." In 1984, in tribute to his pioneering contributions to the small screen, Berle was one of the first seven people inducted into the newly formed Television Academy Hall of Fame.

Born Milton Berlinger on 12 July 1908 in New York City, he was the son of a painter (his father) and a store detective (his mother, who later took the name of Sandra and became a renowned stage mother whose "piercing, compelling laugh cued audiences in almost every city in America"). Little Miltie started winning Charlie Chaplin contests at age six and peddled the $2 loving cups he won for 25 cents for pocket money. In his early vaudeville days, it is recorded, "he developed a stage practice that was to become a hallmark of his career—he began to collect his colleagues' jokes, songs, and bits of comedy business in the belief that all jokes are public property." At the height of his career, he had a repertoire of well over 50,000 gags.

And those gags have grown right into the 90's. In 1987, Berle's memoir *B.S. I Love You* became a bestseller ("I've been saving up these stories since I was about 14.") At the start of 1988, Berle celebrated his 40th year in television with some new bags of tricks. First he starred with fellow friends Sid Caesar and Danny Thomas in a CBS TV-movie "Side-By-Side," which featured three men who "will not be called too old." During an interview with *People,* Berle proclaimed, "A whole new generation is beginning to appreciate me." Then, in typical Uncle Miltie tradition, he graced the cover of *Spy* magazine (March, 1988) with an unforgettable pose—"That Filofax Girl." Clad in a businesswoman's attire, Milton portrays a yuppie complete with portfolio, filofax, "good legs" and sneakers. In 1990 he participated in a Friars Club roast of Zsa Zsa Gabor.

Twice married and twice divorced from actress Joyce Matthews (who later was also twice married and divorced from the late Billy Rose), he married Ruth Cosgrove in 1953 (she died in April 1989). They have one adopted son.

Corbin Bernsen

C orbin Bernsen is a player. Whether he's male-chauvinist divorce attorney Arnie Becker in the long-playing TV series "L.A. Law," or third baseman Roger Dorn in the film *Major League*, he's always acting in top form. This 6-foot, 175-lb, blond-haired, blue-eyed hunk is the subject of many women's fantasies, and the male spokesperson for a brassiere company.

Born 7 September, the son of a popular daytime-television actress Jeanne Cooper of "The Young and The Restless," Bernsen was destined for a theatrical career. Not satisfied as a philosophy student at Humboldt State College, he transferred to the UCLA Theatre Arts Department and earned a Masters Degree in Playwriting. Migrating to New York City, he landed roles Off-Broadway in such plays as *Lone Star*, and in the touring company of *Plaza Suite*. Following in his mom's footsteps, he was cast in a continuing part in the soap "Ryan's Hope." His role on "L.A. Law" brought him back to the West Coast and has earned him two Emmy nominations plus a Golden Globe nomination. His character tied the knot at the end of the 89-90 season.

Bernsen's good looks and proven acting ability have paved the way for motion picture offers. He has appeared in *The Sofia Conspiracy* (1986), *Hello Again* (with Shelley Long in 1987), *Bert Rigby, You're a Fool* (1989), *Major League* (1989), and *Disorganized Crime* (with Lou Diamond Phillips in 1989). Divorced from his first wife, Corbin married actress Amanda Pays 19 November 1988. The couple have a son Oliver born 14 March 1989.

Bernardo Bertolucci

"I don't follow a script," asserts the Italian film director whose 1972 film—*Last Tango in Paris*—earned him a conviction for obscenity. "I write one, mostly for producers, and then close it. I prefer to go on the memory of what I've written rather than film an illustration of words. All film for me is cinema *verité*, and that means capturing what happens naturally between two actors in front of the camera, unrehearsed and unprepared." Though this may be so, the director of the well-received *Before the Revolution*

(1964) and *The Conformist* (1969) careful-ly crafts his films to shock bourgeois sensibilities by flouting social taboos and touting Marxism.

This aging enfant terrible has long been obsessed by the theme of intergenerational conflict, and he regu-larly sets his highly personal screen dramas in and around his native Parma, in the Po Valley. His monumental *1900*, released here in 1977, covers 45 years of Italian history in slightly over four hours. It is, wrote Vincent Canby, "essentially a Marxist romance," and "an antholo-gy of various kinds of indecision." ("It is a great film," *Newsweek* concluded, "but it is also a great 'Yes, but' film.") *Luna* (1979), about an American singer and her heroin-addict teen-age son, is a "no-holds-barred probe of mother-son incest" (*Women's Wear Daily*). Andrew Sarris noted that the director "has shown once more that he is not afraid to take chances," but Donald Barthelme (*The New Yorker*) felt that he "slips badly here" and called the film "near-ludicrous."

In *Tragedy of a Ridiculous Man* (1982), a "cerebrally tantalizing" story of the kidnapping by terrorists of the wealthy "Ridiculous Man's" son, the director for the first time sided with the father. But the fact that the viewer never learns who perpetrated the kidnap-ping caused an impatient Pauline Kael to brand it "a dopey movie—complex yet undramatic . . . like an old man's movie."

Bertolucci traveled to China to film 1987's *The Last Emperor*. He was fascinated with the story of Pu Yi, "an extraordinary anti-hero of modern times. He had been kidnapped on a gust of wind by history and at the age of 3 set on the throne of China." Bernardo's intense interest in seeing this story on the screen ensured that this film would be a huge success. *The Last Emperor* won the Golden Globe Awards across the board—Best Dramatic Picture, Best Direc-tor, Best Screenplay and Best Original Score. The 1987 Academy Awards honored the film with two Oscars: Best Director and Best Screenplay Adaptation. Bertolucci served as head of the Cannes Film Festival jury in 1990.

Born 16 March 1940, the son of a respected poet and film critic, Bertolucci won early fame for his poetry but then switched to film-making. His mentor was Pier Paolo Pasolini, and he completed his first film, *The Grim Reaper*, at 21. He is married to Clare Peptoe, and—oddly, for one so concerned about generation gaps—has no children.

Jacqueline Bisset

She always seems a bit put out by being beautiful. When writers refer to her "luminous" gray-green eyes, mane of copper-gold brown hair, her "classic cheekbones" and "sensuous" mouth. Bisset pooh-pooh's her image. "Producers aren't necessarily interested in beautiful women but those who are pleasant-looking, and I just happen to fall into that category along with dozens of other actresses. . . . I'm just an average woman who has worked hard all her life. My folks weren't rich, and I never made any conscious effort to be glamourous. I avoided Hollywood parties. They are abysmal. . . . I happen to like good quality, and never wore cheap clothes even in those days when I worked as a waitress."

Born Jacqueline Fraser Bisset in Weybridge, England, 13 September 1944, she wanted to be a ballet dancer, but had to give up her ambition because she was "to tall and had too many bones." She left her home, a centuries-old thatched-roof cottage where she was the only daughter of a general practitioner and a mother who had been a barrister in Paris. After attending a private girls' school, Bisset began modeling. She posed for famed British photographer David Bailey in British *Vogue* and *Queen* layouts, and appeared in many TV commercials. When she was broke, she toiled as a waitress in a less-than-fancy London coffee shop.

Her first film was a bit part in *The Knack*, followed by several more small parts, including a featured role in Roman Polanski's *Cul-de-Sac*. Then, by landing a slithering part in *Casino Royale*, playing "Giovanna Goodthighs," a sexy spy whose mission was to seduce and then do away with a secret agent played by Peter Sellers, she won the attention of Twentieth Century-Fox, which signed her for a long-term contract. Her first Fox film was *Two for the Road*. She replaced Mia Farrow as Frank Sinatra's co-star in *The Detective* when Farrow and Sinatra announced the end of their short-lived marriage. This sparked much publicity heat and set Bisset on the path of overnight, spontaneous celebrity.

Her other films include *Bullitt*, *Airport*, *The Mephisto Waltz*, and Francois Truffaut's *Day for Night*, a performance critic Vincent Canby called "hugely funny" and "hugely affecting." The part allowed her to be taken seriously by Hollywood as an actress. She has since starred in *The Deep* (that shot of her in her wet T-shirt was a sexy lucky-fluke nobody had planned on), *The Greek Tycoon, Who is Killing the Great Chefs of Europe?, Under the Volcano, Class, Rich and Famous* (an MGM release with Candice Bergen), plus the TV movies "Forbidden" and a remake of "Anna Karenina". In 1987 she played Josephine to Armand Assante's Napoleon in ABC's historical three-part mini-series "Napoleon and Josephine: The Love Story." Movies in 1989 include *L'amoureuse* and *Scenes From the Class Struggle in Beverly Hills.* In 1990 she appeared in the steamy, controversial *Wild Orchid.*

Switching to real life, Bisset remains in a continual struggle with her main squeeze, ballet dancer Alexander Godunov. Their on-again, off-again romance attracts tabloid headlines, but Bisset maintains, "I'm fascinated by a man with a twinkle in his eye, someone with irony and humor. A certain kind of chutzpah or cheekiness is also very appealing—a daring or courage in their manner."

Karen Black

She was the acid-tripping whore of *Easy Rider* in 1969, the warm and unforgettable waitress in *Five Easy Pieces* (for which she was nominated for an Oscar in 1970), and a nymphomaniac in 1972's *Portnoy's Complaint.* After several uneven box office flicks she again drew important roles in such cinematic trailblazers as *The Day of the Locust* (1975) and Robert Altman's *Nashville* (1975). She has even added a cabaret performance to her talents. The woman once said to have a "lopsided caricature of a pretty face" because of her close-set eyes, is the attractive, one-time Karen Blanche Ziegler, born near Chicago in Park Ridge, Illinois, on 1 July 1942. Although she decided to become a movie star at age seven, she dropped out of high school to marry. Soon divorced, she attended Northwestern for two years before at last taking steps to "get on with it" by going for broke as an actress in New York. She found herself performing in two Off-Broadway revues and she studied with Lee Strasberg at Actor's Studio. ("I'm pretty impatient with all these acting teachers who can't act themselves and therefore don't have the slightest idea of what you're going through.") She was a night clerk, a waitress, then got a role in the thriller, *The Playroom*, called "one of the best and least attended Broadway productions of 1965." Next? Hollywood and a part in a film, many TV dramas, and finally a call from Dennis Hopper concerning something or other called *Easy Rider* he wanted to do. In 1982 she returned to Broadway as a Texan transsexual in *Come Back to the Five and Dime, Jimmy Dean,* with Cher and Sandy Dennis.

A glance at some Karen Black film titles from the 80's alerts the audience to an interesting viewing experience. They include: *Invaders From Mars* (1986), *Night Angel* (1988), *Home and Eddie* (1988), *Out of the Dark* (1988) and *The Invisible Kid* (1988). She branched out in a different direction in 1988, making her cabaret debut at the Los Angeles Cinegrill.

Thrice divorced, she married her fourth husband, Steven Eckelbery (film editor), in 1987. The couple live in California with their daughter, Celine (1987). Karen also has a son, Hunter Minor Norman (1975) from a previous marriage. She says: "A lot of love now occurs in this business: people helping each other to do good work, getting high on each other's success. Isn't that great?"

Shirley Temple Black

Responding on cue when mother said, "Sparkle, Shirley," she became the movie miracle of the Depression years, the most successful child star in Hollywood history, and the biggest box-office draw of her day. "I stopped believing in Santa Claus at an early age," she recalled later. "Mother took me to see Santa Claus in a Hollywood department store and he asked for my autograph." Unlike many other toddler stars, she emerged from her Hollywood years with both psyche and bankroll intact and became the model of a modern suburban woman, dedicated to home, family, good works, and conservative politics. Credited with raising almost $1 million for the Republican Party, she made an unsuccessful bid for Congress in 1967, was named Ambassador to Ghana (1974-76) by President Nixon and was chief of protocol at the Ford White House 1976-77.

Born 23 April 1928 in Santa Monica, California, the daughter of a bank clerk (her earnings were later to total half the bank's total assets), she was spotted by a talent scout in dancing school and was firmly entrenched as a superstar by the time she was five—relentlessly adorable in such films as *Little Miss Marker, The Little Colonel,* and *The Littlest Rebel.* She still avows it was a "perfect childhood" marred only by the shock of discovering her 12th birthday was really her 13th. (Her parents had cooperated with the studio press department in lopping off a year from her real age.) After a few modest junior miss roles, she retired from the screen, married actor John Agar (one daughter), and then the wealthy Socially-Registered Charles A. Black, whom she met while recuperating from her divorce in Honolulu. Their children (two) are now grown. While Black went to work as a $1-a-year man in the administration of then-governor Ronald Reagan, Shirley became more and more interested in civic affairs.

She needed an extra measure of determination when in late 1972 she not only underwent surgery for breast cancer, but publicly announced the operation so that "women will not be afraid to go to their doctors for diagnosis when they have unusual symptoms," adding that she was "grateful to God, my family, and my doctors for the successful outcome, because I have much more to accomplish before I am through."

Shirley published her appropriately titled autobiography, *Child Star,* in 1988. The book was a national bestseller, bringing back highlights of that little girl who encouraged everyone to join her "On the Good Ship Lollipop."

Earl Blackwell

He has been called the present-day Ward McAllister (by columnist Suzy). "The Celebrity pied piper" by Palm Beach's *Shiny Sheet,* "The Ringmaster" by *Women's Wear Daily* and "Mr. Celebrity" throughout Europe and the United States. Each of those designations is correct . . . yet incomplete. For in addition to Earl's friendship with some of the 20th century's most celebrated movers and shakers—from Winston Churchill to President and Mrs. Reagan, from Brooke Shields to Lillian Gish—and his chairmanship of the world's foremost information bureau on celebrities (with offices in New York, Hollywood, London, Paris and Rome), the peripatetic courtly southern gentleman is also actively involved on a number of other fronts. Co-author of *Crystal Clear* and *Skyrocket*, he and longtime friend and companion Eugenia Sheppard completed their third novel—*All About Love*—shortly before her death in 1984. In 1975 Blackwell endowed a scholarship at his alma mater, Oglethorpe University in Atlanta, for deserving journalism students. Each year he supervises the induction ceremonies for the Theater Hall of Fame (honoring Broadway notables) which he originated in 1971 and of which he is chairman. He is also founder and president of Gotham's exclusive social club the Nine O'Clocks of New York. Each day he dictates a few more pages of his autobiography, which he expects to complete within the next few years. He served as editor-in-chief of the previous edition of *Celebrity Register*. The breakneck pace is maintained in spite of the fact that in 1988 Earl celebrated his 75th birthday and has been waging a spirited battle against Parkinson's disease since 1981. A product of southern gentility, Earl Blackwell was born 3 May 1913 in Atlanta, the son of cotton broker Samuel Earl Blackwell and the former Carrie Lagomarsino into whose Roman Catholic faith he was baptized (he was made a Knight of Malta in the early 1980's). After graduating from Oglethorpe, which he entered at 16, he made his way to Hollywood, was offered a contract by Louis B. Mayer, but had more success making friends—among them Joan Crawford, Tyrone Power, Merle Oberon and Ginger Rogers—than in achieving film stardom.

In 1938 Earl came to New York with a play he had written, *Aries is Rising*. It opened at the John Golden Theatre in November, 1939, starring Constance Collier, and closed two weeks later. In a *Cosmopolitan* profile (1985) he recalled, "I had failed on Broadway and I hadn't set the woods on fire in Hollywood either. Then along came a journalist from Atlanta who mentioned she had to contact a celebrity. I immediately furnished her with the star's telephone number." After this was repeated several times Earl realized he had always been interested in famous people, ever since childhood when he caddied for Bobby Jones. That's how Celebrity Service was born. Today, celebrating his 50th Anniversary in the business, Earl is Chairman of the company owned by Vicki Bagley (purchased in 1985). Celebrity Service's international network knows how to locate a half million celebrities—stars of stage, screen and TV, ballplayers, ballerinas, writers, wrestlers, opera singers, Olympians, politicians and pedagogues, heart surgeons and historians—throughout the world.

Earl Blackwell's fame rests as well with his memorable—and newsworthy—special events. When the organizers of JFK's 1962 birthday party at Madison Square Garden wanted someone to sing "Happy Birthday Mr. President" they turned to Earl, and he produced Marilyn Monroe. Earl organized the opening of the art museum in Oslo (1968) for Sonja Henie, the legendary Norwegian queen of the ice. When Israel celebrated its 25th anniversary in 1973, he staged a cast of a thousand at the Tower of David for his friend, Golda Meier. He is also well known as a host. The stately London *Times* dubbed his fabulous costume ball in Venice (1967) "the party of the century".

Claire Bloom

"**I** think that few professions— from the beginning of a career until the end—have so much to do with chance and so little to do with the calculation of will," wrote this actress in her memoir *Limelight and After* (1982). Throughout her career, chance has complemented the considerable talent of this British-born actress who (in the words of critic Walter Kerr) "could not be more beautiful without upsetting the balance of nature." She made her Old Vic debut as Shakespeare's Juliet at age 21 and a few weeks later was catapulted to international fame co-starring with Charlie Chaplin in his 1952 film *Limelight*. Since then, she's become a regular Atlantic-hopper, appearing in classics on stage, film, and TV with a veritable Who's Who of the British and American theater. She's also one of the foremost Shakespearean actresses, gaining her reputation playing opposite the three great "Sirs" of the British theater: John Gielgud, Ralph Richardson, and Laurence Olivier.

Born in London, 15 February 1931, Claire Bloom is the product of the great tradition of British acting—with a disordered childhood thrown in. Her family was constantly on the move, due mainly to her irresponsible father. With the coming of the World War II blitz, Claire, her mother and brother, moved to Florida and it was there that she began to perform—first in Miami resort hotels to raise money for British War Relief, and then on radio in New York. But already pointed toward a stage career ("I wanted to be an actress ever since I was three"), and homesick for London, she returned to England to study despite the buzz bombs, and soon became a teenaged regular on the BBC, debuting as a prostitute ("I hardly knew what the word meant") in *Diary of an Opium Eater*. After her stage debut at age 16 with the Oxford Repertory Company, her first major role came a year later—as Ophelia at Stratford-upon-Avon.

Her first London appearance was in Gielgud's production of *The Lady's Not for Burning*.

Among her notable stage roles at the Old Vic was Cordelia to Gielgud's *Lear*. She's appeared in such films as *Richard III*(with Olivier) and *The Spy Who Came in from the Cold* (with Richard Burton). Recent highlights include a stunning turn in the sexual-political Brit pic *Sammy and Rosie Get Laid* (1987). In New York, she's had leading roles in *A Doll's House* and *Hedda Gabler* among others. She and Olivier starred as Lord and Lady Marchmain in the 1982 TV series "Brideshead Revisited"; and in 1983 she was in theaters with her one-woman show, *These Are Women: A Portrait of Shakespeare's Heroines*. Says Bloom of the Bard: "Shakespeare is really our contemporary. His works are extremely personal, depending on your stage of life. When you're in first love, there is the glory and poetry of *Romeo and Juliet*. In confusion, you can find rhyme and reason in *Hamlet*. And what better touches the problems of rejection and loneliness in old age than *King Lear*?"

Married first to actor Rod Steiger after appearing with him on Broadway in *Rashomon* (one daughter), she wed producer Hillard Eikens in 1969. That marriage, too, ended in divorce. She now lives, partly in the U.S., partly in London, with novelist Philip Roth.

Dirk Bogarde

Number-one box-office draw in postwar pre-Beatles Britain (as the star of light comic films), Dirk Bogarde emerged in the 1960s as a serious actor (*The Servant, Darling*, then later in the 1970s in *Justine* and *Death in Venice*). The turning point, as he sees it, came with his appearance in the film *Victim*. Until then, he reflected, "all the British ever did" about his success was call up and ask "How did it happen?" But after *Victim* the press was "wonderful." "They accepted the film as a thriller hung on a serious theme," he told the *New York Times*. "It was a tremendous departure, playing my first queer . . . the fanatics who had been sending me 4,000 letters a week stopped overnight . . . not because I was playing a homosexual, but because I was playing a middle-aged man."

Born Dirk Niven van de Bogaerde, 29 March 1921 in London, England, he made his film debut in *Esther Waters*, over which he thinks it best to "draw a cool veil" ("I was billed as Burke Gocarte"), played in the stage version of *The Power and the Glory* ("I had a great scene in the third act where I screamed my head off. That's where I got notices"), and later came to harbor great admiration for the plays of Harold Pinter ("Harold has said I am one of the best players of his work"). Though cast in serious roles, Bogarde does not see the cinema as an educational force. "You're never going to change anything by making a film, saying 'Look, this is what you shouldn't do, dears!'. . . . People like being bad. If you learn anything from a movie, it's up to you." Audiences may or may not have learned anything from *Despair* (1977) or *A Bridge Too Far* (1976). Bogarde has also written three highly-praised books, generally autobiographical: *A Postillion Struck by Lightning* (1977), *Snakes and Ladders* (1979), and *A Gentle Occupation* (1980). He appeared in *The Vision* in 1988.

Sonny Bono

"**H**e was tough/he was hard/ but he was kind. And he was loved cause guys like him were hard to find." Sonny sang his song "A Cowboy's Work Is Never Done" with his ex-wife and partner Cher in 1971, never realizing that over 18 years later he would be running a city. Elected Mayor of Palm Springs, California, on 12 April 1988, Sonny could use for a slogan his other original composition, "United We Stand." He cheers: "Palm Springs has earned and maintained its status as a premier resort destination for decades. We must continue to grow and offer the services and facilities visitors expect in a glamorous resort—and to promote our assets—so we can retain that reputation of excellence."

On 16 February 1935, Salvatore Bono debuted into the world in Detroit, Michigan, as the son of Santo and Jean Bono. His family had very little money but they tried to make ends meet during the early years. When Sonny was seven, the Bonos moved to Los Angeles and his parents eventually divorced. Finding his forte was writing songs, not doing his homework, young Bono dropped out of high school. While songplugging, he worked such odd jobs as grocery store delivery boy, waiter, construction worker, butcher's helper, and even truck driver. His demos finally hit pay dirt when he landed a job in 1957 as a songwriter/producer for Sam Cooke, Little Richard and Larry Williams. His first minor hit was "Koko Joe," performed by the Righteous Brothers in 1964. His first big success was the popular "Needles and Pins," for Jackie de Shannon. Moving onward and upward, Bono switched over to work as an A&R man at Phillies Records (associated with Phil Spector's "wall of sound" techniques) and used the job as a learning experience. Bono received the chance to write, sing and play with such artists as Darlene Love and the Ronettes. While maturing musically at Phillies, he met his future wife, Cherilyn Sarkisian LaPiere, a teenager trying to launch her own singing career. The couple were married within a year, on 27 October 1964. In an interview with the *New York Times* Bono said, "I thought Cher was a natural star immediately. She was a real generator for me." Originally billed as "Caesar and Cleo," they decided to use the nicknames "Sonny & Cher" on recordings. Their life together was a blast; the duo's debut single "The Letter" fared well and their next record "Baby Don't Go" zoomed to the top of the pop charts, followed by the classics "I Got You Babe," "Bang Bang (My Baby Shot Me Down)", and "All I Really Want To Do." They had sold over 40,000,000 records by 1967. Rock stars sometimes don't last forever, and the singers stumbled out of popularity in 1968. Investing in a campy film, *Good Times*, in which husband and wife played themselves—an affluent pair of singing stars— they lost money. By 1969 they were broke, but Bono had the insight to reshape their image, forming a nightclub act to attract an adult audience. CBS television executive Fred Silverman flipped over their new act and signed them to do a summer replacement show.

The "Sonny and Cher Show" was a ratings success, propelling a pick-up as a continuing weekly variety hour. Everything seemed sensational, until the couple's personal and professional split in 1974. Their divorce became final in 1975. Going forward, Sonny had a short-lived solo television show, "The Sonny Comedy Revue," and many special guestspot appearances, including an episode of "Love Boat." As an actor he appeared in such films as *Airplane II, Troll, Escape to Athena, Wipeout,* and *Hairspray.* Searching for his new niche, Sonny went into the restaurant business and opened the "Bono" restaurant in Hollywood, followed by one in Houston. He eventually sold those two and opened the "Bono" restaurant in Palm Springs, serving Sicilian-style Italian cuisine. He insists, "This is not California nouvelle cuisine; it's real, hearty peasant food." As everyone knows, his other speciality lies in pleasing people. Hence, Bono's role as Mayor. Almost fifteen years after their split, Sonny and Cher delighted their fans with an impromptu reunion on the "Late Night with David Letterman" show, during which they performed an emotionally-charged "I Got You Babe."

There is a soft side to Sonny; in his song "You'd Better Sit Down

Kids" he tells a heart-tugging story about divorce. Married four times, Sonny's teenage first marriage produced one child, Christine. Sonny and Cher's union produced a daughter, Chastity. He married model/actress Susie Coelho in 1981; they split in 1984. Finding stability, Sonny married model/champion gymnast Mary Whitaker of Pasadena in March 1986. They have a son, Chesaré Elan (born 25 April 1988). "And the beat goes on. . . . "

Marlon Brando

"**Y**ou see that," he said to a companion when two fans wanted to shake his hand, "they are preconditioned. I'm just another S.O.B. sitting in a motor home and they come looking for Zeus. I could have been a Malaysian orangutan. . . . You know. I don't mind what people think about me; they can write whatever they want. I've been devotedly indifferent, I don't even bother suing them. . . . Personally, I'm not interested in making an assessment of myself and stripping myself for the general public to view. We put to sleep our notions about ourselves that are real and dream others."

Born 3 April 1924 in Omaha, Nebraska, he moved with his family to Evanston, then Libertyville, Ill., attending and getting expelled from schools in each town. When he finally turned to ditch digging, his father offered to finance training in any field he chose, so Brando followed older sisters Frances (an art student) and Jocelyn (an actress) to New York, where he enrolled first in Erwin Piscator's Dramatic Workshop and then in the Actor's Studio. His Broadway debut was in *I Remember Mama*(1944) and then he was directed by Elia Kazan for the first time in *Truckline Cafe,* which he followed with a much discussed Marchbanks to Katharine Cornell's 1946 *Candida.*

He was directed again by Kazan as Stanley Kowalski in *Streetcar Named Desire,* a performance that continues to influence subsequent generations of actors. He went to Hollywood after *Streetcar* in 1950 to play a paraplegic in *The Men,* followed by the film version of the Tennessee Williams classic. For a long time it seemed he was brilliant under Kazan's direction (e.g., *Streetcar, Viva Zapata,* and *On the Waterfront*) and bad to mediocre when directed by almost anyone else (*Desire, Guys and Dolls, The Ugly American, Julius Caesar, A Countess from Hong Kong, Morituri, Bedtime Story, Sayonara, Teahouse of the August Moon, Nightcomers, The Missouri Breaks* and *Superman*; exception: *The Wild Ones.*)

Said colleague Rod Steiger: "Marlon was in a unique position. He could have done anything. But he didn't choose to." He insisted that his role in *The Young Lions* be rewritten as more sympathetic, which weakened the film; he took over as director of *One-Eyed Jacks*, bringing the film in late and over budget. *Mutiny on the Bounty* was renamed "The Mutiny of Marlon Brando" as he battled several directors, most of the actors, and the scriptwriter.

Brando married and divorced Anna Kashfi and then Motiva Castenada and was involved in a well-publicized custody fight for his three children—Christian Devi, Miko and Rebecca. He fathered Simon (Tehotu) and a daughter Cheyenne with his third wife Tarita who played his lady-love in *Mutiny on the Bounty*. He settled with her on Tetiaroa, a South Sea atoll of 13 islands that he bought in 1966. Brando's career seemed in serious decline until his stunning performance as Don Corleone in *The Godfather*. Next he shocked the world in the controversial *Last Tango in Paris*, but his performance as a grief-stricken widower who plunges into a bizarre, sexually complicated affair with a young woman about whom he knows nothing (played by Maria Schneider) won him a whole new generation of international fans. (Brando exposed more than his body in *Last Tango*—the sex may be staged but the dialogue is real; director Bernardo Bertolucci insisted not only on improvisation but on Brando making himself the character Paul.) Awarded the Oscar in 1972 for his role in *The Godfather*, Brando asked a young American Indian actress to appear at the award ceremony on his behalf and refuse the award as a protest against America's and Hollywood's treatment of the American Indian. In 1979 Brando gave what some critics consider his finest performance in Francis Coppola's *Apocalypse Now*. Controversy continued to stalk the American Olivier, however, and in 1990 his son was charged with commiting murder in the famed actor's L.A. home.

Recent films include *A Dry White Season* (1989) and *The Freshman* (1990). He was the narrator for a 1986 film titled *Raoni*.

Jeff Bridges

Once upon a time he was known as Hollywood's playboy hippie, a reputation that came from his widely publicized

experiments with est, marijuana and LSD—not to mention Candy Clark, Valerie Perrine and Cybil Shepherd. He'd become a star in 1971 via his appealing portrayal of a troubled Texas youth in *The Last Picture Show* and was nominated for the first of three Oscar nominations. (The others were *Thunderbolt and Lightfoot* in 1974 and *Starman* in 1985.) But by playing the first beefcake extraterrestrial in the history of Hollywood flicks in 1984's *Starman*, Jeff Bridges emerged from past critically-appreciated, quirky, but oftentimes noncommercial parts to become as well-beloved and desired as the Teddy Bear (who also enjoyed a wide-spread revival in 1984-85).

The son of actor Lloyd and kid brother of Beau, Jeff Bridges was born in Los Angeles, California, 4 December 1949. He made his acting debut at age eight on his father's popular TV series "Sea Hunt" and at age 14 toured in summer stock with his dad. As a teenager he recalls improvising scenes from J.D. Salinger's *Catcher in the Rye* with brother Beau on the platform of a flatbed truck which they would rent and park in different L.A. grocery store lots, their audience made up of shoppers and children. "If the cops came," Bridges says, "we'd just jump into the cab of the truck and zip off to the next one." After studying acting at N.Y.'s Hagen-Berghof Studio and a stint in the Coast Guard, he made his film debut in *Halls of Anger* (1970). After his success in *The Last Picture Show* he appeared in *Fat City*, *Bad Company* (both 1972), *The Iceman Cometh* (1973), *Rancho Deluxe* and *Hearts of the West* (1975). He was also in a couple of celebrated fiascos: the remake of *King Kong* in 1976 and *Heaven's Gate* in 1980. In 1976 he was in *Stay Hungry* and in 1984 the sexy *Against All Odds*. In 1985 he filmed *The Jagged Edge* and *Eight Million Ways to Die*. More movies followed: *The Morning After* (1986), *Nadine* (1987), *Tucker: The Man and His Dream* (1988), *See You In The Morning* (1988) and *The Fabulous Baker Boys* (1989). For 1990 release he filmed the sequel to *The Last Picture Show*, reprising his role for *Texasville*.

Bridges is married to the photographer Susan Gaston, and with their two daughters, they live in Santa Monica and on a ranch in Montana where the actor relaxes between movies and composes music, paints and writes. He is involved in several social causes; foremost among them is the End Hunger Network, and organization he helped to found that intends, via the media, to end hunger on the planet.

Lloyd Bridges

P laying a patriarchal tycoon on the 1984 series "Paper Dolls" was just his latest tube adventure. "Damp good," said one critic dryly of his performance as "Sea Hunt's skindiving Mike Nelson, a million-dollar role in which he submerged himself for 156 watery TV weeks in the late '50s and early '60s. Later, waterlogged but not weary, he surfaced for his own TV anthology show, a western series called "The Loner," a Broadway run in *Cactus Flower* and such films as *The Happy Ending* (1969) and the hit *Airplane!* (1980). The younger generation knows him best as the father of actors Beau and Jeff.

A native Californian, born 15 January 1913 in San Leandro, he arrived before the cameras of Hollywood and Marineland via Broadway. After studying dramatics at UCLA, he met and married his leading lady, Dorothy Simpson. They taught drama briefly on the East Coast and he made his Broadway debut in *Othello*. During the WW II years he appeared in over two dozen 'B' films for Columbia. His tall, blond, rugged good looks suited him for westerns and action movies, sometimes as a heavy. After leaving his studio in 1945, he began freelancing and his roles improved. His better films include: *A Walk in the Sun* (1945), *Canyon Passage* (1946), *Home of the Brave* (1949), *The Sound of Fury* (aka *Try and Get Me*, 1951), *High Noon* (1952), *The Rainmaker* (1956) and *The Goddess* (1958). Occasionally he has returned to the stage, including a two-week stint in *Man of La Mancha* ("What a ball I had singing"). Recent roles include appearances in "North and South Book II" (1986 TV movie) and films *The Devil's Odds* (1987) and *Winter People* (1989). In 1988, he played the bad guy opposite his son Jeff in the film *Tucker*.

Lloyd Bridges lives with his wife near UCLA, where they first met, as well as in the High Sierra Mountains and at Malibu Beach. Besides Beau and Jeff, they have a daughter, Lucinda. He enjoys traveling and playing tennis for charities. In the early 1950s he had been a key witness before the House Un-American Activities Committee after affirming his past membership in the Communist Party. His career suffered no setback after his testimony. Like his son Beau (Lloyd 3rd), he doesn't much like his given name. His father called him Bud.

Matthew Broderick

"**A**t times I wanted to be a fireman, a baseball player and a veterinarian, but never an actor. Actually, between the time I was 3 until the age of 13, acting was the last thing I ever wanted to do." But the only son of the late James Broderick (best remembered as the gentle, thoughtful father on the award-winning "Family" TV series) changed his mind in time to become a star, at 21, of both stage and screen. In *War Games,* one of the biggest box office draws of 1983, he played a 16-year-old computer whiz who unwittingly taps into a Defense Department computer and brings the world to the brink of nuclear disaster; in his Broadway debut in Neil Simon's *Brighton Beach Memoirs,* he collected a Tony as the playwright's boyhood alter-ego. He essayed the same role in 1985 in Simon's *Biloxi Blues.*

Matthew Broderick was born in New York City on 21 August 1962. When he was 5, his dad wanted him to do a small role in a play, but "it really scared me," he recalls. "I remember kicking and screaming. I just couldn't do it." Later, he spent a number of school vacations touring with his father on the summer stock circuit and got hooked. "My sisters would be bored, but I would just hang around and watch rehearsals. I just liked being backstage and I loved watching my father work." His decision to take up acting himself came during his final years at NYC's Walden School and, just prior to graduation in 1979, he made his professional debut appearing with his father in an Off-Off-Broadway production of Horton Foote's *Valentine's Day.* He was first spotted as an actor "with a distinctive presence that argues a bright future" in the original Off-Off-Broadway incarnation of Harvey Fierstein's *Torch Song Trilogy* and made his film debut in a not-so-successful Neil Simon film, *Max Dugan Returns.*

Broderick appeared in a steady stream of films throughout the '80s: *Ladyhawke* (1984), *Ferris Bueller's Day Off* (1986), *Project X* (1986), *Biloxi Blues* (1987), *Torch Song Trilogy* (1988), *Family Business* (1989), *The Freshman* (1990) and *Lay This Laurel* (1989). He starred Off-Broadway in *The Widow Claire* (1986) and was seen in Athol Fugard's drama "Master Harold . . . and the Boys" (1985) on PBS television. He helped present the Tony awards in 1990. While on a visit to

Ireland, Broderick was involved in a car accident that landed him in a hospital in Belfast (August 1987). He was later charged with reckless driving.

Once the steady date of Jennifer Grey, Broderick is currently single; he maintains apartments in Los Angeles and New York City.

James Brolin

Known best for many seasons as the eager young associate of Robert Young on the doctor-knows-best series, " Marcus Welby, M.D.", James Brolin has been by choice one of Hollywood's underemployed actors. After hanging up his stethoscope, he bided his time with occasional film and TV roles, until he was lured back to series television in 1983 to play the swinging, laidback manager of the St. Gregory on ABC's glossy "Hotel".

The son of a Los Angeles builder, Brolin, born 18 July 1940, had early ambitions as an aviator but was sidetracked by the lure of Hollywood. "I was also a big moviegoer. One day I got a tour through a studio and I was hooked." After leaving UCLA in 1958 to pursue auditions, he landed a contract with 20th Century-Fox, and later with Universal. "I never really starved." He appeared in the 1964 ABC series "The Monroes" before being cast as Dr. Steven Kiley on "Marcus Welby" in 1969. For six years he argued medical ethics, rode a tame motorcycle, and fell in love with women patients who invariably succumbed to disease before the hour was up, leaving him free to love once more. He recapped the role lightheartedly for a good cause on the 1990 Earth Day Special.

Brolin's film credits include the generally panned *Gable and Lombard* (in which he played the screen idol), the supernatural thriller *The Amityville Horror*, and *Capricorn One*. *He also showed considerable panache as Pee-Wee Herman's alter ego in Pee Wee's Big Adventure* (1985), playing opposite sex bomb Morgan Fairchild. Brolin and his wife, Jane Agee, a wildlife enthusiast whom he married in 1967, dissolved their marriage in 1985 (two sons: Josh James, Jess). He took up with "WKRP" actress Jan Smithers and married her in a nonlegal ceremony (June, 1986) in Nova Scotia. The couple actually made their union legal later that year when they remarried in Carmel, California. They have one daughter, Molly Elizabeth, born 28 November 1987.

Charles Bronson

"I'm not making pictures for messages, nor do I do parts where I would get some self-satisfaction," says this actor who's been likened to "a college wrestler with the face of an Inca mask." "It's the quality of the work that I strive for. And when I say quality, I mean quality that satisfies me, not some fat-ass critic in New York in a swivel chair." Never the conventional Hollywood matinee idol, he became a world-wide superstar at fifty after nearly twenty years of playing bit parts, heavies, or the hero's friend. It wasn't until he transferred operations to Europe that the magic happened and, in 1972, a poll of Hollywood's Foreign Press Association showed him to be the actor with biggest box-office appeal outside U.S. borders. He was the number-one sex symbol in Spain, *Le Sacré Monstre* in France, *Il Brutto* ("the ugly one") in Italy, and in 1979, he received the Gold Star Award as the film industry's top international star, renowned the world over for his screen image of "strength and determination." Actually, these qualities are much more than mere image, for they are the very roots of his early life.

Born in the scrubby Pennsylvania coal town of Ehrenfield (in a section known as Scooptown) on 3 November 1921, Charlie Buchinsky followed his dad and two elder brothers into the mines helping to support twelve younger siblings and their mother after their father's death. He worked underground until he was drafted into the Army during World War II and didn't hit on the notion of becoming an actor until he was 27. Enrolling in the Pasadena Playhouse in 1950, he was soon spotted on stage by director Henry Hathaway and offered a small role in the 1951 Gary Cooper film, *You're In the Navy Now*, in which his one big scene involved belching on cue. He made a number of films in Hollywood but didn't become a bona fide star until 1968 when he began making pictures in France and Italy, most notably Sergio Leone's "spaghetti western" *Once Upon a Time in the West*. He finally was accepted as a U.S. star after the hit *Death Wish* (in which he played an architect-turned-vigilante) in 1974. Subsequent films (he'd made a total of 63 by 1984) include *Hard Times*

(1976), *St. Ives* (1976), TV's "Raid on Entebbe" (1977) and sequels to *Death Wish* in 1981, 1986, and 1987. More Bronson movies include *Murphy's Law* (1986), *Messenger of Death* (1988), *Kinjite* (1989) and *The Golem* (1989). He also appeared in the HBO presentation "Act of Vengeance" (1986).

It was in 1963, during the filming of *The Great Escape*, that Bronson met future wife Jill Ireland (his first wife was Harriet Tendler, Jill's first husband was actor David McCallum). After their marriage in 1969, they appeared together frequently on the big screen (e.g. *The Valachi Papers*, 1972.) "After being in five pictures with him," Ireland once said, "I'm prepared to have him come home still playing the role. It's like making love to five different guys." The parents of five children, they made their home in a Bel Air mansion. Ireland died 18 May 1990 after a six-year battle with cancer, during which she provided inspiration for many through her books and personal appearances.

Mel Brooks

N amed one of "the official satirists of a world that badly needs a hot needle in the posterior," by writer Arthur Cooper, born sometime in 1926, '27, or '28, with the real name of Mel Kaminsky, he remembers his childhood this way: "My father died when he was 34. I was 2. I think that unconsciously, there's an outrage there. I may be angry at God, or at the world, for that. And I'm sure a lot of my comedy is based on anger and hostility. Growing up in Williamsburg, Brooklyn, I learned to clothe it in comedy to spare myself problems—like a punch in the face." On the Borscht Belt, he met fellow comedian Sid Caesar who asked him to help write material for a TV show called "Broadway Revue" (on which Caesar debuted in one of his most famous roles—the daffy German professor).

When Caesar launched "Your Show of Shows," Brooks was hired as one of the writers and sometimes appeared on camera.

By all descriptions this was a wonderful, madcap period in his life. "For 18 months after the show went off, I'd wake up at 6:30 every morning and bang my head against the bathroom wall." In 1960, with pal Carl Reiner, Brooks launched his ad-lib interviews with hilarious "2,000 Year Old Man"—a guy who'd been around and around, seeing it all. He said when asked if he'd known Christ: "Yes, thin, nervous, wore sandals. Came into the store a lot. Never bought anything."

Broadway shows, TV commercials for Ballantine Beer ("My tongue just threw a party for my mouth") the TV show "Get Smart," and hit comedy films *The Producers* and *The Twelve Chairs* all made him the master of intelligent farce with a decidedly *oy vey* twist. His 1974 hit *Blazing Saddles,* a jaundiced, giggly view of westerns, won him America's funnybone for life. More movies, more laughs, even a controversial rap video in which he played Hitler, and his own production company (*Frances, My Favorite Year, History of the World Part I,*) make him one of Hollywood's most formidable figures. The year 1986 saw the release of *84 Charing Cross Road,* with his wife in the leading role. Keeping ahead of the times, Mel's recent movies were *Solarbabies* (1986) and *Spaceballs* (1987).

To his wife, Anne Bancroft (married 1964), and kids, Maxmillian and (from his first marriage to Florence Baum) Stefanie, Nicky and Edward, he is just the 2,000-year-old love of their lives.

Pierce Brosnan

"**I** don't see myself as a hunk of the month," he says modestly. "I don't think anyone is going to ask me to take off my shirt. My chest is rather pale." But this dark, 6'1" Irishman became a TV heartthrob of the first rank in 1982 as the sexy shamus, "Remington Steele," and was soon heralded (by *People*) as a "new Cary Grant—sexy but suave, funny with subtlety instead of slapstick, manly but mannered." He and co-star Stephanie Zimbalist, alternating between on-screen flirting and fighting, approximated "a modern Nick and Nora Charles," in the sophisticated tradition of William Powell and Myrna Loy in the old *Thin Man* movies of the 1930s.

Born 16 May 1952 in Limerick, Ireland, he was an altar boy taught by no-nonsense nuns in a school where the slightest deviation from the straight and narrow got one "strapped with a paddybat." Moving at eleven to the less-restricted atmosphere of London, he had his first taste of acting at a theatre club and joyfully felt "the veils lifting off all those years of inhibitions." After studies at London's Drama Centre, he made his on-stage debut in 1976 in a local production of *Wait Until Dark* and later played numerous roles in repertory. American TV audiences first saw him in the 1981 series "The Mansions of America."

Caught in a commitment to continue as "Remington Steele," Brosnan was unable to pursue an offer to become the new James Bond. His pledge to remain as Remington proved disappointing and a short-season resurge ended with cancellation. Major films followed, including *Nomads* (1986), *The Fourth Protocol* (1987), *The Deceivers* (1988) and *Taffin* (1988), along with TV miniseries roles in "Noble House" (NBC, 1988) and "Around the World in Eighty Days" (NBC, 1989).

He and his English actress wife Cassandra Harris (nominated by photographer Lord Patrick Litchfield as one of "the world's most beautiful women"), have three children: Charlotte, Christopher, and Sean William. How close is he in real life to the insouciant Remington Steele? "I panic more than he does," says Brosnan. "He doesn't take a lot of things seriously. I do."

Genevieve Bujold

"Her hair is shiny and gleaming as a stallion's mane," wrote Rex Reed in 1976. "Her eyes big and brown as chocolate jawbreakers, her tiny mouth a rosebud of surprise. Packed into her 5-foot 4-inch doll's frame is an intriguing mixture of purloined innocence, succulent sexuality and guerilla warfare." Also, for many recent years, a resistance to work before the cameras. After enchanting audiences in such well-received films of the 60's as *Anne of a Thousand Days* (for which she was nominated for an Oscar in 1969) and *King of Hearts* (the antiwar parable starring Alan Bates, set in a French insane asylum, which has become a cult favorite), she opted during the early '80s for motherhood over movies. She told Joanne Mattera of *Women's Wear Daily* in 1984, "I'm an actress—I'm good at it—but I'm also a mother. Being at home with the kids is what I'm most comfortable doing." Result: rather slim pickings in the way of movie-making, limited to a TV version of *Caesar and Cleopatra* (in which she played the African queen to Alec Guinness's noblest Roman of them all), *Coma,* and such turkeys as *Monsignor* and the low-budget *Choose Me.*

A busdriver's daughter, born in Montreal, Quebec, 1 July 1942, Genevieve Bujold was reared in the French-Canadian tradition. ("For twelve years I was in convent school. Everything was very *comme il faut*, very strict, but I remained myself.") Encouraged by the sisters to depart after she was caught reading an outlawed volume of Marcel Pagnol's *Fanny*, she studied at the Province of Quebec Conservatory of Drama but dropped out before graduation when she was offered a job touring with the Green Curtain theater company. While performing in France, she was "discovered" by the mother of director Alain Resnais who promptly cast her in *La Guerre Est Finie*, the 1966 film that launched her screen career.

Ever the rebel, she married (in 1967) a divorced Protestant English-Canadian, Paul Almond, who directed her in *Isabel* and *The Act of the Heart*. Later, after spending three months filming near Malibu following their divorce, Bujold decided to settle and build there. Recent movies include *The Suspect* (1987), *Dead Ringers* (1988), *The Moderns* (1988) and *Thank You Satan* (1988). Her 1990 film *False Identity*, also starring Stacy Keach, was the first US film to have its world premiere in the Soviet Union.

Carol Burnett

"How many people do you know who earn a lot of money by crossing their eyes and taking pratfalls?" asked Carol Burnett, who was born on 26 April 1933 in San Antonio, Texas, where her father managed a movie theater. ("I was almost born during the matinee of *Rasputin and the Empress*.") Because her parents were chronically alcoholic, she was sent at age eight to L.A., where she and her younger sister were reared by their grandmother. After Hollywood H.S. she enrolled in a theater arts course at UCLA and was briefly married to fellow actor Don Saroyan.

Later, living at the Rehearsal club in N.Y. and scrounging for jobs, she organized *The Rehearsal Club Revue of 1955*, which resulted in 13 weeks as the girlfriend of Jerry Mahoney, the dummy on ventriloquist Paul Winchell's TV show. In 1957 she appeared on the Jack Parr show singing, "I made a Fool of Myself over John Foster Dulles," which led to an engagement on the Garry Moore show, on which she appeared regularly from 1959-1962. In 1959 she was cast as Princess Winifred the Woebegone in the Off-Broadway musical *Once Upon a Mattress*, which moved to Broadway, where it ran for a year. When she left Moore, CBS-TV signed her to a ten-year million-dollar contract, which resulted in the tremendously successful "Julie (Andrews) and Carol at Carnegie Hall" and "Calamity Jane," the first TV special to try out before a live audience.

In 1963 (the year of her film debut in *Who's Been Sleeping in My Bed?*) she married Moore's executive producer, Joe Hamilton. They have three daughters: Carrie, Jody, and Erin. There were also eight step-children from Hamilton's previous marriage, all of whom she took in her stride, calling herself "activity director of Camp Hamilton." The Hamiltons divorced in the early '80s.

In 1964 she returned to Broadway in the musical *Fade Out-Fade In*, while simultaneously taping the TV series "The Entertainers." Both projects were plagued with injuries, ill health, lawsuits, and breach-of-contract charges, all of which were dropped when she announced that she was pregnant. Burnett bounced back in 1965-66 with the special "Carol and 2" with Lucille Ball and Zero Mostel. From 1966-77 she was hostess-star of "The Carol Burnett Show," the longest-running musical-comedy series in TV history and the winner of 22 Emmys. Her other TV specials include "Carol and Company" with Rock Hudson, "Julie and Carol at the Palace" and, in 1972, a 90-minute version of *Once Upon a Mattress.* In a change of image, she starred in the dramatic Vietnam-theme TV film, "Friendly Fire" (1979). For HBO she co-starred with Elizabeth Taylor in "Best Friends" (1983). That year she played Miss Hannigan in the film version of the musical *Annie*, was named by *Good Housekeeping* magazine as one of the world's ten most admired women, and successfully sued the *National Enquirer* for libel. Her other theatrical films include: *Pete 'n' Tilly* ('72), *The Front Page* ('74), *A Wedding* ('77), HEALTH ('79-release delayed) and *The Four Seasons* ('81). She played opposite her daughter Carrie Hamilton in a television movie, "Hostage" (1987), and published her autobiography, *One More Time,* in 1986. In 1990 Burnett returned to network television with another comedy series.

She's frank; about her parents' fatal alcoholism, her daughter Carrie's successful battle with drugs, and her early '80s osteotomy—a surgical operation she (and her daughter Jody) had to relieve headaches and improve her recessed chin and overbite ("what my family used to call the Burnett lower lip"). The physical results were remarkable. "And you know what's the greatest thing of all?" she marvels: "Feeling the rain on my chin for the first time."

On being a celebrity: "I certainly like it, (but) I don't really think about it. It was a long time in coming; it will go away. Everything goes away. So I don't dwell on it." In 1985 she was inducted into the Television Academy Hall of Fame.

George Burns

"I 've got all these age jokes," he deadpans, "and I've got to use them—they're funny. Like when I talk about becoming a country singer and I say, 'Why shouldn't I be a country singer? I'm older than most countries.'" After 85 years in show business, the comic with the cigar, toupee and often risqué jokes is still at the top of his form. In his debut as a dramatic actor in *The Sunshine Boys* at the age of 79, he won an Oscar. At 81, he played God for the first time on screen; at 84, he launched a career as a country singer; at 87, he published his "ultimate diet, sex and exercise book," *How to Live to be 100—Or More*.

Born Nathan Birnbaum, one of 13 children, on 20 January 1896, George Burns launched his career at the age of seven in the PeeWee quartet, a foursome of Lower East Side youngsters who sang on New York street corners, in saloons, in front of theaters, and wherever a passed hat would bring a few pennies. Before he was 20 he had been a trick roller skater, dance teacher, and vaudeville comedian. ("In those days, a 'switch' was when you took a gag out of *College Humor* and said you got it out of *Whiz Bang*. Even the suit I wore was stolen from another comic.") He met Gracie Allen in 1923 and the two were partners on the vaudeville circuit for three years before deciding to become partners for life (two adopted children, Sandra and Ronnie). As the team of Burns and Allen, they broke virtually every record in the business until Gracie retired in 1958. (She died in 1964.) George made funny as a single for a season on NBC-TV and since then as worked busily in guestshots and clubs as well as films. (He's made, so far, three *Oh, God* comedies.)

Burns admits that he *is* slowing down in a few respects. "My cuticles," he confesses, "are not what they used to be." And when he smokes a cigar, "the smoke rings are smaller." But over-all, things are fine. In 1982 *Harpers' Bazaar* ranked him as one of six of "America's Sexiest Bachelors"—a step up from being a mere "sex symbol," which is what the *New York Times* called him when he was 86. In 1985 he returned to television as the host of the anthology series, "George Burns' Comedy Week," in 1987 he starred in the film, *Eighteen Again*, and in 1988 he published his touching story *Gracie: A Love Letter*; a special home video, *George Burns: His Wit and Wisdom* was scheduled for 1989 distribution.

Ellen Burstyn

"**A**cting feels like a congenital condition to me—it's in my genes," says Ellen Burstyn. "I can't ever remember not having that idea. I didn't decide to do it till I was 24, but it had been kinda in the back of my mind. I always felt like an actress." The year 1975 was an exciting one for Burstyn; she had the distinction of winning both the Tony (*Same Time, Next Year*) and the Oscar (*Alice Doesn't Live Here Anymore*) in the same year. In 1982 she became the first female president of Actor's Equity in its 69-year-history, "the most overwhelming job I've ever taken on." (Too overwhelming, apparently; she resigned the post in 1985.) Also in 1982 Burstyn was named co-artistic director (with Al Pacino) of the Actors Studio, succeeding the late Lee Strasberg, the father of Method Acting in the U.S. "We want to keep the Actors Studio a safe place where actors can stretch and grow and take risks they can't take in the commercial world. I've used it like that for 17 years—as a gymnasium." In December of '82, continuing to pursue her first love, acting, Burstyn opened on Broadway in *84 Charing Cross Road*. ("When rehearsals started for the play, I locked the Studio and the union out of my mind and concentrated on the play. It's the only way I can do three things at once. . . . I think there's a time in your life when you've got to be of service to other people. I've been very lucky in life and feel I should start giving back.")

Born Edna Rae Gillooly in Detroit, Michigan, 7 December 1932, the daughter of middle-class Irish Catholic parents who divorced when she was quite young, Burstyn grew up hopelessly movie-struck ("I wrote my first Academy Award acceptance speech at the age of 7"). Flunking most courses at Cass Technical High School (cheerleading and student council took up most of her time), she dropped out of school and got married in 1950 ("to a poet"). She eventually worked her way to New York where she had as many different jobs (model, soda jerk, short-order cook, fashion coordinator) as names (Keri Flynn to Erica Dean to Edna Rae). After a year as a "Ziegfeld-type" show girl on the Jackie Gleason television show, she made her Broadway debut in *Fair Game* (1957) with Sam Levene ("I got the part because I sparkled, and I smiled good, but I didn't know how to act, and the rest of company resented it"). She went to Hollywood (as Ellen McRae) and in 1969 appeared in the film of Henry Miller's *Tropic of Cancer* as Ellen Burstyn (her married name). Subsequent movies include *Alex in Wonderland* (1970), *The Last Picture Show* (1973), *The King of Marvin Gardens* (1972), *The Exorcist* (1973), *Harry and Tonto* (1974), *Alice Doesn't Live Here Anymore* (1975), and *Same Time, Next Year* (1978). More recent movies include: *Resurrection* (1980), *Silence of the North* (1980), *The Ambassador* (1984), *Twice in a Lifetime* (1985), and *Innocent Heroes* (1987). She starred in her own television show for ABC, *The Ellen Burstyn Show* (1986); a HBO presentation, *Act of Vengeance* (1986); and a CBS TV-film, "Pack of Lies" (1987). Burstyn also played the title role in the television drama "Jean Harris" (about the headmistress convicted of killing her lover, Scarsdale Diet doctor Herman Tarnower).

Each of Burstyn's three marriages ended in divorce (#2, director Paul Roberts); (#3, actor Neil Burstyn). ("It's not one of the things I'm good at.") She lives in a house near the Hudson River in New York's Rockland County with her son, Jefferson Burstyn. "I love my age," smiles Burstyn, "I enjoy my son thoroughly. I am as happy now as I have ever been. I think not becoming famous until I was past 40 helped a lot; fame was easier to accept."

David Byrne

Pauline Kael, reviewing the 1984 rock documentary *Stop Making Sense*, a concert film with the New York-based new wave group The Talking Heads, wrote: "a continuous rock experience that keeps building, becoming ever more intense and euphoric . . . David Byrne is a stupefying performer who gives the group its modernism—the undertone of repressed hysteria, which he somehow blends with freshness and adventurousness and a driving beat." The aesthetic David Byrne applies no glitter, no sleaze to his performing, and that, in part, is why he has been called "The New Wave Nijinsky." Born in Dumbarton, Scotland, 14 May 1952, Byrne moved with his family to America in 1958. An artist as well as a musician and a composer, with drummer Chris Frantzx and bassist Tina Weymouth, Byrne formed The Talking Heads in 1975, shortly after the threesome arrived in Manhattan. They all had attended the prestigious Providence art school, The Rhode Island School of Design. "We felt there was this big hole," Byrne recalls. "Very little we were hearing appealed directly to us. It appealed to kids younger than us or to other people. We felt nobody's doing anything for our crowd—we'll have to do it ourselves." With its early appearances at clubs like CBGB in the Village, along with the Ramones and Blondie, The Talking Heads became the vanguard of what was known, then, as "punk rock" or "new wave." With producer Brian Eno, The Talking Heads released three LPs. Their first album included the FM hit "Psycho Killer." 1983's album *Speaking in Tongues,* included the superhit "Burning Down the House." Before *Stop Making Sense* was released, Byrne received critical acclaim for the music he composed for Twyla Tharp's "The Catherine Wheel." He has also composed music and helped design the staging for Robert Wilson's *CIVIL warS* and he played an actor on PBS television's "Survival Guides."

Expanding his artistic talents to the fullest, Byrne became active in motion pictures. He co-wrote the screenplay and directed *True Stories* (1986), appeared in *Checking Out* (1988) and composed the film scores for *The Last Emperor* (co-recipient Academy Award for best original score, 1987) and *Married to the Mob* (1988). David took on the role as husband in 1987 when he married Adelle Lutz.

James Caan

"**G**ive the cowboy a big hand!" the barker chants at California's Antelope Valley Fair and Alfalfa Festival. The cowboy is blond, blue-eyed, tough-guy star James Caan, Hollywood's Sonny Corleone of *The Godfather,* who has just roped a running steer around both hind legs. "This ain't my hobby; the other is my hobby," says Caan in a Sunnyside Queens accent. (His family moved to Queens soon after he was born in the Bronx, the son of a now-retired kosher meat dealer.) "I have to do that acting to pay for this."

Born 26 March 1939, Caan came to films by way of the theater and TV, having studied at the Neighborhood Playhouse while

variously employed as a bouncer, waiter, and carrier of hindquar-
ters of beef at a meat market. His first role in the Off-Broadway *La
Ronde* paid him $37.50 a week, supplemented by odd jobs at the
poolroom and Friday night poker, which parlayed his take to about
$600. Married at 21 (divorced four years and one daughter later),
Caan moved to Hollywood in 1962. In 1971 his portrayal of pro-
football player Brian Piccolo in ABC-TV's movie *Brian's Song* made
him hot property, but it wasn't until his performance in Coppola's
Godfather (1972) that he achieved the sure-fire status of superstar.
Caan is not the big bruiser he is often type-cast as. Just a shade over
5'10'' and a slight 162 pounds, his celluloid aura of strength makes
up for what he lacks in actual physical size. (By the time he was
eleven, he had learned how to defend himself with his fists so well
that he was known as Killer Caan. "I was the toughest guy at P.S.
106," he told a reporter for *Time*.) He has, however, played many a
sensitive male role, as in *Cinderella Liberty* (1974), *The Rain People* (1969) and *Chapter Two* (1979). Other films include *Comes a
Horseman* (1977), *Thief* (1980), *Hide in Plain Sight* (which also marked
his directing debut), *Kiss Me Goodbye* (1983), *The Holcroft Covenant*
(1985), *Alien Nation* (1988) and *Dad* (1989). His 1990 film work
includes a cameo role disguised as Ribs in the movie *Dick Tracy*.
Caan's two marriages produced a daughter Tara (1964) and a son,
Scott Andrew (1976). Both mergers only temporarily interrupted his
philosophy of life. "I'm the kind of guy when work is done I've got
to be with my friends. I've got to blow it off like going to the rodeo,
drinking or whoring."

Sid Caesar

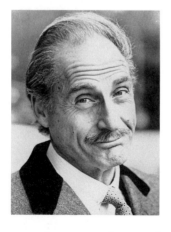

Rendering unto Caesar what is
Caesar's, audiences have paid
him tribute with everything from genial giggles to gargantuan guffaws, plus
roars, raves, rants, rails and mixed ratings. One of the rare comedians without a joke file, he emerged in 1949 as
one of TV's first and finest satiric talents on the "Admiral Broadway Revue" and made "Your Show of Shows"
and "Caesar's Hour" a Saturday night
viewing habit in the 1950's. Critics saluted him as the "funniest man in America." However, behind his classic satiric
comedy were real tears of rage and despair: He was an alcoholic and

barbituate addict skidding into disaster. During his self-described "20-year blackout" on booze and pills, he continued working. "But I wasn't really there," recalled Caesar in his 1982 autobiography, *Where Have I Been*, which describes his harrowing experience and recovery. He relates his gradual awakening to the suffering he has caused people in his life, and especially himself. The hard road back to sobriety began in 1978 when he collapsed at a dinner-theater show and entered a hospital for detoxification. "A man is only a grown-up child, but if you let the child control you, you wind up like John Belushi," he said. "I finally realized there weren't going to be any more hands on the carriage. I'm in control now."

Born 8 September 1922 in Yonkers, New York, he acquired his ability to reproduce dialects and accents while toiling in his father's luncheonette, patronized chiefly by Polish, Russian and Italian laborers. He also acquired the wherewithal to invest in saxaphone lessons, after which he worked "from 9 p.m. till unconscious" swinging with a local combo. His first New York showbiz job was a $15 a week movie usher. "But I rose rapidly from the ranks," explains Caesar. "In practically no time I rocketed to doorman and $18 a week. It wasn't the money so much as the prestige—and the overcoat." He served as sax and clarinet sideman with the bands of Charlie Spivak, Claude Thornhill and then, after enlisting in the Coast Guard during World War II, wound up in the C.G. stage hit *Tars and Spars*. In 1948, in *Make Mine Manhattan*, he won a Donaldson Award "for the best debut of an authentic clown." He launched his TV career the next year, later winning five Emmy Awards as star of "Caesar's Hour" on NBC-TV. His more recent TV projects include NBC's "30 Years of Comedy," "Alice in Wonderland" (1985) and "Side By Side" (1988). On the stage, he appeared as "Frosch" in the Metropolitan Opera's performance of "Die Fledermaus" (1988). In movies, he starred in Stanley Kramer's 1963 comedy epic, *It's a Mad, Mad, Mad, Mad World*. His Broadway credits include *Little Me* (1962-63), in which he played seven different characters. He is married to the former Florence Levy; they have two sons and a daughter. In 1985 Caesar was inducted into the Television Academy Hall of Fame.

Nicolas Cage

In just a few short years, and less than a dozen movies, Nicolas Cage has flown into the limelight. Fearing he might be judged on his name, rather than his talents, he decided to hush the fact that his uncle is famous director Francis Ford Coppola. It was his consistent performances that prompted the respect he

deserves. In many interviews Cage compares his craft to that of a magician and refuses to talk about his specific acting techniques. He insists, "If you give away your tricks, you lose the illusion."

Nicholas Coppola was born in Long Beach, California, on 7 January 1964. One of his first roles was in the "like-a, well, like, y'know," flighty movie *Valley Girl* (1983). Given a shot by his uncle, Nicolas was cast in Coppola's 1983 film *Rumble Fish* as a rebellious teenager, playing opposite Matt Dillon. On a roll, he was cast as a disabled Vietnam vet in Alan Parker's powerful *Birdy* in 1984. More parts surfaced as he played Richard Gere's kid brother in *The Cotton Club* (1984), followed by Kathleen Turner's present-day middle-aged husband/back-in-time teenaged boyfriend in the comedy *Peggy Sue Got Married* (1986). He also appeared in *Racing With the Moon* (1984), *Raising Arizona* (1986), *The Boy in Blue* (1985), *Gardens of Stone* (1987), *Vampire's Kiss* (1987), *Moonstruck* (1988), and the 1990 Cannes Film Festival winner *Wild at Heart*. His other 1990 release is *Fire Birds*, with Tommy Lee Jones and Sean Young. It was his role as the love-struck thirty-year-old brother of Cher's fiancé in *Moonstruck* that had the critics writing praises. Of this romantic role he says, "It could be a medicine for couples that are falling apart. They would see *Moonstruck* and say, 'See? It's alright to be angry with one another, it's alright to argue.' Love is not just holding hands." Fans continue to be eager for the rumored *Moonstruck* sequel.

Michael Caine

O ne critic put it thusly: "Like the Beatles, Caine is a product of Britain's lower class popular arts revolution," Caine says, "A Cockney used to be looked upon kindly, like Mickey Mouse, but we decided to be people instead. I just couldn't see getting up at dawn to schlep iced fish." He burst through the rigid British caste system to both fame and fortune via such vehicles as *The Ipcress File, Alfie, Sleuth, The Man Who Would Be King;* later: *Deathtrap, Dressed To Kill, Blame It on Rio, Hannah and Her Sisters* (recipient Academy Award—Best Supporting Actor, 1987), *Sweet Liberty, Half Moon Street, The Fourth Protocol* (also executive producer), *Dirty Rotten Scoundrels* and *Without a Clue.*

Caine was born Maurice Micklewhite on Old Kent Road in

London, 14 March 1933; his father was a Billingate Fish Market porter, and his mother a charwoman. ("I was rich from the day I was born, I just didn't have the money.") World War II forced a breakup of his family for a year until Caine's mother was able to gather them all again under one roof. At 18 he was drafted for National Service, serving in Berlin and Korea—"a lot of very heroic-looking guys shot their toes off while cleaning their rifles,"—and at 20 went back to London working at the Smithfield Meat Market while taking acting classes at night. Landing a job at Lowestoft Theatre, he met and married his leading lady, Patricia Haines. "I can't remember one single moment that was happy," his ex-wife later said of their three-year marriage. There was one daughter, Dominique, born in 1956. In 1973 he married Shakira Baksh, a former Miss Guyana in a Miss World beauty pageant, and they have a daughter (Natasha, born in 1973).

While working night shift in a laundry, he got his first film part, which eventually led to an appearance in *Zulu* as—of all things—an English patrician. ("All those idiots went to Oxford just because they were lords' sons, but now their day is over. Nobody stands for that bourgeois junk any more.") From that point on, Caine was established as a film actor and continues to chalk up credits. "Money buys independence. I don't like being told what to do, especially by people who know less." 'E 'as a point there, 'e 'as.

Zoe Caldwell

"I was a late bloomer," says this raven-haired actress from down under. "I knew once I turned 30 I could play the Madwoman of Chaillot, Mother Courage, Cleopatra . . . all those marvelous over-thirty women. . . . I always knew that everything about me—in acting and in private life—would come to a sort of fullest bloom from my 30s on." As if to prove the point, after hitting the high side of the generation gap Miss Caldwell copped three of Broadway's much coveted Tonys: the first in 1966 for her role in Tennessee Williams' short-lived *Slapstick Tragedy,* the second, two seasons later, for her portrayal of a dowdy middle-aged school mistress in *The Prime of Miss Jean Brodie.* And shortly thereafter she married for the first time (producer Robert Whitehead; two children). "I think," Miss Caldwell concludes, wrapping up her thesis,

"the later you bloom, the longer the bloom stays on." In 1970, she was drenched in huzzahs for her off-Broadway portrayal of *Colette,* was honored by Queen Elizabeth II with the Order of the British Empire, and received bravas for her portrayal of Lady Hamilton in *Bequest to the Nation* in London. She marked her directorial debut with Colleen Dewhurst in *An Almost Perfect Person,* which played on Broadway in 1977. Soon after, she directed *Richard II* at Stratford, Ontario. Her third Tony was for her performance as *Medea,* directed by her husband, in 1983.

Born 14 September 1933 in Victoria, Australia, Zoe Caldwell acted first with Australian repertory companies and at 24 won a scholarship to Stratford-on-Avon. There, the late Tyrone Guthrie saw her and invited her to appear with his company in Minneapolis. Broadway took notice in 1965, when she subbed for Anne Bancroft in *The Devils.* "I think I was born an actress," Miss Caldwell once mused. "Some people are addicted to drugs. I've got a creative addiction. I could have been an appalling mother or maybe a nymphomaniac if I hadn't become an actress," she adds, "so isn't it fine that I did?" In 1985 she toured with *Lillian* (based on the life of the late playwright Lillian Hellman), and brought the one-woman show to Broadway in 1986.

Kirk Cameron

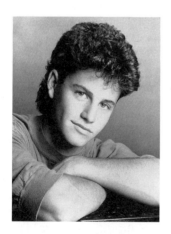

At only 20 years old, he is already a success story in the world of show business. This young actor has made the switch from popular teen idol and heartthrob, to celebrated television and film star. He has performed with such greats as Dudley Moore, Robin Williams, and Kurt Russell.

Kirk Cameron was born on 20 October 1970, in Canoga Park, California. He began acting professionally at age 9, appearing in TV commercials. Several years later he appeared in the short-lived series "Two Marriages," and the made-for-TV-movie "Goliath Awaits." But it was his role as Mike Seaver in the popular ABC series "Growing Pains" that brought him his star status recognition. Since then he has received several awards including the Favorite Young Television Performer in both the 1987 and 1988 People's Choice Awards, the Best Actor Award presented by the Family Television and Film Awards Organization in 1988, and a Golden Globe nomination for his performance in "Growing Pains." His film credits include *Like Father Like Son* co-starring with Dudley Moore, *Mismatch, The Best of Times* with Robin Williams and Kurt Russell, and *Listen to Me* co-starring with Jami Gerz. Kirk is also actively involved in the "Just Say No" anti-drug campaign, using his influence as a role model to act as a spokesperson. He has appeared in several television commercials proclaiming his views against the use of drugs. "The most rewarding results of my participation is when parents stop and thank me for the positive messages I've been able to get across to their children," says Kirk. "If my positive outlook and moral values help others, that's great."

Kirk resides in California, and in his spare time he enjoys working out at the gym and playing the guitar.

Glen Campbell

Campbell's rise from obscure recording artist and studio musician to TV star ("I'm really sittin' in the high cotton now") was largely the result of two recordings in 1968: "Gentle on My Mind" and "By the Time I Get to Phoenix," both of which won Grammys. "I'm busier right now'n a three-headed woodpecker," he said at the time. "They call me an overnight success, but mah night's been 15 years long. That's just about how long I've been strugglin' in this business. I'm gettin' some of the gravy now, but it sure ain't been a picnic."

When the outdoorsy six-footer weighed in at seven pounds, two ounces (22 April 1938), first filling his lungs with Delight, Ark., air, a neighbor looked him over and said, "That boy's goin' to amount. Got to be. His paw, Wes, he's a seventh son. And Glen is the seventh son of a seventh son." "The thing I remember most about Glen," recalls a former schoolmate, "was that he was always singin' or playin' the guitar. He didn't pay any attention to us girls in the class. He weren't sweet on any of us. He was jest in love with that ol' guitar." He left school and the farm when he was 14. ("I was tired of lookin' at the north end of a southbound mule.")

TV director Roger Gimbel explains Campbell's popularity: "He's a fresh, attractive performer who fits the times. . . . It's almost a return to the same kind of nationalism that comes between wars; you know, when you're kind of proud of what your country's all about." Glen adds, "I'm strictly Joe American. I'm the apple-pie kinda guy." It is this kind of hokey sentiment and hillbilly dialect that has propelled Campbell to stardom. On the screen he appeared in *Any Which Way You Can* (1980) and two years later the "Glen Campbell Show" aired on prime time. Recent recordings include *It's Just a Matter Of Time* (1985), *Still Within the Sound of My Voice* (1987) and *Light Years* (1988). The latter album was produced by his long-time friend Jimmy Bowen and songwriter Jimmy Webb. "I think this album is one of the best I've ever done," claims Campbell. "The songs are consistently good—that's what I always look for. I judge a tune by the melody and what it says. That's what counts with me."

Campbell has been married four times and has nine children, the youngest a son born in 1985 to wife Kim Woollen, whom he married in 1982.

John Candy

"Working with John Candy has been one of the greatest delights of my career," remarked director Carl Reiner, who guided the young comedian in his first starring role in *Summer Rental*, the 1985 film comedy hit. "I've been very lucky in my career," continued Reiner, "I've worked with some of the best: Sid Ceasar, Mel Brooks, Dick Van Dyke, George Burns, Steve Martin, and now, John Candy."

Born in Toronto in 1951, the moon-faced Candy, an avid sports fan, played football and hockey in high school before a knee injury ended his hopes for a professional sports career. He started acting in the eleventh grade and the urge continued during his journalism studies at Centennial Community College near Toronto. Candy's first professional job was with a children's theatre group that produced such classics as *Rumpelstiltskin* and *Treasure Island*, in which the four-member cast played a lot of different roles. By 1971 he was a fixture in Toronto's underground theatre scene performing in the popular satirical revue *Creeps* at the time he met another struggling Canadian actor from Ottawa, Dan Aykroyd. He also had roles in several low-budget Canadian films, including *Faceoff*, which he describes as "a real stinker about hockey." In 1972 with Aykroyd's urging, Candy joined Chicago's famed Second City Theatre, which at the time included young comedic talents John Belushi, Shelley Long, Gilda Radner and Bill Murray. After two years there he returned to Toronto and joined the Canadian-based Second City group. This evolved into the "SCTV" television series, which was syndicated throughout the United States and Canada and finally picked up by NBC. Candy was performer/writer for the show, and garnered two Emmys for the latter. He was part of "SCTV" until 1981. His films include Steven Spielberg's *1941*, John Landis's *The Blues Brothers*, and *Stripes*, with Bill Murray. He was featured in *National Lampoon's Vacation* and was Tom Hanks's lecherous sibling in *Splash*. Other films include *Brewster's Millions* with Richard Pryor, *Volunteers*, *Spaceballs*, *Planes, Trains and Automobiles*, *Hot To Trot*, *The Great Outdoors*, *Speed Zone* and *Uncle Buck*. He starred as the bumbling private eye who "always manages to get his man" in 1989's *Who's Harry Crumb?* "I find that there's a common denominator that runs with all creative comedians," says director Reiner. "They're a pleasure to work with because they not only come in prepared but they come with creative ideas which makes everything better, easier. . . . Put somebody like John Candy in it and little goodies happen every day."

Dyan Cannon

S he once claimed that it was almost a career unto itself having people call her "The ex-Mrs. Cary Grant." After the movie idol saw her performance in a television series, "Malibu Run," he was so impressed that he asked her to test for his next film. They married in 1965 after a four-and-a-half year courtship and had one daughter, Jennifer (Jennifer can be seen in the 1990 TV movie "Jailbirds"). Then in the best of Hollywood traditions (high drama) they divorced in 1968. She accused him of taking LSD. His shrink claimed that Cary spanked Cannon "for reasonable and adequate causes." All the while, Cannon was one of the grooviest gals in Hollywood, from Primal Screen to a three-year state of celibacy, so "California" that *People* magazine said at times "she seemed a parody of the film that was her breakthrough, 1969's *Bob & Carol &*

Ted & Alice." She's much more than Cary Grant's ex, the mother of his only child. She's one of the finest comedic actresses around as her many fans will readily attest. Her films include *Deathtrap; Heaven Can Wait; Such Good Friends; Author, Author; Honeysuckle Rose,* a cult classic among puzzle lovers titled *The Last of Sheila,* and *Caddyshack II.* In 1989 she wore a triple hat when she wrote the screenplay for, directed and starred in *One Point of View.*

Born 4 January 1937, in Tacoma, Washington, she was named Samille Diane Friesen. ("After my grandfather Sam.") Her father was a life insurance salesman and a Baptist, her mother was Jewish and "a great bowling champion." She was raised Jewish and was once Miss Seattle. She considered becoming an actress only when she was "discovered" by a producer in a Los Angeles restaurant and given an "explosive" new name. ("I thought they were putting me on.") She decided she needed a nose job and phoned home to dad and said, "I don't want that mink stole you promised me, but I want a nose job." Luckily, a Hollywood plastic surgeon realized that her slightly flat nose was one of her most distinguishing features. That was in 1957. She'd been working for a dress manufacturer, modeling and helping to run his showroom. She studied for a year with Sandy Meisner and made her professional debut in television's Playhouse 90 production of "The Ding-A- Ling Girl," which starred Art Carney, and that led to roles in "Matinee Theatre" and other TV series. She made her film debut in *The Rise and Fall of Legs Diamond,* and her Broadway debut in *The Fun Couple,* a flop that also starred Jane Fonda.

Nominated twice for Academy Awards, she won one the third time in 1976 for a 42-minute film, *Number One,* an examination of the lives of two five-year-old girls, which she produced. She also was applauded for her portrayal of famed San Francisco madam Sally Stanford in a television film, and for playing a hip rock star mother in the ABC-TV movie *Rock and Roll Mom* (1988).

Cannon lives in Malibu, swims daily in her pool and begins each morning reading metaphysics. About Einstein she says, "Now there's a sexy man!" "All I know," she said in 1984, "is that I've never had as much to share or as much to express as right now, at this point in my life. I'm happy most of the time now. I'm a happy lady." She was happier still in April of 1985 when she married attorney Stanley Finberg, but they separated in 1990.

George Carlin

Did you know that there are actually some phrases in the English language that have never been uttered? For example, nobody, in the history of speech, has ever said, "hand me that piano," or "please cut off my legs." Isn't it funny how the phrases, "military intelligence" and "jumbo shrimp," are contradictions in terms? And why is there no blue food? Such are the ponderings of George Carlin, a comic with a face like a Doonesbury cartoon character who has made a career out of his fascination with language, his outrage at convention, and his loathing for political doublespeak. His seventh HBO comedy special, which aired in 1990, lampooned the lingo characterizing the dawn of the 90s: class act, happy camper, bottom line, game plan, etc.

George Denis Patrick Carlin was born in the Bronx, N.Y. 12 May 1938. After playing the role of class clown, he dropped out of high school to observe life in the Air Force and in odd jobs before becoming a radio announcer in Shreveport, La. From his early years in broadcasting, Carlin garnered material for some of his funniest bits: the fast-talking radio DJ on "Wonderful Wino" radio; "Al Sleet, your hippy, dippy weatherman;" and the host of a TV divorce show, in which contestants spin a wheel to determine alimony and child custody rights.

Carlin came to comedy prominence in the 1960's, working Las Vegas and television, eventually becoming a regular on the "Tonight Show" in 1967, delivering mock newscasts. But in the early 1970's, tired of the restrictions placed on his imagination by the confines of TV, he grew his hair long and began a second career, gearing his routines to a younger, more politically-conscious audience, with jokes about drugs, government, and censorship. "I was just sick to my stomach of wearing the dumb tuxedo and entertaining middle-class morons."

Through the years, Carlin produced many popular comedy albums, including, *FM/AM,* (1972); *Class Clown,* (1972); *Toledo Window Box* (1974); and *What Am I Doing in New Jersey?* (1988). He recently extended his comedic talents to the big screen, starring in Disney's *Outrageous Fortune* (1987) and *Bill and Ted's Excellent Adventure* (1989).

George's famous routine, "Seven Words You Can Never Use on Television," got him arrested on a charge of public profanity in 1972. Undaunted by his arrest (the charges were dropped), Carlin continued to write material attacking censorship and government controls. This explains his preference for cable television as the medium for his comedy. "You get to do your act uninterrupted. The subject matter isn't censored." Despite his outrage, audiences were warmed by the underlying message of his madness: a plea for humanity. An automobile accident in 1981 and a heart attack in 1982 haven't taken the edge off Carlin's sharp satire.

Art Carney

The name on his birth certificate (4 November 1918) reads Arthur William Matthew Carney, but for a generation of TV watchers, he'll always be Ed Norton, "the underground sanitation expert" of Jackie Gleason's "The Honeymooners." In reruns in the 1980s, the program was so popular that it spawned a cult of diehard devotees (The Royal Association for the Longevity and Preservation of the Honeymooners, or *RALPH*, founded in 1982 for Ralph Kramden, the portly busdriver played by Jackie Gleason in the 1950's television series). The many critical plums (including multitudinous Emmys) he received during his long and fruitful second-banana years make some people forget that the comic genius has also proved his mettle in tragedy. But whatever the genre the successes speak for themselves, like *Harry and Tonto* (1974), for which Carney received the Golden Globe Award as well as the Oscar for best performance by an actor. In 1985, he teamed up again with Gleason for a TV movie, "Izzy and Moe," about the legendary Prohibition agents.

The man who brought sewer-dweller Ed Norton to life started polishing his comedic craft early. The youngest of six boys, he staged his first one-man-show in the family living room in Mount Vernon, N.Y., artfully titling it "Art for Art's Sake." After touring as a $50-a-week funnyman with Horace Heidt's band, he did light-hearted second-banana duties for the likes of Fred Allen, Bert Lahr, and Edgar Bergen, but faced some rather dark days during World War II when he was wounded shortly after landing at Normandy's

Omaha Beach. (His right leg is still an inch shorter than the left.) A chronic brooder ("I'm always worried about what's going to happen in the next six months"), he had another dark period in the 1960s when he departed from his highly successful Broadway run in *The Odd Couple* to enter a psychiatric hospital.

The '80's were good to Art; he played a wonderful grandpa to Brian Bonsall in a touching Coca-Cola commercial, and guest-starred on the 1987 television series "The Cavanaughs." He played Santa Claus in a television film with Jaclyn Smith, *The Night They Saved Christmas* (1986), and received a TV award from the National Board of Review in 1989.

His marriage to Jean Meyers ended in divorce in 1966 after 26 years and three children, but was reinstated in 1977 (after an interim marriage to Barbara Isaac).

Leslie Caron

Beginning her professional career at the age of 16 as the youngest petit rat of Roland Petit's Ballet des Champs Eliseés, she so impressed David Lichine with her dancing that he gave her the leading role of the Sphinx in his ballet "La Recontre" in 1946. Her good fortune continued when Gene Kelly starred her opposite himself in the 1951 Oscar-winning film *An American in Paris*, which launched her Hollywood career. Today, however, she bears only a slight resemblance to *Lili* (1953), or *Gigi* (1958), or *Fanny* (1961), or the girl-woman who fell in love with *Daddy Long Legs* (1955). "Most miserable period in my life," she declares. "I hate musicals. I had toe shoes on from eight thirty in the morning until six every night. I was constantly in agony. . . . I had bruises and sprains that couldn't heal. When I walked out of Hollywood, after years of unhappiness, Fred Astaire and Gene Kelly both told me. 'Leslie, you're so smart to quit while you can still walk.' I'm glad those days are gone forever." (An attempted dancing comeback failed when in 1984 injuries prevented her from starring in the touring company of *On Your Toes*.) She gained new status as a dramatic actress in *The L-Shaped Room* (1963) and *Is Paris Burning?* (1966). Of the latter she says, "I said hell before I did the scene and giggled right after. Dramatic scenes. I don't enjoy them." Despite her reservations regarding her movie roles, she never completely disappeared from the Hollywood scene. She appeared in *Valentino* (1977), *Goldengirl* (1979), *Dangerous Moves* (1984), *The Train* (1987), and *The Man Who Lived at the Ritz* (1989). Her book of short stories, *Vengeance,* was published in 1982. Kicking up her heels again, Leslie danced with Nureyev and Baryshnikov in a gala performance at the Met in 1986.

Born 1 July 1931 in Paris, France, Caron is the daughter of a French chemist and an American-born dancer. She was first married to American meat-packing heir George Hormel II and then to British producer-director Peter Hall (two children). The second marriage ended in divorce, with Warren Beatty named as correspondent. She married producer Michael Laughlin in 1967. When asked if she thought she had profited from her mistakes, she curtly replied, "What mistakes?" She divorced Laughlin in 1977. Caron is hardly reticent and speaks her mind on a myriad of subjects: "An actor I worked with . . . came up and asked me to go to bed with him. If I did, he said, it would make him act better the next day. Well, I only go to bed with people I'm in love with. I'm not bragging. I haven't the slightest idea what the public thinks of me and I don't care."

John Carpenter

"**T**he first movie [my parents] ever took me to was *The African Queen* and what I remember most is Humphrey Bogart coming out of the water covered with leeches. But my monumental experience with films was in 1953, when I was five. My parents took me to *It Came From Outer Space,* in 3-D. You had to wear special glasses. The first shot was of this meteor—it came right off the screen and exploded in my face. I couldn't believe it! It was everything I'd ever wanted! After that I was addicted to films. I made movies in my head. . . . I made up little stories. When I was eight, my dad gave me an 8-mm movie camera." The grown-up film addict, following several failures, eventually made—in 20 days—the hit film *Halloween* (1978), thereby carving a niche for himself as a key suspense/horror director of the '80s. "When success comes, it's a frenzy—wham! People start running; they get a fever. I remember a producer saying to me, 'You're hot!' Everybody's overreacting. I haven't changed that much; the only difference is that the film has made money. This is how you're judged."

He was born in Kentucky in 1948 and raised there in Bowling Green, the only child of a violinist/music professor. Encouraged in creative endeavors by his parents, he studied violin, piano and guitar, playing the last and singing in a 60s rock band. ("If I'd stayed in Kentucky, I'd still be playing rock and roll today. I have a tremendous love for music.") He attended Western Kentucky University and U.S.C. film school. As a youngster, "I felt I was quite a bit the outsider, a little weird. I was pretty single-minded. As a matter of fact, my movies now are pretty single-minded movies. I'm a little obsessive. . . . I have a great feeling for physical movies. I don't like intellectual films. I love suspense. I want the audience to laugh and cry—an emotional response. The medium *is* emotional, not so much like a book or a play really, as like music. . . . Movies are pieces of film stuck together in a certain rhythm, an absolute beat—like a musical composition. The rhythm you create affects the audience." The intense director also composed *Halloween's* music score. His subsequent films—most but not all in his special genre—include: *Elvis* (1979—originally for TV), *The Fog* (1980), *Escape from N.Y.* (1981), *The Thing* (1982—a remake of the classic by Howard Hawks—"My favorite director"), *Christine* (1983), *Starman* (1985), *Black Moon Rising* (1986), *Prince of Darkness* (1987) and *They Live* (1988).

He is the father of a son, John Cody, by his marriage to actress Adrienne Barbeau, who has appeared in some of his films. He has no illusions about his company town: "There's very little honor here—maybe anywhere. People lie, cheat and steal. All the clichés about Hollywood have a basis in truth. It can be very disgusting. But I live by my decision to make Hollywood films."

Diahann Carroll

"I was a big girl before I found out my name was spelled that way. I had to get a work permit and I saw my birth certificate spelled Diahann. 'Who's that?' I asked. 'That's you, Charlie,' said my mother."

Carol Diahann Johnson was born in the Bronx, N.Y., 17 July 1935, the elder daughter of a subway motorman and a nurse for retarded children. She won a Metropolitan Opera Scholarship at the age of ten and was accepted at Manahattan's prestigious High School of Music and Art. While studying sociology at N.Y.U., she auditioned for a Lou Walters black revue, *Jazz Train*. From that point

her nightclub career took off; she dropped out of college and went on tour. "At first when I worked in Miami they put me in a smaller hotel down the street. I felt like garbage." She appeared on Broadway in the critically acclaimed musical *House of Flowers* (1952) and "Sleeping Bee" became her signature tune. In Hollywood she appeared in *Carmen Jones, Porgy and Bess,* and in non-singing roles in *Paris Blues, Hurry Sundown* and *Claudine.*

Richard Rodgers wrote *No Strings* to bring her back to Broadway and in 1962 she won a Tony for her portrayal in the musical of a Paris mannequin; "Sweetest Sounds" became her new signature tune. In 1968 she became the second black to star in her own TV series, "Julia" (Hattie McDaniel in "Beulah" in 1947 was the first), which ran for three seasons, with the general consensus deeming it just another sit-com. Her past husbands include TV producer Monte Kay (one daughter, Suzanne Ottilie), Freddé Glusman, and Robert DeLeon (who was found dead at the wheel of his wrecked sportscar). She was engaged to David Frost for a brief while, then married her fourth husband, Vic Damone, in January, 1987. The couple took their marriage on the road, and developed a pleasant niteclub act. Recounting her life and loves, Diahann published *Diahann: An Autobiography* in 1986. Additional television performances include: "I Know Why the Caged Bird Sings" (1978), a regular role on TV's "Dynasty" (1984/85) and a role in the NBC 4-hour miniseries "Walkers," with Lindsay Wagner. On Broadway, she played the psychiatrist in *Agnes of God* in 1982.

Diahann and Vic switch off among 3 homes: Beverly Hills, Palm Springs and New York City. She likes cooking, entertaining and designing her own clothes.

Johnny Carson

When a reporter asked "What made you a star?" Johnny Carson replied, "I started out in a gaseous state, then cooled." Actually, he's hotter then ever since becoming television's undisputed Captain Midnight, in the host's chair (vacated by Jack Parr in 1962) on NBC-TV's "Tonight" show. His impudent on-camera activities over the years have won out in the ratings over a gaggle of rival nighttime chatterboxes, and he's now on the NBC payroll for what is rumored to be "millions" of dollars a year. "His success is due in great measure to his quick wit, his ability to seize absurdity and run with it," observed *TV Guide* in 1984. "He is Johnny-on-the-spot with an instant retort. His timing and delivery are expert. His face speaks more eloquently than his writers' scripted words. He is a master of the slow take, the mock-affronted expression, the blank stare at the camera."

John William Carson was born 23 October 1925 in Corning, Iowa ("No cracks, please"), but blossomed as a neophyte performer in the town of Norfolk, Nebraska, where he grew up. He sent away for a mail-order course in ventriloquism and magic, emerged as "The Great Carsoni" and did very well ($3 a performance) on the local Elks-Moose-Redmen circuit before heading off for the Navy. As a University of Nebraska grad after the war, he went to work on Omaha radio station WOW ("I wasn't"); when the TV era arrived, he ad-libbed his way through a local show called "The Squirrel's Nest." While working as a comedy writer for Red Skelton, he was called in on two hours' notice as a replacement when Skelton was injured. The response to that appearance put him on the road to the quiz show, "Who Do You Trust?" where Carson cavorted for five years before moving to the "Tonight" hot seat.

Always accused of being something of a Little Boy "Blue," Carson has kept pace with the enormous social changes in this country in the last 20 years. "Grown older, he has grown bolder; as sexual taboos have relaxed, he has become more permissively risqué," wrote Bill Kaufman in a 1984 *TV Guide* story. When Mr. Universe appeared on his show, he told Johnny, "Your body is your home, you know, your house." Replied Johnny: "Well, my house is a mess, but I have a woman that comes in twice a week." In response to criticism of such "off color" humor, Carson says: "If you can't talk about anything grown-up or sophisticated at midnight without being called immoral and dirty, then I think we're in trouble."

In regard to his marital-go-round, the similar names of his three ex-wives—Joan "Jody," Joanne and Joanna—have caused more than one jokester to observe that Carson has never had to change the monograms on his towels. With his first wife, Jody Wolcott (they met at the University of Nebraska), he had three sons. Wife number two was Joanne Copeland, whom he divorced in 1972. Number three was Joanna Holland, whom he married later that year. They filed for divorce in 1983 after ten years of marriage. Carson's ex-wives became the subject of an exposé on "A Current Affair" when his first wife brought suit against him for more alimony. When asked about weddings, Carson joked: "My giving advice on marriage is like the captain of the *Titanic* giving lessons on navigation. . . . I resolve if I ever get hit in the face again with rice; it will be because I insulted a Chinese person." Carson started from scratch again in 1987 when he married his fourth wife, Alex Maas, in Malibu. Off to a new beginning (her first name starts with an "a"), the couple reside in California.

"That he managed to survive for so long is one of the most interesting things about prankish, puckish Johnny," Bill Kaufman observed. "We have been a part of his survival; we made him, he is ours. . . . As long as he makes his audiences laugh at what they consider funny and dares to criticize what they would like to, he will continue to be No. 1, the King of the Talk Shows, the nice boy from Nebraska who made good, but real good, in the Big City of America."

Lynda Carter

This indefatigable "Wonder Woman" power-glided over American air-waves from 1976-70 after winning the Miss World-U.S.A. title in 1973. As amazons go, she can surely hold her own against Godzilla, but she can also score with an audience. Witness all the Lynda Carter specials and celebrations ("Body and Soul" which aired March of '81 was a typical example of a ratings clean-up) and TV movies as well: ("Born To Be Sold," 1981; "Rita Hayworth: The Love Goddess," 1983).

Born in Phoenix, Ariz., 24 July circa 1950 the youngest of three children, Lynda made her professional singing debut at fifteen and is as adept at singing and dancing as she is at situation comedy or realistic drama. Co-starring in the 1984 series "Partners in Crime" with Loni Anderson, the two actresses played the widow and ex-wife of the same man. After his death, they jointly inherited his detective agency. In 1987, Lynda appeared in the made-for-TV film "Stillwatch." When not doing television, the "shazam superstar" makes believers out of all who see her Vegas act, "slinking and sizzling" as one reporter puts it, her way through a battery of songs.

Carter also serves as Beauty and Fashion Director of Maybelline cosmetics, appearing in the company's advertising and serving as a consultant in the development and marketing of new products. In the 18 months following her signing by Maybelline, the company's sales tripled, skyrocketing from $70 million to over $200 million. Also championing social causes, Carter appeared at a White House hearing in 1990 to speak out in favor of breast cancer research, detection, and education.

Carter was named one of "Ten Most Exciting Women in the World" by the International Bachelors Association. That group is out of the running since she married Robert Altman (not the director) in January of 1984. Carter's Altman is a partner in a Washington, D.C., law firm. The couple are the proud parents of son, Jamie, born 14 January 1988.

Nell Carter

Although she survived as she attempted to follow that familiar trial of stardom—going to New York—it took ten years before the ironically-ill-timed pieces finally fell into place. While working as a nightclub singer at Dangerfield's, The Apartment, and even in Mayor Lindsay's campaign, she occasionally went into one production when she had the opportunity to take more fruitful offers, "I was in the original cast of *Bubbling Brown Sugar*," Carter says, "before it came to Broadway. I left it to go into *Be Kind to People Week*. Instead of *The Wiz* I chose *Miss Moffat*, which closed out of town. I chose *Duds*, which lasted one night." But, proving that where there's life there's hope, the woman the *New York Times* describes as "the short, buxom, bubbling woman with a singing voice that has the raw, penetrating quality of a steel-tipped drill" kept at it.

Born Nell Ruth Carter on 13 September 1948 in Birmingham, Ala., this frequent local radio and TV-performing teen had hightailed it north at age 19 when an NBC-TV "Today" show scout encouraged her. In New York she honed the voice that had been inspired by Dinah Washington and Dakota Staton, and studied for three years at Bill Russell's School of Drama. The persistent polishing paid premiums when she won a Tony Award in *Ain't Misbehavin'*. Her lively performance led to scads of offers, and she was soon seen in the film version of *Hair*, as a guest of Johnny Carson's and Merv Griffin's, and as a member of TV specials like the all-black Cinderella story "Cindy," and "Baryshnikov on Broadway." She picked her prized plum, to that point, when NBC-TV gave her "Gimme a Break," her own situation comedy. In 1988, Nell celebrated the tenth anniversary of *Ain't Misbehavin'* in a special new touring production of the show. She was also given the honor of performing at President George Bush's Inaugural Gala in 1989. Nell married George Krynick in 1982 and makes her home in California.

Dick Cavett

"**M** e? People say I come across as wry, subtle, Ivy League, Midwestern. Sometimes I worry about it. I don't have an image of myself," says this former Yale drama major and comedian who rose to fame in the late 1960s as the provocative TV talk show host on ABC's "Dick Cavett Show." A combination comic-raconteur, Cavett was a born talk show host and won three Emmys on his six-year ABC show. That fusion wasn't without friction, however. He was often attacked for the controversial things he said and allowed to be said, and in 1972 his show was relegated to a one-week-a-month schedule—and that only because his fans demanded he stay. He later hosted a five-year public television series, "The Dick Cavett Show," and since 1974 has hosted a number of public television specials. A man of many moods and talents (actor, comedian, writer, award-winning amateur magician, gymnast), Cavett has spread out in various directions. In 1977, he made his Broadway acting debut, starring in the comedy *Otherwise Engaged*. In 1983, he published his second book, *Eye on Cavett*; in 1986 he hosted "The Dick Cavett Show" (ABC-TV), and in 1988 he joined the cast of Sondheim's *Into the Woods* (playing the narrator). He also appeared in the movie *Moon Over Parador*. In 1990 Cavett was featured in the *Spy* magazine television special, "How To Be Famous."

The only child of schoolteachers, Dick Cavett was born in Gibbon, Nebraska, 19 November 1936. ("My mother helped out by taking in washing at night—off other people's clotheslines.") He grew up in Gibbon, Grand Island and Lincoln, Neb., where he garnered local fame as a teenage magician. At Yale, he appeared in many campus radio and stage productions, graduating in 1958 with a major in English and drama. He later spent two seasons with the Williamstown (Mass.) Summer Theater and from 1961-64 was a writer for "The Tonight Show" and "The Jerry Lewis Show." He created comedy for Johnny Carson and Jack Parr, among others. His performing career began in 1964 as a nightclub comedian in such clubs as "the hungry i" in San Francisco and Bon Soir in New York. He made guest appearances on TV shows including "The Ed Sullivan Show." His talk show debut with ABC-TV came in 1968. Beginning in 1979, he hosted "Time Was," a documentary series seen on Home Box Office cable TV, and has done several other HBO series since. During early '80s, he continued appearing on stage, including roles at Williamstown Theater. He collaborated with Christopher Porterfield in 1974 in his bestselling autobiography, *Cavett*, and also wrote his 1983 book with Porterfield.

Cavett lives in New York with his wife, Mississippi-born actress Carrie Nye, whom he met at Yale, courted for eight years and married in 1964. The two have appeared at Williamstown Theater in Noel Coward's *Nude With Violin*. Known for his nasty temper (once shouting to a heckler while on the air, "Shut up!"), Cavett insists he is really shy. His former Yale roommate describes him thus: "He has a quick, lively mind, an eager curiosity in all spheres. And he never loses his quick, light, humorous touch. He has a literate form of humor, yet it doesn't become cliquey or in-group. He'll always be somewhat of an earnest, wholesome Midwestern kid."

Richard Chamberlain

He was Grand Master of the Miniseries by 1983 after "Centennial" (1978), "Shogun" (1980) and "The Thorn Birds" (1982). Chamberlain spent half a year in Japan filming "Shogun" which was based on the James Clavell bestseller. "The Thorn Birds," in which Chamberlain hypnotized his fans with his portrayal of a lust-ridden priest, focused on a pulchritudinous Australian lassie played by Rachel Ward, drew 110 million viewers. According to Chamberlain, making love to Ward in the show was easier said than done: "There's a microphone hidden in the armpit and another in the sheets. There's a wig to worry about, a shadow, an angle. Your arm is giving out because you've been sitting above her for three hours on the same elbow, and you're trying not to smear her lipstick or make slurpy sounds while you're kissing." TV being his medium, he is yet to win an Emmy despite much good work including "Cook and Peary" (1983), "Wallenberg" (1985), "Dream West" (1986), "Casanova" (1986) and "The Bourne Identity" (1988). "You can't be in this business for awards," says a philosophical Chamberlain.

Born 31 March 1935 in Beverly Hills, California, ("a few reels from the studios"), he turned to acting after an Army hitch, and became TV's Dr. Kildare at 26. After five years in the series he shook the clean-cut "apple-pie hero" image by moving to England and studying drama. Applauded there in his role as *Hamlet,* he returned to the States in a well-publicized *Richard II* and bolstered his credibility with general audiences in films like *The Last Wave* (1978) and *Allan Quartermain and the Lost City of Gold* (1986), although one could maintain his credibility had already been established in two 1971 films: *Julius Caesar,* shot on location in Spain and *The Music Lovers* (directed by Ken Russell). Recent films include: *The Return of the Three Musketeers* (1989) and *Say Goodbye To Sam* (1989). He appeared on Broadway in Noel Coward's *Blithe Spirit* in 1987, sharing the stage with the late, great Geraldine Page. In the fall of 1989 he returned to television, starring as another "Dr. K" in the series "Island Son." He resides in Hawaii.

Carol Channing

She has eyes "like baby blue baseballs," a little-girl voice that's like no other on this planet, and she's created a trio of memorable femmes —fatale or otherwise—in the Broadway pantheon. Bursting into bloom first as the Gladiola Girl of 1948's *Lend an Ear,* she metamorphised herself in 1949 into Lorelei Lee, the girl who demonstrated why *Gentlemen Prefer Blondes. Time* magazine said after she debuted in the role of Lorelei: "On Broadway, an authentic new star is almost as rare a phenomenon as it is in the heavens. Perhaps in a decade a nova explodes above the Great White Way with enough brilliance to reillumine the whole gaudy legend of show business." Then in 1964, she started the lines forming to see *Hello Dolly,* and ultimately made theatrical history by playing the role of Dolly Gallagher Levi more than 3,000 times. The kewpie-doll clown has also sparkled in clubs and concert halls with her successful one-woman shows, appeared in films and television specials, and recorded 10 gold albums.

This saucer-eyed nova was born 31 January 1921 in Seattle, Washington, to George Channing, a well-known lecturer and teacher in the Christian Science Church. "At the age of four," she recalls, "I went through a black and blue period, after discovering that a funny fall was always good for a laugh." Leaving Bennington College, she sang in an ill-fated Broadway musical, *I'm Simply Fraught About You*, and the next four years were fameless and largely jobless. She left New York for California to be with her parents. ("My father dragged me home, fearful I would come down with beriberi.") As luck would have it, Gower Champion was auditioning hopefuls for a revue, *Lend an Ear*. The show was transplanted from Hollywood to Broadway success, and Carol was on her way to stardom.

She made her official nightclub debut in 1957 in Las Vegas, then took her one-woman entertainment, *Show Girl*, to Broadway in 1961. In 1970, Carol Channing and Her Ten Stout-Hearted Men invaded London's Drury Lane Theatre. She did four Command Performances for the Queen of England and was immediately elected to "Her Majesty's Royal Order of Comedians." Channing toured with Mary Martin in *Legends!* in 1986 and 1987. Among her films are *Thoroughly Modern Millie* (her favorite assignment) and the award-winning *Archie and Mehitabel*, which she previously recorded on a best-selling album. Her little-girl voice has made her America's number-one best seller of children's records (including her delightful *Winnie the Pooh*). On television, she's appeared on "The Love Boat" and her own specials, including "George Burns and Carol Channing."

Wed twice before, since 1956 she's been married to producer-writer Charles F. Lowe. They have a son, Channing Lowe. Carol is almost as famous for her offstage eating habits as for her stage personality. Allergic to chemicals in food, she carries her own specially prepared dishes, even when dining at places like "21" or Buckingham Palace.

Chevy Chase

"I guess I just look so straight and normal nobody expects me to pick my nose and fall." He frequently did both with great gusto on NBC's irreverent late-night comedy hit "Saturday Night Live." After he left the show at the height of its popularity to

become a film star, his career tumbled with the velocity of one of his spastic pratfalls, made famous as the opener of the comedy program.

He was born Cornelius Crane Chase on 8 October 1943 in New York, the son of a publishing executive and a Crane plumbing heiress. A restless student and self-described "class cutup," he was ejected from one high school and asked to leave his first college for his *Animal House*-type shenanigans, which he admits he has never outgrown. "I'm whatever I was at six, only I make more."

After graduating from Bard College, he formed an Off-Broadway production company in Manhattan's East Village, which created lampoons of advertisements and other TV fare. The best sketches were incorporated in the 1974 video potpourri, "Groove Tube." He appeared Off-Broadway in National Lampoon's revue, *Lemmings,* while penning scripts for "National Lampoon Radio Hour." Hired as a writer by "Saturday Night Live" producer Lorne Michaels—whom he met standing on a movie line—he convinced Michaels to feature him as one of the "Not Ready for Primetime Players," the show's seven-member troupe of regular performers. With his benign manner and Joe College face, he had the perfect deadpan delivery as host of a mock newscast, "Weekend Update." Turning sheepishly to the camera, after being discovered involved in a steamy phone conversation with his paramour, he would intone, "Good evening, I'm Chevy Chase, and you're not," and proceed to read subversively funny stories, aided by a backdrop of doctored news photos: "President Ford pierced his left hand with a salad fork at a luncheon celebrating Tuna Salad Day at the White House today. Alert Secret Service men seized the fork and wrestled it to the ground." He earned two Emmy awards, for writing and performing, before leaving the show in 1976 to debut opposite Goldie Hawn in the 1978 movie *Foul Play.* His other film credits include: *Caddyshack* (1980), *Seems Like Old Times* (1980), *National Lampoon's Vacation* (1983), *Fletch* (1985), *National Lampoon's European Vacation* (1985), *Spies Like Us* (1986), *Three Amigos* (1986), *Memoirs of an Invisible Man* (1987), *Fletch II* (1988), *Funny Farm* (1988), *Caddyshack II* (1988), *Fletch Lives* (1989), and *National Lampoon's Christmas Vacation* (1989).

Chase entered into marriage with a model and with an actress; both unions ended in divorce. He married a production coordinator, Jayni, in 1982, and they have three children.

Cher

"Cher's identity as a famous person has been complicated by the burgeoning acceptance of her screen talent. These roles are startling departures from her earlier ones, and mark a surprising cusp in an already surprising career," wrote Bruce Weber of the *New York Times Magazine*. Earning the respect due a seasoned performer, Cher won the Academy Award and Golden Globe Award in 1988 for *Moonstruck*.

Born 20 May 1946, Cher (whose real name is Cherilyn Sarkisian LaPiere; she is of Armenian, Turkish, French and Cherokee descent) was just a teenager when she teamed up with Salvador "Sonny" Bono to play clubs in the West as "Caesar and Cleo" (their first stage name). Among the first performers to be dubbed hippies by the media in 1965, they performed their first big hit, "I Got You, Babe," wearing sandals, Neanderthal-like fur vests and blue jeans. "The Sonny and Cher Comedy Hour" ran on television from 1971 to 1975, one season after her divorce from Sonny in 1974 (one daughter, Chastity). After the divorce, Cher launched her solo career as what she called "this glamorous, exotic creature." She became a frequent *Vogue* cover girl, wore Bob Mackie clothes, garnered multiple gold and platinum records, appeared in a number of TV specials and had her own "Cher Show." A second marriage to rock singer Gregg Allman (one son, Elijah Blue) also ended in divorce. "She's at the top of her act now," said an admiring Meryl Streep, who has become a close friend of Cher's since *Silkwood*. "Maybe because she's not dependent on any man." Cher made her Broadway acting debut in Robert Altman's *Come Back to the 5 & Dime, Jimmy Dean, Jimmy Dean* in 1982. Before that she'd grinded for a minimum of 20 weeks each year in Las Vegas. "I was always afraid of having no money. But I was dying in Vegas. Francis Coppola once said to me, 'You should do films, you're so talented.' I said, 'Get me a job, find anyone who'll give me a job.' I love comedy but serious is closer to who I am. I know pain, I really know it." After Mike Nichols favored her in *Jimmy Dean* he picked her for *Silkwood* (she received an Academy Award nomination as Best Supporting Actress for her portrayal of Silkwood's lesbian coworker and housemate, Dolly Pelliker). Her third film was the Peter Bogdanovich-directed *Mask* (also well received). These days, on top of the piano in her Benedict Canyon Mansion (for sale in 1984 for a breezy $6.4 million) there is a photo of herself and Streep with an inscription from Nichols: "You are a major actress and a great human being. Love, Mike."

Involved in all aspects of showbiz, Cher continues to record and has several hit songs, accompanied by videos, including: "I Found Someone" and "After All" (duet with Peter Cetera which was the theme song of the movie *Chances Are;* 1989). Other movies with Cher, including *Witches of Eastwick* (1987), *Suspect* (1987), and *Mermaids* (1990) added to her star status. Rumors of a sequel to *Moonstruck* are eagerly embraced by those millions of moviegoers who enjoyed the first one. In addition, she has a hit album *Heart of Stone* (1989). Already floating on air, now Cher has become a part of it, with her fragrance, "Uninhibited", launched in 1988. In 1990, she also conducted a successful concert tour of the U.S. Choosing to remain single at this point in her life, she continues to shine as one of America's originals—an outrageous singing star, glamorous vamp and talented actress. Fans of Sonny and Cher were delighted when, almost fifteen years after their divorce, the couple appeared for an impromptu reunion on the "Late Night with David Letterman" show, during which they joined in an unrehearsed, emotional performance of "I Got You Babe."

Julie Christie

The winner of the New York Film Critics Award and an Oscar for *Darling* in 1965 is focusing her high-powered energy on the peace movement. The blonde, blue-eyed beauty has studied the subject, keeps files on it, quotes impressive statistics and makes a point of doing her homework before speaking. She was the narrator of the half-hour TV documentary "Taking on the Bomb." "I felt it was an important recording of the impressive, amazing activities women have organized to demonstrate for peace and I wanted to contribute. I have done far less than many, many women. There are people whose voices should certainly be heard before mine." Ironically, it's her British accent that always seems to get the publicity, particularly when she lambasted the U.S. government over its nuclear-arms policies. "I get the feeling that the U.S. doesn't really care about the annihilation of Europe and the rest of the world," she said in 1984 after meeting with American weapons negotiator Paul Nitze and other officials in Washington. "I can't believe it, but using nuclear missiles is quite clearly part of the game plan."

Born in Assam, India, 14 April 1940, the daughter of a tea planter, she was sent back to England at the age of eight for schooling. When she was 16, she want off to study art and French in Paris for a year and later attended a technical college in Brighton, before starting drama studies at the Central School of Speech Training and Dramatic Art. "I was a vagrant," she recalls of her three years there. "I used to sleep in attics, even parks. When I got some money I bought one of those air mattresses you blow up. I used to go around to friends' houses carrying my own mattress."

She first attracted real critical notice in a small role in John Schlesinger's *Billy Liar* in 1963 and then went on to play Luciana in the Royal Shakespeare Company's *A Comedy of Errors*, which toured Europe and the U.S. in 1964. After appearing in *Young Cassidy*, she was given her big chance—with Schlesinger once again—in *Darling*, a difficult role that she grew to loathe. She may be best known for her portrayal of Lara in 1965's *Dr. Zhivago*, which also starred Omar Sharif in the title role. Christie later starred in *McCabe and Mrs. Miller* (1971) and *Shampoo* (1975), both with erstwhile off-screen companion Warren Beatty. Writing of the latter, one critic, noting that the film seemed to exploit the much-publicized Beatty-Christie affair of the time, reported, "You've read about Beatty and Christie. Now you can see them screwing—almost." She appeared with Beatty again (more chastely) in *Heaven Can Wait* in 1978. She returned to India in 1983 to make the Ivory-Merchant film, *Heat and Dust*. Other films include: *The Return of the Soldier, Miss Mary*, and *Power*. She made the television mini-series "Mary, Mary" (1986) and starred in the made-for-TV film "Deadly Decision" (1988).

Dick Clark

H ardy television perennial Dick Clark has often been dubbed "the world's oldest teenager," thanks to his ever-boyish face. He was on a roll in the early 1980s with shows on three major networks: celebrating his 30th anniversary on the tube in 1984 as host of "American Bandstand"; the CBS daily quiz show "The New $25,000 Pyramid"; and NBC's weekly "TV's Bloopers and Practical Jokes."

Born 30 November 1929 in suburban Mount Vernon, New

York, Clark was smitten as a teenager with "talk radio." He worked briefly as a news anchorman and later moved to Philadelphia where he hosted the radio version of "American Bandstand." He was made full-time host when the program went to television in 1956. Over the years he developed a long list of production companies that produce over 170 hours of television programming a year. He also supplies the networks and independent stations with dozens of award ceremonies each year. Clark says, "Too many people who produce live television lead guarded, sheltered lives in New York or Los Angeles. I get out and shake hands. I ask people on the street what they would like to see." In 1984 he scored another success for NBC with "The Most Beautiful Girl in the World," a two-hour beauty contest that permitted the television audience to vote for its favorite contestants. The show earned a 19.8 rating and a 29 share, beating or tying the programs on the other two networks.

Rising in the 1980's as a prosperous entrepreneur, he was involved in many projects. His radio roots are responsible for the success of such syndicated shows as: "Dick Clark National Music Survey" and "Dick Clark's Rock, Roll and Remember Show," airing on hundreds of stations and reaching millions of listeners. He was the co-executive producer of CBS-TV's "Promised a Miracle" (1988) and the author of a 1986 book, *Dick Clark's Easy-Going Guide to Good Grooming*. He zeroed in on the home video market and released "Dick Clark's Best of Bandstand" in 1985. Contributing his name and time to a good cause, Dick hosted the "Live Aid" Rock Concert—an internationally broadcast concert that raised money for African famine relief. In another behind-the-scenes venture, Clark was the executive producer for the ABC-TV movie "Liberace" in 1988. Dick lives in Malibu, California, with his third wife Kari, and his three children.

Jill Clayburgh

After appearing in a series of mediocre films during the early 70's (*Portnoy's Complaint, Gable and Lombard, Silver Streak, Semi-Tough*), Jill Clayburgh finally achieved unanimous acclaim in

1978 as Erica in Paul Mazursky's *An Unmarried Woman*. Clayburgh plays an educated, intelligent Manhattan woman whose life is shattered when her husband leaves her. The actress' straightforward, genuine performance earned her a Best-Actress award at the Cannes Film Festival, her first Oscar nomination, and many fans.

The daughter of well-to-do, socially prominent parents, she was born in New York City on 30 April 1944. Her exclusive education included Sarah Lawrence College (Class of '66), where she studied philosophy, religion and literature. In college she also acted in her first film, *The Wedding Party*, which was directed by an unknown Brian De Palma and co-starred the equally obscure Robert De Niro. "I loved the fantasy of movies and theatre," says Clayburgh. By the late 60's, following summer stock, regional theatre appearances and lessons with Uta Hagen, Clayburgh was doing television. Her Broadway debut in October of 1970 was in a musical, *The Rothschilds*. This led to another musical appearance the next year in Bob Fosse's *Pippin*. In 1974 she was in the N.Y. cast of Tom Stoppard's *Jumpers*. A decade later she starred in a Broadway revival of Noel Coward's *Design for Living*. Clayburgh's role as a prostitute in the 1975 TV film "Hustling" earned an Emmy nomination. "I play this whore as funny, sensitive, childlike, and quite mad," she says, "a girl who just doesn't know how to make it, a state I know something about."

After her live-in relationship with Al Pacino ended, Clayburgh married playwright David Rabe in March 1979 (a daughter, Lily). That year she finally played a Rabe role she'd long coveted, Chrissy, a go-go dancer, *In the Boom Boom Room*. (The original Lincoln Center production had starred Madeline Kahn.) The couple have an apartment on New York's West Side and a Pennsylvania country house. "My biggest extravagance is where I live," the actress says. Like her character Erica, Clayburgh jogs regularly. "I support it so wholly," she says, "that I would never think not to talk about it."

Starting Over (1979) brought Clayburgh a second Oscar nomination. She has worked with such noted directors as Bertolucci and Costa-Gavras, but shuns the trappings of stardom, claiming, "I want to be an actress, not a personality." Clayburgh's other films include *The First Monday in October* (1981), *I'm Dancing As Fast As I Can* (1982), *Hannah K.* (1983), *Shy People* (1987) and a CBS-TV movie "Who Gets the Friends?" (1988).

Glenn Close

And she sings! She's a lyric soprano who was nominated for a Tony as the feisty wife of Phineas T. in the 1980 Broadway musical *Barnum*. In 1984 she won the Tony for Best Actress playing opposite Jeremy Irons in Tom Stoppard's *The Real Thing* directed by Mike Nichols. "Twice I sang the anthem at Shea Stadium. It was when I was living with [actor] Len Cariou and he knows lots of sports people, and one day somebody said to me, 'Do you want to do it?' And I said, 'Sure.' It was terrifying. I forgot my pitchpipe and I started too low and I forgot about the echo. You go out into this field, and the mike is right behind home plate, and there are all these people. You start singing, 'oh say can you see,' and you don't hear anything for a second and a half, and then you hear, 'OH SAY CAN YOU SEE,' and you're already on the next line."

Born 19 May 1947 daughter of a Greenwich, Conn., surgeon whose family settled in that prosperous New England town sometime around 1682, she began acting while a student at a fashionable girls' boarding school, Rosemary Hall, where she organized a theatre troupe called "The Fingernails—the Group with Polish." After five years of travelling with folksinging ensembles she studied drama at the College of William and Mary and graduated with a Phi Beta Kappa key. She got her first job in New York soon thereafter as understudy in a Phoenix Theatre production of *Love for Love;* she was even luckier when the leading lady backed out during dress rehearsal and Close went on although she'd never walked through the part. As she says, "it was trial by fire." She spent a very successful season at that theatre before appearing on Broadway in the thriller *Crucible of Blood* and she later collected an Obie for her work in Simon Benmusa's *The Singular Life of Albert Nobbs*. "I'm a very competitive person, but I don't believe in competing with individual people because it's destructive. The best piece of advice I got on the first job I had was: 'Never compare your career with anybody else's. You'd jump out a window.'" Her screen debut was as the outspoken feminist mother in *The World According to Garp*, for which she received her first Academy Award nomination; the second came in 1984 for *The Big Chill*. That same year she played in "Something About Amelia." About incest, it was one of the most viewed TV shows of that season. She played opposite Robert Redford in the film of Bernard Malamud's *The Natural* and she jokingly lamented to *Vogue* interviewer Aimee Lee Ball that she had to play the "good woman" in the film and was allowed only one very chaste kiss. "I kept saying 'This is the one man who's everyone's fantasy, and she never gets to kiss him.' But that's my image."

Close, who says that the only thing she hates about making movies is coffee "in styrofoam cups," lives in Greenwich Village. In 1984 she wed venture capitalist James Marsalis whom she met after the opening of *The Real Thing*. The couple later divorced. In 1985 she appeared Off-Broadway in *Childhood*, based on the memories of French writer Nathalie Sarraute, and made the films *Maxie* and *Jagged Edge*. She returned to Broadway in the 1985-86 season in *Benefactors*. Playing the role of Alex Forrest in the 1987 film *Fatal Attraction*, Close received an Academy Award nomination, but was edged out by Cher for the highest honor. Nevertheless, Glenn received her own prize, daughter Annie Maude, born 26 April 1988. Not married to Close at the time of her baby's birth, the child's father is John Starke. Continually active, Close has taken on recent projects that include the films *Dangerous Liaisons* (Academy Award nomination—1989), *Immediate Family* (1989), and *Reversal of Fortune* (1990) about the Sunny Von Bulow case.

Claudette Colbert

Hailed as "the cinema's most sparkling and deft comedienne" during Hollywood's Golden Age, her exquisite light touch and "civilized sexiness" refined and defined sophisticated comedy. "If you live long enough, everything happens to you," chirped the radiantly ageless actress who made her debut in 1923 and was still charming audiences in the 1980's. "I just tell myself I'm 60 and that I have 30 years to go," joked Colbert, an elegant 81 in 1984 when she was saluted by The Film Society of Lincoln Center for her 64-film career. Also in '84, she returned to the London stage (and a year later to Broadway) amid praise and applause, co-starring with Rex Harrison in a revival of Frederick Lonsdale's 1923 comedy of manners, *Aren't We All?* One critic noted Colbert had "kept her looks, her dimples, and her cute and cuddly naughtiness." A versatile dramatic actress, she's played a broad range of roles, though breezy comedy became her specialty. In 1934 she won a Best Actress Oscar for *It Happened One Night,* a landmark in sophisticated comedy that also won Oscars for co-star Clark Gable and director Frank Capra. She's also vamped her way seductively through serious roles such as the wicked Poppea in Cecil B. DeMille's 1933 spectacular, *The Sign of the Cross* and his 1934 epic, *Cleopatra.* Directors have found her demanding. (She was said to be bossy, stubborn, fickle about her clothes, and wanted only her left profile photographed.) However, as one actress observed, "That's why she *is* Claudette Colbert."

Born Lily Claudette Chauchoin in Paris, 13 September 1903, Colbert came to America in 1910 and grew up in New York City. She started her acting career in 1923 on the New York stage and still considers the stage her first love ("I never thought of movies, God knows, until the 1929 crash. When that came, the money seemed to dry up on Broadway"). Paramount snatched her up, and she went to Hollywood, not returning to the theatre until the 1950s. During her 34 years in Hollywood, she evaded being typecast, alternating between serious drama and high comedy in a succession of film classics.

After her breakthrough year in 1934 (*Cleopatra, Imitation of Life, It Happened One Night*), she went on to such laugh classics as *Bluebeard's Eighth Wife, Tovarich,* and the wartime tearjerker, *Since You Went Away.* Her last film was *Parrish* in 1961. She's returned periodically to the stage, pleasing Broadway audiences with such light comedies as *Marriage-Go-Round* with Charles Boyer in 1958, and *The Kingfisher* with Rex Harrison in 1978. She also appeared in the 1981 suspense comedy, *A Talent for Murder.* Says Colbert of her love for the stage: "There's really nothing like that wonderful feeling of facing your audience." On television she's starred in "The Royal Family" with Helen Hayes and Fredric March, and "Blithe Spirit" with Noel Coward and Lauren Bacall. She earned a Golden Globe Award for Best Supporting Actress in 1988 for her role in the TV adaptation of "The Two Mrs. Grenvilles."

Married first to Norman Foster, but more compatibly to ear-nose-and-throat specialist Dr. Joel Pressman (who died in 1968), she once gave this secret for the success of that 35-year partnership: "A wife shouldn't bore her husband with her petty ills. He never knew what picture I was in from one year to the next." She offered some further insights into the off-screen world of Claudette Colbert to columnist Hy Gardner: "Q. What keeps you looking and feeling so young? A. Not worrying about looking and feeling so young. Q. What kind of sleep do you get? A. I don't know. I'm asleep at the time. Q. What do you worry about most? A. I devote the same amount of worry to all problems. I don't play favorites. Q. Do you take exercise? A. My dog walks me twice a day. Q. Do you use any alcohol? A. Only in my drinks. Q. Are you bitter about anything? A. No, but I'm open to suggestions. Q. Do you ever expect to retire? A. Don't call me after midnight." Colbert divides her year between her New York apartment and a house in Barbados.

Dabney Coleman

"I 've played good guys and nice guys, but the truth is that I'd rather be nasty than nice," he says. "The bad guys are always better written and more fun to play. If I do villains well, it's because I play them straight. I resist cliches. I always try to make my good guys a little bad and my bad guys a little good." A master at portraying shifty schemers, Dabney Coleman manages to turn heels into heroes by making them funnier than they are mean. After years of anonymity playing bland doctors and lawyers in TV guest stints (and a sojourn on Marlo Thomas' "That Girl"), his breakthrough came in 1976 as the lecherous, sanctimonious Rev. Merle Jeeter on "Mary Hartman, Mary Hartman," television's soap opera parody. Following a string of hit films, his own TV series, "Buffalo Bill," attracted a whole new following in 1982-83 for his character Bill Bittinger, a repugnant yet perversely bearable Buffalo talk-show host that seemed the ideal Coleman role. There was mourning in many households when the show was cancelled. Coleman received another shot at his own series, "The Slap Maxwell Story," and for his work on this show was presented with a Golden Globe Award (1988) for "Best Actor in a Comedy."

He was born in 1932 in Austin, Texas, and raised in Corpus Christi, never quite losing his southern drawl. He attended Virginia Military Institute, served in the U.S. Army, and dropped out of the University of Texas Law School to study acting at N.Y.'s Neighborhood Playhouse. His caddish employer in *9 to 5* (1980) was his first important film role. He was nicer as Jane Fonda's fiance in *On Golden Pond* (1981) but the next year in *Tootsie* found him back in his exasperating image. In 1983's *War Games* he was a maniacal computer expert. By the mid-1980s he was the screen's most popular comic heavy, in such films as *Dragnet* (1987), *Hot To Trot* (1987) and *Meet the Applegates* (1989). Dabney has also starred in two acclaimed real-life-stories-turned-television movies: "Guilty of Innocence: The Lenell Geter Story" (1987) and "Baby M" (1988).

"There is a lot of anger in me," he confesses. It's sublimated in his acting and also on the tennis court (sometimes up to four hours a day), where he has a reputation as a formidable opponent. He also lifts weights in his California beachfront condominium, chainsmokes, has a courtly manner and dislikes discussing himself. He's twice divorced (one marriage lasted 21 years), with three children. Wryly humorous off the set, he's a perfectionist at work. He could play heroes, he maintains, but "I just couldn't play a placid hero. Heroes are usually straight and without color. . . . I always look for something specific in a part—some rebelliousness, maybe, or eccentricity—and it usually comes in the form of a villain. That makes it fun for me to play." He excels at bringing out the best in the worst of people.

Joan Collins

Although she acted for over 30 years—in more than 50 movies and 30 TV series—it was not until her role as the beauteous bitch Alexis Carrington Colby on television's *Dynasty*, the super-successful sentimentalization of the endless ups and downs and groin pains of the super-rich, that Collins became a Nielsen-proclaimed rhinestone icon here and abroad. Her campy numbers (escorting her episodically brain-damaged stepson Jeff via private jet to a hospital in Gstaad wearing as her skiing outfit white jodpurs, white boots, white shirt, white fox fur jacket, fox hat and fox muff; hitting husband-to-be Cecil as he was having a massive coronary attack) have dulled Joan Crawford's iceberg and shoved Liz Taylor off her "I-got-there-first" pedestal. Collins used to be referred to as "a poor man's Liz Taylor," but no longer. Her company produced and she starred in the fall 1985 miniseries "Sins," and her novel *Primetime* (1988) became a bestseller.

Jaunty Joan (a reporter once joked that she would "gussy herself up for a smog alert") was born in London 23 May 1933. She grew up surrounded by show biz sorts since her father was a theatrical agent. She left school at 15 to attend the Royal Academy of Dramatic Art, but withdrew to make her screen debut, at age 17, in

I'll Be Leaving You, opposite Laurence Harvey. After gaining recognition as "Britain's Best Bad Girl," she headed for Hollywood where her first film was *Land of the Pharoahs,* directed by Howard Hawks. She appeared in about a dozen movies as the sultry sexpot with an impressive assortment of cinema studs, including Richard Burton, Harry Belafonte, Robert Wagner, Gregory Peck and Paul Newman. Among her later credits: *The Stud* and *The Bitch,* both based on novels written by her younger sister, Jackie Collins. Joan has spawned a cottage industry of Alexis-inspired products (from furs to jewelry to perfume and bed linen), all hot-sellers helped by her "50 is beautiful" spread in the buff for *Playboy.* According to her bestselling autobiography, *Past Imperfect,* her life has been just that: a roller coaster ride of highs and lows. Her first brief marriage, at 18 to British actor Maxwell Reed, began and ended disastrously. She claimed that on their first date, he slipped a mickey into her drink and raped her; the marriage was finished when he tried to sell her to an Arab sheik for one night of 10,000 pounds. She put her career on hold for seven years when she was married to Anthony Newley in the early 1960s and tried to be a good Hollywood wife. The Newleys had two children. Joan has a third, a daughter Katy from her marriage to American record producer Ron Kass. When Katy was eight she was hit by a car and lay in a coma for eight days. Doctors predicted that she would be permanently brain damaged, but Collins' resolve to nurse her daughter back to life effected a miraculous recovery. Joan's fourth marriage to Peter Holm fizzled fast (married November, 1985; filed for annulment in December, 1986) and their divorce trial lit up the tabloids. The courtroom antics seemed to pop right out of a soap opera, even to the introduction of Peter's "passion flower."

Thrilled but not deluded by her success in a profession where she's "been down for the count more than once," she says: "Even when you win the rat race you're still a rat." "I've had to give up certain things in my life," she adds. "One is shopping. Two is lunch with the girls. Three is cocktail parties and four is studying my lines . . . but I know Alexis so well, I know her better than I know myself."

Sean Connery

"**T**here's no question that I'm not so enamored of throwing myself around as much," he said when he returned to filming his sixth James Bond film, *Never Say Never Again* in 1983. "I'm not too mad about the underwater stuff, either, because suddenly I feel I'm out of my element. I was a bit nervous, but one

ends up doing as much as is physically possible and the insurance will allow." It was his first Bond film in 12 years, and it required him to train hard in order to return his brawny body to Bond perfection. Connery, the veteran of over 35 films besides the Bond epics (including *Robin and Marian* and *The Great Train Robbery*) was showing the signs of mellow middle age. During his stunts he had to worry that his short-cropped toupee might slip. In 1985, Sean broke out of the Bond mold and starred in the film version of the best-seller *The Name of the Rose*. It's been a steady rise with continual good roles: *Presidio* (1988), *The Untouchables* (Oscar for Best Supporting Actor, 1988), *Indiana Jones and the Last Crusade* (1989), *Family Business* (1989), and *Rosencrantz and Guildenstern are Dead* (1989) with Robert Lindsay and Sting, and the cold-war thriller *Hunt for Red October* (1990).

"I had no idea acting would by my career, but I didn't have many alternatives, mind you." Born in Edinburgh, Scotland, 25 August 1930, a truck driver's son, he dropped out of school at 13 and "took many jobs . . . it was a gradual progression before I found out what I wanted to do." He enlisted in the British Navy for three years and then worked as a milkman, trucker, cement mixer, bricklayer, and steel bender—but it was bodybuilding that eventually brought him to acting. In London in 1950, representing Scotland in the Mr. Universe contest, Connery got a part in the chorus of a West End production of *South Pacific*. Joining a small suburban London repertory company ("I learned enough to know that I didn't know enough"), he was singled out to play James Bond by producer Harry Saltzman during a London *Daily Express* reader-popularity poll. Connery first portrayed Agent 007 in the 1963 film version of Ian Fleming's *Dr. No* and repeated the role in *From Russia With Love* (1964), *Goldfiner* (1965), *Thunderball* (1965), *You Only Live Twice* (1967) and *Diamonds Are Forever* (1971), before satisfying his Bond fans once again in *Never Say Never Again*.

Connery split from his first wife, actress-author Diane Cilento, in 1971 (one child). In 1975 he married French-Moroccan artist Micheline Roquebrune. In the late 1960s the pressures of being James Bond got to the actor, and he disappeared for a while in Norway under the care of famed psychiatrist, Professor Ola Raknes, to divorce the real Sean Connery from the indigestible gun-waving sex symbol. "It's very difficult for people who haven't been exposed to the public eye to appreciate what one is talking about," Connery has said by way of explaining why he chooses to live on Spain's Costa Del Sol and in the Bahamas where he is an avid golfer and tennis player. Tough, craggy-faced, a greying six-foot-two Adonis, he is atypically attached to home and hearth. On his muscular arms are two tattoos: One says, "Scotland Forever," the other "Mum and Dad."

Francis Ford Coppola

From his composer-flutist father, Carmine, he inherited a Bohemian indifference to financial stability, as well as a yearning for artistic achievement. "So what if my telephone is turned off again at home? Or my electricity is shut off? Or my credit cards cancelled? If you don't bet, you don't have a chance to win. It's so silly in life not to pursue the highest possible thing you can imagine, even if you run the risk of losing it all, because if you don't pursue it you've lost it anyway. You can't be an artist and be safe." Some of his gambles he's won, others lost. Chief among the former: 1972's *The Godfather* (his screenplay Oscar joined the one he'd won two years earlier for co-scripting *Patton*), 1974's *The Godfather, Part II* (that rare breed, a critically acclaimed sequel, it earned him Oscars for his screenplay and direction and, like its predecessor, was named Best Film by the Academy), the same year's *The Conversation* (a taut and intelligent inner view of the bugging business, which won him high critical praise as well as the Cannes Film Festival Golden Palm) and 1979's *Apocalypse Now* (which received both the Grand Prix and Best Director awards at Cannes).

Born 7 April 1939 in Detroit, Michigan, and raised in NYC's Queens, Coppola was bedridden and almost paralyzed for a year at age nine after contracting polio. While studying drama at Hofstra, he wrote the book and lyrics for a couple of school musicals, but returned to his first love, movies, in graduate school at UCLA. His breakthrough came via his association with Roger Corman. After helping the producer-director in various capacities on a number of films, he was awarded the opportunity to direct a low-budget horror film, *Dementia 13* (1963), made in Ireland in three days. Three years later he achieved his first artistic success with *You're A Big Boy Now*, an expanded version of his M.F.A. thesis. His career over the next few years was eclectic, scripting *This Property is Condemned* (1966) and *The Great Gatsby* (1974) and directing such varied films as 1968's *Finian's Rainbow* (a big-budget flop adaptation of the Broadway musical classic) and 1969's *The Rain People* (a low-budget grim slice of Americana). In the late '60s he was in deep financial trouble and his own newly-formed San Francisco-based production company, American Zoetrope, was on the verge of bankruptcy—not for the last time. (In 1980 it became the expanded L.A. facility, Zoetrope Studios.) In 1975 he devoted much of his energies to publishing *City* magazine (also S.F.-based), which folded the next year. Like his mentor Corman before him, Coppola has been instrumental in aiding the careers of fledgling filmmakers.

He had three children from his marriage to artist Eleanor Neil. The youngest—and only daughter—Sophia, appeared at one month old as the baby in *The Godfather's* baptism scene. His son Gian Carlo died in a boating accident in Maryland in 1986.

Along with his even more ambitious *Apocalypse Now, The Godfather* saga remains the director's crowning achievement. "I feel that the Mafia is an incredible metaphor for this country," he says. Since *Apocalypse*, his movies include: *One from the Heart* (1982), *The Outsiders* (1983), *Rumblefish* (1983), *The Cotton Club* (1984), *Gardens of Stone* (1986), *Tough Guys Don't Dance* (1987), a segment in *New York Stories* (1988) and the critically acclaimed *Tucker: The Man and His Dream* (1988). 1990 saw the release of *The Godfather, Part III*.

Roger Corman

Sometimes called the "King of Schlock," he produced and/or directed an unbroken string of (financially if not critically) successful "quickies"—low budget exploitation films. The "graduates" of his unofficial film school (lending and honing their talents for a pittance before they achieved fame) include actors Jack Nicholson, Robert DeNiro,, Ellen Burstyn, and Bruce Dern and directors Francis Ford Coppola, Peter Bogdanovich and Martin Scorsese. From his first critical success, 1958's *Machine Gun Kelly*, to his celebrated eight-film Edgar Allan Poe cycle of the early '60s, Corman savvily exploited trends and headlines, working in a variety of genres (action-adventure, monster, western) aimed chiefly at the youth market.

Born in Detroit on 5 April 1926, he moved with his family around 1940 to California and attended Beverly Hills High School. "There was no way I couldn't be interested in movies, growing up where I did," he says. "Movies just fascinated me." He was preoccupied with fantasy and horror, devouring Poe's tales and sci-fi. He enlisted in the Navy, serving for the last years of WW II, and graduated from Stanford in the late '40s with an engineering degree. After two years (spent partly in Europe) as a self-confessed "bum," he held a variety of Hollywood odd jobs. His stint as a script reader inspired him to write one. Using a "learn while you work" approach, he made an amazing 32 films for American International Pictures between 1955 and 1960. In '60 he made his first color film, *House of Usher*. (*The Masque of the Red Death* and *Tomb of Ligeia* are considered his best Poe-inspired-films.) His 1960 cult classic *Little Shop of Horrors* (which Corman says was shot in only two days) inspired one of Off-Broadway's biggest musical hits of the 1980s. His 1962 *The Intruder* was an uncharacteristically grim study of racial prejudice and social injustice. Self-financed, it was his first message film and first boxoffice flop. "I was devastated," he says. "I decided, then and there, that I would never again make a movie that would be so obviously a personal statement."

Tall, slender, youthful, a tennis buff, he's been married since the early '70s to Julie Halloran. They live with their three children in Pacific Palisades, an affluent L.A. suburb. Recent releases include: *Munchies* (1987), *Stripped to Kill* (1987), *Don't Let Go* (1987), *Matar es Morir Un Poco* (1988), and *Not of this Earth* (1988).

Bill Cosby

Born in Philadelphia, 12 July 1937, the son of an eight-dollar-a-day domestic and a father "who liked his booze," he is now Dr. William Henry Cosby, Jr. He is something of a child expert, as well as a successful actor, producer, comedian, author, tennis buff, and former bartender. He's been by Sidney Poitier's side on-screen and as co-producer in the *Uptown Saturday Night* sequels and has some half-dozen movie credits to add to those. Having received enough Grammys, Emmys, and People's Choice Awards to fill a few bookshelves, Cosby struck gold again in 1984 with the debut of the long-running NBC-TV series "The Cosby Show."

Cosby attended grammar school along with his pals Fat Albert, Old Weird Harold, Dumb Donald, and a host of others made famous by Bill in his comedy routines, as well as serving as inspira-

tion for his Saturday animated cartoon series. During his freshman year at college he went to California to look for a summer job. ("I got some of the worst excuses for not hiring me. I got so tired of riding buses and spending money to hear some guy say, 'Well—'. Finally I just called and said over the phone, 'Do you hire Negroes?' 'No.'") Temple University was later to lose one of its finest two-year-scholarship gridders when Cosby decided he'd rather tackle show biz, although he says his dad greeted the proposition with the question, "Do you want to play for the New York Giants and be a man, or do you want to make a damned fool of yourself?" When he was singled out by a *New York Times* reporter while he was appearing at the Gaslight in Greenwich Village, his career was launched. In 1964 he married University of Maryland student Camille Hanks, by whom he has five kids whose first names all begin with the letter "E."

The first black to star in a dramatic TV series ("I Spy"), he refused to exploit his color. ("Why should I go out there and say, 'Ladies and gentlemen, I grew up in a Negro neighborhood?'") In fact, in his next series, "The Bill Cosby Show," which began in 1969, black characters were impeccably normal while the whites were stereotypical. "That's done on purpose," he said. He meant to alter other, historical prejudices when he produced, starred in and poured $350,000 of his own money into *Man and Boy,* his movie debut, about a black Wild West family and gun-slingers. Cosby is universal enough to be a sought-after commercial pitchman, however. He's an enthusiastic spokesman for Ford, Del Monte, and Jell-O.

This broad-chested funnyman who once could set hearts aflutter by taking off his shirt in his TV roles, has eased into middle-aged exasperation, which only becomes a source for more mirth material. A children's television genius who's got a Ph.D. in education from the University of Massachusetts, he gave 1984 grads of Harvey Mudd College their commencement address. In addition to his role as Dr. Cliff Huxtable on "The Cosby Show," Bill's been a very busy man. His album *Cosby and the Kids* was released in 1986, two books—*Fatherhood* (1986) and *Time Flies* (1987)—hit the bookstands, and he co-produced, as well as starred in a movie *Leonard: Part VI* in 1987 with Tom Courtenay. On the heels of his sitcom success, Bill created the spin-off series "A Different World," which also became a top-rated comedy show. His 1990 film work includes *Ghost Dad*.

Costa-Gavras

"A camera is not a gun. In fact, a camera is the anti-weapon *par excellence*, because it can express. A gun expresses nothing." Thus does this Greek-born, French-based *"agent provocateur* of films" make a distinction between his own politically *engagé* products and those of self-styled revolutionary filmmakers. While unveiling the blacker aspects of some of the major forces of our time, Costa-Gavras has shifted the political film from a genre with only sectarian appeal to one with a mass audience. His *Z*, about the assassination of a Greek parliament member, was a phenomenal success throughout the world, "changing the image of Greece from that of a country with colorful islands, sun-baked beaches, and evzones in pleated skirts to that of a harsh, militant state." It also won an Oscar in 1970 as Best Foreign Picture.

He was born Konstantinos Gavras in Athens in 1933, the son of a resistance leader, and shortened his name to Costa-Gavras when he moved to Paris as a 19-year-old to study comparative literature at the Sorbonne. ("All this time I was going to Latin Quarter movie houses and to the Cinemathèque, where I saw the possibilities that filmmaking offered.") An insatiable movie buff from early childhood, he at last bowed to the inevitable and enrolled at the French Cinema School to prepare for a film career. After a series of jobs as assistant to some of France's leading directors, he struck out on his own in 1964, writing and directing *The Sleeping Car Murders*, a Hitchcockesque thriller which starred Yves Montand and became an instant hit. Montand also appeared in such subsequent Costa-Gavras efforts as *Z* and *State of Siege;* Jack Lemmon starred in 1982's *Missing*, the director's first film for a major American studio; his 1983 *Hannah K.* was a tour-de-force for Jill Clayburgh; he wrote the screenplay and directed 1987's *Family Business;* and his *Betrayed* (1988) starred Debra Winger and Tom Berenger. In 1990, he directed *The Music Box*, a political thriller about an attorney who defends her father from charges of Nazi war crimes, starring Jessica Lange.

Costa-Gavras was wed in 1968 to French fashion-model-turned-journalist Michele Ray, who made news herself during the Viet Nam war when she was held as a prisoner for 20 days by the Viet Cong. They have a son, Alexandre, and a daughter, Julie.

Bob Costas

An expert in the field of sports, Bob Costas has crossed over to become a well-respected talk-show personality. His twinkling eyes and boyish grin lend a special dimension to his broadcast qualities. Working for over five seasons as host of NBC's pre-game show, "NFL LIVE," Costas has paid his dues along the way.

Born 22 March 1952 in Queens, New York, Bob's father was Greek and his mom was Irish. Always interested in sports and communications, Costas actually began his professional career at WSYR-TV/Radio while still an undergraduate at Syracuse University. After graduation, he moved to St. Louis where he did play-by-play announcing of the ABA Spirits of St. Louis on KMOX Radio (1974). Breaking over to network, from 1976 to 1979 he had the responsibility of regional NFL and NBA assignments for CBS Sports. He was also the radio voice of the University of Missouri basketball from 1976 to 1981. Finding his niche with football broadcasts, he and Bob Trumpy were considered the most outspoken NFL announcing team from 1980 to 1983.

At the top of his field, Costas served as late-night anchor for NBC's coverage of the 1988 Olympic Games from Seoul, Korea. He has won an Emmy Award as Outstanding Sport Personality, has been twice honored as "Sportscaster of the Year" (1985 and 1987), and is frequently seen as fill-in co-anchor of NBC's "Today" show. Presently the host of "Later With Bob Costas," a nighttime talk show, he has the savoir faire and experience to compete in this format. He added pro-basketball play-by-play to his roster of duties at NBC for the 1990-91 season. He is also known for his nationally syndicated sports talk show "Costas Coast-to-Coast." Married to Randi Krummenacher since 1983, Costas and his wife have one son, Keith. They recently built a house in St. Louis, in addition to a home in New York.

Kevin Costner

" **J** ust standing there and delivering his lines Costner projects a fascinating volatility. You don't know what he might do next: grab the gun, grab the girl, or do a backflip. He is something the movies haven't seen for a while . . . a leading man." *Vanity Fair's* evaluation of Kevin Costner was right on the money (as in, box-office draw). Playing a variety of parts ranging from the free-wheeling, fun-loving cowboy Jake of *Silverado* to the incorruptible Eliot Ness of *The Untouchables*, from the duplicitous naval officer Tom Farrell in *No Way Out* to the veteran catcher Crash Davis in *Bull Durham*, Costner has been a leading man in character parts that women could swoon over and men wanted to emulate. Ironically, Costner began his career as king of the editing room floor. His roles in the films *Frances, Table for Five* and *Night Shift* were either edited out or cut to nothing. Cast for a key role in John Badham's *Wargames*, he was graciously released to assume the pivotal role of the suicide victim Alex in Lawrence Kasdan's *The Big Chill*, only to have his sequences (he appeared in flashback) edited out. Another character from a film made in Greece was cut before he even stepped off the plane. Undaunted, Costner prevailed.

Kevin Costner was born 18 January 1955 in Compton, California. Growing up in various Southern California communities as his utility executive father travelled the state, Costner was the class jock, lettering in high school baseball and basketball and playing on the football team. His creative side was expressed through singing in the choir, performing in church musicals and writing poetry. Enrolling in California State University, Fullerton, as a marketing major, he was halfway to a degree before acknowledging his acting interest. While continuing his college courses he enrolled at the Southcoast Actors Co-op and appeared in a number of community theatre productions. Between honing his acting skills and earning his marketing degree, he married his college sweetheart, Cindy. Landing a marketing slot with a major national firm after graduation, he resigned after 45 days, determined to break into movies. Jobless for six months, he accepted a job as a stage manager for a small independent film studio. It afforded him the opportunity to attend drama workshops, study with private coaches and perform in student films. A part in the low-budget, non-union film *Stacy's Knights* preceded his string of edited parts. Finally represented by a major agency, Costner landed a role in PBS's "Testament." Its strong reviews helped Costner nail down the lead role of the smoothly manipulative Gardner Barnes in *Fandango.* Understandably, his reaction to being in virtually every scene was, "They're going to have to stay up nights thinking how to cut me out this one." Restitution for earlier wrongs occurred when Lawrence Kasdan— who felt he owed "this amazing young actor" a part—tapped him for Jake in *Silverado.* "I've waited all my life to do a Western," Costner exclaimed as he dedicated his performance to everyone who ever dreamed of being in Western. John Badham then cast him as the doomed doctor in *American Flyers* and Costner was on a roll. He appeared on Steven Spielberg's television anthology series "Amazing Stories" as the Captain in "The Mission," a special hour-long segment. Voted the "Star of Tomorrow" by the National Association of Theatre Owners in 1986, Costner quickly proved their choice correct. *The Untouchables* (1987) scored with audiences and was going strong when *No Way Out* (1987) cemented his reputation as a leading man and sex symbol. It was a box office smash. His athletic ability served him well as Costner accomplished the impossible. He made a baseball film, historically box-office deadwood; *Bull Durham* was one of 1988's biggest hits. He out-hit himself with 89's *Field of Dreams,* based on W.P. Kinsella's novel about a man's devotion to baseball's "Shoeless Joe" Jackson. Other films include *Revenge* (1990) and his directorial debut with the independent film *Dances With Wolves* (1990).

Costner resides with his wife Cindy and their three children— daughters Annie and Lilly and son Joe—in California. With his All-American good looks, incredible acting ability and proven box-office drawing power, it seems fair to assume he's seen the last of the cutting room floor.

Michael Crawford

White mask, tenor tones, and tender inflections transmit a mental image of this Tony Award winning actor. *Time* magazine asserted: "As the phantom, Michael Crawford gives the most compelling performance currently to be found on any Broadway stage." He not only won the Tony Award for his riveting role, but he also took home Outer Circle Critics Award for Best Actor in a Musical, and the Drama League Award for Unique Contribution to Musical Theater. For his London rendition of the love-sick masked man, he was honored with the Laurence Olivier Award.

Born in Salisbury, Wiltshire, on 19 January 1942, Michael Crawford began his career at a young age. As a boy actor, he starred in children's films and was featured as the boy soprano in Benjamin Britten's *Let's Make an Opera*. Later, he went on to make many TV appearances and over 500 radio broadcasts. He landed a continuing role on the British TV series "Not So Much a Programme, More a Way of Life," and he won the Variety Club Award for "Most Promising Actor" (1965). The same year, he was given the British

Film Academy Award as "Best Newcomer" for *The Knack*. More television parts followed, and Michael had a steady stream of work on the British tube. Some shows included: "Private View," "Audience," "Play for Today," "Chalk and Cheese" and the long-running BBC comedy series "Some Mothers Do 'Ave 'Em." Crossing his popularity over-the-ocean, Crawford became known to American film audiences in: *Hello Dolly, A Funny Thing Happened on the Way to the Forum, The Jokers, The Games, Hello and Goodbye, How I Won the War* (with John Lennon), *The Adventures of Alice in Wonderland* and *Condorman*.

Known to theater audiences in London and New York, Michael has starred in many attractions: *Barnum* (won his first Olivier Award), *Billy, Flowers for Algernon*, and his latest claim to fame, *The Phantom of the Opera*. How does the phantom follow-up on his phenomenal success? Crawford released a wonderful record album, *Songs From the Stage and Screen*, in 1988. Divorced from his wife, Gabriella Lewis, Michael has two children: Lucy and Emma.

Hume Cronyn

To *Promenade All* (1972) of his activities on the boards would take a full book. In brief, the parade of characterizations moves from a lone janitor in *Hipper's Holiday* back in 1934 through *Fourposter* in 1951 to Polonius in *Hamlet* (Tony 1964). He has graced the stage with his wife, Jessica Tandy, many times since their first Broadway outing together in 1951; including *Noel Coward in Two Keys* (1974), the Pulitzer-Prize winning *Gin Game* (1978), followed by *Foxfire* (1982). The man who says he was "puny and lonely as a child" (born 18 July 1911 in London, Ontario) was actually nominated for the Canadian Olympic boxing team. After his pugilistic

period, he wavered between law and Shaw, finally studying at the American Academy of Dramatic Arts. He has portrayed both Milquetoast-Mitty types and sadistic heavies, and has been married since 1942 to Tandy (three children). "Whenever anyone compares us with the Lunts, we're delighted. It's music and we cannot hear enough of it."

Winner in 1961 of the Barter Theatre Award for his performance in *Big Fish, Little Fish,* he is also a director, screenwriter (Hitchcock's *Rope,* 1947), and producer (*Slow Dance on the Killing Ground,* 1964) and has appeared in many films. Sean O'Casey once told him, "The theatre is no place for a man who bleeds easily," and he himself groans, "Perfectionism is a terrible burden. It's a drive I wish I didn't have." For his outstanding contribution to American theatre over a 25 year period he was inducted into the Theatre Hall of Fame in 1974. Says wife Tandy of Cronyn, "When I first met him, he was very naughty because he led me to believe, before I saw him act, that he only got jobs in plays because he would put money into them. I was in fear and trembling that this was a very bad actor, and I didn't like that at all. And then I went to see him in a play by Irwin Shaw and I was so relieved. He was the best thing in it." He and Tandy appeared in the 1985 blockbuster film, *Cocoon* and they returned to Broadway in 1986, starring in *The Petition.* Hume also appeared in the film *Batteries Not Included* (1987) plus *Cocoon II* (1988).

Tom Cruise

He's rocked in his briefs, flown through the skies, highjinxed with a hustler and flipped jiggers in mid-air. He broke many-a-girl's heart when he married actress Mimi Rogers on 9 May 1987, but his sex appeal still stands. Labeled as one of Hollywood's "brat pack," actor Tom Cruise has proven to be more than a one-time box-office hit. His list of movie credits reads like a line-up of the leading popular movies of the 1980s. An article in *Cosmopolitan* stated, Tom "projects a potent wholesomeness . . . an optimistic air of knowing how to survive."

The only son of Thomas Cruise Mapother III (electrical engineer) and Mary Lee Mapother (teacher/actress), Thomas Cruise

Mapother IV was born in Syracuse, New York, on 3 July 1962. When his parents divorced, Tom moved with his mother and sisters to Louisville, Kentucky. These were struggling years for the Mapothers; Mary Lee was attempting to make ends meet, while Tom battled to read correctly. Suffering from dyslexia (his mother and sisters did, too) he recalls the trouble he had determining "whether letters like c or d curved to the right or the left." Longing to be accepted by his peers, Tom became a sports enthusiast, participating

in lacrosse, football, hockey, wrestling, skiing and tennis. After being injured during a wrestling match, Cruise sought other extra-curricular activities and discovered acting. Cast as Nathan Detroit in his high school's production of *Guys and Dolls,* Cruise decided that he was destined for a theatrical career. Moving in with a friend in New York, he was cast in a local dinner theatre production of *Godspell,* followed by a small role in the Brooke Shield's film *Endless Love* (1981). With the word out on Cruise, he won the role of a psychotic cadet in *Taps* (1981) followed by *Losin' It* (1983), *The Outsiders* (1983), *All the Right Moves* (1983) and *Risky Business* (1983). The latter film shot him to stardom, as his memorable "underwear, white socks, dark sunglasses" sing-a-long to "Old Time Rock & Roll" became a favorite scene for teenagers. As Cruise says, "When their parents leave, they turn the music up." When producers Don Simpson and Jerry Bruckheimer were seeking "Tom Cruise types" for their movie *Top Gun* (1986) they decided to approach the real person. Tom's star contribution to the film earned an incredible $8.1 million during its debut weekend at U.S. theatres. Next up, he paired with veteran actor Paul Newman in *The Color of Money* (1986). Not only did he pick up some good hustling tips, but the magic that these two actors created on the screen together touched all. Director tMartin Scorsese explains there was a kind of "mentor/protege relationship" between the two men. It's where "the older guy [is] passing on the torch to the younger actor." Tom was fortunate to share another artistic experience by filming the Academy Award-winning film *Rain Man* with Dustin Hoffman. Portraying Charlie Babbit, a wheeler-dealer, he turns the role into an outstanding character study. Other Tom Cruise films include: *Legend* in 1985 and *Cocktail* in 1988. In 1989, Cruise was set to star in *Born on the 4th of July.* He and his actress wife, Mimi Rogers, parted ways in 1990, a year that saw the release of Cruise's race-car drama *Days of Thunder.*

Billy Crystal

"I'm comfortable being old . . . being black . . . being Jewish," wrote Billy Crystal, the gifted mimic who feels "at home in other bodies." "And I look very good in dresses" he also admits. The comedian, sometimes described as "straight as a baseball bat" in his lifestyle, made quite a stir when he first appeared before a national TV audience in 1977 as Jodie Dallas, the first openly homosexual character in the history of television, in the prime-time ABC weekly sitcom "Soap." But the security of a successful series wasn't paramount to this energetic talent, who left "Soap" after four years because he was bored with playing the same character season after season. "It wasn't what I wanted," Crystal says in retrospect. "It wasn't me." However, the exposure was just what the 5'6", 130-pound Crystal needed. It landed him the role of Lionel, the world's first pregnant man, in the Joan Rivers film *Rabbit Test* (1978), which was followed by a number of TV movies, both comedic and dramatic. But live comedy had always been Crystal's love, and he showed his immense talents as a regular of "Saturday Night Live" during its 1984-1985 season. Writing all his own material, Crystal created the character Fernando, which helped earn him an Emmy nomination for "Best Actor in a Variety Program," and coined the expression "You look mahvelous." Crystal then parlayed his character's theme into a hit song ("Marvelous") and into the title of his slim autobiography (*Absolutely Mahvelous*, 1986). Crystal co-wrote and hosted "A Comedy Salute to Baseball" (NBC, 1985) before going on to do his own special, "On Location: Billy Crystal—Don't Get Me Started" (HBO, 1986) which garnered two Ace Awards and five nominations. Keeping busy, the multi-talented Crystal starred in such films as *Running Scared* (1986) and *Throw Momma From the Train* (1987) before writing the screenplay of *Goodnight Moon* (1987)—in which he also acted—and co-writing, producing and starring in *Memories of Me* (1988). Whether it's hosting the Grammy Awards (which also earned him an Emmy nomination), working on a new live act or preparing another edition of Comic Relief to benefit the homeless (edition III was aired in early 1989) Crystal's star is definitely rising. Another hit is *When Harry Met Sally* (1989), the popular romance-comedy. He is also popular as the Oscars host.

Born 14 March 1948 in New York city to mother Helen (who loved theatre and performed in shows at temple) and father Jack (who produced jazz concerts at a lower East Side Jewish catering hall and managed his uncle Milt Gabler's Commodore Music Shop in New York City), Crystal, the youngest of three sons, says he was "bred for show business." "My father used to bring home jazz musicians at Passover. We had swinging seders." Crystal recalls meeting Billie Holiday when he was five years old ("Miss Billie called me Mister Billy") and having jazz musicians play at his bar mitzvah. Loving the musicians' "jive talk," Crystal started imitating them and doing impressions of adult visitors by donning their hats and coats. Guiding the boys' comedy viewing, Dad chose "tasty things" on TV like Laurel and Hardy movies and brought home recordings of Bill Cosby, Woody Allen, Elaine May, and Jonathan Winters. After listening to Cosby's family stories, Crystal realized that he had his own "relative stories." Encouraged by their mother, the boys (Joel, now a high school teacher and Richard, a TV producer who had the idea for Fernando's character) performed in their living room, lip-synching to Spike Jones' records or imitating Mel Brooks, Sid Caesar or Ernie Kovacs routines. Crystal was voted the wittiest student in his class at Long Beach High School where he emceed their 1964 annual variety show, contributing his own rendition of Cosby's "Noah." Starting at Marshall University on a baseball scholarship, Crystal hosted a campus call-in radio show. A year later he transferred to Nassau Community College when Marshall's baseball program was eliminated due to lack of funds. Majoring in theatre, he spent three summers acting in the school's alumni theatre group. After graduation Crystal studied television and motion picture directing with Martin Scorsese at New York University. He also worked as stage manager for the Off-Broadway hit musical *You're a Good Man Charlie Brown*. In 1969, along with two Nassau alumni, Crystal formed his first improvisational comedy troupe, playing Greenwich Village, small Eastern colleges and trade shows. By then the father of an infant daughter, Crystal also worked as a part-time high school teacher to make ends meet. Turning to a solo act, Crystal played his first "gig" at a N.Y.U. fraternity party. Later, doing night solos at such places as "Catch a Rising Star" and the Playboy Clubs, Crystal spent his days watching his daughter Jennifer so that his wife Janice (whom he met a Nassau Community College, and married in 1970) could work as a secretary. After walking off the set of "Saturday Night Live" in October 1975 over a dispute about cutting his monologue from seven minutes to two minutes, Crystal finally appeared on the show April, 1976, doing "Face," his monologue of a composite of old black musicians. Even though he received good reviews, it would be eight years before he would return to the show. Moving with his wife and daughter to Los Angeles, Crystal performed at the "Comedy Store" where he was seen by Norman Lear. He was cast in a guest spot in the hit "All in the Family" before being chosen as Jodie Dallas in "Soap." After his success, NBC gave Crystal his own show, "The Billy Crystal Comedy Hour," which premiered in 1982 and was cancelled after five airings. Reviewing the first program, which had Robin Williams as a guest, Marvin Kitman said in *Newsday*, "He [Crystal] seems to be able to do everything. . . . He seems to be, underneath the nice guy image, a nice guy." In 1984 and 1985 Crystal performed regularly at the Sands Hotel in Atlantic City and at the Bottom Line in New York City when not working on "Saturday Night Live."

Currently residing with his wife Janice and their two daughters, Jennifer and Lindsay, in Pacific Palisades, California, Crystal hopes to be able to move back to New York again.

Jane Curtin

After moderate early success in showbiz, this actress-comedienne found her father singularly unimpressed. He told her, she says, that "it's a silly-ass business and that I should work in the John Hancock death claims department, something steady. But I happen to know he shows off about me to his friends on the golf course when I'm not there." If Mr. Curtin glowed with silent pride back in the early 1970's when Jane was playing in a little-known New York and Boston-area improvisational comedy production, *The Proposition*, he must be positively bursting now that she's had her very own weekly sitcom, *"Kate and Allie"* (with co-star Susan Saint James) on national TV. She returned to sitcoms in 1990 as a divorcée in love on "Working It Out." Not to mention her extended stint as one of the first-generation jokesters on NBC-TV's weekly laughfest, "Saturday Night Live." She shone as the alien Conehead housewife, in parodies of TV talkshow hosts, and as an uptight news anchorwoman. When the National Endowment for Arts began asking grant recipients to sign an anti-obscenity pledge, Curtin joined others in the performing arts to protest the action. She testified before a congressional subcommittee on a proposal to reorganize the NEA in May, 1990.

Born 6 September 1947 in Cambridge, Mass., Jane Curtin was brought up the Catholic-reared, middle-class daughter of an insurance agency owner and "a Radcliffe graduate who . . . wanted to do something worthwhile, but . . . had four kids instead." Jane became the first of her siblings "who ever moved out without moving out to get married." After dropping out of Northeastern University, she spent four years with *The Proposition*, did numerous commercials and a tour with *The Last of the Red Hot Lovers* before signing on with "SNL" in 1975. Since going off on her own, she's appeared in a number of movies for both the big and small screen. She married Patrick Lynch in 1975; the couple have a daughter.

Jamie Lee Curtis

"**I** 've worked so hard to find my identity," frets Jamie Lee Curtis. "Now all they want to know is where I got my body." The terrific body was finely tuned (which meant months of aerobic training, weight lifting and swimming) for her role in the 1985 film *Perfect*. Though serious roles are coming her way, Jamie Lee is still known as the "Scream Queen" (*Halloween, The Fog, Prom Night* and *Terror Train*), dodging knives and sadistic killers. She graduated from horror films and then played junkie-sluts on TV before landing the lead role in the made-for-TV movie "Death of a Centerfold: The Dorothy Stratten Story." Other films include *Trading Places, Love Letters, Grandview U.S.A., A Fish Called Wanda, Amazing Grace and Chuck,* and *Blue Steel*. In 1989 she hit sitcom success playing a writer for a magazine in the ABC-TV series "Anything But Love" opposite Richard Lewis.

The daughter of Tony Curtis and Janet Leigh (born 22 November 1958) had, by her own account "a very abnormal childhood." Says Curtis of her parents, "My father was sort of a stranger, then a real stranger, then an enemy. Now he's a friend." (She considers her stepfather to be the real father figure in her life). "My mom was very good about reminding me that if I was to be successful, it would be because I was true to myself." Yet the young Jamie Lee is finding it very difficult to emerge from the pressures of Hollywood as a whole person. As a youngster, "I didn't want to be an individual; I just wanted to fit in and be normal," she remembers. Curtis spent most of her youth trying to conform. "I learned early to be a chameleon, to turn whatever color was needed." Her true colors are managing to surface now she's given up smoking, drinking and drugs, and trying to please all of Hollywood. Married to Chris Guest ("Saturday Night Live"), they live with their daughter, Annie, in a historic apartment in L.A. and when not pursuing stardom, Jamie Lee practices yoga and dreams of future plans to produce and direct.

Tony Curtis

His acting range covers everything from *Houdini* to *The Boston Strangler*. His lively transvestite capers (with Jack Lemmon and Marilyn Monroe) in *Some Like It Hot* (kissing Monroe, he says, "was like kissing Hitler") in 1959, uncorked his bubbly comedic talents; his gutsy portrayal of a chain gang fugitive in *The Defiant Ones* (1958) had already proven he could handle drama.

The Great Imposter came into the world as Bernard Schwartz on 3 June 1925 in the East Bronx. In his first screen appearance he was billed as Jimmy Curtis. Remembering his "hungry childhood," he suggested "Anthony Adverse" as an alternative; compromised on Anthony Curtis. He drew on his own tough Hunt's Point background when he played a juvenile gang member in *City Across the River* ("Where I come from, being good-looking was a passport out of a garbage can"), but didn't have much personal precedent for the spate of swashbuckling "Ali Baba" roles that followed. He married actress Janet Leigh (two daughters, one of whom, Jamie Lee, became a successful actress). After their 1962 divorce he married Christine Kauffman (two more daughters), and with his third wife, model Leslie Allen, became the father of a son. (He divorced Allen in 1981.) The '80s saw Curtis in *Title Shot* and *The Mirror Crack'd* (both released in '80), *Where is Parsifal?* (1984), *Insignificance* (1984), the TV film "Mafia Princess" (1985), CBS's "Murder in Three Acts" (1986) and "Harry's Back" (1987), and the motion pictures *Midnight* (1988) and *Lobster Man From Mars* (1989).

Arlene Dahl

This Hollywood alumna turned beauty expert added another career notch in the 1980s based on her expertise in astrology. "Arlene Dahl's Lovescopes" became a cable TV staple in 1982 and she published a book of that title in 1983. The redheaded leading lady of such films as *Three Little Words* (with Fred Astaire, 1950) and *Here Come the Girls* (with Bob Hope, 1953) first made it as an author in 1965 with the bestseller *Always Ask a Man*, later followed by a series of beauty-advice tomes.

Women born under the sign of Leo, says Arlene, have "a flair for the dramatic and a regal bearing" and "combine authority with elegance"—a description which aptly fits the Leo-born Dahl. Born 11 August circa 1927 to a Minneapolis family of Norwegian heritage, she began performing on a local children's radio series and had her initial taste of fame as a New York Cover Girl in the 1940s.

After making her Broadway debut in the musical, *Mr. Strauss Goes to Boston*, choreographed by George Balanchine, Arlene was tapped by Jack Warner for the leading role of "Rose" in Warner Brothers' 1947 Dennis Morgan musical, *My Wild Irish Rose*. She made a total of 28 films before returning to New York and carving a niche in the fashion/beauty biz as a consultant, ad exec and designer. (Her pet invention is the patented "Dahl" boudoir cap.) In 1983 she made her soap opera debut on ABC's "One Life to Live."

The six-times-wed Arlene is pleased that all three of her children were "born under Sun signs compatible with mine." The eldest, Lorenzo Lamas (son of the late Fernando Lamas and a regular on the blockbuster TV series, "Falcon Crest") is an Aquarian; daughter Carole Christine Holmes (father: Christian R. Holmes, III) is a Leo like her mom; Sonny Schaum (father: Rounseville W. Schaum) is a Sagittarian. Other husbands include the late Lex ("Tarzan") Barker, Alexis Lichine, and, currently, cosmetic executive Marc Rosen, whom she wed in 1984 aboard the "Sea Goddess."

Jim Dale

Called the "Toast of the Town" (*N.Y. Times*) and "One of the five or six funniest comedians [he] had ever seen" (John Simon of *New York*), Jim Dale is riding the crest of Broadway's wave of popularity. From his 1974 Broadway debut performance as the swashbuckling rogue "Scapino" (which earned Dale his first Outer Critic's Circle Award for Best Actor, a Drama Desk Award and a Tony nomination) and his Tony Award-winning performance as the flamboyant Phineas T. Barnum in the musical *Barnum*, through his appearance in the revival of *Joe Egg* (which won Dale his second Outer Critics' Circle Best Actor Award and nominations for both the Tony and Drama Desk Awards), to his twenty-month run as the star of the number 1 musical comedy hit *Me and My Girl*, Dales has shown audiences and critics alike the talents that made and keep him a star in this, his adopted country. But the British-born singer, dancer and comedian was not new to stardom and popularity when he arrived on our shores. A pop singer in the late 1950's, Dale sang for three years on British TV's first and most popular rock and roll show, BBC's "6:05 Special," before returning to comedy with his own TV program, "The Lunchtime Show." For two years he wrote and performed comedy sketches three times a week. Switching in the 1960's to the large screen, the energetic comedian appeared in British films including a dozen of the bawdy "Carry On" films while indulging in his lyric-writing "hobby," earning an Oscar nomination for his lyrics to the title song "Georgy Girl" (1966). Always wishing to expand the showcase for his talents, Dale branched into performing Shakespeare remarking that "the laughter of a Shakespeare audience was just the same as the laughter in a music hall." Performing with the National Theatre Company, for five years, Dale took time out to host England's most popular TV variety show "Saturday Night at the Palladium" for a fifteen week season (1973-74) asides from filming three movies (1972-74). With these credits behind him, Dale arrived on American shores with the National Theatre Company, doing *The Taming of the Shrew* at the Brooklyn Academy of Music before moving to Broadway with *Scapino*, appearing in a variety of films, including Disney's *Pete's Dragon* and stage performances in New Haven (*Privates on Parade*, 1974) and Los Angeles (*Comedians*, 1977).

Born 15 August 1935 in the small industrial town of Rothwell, Northamptonshire, England, Jim Smith (he changed his name when he entered show business in order to not be confused with the British entertainer Jim Smith) was not exposed to any theatre in his early years. Rothwell had neither a theatre nor a cinema. "But when I was nine," he recalls, "I went to a show at the Victoria Palace in London and saw a comic." Sitting in the audience, hearing the laughter, Dale was instantly stage struck. His first exposure to a musical, which coincidentally was *Me and My Girl*, changed Dale's life. He knew then and there that what he wanted to do in life was "to make people laugh." The very next day Dale started dancing lessons. For the next six years he spent most of his free time learning ballet, tap and "eccentric" dancing which Dale describes as "learning to move the body as if it has no joints, like an Indian rubber doll." Dale also studied judo and tumbling. At 16, Dale dropped out of school and took a job in a shoe factory. Fortunately, that career was cut short by the appearance of Carroll Levis and his Discoverers, a traveling vaudeville troupe. Catching the owner's attention by falling when running on stage to audition, Dale spent the next two years touring England's music halls as a comic tumbler with the troupe. After a six month disc jockey job at BBC, Dale was asked to do the warm-up comic routine on "6:05 Special." The 22-year-old picked up a guitar, did some singing and became an overnight sensation. From that point on it's been one challenging role after another for the lean comedian with the aqua eyes, weathered face and smiling disposition. "When I say challenge, I'm not talking about dangerous things," says the diversified performer. "It's the knowledge that each day, when the show begins, you and the audience are all, in a sense, starting from nothing."

Dale is the father of four children by his first wife, British born Patricia Gardine. Dale and his second wife, New York gallery owner Julie Schafler (23 March 1981), reside in New York City where he collects puppets, dolls in bell jars and antique toys when not writing or preparing for his next challenge.

Timothy Dalton

M usic up . . . "My name is Bond, James Bond." The pumping underscore paves way for the unexpected happenings about to invade the screen. "What I find so appealing is that Ian Fleming tapped into a mythological figure—a 'George and the

Dragon' type of hero who single-handedly takes on the forces of evil. I hope that I've captured the spirit of the man the essence of Fleming," says the current 007, Timothy Dalton. Following in the footsteps of predecessors Sean Connery and Roger Moore, Dalton fit into his role with enough debonair to capture any Bond fan.

Born in Colwyn Bay, North Wales, 21 March 1946 to English parents, Timothy came from a theatrical heritage. His father is an advertising executive; one grandmother performed at English music halls with Charles Chaplin; and his other grandmother was a theatrical manager. At 16 years old, he debuted in an Old Vic production of *Macbeth*. After completing his studies in Manchester and Belper, he joined the National Youth Theatre in 1964 and appeared in Shakespeare's *Coriolanus*. Pursuing his career, the future James Bond trained at the Royal Academy of Dramatic Arts, joined the Birmingham Repertory Theatre Company, and appeared in many Shakespearean productions.

Not a stranger to films, Dalton has starred in an outstanding array of movies: *A Lion in Winter, Cromwell, Wuthering Heights, Mary, Queen of Scots* (received a British Film Award nomination), *Permission to Kill, Sexette,* and *Agatha*. Recent releases include: *Brenda Starr* (with Brooke Shields), *Flash Gordon, Chanel Solitaire* and *The Doctor and the Devils*. He also appeared in a number of television roles: "Sins," "Mistral's Daughter," "The Master of Ballantrae," "Centennial," "Jane Eyre," "Candida" and "Five Finger Exercise."

Originally skeptical about signing a contract and becoming the suave screen hero, he turned down the first Bond offer: "When I was about 25, Mr. Broccoli very kindly asked me if I'd be interested in taking over the role of James Bond from Sean Connery. Frankly, I thought it would be a very stupid move—I considered myself too young and Connery too good. I was approached again several years later, but had already been asked to appear in 'Flash Gordon.' So when the schedules came back together this time, I was delighted to accept and embraced this film with a lot of joy and enthusiasm." Dalton's first Bond film, *The Living Daylights* (1987), established him as this principal male character, and the sequel, *Licence to Kill* (1989), cements his position. Still single, Timothy lives in the quiet town of Chiswick in London. His best friend, actress Vanessa Redgrave, resides in the same neighborhood. When he's not filming, he likes to go fishing or relax listening to classical music and opera.

Timothy Daly

"**W**hen I was a kid, I wanted to be a brain surgeon, a plumber, an athlete, a fireman—all these things. But somehow I realized that I didn't have the stamina or the ability to be all those things at once. So I decided on the next best thing. An actor. That way I could at least pretend to be all these things." Timothy Daly has skillfully "pretended" in theatre, film and television, embellishing the Daly family reputation that originated with his father, the late James Daly, and continued with his Emmy-award-winning sister, Tyne Daly.

Born 1 March 1956 in New York City, Daly grew up in Suffern, N.Y. Although he made his acting debut at age nine in PBS's "Enemy of the People," he truly began his career after graduating from Bennington College with a bachelor's degree in theatre. He made his screen debut in the 1982 critical and commercial success *Diner*. Initially he felt all future films had to live up to the standards set by *Diner* but he soon realized that was impossible and in the long run an unimportant task. Other films include *Made In Heaven, Just the Way You Are, Love Or Money* and *Spellbinder*. Daly found himself a home in television and on stage in between features. He was a series regular on the short-lived ABC series "Ryan's Four" during the 1982-83 season. Television appearances followed on NBC's "Hill Street Blues," PBS/American Playhouse's "The Rise and Rise of Daniel Rocket," the NBC Movie of the Week "Mirrors" and "I Married a Centerfold" and the CBS Movie of the Week "Red Earth, White Earth." Daly received excellent notices portraying Valerie Bertinelli's blind brother on the CBS miniseries "I'll Take Manhattan." The raves continued when Daly created the role of Norman Foley on the 1988-89 CBS series "Almost Grown." Although the series was cancelled after a short run it showcased Daly's ability as it afforded him the opportunity to play Norman at different stages of his life. Daly aged from a clean cut high school senior to a rebellious 1960's disc jockey to a family man of the '70's who becomes a fortyish divorced father of two in the 80's. Whatever the age group, Daly convinced viewers and reviewers alike that he was Norman Foley in a truly inspired performance.

Daly debuted Off-Broadway in 1984 in *Fables for Friends* followed by *Oliver Oliver*. He made his Broadway debut in 1987 with *Coastal Disturbances*. It earned him a Tony nomination and he received a Theatre World Award for the role. Daly treated TV audiences again when he played a pilot at a small airport in a 1990 offering.

Daly met his wife, actress Amy Van Nostrand, in 1981 when they performed with the Trinity Repertory Company in Providence, Rhode Island. They were married 18 September 1982, and their son, Sam, was born in 1984. The family resides in New York where Daly pursues his hobbies. Besides being a talented actor, he is an accomplished guitarist and an excellent cook.

Tyne Daly

For Tyne Daly, being the daughter of an actor and actress did not necessarily mean an automatic ticket to stardom. The brown-haired actress who has won Emmys as Outstanding Actress playing the "warm, pizazzy, tough but vulnerable" Mary Beth Lacey on the CBS series, "Cagney and Lacey," the story of two New York policewomen, went through a slow process of paying her dues with small roles in regional theater and television. "The fact that I'm an actor's kid means simply that my dad [the late James Daly] was an actor and I'm his kid. I consider myself a very privileged person. I grew up with people like Helen Hayes sitting in my living room. It was glamorous." Nevertheless, Daly is quick to remind one that privilege must not be mistaken for wealth. "My father didn't always work and we didn't always have money."

Born in Madison, Wisconsin, 21 February 1945, Tyne Daly made her performing debut in the second grade, playing the role of the Virgin Mary in a school Christmas pageant ("I was sure Mary Magdalene was the better role"). Her professional start came during her sixth, seventh and eighth grade summer vacations when she took part in productions like *H.M.S. Pinafore* with the Antrim Players at the Antrim Playhouse in New Hampshire. There followed an apprenticeship with the American Shakespeare Festival in Stratford, Conn. While still in high school, she attended a reading for an English play at Rockland Community College in Rockland, N.Y., and wound up serving as stage manager, moving scenery, working on costumes and doing whatever else had to be done. Eventually, she also had a chance to act.

After high school graduation, Tyne was sent off—under protest—to Brandeis University to major in liberal arts and humanities. She begged her parents to let her pursue an acting career and they finally agreed to her entering the American Musical and Dramatic Academy only if she continued to live at home in Suffern, N.Y. (Although her family moved around, she considered Suffern her "real home.") In her first year at the Academy, she met Georg Stanford Brown, who was working his way through classes as the institution's janitor. "We wound up scrubbing the school's dance floor together," she says. The couple was married in June 1966 and now have three children (Elizabeth, Katherine, Alyxandra). Roles on TV's "The Virginian" and a three-month stint on "General Hospital" preceded Daly's breakthrough film role in 1976 as Clint Eastwood's "Dirty Harry" Callahan's partner in *The Enforcer*. With "Cagney and Lacey" in syndication, the actress is seen daily in reruns. Breaking out of her stereotype, Tyne appeared in a television film "Kids Like These" (1987) and starred in *Come Back Little Sheba* (1987) at the Los Angeles Theatre Center. In 1989 she was Broadway-bound with the musical *Gypsy*, for which she won the Drama Desk best actress award in 1990.

Rodney Dangerfield

"I once played a club that was so far out in the sticks, the only review I got was in *Field and Stream*. I started at age 19," explains the comic, "and at age 40, I was still just a businessman going to the office during the week to support my weekend career as an entertainer. Hey, I just don't get no respect." Perhaps not, but the comedian has parlayed his tagline wail into the hearts of millions of empathetic fans, becoming the nation's most famous anti-hero.

Born 22 November 1921 in Babylon, Long Island, he went on the road as a comedian under the name of Jack Roy, a switch from his real name, Jacob Cohen. He stuck with the road for ten years but the constant travelling and not-so-constant income made it tough for a married man with responsibilities. Eventually, except for small club dates on weekends, he left show business for plain old business . . . any business. His fortune changed at age 40 when he launched a new career not only as a performer but as a comedy writer. Recognized at last, he won bookings at such New York clubs as Upstairs at the Downstairs, the Duplex and the Living Room. In 1969 he opened his own nightclub, Dangerfield's, on Second Avenue in Manhattan. Well known to audiences because of his many appearances on talk and television variety shows, including the late night chuckler "Saturday Night Live," Dangerfield's debut record was called, what else, *I Get No Respect* and won a Grammy in 1981 for best comedy album. He starred in the hit films *Easy Money, Caddyshack, Back To School*, and *The Scout,* and was one of the first comedians ever to headline his own show at the Radio City Music Hall. In 1988 he packed the Mark Hellinger Theatre with a special 2-week engagement. The icing on the sadsack cake was the tremendous success of his rap-disco song and video called "Rappin' Rodney"—which got "heavy rotation" on MTV in 1983. Dangerfield and his wife Joyce live in the kingdom of no respect itself—New York City. They have two children, Brian and Melanie.

Blythe Danner

Calling her "one of the best American actresses," *Newsweek's* Jack Kroll observed (after seeing her in repertory in 1977) that "with a face like truth, a golden intelligence and a superb stage voice, [Blythe Danner] is pure delight from the moment of her entrance." Aside from similar rave reviews, Danner has a Tony award and nominations for her Broadway efforts. However, the *New York Post* pegged her (back in 1975) as "the most underrated comedienne in American movies right now." And the *New York Times* completed the circuit by praising her role on TV in the John Updike-adapted "Too Far to Go" as helping to make it a "landmark in television programming." Having won unanimous accolades in all three acting mediums, she's still probably best described, as critic John Simon did, as "the most underrated and underused major leading lady of our screen and stage."

Tall, willowy, and interview-shy Blythe Katharine Danner was born circa 1944 and grew up in a house on Philadephia's Main Line;

she earned a B.A. in drama at upstate New York's Bard College and served her theatrical apprenticeship playing repertory in New England and New York. Her portrayal of the free-spirited young divorcee in her Broadway debut, *Butterflies Are Free*, in 1969, led to a Tony, and a stream of jobs in both movies and in TV. In addition to catching her in her own TV series in 1973, "Adam's Rib," New York theater-goers saw her in 1980 in the Lincoln Center revival of *Philadelphia Story*, and on Broadway in *Blithe Spirit* (1987). She also appeared on stage in *A Streetcar Named Desire* (1988) and in the New York Shakespeare Festival's rendition of *Much Ado About Nothing* (1988). On film, her memorable screen roles are as the singing-dancing bride of young Thomas Jefferson in *1776* (opposite Ken Howard in 1972), the wife and mother in *The Great Santini* (1980; opposite Robert Duvall), a jewish mother/housewife in Neil Simon's *Brighton Beach Memoirs* (1985) and in Woody Allen's dramatic *Another Woman* (1988). Surfacing again in her own television series, Blythe starred in the NBC-TV show "Tattinger's" (1988/89) with Stephen Collins.

Another of today's bi-coastal performers, Danner has been married to TV producer Bruce Paltrow ("The White Shadow," "St. Elsewhere") since 1969 and has two children.

Ted Danson

This square-chinned TV star holds the singular distinction of having had the male lead in both an Emmy-winning dramatic television movie, "Something About Amelia," and in an Emmy-winning comedy series, "Cheers," in the same double-barrelled TV season: 1983-84. It was well-deserved recognition for the dedicated family man whose wife, Casey, suffered a massive, left-side-paralyzing stroke while delivering their child, Kate, on Christmas Eve 1979. (Danson has another daughter, Alexis.) Told she'd be lucky ever to walk again, Danson stuck by her, sleeping on her hospital room floor for nearly the whole first month after the stroke, and using humor and their shared training in *est* (over which they met in 1976) to nurture Casey back to full health. Meanwhile, Danson's series in which he plays a slightly macho, lovable, bar-owning ex-jock, was slowly climbing to a cult-loyal status whose followers included U.S.

House Speaker Tip O'Neill, who once made a personal appearance on the show. (The "Cheers" bar is based in O'Neill's hometown of Boston.) Already the star of a glamorous Aramis cologne commercial, Danson was now being widely deemed a sexy hunk, and he found himself being photographed with "all the ladies of the world." They apparently knew to separate him from his character; in the arresting "Something About Amelia" he played a father guilty of incest with his teen-age daughter. The movie led to national discussion of the problem, and in the wake of public interest, also led to the resolution of a few pending cases.

Danson (born 29 December 1949) has been near important acting action off and on ever since he got a part in the 1979 movie *The Onion Field*. Prior to that, the Flagstaff, Arizona-reared son of an archaeologist had gone to the elite Kent School in Connecticut before flunking out of Stanford. He finished up at Carnegie-Mellon University in 1972, then went on to New York and small stage roles and commercials and eventually soaps. After he and Casey moved to L.A. in 1978, the two managed to make ends meet through his teaching at the Actors Institute while snaring TV parts on "Laverne and Shirley," and "Magnum P.I.," and movie roles in *Body Heat* and *Creepshow*. Some recent works include the films *Something in Common* (1985), *A Fine Mess* (1986), *Three Men and a Baby* (1987), *Cousins* (1988), and *The Hard Way* (1989). He co-starred with Olympia Dukakis and Jack Lemmon in 1989's *Dad*. He also starred in the NBC-TV movie "When the Bough Breaks" in 1986. Thus, with TV, movies and commercials he's been able to make his calling pay the bills, while finding pleasure in family. "What we like best is playing house," Danson says.

Tony Danza

"I t's been 10 years since I came to Hollywood," smiles Tony Danza. "I never dreamed of such success. The best part of it all, is that I'm enjoying it." With two hit sitcoms back to back, Danza can smile. The professional boxer-turned-actor went from the hit show "Taxi," which ran for 5 seasons, to the ABC sitcom "Who's the Boss?," which, in its fifth year on the air, was the sixth highest rated show of the TV season. Branching out from his role as "Tony" (he was Tony Banta in "Taxi" and is "Tony Micheli" in "Who's the Boss?"), the Brooklyn-born Danza has appeared in TV movies ("Wall of Tyranny" and "Single Bar, Single Woman") and feature films (*Hollywood Knights, Cannonball Run II* and *Going Ape*). Showing his abilities on the other side of the camera, Danza has directed episodes of "Who's the Boss?" and been the executive producer as well as the star of NBC-TV movies "Freedom Fighters" and "Doing Life." The smiling, gregarious actor is also in demand as a host. Aside from hosting various TV shows and charity benefits, the 5'11" ex-middleweight also co-hosted the show "99 Ways to Attract the Right Man." "It's an exciting time. Everything is so positive. I'd like to bottle it up and share it with friends."

Born Anthony Iandanza on 21 April 1951 in Brooklyn, New York, Danza never took his education seriously. Nonetheless, he graduated from the University of Dubuque, Iowa, with a history degree. Supporting himself with such jobs as selling jeans out of the trunk of a car and tending bar, Danza had found his niche when he turned to boxing, or so he thought. As if out of a Hollywood script, a boxing match was to change young Danza's life. Like a scene from *Rocky*, the middleweight was knocked down twice in the first round, but managed to nail his opponent at the end of the round with a one-punch knockout. In the arena that night was director James Brooks, looking to cast an Irish heavyweight for his new sitcom "Taxi." After watching Danza, the director decided to use an Italian middleweight instead. With a record of 12 and 3—all decisions via knockout—Danza left the ring for Hollywood and stardom. "I thought I was going to be middleweight champion of the world and a great actor at the same time," recalls Danza. Hollywood was good to Danza so he never returned to the ring. Thinking about the old life, Danza misses the ring, "being in shape, the discipline and the guys in the locker room."

To stay trim, Danza still runs in the morning and uses an exercise bike. He plays softball on the weekends when he's not sharing the cooking honors at home with his second wife, Tracy Robinson (married 29 June 1986) or playing daddy to daughter Katherine ("Katie," born 8 May 1987) or 18-year-old son Marc Anthony (one of the two children of his first marriage to Rhonda, divorced in 1974) who has lived with his father since 1984. "My family is my life," says Danza whose latest film, *Daddy's Little Girl* was released in 1989. The successful actor is also creating and producing projects under his Katherine Anne Production banner. Daddy, who worked with son Marc on an episode of "Taxi," explains, "I'm nervous about the future. With success you have to live up to things. The levels are higher. In my case, I want to make my family proud of me."

Geena Davis

Equally at home in a comedy or a drama, screen actress Geena Davis won an Academy Award for Best Supporting Actress in 1989 for her role in the "comedy-drama" *The Accidental Tourist*, based on the bestselling novel of the same title by Anne Tyler. Geena plays Muriel, an unusual dog trainer who befriends Macon Leary (William Hurt), whose world is turned upside down when his wife, Sarah, leaves him.

Born 21 January 1957 in Wareham, Massachuetts, Geena Davis studied music as a child. She spent her senior year in high school in Sweden as an exchange student and switched her focus from music to theatre. Davis graduated from Boston University's Professional Actors' Training Program, and spent some time with the Mount Washington Repertory Theatre Company in New Hampshire. Once in New York, she became a model, which led to television commercials and eventually to her screen debut in *Tootsie* (1982), when she appeared as the girl in her underwear who shared a dressing room with Dustin Hoffman. Her first starring role was in 1986 when she appeared opposite Jeff Goldblum as a free-lance science reporter in the successful remake of *The Fly*.

More recently Geena Davis starred in the frightening and funny ghost story *Beetlejuice* (1988) and in *Earth Girls Are Easy* (1989). Davis co-starred with Bill Murray and Randy Quaid in *Quick Change*, released in 1990. She was also in the films *Fletch* and *Transylvania 6-5000*. Davis has also appeared in her own NBC series, "Sara"; with Dabney Coleman in the much-talked-about "Buffalo Bill"; and in two memorable episodes of "Family Ties," in which she played a character hired to be the Keatons' maid although she was incompetent. After a failed marriage to Richard Emmolo, she married actor Jeff Goldblum on 1 November 1987 in Las Vegas.

Ossie Davis

"There's a tremendous hunger among blacks and whites, for truth about the black experience in this country," says the author-star of the *Non-Confederate Romp Through the Cotton Patch*, *Purlie Victorious* (1961), and its musical version, *Purlie* (1970). "This is a way I can increasingly be part of the cultural arm of the revolution that Martin Luther King was all about. The revolution of regeneration, building a new set of values through an art that is revolutionary in that its concern is building beautiful human beings. . . . I'm for a moral regeneration of this country for everybody," he observed in the late 1960s.

Born in Cogdell, Ga., 18 December 1917, Ossie Davis decided to be a playwright as a child, although he had seen only a "few cowboy movies" and had never seen a stage. "We read Shakespeare in the school," he says. In New York he attended a Harlem actors' theatre by night, and worked in the garment district by day. ("If the money ran out, we slept in the park. I was young and romantic then.") He finally made good in *Jeb* in 1946. "David Merrick signed me," he says dryly "so I guess you could say he discovered me." Davis is married to his frequent co-star Ruby Dee (three grown children, three grandchildren). His Broadway credits include *The Royal Family*, *No Time for Sergeants*, and *Raisin in the Sun*. Screen credits include: *Let's Do It Again* (1975), *Hot Stuff* (1979) and *Nothing Personal* (1979). He appeared in and directed *Countdown at Kusinj*. His recent films include *Harry & Son* (1984), *Avenging Angel* (1985), *School Daze* (1988) and *Do the Right Thing* (1989). He was rumored to be slated to co-star in Burt Reynold's 1990-91 TV series, "Arkansas," for CBS.

Pam Dawber

When "Mork & Mindy" premiered on television in 1978, a nationwide audience was given its first glimpse of the bright-eyed, sweet smiling co-star. Pam Dawber has been a busy actress ever since. After four seasons opposite Robin Williams on the ABC hit series, Pam has stayed in television, acting in a TV movie every year from 1982 through 1986. These movies ran the spectrum, showing the diversity of Pam's talents: "Naked Eyes," a mystery/thriller; "Last of the Great Survivors," a romantic comedy; "Wild Horses," a Western; and "American Geisha," based upon a true story of anthropology student Liza Dalby. Returning to her first love, Pam starred in another TV series, "My Sister Sam," which was co-produced by Pam's company Pony Productions in association

with Warner Brothers. Her TV movie "Face of Fear" aired in the 1990-91 season, when she also signed with CBS for a half-hour comedy and more movies. Not wishing to limit herself nor lose out on one of her talents, Pam took time out to appear in musical theater productions. Her credits include such roles as Eliza in *My Fair Lady* (1980 production by Kenley Theatre) and Mabel in *The Pirates of Penzance* (1982 Broadway and 1981 L.A.). Pam also sang and danced as Marion the librarian in the 1984 three-city mid-west tour of *The Music Man*.

Born on 18 October 1954 in Detroit, Michigan, Pam admits that musical theatre was always her first love. As a teenager she performed in musicals at her high school and studied art and vocal music at Oakland Community College near her home. With her good looks, it's not surprising that modeling followed.

At the suggestion of a friend, Pam packaged her portfolio and left Michigan for the bright lights of New York City where, in 1974, she decided to devote herself to her two loves, acting and singing. Offered a part in the play *Sweet Adeline,* Pam grabbed it and went to the Tony Award-winning Goodspeed Opera House in East Haddam, Connecticut, for the production. It was there that the call came from the West Coast that changed her life. Dawber flew west, and after not being chosen for the part of "Tabitha" was seen and screen-tested by Robert Altman, which prompted ABC to give her a one-year contract.

Pam and husband, actor Mark Harmon, married 21 March 1987 and are the parents of a son, Sean, born 25 April 1988. The family resides in Los Angeles and maintains a solar home in New York.

Doris Day

In the 1950s and '60s, she was the top box-office draw in America, often voted the world's most popular actress. In such light comedies as *Pillow Talk* (1959), *Lover Come Back* (1961), and *Please Don't Eat the Daisies* (1960), her sunny on-screen personality earned her a comfortable niche as "America's Sweetheart" and everybody's favorite "girl-next-door"—as well as a *not*-so-comfortable niche as a too-pure-to-be-true perennial "Goody Two-

Shoes." (The sardonic pianist Oscar Levant once remarked, "I knew her before she was a virgin.")

Doris von Kappelhoff was born 3 April 1924 in Cincinnati. Her first daydream was to be a dancer and she succeeded to the point of being en route to Hollywood when an auto accident sidelined her into singing. When she warbled "Day by Day" at a club in her hometown, the owner changed her name to Day. ("I'm glad," she said later "he didn't catch me singing *Gotterdammerung*.") Soon she was a band singer with Les Brown, then belting out the big ones on record (e.g. "Que Sera Sera" and "Secret Love"). The big Day-break on film came in 1948 when she replaced a pregnant Betty Hutton in *Romance on the High Seas* and from then on, she shone in a series of musicals (*The Pajama Game*, 1957), mysteries (*The Man Who Knew Too Much*, 1956) and the country-fresh, cider-sweet girl-who-can't-be-seduced-but-still-gets-Rock-Hudson-or-Cary-Grant-anyhow romances cited above. Married first to "the trombone player" (Al Jordan; son Terry has followed her to the music biz), second to "the saxophone player" (George Weidler), number three in 1951 was agent Marty Melcher, whom friends called "executive seeing eye dog" and she described as "my husband and best friend." She was widowed in 1968 and during the first "big black void" threw herself into work on a popular TV series which continued until 1972. Her 1976 marriage to restaurateur Barry Comden (according to friends "perhaps the most unfortunate of the lot") was later dissolved. From now on, she said in 1982, "marriage is a no-no. For some reason, it gets old. I do love seeing it work for others, and I suppose it does work for many people, but goodness knows it doesn't work for me."

In the 1980s, retiring from performing, the erstwhile superstar occupied herself primarily with her Doris Day Pet Foundation, helping animals who are hungry, homeless or hurt. (She once reprimanded a man in Malibu who was beating to death a man-eating shark.) Her Carmel Valley home houses a family of dogs and cats (mostly strays) plus a bird. "There are things you get from the silent, devoted companionship of pets," she says, "that you can get from no other source. Perhaps there are people who don't understand my devotion. I would like them to know it is something rich and simple and beautiful. A love as soft and gentle as the summer rain."

Ruby Dee

Stereotyped for years as "the Negro June Allyson," this pretty, petite former Harlemite scored a big breakthrough as a dramatic actress Off-Broadway in 1970 in the South African-set drama *Boseman and Lena*. Asked, after the raves, if she felt she was really "on her way," she retorted, "I've been 'on my way' for the past twenty years, honey. Maybe now people will believe I've actually arrived."

Born Ruby Ann Wallace in Cleveland, 27 October circa 1924, daughter of a Pennsylvania Railroad porter, she grew up in Harlem and in 1941 got her feet wet as an actress in the American Negro Theatre, then operating in the basement of the West 135th Street branch of the New York Public Library. (Among her classmates: Hilda Simms, Harry Belafonte, and Sidney Poitier.) One of her first important Broadway roles was in *Jeb* (1946), opposite Ossie Davis whom she later married (three children) and with whom she appeared in his hit play *Purlie Victorious* (1961). She appeared in both the stage (1959) and screen (1961) versions of *Raisin in the Sun* and in 1965, playing Kate in *The Taming of the Shrew* and Cordelia in *King Lear*, was the first black actress to appear in major roles at the American Shakespeare Festival at Stratford, Conn. In 1988 she appeared in the Broadway play *Checkmates* and was inducted into the Theatre Hall of Fame. She also appeared in the television film version of Sidney Sheldon's novel "Windmills of the Gods" that same year. Movie credits include *St. Louis Blues, Wedding Band, Cat People* and *Do the Right Thing*. A literal lightweight in frame (5'1", 108 lbs.) she's proved herself a heavy-weight in the fight for civil rights and, together with Davis, was honored in 1970 with the Frederick Douglass Award of New York's Urban League for bringing "a sense of fervor and pride to countless millions." From 1974 to 1978, she was heard on sixty-five radio stations nation-wide on the weekly series, "The Ossie Davis and Ruby Dee Story Hour" broadcast over the national Black Network. She is also a poet and a writer, with a play (*Take It From the Top*) a poetry anthology (*Glow-child*) and a column in the *New York Amsterdam News*. In 1983 she made her debut as a director in the Howard University Production *Zora Is My Name*. In 1990 she joined Joseph Papp and Jessica Tandy in testifying before a Congressional subcommittee examining the National Endowment for the Arts and its role in censoring grant recipients.

Olivia De Havilland

The demure, gentle Melanie of *Gone With the Wind* never had it so tough as the torn and tattered Olivia of the 1960s. Trapped in an elevator (*Lady in a Cage*), driven crackers (*The Scream*), and crucified (*Pope Joan*), Errol Flynn's longtime light-hearted screen ladylove (*Captain Blood, The Adventures of Robin Hood,* et al) joined her old Warner Brothers stablemate Bette Davis in Hollywood's violent era in becoming a Grand Duchess of the Gruesomes. They actually appeared together in *Hush, Hush Sweet Charlotte*, released in 1964 and still a TV late-show favorite.

The smaller, darker half of one of the most famous sister feuds in histrionic history, Olivia by the 1970s was pooh-poohing all those nasty stories about her rivalry with Joan Fontaine as mere grindings of the publicity mill. Born 1 July 1916 in Tokyo, Japan, she preceded sister Joan to Hollywood but lagged behind her in snaring her first Academy Award (*To Each His Own*, 1946), then surged into front position again by winning a second Oscar a few years later (*The Heiress*, 1949). She broke ground for her later incarnations in the horror flicks in such epics of travail as *The Dark Mirror* and *The Snake Pit* (both 1948). After divorcing her first husband, Marcus Goodrich, in 1952 (one son), she met and married Pierre Galante, editor of *Paris-Match* (one daughter) in 1955, moved to France, and wrote a bestseller about her bilingual tribulations (*Every Frenchman Has One;* the title referred not to a mistress, but to the typical Frenchman's greatest concern, his liver.) On the loose again in 1972, she had a brief, highly publicized fling with Great Britain's bachelor prime minister, Edward Heath.

Olivia's been visible on the big screen in *Airport '77* and the horror flick *Swarm*. On the little screen, she appeared in "Roots: The Next Generation" (1978), "Charles and Diana: A Royal Romance" (1982), "North & South Book II" (1986), and received an Emmy Nomination and Golden Globe Award as Best Supporting Actress for the NBC miniseries "Anastasia: The Story of Anna" (1986). In

1989 she had the honor of accepting the People's Choice Award given to *Gone With the Wind* as the favorite film of all time.

Dino De Laurentiis

"**T**he critics say my movies bad, but the audience is my boss. They pay me. They tell Dino what to do. I am entertainer, showman. I can always smell a good story. I read one page sometimes, think, 'is a good picture there, we make.'" Thus, in 1977, did the Italian filmmaker describe his work, spelling it out seven years later as follows: "I select the story, I select the director, I approve the script, I select the cast. I see the way the shooting is going and I see the dailies [rushes] every day. I talk to the director, I talk to the editors. I check every moment, every stage of the movie." He also somehow finances projects, juggling "private investors" and complex deals with the studios, and sells films worldwide. ("Here," actor Charles Bronson told *People*, "Dino really shines. . . . He can pick up the telephone and book pictures even before they're made— he has such a good reputation for success.")

Born 8 August 1919 in Torre Annunziata, Italy, the son of a Neapolitan pasta manufacturer, Dino enrolled at 17 in Rome's Centro Sperimentale di Cinematografia and at 20 produced his first film. After World War II he espoused Italian Neorealism, in 1948 producing an international hit, *Bitter Rice*, whose star, Silvana Mangano, became his wife the following year. In the '50s he and Carlo Ponti jointly made two Federico Fellini films, *La Strada* (1956) and *Nights of Cabiria* (1957), both winners of Academy Awards for Best Foreign Film, and King Vidor's *War and Peace*, regarding which he recalled 20 years later that "my partner say he no believe in it, is too big. I say, 'Carlo, you no believe in "La Strada," is too small.' Then I say, 'You go your way, I go mine.'" Among the dozens of pictures he has produced solo have been such spectaculars as *The Bible* (1966), *King Kong* (1976) and *Conan the Destroyer* (1984), of which *Variety* wrote, "The sensibility is Southern California Suburban, the meat on the spit is likely to be an unfriendly barbarian." Other films include Michael Cimino's *Year of the Dragon*, *Red Sonja* and the Sissy Spacek starrer, *Marie*.

Dino, who moved to the United States with his family in 1973, is no mean cook himself. "I cook," he once said, "as Picasso paints." He also likes to eat, and out of his passion for gastronomy has come the modishly lower-cased "ddl Foodshow," a dazzling restaurant-cum-snackbar in Manhattan's superchic Trump Tower. He has three daughters; the death in 1981 of his 26-year-old son Federico was, he says, "the great tragedy of my life." But if he enjoys the give-and-take of family life in his rare hours of relaxation, at work he insists on sole command. "I make a movie," he says, "I want to control everything. I no see why not."

Catherine Deneuve

Women admire her, men desire her. Once hailed by *Esquire* as "one of the most remarkably beautiful actresses of out time," Catherine Deneuve has become for many middle-aged women the symbol of outspoken independence. Says the ageless beauty on the subject of encroaching time, "Forty is not so old anymore—not what it used to be fifteen or twenty years ago. One is old the moment she is no longer desirable. That's not to say there aren't days when I don't feel beautiful, when I don't look like the person I'm suppose to be. It's unfair, when it's expected that you're to look a certain way, you just have to work a little harder." In addition to the long list of films she's played in (among them—*Belle de Jour*, *The Umbrellas of Cherbourg*, *Mayerling*, *April Fools*, *The Last Metro*, *The Hunger*, *Fort Saganne*, *Scene of the Crime*, *Love Songs* and *Agent Trouble*) she is also into very different lines of work: jewelry design and fragrance. The "archetype of patrician grace,"so dubbed by *Newsweek*, came out with her own line of jewelry complete with chic "CD" logo. In 1984, she created her own perfume, "Deneuve," which she tested for three years before a retail introduction in March, 1987. She explains, "I wanted my perfume to be a classic—to defy trends, but never bore. And it is." Deneuve has replaced Brigitte Bardot as the inspiration for the Marianne statues that adorn many town halls in France.

She was born in Paris on 22 October 1943 to a family with theater in their blood; Deneuves's father, Maurice Dorléac and mother, née Deneuve, were both actors. Her sister Françoise Dorléac, eighteen months older than Catherine, brought her into the profession, appearing with her in Deneuve's first film, *Les Petits Chats*. The volatile French actress has since appeared in over fifty films, many under the tutelage of some of the most illustrious directors in the world. ("Bunuel is a genius. His method is to explain nothing. Here, actors think too much about why a character does this or that. . . . Polanski is brilliant. He works by talking a great deal to the actors and analyzing emotions, yet he did not wish me to think about why the girl in the film [*Repulsion*] was crazy. . . . Vadim [who is the father of son Christiaan] saw me as a sex symbol. He is talented.") Roman Polanski has said of her, "When you work with an actor, you have good moments and bad moments, but at the end you remember only the pattern. With Catherine it was the best I've ever had." Though constantly beseiged with and enraged by undignified questions from the press; about: (1) her illegitimate son and daughter (fathered by Vadim and Marcello Mastroianni respectively) (2) her dissolved marriage to British fashion photographer David Bailey and (3) the flaming car-crash death of her beautiful actress sister, in recent years Deneuve has softened especially on the subject of her children. She admits both kids are concerned about what people think and that, of course, is of great concern to her.

Robert De Niro

An intensely private man loath to give interviews, the brown-haired, green-eyed actor has all of this to say about the greening of his thespian inclination: "My father is a painter. My mother used to be a painter. I was lucky. They never bothered me about wanting to be an actor." And about that desire to act? "Well . . . it's complicated. Getting into it . . . it's a personal thing. Is that okay?" Having nearly filled Brando's footprints in the 1970s, a segue into doing his own thing made this renegade's talents both highly respected and dearly coveted by his celluloid peers on the silver screen.

An only child, De Niro was born 17 August 1943 on Manhattan's lower East Side. His parents (painter Robert De Niro of Irish-Italian descent and former painter Virginia Admiral, a Berkeley, California, "golden girl") separated when he was just two. Nervous and rail-thin, he was a drifter and a loner, although for a while he ran with a street gang. (His mother once said her son's idea of high school "was not to show up.") At 16, he found Stella Adler and acting became his haven. For 14 years he plugged away in low budget films made by top talents like Brian De Palma and Martin Scorsese, as well as Off-Off-Broadway shows such as *One Night Stands of a Noisy Passenger,* written by his then mentor, actress Shelley Winters. The play closed after seven performances. He was catapulted into instant stardom with his heart-wrenching perform-ance as Bruce Pearson, a crude but endearing second-string baseball catcher dying of Hodgkin's disease in the film *Bang the Drum Slowly* in 1973. Dedicated to building what he calls "a body of work," De Niro has chosen his parts with great selectivity. They include Johnny Boy in Scorsese's *Mean Streets* (1973); the young Vito Corleone in *Godfather Part 11* (the older Corleone was played by Brando); the sexual maniac Travis Bickle in *Taxi Driver* (1976); as well as star turns in Bertolucci's *1900* (1977); *The Last Tycoon* (1976); *New York, New York* (1977); *The Deer Hunter* (1978); *Raging Bull* (1981 Academy Award as Best Actor); *King of Comedy* (1983); *Falling in Love* (1984); *Brazil* (1985); *The Mission* (1986); *The Untouchables* (1987); *Stanley & Iris* (1988); *Midnight Run* (nominated for a Golden Globe Award as Best Actor— 1988); *Jacknife* (1988); *We're No Angels* (1989); and Scorsese's gangster eipic *Good Fellas* (1990).

In the spring of 1976, De Niro married actress and singer Diahnne Abbot and the couple divorced in 1978 (one son, Raphael). He also has a daughter, Nina Nadeja, with singer Helena Springs.

Sandy Dennis

With her advancing maturity, this stage and screen actress who, uh, stutters has gotten even more flappable. She may also go down in the annals of show biz history remembered more for her spirited recitations of the names of her more than 30 cats (all of whom occupy her Connecticut house) than for her Academy Award winning performances in *Who's Afraid of Virginia Woolf,* or Tony Award performances in *Any Wednesday* and *A Thousand Clowns.*

Born 27 April 1937 in Hastings, Nebr., the daughter of a postal worker, she dropped out of Wesleyan College at 19 to become an actress in New York. For seven years she lived with actor Gerald O'Loughlin.

Next she shared a place with saxman Gerry Mulligan. Her first New York appearance was in a three-week run of Ibsen's *The Lady from the Sea;* her first Broadway play was *Face of a Hero.* She made a big mark in 1962's *A Thousand Clowns* with Jason Robards, followed in 1964 in Muriel Resnik's *Any Wednesday.* Though it supposedly infuriated her co-actors and directors, her tendency to mutter, stutter, and flutter her hands about often led to highly original improvisations in the midst of a scene. Since her early days she has toned down her style. ("I think the mannerisms offended a tremendous number of people," she now confesses. "They were due to the fact that I didn't know what I was doing.") About acting she says: "It isn't like painting a picture or writing a book. When you finish an acting stint, there's nothing except money. You have to keep going, giving the best you've got, to get something intangible." Sandy has pouted, yelled, muttered, stuttered and fluttered through such other plays as Robert Altman's *Come Back to the Five & Dime Jimmy Dean, Jimmy Dean; Buried Inside Alive* and *Absurd Person Singular* in films *The Fox, The Out-of-Towners, Thank You All Very Much, Nasty Habits,* and *The Four Seasons.*

Brian De Palma

"**E** ither I'm getting too old or they are getting worse or I've seen too many, but I rarely go to the movies. Mainly I'm disappointed." Not scary enough for his taste no doubt; Hitchcock's inheritor of fright operates on what he calls "the principle of escalating terror. My films deal with a stylized, expressionistic world that has a kind of grotesque beauty about it. I don't think you necessarily have to have blood flying across the screen and guts coming out of stomachs and stuff like that. But I think you should be able to use what you consider effective within certain limitations. There can be something very poetic about violence in film. I think movies are about action—you know, bodies falling, knives sweeping through the air. That has a lot to do with what one can do in cinema so effectively."

Brian Russell De Palma was born 11 September 1940, in Newark, New Jersey, the youngest of three sons of an orthopedic surgeon and his wife. In the mid '40s the family moved to Philadelphia where Brian attended the private Friends School. He enrolled in Columbia University's Class of 1962 intending to major in physics but instead became obsessed by movies. Becoming a filmmaker meant taking his masters degree at Sarah Lawrence, where he made a film using two then-unknown New York actors, Robert de Niro and Jill Clayburgh. After graduation he supported himself making short commercial films for corporations and cultural institutions such as the NAACP. His two independent films made at this time— *Greetings* and *Hi, Mom,* both dealing with the climate of the 60s— earned him a reputation as something of a counterculture hero. Not terribly fond of "big brother" movie studios, De Palma bolted just two weeks before completing a film for Warner Brothers starring Tommy Smothers. On his own he made *Sisters,* a tale of a Siamese twin possessed by the murderous spirit of her dead halved sister. Then came the horror classic *Obsession,* followed by *Carrie,* based on Stephen King's story of a high school girl with telekinetic powers of revenge. The film earned big dollars at the box office and confirmed King's career as a horror writer and De Palma's career as an independent director. He followed *Carrie* with *The Fury, Blow-Out, Dressed to Kill, Wise Guys, The Untouchables,* and *Casualties of War.* His most recent work is as director of the controversial *Bonfire of the Vanities* (1990). In 1979 De Palma married Nancy Allen, the actress who appeared in several of his films. They divorced in 1984. De Palma prefers New York to Hollywood. His cooperative apartment looks over gothic Washington Square Park in Greenwich Village.

Gérard Depardieu

Looking like a survivor of one too many go-arounds with Muhammad Ali, France's rugged, hefty and compellingly photogenic box office superstar is the latest of the sexy pug types French cinema has sent our way beginning with the incomparable Jean Gabin. Moreover, Gérard Depardieu's captivatingly irregular features were achieved by means not altogether genetic in origin: "I started [at 12] leading a wild life, attacking jewelry stores, stealing cars. . . . I became familiar with courtrooms, judges, detention and parole." Paradoxically, it's been in courtroom settings that he's achieved some of his major cinematic triumphs—as the titular defendants in

The Return of Martin Guerre and *Danton,* and as a crack defense attorney in the 1984 romantic thriller *Right Bank, Left Bank.*

Born 27 December 1948 at Châteauroux ("in the heart of France"), the third of six children of an illiterate metal worker, Gérard says his occupation of convenience during his youthful days as a petty criminal was "an actor . . . I said I was playing at the Théâtre National Populaire because it was the only theater I was acquainted with." Realizing that "having to confront policemen and judges is an excellent way to train your imagination. . . . In a few seconds, you have to improvise a role with talent and emotion," it was to the TNP that he turned when he decided to pursue an acting career in earnest. After studies there and private lessons, he made his motion picture debut in a short, followed by an unfinished Agnes Varda feature. A role in a television series led to a stage career in the French versions of *The Boys in the Band, A Girl in My Soup* and *Home,* among others. After a number of supporting roles, he achieved his first major film success co-starring with the late Patrick Dewaere in Bertrand Blier's *Going Places,* as "a guy who has the urge to experience all kinds of emotions at 100 miles an hour." It's that astonishing range of emotions in a wide variety of roles that sets him apart from the usual run of French hearthrobs. Of his more than 50 films, among the more popular are Blier's *Get Out Your Handkerchiefs* and *Buffet Froid;* Alain Resnais' *Mon Oncle d'Amérique;* the late François Truffaut's *The Last Metro* and *The Woman Next Door; The Moon in the Gutter, La Chevre* (in her 1985 review of the film's U.S. release, the *New York Times'* Janet Maslin wrote, "There appears to be nothing that Gérard Depardieu cannot do well on the screen"), *Les Compères,* the title role in the film of a stage production of *Tartuffe* (which he also directed) and *Police* (for which he was named best actor at the 1985 Venice Film Festival). In 1987 he starred in the acclaimed *Jean de Florette,* opposite his wife, Elisabeth. He also appeared in *Sous le Soleil de Satan* that same year, followed by *Traffic Jam* in 1988. He won best acting honors at the 1990 Cannes Film Festival for his performance in the title role of *Cyrano de Bergerac.* Married to Elisabeth Guignot (an actress he met at the Theatre National Populaire), Depardieu is the father of a son Guillaume and a daughter Julie. The Depardieus have a home in Bougival (near Paris) and a farm on the coast of Normandy, where Gérard raises his own livestock.

William Devane

"**I**'m a damn good actor. . . . I only like to play roles that are good and meaty. Usually, those are character parts or villains." William Devane's matter-of-fact description of his acting was expressed in a 1979 press release for his role as St. Milt Warden in "From Here to Eternity: The War Years." Over ten years later, Devane was still playing a sleazy-type character on the nighttime soap "Knots Landing." In his role as Gregory Sumner, he divorced his first wife, ran for Senator, gave away the daughter of his late-second wife, stepped down from the Senate, ran and lost for Mayor, had an affair with his good friend's younger daughter, and then married the neighborhood manipulator for political prestige rather than love. Of his role, he explains: "Sumner is a man caught up in a struggle with power and notoriety."

William Devane was born 5 September 1939 in Albany, New York. In and out of four different high schools in four years, he eventually moved to Manhattan to seek stardom. In a 1970 interview he claimed he started out as an iron worker, but says "I decided I'd never become a millionaire that way." He studied at the New York Academy of Dramatic Arts and worked for Joseph Papp as a carpenter-electrician. Persistance paid off, and Devane wound up as a mainstay of the New York Shakespeare Festival.

It's hard not to notice the physical resemblance between him and the Kennedy brothers, so it was only natural for him to be cast as President John F. Kennedy in "The Missiles of October," a part that sterotyped Devane yet brought him an Emmy Award nomination. He told Ted Morgan of the *New York Times* in 1975 how he prepared for such a demanding role. "I got me a back brace, which gave me a slight stoop. I bought me a pair of those Florsheim $60 black wing-tipped shoes, which slowed down my walk and gave me the weight of high office. I got me the record 'The Kennedy Wit,' and played it until the grooves wore out and I had that Irish attack on things that was so relaxed and so clear." More meaty roles followed, including a lead in the telefilm "Fear on Trial" and in the miniseries "From Here to Eternity" with Natalie Wood. He repeated his role as Sgt. Milt Warden in the series "From Here to Eternity: The War Years." He has also appeared in feature films; some Devane movies are: *Marathon Man, Yanks, Family Plot, The Bad News Bears in Breaking Training, Rolling Thunder, The Dark, Report to the Commissioner,* and *Testament.* In addition to his work with Joseph Papp, Devane appeared in a Broadway revival production of "One Flew Over the Cuckoo's Nest."

The sought-after actor has been married to the same woman for over 20 years. He and his wife Eugenie have two sons: Josh and Jake; the family resides in Sherman Oaks, California, and on their Arabian horse ranch in Sundance, Utah. An avid sportsman, Devane likes to relax by riding or playing a good game of polo.

Danny De Vito

"I usually try to find the redeeming qualities in the guys I play so that I can have a good sleep at night," Danny DeVito explained in a *People* magazine article. This approach could be considered a difficult task, knowing the various characters he has portrayed, both on the big and little screen. Whether he's an aluminum-siding salesman being chased by the government, a middle-aged momma's boy, a mental patient, or a cab dispatcher, DeVito becomes "one of those guys you love to hate."

He was born at Fitkin Hospital in Neptune, New Jersey, on 17 November 1944 to Julia and Daniel DeVito, Senior. He had a happy childhood in Asbury Park. He told the *Daily News* in an interview that it "was the greatest place in the world to grow up. . . . We were thirteen blocks from the beach. . . . Every woman for a five- or six-block radius was my 'aunt'. . . . In the summer everything changed. There was an incredible influx of new blood. All the city girls would come down and the place would turn these brilliant colors." After graduating from Our Lady of Mt. Carmel grammar school and Oratory Prep in Summit, Danny headed for Manhattan. He studied for two years with the Academy of Dramatic Arts. He also learned the haircutting trade at the Wilfred Academy of Hair and Beauty and at age 18 worked as a hairdresser for one year at his sister's shop to bring in money. Determined to make it as an actor, he traveled to California with hopes of appearing on the big screen. Unable to click, he was down to his last $10 in Los Angeles; he had previously purchased a round-trip plane ticket which he used to return to New York. Then the doors opened.

Landing a role in the Off-Broadway play *The Man With the Flower in His Mouth* set his career in the right direction. More offers followed, and he appeared in the stage productions of *Shrinking Bride* and *One Flew Over the Cuckoo's Nest*. As a result of his performance as Martini in the latter play, he was cast in the film version, which became the Academy Award picture of that year (1975).

DeVito's been active ever since. Perhaps his most popular part was that of Louie De Palma in the ABC sitcom "Taxi." The show brought him immediate national exposure and enabled him to work with his wife, actress Rhea Perlman. A large majority of 1980's box-office smashes were DeVito's films; in addition to *Cuckoo's Nest*, he also appeared in another Academy Award Best Picture, *Terms of Endearment* (1983). Other films include: *Romancing the Stone* (1984) and its sequel, *Jewel of the Nile* (1985); *Ruthless People* (1986); *Tin Men* (1986); *Head Office* (1986); *Throw Momma From the Train* (1987); *Twins* (1988); and *The War of the Roses* (1989). Although Danny had been associated professionally with Rhea Perlman for many years (produced two short motion pictures together in their early careers: *The Sound Sleeper* and *Minestrone*), they actually tied the knot in 1982. They appeared together in the television special celebrating Earth Day 1990. Living in California, the couple have three children: Lucy Chet, Gracie Fan and Jake Daniel. A man of many talents, DeVito likes to unwind by playing the piano and the violin.

Colleen Dewhurst

"**I**t's a cameo role, but Miss Dewhurst, functioning as a cleanup hitter, knocks every laugh line clear out of the park," praised Frank Rich in his *New York Times* review of the 1983 revival of *You Can't Take It With You*. "Jason [Robards] and I are so used to doing heavies," beamed Dewhurst in an interview during the show's run, "that the cast broke up the other night when I said, 'Gee, it's wonderful to be in a play where the audience smiles back at you when you take the curtain call.'" Because of those "heavies" she became and remains one of the theatre's undisputed queens. Some of her memorable roles include Camille, Portia, Cleopatra, Kate, Eleanor of Aquitaine, Lady Macbeth, Medea, Miss Amelia in *Ballad of the Sad Cafe*, Sara in *More Stately Mansions*, the Albee shrikes in *Who's Afraid of Virginia Woolf* and *All Over*, Christine Mannon in *Mourning Becomes Electra*, and Josie in *The Moon for the Misbegotten*. She's won three Obies, two Tony Awards and one Emmy.

Born in Montreal, Quebec, 3 June 1926, the daughter of a hockey player, she wanted to be an aviatrix at five. Years later, the dean of Milwaukee's Downer College (now Lawrence U.) wrote to her parents saying that life was an endless party to which Colleen had been the only one invited and requested her removal. There followed a $25-a-week elevator operator's job in Gary, Ind., and she later worked as a gym instructor "teaching fat old ladies how to shape up." Trekking off to New York, she enrolled at the American Academy of Dramatic Arts, made her professional acting debut in 1946 in *The Royal Family*, and in 1952 her Broadway debut in *Desire Under the Elms* by Eugene O'Neil, the playwright whose work she has so brilliantly illuminated. Varied theatrical activities have moved her on and off stage. Appearances include *An Almost Perfect Person* (1977), *The Queen and the Rebels* (1982) and as O'Neill's wife Carlotta in the 1985 Off-Broadway play, *My Gene*. She joined the ranks of women directors when she took over the reins (for a very short ride) of *Ned and Jack* (1981). Later she directed the National Theater of the Deaf's '84-'85 production of *All the Way Home* (for which she won an "actress" Tony in 1961). Elected president of Actor's Equity in 1985, she is vice-chairman of the Save The Theater movement (preservation of Broadway theatres) and is on the board of the Actor's Fund. The diversified actress continues to spread her wings across all mediums. Recent roles include: *Ah! Wilderness!* and *Long Day's Journey* on stage in 1988; the films *The Boy Who Could Fly* (1986), and *Hit & Run* (1987) and television appearances in "Moonlighting" and "Murphy Brown" (playing Candice Bergen's mother). Her mercurial marriage to George C. Scott in 1960 finally ended in 1972, *two* marriages, two divorces and two children (Campbell [the C. in George C.] and Alexander) later. She now lives in her farmhouse in South Salem, N.Y. with her two grown sons and a flock of animals and birds. She prefers the casual comfort of country life, and her passions are antiques and paintings. She once told an interviewer she'll never marry again. "Those might be famous last words," she admits, "I could live with a man without having to get married. But I have all I need—a career, children, and a house."

Susan Dey

While a "Partridge," this model-turned-actress discovered the true meaning of being a professional. She told *TV Guide* in a 1973 interview that "what I learned this year is that a set is not a home; if you're bored, too bad—get unbored in a hurry. If you're tired, wake up fast. If you're upset about something, the set is not the place to work it out." This strong sense of self and understanding of her trade have enabled Susan Dey to become one of the most popular television personalities of the 1970's, and the 1980's, and beyond. Her present role as Grace Van Owen in the

Award-winning NBC-TV show "L.A. Law" has brought her respect, honors and a secured standing as a favorite actress of the era.

One of four children, Susan was born 10 December 1952 in Pekin, Illinois, to Robert Smith Dey (city editor, *New Rochelle Standard-Star*) and his wife Gail. The aspiring actress grew up in Mt. Kisco, New York, and graduated in 1970 from the Fox Lane High School in Bedford. Her career began in modelling, when her mother submitted pictures of her and her sister, Lesley, to a modeling agency. Dey's fresh, young look graced the covers of many magazines at the time, including *Seventeen, American Girl,* and *Simplicity.* Winning the role of "Laurie" in "The Partridge Family" during a New York audition, she later flew to Hollywood to make the pilot. While making the series she lived in California with a chaperon and completed her education by correspondence courses. Her fame skyrocketed and her name was popping up all over fan magazines with articles like "Susan's Popularity Secrets," "Ten Ways to Get Him to Kiss You," and "Susan Reveals All." She told *TV Guide* that she was bothered by the way her younger sisters reacted to her instant stardom. "The very first time I went home, my own little sister really surprised me by asking for my autograph— not as a joke or on a blank check or anything; she really wanted Laurie Partridge's autograph. I was very disturbed by that." Springboarding from the series to feature films, Dey acted in *Skyjacked, First Love,* and *Looker.* She also starred in the telefilms "Loves Me, Loves Me Not," "The Comeback Kid," "Little Women," "Cage Without a Key," "Mary Jane Harper Cried Last Night," "The Gift of Life," and "Angel in Green," plus the 1983 TV series "Emerald Point N.A.S."

On a hiatus from acting when she gave birth to her daughter Sarah, Susan says "It was a period of change in my life, and I needed time to ground myself." Her marriage to agent Leonard Hirshan ended in divorce and her career hit a standstill. Then, as her NBC biography stated, a chance meeting became the slingshot to her current success. "Timing—and bumping into the right person— was everything for Susan Dey, whose serendipitous first meeting with 'L.A. Law' executive producer Steven Bochco at a private school function for their children paid off in a starring role just as the series was to begin its first year of production." Happily matriculated with a fine ensemble of players, Susan also finds time to branch out in other areas. She appeared in the movie *The Trouble With Dick* (1988) and the TV film "A Place at the Table" with David Morse. In 1988 she married Bernard Sofronski and the couple live, along with her daughter, in Los Angeles. During her spare time, she likes swimming or sailing, and just walking on the beach.

Angie Dickinson

"**I** love hot weather," she once purred on "The Tonight Show." "I like to take my clothes off in the heat." In the next breath, she asked Johnny Carson to describe his erotic fantasies. (He just blanched and cut to a commercial.) The steamy star was certainly in her element in Brian De Palma's *Dressed to Kill* (1980) in which she played a suburban matron hungry for love in the backseat of a taxi. "I am not Doris Day," she quips. Lucky for her; *Dressed to Kill* was the biggest movie smash of her checkered career. "This is the first time I've had this instantaneous reaction, the feeling I am a hot number." (The sex and violence in the film earned the thriller $25 million and cries of exploitation from the feminist community.) Forced to retire as NBC's "Police Woman" after its abrupt cancellation in '78, she laid low until cast for *Dressed to Kill*. De Palma however, used a 23-year-old neck-to-knees stand-in for the nude scenes, and made no bones about telling the public just that. "I was shocked," says Dickinson. "Why destroy the illusion? Let them think it's Tahiti, even if it is Burbank."

Born Angeline Brown in Kulm, N.D., 30 September 1932, she became Dickinson while attending Glendale College. (Her first husband was college football star Gene Dickinson; "I was just wrong for him as wonderful as he was.") She got her first break when producer Howard Hawks spotted her, and she subsequently starred in *Rio Bravo, Point Blank,* and *Pretty Maids All in a Row*. A onetime Mayor of Universal City ("My community covered 408 acres, eight acres bigger than Princess Grace's Monaco"), she has, in the past, been courted by Frank Sinatra, the late David Janssen, even JFK, but at the moment her romantic involvements are being kept at bay since her split in '76 from husband Burt Bacharach (one daughter Nikki).

Marlene Dietrich

Mike Todd called her "the world's greatest" entertainer. In the 1950s, as her film career waned, she became a recording star and cabaret performer, singing to packed houses internationally (including her native Berlin). Facing audiences in Paris, London, Las Vegas, and New York, she could, with the measured enunciations of a single syllable, evoke a seamy Berlin honky-tonk of the 1920s. "Look me over closely," she would huskily intone while gowned in a Jean Louis dazzler, her voice ironic even in solicitation. So the legend lives; on a column in the Café de Paris against which she learned singing is a bronze plaque inscribed, "Dietrich rested here." Her legs were insured by Lloyd's of London and she had the pleasure of seeing them banned from posters in the Paris subways (too demoralizing to the customers).

She was born Maria Magdalena Von Losch, 27 December 1901, into a strict Berlin family. Aside from her basically upper-middle class conservative background, her early life is shrouded in mystery. Seriously bent on a musical career as a violinist, she was reportedly unable to perform in concert because of a chronic wrist ailment. Turning to the theatre, she coaxed Berlin's famed theatrical dictator Max Reinhardt into giving her a part in *The Taming of the Shrew*. When Josef von Sternberg brought her to America in 1930, she was regarded as Paramount's answer to MGM's Garbo. (Dietrich had appeared in a bit part five years earlier in G.W. Pabst's *The Joyless Street*, starring Garbo.) Of the two, Dietrich had vastly more theatrical experience: she had appeared in Shaw, in revues, in musical comedy, and in a dozen films. Auditioning for the 1929 UFA film that was to bring her international celebrity, she was advised by Sternberg to "learn a vulgar song"—and she walked into the sordid erotic twilight of *The Blue Angel* and film history in 1930 belting a jazzy American lunacy, "You're the cream in my coffee, You're the salt in my stew." Most of her early American films (half a dozen directed by her mentor Sternberg, whose reputation was later considerably elevated by revisionist auteurist film critics like Andrew Sarris) were criticized as so much visual rhetoric draped around a fabulous face and figure. (At the height of her fame, she was credited for starting the vogue among women for wearing slacks.) In her first, *Morocco* (1930—her sole Oscar nomination), Sternberg sent her stalking Gary Cooper across broiling Sahara sands in billowing chiffon and six-inch heels. Her subsequent films were at times even less coherent; nobody seemed to mind. Her other Sternbergs are: *Dishonored* (1931), *The Scarlet Empress* (as Catherine the Great; 1934), *Blonde Venus* (in which she sang "Hot Voodoo" while dressed in a gorilla suit; 1932), *Shanghai Express* in 1932 ("Oh, why are they always talking about those old movies of mine?") and *The Devil is a Woman* in 1935 ("I was more beautiful in that than in anything else."). Other memorable films include: *Garden of Allah* (1936), *Destry Rides Again* (1939), *A Foreign Affair* (1948), Hitchcock's *Stage Fright* (1950), *Witness for the Prosectuion* (1957), Welles's *Touch of Evil* (1958) and *Judgment at Nuremberg* (1961). While filming *Knight Without Armor* in England in '37, she received a generous, personal offer from Hitler to return to German films. She refused and, as a result, her films were banned in her native country. In '39 she became an American citizen. During W.W.II she entertained U.S. troops, participated in war bond drives and made anti-Nazi propaganda broadcasts in German. She was decorated by the U.S. and France.

A longtime friend, Ernest Hemingway, said of her, "Brave, beautiful, loyal, generous . . . I value her opinion more than professors." Her only husband, Czech-born chicken farmer Rudolph Sieber (they were married in 1924 and, except for a few days each year or so, lived apart for nearly four decades until his death in 1975) said, "When I had a heart attack she flew to my bedside and nursed me to health. This is what lasts. She is basically a regular guy." She has one daughter, onetime actress Maria Riva, to whom her devotion is legendary, and four grandchildren. When Maria's first child was born, Dietrich was called "the world's most glamorous grandmother." Now she is a recluse, confined to a wheelchair in her Paris apartment. Her 1979 autobiography *My Life Story* was published in Germany. In 1984 actor-director Maximilian Schell (whose appearance with her in *Nuremberg* earned him an Oscar) filmed a documentary on her life and career. Her autobiography, translated by Salvator Attansio was published in 1989.

Phyllis Diller

S he can deliver as many as 12 punchlines per minute and not all about "Fang" either ("Fang is SO-OOOO dumb that a brain operation on *him* would be minor surgery")—in point of fact

"Fang" is a dreamed-up figure and "bears no resemblance to either of my former husbands." Her hair may look as if it might have been styled by a food processor but her bankbook looks beautiful. She remains one of the busiest and most popular female comics around, headlining in six countries for over thirty years.

Born in Lima, Ohio, on 17 July 1917, as Phyllis Driver, she met her first husband Sherwood Anderson Diller at Bluffton College in Ohio. Married in 1939, she became the mother of five children, worked as an advertising copywriter, but did most of her joking at the laundromat. In 1955 her rep as a neighborhood cut-up led to a trial engagement at San Francisco's *Purple Onion;* it stretched on for 89 weeks. Since then Phyllis has been in 11 movies including a dramatic role in Elmer Rice's *The Adding Machine* and three co-starring roles with Bob Hope. ("We have an agreement," she says, "I don't make fun of his nose and he doesn't ridicule my body.") She's played Dolly Levi in a Broadway revival of *Hello Dolly* and as an accomplished pianist has appeared with some top-notch symphony orchestras in the U.S. In the early '80s she had already published four books and *The Joys of Aging and How to Avoid Them* (1981) was destined to become a bestseller if only because she looked better in '81 than she did in '61. Much better. She is a former honorary mayor of Brentwood, California, and received a Ph.D. ("Is that an abbreviation of Phyllis Diller?") from National Christian University. Divorced from Diller in 1965, she later married actor Warde Donovan whom she also divorced. Phyllis lives in a large English-style home in West Los Angeles. "The place used to be haunted," she says, "but the ghosts haven't been back since the night I tried on all my wigs."

Matt Dillon

Here's how Maura Moynihan in *Interview* gilded this teenage pistol noted for his reform-school-tough-outside and heart-of-gold inside, sort of a poor boy's knight-in-shining-armor: "The magnetism he radiates is very powerful; it is something tangible. On his taut physique clothing falls in loose disorder.

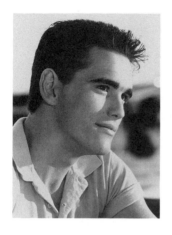

Buttons seem to come undone and fabric slackens. He is blessed with dramatic Gaelic coloring: glossy black hair, luminous skin with flushed cheeks and enormous liquid eyes. His attention is elusive but once captured, focuses with great intensity. He explores his thoughts more with instinct than intellect; often his movements convey his meaning more effectively than his words. He loves rock music and speaks with jargon comprehensible to any teenager. The qualities of maturing self-possession and ingenuousness are gracefully co-mingled."

In other words, he's a big heart-throbber, another one of the "sons of DeNiro." Matt Dillon, born 18 February 1964 in New Rochelle, N.Y., (where, TV trivia fans, Dick Van Dyke lived with Mary Tyler Moore), was discovered in the halls of his high school while he was cutting class one afternoon in 1979. Talent scouts were combing the area for some fresh young skin for the film *Over the Edge*. After a mere five minutes with Matt, casting director Victor Ramos pencilled in his notebook: "Should be a movie star." Soon thereafter, Ramos became Dillon's personal manager. Following *Over the Edge*, Matt appeared in *Little Darlings* and overnight became the honey to an adoring teeny-bopper population, receiving up to 7,000 pieces of fan mail a week. His subsequent films such as *My Bodyguard*, *Liar's Moon* (as the naive farmboy), *Tex* and the PBS production of Jean Shepherd's satirical "The Great American 4th of July and Other Disasters" brought him full star status and established him as an actor of depth and both dramatic and comedic versatility. Two of his best performances have been in the film adaptations of novels written by one of his favorite writers, S.E. Hinton, whose fan he was long before his film career took off; *The Outsiders* and *Rumble Fish* were both directed by Francis Coppola. Dillon garnered rave reviews for his starring roles in *Flamingo Kid*, *Target*, *Native Son*, *The Big Town*, *Kansas*, *Bloodhounds of Broadway* and *Drugstore Cowboy* (1989).

Into astrology, reading, girls and more girls, the young actor finds it difficult "to keep a relationship together. I fall in love really hard," he says, "I get myself into trouble. For some reason I do, but I have a hard time keeping it going. . . . commitment . . . my work has to be first. . . . I've had my heart smashed, stepped on, crunched, everybody has. Vice-versa, too. I know that. I don't screw anybody over, but I know that happens. It's tough."

Kevin Dobson

This 6-foot, brown-haired, blue-eyed actor is perhaps one of the most sought after husbands on television. Sharing a Soap Opera Award with his co-star Michele Lee, Kevin Dobson was named as part of the "Best Couple" for playing honorable M. Patrick MacKenzie on the popular nighttime series "Knots Landing." His rugged good looks and endearing personality assure certain screen stability, but Dobson is a trained actor who has paid his dues along the way to stardom.

Born in Jackson Heights, New York, on 18 March 1944, young Dobson was initially interested in sports. While attending high school he was offered a professional baseball contract with the San Francisco Giants. He passed on the tempting proposition in order to fulfill a military term in the U.S. Army. After his military obligation he found work as a ticket-taker for the Long Island Railroad to save enough money for college. In the interim his girlfriend (and future wife), along with his sister, prodded Kevin to try out for commercials. A short time later he appeared in his first stage play, *The Impossible Years*, which toured throughout the United States. When he returned to New York, he studied under the direction of Sanford Meisner while working odd jobs as a waiter, bartender and taxi driver. Eventually fielding offers, Dobson appeared in some Off-Broadway plays and major films: *Love Story*, *Bananas*, *Klute*, *The Anderson Tapes*, *The French Connection*, and *Carnal Knowledge*. Crossing the coasts for a swing at Hollywood, he landed some guest roles on established television shows such as "Mod Squad," understudied for Jon Voight in an LA stage production of *A Streetcar Named Desire*, and then hit the bigtime hooking the recurring role as Detective Bobby Crocker on "Kojak" (1973-1978). With over 100 episodes behind him, Dobson became a popular choice in 1979 to add to the mostly female cast of "Knots Landing." As the justice-seeking Federal prosecutor, Dobson's character added bite to the soap opera. In 1989, "MacKenzie" tried it solo as an independent lawyer on the show and his relationship with his wife "Karen" (Michele Lee) was sprinkled with some teasing indiscretions. Other TV credits include the telefilms "Transplant," "Orphan Train," "Hardhat and Legs," "From Here to Eternity," "Mickey Spillane's

Mike Hammer," "Reunion," and "Sweet Revenge," and the series "Shannon" (1981-1982).

Kevin and his wife, Susan, have three children. They enjoy family outings and family-oriented sports. Kevin is associated with many charities; he was the recipient of the United States Jaycees Outstanding Young Men in America Award for Professional Achievement and Community Service in 1979, and he finds time to get involved with the Retinitis Pigmentosa Foundation, Muscular Dystrophy Association, Easter Seals and the Special Olympics. An active sportsman, Dobson likes to play tennis and racquetball on his own backyard court.

Phil Donahue

"What we do," he says, "is provide on daytime TV a relief from the soaps and game shows. . . . I honestly believe we have spoken more thoughtfully, more honestly, more often to more issues about which women care, than any other show." His Emmy-Award-winning program, "Donahue," which moved from Chicago to New York, is unique in tackling contemporary and often controversial (e.g., lesbian nuns; women involved with priests) topics in an innovative discussion format that encourages active audience participation. The audience is mostly female. Erma Bombeck has said, "He's every wife's replacement for the husband who doesn't talk to her. They've always got Phil who will listen and take them seriously."

Born in Cleveland on 21 December 1935, Donahue gained his initial broadcasting experience at his *alma mater,* Notre Dame, where he became an announcer on the university-owned commercial TV station. Eventually he did newscasts and phone-in talk shows. "Donahue" began as a local show in Dayton, Ohio, in 1967. From the start, it was especially popular among housewives. His first guest was atheist Madalyn Murray O'Hair, whose successful 1963 Supreme Court suit had outlawed prayer in public schools. "We were flooded with letters, calls," her host says. "Some were furious, threatening, while others were very positive. We were getting people excited, upset, thinking and expressing themselves. And this is just what we wanted." In 1969 "The Phil Donahue Show" began syndication, and in April 1974, moved to Chicago, where it had its name shortened. Today it's one of the most watched syndicated TV talk shows, with an 18-month waiting list for studio tickets.

Offscreen, Donahue says, he's a "shy, insecure, vulnerable manchild." His first wife (married 1958; divorced 1975) was his college sweetheart, Margaret Mary Cooney, by whom he has four sons and a daughter. In May 1980, he married actress/feminist Marlo Thomas. They live in New York and Connecticut. Donahue's annual salary is reported over $500,000. A "lapsed Catholic" who blames his former sexism on Roman Catholic theology, he's an ardent feminist and member of NOW. In his 1980 best-selling autobiography, *Donahue: My Own Story*, he states, "Television's problem is not controversy. It is blandness." Donahue's 1985 book *The Human Animal* explores human behavior, "the brightest and darkest corners of human nature."

Increasing his visibility, Donahue has co-hosted NBC's "Today" show (April 4-8, 1988) with Jane Pauley, and he made broadcasting history when he became the first American talk show host to tape shows inside the Soviet Union. He has received many awards, including the prestigious George Foster Peabody Broadcasting Award. Of his job, Donahue says, "Having your own talk show is an opportunity afforded very few people. It should happen to everybody. . . . This business of asking the questions and being involved in conversation they stimulate is the most personally satisfying part of all that has happened to me in my career."

Kirk Douglas

"I came from the east end of Amsterdam, N.Y. and the farther east you went the tougher it got. . . . To mention to anybody around there you wanted to be an actor was to lay yourself open to a punch in the nose." It's no surprise, then, that the lantern-jawed actor first made his mark on screen (and collected an Oscar nomination) as a tough, wrong-side-of-the-tracks fighter in *Champion* (1949). Also, as someone his second wife once described as "a volcano . . . with tension spitting out of him like sparks," it's no wonder that he delivered one of his best performances as the tortured Dutch painter Vincent Van Gogh in *Lust for Life* (1955). His dimpled-chin hallmark has been on view in over 70 films including such semi-classics as *The Bad and the Beautiful, Detective Story, Gunfight at the O.K. Corral, Paths of Glory* and *Seven Days in May.*

Born Issur Danielovitch (the name was temporarily "American-ized" to Isadore Demsky) on 9 December 1916 in upstate New York, he was the only boy among six girls in the family of a Russian peddler. Working his way through St. Lawrence University and New York's American Academy of Dramatic Art, he toiled at well over 50 different jobs. ("My life is a B script," he once said. "I'd never make it as a picture—too corny.") Given a pep talk by one of Douglas' AADA classmates, Lauren Bacall, a Hollywood producer took a look at the young actor in a flop play and signed him up to play opposite Barbara Stanwyck in the 1946 drama *The Strange Love of Martha Ivers.* The not-so-wee Kirk has been a Hollywood fixture ever since, and a ranking member of the local hierarchy of actor-producers starting in 1955. His Bryna Productions (*Spartacus, The Vikings*) is named for his late mother.

Married first to drama school classmate Diana Dill (sons Mi-chael and Joel), Douglas then wed photographer Anne Buydens (sons Peter and Eric). He detailed much of his career and personal life in his 1988 autobiography *The Ragman's Son.* He made his fiction debut in June, 1990, with the novel *Dance with the Devil.* Michael Douglas has been a familiar face in the Tinseltown crowd since appearing on the TV series "The Streets of San Francisco" and, following in his dad's footsteps as an actor-producer, put out *One Flew Over the Cuckoo's Nest* (1975) and *Romancing the Stone* (1984), among others. Kirk says now he's identified as "the father of Michael Douglas" as often as the other way around.

Michael Douglas

This green-eyed, cleft-chinned actor-producer has carved his own secure niche in the entertainment industry, but some critics and fans still try to credit a part of his remarkable success to his father, Kirk Douglas. "One never gets full credit for anything you do. Like with *One Flew Over the Cuckoo's Nest*, people will say: "Well, it's his father's project."

Douglas *père* has helped him with advice and other favors Michael admits, but he will cherish the day when "I can be indepen-dent, someone more than Kirk Douglas' son. My father and I are very different." Kirk lived in poverty as a youth, Michael points out, whereas *he* attended prep school, owned a motorcycle and lived three years in a commune before deciding to work. Professionally,

Douglas *fils* considers himself "a late bloomer." It wasn't until he was a senior at University of California when "they forced me to choose a major" that he decided to pursue acting.

From 1972 to 1975, Douglas starred with Karl Malden in TV's "The Streets of San Francisco," in the role of Assistant Inspector Steve Keller, the youngest man ever to achieve that rank in the San Francisco police department. "Michael is an ambitious young man, and I used that in the best sense of the word," said Malden at the time. Douglas hit the jackpot in his film producing debut in 1975 when *One Flew Over the Cuckoo's Nest* tallied a whopping $130 million at the box office and pulled in five Academy Awards. His 1979 *China Syndrome* grossed $75 million (helped no doubt by the Three Mile Island fiasco which occurred just as filming was completed) and his 1984 romp, *Romancing The Stone* grossed $63 million in its first six months in spite of mixed reviews. One critic described *Romancing The Stone* as a "slapstick comedy" and contended that Douglas was not right for his role because he was not a comedian. "No matter how fast he moves," quipped the reviewer, "he seems to slow down whatever is going on around him." Undismayed, Douglas produced a sequel in 1985, *The Jewel of the Nile,* with his *Stone* co-star, sultry Kathleen Turner, once again along for the fun and adventure. Bouncing off from the movie bomb version of *A Chorus Line* (1985), Douglas hit it big with *Wall Street* (1987). As *Wall Street's* unscrupulous corporate raider Gordon Gekko, Michael walked away with both the Academy Award and Golden Globe Award for Best Actor in a Motion Picture. He also scored high that year with Paramount's alarming film *Fatal Attraction* (1987). Continually on the move, Michael next took on films that included *The Tender* (co-executive producer, 1988) and *The War of the Roses* (1989).

Born in New Brunswick, N.J., 25 September 1945, Michael is the elder son of Kirk and English-born actress Diana (Dill) Douglas. His parents were divorced when he was 6. In the 1960s Michael was a hippie in California, and remains active on behalf of liberal political causes, including membership in the Committee on Concern, a group of Hollywood activists involved in Central American issues. He is also part owner of the *L.A. Weekly,* an alternative newspaper. Nevertheless, his major concern is his movie career. "Finding a good script is like falling in love with a girl. You read a script like you see a girl. You flirt with her a little bit and then you're hooked."

Michael got "hooked" the same way when he met Diandra Lucker, whom he married in 1977 after a courtship of just two weeks. They have one child, Cameron Morrell.

Robert Downey, Jr.

Named *Rolling Stone* magazine's Hottest Actor for 1988, Robert Downey, Jr. doesn't take all the attention to heart. After an audition for "Saturday Night Live" he replied, "I was extremely nervous when I auditioned but some things are too important to take seriously." When asked what it meant to be hot, he answered, "destined to be cold." But this young, multi-talented actor is anything but cold.

Born 4 April 1965 in New York, the son of an actress/singer mother and a filmmaker/writer father (Robert Downey, Sr.), Robert was destined for show business. Although born in New York, Downey was raised in California, New Mexico and London. He debuted at the age of five in the motion picture *Pound*, which was produced by his father. Shortly after his debut, Downey starred in three more films produced by his father: *The Greasers Palace* (1972), *Up the Academy*, and *This is America the Movie, Not the Country*. Downey attended Santa Monica High School, but left in the eleventh grade to perform in the movie *Baby It's You*. Proving that he is as comfortable doing drama as he is doing comedy, Downey has tackled such diverse leading roles as a girl-crazy teenager in the comedy *Pick Up Artis* and a cocaine addict in the film *Less Than Zero*. Other films Downey has starred in include: *Firstborn, Tuff Turf, Weird Science, Back to School, Johnny B. Good, Rented Lips, Chances Are,* and *Air America* (1990). His TV appearances include one season of "Saturday Night Live," and a feature role playing George C. Scott's son in the miniseries "Mussolini: The Untold Story."

Still single, Downey resides in both New York and Los Angeles.

Richard Dreyfuss

"I have no memory of not wanting to be an actor," says Richard Dreyfuss, whose stage and screen performances convey charm, intelligence and sensitivity. "It was emotional," he says of his chosen career. "It stemmed from my personality. . . . I'm an egoist. . . . I believe everyone is unique, everyone has within him a universe of things never adequately described. Behind all art is ego, and I am an artist and I am unique."

Born in Brooklyn on 29 October 1947, Dreyfuss was raised in Queens and L.A. His first stage experience occurred in Hebrew school productions and he began acting professionally at L.A.'s Gallery Theater. Intending to major in theatre arts at San Fernando Stage College, Dreyfuss "got kicked out of the drama department" for arguing with a professor over Marlon Brando— "the greatest actor in the world, period, bar *none*." Dreyfuss switched majors to political science, and doesn't rule out a future run for the Senate or another elective office. As a conscientious objector, he had to leave college in his sophomore year to do two years of alternative service as a file clerk on the midnight-to-morning shift at L.A. County General Hospital. TV work and few bit parts in films followed as did stage performances in N.Y. and regional theatres. After seeing Dreyfuss in Shaw's *Major Barbara* at L.A.'s Mark Taper Forum, the screenwriters of *American Graffiti* (1973) recommended him to the film's director, George Lucas. Following *Graffiti* stardom, Dreyfuss won acclaim for *The Apprenticeship of Duddy Kravitz, Jaws, Close Encounters of the Third Kind*, earned an Academy Award for *The Goodbye Girl* (1977) and he played a paraplegic in the 1981 film *Whose Life Is It, Anyway?* More 80's films include *Down and Out in Beverly Hills* (1986), *Tin Men* (1987), *Stakeout* (1987), *Nuts* (1987) and *Moon Over Parador* (1988). Films released in 1989 include *Fifty, Let It Ride*, and *Always*. In addition to his motion pictures, Dreyfuss created, produced, wrote, and hosted "Funny, You Don't Look 200!" on ABC-TV.

At 5'6", Dreyfuss tends toward chubbiness. Outspoken in his opinions, Dreyfuss asserts that the "motion picture business is run by corporate thieves," with "the level of corruption . . . taken for granted all over the place." Richard married Jeramie Rain (real name: Susan Davis) on 20 March 1983. They have two children: Emily and Benjamin.

Patrick Duffy

"Who shot Bobby Ewing?" the cliffhanger at the close of the 1983-84 "Dallas" season, didn't set off the media fireworks of "Who shot J.R.?" in 1980, but the future career of Patrick Duffy as a leading television light nevertheless seemed secure. He was in at the start of the CBS-TV blockbuster in 1977, playing the straight-arrow "good brother" (Larry Hagman was the bad one) in the squabbling family of oil millionaires and, like the show, was an immediate hit. Says the classically-handsome 6'2" actor about his small-screen alter ego: "He is sentimental but a realist, determined but passive. He is also a happy person with a good temper and a principled set of mores and values. About 80% of Bobby is me." At Duffy's request, "Dallas" writers bumped off Bobby at the end of the 1984-85 season. Duffy returned to "Dallas" in the fall of 1986.

Born (and christened) on St. Patrick's Day, 1949, Duffy was raised by his tavern-owning folks in, first, Townsend and later Boulder, Montana, and eventually, Seattle. (Both his parents were murdered in the mid-eighties during an unexpected act of violence in their quiet tavern.) Patrick's career decision to become an actor was clinched when he was accepted into the Professional Actors Training Program at the University of Washington, one of 12 students selected out of 1200 applicants. ("I was incredibly fortunate . . . when we weren't involved in a project, we were studying with mime teachers from France, gymnasts from the Olympics, and even jugglers from Barnum and Bailey's Circus.") His first job after graduation was as "Actor in Residence" at Washington State, where he met his ballet-dancer wife, Carlyn. Later, while going through the mandatory making-the-rounds lean period in both New York and Hollywood, he supported himself with construction jobs and architectural work between acting jobs. Fittingly, he was remodeling a boat in 1976 when he was signed for his first starring TV roles as "The Man from Atlantis" in which he learned to talk underwater and outswim dolphins. In addition to his long-running Bobby Ewing role on "Dallas," Duffy also directed a number of episodes and has appeared in TV movies: "Strong Medicine" (1985), "Alice in Wonderland" (1985), "Too Good To Be True" (1988). He was also seen in the big-screen release *Vamping*. He is a favorite host of the Thanksgiving Day Parade. He and his wife (two sons) are active followers of Nichiren Shoshu of America, a form of Japanese Buddhism.

Olympia Dukakis

"People would see my name, at least at first, and assume that I must have been born in Greece and spoke English with a heavy accent. The fact was, I was born in Massachusetts and had a bit of a New England accent. Later, I was styled an 'ethnic' actor, meaning I got to play a lot of ethnics, Italians and so on. My big breakthrough in TV was that I was 'Aunt Millie' in the spaghetti sauce commercials. And for a while there, I played so many prostitutes that my resume looked like I ran a house of ill repute," Olympia Dukakis recalled during a 1988 interview with *The Record*. Her portrayal of the unsentimental mother in *Moonstruck* brought her worldwide recognition and numerous awards (L.A. Film Critics, Golden Glove, Academy Award). When talking about her performance in the movie *Moonstruck* she says: "Who is this woman to compare to some of the really challenging characters I've played on the stage? Try Hecuba [in Euripides' "The Trojan Woman"]; try Luba [Ranevskaya in "The Cherry Orchard"]; try Mother Courage [in Bertolt Brecht's "Mother Courage and Her Children"]. But then my friend Austin Pendleton tells me, 'Olympia, you're not understanding what it's all about. You're getting these awards because all those other, more challenging women you've played shine through in Rose.' Any maybe that's the truth of it." Rumors abound for a sequel to *Moonstruck*.

Born in Lowell, Massachusetts, on 20 June 1931, she is the cousin of Michael Dukakis, the Governor of Massachusetts and the defeated 1988 Democratic candidate for president. Centering her career on the theatre, Olympia studied for the stage. She graduated from Boston University with a Bachelor of Arts Degree. Getting started was not that easy. She told *The Washington Post*, "If your name is Olympia Dukakis, that's it, bang. The doors close, the shades come down. You play Italians. . . . I've been 'discovered' about six times, y'know." With her husband, actor Louis Zorich, she launched the Whole Theatre, involving some actor friends. Today, it is a well-respected Equity company. Between "discoveries," Dukakis worked as an acting teacher at NYU from 1967 to 1979, then as a master instructor from 1974 to 1983. She also taught at Yale University in 1976.

Other significant Olympia performances include, on stage: *Social Security* (Broadway), *The Marriage of Bette and Boo* (Obie Award), *Curse of the Starving Class, A View From the Bridge* (Theatre World Award), *Peer Gynt,* and *A Man's a Man* (Obie Award); on television: "FDR—the Last Days," "One of the Boys," "The Seagull," "King of America," and a continuing role on the daytime soap "Search for Tomorrow"; on screen: *Steel Magnolias, Dad, In the Spirit, Daddy's Home, Working Girl, Made for Each Other, The Idolmaker, Rich Kids, Deathwish,* and *John and Mary.*

Patty Duke

There wasn't much time for hopscotch or any other childhood diversions. From the time she was discovered at seven, Patty Duke was a working actress making the rounds. By age twelve, she had starred in more than 50 TV shows and played on stage opposite Kim Stanley, Helen Hayes and Laurence Olivier. She was 13 when she exploded as a superstar playing the young Helen Keller in *The Miracle Worker.* Wrote Walter Kerr: "She is a very great actress who only happens, at the moment, to also be a child." Duke followed it with the film version and at 16 collected an Oscar as best supporting actress. Then came her own Emmy Award winning sitcom series, "The Patty Duke Show." In her early twenties in 1968, she could sum it all up by telling writer Rex Reed, "I had days when I did nothing but cry for nine hours straight." And no wonder; her life (which began 14 December 1946) in Reed's words "reads like Elsie Dinsmore." Her cabdriver father and restaurant-cashier mother called it quits early with their marriage, and Patty's budding dramatic gifts were urged into bloom by the John Rosses, a husband-wife manager team who had no children of their own and so took in their young protégée. Diction, singing lessons and drama classes were interspersed with toothpaste commercials, TV shows and theatre appearances. (To rid her of her heavy New York accent the Rosses made her sit for hours with a tape recorder trying to learn a British accent.) Preparation for the Helen Keller role took 15 months of learning what it was like to be deaf (ear plugs), then blind (eyes closed), and then mute. The play, which opened in 1959, lasted two exhausting years. Eventually the girl beloved by tube regulars as "The All-American teenager" wound up on the big screen as a ravaged alcoholic in *Valley of the Dolls* and offscreen, on a psychiatrist's couch. She was married and divorced first from director Harry Falk, Jr., second from rock promoter Michael Tell.

She married actor John Astin in 1973 ("I inherited John's three sons") and had two children with him (Sean, born a year before their marriage, and Mackenzie, born in 1973) while continuing to act in TV movies such as: "Me, Natalie" (1969), "My Sweet Charlie" (1970), "Captains and the Kings" (1976), "Having Babies" (1978) and "The Women's Room" (1980). That marriage ended in 1985. During the filming of a television movie Patty fell in love again, and married Michael Pearce on 15 March 1986 in Lake Tahoe. They have a son, Kevin Michael Pearce. In 1983, she won "most popular actress in a new TV series" in the short-lived "It Takes Two." In 1984, she was warm and motherly Martha Washington to Barry Bostwick's George on the CBS miniseries about the Father of Our Country, and in 1985 starred as the first woman president in the TV series, "Hail to the Chief." The green-eyed snappy five-footer is charged with "positive think": "The one constant . . . is to try to keep a sense of humor about everything in life. . . . In some infinitesimal way, I would like to believe that I could leave things a little better than when I found them." Elected in 1985 to head SAG (Screen Actors Guild), she held that position through the middle of her second term. In 1987 her revealing autobiography *Call Me Anna: The Autobiography of Patty Duke* hit the bookstands.

David Dukes

Typecasting has never been a problem for actor David Dukes. He has established himself in theater, television and feature films by playing a variety of characters. From Edith Bunker's would-be rapist on the CBS series "All in the Family," to helpful diplomat Leslie Slote in the ABC miniseries "The Winds of War" and its sequel "War and Remembrance," to Dr. Frankenstein in *Frankenstein* on Broadway, Dukes has been a working actor whose face is probably better known to the public than his name.

David Dukes was born 6 June 1945 in San Francisco, California. He attended Mann College. The successes of the 6-foot, 175-pound actor with dark brown hair and hazel eyes must be attributed to his

chameleon-like ability to maneuver easily between the fields of stage, television and screen, creating memorable characters along the way. Dukes made his Broadway debut in 1971 in *School for Wives*. Other theater appearances include: *Don Juan, The Play's the Thing, The Visit, Holiday,* and *Rules of the Game.* He also appeared in *Key Exchange* with Kate Jackson and Peter Riegert at the Westwood Playhouse, *Another Part of the Forest* at the Ahmanson, and *Every Boy Deserves Good Favor* at the Dorothy Chandler Pavillion. *Travesties,* in which he performed on Broadway and in Los Angeles, earned him a L.A. Drama Critics Award. Other Broadway performances were *Amadeus,* in the role of Salieri; *Dracula, Bent,* with Richard Gere; and role of the French diplomat in *M. Butterfly.*

Television has cast Dukes in different eras, from the 1700's to modern day. He appeared on the series "Beacon Hill" and in the TV movies "The Triangle Factory Fire" and "Sentimental Journey," but it is in the miniseries format that Dukes has found his niche. He co-starred with Lesley Ann Warren as the "nice guy" Michael in "79 Park Avenue" and with Barry Bostwick in "George Washington." Dukes portrayed a slick con man in "Space" co-starring Bruce Dern, played Leslie Slote in "Winds of War" and "War and Remembrance," and had roles in "Kane & Abel" with Peter Strauss and in the PBS miniseries "Strange Interlude." Dukes managed to fit in feature films between miniseries and theater roles, appearing in *The Wild Party* with James Coco and Raquel Welch, *A Little Romance, The First Deadly Sin* with Frank Sinatra, *Only When I Laugh, Without a Trace, The Men's Club, Date With an Angel, Deadly Intent* and *See You in the Morning* with Jeff Bridges.

Dukes married poet and writer Carole Muskes on 31 January 1983. They have a daughter, Annie Cameron.

Keir Dullea

He is an ancient Jon Whitcomb illustration come to life (6'1", Nordic-looking). His first two films, *The Hoodlum Priest* and *David and Lisa* cast him as an immature, repressed upper-middle class kid. ("*The Fox* was really the turning point. It was a sexual role and the women were the ones who had the problem. . . . And I looked older.") Other films include *Madam X, De*

Sade, Black Christmas, Bunny Lake is Missing, The Thin Red Line and Stanley Kubrick's *2001, A Space Odyssey* (he also appeared in the sequel *2010* released in 1985). Of *2001* he says, "It is the only movie I have made which I grew to like better and better. It created a brand new vocabulary in film making." His Broadway credits include the Tony Award winning *Butterflies Are Free* (1969) followed by a revival of *Cat on a Hot Tin Roof* and *Doubles* (1985), and his TV films include "Law and Order," "The Hostage Tower," "No Place To Hide," and a miniseries based on Aldous Huxley's *A Brave New World*.

Although he was born in Cleveland (30 May 1936), Dullea (pronounced Delay) considers Greenwich Village his native habitat. For 25 years his Scottish-Irish parents ran a bookstore there. After attending private schools in New York, he studied briefly at Rutgers University, then hitchhiked to San Francisco, where he worked as a carpenter before enrolling at San Francisco State college in 1955. ("I had decided to be an actor, I hurried back to New York and studied with Sanford Meisner.") He seldom discusses his first wife, actress Margo Bennett. His present wife is former fashion director Susan Coe, whom he married in 1971. The pair reside in Connecticut where they run a professional workshop for actors, writers and directors, *The Theatre Artists Workshop of Westport*.

Faye Dunaway

Try to find the real woman aside from her powerfully dramatic and disparate on-screen portrayals. She's been a gangster in *Bonnie and Clyde* (for which she was nominated for an Academy award); the despotic Eva Peron in the TV drama "Evita Peron"; the silently suffering yet anxiously ambitious Wallis Simpson (on her way to becoming the Duchess of Windsor) in TV's "The Woman I Love"; the evangelist Aimee Semple McPherson in "The Disappearance of Aimee." She won her second Oscar nomination for her performance in Roman Polanski's *Chinatown*, and she won the award itself as the driven career woman in Sidney Lumet's *Network*. So who is she?

"No more . . . "

"Say what mommie?"

"Christina, I said—no more . . . "

"What *Mommie Dearest?*"

"Christina, no more wire coat hangers!" Screech, bang, wham . . . what a part: the ghost of Joan Crawford played to lights-camera-action perfection, the egomaniacal actress and monstrous child abuser, depicted with amphetamine alacrity by Dunaway in the 1982 film.

"I felt I needed to break into a simpler woman," she said when she accepted the lead on Broadway in 1983 of William Alfred's *The Curse of the Aching Heart*. In Alfred's *Hogan's Goat*, her first stage appearance at age 25, she earned high praises and attracted the attention of movie mogul Sam Spiegel, who launched her career in Hollywood. Born in Florida 14 January 1937, the daughter of a career Army man, Dunaway lived with her parents in such diverse places as Utah, Germany and other countries overseas. After majoring in drama at the University of Florida, she attended the Boston University School of Fine and Applied Arts, where her work led her to audition for New York's Lincoln Center Repertory and a role in Arthur Miller's *After the Fall*. Her glowing notices in *Hogan's Goat* were followed by many splendid film parts in *Hurry Sundown, The Arrangement, The Thomas Crown Affair, Little Big Man, The Wicked Lady, Barfly, Cold Sassy Tree, The Burning Secret, Crystal Or Ash, The Handmaid's Tale*, and the TV series "Ellis Island." She donned armor for her role as Queen Isabella in the 1985 miniseries "Christopher Columbus." Her most recent work is the Lina Wertmuller film *Up to Date* (1990), about AIDS.

Divorced from both her songwriter-composer husband Peter Wolf, and second husband Terry O'Neil (a photographer), she has one son, Liam (born 1980). Referring to her haughty reputation among Broadway and Hollywood insiders, she says: "I am a perfectionist, as you no doubt heard. The scariest thing is not the critics or the audience, but the demands I am making on myself."

Sandy Duncan

Sprightly Sandy Duncan has charmed Broadway and television audiences with her dancing, singing and dramatic talents and All-American good looks for over twenty years and shows no signs of slowing down. Her popularity helped her overcome the controversy she encountered in 1987 when she was hired to replace the fired Valerie Harper on the retitled television series "The Hogan Family." The show continues to be a hit with Duncan in the lead. Despite the demanding TV schedule, she continues to polish her singing and dancing talents performing in numerous AIDS benefits with her husband, singer/dancer/actor/choreographer Don Correia.

Sandy Duncan was born 20 February 1946 in Henderson, Texas, and raised in Tyler, Texas, where her family moved when she was nine months old. She made her theater debut at age 12 in the State Fair Music Hall production of *The King and I* in Dallas. It wasn't until 1965, however, after a year of college, that she moved to New York City intent on pursuing an entertainment career. While studying acting at the New York City Center Repertory Company she landed her first jobs as a lead dancer in its various musical productions. Performing in regional theater, summer tours, and Off-Broadway productions, Duncan got her big break in the 1969 Broadway musical *Canterbury Tales*, for which she received her first Tony Award nomination as Best Supporting Actress in a Musical. More awards followed in 1971. Her second Tony nomination came for her starring role in *The Boyfriend*. The role also garnered her a New York Drama Desk Award and the Outer Critic's Circle Award. 1971 also found Duncan starring in her first television series, "Funny Face," which earned her an Emmy nomination. To cap off the year, she was honored with the Gold Medal Photoplay and the Golden Apple Awards. Her second series, "The Sandy Duncan Show," premiered the following season in 1972. It too was short-lived but Duncan appeared on television often, guest-starring on shows, hosting two specials— "Sandy in Disneyland" and "The Sandy Duncan Special"—and "aging" from 20 to 70 years old in the miniseries "Roots" (1977), which earned her another Emmy nomination. She has also been a successful commercial spokesperson. In addition to her television work and film appearances—in Neil Simon's *Star Spangled Girl* and the Disney films *Million Dollar Duck* and *The Cat From Outer Space*— Duncan's theater career was still going strong. She won a Theatre World Award for the Off-Broadway production *Ceremony of Innocence* and Los Angeles Drama Critics nomination for the 1976 Mark Taper Forum production of *Vanities*. Arguably, Duncan's greatest Broadway success occurred when she assumed the role made famous by Mary Martin in the 1980 production of *Peter Pan*. It brought her critical raves and her third Tony nomination. Additional Broadway hits include *My One and Only* (1984) and *Five, Six, Seven, Eight, Dance!*, with husband Don Correia at Radio City Music Hall.

Duncan's native state of Texas honored her as she became the first female recipient of the CoCo Award, the highest honor given to those in the entertainment industry by the Dallas Communication Council. Duncan married Correia, who is her third husband, on 21 July 1980. They have two sons, Jeffrey and Michael. They currently reside on Los Angeles's west side, where in her spare time Duncan enjoys yoga, dance and time with her family.

Robert Duvall

He's risen in the Academy from nominee for Best Supporting Actor to highest Oscar honors as Best Actor and incontestable star status. One of "the most resourceful . . . technically proficient . . . remarkable actors in America today," according to the *New York Times's* Vincent Canby, Robert Duvall is a director's dream because of the way he locks into a character, and because he demands a natural relaxed set. "The actor's the guy that's gotta be given the room, because it's his face that's going up there," he says. "The two worst things a director can say are, 'Pick up the pace,' and, 'Give me more energy.'" But the days when he physically assaults equally headstrong directors appear to be over; he's putting that tension into his roles. "I guess most of my parts have been complex, contradictory. They mostly have a hard side to them, the more interesting side."

Robert Duvall was born in San Diego in 1931 into the family of an admiral who wanted his son to go to Annapolis. The lure of the theatre, however, proved stronger than that of the sea, but he ended up making a mandatory tour of the Army anyway. With his G.I. Bill he took up studies at New York's Neighborhood Playhouse, and made his screen debut in the 1963 *To Kill a Mockingbird*. He made his first major impression on moviegoers with his portrayal of the Corleone family's *consigliere* in *The Godfather* films, for which he was first nominated for an Oscar. His other two nominations came for stunning performances as the American colonel who loved the smell of napalm in the Vietnam flashback *Apocalypse Now*, and as the Marine ace at war with the brass of his own family in *The Great*

Santini. But it was his 1983 role as an ex-country music star in love with a young Texas widow in *Tender Mercies* for which he was awarded an Oscar as Best Actor. More movies followed: *The Lightship* (1986), *Let's Get Harry* (1986), *Colors* (1987), *The Handmaid's Tale* (1989), *A Show of Force* (1990), and *Days of Thunder* (1990).

The protean film, stage, and TV actor has also been recognized as a talented director for his film, *Angelo My Love,* about modern Gypsies. On the sending end of the megaphone, Duvall instructs, "No frigging acting," to his charges; he says the true test of proficiency is not to appear to be at work. His second marriage is to actress Gail Youngs.

Clint Eastwood

He's made a big name for himself as The Man With No Name, Dirty Harry Callahan, and the aptly-named Rowdy Yates in TV's "Rawhide." He created one of the catchphrases of the 80s; even President Ronald Reagan once invited a recalcitrant Congress to "make my day." Usually playing the anti-social anti-hero, this box-office lodestone now also produces and directs films that, following the hit spaghetti western *Hang 'Em High*, have grossed nearly a billion dollars. But the law-and-order-keeping actor with the screen's most famous glare says, "I really don't like to be the focus of attention. . . . Maybe being an introvert gives me, by sheer accident, a certain screen presence, a mystique. People have to come and find out what's inside me. If I threw it all out for them to see [off-screen], they might not be interested." Eastwood's tough, snarlingly-silent, gun-blasting characters have kept moviegoers interested enough, however, to support him in 40 plus movies in over 35 years of minimalist acting.

The tall (six feet four, 190 pounds) and rugged Eastwood was born in San Francisco, 31 May 1930. He grew up during the Depression, trailing a father who pumped gas in towns along the West Coast. "My family was too busy moving around, looking for work, for me to know what I wanted," he says. "Then I was drafted into the Army and was sent to work in Special Services where I met a lot of actors, so I thought I'd give that a shot." In Los Angeles, having "tripped across the movie business," he endlessly auditioned for commercials and was thrown off the Universal studios lot in the late 1950s only to land on his feet as he lassoed his cowpunching role on "Rawhide" from 1959 to 1966. Like most Western heroes, he's a political conservative, although he asserts that his acting shouldn't be taken too seriously. "When I go to the movies . . . I don't worry about social injustice." Neither have most of his characters. While Eastwood calls to mind former Hollywood tight-lipped heroes like Gary Cooper and John Wayne, the German-Spanish-Italian sequels *A Fistful of Dollars, For a Few Dollars More, The Good, the Bad and the Ugly,* and *Hang 'Em High* froze him into the public consciousness as a lone gunman at odds with the law. His Dirty Harry series, about the San Francisco detective who frequently cuts procedural corners and kills aplenty, didn't tarnish the image. But Eastwood has also lightened up with comedic modern cowboy parts, and an occasional cop role in which he doesn't have all the answers, even with a .356 Magnum tucked under his jacket. He's had a reputation as an on-schedule, on-budget producer-director ever since his first try at it, *Play Misty for Me.* Now divorced from long-time wife Maggie (to the tune of a $25-million settlement), he runs the Hog's Breath Inn in Carmel, the town where he served as mayor for two years (1986-1988) and where he lives when not at his Sherman Oaks home. The physically trim and well-disciplined Eastwood believes the same qualities ought go into making movies. "With Francis Coppola's budget," he remarks, referring to the $31.5 million that went into *Apocalypse Now,* "I could have invaded some country." Son Kyle was seen in his 1982 film, *Honkytonk Man,* and ex-longtime companion Sondra Locke graced a number of Eastwood films. More popular movies include: *Pale Rider* (1985), *Heartbreak Ridge* (1986), *The Dead Pool* (1988) and *Bird* (1988). The latter film about jazz great Charlie Parker won an Academy Award for best sound in a motion picture. Eastwood's 1989 film is *Pink Cadillac.*

Roger Ebert
(see Siskel & Ebert)

Blake Edwards

H is first hit film, *Breakfast at Tiffany's* (1961), containing a mixture of moods ranging from slapstick to poignance, typifies his versatility. He followed this romance with the suspenseful *Experiment in Terror* and the devastating *Days of Wine and Roses* (1962). Then came his biggest success, the original *Pink Panther* (1963), which established him as a master of a kind of physical comedy seldom seen since the days of the silents. An equally popular sequel, *A Shot in the Dark* (1964) quickly followed, again featuring Peter Sellers' incomparably inept Inspector Clouseau character.

Born in Tulsa, Okla., 26 July 1922, he as raised from the age of three in California, where his stepfather was a Hollywood production manager. Much of his childhood was spent on film sets. After graduating from Beverly Hills H.S. he acted in films in the early 40s. He served in the Coast Guard during WWII, and by the late 40s was acting in his own film scripts. In 1949 he created the Dick Powell radio series, "Richard Diamond, Private Detective." Following more low-budget screenplays in the early 50s, he got to direct two Frankie Laine 'B' films. *Mister Cory,* a 1957 Tony Curtis vehicle, established him as a promising writer-director, and he fulfilled that promise directing two popular TV series: "Peter Gunn" and "Mr. Lucky." As early as this period, he was collaborating with composer Henry Mancini, who has scored most Edwards films. A temperamental man devoted to yoga, judo, mystery stories and jazz, he has a son and daughter from his first wife Patricia, whom he divorced in 1967 after 14 years of marriage. His second wife (since 1969) is Julie Andrews, who has starred in several of his films: *Darling Lili* ('69), *The Tamarind Seed* ('74), *10* ('79), *S.O.B.* ('81), *Victor/Victoria* ('82) and *The Man Who Loved Women* ('83), a Truffaut remake. Together they adopted two Vietnamese orphans, who reside with them in California and also in their Swiss chalet. His self-imposed European exile resulted from his feeling that his films of the late 60s and early 70s were sabotage by studio executives. "I thought I was going to have a nervous breakdown," he says. "Withdrawn and very, very, angry," he revived the *Pink Panther* series to continued success in the mid-70s and—once again "bankable" after these films and *10*—made his scathing Hollywood satire, *S.O.B.* which constituted an act of revenge. He wrote and directed *A Fine Mess* (1985); directed and co-wrote the screenplay for the Bruce Willis vehicle *Blind Date* (1986); and directed, executive produced and wrote "Justin Case" for an ABC-TV movie (1988). His 1988 work includes the film *Sunset.*

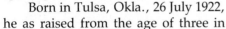

Ralph Edwards

The man has an affinity for success. He took an unknown retired judge, surrounded him with a format that fit him like a glove and parlayed it into a most remarkable television success: "The People's Court," a syndicated series. The show was further immortalized in the award-winning film *Rain Man*.

Born Ralph Livingston Edwards, 13 June 1913 in Merino, Colo., he began his radio career in Oakland, California, when, as a 15-year-old, he went to work as a writer on a local station for a dollar a script. Later working his way through the University of California, he was an announcer, actor, producer, writer, effects man—and janitor—at Oakland's Station KTAP. He spent a year with various San Francisco stations before heading for New York on the shaky promise of a small part in a Broadway play. He arrived and found the show closed but things picked up when he talked himself into a staff announcer's job at CBS, and by 1939 he was doing as many as 45 network shows a week. In 1940 he parlayed an old parlor game into the popular "Truth or Consequences" (1984 marked its 43rd consecutive year), thereby launching his lucrative career as a producer of such entertainment packages as "Place the Face," "It Could Be You" and the perennial favorite, "This Is Your Life" (radio debut 1948) which had a 23-year run. Married in 1939 to the former Barbara Jean Sheldon (three children), he's pleased to have made his mark not only in TV history but also on the map of the U.S.: on the tenth anniversary of his first radio success, the town of Hot Springs, N.M., officially changed its name to Truth or Consequences, the first and probably last time a radio show has ever been honored in such a way. Edwards has made substantial contributions to the Heart Association and the March of Dimes via his radio and TV shows. He is the recipient of three Emmys and the Eisenhower Award (1946).

Emilio Estevez

A member of the "Brat Pack" Emilio Estevez joins his peers Rob Lowe, Judd Nelson, and Andrew McCarthy as a rising young superstar of the screen. His early movies hinted at his appeal, paving the way for major roles in feature films. Born in Manhattan, New York, (1962) into a theatrical family, it's no wonder that talent runs in his genes. The oldest son of actor Martin Sheen and his wife Janet, Estevez was set from the start for a theatrical career. He graduated from high school in Santa Monica, California, and with his brother, actor Charlie Sheen, chose to follow in his father's footsteps. With teenage roles in the movies *The Outsiders* (1982), *Tex* (1982)

and *Repo Man* (1984), Emilio became a recognizable face. *The Breakfast Club* became an even more popular film; his performance as an athletic student forced to stay for detention with fellow cast members Paul Gleason, Anthony Michael Hall, Judd Nelson, Molly Ringwald and Ally Sheedy made him the toast around the town. Not only was his next film, *St. Elmo's Fire* (1985), a hot movie ticket, but the theme song was a pop hit. Expanding his creative energies, Estevez wrote the screenplays and starred in *That Was Then This Is Now* (1985) and *Wisdom* (1986). The latter film showcased a spellbinding performance as a young man obsessed with robbing from the rich and giving to the poor. More films followed, including *Maximum Overdrive* (1986) *Stakeout* (1987), *Young Guns* (1988), and *Young Guns II* (1990). He also appeared in a couple of stage productions (*Mister Roberts, Burt Reynolds Dinner Theatre*), in addition to various television movies. Some TV works include: "Seventeen Going on Nowhere," "To Climb a Mountain," "ABC," "Making the Grade," and "In the Custody of Strangers." He filmed a special telefilm "Nightbreaker" with his dad, Martin Sheen, for the TNT network.

Estevez is the father of two children, Taylor and Paloma; his ex-companion, model Carey Salley, filed a paternity suit against him in 1986.

Linda Evans

As Krystle Carrington in "Dynasty," television's hit series revolving around the wealthy Carrington clan of Denver,

Linda Evans has become one of the most publicly applauded stars on the small screen. Not only have her devoted fans suffered with the most virtuous and patient woman on television (who gradually got "claws" written into character) but her women viewers (and men, too) have been awed by the beauty and appeal of the "over 40" actress.

Born Linda Evenstad 18 November 1943 in Hartford, Connecticut, she moved with her parents to North Hollywood when she was six months old. Her father was a decorator and painter, her mother a housewife. Painfully shy as a child ("I grew up just trying to cope"), she attended Hollywood High, and while there a friend dragged her to a casting session of a television commercial, which she got. After appearing on TV's "Bachelor Father" she signed an MGM contract. She later studied with Lee Strasberg. In 1965 she won a continuing role on ABC's "The Big Valley." She also appeared in the TV series "The Hunter." By choice her movies, in which she invariably played a glamour girl, have been few. "I'm simply not an aggressive type," she once admitted, "If I get a role that's fine. If not, that's all right, too. I've worked in show business only when I wanted to." Since the "Dynasty" success, she has taken a different approach to her career. She has formed her own production company and is negotiating to produce television movies.

Evans has been married twice. Her first well-publicized marriage to Producer John Derek began when she was in the "Big Valley" series. "It was the most wonderful life I can imagine any woman having." Evans recalls, "he cares about beauty more than anyone I've ever known. He would have a wonderful knight of the Round Table." They separated in 1973, divorced two years later, and in 1976 Evans married real estate tycoon Stan Herman; it ended three years later. "I had marriages that didn't work," Evans says candidly. "In doing the thing that I least wanted to do—be by myself—I've discovered something really beautiful, which is I'm going to make the best partner for someone in the whole world now because I've found myself. The character Krystle is learning this, too."

Keeping busy, Evans appeared in the ABC-TV epic "North & South Book II" (1985), in CBS's "The Last Frontier" (1986), and the film *Dead Heat* (1988).

Douglas Fairbanks, Jr.

"**B**esides Alistair Cooke, no man is as skilled at hosting a TV series as the tanned debonair Douglas Fairbanks, Jr. He has style, sophistication and knowledge, qualities that are rare in the medium," wrote Kay Gardella in the *New York Daily News* when Fairbanks began the PBS "Gilbert & Sullivan" series in 1989.

He was born in New York City 9 December 1909, son of the swashbuckling silent film star Douglas Fairbanks and Anna Beth Sully, who were divorced when he was nine (whereupon his father married Mary Pickford). He attended private school in Pasadena, and was tutored in Paris until he made his first film for Jesse Lasky, *Stephen Steps Out,* at age 14. It was not until 1927 that he came into his own as an actor, playing *Young Woodley* in Los Angeles. This led to a meeting with Joan Crawford and eventual marriage (1928). They were divorced five years later and it was not until 1939 that he married Mary Lee Hartford (she died in September, 1988). The couple had three children together, Daphne, Victoria and Melissa. In World War II Doug earned the British D.S.C. as the only U.S. officer to command a flotilla of raiding craft for Mountbatten's Commandos and in 1949 the Queen invested him with an honorary knighthood.

"One of the problems of acting today," Fairbanks says, "is that too many people want to be overnight successes." Among his many films: *Morning Glory* with Katharine Hepburn (1932), *Stella Dallas* with Barbara Stanwyck (1935), *The Joy of Living* with Irene Dunne (1940) and *Ghost Story* (1981). He lectures occasionally, divides his time between homes in Palm Beach and New York, and summers mostly in England (when not touring in the straw-hat circuit). His autobiography, *Salad Days,* was published in 1988. His work for social causes includes an appeerence at the Art Against AIDS gala benefit held in May, 1990.

Peter Falk

"**T**here is," says a friend of this tough talking actor, "something absolutely terrifying about the courage, the naked-

ness and the honesty of his work." There is also something of the candid maverick about a man who has starred in dozens of films and TV shows, has twice been an Oscar nominee (*Murder, Inc.*, 1961; *A Pocketful of Miracles*, 1962), has won three Emmys (he won in 1962 for his portrayal of a truck driver in "Price of Tomatoes" and a decade later for his "Columbo" series) and who bluntly declaimed from the height of his cinematic celebrity, "You really can't be an actor unless you act on the stage." So in 1972 he won a Tony Award for his performance in Neil Simon's *Prisoner of Second Avenue.*

Born 16 September 1927 in New York City, Peter Falk grew up in Ossining, N.Y., where his parents ran a clothing and dry goods store. Despite potential handicaps—as an only child with a glass eye—he became a three-letter high school athlete, an A-B student and a member of the Merchant Marine. Also a pool shark, which he says was part of the reason he flunked out of school—"Most of my studying was done in the poolroom . . . it was a pretty classy college and I didn't fit in with the silver spoon set." He craved excitement and described it this way: "When you're a kid the real world seems dull and ordinary compared to the dream. Some of the things we do when we rebel as kids comes from a desire to put some of the dream into the real world." Armed with a B.A. from the New School and an M.B.A. from Syracuse, Falk greeted the real world scanning figures for Connecticut's Budget Bureau. Lonely, seeking companionship, he began reading scripts for local theatre groups in Hartford and in 1955 Eva Le Gallienne encouraged him to turn professional. His first work opened "at 8:45 and closed permanently two and a half hours later." But his luck changed when he landed the bartender's role in an Off-Broadway production of *The Iceman Cometh* which led to Broadway, movies and TV. The latter made his career and he was widely popular with audiences as the gruff but adorably sloppy police detective Lieutenant Columbo. Falk revived the character for television movies from time to time, and the series was back on prime-time in 1989. Falk financed and starred with his close cronies John Cassavetes and Ben Gazzara in the Cassavetes' film *Husbands*, a triumph in 1970. "I've got a weak stomach for lousy scripts," says he, so he keeps his activity down to a minimum. He and his wife of 16 years, Alyce Mayo, divorced in 1976. The couple had two daughters, Jackie and Kathryn. Falk married actress Shera Danese in 1977; they separated in 1985, then reconciled in 1987. More movie credits include: *Happy New Year* (1985), *The Princess Bride* (1987), *Vibes* (1987), *Sky Over Berlin* (1987), *In the Spirit* (1987), *Cookie* (1989), and *Aunt Julia and the Screenwriter* (1990).

Mia Farrow

"**F**alling in love is compulsive with me," confides Mia Farrow, who first gained wide audience recognition in 1965 as Allison MacKenzie in television's first night-time soap, "Peyton Place." "I relate to people in such a strong way." She raised eyebrows when in 1966 she eloped to Las Vegas with Frank Sinatra. She was 20; he was 50. They were divorced in 1968. Asked if she suffered a father search, she replied: "I find older men appealing. They can handle so much that I can't."

Born in Los Angeles 9 February 1945, the third eldest daughter of actress Maureen O'Sullivan and late film director John Farrow, she says: "I didn't know my parents very well, but they represent a great deal to me. My mother was a terrific mother, full of fairy tales with a soft voice and soothing manner. She was a mystical figure, and I sort of romanticized her and my father." In London, 1970, she wed conductor Andre Previn several months after making headlines with the birth of their twin sons. They subsequently adopted four Vietnamese children (and she adopted a fifth in 1985). As a film actress, she came into prominence starring in Roman Polanski's *Rosemary's Baby* (1968), and captured the plum role of Daisy Buchanan (opposite Robert Redford) in *The Great Gatsby* (1973). While Previn toiled with the London Symphony, she performed leading roles with the Royal Shakespeare Company (in plays by Chekhov, Gorky, Lorca, Shakespeare). Filming *Hurricane* (1978) on the island of Bora Bora, she became romantically involved with Swedish cinematographer Sven Nykvist. Single again in 1979, she returned to the United States to make her Broadway debut in *Romantic Comedy* with Anthony Perkins. Her filmic association with Woody Allen began in 1982 with *A Midsummer Night's Sex Comedy*, following by *Zelig* and *Broadway Danny Rose*. "I find people who create something and live out of their own purity without fakery the most desirable to be around," she remarks. Thus, her current longtime beau—Woody Allen.

Although marriage doesn't seem to fit into the picture, the couple had a son on 19 December 1987, named Satchel. Other Farrow films, notably Allen productions: *The Purple Rose of Cairo* (1984), *Radio Days* (1987), *September* (1988), *Another Woman* (1988), *New York Stories* (1988), and *Crimes and Misdemeanors* (1989).

Farrah Fawcett

The tousled-haired, statuesque blonde who flew the coop of the 1976 top-rated girl detective show, "Charlie's Angels," stayed just long enough to become an overnight sensation. Farrah Fawcett, flanked by two dark-haired actresses, quickly became the focal point of the action series, described by a critic as "family-style porn, a mild erotic fantasy." Teasing and bouncing her way through non-sensical plots, Fawcett triggered a hairstyle phenomenon in the late 70s sending droves of women to the beauty parlor for "Farrah cuts." Her bathing suit poster—featuring cascading hair and blinding white teeth—rang cash registers to record profits, sparking a resurgence in personality poster sales. Farrah fever had caught. Former manager Jay Bernstein recalls, "I saw in Farrah the possibility of a real legend—baseball, apple pie and Chevrolets."

Born 2 February 1947 in Corpus Christi, Texas, and raised in a strict, working class home, Fawcett learned early to conform to traditional standards. "Catholic girls know how to take good direction," she noted. Fawcett shined as a commercial and print model, hawking Ultra-Brite toothpaste, Noxema Shaving Cream, and Wella Balsam shampoo, before landing her star-making role. Fawcett quit the series to make movies, which she did in rapid succession. *Somebody Killed Her Husband,* released in 1978, provoked one critic to quip, "To buy this film's plot, it isn't enough to suspend disbelief, you have to submit to a lobotomy." The two films that followed were similarly received.

Tiring of the star-making machinery that hyped her as more style than substance, Fawcett parted with her manager, cut her trade-mark locks, and split with husband Lee Majors (formerly TV's "Six Million Dollar Man"; then TV's "The Fall Guy"), in 1979 (divorced 1982). Soon thereafter, she linked up with Ryan O'Neal, by whom she had a son—Redmond James—in 1985.

Against advice, Fawcett tackled a series of unglamorous roles—as a battered husband killer in TV's "The Burning Bed" (1984) and as a battered and terrorized rape victim Off-Broadway in *Extremities* (1983), and received glowing reviews for both; she starred in the film version of *Extremities* in 1986. Recently, Fawcett reflected on her change in life strategies, "I never had a chance to be my own person, find out who I was, what I wanted. I was always trying to please someone else, now I want to please myself." Other works in the late 1980's included: "Between Two Women" (ABC-TV, 1986), "Poor Little Rich Girl" (NBC-TV, 1987), the movie *See You in the Morning* (1988) and a TNT special, "Margaret Bourke-White" (1989). Fawcett returns to network television with live-in Ryan O'Neal, in a sitcom for the 1990-91 season.

Federico Fellini

"He's a monster, a genius, a fraud, and a master, all in one," said an actress who worked for him in *La Dolce Vita* (1959). A leonine-maned burly six-footer with an expansive manner suggesting a friendly bear, he's been bewitching and startling audiences since 1946, when he scripted the Oscar-winning *Open City*. Fellini has directed more than 20 films, including four Oscar winners: *La Strada* (1954), *Nights of Cabiria* (1957), *8* (1963) which raised him to superstar status, and *Amarcord* (1974). (Nineteen years after  it reached the screen the autobiographical *8* inspired the hit Broadway musical *Nine*.) Fellini's penchant for using clowns in his films reflects his lost fantasy world. His documentary *Clowns* (1970) is the study, he says, "of a world which seems inexorable destined for extinction, and therefore all the more melancholy and mysterious, made up more of rarefied memories than of concrete facts." Fellini admits he's also inexorably drawn to themes about women. After the release of his *City of Women* (1981), he observed, "I have the feeling that all my films are about women. . . . They represent myth, mystery, diversity, fascination, the thirst for knowledge and the search for one's own identity. . . . I even see the cinema itself as a woman, with its alternation of light and darkness, of appearing and disappearing images. Going to the cinema is like returning to the womb, you sit there still and meditative in the darkness, waiting for life to appear on the screen. One should go to the cinema with the innocence of a fetus."

Born 20 January 1920, the son of salesman, in Rimini, a small resort on the Adriatic coast, Federico Fellini ran away briefly at age 12 to join the circus. After high school, he broke away from small-town life and worked as a comic-strip artist in Florence. Moving on to Rome, he worked as a cartoonist, journalist, radio scriptwriter and alternated as straight man and comic with the Fabrizzi vaudeville troupe. Hired as a gagman and scenarist for various film producers, he met Roberto Rossellini in 1944 and formed a collaboration that was to last for eight years, during which he wrote the script (in 10 days) for *Open City*. Fellini names Rossellini and Chaplin as the primary influences on his films. "Jesus, Cagliostro, St. Francis and Satan," are the historical figures he finds most interesting. When directing, Fellini becomes Cagliostro, his gift for hamming and clowning it up coming to the fore. He hurls an evenly balanced barage of jokes and insults at his actors as he prods them on into a "portrayal of the truth." Among his recent films are: *The Ship Sails On* (1983), *Ginger & Fred* (1986), *L'Intervista* (1987), and *Voice of the Moon* (1990). "I never know why I choose to shoot one film rather than another," he says. "I could even say that it is not I who choose a theme but the theme that chooses me, and then the film immediately takes shape and acquires images and feelings." Fellini's wife, whom he married in 1943, Giulietta Masina, an actress and the author of a column for the love lorn. In June, 1985, Fellini was honored by the Film Society of Lincoln Center at Avery Fisher Hall.

Jose Ferrer

This gifted theatrical gamut-runner (Iago to Toulouse-Lautrec to Cyrano to Charley's Aunt) has never been typecast. Flipping with ease from sober tragedy to wild farce, he's demonstrated his performing talents in plays, films and even on the nightclub circuit and as a director and producer as well. In once blockbuster season (1951-52) he was star of Broadway's *The Shrike*, Hollywood's *Moulin Rouge* and director-producer of both *Stalag 17* and *The Fourposter* on Broadway. Other noteworthy acting credits include: *Richard III*, *Volpone*, *Angel Street*, *Twentieth Century* and *Man of LaMancha* on stage, and such films as *Joan of Arc, The Caine Mutiny, Lawrence of Arabia, Ship of Fools,* Woody Allen's *A Midsummer Night's Sex Comedy* and *Dune.* He directed, among others, *Oh, Captain* (which he co-wrote)*My Three Angels* and *Andersonville Trial.*

Born Jose Vincente Ferrer de Otero y Cintron on 8 January 1912 in Santurce, Puerto Rico, of well-to-do parents, he was brought to the mainland United States as a child by his father ("I'm always trying to live up to him") and discovered dramatic arts at Princeton's undergraduate Triangle Club of which James Stewart and Joshua Logan were the leading lights. Married first to actress Uta Hagen (one daughter, Lauitia), he subsequently married second wife Phyllis Hill and third, singer Rosemary Clooney, with whom he had five children, Miguel Jose, Maria, Gabriel, Monsita Teresa and Rafael. They divorced in 1962, remarried in 1963 and then divorced a second time in 1966. A performer who consistently gives his all (during the run of *Charley's Aunt,* he trapezed about the stage, lost five pounds at each performance), he admits to occasional bouts of battle fatigue. "I had to do it 8 times a week," he recalls of one emotional scene, "and you should know some of the things I did in my own mind. At one point or another I think I killed every single person that I loved—and I saw them lying there bleeding before me—to work myself to the point where I was moved. I killed my father and my daughter and my best friend and his wife and my pet dog and my rabbit and my canary. I even," he concluded sorrowfully, "ran over strangers." Ferrer, who was inducted into the Theater Hall of Fame in 1980, lives in Manhattan with his fourth wife, the former Stella Daphne Magee.

Sally Field

Once upon a wave she rode her TV audiences wild with her giggly "Gidget" act, then the faithful fellows at ABC flew her up to God as Sister Bertrille, "The Flying Nun." She left the prime time box of worship and went into her own orbit as a powerfully gifted performer in such quality projects as her Emmy-award winning, made-for-TV "Sybil," the story of a woman with no less than 16 personalities, and the 1979 feature film *Norma Rae,* about a Southern textile worker, which won her an Oscar and the Best

Actress Award at the Cannes Film Festival. She won her second Oscar for *Places in the Heart* (1984). In 1985 she starred with James Garner in *Murphy's Romance,* in 1986 she appeared in the telefilm "Three Minutes to Midnight", in 1988 she co-produced and starred in *Punchline* with Tom Hanks, and also starred in *Steel Magnolias* that same year. In 1990 she filmed "Not Without My Daughter."

"I grew up and didn't buckle under when they wanted me to remain cute forever," explains Sally Field, born 6 November 1946, about her unusual switch from ingenue starlet to serious actress. After high school she enrolled in Columbia Pictures Workshop, which developed new talent, and it was there that she was fished out of the talent pool to play television's "Gidget." After years of that show and the "Flying Nun," the mother of two sons, Peter and Elijah, divorced their father Steve Craig, left Hollywood and joined the Actor's Studio in New York. Before that she says: "The truth was that nobody around me had any respect for me; to them I was a joke, so I took the plunge and changed everything at once—I got rid of my agent, my business manager and my husband. For three years I dropped out and studied and did summer stock." Along with many TV and film projects of note are *Smokey and the Bandit* and its sequels, made with erstwhile lover Burt Reynolds. *Smokey* is reported to have grossed one quarter of a billion dollars. A self-described "old fashioned girl," she credits her mother, Maggie Field Mahoney, with inspiring her acting career. "She used to carry me around on her hip to acting lessons with Charles Laughton and she was always reciting Shakespeare to me. I'm sure I didn't understand any of it at that age, but what was communicated was this immense love of what she was doing." In 1985 she took Allan Griesman as her second husband. The couple have a son, Samuel H. Morian, born in 1987.

Harvey Fierstein

"I 've never been secretive about being gay. Never," says Harvey Fierstein. Indeed. The actor-playwright's *Torch Song Trilogy* was the Broadway theatre's first openly homosexual successful play, and—to the happy surprise of many—earned its author-star two Tony awards in 1983. This triumph led to Fierstein's writing the book for the $5 million musical version of the French stage and film hit, *La Cage aux Folles,* which, like *Torch Song* disarmingly blended outrageous "camp" humor with relatively traditional

sentiments. Fierstein is a prime exam-
ple of the 1980s openly gay artist.

The gravel-voiced performer was
born 6 June 1954 and raised in Brooklyn, the son of Easter European Jewish
immigrants. A "misfit" youngster, he
weighted over 200 pounds at age 13.
But also at this age—when most nice
Jewish boys have a Bar Mitzvah—Fierstein
"came out" to his parents. This disclo-
sure of his sexual identity at an unusually early age met with acceptance:
"There was no crying or screaming. It
was what I was—it wasn't a family
decision." With typical wit he adds, "The way I look at it, I'm a
human being first and gorgeous second." Fierstein studied art at
Pratt (he drew the striking eyes logo for *Torch Song*) and made his
professional theatre debut in 1971 at Ellen Stewart's LaMama in an
Andy Warhol production. He worked extensively Off-Off Broadway, acquiring a cult following for his transvestite act. "In drag I
could completely become someone else," he says. "And guess
what? I liked it. That was the kind of power I wanted. And some of
us can't help it if we're ravishing."

Fierstein once considered suicide, until a therapist friend told
him, "Look, you can kill yourself, or you can write a play about it."
Fortunately he did the latter, resulting in *Torch Song*, which straight
as well as gay audiences embraced. According to its author, "The
single most important thing I'm saying is that we have to get the
concept out of our minds that love and commmitment and family
are heterosexual rights. They're not. They're *people's* rights. Hetero-
sexuals can adopt or reject them, gays can adopt or reject them, but
everyone has the right to choose." Rather popular within the theatre
world, Harvey's next work *Safe Sex* (1987) was produced as a play,
published as a book, and a segment was presented on Home Box
Office television. His *Torch Song Trilogy* was made into a film in 1988.

Albert Finney

"All the effort, all the struggle and sacrifice of an actor and
everyone in a theatre company goes into creating a
momentary illusion, it is like a dream and when it's over, it's over.
Gone. Of course, what most people spend their lives doing may not

add up to a hill of beans. But their love, effort, devotion goes into doing it, and it becomes worthwhile." A star at 25 in *Saturday Night and Sunday Morning*, followed by stunning successes in the films *Tom Jones* and in the plays *Luther* and *Joe Egg* on Broadway, Albert Finney asked himself, "What do you do next?" Friends advised; "Strike while the iron is hot or people will forget you." Instead, Finney lit out on a year's voyage around the world and found himself on a tiny island in the Pacific one day, a beachboy with a need to "return to the neurotic society" and decided, "I didn't find any answers, only more questions. But I came out of it more convinced than ever that I wanted to be my own man."

Finney (Albie to his friends) was born in Lancashire, England, 9 May 1936, the son of a bookie. ("We were always illegal.") He remembers a life dominated by hasty moves to avoid the police. ("No security; perfect training for the actor's life.") His North Country heritage, he says, makes him "very suspicious of success," and he turned down the lead role in *Lawrence of Arabia* because he didn't "want to become a Hollywood property or spend two years in the bloomin' desert." Of *Charlie Bubbles*, which he produced, directed and starred in, he says, "the incidents in it are not autobiographical, but the feelings are," adding that "the mood is the feeling that you are no longer living your own life, not holding your destiny in your own hands." He credits variety as the main source of inspiration in his life. This variety is best seen in the different and challenging parts he plays both on stage and in films: Daddy Warbucks in the film of the musical, *Annie;* irate husband in the film *Shoot the Moon,* playing opposite Diane Keaton; "Sir" in the *Dresser*, a movie about life in a touring stage company; the alcoholic Consul in John Huston's film of *Under the Volcano* (Oscar nomination) and "Pope John Paul II" in a television movie. More recent films include *Orphans* (1987) and *Endless Games* (1988).

At present, Finney is not married. A well publicized fling with Audrey Hepburn while making all-time favorite *Two for the Road* resulted in the fizzling of her marriage at the time. Finney was married to Anouk Aimee from 1970 until 1975, and has one grown son from his first marriage (to actress Jane Wenham from 1957-61) named Simon. One bit of Finney trivia for the road: while waiting to open Britain's new National Theatre in the Marlowe play *Tamburlaine*, Finney cut a record for Motown. That's variety.

Carrie Fisher

"You are not allowed to grow up with parents who are famous and then get into one of the biggest movies of all time and run around with famous people—it's resented after a while. And I would always try to emphasize something really wrong with me, so that people wouldn't be put off." More confident now, the daughter of Debbie Reynolds and Eddie Fisher—a self-declared Hollywood brat with "high-velocity-verbiage"—gained her own fame as Princess Leia in the phenomenally successful *Star Wars* (1977) and its equally popular sequels: *The Empire Strikes Back* (1980) and *Return of the Jedi* (1984). "Who's more famous than Debbie and Eddie? C-3PO and Darth Vader, and Jesus Christ and God. There's a whole lot of freight that goes with being movie stars' kids—on the cover of *Life* when you're two minutes old. I remember the press diving through trees to get pictures of me, my brother and my mother. Poor Debbie; that bastard Eddie; and Liz. We've been the public domain all our lives. I was trained in celebrity, so I did the only thing I knew. I went into the family business. . . . My brother and I went in different directions on the Debbie and Eddie issue. He's gotten involved with Jesus, and I do active work on myself, trying to make myself better and better. It's funny."

Born in Los Angeles on 21 October 1956, Carrie Fisher began her professional career at 13 performing in her mother's Las Vegas nightclub act. She dropped out of Beverly Hills H.S. at 15 to join the chorus of *Irene*, Debbie's 1972 Broadway outing. Her film debut as a nymphet in *Shampoo* (1975) was followed by studies at London's Central School of Speech and Drama. Her other films include *The Blues Brothers* (1980), *Under the Rainbow* (1981) and *Garbo Talks* (1984). On TV she appeared in "Come Back, Little Sheba" (1977) and "Thumbelina" for Shelley Duvall's cable "Faerie Tale Theatre" (1983). She returned briefly to Broadway in 1983 in *Agnes of God*. "There was a sort of fear of mine when I started acting that I would come off like Tammy the eternal virgin, and in fact, the opposite has happened. Because I started out with Warren Beatty, asking him 'Want to fuck?' and in *Jedi* I'm in space shooting people and saying, 'Got you, you asshole'. . . . There are a lot of people who don't like [Leia]; they think I'm some kind of space bitch." After playing such a strong character, "part of me goes, 'When does the cooking and sewing and gossiping and, you know, putting on make-up start to happen?'" She lived in a one-room Los Angeles log-cabin until her August 1983 marriage to singer-writer Paul Simon after a five-year on-again-off-again relationship. "Let's just say we had a stormy romance, and the storm's finally over." (Not quite; the couple split in 1984.) Shortly after her marriage, she scoffed, "*The National Enquirer* says I'm . . . pregnant. . . . They also say I've quit show business, so I guess that's my plan for now. . . . Yeah, I believe everything I read." The witty actress muses, "Everybody wants to be a celebrity. But you know what happens to old celebrities. They die or go to Vegas. Star-life duration is getting shorter and shorter. It could be me at the Tropicana Lounge any minute."

Securing her star status, Carrie branched out and conquered the literary field with the release of her first novel, *Postcards From the Edge* (1985). She won the PEN Award for her book, which was filmed by director Mike Nichols with actresses Meryl Streep and Shirley MacLaine for 1990 release. Her 1990 novel is *Surrender the Pink*. Also keeping active in films, she's starred in a variety of pictures throughout the 1980's: *Hannah and Her Sisters* (1985), *Hollywood Vice Squad* (1986), *Appointment With Death* (1987), *Amazon Women on the Moon* (1987), *Bloodshot Lightning* (1988), *The Burbs* (1989), *When Harry Met Sally* (1989) and *Loverboy* (1989).

Geraldine Fitzgerald

She's been called "an enchantingly free spirit who roams . . . fast and far on her facile intellect and voluble Irish charm." Indeed, for over forty-five years she has roamed from theatre to screen and back again capturing both audiences with her artistry. In the last decades not only has she had the opportunity to secure her place as one of the most luminous stars of the American stage, but has become a concert singer of "street songs," a director for the stage, and, especially close to the heart, has worked with young people in New York City in support of street theatre.

Geraldine Fitzgerald was born 24 November 1913 into a family notable for professional and cultural achievements. Her father was a lawyer and her aunt Stet a well-known Irish actress. After completing her early convent school education and several years of art study (her first love), and, encouraged by her aunt, she turned to the stage. She made her debut in Dublin in 1932 and after a few appearances in London, came to America in 1938 production of the newly-founded Orson Welles Mercury Theatre Company. "I looked to America when I was a girl," she says, "I read the *New Yorker* and that was considered very daring, very avant garde in those days."

Her first two Hollywood roles, *Wuthering Heights* and *Dark Victory* (both in 1939) remain among her best. Of the former, Laurence Olivier said: "I saw the film on TV the other night and Geraldine Fitzgerald is the only thing that holds up in that one." Finding the commercialism of Hollywood abrasive she insisted on contracts with six months of every year to work on the stage. She continued her East Coast/West Coast shuttle and in 1969 her stage career took a decided upward swing with the revival of Eugene O'Neil's *Ah, Wilderness,* followed by an entirely different mother role in *Long Day's Journey Into Night,* (for which she won the *Variety* Critics' award in 1970-1971). *Juno and the Paycock* was a further stage triumph. At the age of 55 she started taking singing lessons, and, receiving favorable reviews in *The Threepenny Opera,* made her nightclub debut singing a program of "street songs." "I've only got about 4 tones," she says, "but it's what you do with it that counts." She has sung the songs at Lincoln Center, Circle In The Square, and elsewhere. In 1974 she received New York City's highest cultural award, the Handel Medallion for her achievement in street theatre. Geraldine Fitzgerald is the mother of Michael Lindsay-Hogg, a director of British television and films, son of her first marriage. In 1946 she married Stuart Sheftel, a business executive and chairman of the New York City Youth Board. They live in Manhattan and have a daughter, Susan. Miss Fitzgerald became one of the few American women stage directors when she presented *Mass Appeal* on Broadway in 1981. "I love to wake up in the morning looking forward to doing and experimenting and risking," she has said. "I'm delighted with it all, and I'm going to do as many things as I can and risk it all as often as I can."

In 1987, Ms. Fitzgerald appeared in a CBS-TV pilot "Mabel & Max" and she was in the Dudley Moore move *Arthur II: On The Rocks* in 1988.

Jane Fonda

"**W**hen you are the offspring of a celebrity it is critical to develop your own identity. You have to feel that you

are your own person. And my father was such a powerful . . . figure," says Henry's daughter. "I rebelled against father because I needed my own identity, then I came close to him again. . . . He also mellowed as he got older. I think it's a universal story. . . . It's more complicated when it's played out in public." The controversial, cause-oriented actress graduated from playing sex objects (sometimes in films by her first husband, French director Roger Vadim) to earning acclaim as a serious actress. The turning point (shortly after the ebb of Vadim's *Barbarella*) came late in 1969 with *They Shoot Horses, Don't They?* Her performance as a burned-out marathon dancer brought her a N.Y. Film Critics Award and her first Academy Award nomination. Two years later she received the Oscar and another N.Y. Film Critics citation for her call-girl portrayal in *Klute*. Her second Academy Award was for *Coming Home* (1978), with additional nominations for *Julie* (1977), *The China Syndrome* (1979) and (supporting) *On Golden Pond* (1981). More memorable performances followed: *Agnes of God* (1985), *The Morning After* (1986—Academy Award nomination for Best Actress), *The Old Gringo* (produced and appeared, 1989), and *Stanley & Iris* (1989).

Born 21 December 1937 in NYC, she was told at age 12 that her mother had died of a heart attack. Fonda subsequently learned the truth from a movie magazine: that her mother had actually slashed her throat in an asylum after a mental breakdown. As a child, Jane showed little interest in acting. "When I left Vassar I drifted. I went to Paris and worked for the *Paris Review*. I modeled [twice making *Vogue's* cover]. I tried to act like a lady . . . [but] I was a slob at heart. I did all kinds of things I didn't believe in because I didn't want to disappoint my father. Then I started acting in N.Y. with Lee Strasberg and discovered because I was a Fonda everybody expected me to fall on my face. You'd think it'd be the other way around, but it wasn't. I found incredible resentment from other actors, and I remember one terrible agonizing audition when Tyrone Guthrie said to me, 'What else have you ever done besides being Henry Fonda's daughter?'" She went back to Paris and married Vadim. they had a daughter, Vanessa. Her Broadway and Hollywood debuts occurred in 1960 and despite some good films like 1965's *Cat Ballou* and 1967's *Barefoot in the Park*, her career floundered until the decade's end. At that point, following her return to the U.S. (and divorce from Vadim), she immediately plunged into fervent social activism, championing a variety of anti-Establishment causes and getting into trouble with the authorities over her actions on behalf of Black Panthers, American Indians and rebellious GI's. As part of her campaign to end the war in Southeast Asia, she formed with actor Donald Sutherland the Anti-War Troupe, which toured military camps in defiance of the Pentagon. She co-produced and co-wrote *F.T.A.* (*Free the Army*, 1972), a filmed record of the tour. In 1973 she married antiwar militant and former SDS head Tom Hayden (they separated in September, 1989). With Hayden and cinematographer Haskell Wexler, she co-directed a documentary, *Introduction to the Enemy* (1974), an account of her controversial visit to North Vietnam. Until recently she lived in California with Vanessa, Hayden and their son Troy. "I think there's this problematic tension between art and business which exists nowhere as powerfully as it does in Hollywood," she says. "It is an art form, it is a part of our culture, but the bottom line is business and you're irresponsible if you ignore it. I personally like that challenge. I think it's a healthy tension." Having formed her own production company in the '70s, she expanded her business interests in the '80s, with the staggering success of "Jane Fonda's Workout," which sold records, books and videotapes worldwide. All profits went to support Hayden's political organization, The Campaign for Economic Democracy. "I said to myself [at about age 42] . . . if you look at the history of aging actresses, it's not exactly a bright future. I intend, of course, to change that. Hollywood is not forgiving of gray hair and wrinkles on the big screen. . . . I might not be able to work as much. . . . So I realized that the only business I knew anything about beside acting was exercise." Fonda separated from Hayden in 1989 and has since been seen publically with communications mogul Ted Turner. Her latest releases in the home video department are: "Jane Fonda Presents Sports Aid" and "Jane Fonda's Complete Workout."

Peter Fonda

At age ten he shot himself through the liver and kidneys with a .22 caliber pistol after he learned that his socialite mother Frances Seymour Brokaw, the second of the late Henry Fonda's wives, cut her throat. "Nobody told me the truth about my mother. I was ten years old and I didn't understand. My father won't even talk to me about it today, so he's not going to talk about yesterday," Peter Fonda said years ago before coming to terms with his famous dad just before he died. Arrested on drug possession charges in 1966, this renegade was a symbol of the alienated anti-hero in the late '60s and early '70s. His films *The Wild Angels* and

especially *Easy Rider* brought the hippies battle cry to audiences across America by raising something in every sympathetic young person of those turbulent times. Also a director (*The Hired Hand*) Fonda spoke openly about his countercultural practices including his LSD trips. "After LSD, I have seen the worst and I've seen the best and I know where I am on this planet."

Born 23 February 1939, he attended the University of Omaha. "They were talking about 'art' when just the summer before I had met Picasso," he recalled. Enthusiastically received in his first Broadway part, in *Blood, Sweat and Stanley Poole,* that same year he married Susan Brewer and had two children, Brigitte and Justine. They divorced in 1974 and Fonda married Portia Crockett in 1976. The '70s brought parts in adventure flicks such as *Highballin'; Futureworld, Cannonball Run* and *Wanda Nevada.* Films in the 1980's included *Freedom Fighters* (1987), *Time of Indifference* (1987) and *The Rose Garden* (1989). Peter resides with his family in Montana. When he's not filming, he enjoys being the captain of a full crew aboard his 102' sailboat. He says "I find my time at sea and my time in the mountains of Montana rejuvenating, so that I can dive into Hollywood with increased stamina."

Joan Fontaine

Her sister, Olivia de Havilland, was 16 months older, but *she* may have been the smarter of the two. In *No Bed of Roses*, her 1978 autobiography, Joan tells of the day the two siblings were studied by the Stanford Psychologist who later developed the Stanford-Binet Intelligent Quotient tests. "Olivia, on the day of her test, had a fever. I tested higher than she— so high, as a matter of fact, the examiner called me back. The only thing I can remember was that when asked what I did at night, I answered logically, 'Wet the bed.' For goodness sake, they didn't want some obvious answer like 'sleep,' did they?"

Born Joan de Beauvoir de Havilland, 22 October 1917 in Tokyo, she adopted her stepfather's surname of Fontaine when she arrived in Hollywood so as not to be confused with her already-established sister. Up for many of the same parts, the two were often at odds, although both now say that their famous feuds were more a product of the publicity-mill than real life. Still, in her book, Fontaine tells a poignant story of the encounter that followed Olivia's winning of the 1946 Academy Award. "After Olivia delivered her acceptance speech and entered the wings, I, standing close by, went over to congratulate her. . . . She took one look at me, ignored my outstretched hand, clutched her Oscar to her bosom, and wheeled away." Earlier, in 1942, both women had been up for a Best Actress statuette (Joan for Alfred Hitchcock's *Suspicion*; Olivia for *Hold Back the Dawn*) and Joan won. Among her best-remembered Hollywood efforts: 1940's *Rebecca* (in which she played the un-named "I" character of Daphne duMaurier's Gothic classic); *This Above All* (1942); *The Constant Nymph* and *Jane Eyre* (1943). On stage, she replaced Deborah Kerr in *Tea and Sympathy* in 1954. She was visible to New Yorkers in the 1980s via her own interview show on cable TV. She also appeared in the TV movies "Crossings" (1985) and "Dark Mansions" (1985).

Fontaine's autobiography tells how she swooned over romantic idol Conrad Nagel in the silent version of *Quality Street*. Years later, after she was in the sound remake, she met Nagel in a stage production of *Faust* and shortly thereafter, "you might say I was surprised out of my virginity." Nagel was old enough to be her father and Joan says they ultimately parted company because of her reluctance to "compete" with his daughter. She later married: (1) Brian Aherne; (2) William Dozier (one daughter, Deborah, and one adopted daughter, Martita); (3) Collier Young; and (4) Alfred Wright, Jr. (Multiple marriages are not unusual in the deHavilland family. Her father married for the third time at the age of 89.) As for herself, Joan credits her many marriages for the development of such extra-curricular skills as piloting a plane, ballooning, fishing for tuna and hole-in-one golfing. "If you keep marrying as I do," she once observed, "you learn everybody's hobby."

Harrison Ford

"Acting is basically like carpentry—if you know your craft, you figure out the logic of a particular job and submit

yourself to it. It all comes down to detail." This is not just some weekend handyman pontificating on the mastering of hammer and nail. For nine years, as he struggled for recognition as an actor in Hollywood, he found steady employment as a "carpenter to the stars." He credits the satisfactions of his sideline business for giving him the ego strength to persist as an actor. His persistence landed him in outer space, as a swashbuckling hero of George Lucas' sci-fi thriller, *Star Wars*.

Harrison Ford was born in Chicago on 13 July 1942 the son of an Irish Catholic father and Russian Jewish mother, and raised in the suburbs. Unable to take academia seriously, he "slept for days on end," and flunked out of Ripon College in Wisconsin three days before his class graduated. Relocated in L.A., he was signed by Columbia Pictures for $150 a week. "I did a year and a half and got kicked out on my ass for being too difficult. I was very unhappy with the process they were engaged in, which was to recreate stars the way it had been done in the fifties. They sent me to get my hair pompadoured like Elvis Presley." He repeated the experience at Universal Studios.

Then in 1977, Lucas, who had cast him in a small role in *American Graffiti*, picked him for a lead in *Star Wars*, a kind of Hardy-Boys-in-Space epic that captured the imagination of moviegoers, sparking huge profits, a merchandising campaign, and two sequels, also starring Ford, *The Empire Strikes Back*, in 1980, and the 1983 *Return of the Jedi.* His performance as adventurer Indiana Jones in the 1981 hit movie, *Raiders of the Lost Art,* and its sequels, *Indiana Jones and the Temple of Doom*, and *Indiana Jones and the Last Crusade*, solidified his bankable image as a rugged romantic. Other popular films include *Witness* (1985), *The Mosquito Coast* (1986), *Frantic* (1987), *Working Girl* (1988), and *Presumed Innocent* (1990).

Resistant to publicity, he believes too much fanfare clouds an actor's vision. "The natural state for an actor is that of observer, where you can learn something. Instead, I'm a focus of attention. When you're written about you're stuck with a 'personality'—even if it's your own."

A father of two from his first marriage, which ended in divorce, he married screenwriter Melissa Mathison (*E.T.*) in 1983.

Milos Forman

His gentle comedies of contemporary life, revealing eternal truths in mundane situations, helped create the internationally celebrated mid-1960s new wave of Czech film-making, which flourished all too briefly until his country's invasion by the U.S.S.R. in 1968. Not so coincidentally, that was the year he moved to the U.S. to continue his movie career. Triumphantly, he won the 1975 Academy Award for his direction of *One Flew Over the Cuckoo's Nest*.

Born 18 February 1932 near Prague to parents (one of whom was Jewish) who died in Nazi concentration camps, he was raised with his two brothers by relatives and friends. This gypsy-like upbringing may account for his sharp eye for familial relations. "Because I wasn't emotionally involved," he says, "I became very objective. Most children aren't consciously aware of what is going on around them, but I was always following the action, trying to fit myself into the group." After study at the esteemed Prague Film Faculty, he made his first feature, *Black Peter* (1963), followed by *Loves of a Blonde* (a 1965 Oscar nominee for best foreign film) and the controversial *Fireman's Ball* (1968). His first U.S. film, *Taking Off* (made in 1970 and released the following year) depicted teenage runaways and the generation gap. His adaptation of the Broadway counter-culture musical *Hair* (1979), contained similar themes. In the 70s he became co-director of the Film Division of Columbia's School of the Arts. His recent films are adaptations of huge literary and stage successes: *Ragtime* (1981) *Amadeus* (1984), which won a slew of Oscars, including Best Picture, and the multi-Academy Award-nominated *Les Liaisons Dangereuses* (1989).

His first wife was Jane Brejchova, a popular Czech film actress. He's divorced from his second, singer Vera Kresadlova, by whom he has twin sons who were raised in their native country. He enjoys skiing and basketball.

John Forsythe

Some years ago his pal Gore Vidal told him, "No, I don't think you're square. Just slightly rhomboid." Now that this

"sweet, avuncular, charming establishment man" has become a vintage silver fox, his sex appeal has soared. "Gray hair doesn't mean you're over the hill. It's all in your attitude," says the actor, who was type cast on TV shows such as "Bachelor Father," "The John Forsythe Show" and "To Rome With Love." In the 1980s, as the patriarch on "Dynasty," the sex, money and rage-throbbing ABC-TV nighttime soap set in oil-rich Denver, "Blake Carrington" is capitalism's most attractive symbol, a rock-hard Teddy Bear married to "Krystal" aka Linda Evans who played the pal of his niece on the sitcom "Bachelor Father." "That," smiles Forsythe who also was the disembodied voice of Charlie on ABC's "Charlie's Angels," "says a lot about hanging in."

Born in Penn's Grove, N.J., 29 January 1918, the son of a stockbroker, he worked as an announcer at Brooklyn's Ebbets Field (home of the pre-L.A. Dodgers) and as "the weak younger brother who was always killed in auto accidents" on soap operas. He joined the Air Force production of *Winged Victory* and then studied at the Actor's Studio in New York after the war. ("I was known as the Brooks Brothers bohemian.") He received attention when he replaced Arthur Kennedy on broadway in the Arthur Miller play *All My Sons* and reached star status when he replaced Henry Fonda in *Mr. Roberts;* later he originated his own starring role in *Teahouse of the August Moon.* Next came Hollywood, and all those avuncular years on TV. A devoted family man, he's been married to actress Julie Warren since 1943 (two daughters); an earlier marriage produced a son. In their Bel Air farmhouse he lives the good life, which, according to one close observer, Forsythe has managed to "elevate to a kind of art form all by itself." In 1985 he became the spokesman for a men's scent line—Carrington—inspired by his televison alter ego. In 1987 he was nominated for a Golden Globe Award (Best Actor in a TV series) and in 1988 he appeared in the film *Scrooged.*

Jodie Foster

S eldom does a film role earn both an Oscar nomination and result in a national scandal. But such was the case with Iris, the 12-year-old prostitute played by Jodie Foster in Martin Scorsese's *Taxi*

Driver. "I knew," the deep-voiced actress said, "when the hustler part . . . came up that I had to be really perfect or it would ruin my career. That role was really risque for a child." Her portrayal was so effective that, in addition to putting Foster into the 1976 "Best Supporting Actress" competition, it allegedly inspired John W. Hinckley, Jr., to mount an assassination attempt against President Ronald Reagan 30 March 1981. The disturbed young man attributed his "historical deed" to a desire to impress Foster after becoming obsessed with Iris and the actress who portrayed her.

This unwanted notoriety plagued Foster during her freshman year at Yale, just days before she made her stage debut there as, ironically, a prison inmate in a student production of Marsha Norman's *Getting Out*. By then, Foster had been in films for nearly a decade, following a precocious childhood that saw her speaking at nine months, uttering sentences at one year, and teaching herself to read at three. Her parents divorced before her birth in L.A. 19 November 1962. "I feel lucky in a way that I never knew a father," she says, "that there was never a marital conflict in the house. I've always felt like a replacement . . . that I took the place of a husband, roommate or pal." Foster's mother has astutely managed her career, which has progressed from TV commercials (including the bare-bottom Coppertone child ad) to Disney features to an earlier Scorsese film, *Alice Doesn't Live Here Anymore*, in which she played a wine-drinking street urchin who (according to one critic) "looks like a boy and talks like a man."

At age 13, Foster had the distinction of having three of her films shown at the Cannes Film Festival: *Taxi Driver, Bugsy Malone* (an all-kiddie gangster musical spoof) and *The Little Girl Who Lived Down the Lane* (in which she played a murderess). An instinctive performer, Foster never studied acting. Fluent in French (the language in which she delivered her bilingual high school's valedictory), she concentrated on studying literature and creative writing at Yale, from which she was graduated in 1985. During school vacations she continued making films such as *The Hotel New Hampshire*.

Her mesmerizing portrayal of a young woman gang-raped in the movie *The Accused* brought about Jodie's popular win as Best Actress at the 1989 Academy Awards. A celebrity in demand, Foster has appeared in *Five Corners* (1987), *Siesta* (1988), *Backtrack* (1988) and *Stealing Home* (1988).

Michael J. Fox

"**C**all me cheap, but I wasn't ready to pay $5 to see myself on the screen," says Michael J. Fox about his smashing performance in the Steven Spielberg-produced movie *Back to the Future* which was released in 1985. "I was in London when the movie opened, and I wanted to see it when I got back to town. So I called the Cinerama Dome in L.A. and asked if I could come down. It was actually kind of cool. They even had a spot reserved for me in the parking lot." However, before all the fanfare and good reviews, Fox confided to Robert Basler of the *Washington Post* that "there's never been a Spielberg flop, and God, Lord, don't let it be my movie." He didn't have to worry; the film became the top grossing movie of 1985. The red-hot young dynamo of NBC's hit series "Family Ties" (1982-1989) works around the clock to fit both movie-making and television appearances into his schedule. In a short time span, Fox's face was seen incessantly promoting his latest features. His 1980's movies include: *Teen Wolf* (1985), *Light of Day* (with Joan Jett; 1986), *The Secret of My Success* (1986), *Bright Lights Big City* (1988), and *Casualties of War* (1989). Sticking with a good thing, Michael's next slew of films are sequels: *Back to the Future II* (1989), *and Back to the Future III* (1990).

Born in Edmonton, Alberta, Canada, on 9 June 1961, Fox was raised in a family with five children. He began working at 15 in a regional television series called "Leo and Me." After a small role in a television film with Art Carney and Maureen Stapleton, he moved to Los Angeles on his own and landed a role in a Walt Disney feature, *Midnight Madness*. He won a role in the critically acclaimed CBS series "Palmerstown, USA" by Alex Haley, and made appearances on "Trapper John," "Lou Grant" and "Family." When the part of Alex P. Keaton, the conservative "ultimate Yuppie" son of former 60's peace activists in "Family Ties" came along (he was not the producer's first choice) Fox soon became a network favorite receiving approximately 500 fan letters a week. Before "Family Ties," "I didn't have a phone, a couch or any money," says Fox. "In fact, I was getting all these great letters from collection agencies saying 'This is your last chance' in big red letters." These days he doesn't receive nasty notes from bill collectors but loving scented notes from young girls. Although Michael J. Fox was considered one of the most eligible bachelors, in true show-biz tradition, he married his ex-"Family Ties" girlfriend, "Ellen" (actress Tracy Pollan) in a private guest-list ceremony on 17 July 1988 in Arlington, Vermont. Fox's future looks bright; the long-running "Family Ties" concluded its run by sending Alex P. Keaton to work on Wall Street in Manhattan. The possibilities of spin-offs seem endless. The 5'4", 120-pound heartthrob is an avid hockey, baseball and skiing enthusiast, and resides with his wife, Tracy, in both California and Vermont.

David Frost

A uthor, television producer, columnist and—most formidably—an interviewer, his approach is deceptively casual, almost avuncular. Tight-lipped guests hopped aboard his departed "David Frost TV Show" and a split second later unpeeled their innermost thoughts. "It's odd to be discussing things as frankly as this with you in front of an audience," declared a foreign secretary after suddenly blurting out, "I don't want to be prime minister. I don't believe I've got what it takes to be prime minister." Frost also made television history with his revealing on-camera colloquies in 1977 with former President Richard Nixon and cites this erstwhile talk-partner in his *Book of the World's Worst Decisions*. Nixon, claims Frost, deserves the "Order of the Golden Boot" for "his decision to order voice-activated Sony tape recorders for the Oval Office in the White House," thus cinching his place in history in a much different manner than anticipated.

Frost has made his mark on both sides of the Atlantic for his efforts on the tube. Probably the smoothest, shrewdest, and most amiable interviewer around, he rocketed to the top of the slippery pole at a very early age. ("The most important thing on talk shows is to listen. And I like involving myself with the audience a lot. I like talking to people in all walks of life.") His illustrious guests have included Golda Meir, King Hussein, the Rolling Stones, Prince Charles, Jackie Gleason, Noel Coward, a fellow who sings to a tin tray, someone who blows up hot water bottles until they burst, and you-name-him-or-it. ("The thing I believe in really most of all in TV is this thing called unpredictability.") Frost has been responsible for "Headliners with David Frost" (1978), star of "The Frost Programme," joint founder of London Weekend TV and chairman/managing director of David Paradine Productions (his film-producing credits include *Charlie One-Eye*). He launched "Breakfast Television," also London-based, but the show has been a consistent also-ran behind its cozier BBC competition. He has been decorated with an Order of the British Empire, received many TV-related awards (including 2 Emmys), and been named TV Personality of the Year.

Born in Tenterden, England, 7 April 1939, the son of a Methodist minister, he attended Cambridge, where he took an honors degree in English at Gonville and Caius College ("or as I describe it to people who don't know, 'the ugly one on the right'"). Popping out of Cambridge in 1961, he found himself connected with the network called Associated Rediffusion. There he met Ned Sherrin and they cooked up "That Was the Week That Was." He was on hand for the U.S. version, which wasn't too successful. ("I think it could have been funnier and could have had a lighter touch.") Tired of satire, he created "The Frost Report" for BBC, which each week treated subjects like Frost on Money, Frost on Women, etc., then came up with "The Frost Programme," a gabfest similar to his New York show. He authored *Talking with Frost* (1967) and *The Presidential Debate* (1968). For years a confirmed and seasoned bachelor (his romantic involvements included Diahann Carroll and Carol Lynley), in 1981 he wed Peter Sellers' widow Lynne Frederick, a marriage that lasted two years. Then in 1983, this Protestant minister's son wed Lady Carina Fitzalan Howard, daughter of the Duke of Norfolk, the highest ranking Roman Catholic peer of the realm. They are the parents of three sons.

Eva Gabor

Although she allegedly once said that marriage is "too interesting an experiment to be tried once or twice," the youngest and possibly the most talented of the glamorous Hungarian sisters has tried matrimony five times.

Born 11 February circa 1924 in Budapest, Hungary, she yearned early to be an actress, but was discouraged by her well-to-do parents, who viewed the theatre as too vulgar a profession for their daughters. Eva finally got her chance after a runaway marriage (1939) to Dr. Eric Drimmer landed her in Hollywood and she was signed by Paramount. Her first film, shot in ten days in 1941, was called *Forced Landing*. She said later, "It was a B picture but only to those too lazy to look down the alphabet." Divorced from Drimmer in 1942, she married millionaire realtor Charles Isaacs, appeared in a number of undistinguished films and finally found her first real success as the Hungarian housemaid in the Broadway production of *The Happy Time* (1950). She scored on Broadway again in Noel Coward's *Present Laughter* and as Vivien Leigh's replacement in *Tovarich,* acquired a third husband, surgeon John E. Williams (1956), and continued to fracture the English language on TV guest spots, cheerfully admitting. "I know four languages and misspell in them all." She

wed husband No. 4, Richard Brown, in 1959 and No. 5, aeronautics tycoon Frank Jamieson, in 1973. Her long-running TV comedy "Green Acres" opposite Eddie Albert was on the tube for seven years and is still seen daily in 52 countries. "Green Acres" was a spin-off from "Petticoat Junction," which was a spin-off from "Beverly Hillbillies." Gabor and Albert reunited with most of the rest of the cast for the 1990 TV movie *Return to Green Acres.* In 1983 Gabor and Albert also appeared together on Broadway in a revival of *You Can't Take It With You.* Her many films include *Gigi, Don't Go Near the Water, The Last Time I Saw Paris* and two Walt Disney classics, *The Aristocats* and *The Rescuers.* In 1985 she appeared in the CBS telefilm "Bridge To Cross." Outside show business, Eva is chairman of the board of the world's largest wig company, Eva Gabor International. "We Gabors are supposed to do nothing but take bubble baths and drip with jewels, but I've worked like a demon. I didn't have time to sit in the bubbles." She is currently single; her constant companion is Merv Griffin. Eva's autobiography hit the bookstores in 1989.

Zsa Zsa Gabor

"Darling," intones the hot Hungarian beauty-at-any-age who has been married a mere eight times, "I am a wonderful house-keeper. After every divorce, I keep the house." Less famous for her acting than her jewels and her sharp-tongued barbs on television talk and game shows, she was once described by a U.S. congressman as "the most expensive courtesan since Madame de Pompadour" when she received some rather pricey gifts from General Rafael Trujillo, the former Dominican strongman.

Born Sari Gabor on 6 February in either 1921 or 1923, she

received her first big boost into the International Beauty League when she was named Miss Hungary in 1936. She has since then adorned films (*Moulin Rouge* and *Lili*, 1953; *Arrivederci, Baby*, 1966; *Up the Front*, 1973), stage (*40 Carats* on Broadway in 1970 and, co-starring with her sister Eva, *Arsenic and Old Lace* in 1975), and contributed her hard-won wisdom to such tomes as *Zsa Zsa Gabor's Complete Guide to Men* (1969), *How to Catch a Man, How to Keep a Man, How to Get Rid of a Man* (1970) and her autobiography *Zsa Zsa Gabor: My Story* (1976). When she was the guest of honor at L.A.'s Friar's Club roast in 1990, she braved barbs by Henny Youngman and Milton Berle and boos from the crowd due to her year-long battle in and out of the courts over a cop-slapping incident that she claims has been unfairly handled.

"My father liked to tell me that when I was six months old, if a woman bent over my crib I cried, but if a man—I cooed," she recalls. Her first husband was Burhan Belge, press director of the Foreign Ministry of Turkey. "He was sweet but I did not like to live in Turkey." Arriving in America, she lunched her very first day at "21," and met hotel tycoon Conrad Hilton, who became husband No. 2. ("We both had one thing in common. We both wanted his money.") They had one daughter, Francesca. Hubby No. 3 was George Sanders. ("I believe in big families," she said. "Every woman should have three husbands.") But after a torrid affair and a big black eye from international playboy Porfirio Rubirosa, she had another divorce. Husband No. 4 was Herbert L. Huntner, board chairman of Struthers Wells Corp.; No. 5 was oilman Joshua Cosden, Jr.; No. 6 was Jack Ryan and No. 7 was Michael I. O'Hara from whom she was divorced in 1982. Zsa Zsa married No. 8, Prince Frederick Von Anhalt (Duke of Saxony), on 14 August 1986 in Beverly Hills.

Art Garfunkel

The harmony of his pristine tenor voice and the pop stylings of songwriter Paul Simon made them one of the most popular folk-rock duos of the 1960s. Their reunion tour in 1982, after an eleven-year split, was sparked by the turnout of nearly half a million fans for a joint concert in New York's Central Park. Said an associate, "I think they both underestimated how many people cared about their reunion, how important it was to so many people. It was the right time, and they both sensed that."

Art Garfunkel was born 13 October 1941 in Forest Hills, N.Y. He met Simon when they appeared together in a sixth grade production of *Alice in Wonderland*, he as the Cheshire Cat, and Simon as the White Rabbit. Finding a mutual interest in music, they began singing together locally, backed by Simon's acoustic guitar. Signed by Big Records, and renamed Tom and Jerry, they produced only one mild hit, and upon the demise of the company, they split. After attending Columbia University, Garfunkel hooked up with his former partner once more to perform at popular New York clubs. Their 1964 debut album for Columbia Records, *Wednesday Morning, 3 A.M.*, netted the top single, "Sounds of Silence." Among the six popular albums that followed were *Parsley, Sage, Rosemary and Thyme*, the music to the 1969 hit movie, *The Graduate, Bookends*, and their 1970 *Bridge Over Troubled Water*, which brought them six Grammy awards. After personal and artistic friction caused their split in 1970, Garfunkel produced several pop albums with moderate success, but failed to reach the commercial heights achieved by Simon. Garfunkel's solo recording efforts include the 1973 "Angel Clare," and the albums, *Scissors Cut, Good To Go, The Animal's Christmas* (with Amy Grant), and *Lefty*. His singles include, "Second Avenue," and "I Only Have Eyes for You."

An introspective person prone to depressive moods, Garfunkel found stability through acting. "You are hired to search your soul and come up with aspects of who you are for presentation. So it behooves you to find out who you are." He debuted in films in *Catch 22*, and was favorably reviewed as a sensitive collegian evolving toward middle age in *Carnal Knowledge* (1971). After an unsuccessful marriage to Linda Marie Grossman, Garfunkel married Kim Cermak (of the Lime rock group) on 18 September 1988.

James Garner

Although he has starred in four TV series, this perpetually quizzical anti-heroic actor once said, "If you have any pride in your work, you don't go on TV. If you want to sell

underarm deodorant . . . you do." Yet James Garner's multimillion dollar contract was with Polaroid Cameras, not a deodorant company, and after having won an Emmy and a People's Choice Award for "The Rockford Files" series, he's unquestionably one of the medium's most popular stars. *Esquire* characterized him as "a master at playing dumb while maintaining a sense of shrewdness and dignity. He always throws us off guard. He is the macho stud who makes fun of himself; he is the scaredy-cat who we know will not let us down in the end."

Garner, who says, "I became an actor by accident, but I'm a businessman by design," was once vice president of the Screen Actor's Guild when Ronald Reagan was its prez. "We used to tell him what to say," Garner reflects. "He can talk around a subject better than anyone in the world. He's never had an original thought that I know of." As for himself, Garner (born 7 April 1928 in Norman, Okla.) grew up as James Baumgarner before changing his moniker. Domestic troubles led him to become a high school dropout, and he arrived in Hollywood via the Army and Merchant Marines. A pesky aunt and an acquaintance-turned-producer helped him out of odd-job employment into a $175-a-week contract with Warner Bros. He married actress Lois Clark (two daughters) after a two-week courtship, and after a quarter-century together she says, "I think the key is that at some point Jimmy decided that he was going to stay married to me and at some point I decided that he was going to stay married to me. . . . I feel threatened all the time. I am never complacent."

Garner became an instant, though low-salaried, star on "Maverick" in 1957; while the show topped Ed Sullivan in the ratings, the actor says, "I made more money in eight weeks in summer stock than I did in three years on 'Maverick.'" Movies are more to his liking, and since buying his way out of video bondage from two of his series, he's made more than thirty-five flicks. Some have been forgettable (*Boys' Night Out, Grand Prix*) while others have been memorable (*The Americanization of Emily, The Great Escape, Victor/Victoria*); either way he prefers "clean to dirt." However, he loves real estate dirt, and owns 375 acres in Carmel with Clint Eastwood, and "one of the ten most beautiful houses in LA," to go along with other land holdings. The one-man mini-conglomerate also owns apartments, oil wells, race cars, and a production company improbably dubbed "Cherokee" after his maternal grandfather, who claimed he was, partly. He has also softened somewhat on his harsh opinion of tube-toiling. Now he says, "I'd do any script if the people were right. I am an actor. I hire out. I do commercials, television, movies, stage. I am not afraid of hurting my image." Recent films include *Murphy's Romance* (1985), *Tank* (1985), and *Sunset* (1987). He also starred in the Hallmark Hall of Fame CBS-TV movie, "My Name is Bill W" (1989) and is the commercial spokesperson for Mazda.

Richard Gere

An eighties version of the tradi-tional, darkly handsome Hollywood leading man, Richard Gere has a brooding mien that may recall James Dean. Despite his popularity with audiences, Gere shuns fame and lives out of the proverbial actor's suitcase. "The only way I can figure to keep it together," he says, "is not to accumulate materially anything and to keep people around me—my friends from way back—who still have their heads in the clouds, in the ozone; you know, who are still visionaries, poets, dope freaks, dropouts, actors, musicians. I'll be very disappointed in myself if I become just an actor."

Born 29 August 1949 in Philadelphia, Gere was one of five artistically talented children raised by their parents on a farm near Syracuse, New York. An early interest in music had him composing scores for student theatrical productions and studying piano, guitar, trumpet and banjo. He left the U. of Massachusetts following his sophomore year and, after work at the Provincetown Playhouse and Seattle Repertory Theater, joined a commune of rock musicians in Vermont in 1970. He played guitar and keyboard in a band there, but found musicians "even harder to get along with than actors." Theatrical forays in London and N.Y.—in *Grease*—preceded his film debut in 1975. Two years later he attracted much attention as the doped-up psychopath who menaced Diane Keaton in *Looking for Mr. Goodbar*. This led to starring roles in *Days of Heaven, Bloodbrothers, Yanks* and *American Gigolo*, in which he played the title role of a narcissistic male prostitute.

A bachelor, Gere, whose theatrical training includes the classics, scored a great success in December, 1979, when he ended a five-year absence from the New York stage in the controversial play, *Bent*. His performance as Max, a homosexual concentration camp inmate, earned Gere more praise than most of his movie portrayals. The subsequent *An Officer and a Gentleman* kept the Gere film career in high gear and some of the films that followed were *Breathless*, the 1984 Coppola extravaganza *Cotton Club*, the 1985 less than impressive *King David, Power* (1985), *No Mercy* (1986), *Miles From Home* (1989), *Internal Affairs* (1990), and *Pretty Woman* (1990).

Estelle Getty

"I know this lady I'm playing," Estelle Getty says about her character Sophia, the fiesty, irreverent and intractable mother of Dorothy in the hit TV sitcom "The Golden Girls." "She's partly me and partly my imagination, but she's an original and that's what I've been playing all my life, original characters." Her originality and talent were not overlooked. "The Golden Girls" first aired in the fall of 1985 and during that season Getty won the Golden Globe Award for Best Actress in a Comedy Season. Two years later, she was awarded the 1988 Emmy for Best Supporting Actress in a series. Getty, an original herself, has performed in contemporary as well as experimental theatre for over half a century.

Born on 25 July 1923 in New York City, Getty was raised near the bright lights and felt the lure of the stage. She trained at the Herbert Berghof Studio and with Gerald Russak. After a long stage career, Getty blossomed into national prominence with her much-heralded performance as Mrs. Beckhoff in the Tony Award winning show "Torch Song Trilogy," gaining her the first-ever Helen Hayes Award as Best Supporting Performer in 1982. Traveling to Los Angeles with the show, Getty was "discovered" by Hollywood. While performing in the play at night, Getty was filming movies during the day. Within her first six months on the West Coast, Getty filmed the NBC pilot "No Man's Land." She went on to appear as Cher's mother in *Mask* (1984) and Barry Manilow's mother in the telefilm "Copacabana" (1986) and in *Mannequin* (1986). Even though still in demand, Getty took time out to write her book, *If I Knew Then What I Know Now . . . So What*, published in 1988. Enjoying her new-found popularity, Getty looks forward to new challenges and the release of her latest movie, *The Little Old Lady From Pasadena*.

Mel Gibson

The handwriting was on the wall when this "dish from Down Under" followed screen legends Clark Gable and Marlon Brando in the role of mutineer Fletcher Christian in the remake of *Mutiny on the Bounty*. Sure enough, like those predecessors, he soon exploded to supernova status—including the impramatur of a *People* cover in 1985 certifying him as "the sexiest man alive." Plain ordinary stardom came for Mel Gibson in 1981 playing a World War I Aussie soldier in Peter Weir's *Gallipoli*. In 1983 he took a giant step toward becoming an international sex-symbol in the same director's *The Year of Living Dangerously*, a romantic adventure story set in Indonesia in which his love scenes with Sigourney Weaver (every scene they had together but one, as pointed out by sharp-eyed *New Yorker* critic Pauline Kael) were notable for what Kael called their "new-style-old-time 'dangerous' steaminess." Subsequently loving it up with Sissy Spacek (*The River*) and Diane Keaton (*Mrs Soffel*), his sizzling screen presence thrust him up front as what one critic called "the putative star of the decade." More popular films followed, including *Lethal Weapon* (1987), *Tequila Sunrise* (1988), *Lethal Weapon II* (1989), *Bird on a Wire* (1990), and opposite Glenn Close in Franco Zefferelli's film of Shakespeare's *Hamlet* (1990). He co-starred with Robert Downey, Jr., in *Air America*, also released in 1990.

The sixth of eleven children, born 3 January 1956 into the Catholic family of a railroad brakeman in Peekskill, N.Y., Mel Gibson first heard about Australia in stories about his paternal grandmother who'd come to the U.S. from Kangarooland to find fame and fortune as an opera singer. When Mel was 12, his dad, injured on the job, decided to use the insurance settlement to move his family back to Australia—partly so the boys in the family could avoid being drafted to fight in Vietnam. Mel was treated as an outsider at first (schoolmates sneeringly called him "Yank") and he grew into a chip-on-the-shoulder loner. Eventually, he drifted into acting via studies at the National Institute of Dramatic Arts and, in

1976, gave his first hint of sex-symboldom-to-come when he was cast as Romeo to Judy Davis's Juliet in a school production of Shakespeare's romance.

Gibson made his film debut while still a student in an Australian quickie called *Summer City* but made a bigger impact in 1980 playing a scurvy vigilante in leather in the futuristic fantasy, *Mad Max*, a $300,000 production which Gibson calls "very classy grade-B trash" but which eventually grossed $100 million. (He later appeared in the sequels, *Road Warrior* and 1985's *Mad Max Beyond Thunderdome*, in which he teamed up with Tina Turner.) Uncomfortable with his "sex object" image, Gibson ruffled reporters' feathers in 1985 with biting, negative comments about the press and the price of fame. ("I have a very bad habit of saying embarrassing, goofy things," he said later. "The next day I could kill myself.") Married to former Robyn Moore (daughter Hannah, twins Edward and Christopher, sons Will and Louis), between pictures he escapes adulatory female fans at a beachside retreat in the Sydney suburb of Coogee. Although he retains his American citizenship ("despite all the cynicism in the world today, I'm proud of it. You have to be."), he thinks of himself primarily "as an Aussie." "I think it's good to be a hybrid," he told *Interview* magazine. "You can be more objective. If you get shifted from one culture to another, you look at something unusual and say, 'What is this?'"

John Gielgud

"**O**ne of the joys of owning a TV set right now," observed James Fallon in *Women's Wear Daily* in July, 1984, "is the variety of chances to observe the elegantly active octogenarian, John Gielgud." Sir John (he was knighted in 1953) has appeared on TV in HBO's "The Far Pavilions," as the brave but bigoted Major Sir Louis Cavagnari; as the blind hermit in Showtime's "Frankenstein"; as the host-narrator of the German series on PBS, "Buddenbrooks"; as Albert Speer's father in ABC's "Inside the Third Reich"; as Pope Piux XII in CBS's "The Scarlet and the Black"; as a doge of Venice in NBC's "Marco Polo"; and most wonderfully as Charles Ryder's papa in "Brideshead Revisited." Then, of course there are those TV commercials for Paul Masson wine, bits which *Time*

magazine feels show how he is perceived around the world: "bright blue eyes looking condescendingly down a luxuriant nose at the unruly, almost always inelegant world around him." In fact it seems impossible to make anything without him these days. His films include *Chariots of Fire, Priest of Love, Gandhi, Scandalous, Arthur* (Best Supporting Actor Oscar), *The Shooting Party, Plenty, The Whistle Blower, Appointment with Death, Arthur on the Rocks, Getting It Right* and *Loser Takes All.* He also appeared in the television miniseries "War & Remembrance" on ABC in 1988.

Claiming to be "a very timid, shy, cowardly man out of the theatre . . . acting has proved a great release for me," (the late Ralph Richardson contradicted Sir John's claim: "You needn't say a word with him, sometimes I will say yes or no or really?. . . afterward he will say to someone, 'I had a wonderful talk with Ralph,' and I didn't say anything . . . he's a continual firework of words."), he admits to loving junk novels and finds TV, if it is done with sufficient sincerity, skill and expertise, "Very enjoyable escapist entertainment. . . . I was born into a time when the theatre was very escapist, and I have always been an escapist in my own life and work. The romance of being in another century, in another situation, had always appealed to me because it enabled me to escape from my own emotional frustrations."

He was born in London on 14 April 1904 to Frank Gielgud and Kate Terry-Lewis, whose family, the Terrys, were the royalty of Britain's stage. Gielgud grew up in upper-middle-class comfort, and his ambition was always to become an actor. He promised his conservative stockbroker father that if he didn't make a success by 25 he'd become an architect. He went on the stage at 17 and made his first appearance at the Old Vic in 1921 as the herald in *Henry V*. With his voice, which Sir Alex Guinness says sounds like "a silver trumpet muffled in silk," Gielgud made his greatest marks in the 1920s and '30s playing Shakespeare. Many critics thought he was the best *Hamlet* of his generation. He considers his *Richard II* to be his finest performance. His contribution to Shakespearean acting was that he made it more natural and less declamatory. As the '30s came to a close, Britain's triumvirate of its finest actors were Laurence Olivier, Richardson and Gielgud, about whom British producer Derek Granger drew this distinction: "Larry is the lion, the hero who can play Oedipus, Henry V and Lear. . . . Ralph is the transmuted common man, John is the poet, the one with the finest and most aristocratic sensibility." He has had his flops, of course, but by the end of the '40s he says that he played so many Monarchs his management would say: "Just stick a crown on his head and send him onstage." In 1950 under the direction of Peter Brook, he interpreted Angelo in *Measure for Measure* not as a sensualist, but as a repressed Puritan. The role sparked his career to do the opposite of what most careers do in the golden years—glow rather than dim.

Gielgud moved from his London home behind Westminster Abbey to reside year-round in a 17th Century house in Buckinghamshire more than fifteen years ago. This he says changed his life because now he goes out less. "London is too full of ghosts for me," he says. He reads avidly, watches TV and keeps an aviary of parakeets and cockatoos. "I'm a very contented man." When he turned 80 in 1984 the occasion was duly noted. Several books were published to mark his birthday, including his own *Gielgud: An Actor and His Time.* About turning 80, Gielgud—the star of over 50 films (including earlier in his career *The Barretts of Wimpole Street, Saint Joan, Becket, The Loved One* and *Chimes at Midnight*) and, besides the classics, such modern plays as *Home,* for which he shared the Tony award for best actor with Richardson, and Edward Albee's *Tiny Alice*—told the *London Daily Mail,* "Ideally, what I'd like to do is die on stage in the middle of a good performance—and with a full house."

Kathie Lee Gifford

As Regis Philbin's perky co-host on the daytime talk-show ratings champion "Live with Regis & Kathie Lee," Kathie Lee Gifford keeps up admirably on the wacky, anything-can-happen show. A professional performer since the age of 14, she's been an actress and singer as well as a television journalist and talk-show host.

Kathie Lee Gifford was born 16 August in Paris, France, where her father was stationed as the Naval attache to General Eisenhower. The family moved to Annapolis, Maryland, when she was five years old, soon relocating to Bowie, Maryland. Her parents encouraged creativity so Kathie Lee grew up putting on plays and carnivals with her older brother and younger sister. Gifford started her professional career at age 14 when she and her sister formed a folk group called Pennsylvania Next Right's. They arranged the music and even booked their own gigs at coffee houses. At the age of 17, Gifford became Maryland's Junior Miss and landed her first commercial by winning the national competition's Kraft Hostess Award. Following high school, Gifford studied communications, drama and arts in college but at age 20, a few credits shy of a degree, opted to take her chances in Los Angeles. In true Hollywood fashion, while on the set of "Days of Our Lives" she was spotted by the producer and appeared as an extra the next day. She moved up to "under fives" and voice-overs, eventually portraying the minor role of Nurse Callahan for one year, while doing a slew of commercials. Turning down a two-year contract, Kathie Lee continued to do commercials while shooting countless network pilots. In 1977 she was a featured singer on the game show "Name That Tune." That exposure launched her nightclub act as she opened for such headliners as Bill Cosby, Rich Little and Bob Hope. She also costarred on "Hee Haw Honeys," a musical sitcom spinoff of "Hee Haw." Her journalistic career began when "Good Morning, America" producers saw her gueststinting on "A.M. Los Angeles." Within five weeks of arriving on "GMA," she was substitute anchoring for Joan Lunden. As special correspondent, she logged over a quarter million air miles covering human interest stories. She continued her "GMA" work for the first year of her co-hosting duties with Philbin in 1985. Gifford has never been one to sit back and relax. In addition to "Live," she has co-hosted the "Miss America" pageant for three years, performed at the 1985 Inaugural Ball for President and Mrs. Reagan, co-hosted nightly half-hour reports with her husband, Frank Gifford, from the 1988 Winter Olympics at Calgary, and performed with Philbin in a nightclub act.

The Giffords devote a great deal of time to charitable causes like Multiple Sclerosis and the Special Olympics. She is also very involved in The Children's Charity through Variety Clubs, International, and often sings for various charity benefits. In her spare time, Gifford has supervised the interior refurbishing and decor of her historical country home. She enjoys entertaining good friends and family, cooking, searching for American pine antiques and relaxing at home with her husband and her dog, Chardonnay.

Melissa Gilbert

A t 12 years old, Melissa Gilbert stated in her NBC biography, "When I get big I'm going to be an actress. Or maybe a dancer—or a doctor, or a lawyer. But I might be a nurse." Over a decade later, it seems she stuck with her first idea. Presently a star of television, stage and screen, Melissa has matured into a stunning young woman who can tackle any role.

Born in Los Angeles on 8 May 1964, she was a product of a show-biz family. Her father was the late entertainer Paul Gilbert. Her mother Barbara Crane Gilbert was a former dancer/actress, and her grandfather, Harry Crane, was a television comedy writer.

Melissa's debut in front of the camera at two-and-a-half for a Carter's baby clothes commercial provided her with the first item on her theatrical resume. Retiring until age seven, she returned to work by doing over thirty commercials. These sixty-second spots led to guest appearances on such shows as "Gunsmoke," "Emergency," and "Tenafly," then eventually the reprising role as Laura Ingalls in "Little House on the Prairie" (1974-1981). Her part as an engaging nine-year-old progressed into an appealing teen-age wife and mother in weekly TV view of millions of adoring fans during her eight-year run in NBC's homespun hit. Although she is probably most widely known for her moving portrayal of young Laura on "Little House on the Prairie," she has also demonstrated her considerable talents as Helen Keller in a TV movie of "The Miracle Worker" (1979), and in the title role of a TV rendition of "The Diary of Anne Frank" (1980). Manifesting a more adult (and considerably sexier) side, she also starred in a small-screen movie of the William Inge classic, "Splendor in the Grass" (1981), playing the role originated on the big screen a generation earlier by the late Natalie Wood. On 29 October 1987, Gilbert made her official New York stage debut in a new play by Barbara Lebow called *A Shayna Maidel*. Set in Manhattan in 1946, with glimmers of Chernov, Poland, before World War II, the drama focuses on two sisters, their father and the circumstances that have torn the family apart and brought it back together. In 1987 she appeared in the telefilm "Blood Vows" and has starred in two major motion pictures: *Sylvester* (1984), and *Ice House* (1988). Other television specials include participation in "Battle of the Network Stars" (1978-1982), "Celebrity Challenge of the Sexes" (1980), and "Circus Lions, Tigers and Melissa, Too" (1977).

After a long, well-publicized affair with fellow actor Rob Lowe, Melissa married actor/director Bo Brinkman on 21 February 1988. The couple live in Manhattan and have a son, Dakota Paul (born 1 May 1989).

Lillian Gish

"We didn't have unions in those days. We worked 12 hours a day seven days a week," recalled Lillian Gish, who started in films in 1912, following eight years on the road barnstorming in old melodramas with her mother and sister, Dorothy. The fragile heroine of D.W. Griffith's epic film, *Birth of a Nation* (1914), *Intolerance* (1916), and *Broken Blossoms* (1918) has proven herself to be indestructible in audience appeal. On tour in the 1970s with her own one-woman show, *Lillian Gish and the Movies*, she could reminisce about a nonstop performing career on stage, screen and TV spanning nine decades, all the way back to her theatrical debut at the age of five in a drama called *In Convict Stripes*. "I was merely taught to speak clearly and loudly so the audience could understand."

The elder of the two precociously performing Gish sisters (Dorothy died in 1968) was born 14 October 1896 in Springfield, Ohio. The two moppets were allowed to go on the stage as a means of helping family finances after their father deserted them, and, in such silent film spellbinders as *Orphans of the Storm*, they became, as Brooks Atkinson put it, "as much a part of American folkore as Jack Dempsey or Harry S Truman." In 1969, looking back with wry amusement on the old Hollywood days, Miss Gish (who never married) penned a book, *The Movies, Mr. Griffith and Me*. In 1971 she was presented with a special honorary Oscar for her "distinguished contributions to and service in making motion pictures." In 1982 she received the Kennedy Center Honors, and in 1984 the coveted Life Achievement Award from the American Film Institute. That same year she fulfilled a lifelong dream when she was partnered by Paris Opéra Ballet sensation Patrick Dupond in *Le Spectre de la Rose* on the stage of the Metropolitan Opera House during the Met's centennial celebration of the performing arts. Continuing her presence on the screen, Gish appeared in the Alan Alda film *Sweet Liberty* in 1985, followed by *The Whales of August* in 1987.

Alexander Godunov

I t was an airport scene that rivalled the one in *Casablanca* for suspense and international intrigue. For 73 hours in August of 1979 U.S. authorities delayed the departure of an Aeroflot jetliner until one of its passengers, ballerina Lyudmila Vlasova, gave him assurances that she most assuredly did not wish to join husband Alexander Godunov as the latest member of the jeté set (and the first from the Bolshoi) to defect to the West. By April of 1980, the

powerful six foot two *premier danseur*, who had been the legendary and formidable Maya Plisetskaya's preferred partner at the Bolshoi, utilized his dazzling technique and magnetic stage presence to partner Natalia Makarova to "the most passionate Giselle" of her career, according to *The New York Time's* Anna Kisselgoff. He felt even more at home at American Ballet Theatre, the classically oriented company he joined on his arrival in America, when his old classmate Mikhail Baryshnikov took over as artistic director in 1980. So it came as a seismic shock to dancer and public alike when after the 1982 season he was fired. "He threw me away like potato peel. . . . I really don't know why . . . nobody talked to me, nobody had the guts to face me personally," he told John Gruen in *Dance* magazine, adding that it reminded him "of the Russian way of behavior," thereby decisively burning his second bridge in three years. With characteristic resilience, however, Godunov quickly lined up a series of guest appearances, formed his own touring company of dancers and romantic alliance with actress Jacqueline Bisset (he divorced Lyudmila in 1982) and made his American motion picture debut in 1985 in *Witness* with Harrison Ford (to favorable notices), followed in 1986 with *The Money Pit* and *Die Hard* (with Bruce Willis) in 1988.

Boris Alexander ("Sasha") Godunov was born 28 November 1949 on the island of Sakhalin, and moved (after his parents' divorce) with his mother to Riga, in the republic of Latvia, where she enrolled him in the Riga State Ballet School in 1958 to keep him from becoming "a hooligan." He and classmate Mikhail Baryshnikov were denied partnering classes because of their short stature, so they concentrated all the more on developing their superb techniques, while resorting to a variety of folk remedies to induce the growth that would be their ticket out of the character dancer category. (By the time he graduated in 1967 Godunov had reached his present height.) After three years touring with the Young Ballet, he auditioned for the Bolshoi and was promptly hired as a principal dancer in 1971. His debut in *Swan Lake* ("It wasn't about *pirouettes* or *cabrioles*—it was about acting," he recalled about preparing for the role) was hailed as "an evening of poetic discovery" and an accomplishment that usually results only after "years of work and many performances." He continued to expand his repertory, adding such contemporary pieces as Roland Petit's *La Rose Malade* and Plisetskaya's own *Anna Karenina*. As one of the Bolshoi headliners in a U.S. tour in 1973, he astounded audiences with his astonishing pyrotechnical display of blindingly fast multiple *pirouettes* and whiplash *tours à la seconde*. But he *captured* them with his strongest asset, a spellbinding dramatic ability. From 1974 to 1979 the rock-ribbed Bolshoi management refused to let him travel abroad, lest his affection for things American expand to include its geography. But in 1979, strapped for high-calibre *premiers danseurs* for its scheduled American tour, the company reluctantly added him to its roster, and the ever-opportunistic Godunov confirmed their worst fears by strolling out of his upper West Side of Manhattan hotel on the evening of 21 August 1979 to begin his American odyssey.

Whoopi Goldberg

"It's a Cinderella dream come true. It's a gas. . . . It's amazing. . . . Everyone should have this luck. . . . This is the last thing I expected to happen." Whoopi Goldberg—actor (as she prefers to be called), comedienne extraordinaire, was introduced to Broadway in 1984 (with the help of producer/director Mike Nichols) and met with rave reviews. Says Nichols of his "discovery," "I went backstage to . . . meet her and I burst into tears, made a complete fool of myself. . . . Her compassion and her humanity are enormously moving and quite startling in somebody that funny." Goldberg's one-woman sketches, all of her own creation, "walk a fine line between satire and pathos, stand-up comedy and acting," observed a *New York Times* critic. Midway into her act, Whoopi coaxes the audience to link hands and form a bonded chain from row to row. "They told me not to try this, said it was too risky. . . . They called it the sentimentality of the 60s. I call it the sensibility of the 80s. . . . The most wonderful thing about touching somebody is you never know who your fairy Godfather might be."

Born circa 1950, Whoopi Goldberg came by her moniker when (according to Whoopi) a burning bush with a Yiddish accent suggested that her own name (which she refuses to divulge) was boring and convinced her to change it. A native of Manhattan's Chelsa district, Whoopi attended a local Catholic school and began her theatrical career at age eight at Helena Rubinstein's Theatre at the Hudson Guild. A 60's hippie "on the fine line between the lower East side and something spiritual, I asked myself am I going to keep doing drugs or figure out what I'm going to do with my life?" She decided: straight theatre, improvisation, and chorus bits on Broadway (*Pippen, Hair, Jesus Christ Superstar*) followed. In between she supported herself with a variety of jobs—bricklayer, bank teller, cosmetician in a morgue. In California Goldberg worked with the San Diego Repertory Theatre and the Balke Street Hawkeyes. Whoopi dreams of being cast as Shaw's St. Joan. She embraces her success, yet takes it in stride. "It's not so much that my life has changed, it's that I'm now able to experience things that were not accessible to me before. . . . What I enjoy most, though, are the simple things fame provides. I can stay at interesting places when I travel. I can get lost of pants, buy groceries and pay the rent and phone bills." Whoopi shares her California home with her daughter, Alexandra, and is seen around town with cameraman Eddie Gold.

In 1985 Goldberg made her film debut as the protagonist of Alice Walker's *The Color Purple*, with Steven Spielberg in the director's chair. Her performance earned her an Oscar nomination and a Golden Globe Award. Very much in demand, Whoopi's comedic talents are frequently seen on cable and television specials such as "Whoopi Goldberg's Fontaine . . . Why Am I Straight," "Funny, You Don't Look 200," "Carol, Robin, Whoopi and Carl," and "Comic Relief." She landed a recurring role on "Star Trek: The Next Generation," playing Guinan, the alien humanoid hostess. She received an Emmy nomination in 1986 for her guest appearance on the hit television series "Moonlighting." Always returning to her stage roots, Goldberg toured with a new one-woman show *Living on the Edge of Chaos* in 1988, and was presented with the 12th annual California Theatre Award for Outstanding Achievement on stage. Her recent films include *Jumpin' Jack Flash* (1986), *The Telephone* (1987), *Fatal Beauty* (1987), *Clara's Heart* (1988), *Homer & Eddie* (1988) and the CBS-TV telefilm "Bagdad Cafe" (1989). In 1990 she appeared at another *Comic Relief*. For her contributions to charity, the comedian/actress was honored in March, 1989, by the Starlight Foundation as their Humanitarian of the Year.

Jeff Goldblum

Jeff Goldblum is both a talented and resourceful performer. He is every bit "the chameleon," his persona transforming itself for his variety of roles. Although he began his career in the theater, he is most well known for his eclectic characterizations in film.

Jeff Goldblum was born 22 October 1952 in Pittsburgh, Pennsylvania. At the age of seventeen, he left home to study acting. He landed in The Neighborhood Playhouse in New York under the tutelage of Sanford Meisner. Joseph Papp was first to spot his talent, and cast him in *The Two Gentlemen of Verona*, a resounding Broadway success. The stage gave way to the camera in Goldblum's priorities. His film career began in 1974 with both *California Split* and *Death Wish*, soon to be followed by the cult film *Nashville* (1975). He seems to have mapped out his film career very carefully. His choices of scripts were as daring as they were varied. He quickly understood the danger to typecasting, and deliberately chose to play very diverse characters in films such as Woody Allen's *Annie Hall* (1977) and Phil Kauffman's *Invasion of the Body Snatchers* (1978). He made it a point to alternate between serious and dry comedic roles. He is perhaps most remembered by the public for two performances: his participation in *The Big Chill* (1983) and the cult classic *The Fly* (1986). Other notable performances came in *The Adventures of Buckaroo Bonzai (1984), Into the Night* (1985), *Silverado* (1985), and *Beyond Therapy* (1987). His most recent film appearance is in the comedy *Earth Girls Are Easy* (1989). He has temporarily resumed his theatrical stage career. He appeared at the Delacorte Theater in Shakespeare's *Twelfth Night*, produced by his old friend Joseph Papp. This 1989 production was not a critical success, but Goldblum will continue to persevere undaunted.

In keeping with Goldblum's wry sense of humor, however, he might agree that his greatest claim to fame just might be that of "Husband of the Year," since his wife, Geena Davis, was the surprise Academy Award winner for her performance in *The Accidental Tourist* (1989).

Louis Gossett, Jr.

The director of *An Officer and a Gentlemen* was looking for a white drill sergeant for the film when this veteran black

actor tried out for the role. He got the job, made the picture, and subsequently walked off with a Best Supporting Actor Oscar in 1983. That says something about today's Hollywood, he believes, where "the racism is not conscious as much as it's an omission of thought. Black actors will look at the trade papers and if the casting list doesn't say 'black sergeant,' they won't go out for the part. And if the script doesn't say 'black sergeant,' the producers and directors won't look for one."

Born 27 May 1936 in Brooklyn, New York, son of a porter and a maid, Louis Gossett, Jr., began acting at 17 when a leg injury temporarily sidelined the tall, lanky youngster from his first love, basketball, and he turned to the theatre. Chosen over 445 contenders for the role of a coming-of-age black youngster in *Take a Giant Step* on Broadway in 1953, he won a Donaldson Award as Best Newcomer of the Year and looked back only once. While performing in *The Desk Set* in 1958, he was drafted by the New York Knicks to play pro ball, but discovered "the others were bigger, stronger, faster and smarter," and returned to the theatre. He has appeared in more than 60 stage productions (*Lost in the Stars, A Raisin in the Sun, The Blacks, Murderous Angels*) and played character parts on a number of TV series ("The Nurses," "The Defenders," and "East Side, West Side") before winning an Emmy for his 1977 performance in the TV mini-series "Roots" as Fiddler, the old slave who befriends Kunta Kinte. He starred in TV's "The Father Clements Story" in 1990. He has also been in the cast of such films as *Skin Game* and *The Deep*, filled the title role in *Sadat* (which generated headlines when the Egyptian president banned the film because, among other things, the late Egyptian president was played by a black), and received star billing in *Firewalker* (1986), *Iron Eagle* (1986), *The Principal* (1987), *Iron Eagle II* (1988), *The Punisher* (1989) and *Gideon Oliver* (1989). Married and divorced from Hattie Glascoe and actress Christina Mangosing (one son), he favors offstage pursuits such as composing (his antiwar anthem, "Handsome Johnny" was played by Richie Havens at Woodstock), his African art collection and traveling. He tied the knot again in 1987 by marrying Cyndi James-Reese (an actress). The couple have a son, Sharron. Despite his own impressive list of credits, he believes the situation for black actors is generally "terrible—no writers are writing for us, and no producers are producing. . . . We should be represented in the overall fabric of America."

Elliott Gould

He refers to the period between 1971 and 1985 as "the debacle." Gould was behaving like some sort of wild man. In 1984, *TV Guide* quoted one observer: "Whether it was from drugs . . . Elliot went *crazy*. Not crazy enough to commit, but enough to think he had such unbridled power he could rule the universe. When he couldn't, he got terribly paranoid." So paranoid, in fact, that Warner Bros. was forced in 1971 to halt production of the film *A Glimpse Of the Tiger*, a decision that labelled Gould's career: on hold. Even when he was approached two years later to make *The Long Goodbye*, he was required to submit to a battery of psychiatric tests before he was given the part. "I took all the tests, and finally they put 19 needles in my head to study my brain waves," Gould explained. "At last I was certified sane. How many of us are certified by document as being sane?" Gould's "debacle" was transformed by the debut in 1984 and subsequent popularity of the TV sitcom "E/R" in which he played the cigar smoking emergency-room physician Dr. Howard Sheinfeld, a man who must work 48-hour shifts to keep up his alimony payments to his ex-wife.

Called in the 1980s "America's answer to Jean-Paul Belmondo," the beefy, brown-eyed 6-foot-3 actor was born an only child in Brooklyn, New York, 29 August 1938, the product of a frustrated middle-class Jewish household (his real name is Elliott Goldstein). The son of a garment center employee and driving "stage mother" (it was she who changed his name to Gould without telling him, thinking it sounded better for television), he began studying drama, diction, singing and dancing at age eight. As a child he appeared in song-and-dance routines in temples and hospitals, modeled and "danced with Josh White when I was ten." On summer vacations from Manhattan's Professional Children's School, he performed in the Catskills's "borscht belt." Because he could dance, his first "real TV job was on the old 'Ernie Kovacs Show' just out of high school. I was one of 50 guys who tap-danced in the chorus as Edie Adams sang 'Lullaby of Broadway.'" Living in New York he ran up debts and pawned his father's jewelry, sold vacuum cleaners and ran a hotel elevator, among other odd jobs. He made a small name for himself playing several parts in *Irma La Douce*, which led to his lead part in the Broadway musical *I Can Get It for You Wholesale* (1962). Also in that show was a certain odd duckling with an incredible voice named Barbra Streisand. Although they were almost fired by David Merrick before it opened, the show was both a box office hit and a romantic hit as well. Streisand and Gould were married in 1963 and three years later they had a son Jason (who, at age 18 months made his first, short, non-commercial film, which starred his Pop). As Streisand's fortunes soared Gould's sunk. Known as "Mr. Streisand," he was tolerated by Hollywood to please the Mrs. He dove into deep despair and was resurrected in psychoanalysis. His stardom coincided with his separation and divorce from Streisand. The 1968 film *The Night They Raided Minsky's* led to the super-popular *Bob & Carol & Ted & Alice* (for which he won an Oscar nomination as Best Supporting Actor), *M*A*S*H* (1970), *Little Murders* (1971), *The Long Goodbye* (1973, as private eye Philip Marlowe), *California Split* (1974) and *Nashville* (1975, as himself in a cameo appearance). All of these, except for *Murders*, were directed by Robert Altman. In 1970 he was chosen by Swedish director Ingmar Bergman as his first American lead for the film *The Touch*. Gould recalls his experience after making the Bergman film: "I thought when I came home from Sweden, I'd be met with a ticker-tape parade. . . . I'd proven I was a worldclass actor—I could not accept the torch. But *oy vey* . . . I was so naive. I call it 'The Debacle' because I wasn't stable enough to take the reins of my own life." Gould has two children with his wife Jennifer Bogart, whom he has married twice, in 1974 and 1978. Recent movies include *Inside Out* (1985), *The Myth* (1986), *Joker* (1987), *The Big Picture* (1988) and *Act of Betrayal* (1988).

Robert Goulet

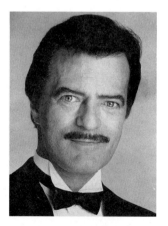

J udy Garland once described him a living eight-by-ten glossy, while critics complained that he was as stiff as the cardboard backing. Nevertheless he made women swoon as Lancelot back in 1960 in Lerner and Lowe's *Camelot* and drove them crazy with his nightclub act. Not too shabby for a guy who once categorized himself as a "lousy middled-aged baritone."

Robert Goulet was born 26 November 1933 in Lawrence, Massachusetts, but grew up in Edmonton, Alberta, Canada, and prepared for a singing career at the Royal Conservatory of Music in Toronto. His first attempt at taking New York by the horns ended up benignly enough ("I wound up selling writing paper at Gimbels"). Then came *Camelot*, followed by a couple of movies (*Honeymoon Hotel* and *I'd Rather Be Rich*) and a stint on TV's "Blue Light." Notwithstanding, this beefcake baritone with the "sullenly sexual face" has fared well on TV guest stints, records, in clubs, and (together with the late Judy Garland) on the soundtrack for the 1962 filmusical *Gay Purr-ee.* Divorced from Louise Nicole (one daughter), he married singer-dancer Carol Lawrence (*West Side Story*) in 1963 and they had two sons. Vera Novak is his third wife (married 1982) and the two of them divide their time between homes in Las Vegas and Los Angeles, his L.A. quarters being his 71-foot cruiser "Roger" docked in Marina Del Rey. In 1988 he toured with the national company of *South Pacific.*

Lee Grant

The raven-haired actress, acclaimed for her portrayals of coarse, sultry women of steely dispositions, proved that she was similarly indomitable when her promising career was nearly halted by a powerful accusation. When her name, in association with that of her first husband, playwright Arnold Manoff, was added to Senator Joseph McCarthy's insidious list of suspected communists in 1952, an intimidated Hollywood slammed its doors on her. Barred from any major film work for a frustrating twelve years, she took refuge in the theatre while resisting pressure from authorities to name her husband and others as subersives. Grant returned to memorable roles in television and movies in the mid 1960s, and overcame another prejudice, of sorts, to join the elite ranks of women directors.

Born 31 October 1929, Grant is remembered by TV audiences for her long-running featured role in the popular nighttime soap opera, "Peyton Place." She was gritty and intense as the justice-hungry wife of a murder victim in *In the Heat of the Night* (1968), the steamy detective drama of racism and murder in a Southern town. Referring to the stature of roles available during this era, she said, "At that time, women's parts were supportive of men's roles. I played ladies who just bore up when their husbands were murdered or stuck in outer space" (a reference to *Marooned*, 1970). Other film credits include *Plaza Suite, Airport '78, Damien: Omen II, Valley of the Dolls*, and *The Big Town*. She appeared in the telefilm "The Hijacking of the Achille Lauro" (1989) and the NBC miniseries "Mussolini: The Untold Story" (1985). On another level, Grant has blossomed into a well-respected director for stage and screen. She made her directorial debut with *Tell Me a Riddle*, from the Tillie Olson novel (1980). The film was well received, although sparsely released. Her directing credits include the film *A Private View* (1983); "The Willmar 8," and "A Matter of Sex" for NBC; and three documentaries—*When Women Kill, What Sex Am I? Down and Out in America* (won an Academy Award in 1987). She also directed the CBS-TV film "Nobody's Child," starring Marlo Thomas, and received the Directors Guild Award for the 1987 production. Grant directed Vaclav Haval's *A Private View* for the stage and was presented with a New York Drama Critics Award nomination. In 1989 she directed Strindberg's *Playing With Fire* for the Public Theatre.

Widowed in 1965, she is now married to independent filmmaker Joe Feury (one daughter). Her other daughter, actress Dinah Manoff, was born in 1958.

Jennifer Grey

A third-generation performer, Jennifer Grey made a name for herself with the role of "Baby" in the box office phenomenon *Dirty Dancing*. The physically demanding role required the skills of a professional dancer which Grey was not, although she had studied dance since the age of five and began her career as a dancer in a Dr. Pepper commercial. Her co-star, Patrick Swayze, cited Grey's "incredible natural talent" that allowed her to "come out with a sensuality in her dancing that has just staggered everybody." The film made the 5'4", brown-haired, grey-eyed actress a household name.

Jennifer Grey was born in 1960, the daughter of Academy Award winning actor-dancer-singer Joel Grey and singer Jo Wilder, and the granddaughter of famous Borscht Belt comedian Mickey Katz. A graduate of the Neighborhood Playhouse School of Theatre where she studied with Sanford Meisner and Wynn Handman, Grey was cast as an understudy in the Off-Broadway production of *Album* directed by Joan Micklin Silver. She followed it up with the role of Shirley in *Fifth of July* at the Portland Stage Theatre. Her brief television appearances include roles in the PBS production of "Media Probes," the ABC Afterschool Specials "The Great Love Experiment" and "Cindy Eller: A Modern Fairy Tale" and the CBS series "The Equalizer." Grey was introduced to movie audiences in James Foley's *Reckless* (1984) playing Darryl Hannah's wild Italian friend. She went on to play Nicholas Cage's wife in Francis Ford Coppola's *The Cotton Club*. She then was cast in John Milius' controversial film *Red Dawn* opposite Patrick Swayze and John Badham's *American Flyers* starring Kevin Costner. Her role as the young frustrated sister in John Hughes smash comedy *Ferris Bueller's Day Off* opposite Matthew Broderick earned her critical notice. It was followed by *Dirty Dancing*, about which David Ansen of *Newsweek* declared, "Jennifer Grey is a knockout." The independent film became a surprise international hit, spawning hit albums, concert tours, videos and even a short-lived television series (without Grey). While it seems difficult to surpass *Dirty Dancing's* success Grey continues to work. Her latest features include a Damon-Runyonesque romantic comedy *Bloodhounds of Broadway*—with Madonna, Matt Dillon, Randy Quaid and Rutger Hauer—and *The Sixth Family*.

Romantically linked with actors Matthew Broderick and Johnny Depp, Grey is currently single.

Joel Grey

He admits he isn't Captain Nice to work with. Some actors consider him self-serving and capricious. He says "I'm impatient. I have a quick temper. I don't hold grudges though. There's no point in keeping negative stuff." This compact, 5'5" and "wispish enough to pack in a theatre trunk," crackerjack entertainer trained hard for 24 years before coming upon the resounding click that signals full-fledged stardom. The time was the decadent Berlin decade of the 1930s. The place: a soulless cellar called The Kit Kat Klub, setting for much of the action in the 1966 Broadway musical, *Cabaret*. His George Grosz-inspired characterization of the red-lipped, white-faced, blue-humored MC won him critical flips, a Tony, and a follow-up role in the equally cheer-winning but totally different *George M!* ("Hooray," headlined the *Daily News*, "for the Red, White and Grey!") The Kit Kat Kaper was immortalized on film in 1972, and netted Grey an Oscar. He stayed with films for a while (*Man on a Swing, Buffalo Bill and the Indians, The Seven-Per-Cent Solution*) before returning to Broadway in 1975 as Charles VII in the musical *Goodtime Charlie*. 1979 marked a reappearance on Broadway in Larry Kramer's *The Normal Heart*.

Born in Cleveland on 11 April 1932, into the family of Yiddish comic Mickey Katz, Joel Katz (he changed his name to Grey in his teens) made his official debut at ten in a hometown production of *On Borrowed Time*, became a teen-aged protégé of Eddie Cantor on the basis of his skills as an impressionist, and was a Copa headliner at 19. Unfortunately the cabaret life "hit him below the belt" and he developed gastric as well as psychic problems. "It took many years and dollars and hours in therapy to work them out"—and a special interest in legit theatre which he "acted upon" at New York's Neighborhood Playhouse. For an extended time period, Grey began what he now refers to as his "replacement epoch"; coming to Broadway to join shows in mid-run (*Stop the World I Want To Get Off, Half a Sixpense* et al). Subsequently he developed a "benchwarmer mindset" which didn't last long, thanks to Hal Prince casting him in *Cabaret* and making him an overnight star. Showing his diversity, Grey appeared in the acclaimed ABC telefilm "Queenie" and was in the 1985 film *Remo Williams: The Adventure Begins*. Complying with a continual demand to see him "live" in *Cabaret*, Grey reprised his role in 1987 on Broadway and in a National Tour of the musical. Interviewed in *People*, he admitted, "I don't love the theatre. People ask, 'do you get a lot of pleasure when you perform?' and I say, 'Occasionally.' If I'm enjoying it, chances are the audience might not be."

Merv Griffin

"I'm afraid of becoming a huge machine." But confessions of fear do not match his ruddy cheeks and steady blue eyes. Singer/talk-show host turned mogul is now competing with such wheeler-dealers as Donald Trump in the high-stakes world of real estate. Making his millions through the ingenious creations of the game shows "Jeopardy" and "Wheel of Fortune," Merv has become financially secure enough to play his own game of Monopoly.

Griffin was the first to introduce the "theme" format to television talk programs which *de temps en temps* he taped from Cannes or

Venice or even the Belmont Race Track. Although he no longer has a daily show, he occasionally hosts a nighttime special. Merv Griffin maintains he gee-whiz boyishness with whomever he happens to be interviewing and this accessibility has won him a sizeable audience and Emmy Awards. Past forays include stints as a band singer (Freddie Martin's orchestra), TV quiz-show host, nightclub performer, hit vocalist on such records as "I've Got a Lovely Bunch of Coconuts" and Hollywood contract player in such epics as *So This Is Love, The Boy From Oklahoma*, and *Cattle Town*.

Merv was born in San Mateo, California, 6 July 1925 and studied music at the University of San Francisco. His first job was singing for a San Francisco radio station: "I had a high, dreamy Irish tenor. They billed me as the Romantic Voice of America." In 1950 the slow hike to television stardom began when he hosted his own show in Miami. "I remember him hosting the Saturday-night proms," recalls Murray Schwartz, who was then Griffin's agent. "The set looked like an automobile accident." Time passed and Merv "the Good Boy" found himself pitted against Johnny "What-the-Heck's Bad Boy" in a late-night ratings war (1970). Griffin bit the bullet and survived albeit at an earlier hour. He is the author of two books: *Merv: An Autobiography* (1980) and *From Where I Sit* (1981). He married the former Julann Wright, a radio comedienne, in 1958 (they divorced in 1976; one son Anthony Patrick). Griffin's hobbies include solo piloting and tennis. He is frequently seen around Beverly Hills with actress Eva Gabor.

Andy Griffith

H e is long gone from the rustic environs of Mount Airy, North Carolina, but his drawling Blue Ridge accent is still as thick as sow fat, and the country-boy actor is still more comfortable at an RFD address than in the glitzy spots of Hollywood and New York. Operating out of the sheriff's office of mythical Mayberry on CBS-TV's "The Andy Griffith Show," he ambled high in the ratings for five seasons during the 60s; found himself in less clovery circumstances with his short-lived stint as "Head-master" in the 70s. He served as executive producer for "Mayberry RFD" (1970), which took up where "The Andy Griffith Show" left off, but it lasted

just a season. He tried again with "The New Andy Griffith Show" (1970), but that too was short-lived. Griffith, however, remained visible on the tube in such miniseries as "Centennial," "Murder in Texas," and "Fatal Vision." *Hearts of the West*, a feature with Jeff Bridges, was released in 1975. Then, the year 1986 became a comeback of sorts for Griffith. There were two NBC specials— "Diary of a Perfect Murder" and "Return to Mayberry"— and the first season of the hit series "Matlock." Playing the role of a top criminal lawyer, Griffith combines the courtroom series with a perfect blend of country sophistication. His appeal has propelled the drama to still be a ratings winner into the 1990's.

Born 1 June 1926, he hied himself to the University of North Carolina with the notion of becoming a Moravian minister (although he was born a Baptist), but switched to music and drama instead. After graduation he taught school, married a music teacher (Barbara Edwards whom he divorced in 1972; two adopted children), and earned his first showbiz dollars doing a "preacher act" on the Rotary circuit "in a raggedy moth-eaten split-tail coat." He landed on Broadway in 1955 as a star in *No Time for Sergeants*, then to Hollywood in *A Face in the Crowd* (1957), and back to Broadway again in *Destry Rides Again* (1959). City Slickers who discover that for seven seasons in the early part of his career (1947-54) he portrayed English-accented Sir Walter Raleigh in the famed "Lost Colony" pageant, sometimes suspect that the drawl is put on. We know better. He loves to skeet and trap-shoot and married Cindi Knight in 1983.

Melanie Griffith

Having shed the stigma of her party girl image, actress Melanie Griffith rose above the dim future most had predicted for her in triumphant "tragedy to success" movie style. Once a candidate for Hollywood fatality, Griffith, with her lilting childlike voice, vulnerable-yet-tough demeanor, has combated her way from inexperienced actress to accomplished movie star. Hers is a success story that serves as an inspiration to all who have relentlessly struggled to overcome the obstacles that sometimes make success, whether professional or personal, seem impossible.

The charming and determined Miss Griffith was born in New York 9 August 1957 to Tippi Hedron, the grand-dame of Hitchcock films and real estate magnate Peter Griffith. A transplanted Californian at age four, Melanie spent much of her childhood attending private Catholic academies. She worked as an extra at the age of fourteen in the feature film *The Harrad Experiment* in which her mother had a leading role. On the set she became smitten with a struggling young actor by the name of Don Johnson. A rebel, Melanie lived

life in the fast lane. Sixteen years old and estranged from her parents who were divorced, she moved in with Johnson, then twenty-four years old. In 1974 at age seventeen, having never gone through any professional training, she landed a role as a nymphet opposite Gene Hackman in Arthur Penn's *Night Moves*. Mitchell Ritchie's 1975 beauty pageant satire *Smile* placed her name on a billing that included Bruce Dern, followed by a role in *The Drowning Pool* (1975) opposite legendary Paul Newman and Joanne Woodward. Baby-faced Melanie seemed to be taking off at top speed professionally but her personal life was suffering; her marriage to Johnson failed and she was hooked on drinking and drugs. In 1979 Melanie began doing television work. Among her credits: a recurring role in "Carter Country" telefilms: "Steel Cowboy," "Golden Gate," "She's in the Army Now" and opposite Rock Hudson and Suzanne Pleshette in "Starmaker."

Debilitated for months after a drunk driver hit her as she was crossing a Los Angeles street in 1980, Melanie began to put her life in order. Determined to rid herself of her destructive vices, she joined Alcoholics Anonymous. She met and fell in love with actor Steven Bauer, which led to a short-lived marriage. The union produced a son, Alexander, born 22 August 1984. With her personal life in order she began to study acting with Stella Adler in New York. She landed a role as a porn queen in Brian De Palma's *Body Double* (1984) followed by her portrayal of Lulu the flamboyant seductress in Jonathan Demme's 1986 feature film *Something Wild*. In the spring of 1988 she portrayed a weary mistress in the British thriller *Stormy Monday*. That same year she was the wife of a greedy rancher in Robert Redford's *The Milagro Beanfield War*. However it was the latter part of 1988 that brought Melanie to the forefront of the Hollywood thoroughbreds. As struggling secretary Tess in Mike Nichol's *Working Girl* Griffith found herself in a role that paralleled her life in many ways. Both the character and Griffith were vulnerable yet talented and determined to rise above their present status. Tess ended up with an office with her own secretary and Melanie ended up with a Golden Globe for her portrayal and her first Oscar nomination for Best Actress.

Griffith reconciled with former husband Don Johnson; they were engaged again in 1989 and married 6 June 1989, expecting their first child together. The couple reside with Alexander and Jesse (Johnson's son) in Miami, Colorado, and California.

Tammy Grimes

"**S** he lives," observed good friend Roddy McDowall, "on the tilt, half on the earth and half somewhere between the earth and the sky." She was *The Unsinkable Molly Brown* (1961) for which she won the Tony Award for best musical comedy actress and prompted Walter Kerr to write: "She is a genius." She was also a Tony-winning Amanda in Noel Coward's *Private Lives* (1970). It all started when McDowall once invited Noel Coward to a New York City cabaret. Tammy Grimes appeared on stage in silver sequins and proceeded to sing 18 Cole Porter songs. Mr. Coward grinned, rose above it, and offered Miss Grimes her first Broadway role—*Lulu*.

Despite her *veddy* British accent, she was born in Lynn, Mass., 1 January 1934. Even as a child, says her sister, "Tammy never looked like anybody else." Daughter of the manager of a swank country club, she "came out" in Boston society in 1951 ("I was quite fat and wore a dress with spangles"), served her apprenticeship as a performer at Stephens College in Missouri and at the Westport Playhouse. After the flamboyant overnight stardom she gleaned with *Molly Brown*, the 1960s proved more a career period of valleys rather than peaks (with the exception of the 1965 musical *High Spirits*). Her private life she likes to keep that way. Wed for four years to actor Christopher Plummer (daughter, actress Amanda), she had a short and stormy second marriage to Jeremy Slade, also an actor. In 1982 she married musician Richard Bell but on occasion denies the fact that they actually tied the nuptial knot. She worked consistently in both theatre and film throughout the 1980s. Her performances include the shows *Forty-Second Street* (1980), *The*

Waltz of the Toreadors (1985), *Mademoiselle Colombe* (1987) and her one-woman show *Tammy Grimes: A Concert in Words & Music* (1988). She also appeared in the films *The Last Unicorn* (1982) and *Mr. North* (1987). She describes herself as a "fake gourmet cook," likes to live in elegant surroundings, and sums up the essential Tammy this way: "If you're born an overstatement and the world sees you as one, you might as well play it that way. . . . I've always seen myself through other people's eyes, a mirror for the audience."

Charles Grodin

W ho played Aardvark the navigator in the film of *Catch 22*, Mia Farrow's gynecologist in *Rosemary's Baby*, co-authored and directed *Hooray! It's a Glorious Day*, co-produced and directed *Unexpected Guests* and *Thieves?* Why it's *The Heartbreak Kid*, Charles Grodin, "the 1972 American Heel of the Year." Director Elaine May cast him in the film *The Heartbreak Kid* opposite her daughter Jeannie Berlin, as a three-day husband who dumps his wife while on their honeymoon. Since then Grodin has made other major stage and film appearances, e.g., as the engagingly sincere philanderer in *Same Time Next Year* at the Brooks Atkinson in 1975; as the grim and greedy oilman in *King Kong;* as the jocular divorced father in *It's My Turn* (1980) and as Goldie Hawn's husband running for attorney general of California in *Seems Like Old Times* (1980). More films followed, including *The Woman in Red* (1984), *Movers and Shakers* (1985), *Club Sandwich* (1986), *Ishtar* (1986), *Greetings From LA* (1987), *The Couch Trip* (1987), *Midnight Run* (1988), and *Taking Care of Business* (1990).

Born in the East Liberty section of Pittsburgh, Grodin claims to have "no idea" how old he is. (He was born 21 April 1935.) His late father used to work seven days a week selling supplies to cleaners, tailors, and dressmakers; his mother Lana, did volunteer work with disabled veterans and kids. Chuck himself is divorced from his first wife Julia (one daughter) and married Elissa in March, 1985. In 1989 he published a humorous volume, *It Would Be So Nice If You Weren't Here.* Efforts in 1990 include starring in the play he penned, *The Price of Fame.*

A classmate of Dustin Hoffman when both were studying under Lee Strasberg, Grodin married the girl (Julia) Hoffman had been chasing. ("I got my wife and he got *The Graduate*.") Despite his success as an actor, Grodin says, "My main thrust in life is none of this. I am really more interested in educating myself, talking to people and trying to figure out what's going on, than acting, directing or writing any movie." He shifts his weight and in the next breath concludes, "I started off years ago playing bigots on television, even though I'm almost a nut in the other direction, and when someone asked me how I could do it I told them all you needed was strong feelings about these questions, and then you can apply them to the character you're playing."

Alec Guinness

"One became an actor," he says, "to escape oneself." Indeed, on both stage and screen, he is admired as "an actor who makes you forget that he is acting," a tribute to his characteristic, exquisite economy of technique. Playing *Hamlet* in a controversial modern dress version at the Old Vic when he was 24, he proceeded onward and upward to become an international star of films and the theatre, and, offstage, a knight of the realm. (Queen Elizabeth II added the title "Sir" to his name in 1959.) Famed for his versatility, he counts among his stage triumphs roles as startlingly dissimilar as the urbane psychiatrist in T.S. Eliot's *The Cocktail Party*, and the drink-sodden, womanizing Welsh poet in the biographical drama *Dylan*. In motion pictures, his finely detailed characterizations have ranged from a tour-de-force delineation of eight members of an eccentric English clan (including that of an elderly woman) in *Kind Hearts and Coronets* (1949) to an Oscar-winning portrayal of the priggish Colonel Nicholson in *Bridge on the River Kwai* (1957). In 1977 he won new fans among the smallfry set with his characterization of the whiskery wizard Ben (Obi-wan) Kenobi in the super-successful sci-fi spectacle *Star Wars*. In the 1985 blockbuster, *A Passage to India*, he was a Brahmin professor, and he starred in the 1988 film *A Handful of Dust*. For his work in *Little Dorrit* (1988) he received an Academy Award nomination for Best Supporting Actor. His book *Blessing in Disguise* was published in 1986.

Born a banker's son in London on 2 April 1914 (no relation to the Irish brewing family), he was discouraged from participating in student theatricals at boarding school ("You're not the acting type") but eventually nabbed the part of a breathless messenger in a class production of *Macbeth*. He experienced lean years as a copywriter, layout man and acting student before landing his first theatre job in 1934—a stint with John Gielgud's repertory troupe and a later stint at the Old Vic in Shakespearean roles that really established him on the English stage as one of its most promising young actors. His depiction of Herbert Pocket in the 1946 David Lean movie version of *Great Expectations* made him an international film star. Since then the reserved, almost timid actor has turned in brilliant performances in more than a score of major pictures, among them, his deliciously adroit characterization of Fagin in Lean's *Oliver Twist* (1948); as a rogish painter in *The Horse's Mouth* (for which he wrote the screen adaptation; 1958). He also brought immense conviction to the part of Prince Feisal in Lean's 1962 epic, *Lawrence of Arabia*. While "no-flesh-and-blood actor could have stolen the show from the special effects '*Star Wars*,'" by portraying a space-age sage with dignity Guinness added to the 1977 release a potent touch of class. Since *Star Wars* (and its 1980 sequel *The Empire Strikes Back* in which Guinness made a token appearance) ranks as one of the biggest-grossing motion pictures of all times, he—with his two percent of the profits and exposure to massive audiences—has acquired addition "fame and greenbacks."

Active also on the stage on both sides of the Atlantic throughout his career, he held out until recent years where television was concerned. Since September 1981, however, he's received advantageous exposure on the small screen in the U.S. as the rueful middle-aged secret agent George Smiley in the Public Television series based on John Le Carre's novel, "Tinker, Tailor, Soldier, Spy." This impressive debut spawned a sequel, "Smiley's People," in which Guinness again starred, and further TV work included underplaying the crusty but meltable Earl of Dorincourt in the classic "Little Lord Fauntleroy." Guinness believes that he possesses a "chameleon quality" that has been an asset to him as an actor "but not as a person."

Married since 1938, Guinness met his wife, the former Merula Salaman, in a London play called *Noah* in which he played a wolf and she a tigress. After departing from the ark and proceeding to the altar, Mrs. Guinness relinquished the stage but the couple's son Matthew (born during World War II) is following in his father's performing footsteps. When asked if he really enjoys acting, Guinness's reply: "Yes, I do. It's happy agony."

Gene Hackman

His 1971 Oscar-winning performance as tough, hard-edged narco detective Popeye Doyle in *The French Connection* rocketed him to the superstardom he had pursued since his teenage days as a movie usher. ("I had a chance to see Ethel Barrymore in *The Corn is Green*. She inspired me to want to be an actor above all else.") It wasn't easy. Enrolled at the Pasadena Playhouse, he and another student, Dustin Hoffman, were considered the two least likely to succeed. But persistence paid off. Hackman eventually made it to Broadway, playing Sandy Dennis' crude boyfriend in *Any Wednesday*, a sleeper that ran for 983 performances. His screen career began with a bit part in *Lilith*—which was big enough to attract the attention of its star, Warren Beatty, who remembered Hackman two years later when casting his 1967 classic, *Bonnie and Clyde*. Hackman's performance as Clyde Barrow's backslapping brother, Buck, earned him an Oscar nomination. Though best known for his dramatic works and tough-guy roles, Hackman is a versatile actor who has starred in sensitive dramas (*I Never Sang for My Father, Misunderstood*) and in off-beat comic roles (he was Luthor, the arch enemy of *Superman*, and the friendly blind man in *Young Frankenstein*). His performance in *Mississippi Burning* (1988) earned him an Academy Award nomination for Best Actor.

Born Eugene Alden Hackman in San Bernardino, California, 30 January 1931, he spent his early teens in Danville, Ill.; at sixteen, with his parent's blessing, Hackman enlisted in the Marines. He served in China, Japan, Hawaii, and Okinawa before breaking both legs in a motorcycle accident and receiving a disability discharge. His first performing stint was in China, where he worked as an announcer at his Marine unit's radio station in 1947. After returning to the states, he traveled around the country working at various small-town TV stations, then enrolled at Pasadena Playhouse. After a period of summer stock, he moved to New York and worked his way through odd jobs before landing a role in an Off-Broadway revue and finally making it to Broadway.

Hackman has made more than 35 films. Some of his 1980's releases include *Uncommon Valor* (1983), *Misunderstood* (1984), *Target* (1985), *Twice in a Lifetime* (1985), *Power* (1986), *Full Moon in Blue Water*

(1987), *Superman IV* (1987), *No Way Out* (1987), *Bat 21* (1988), *Another Woman* (1988), and *The Von Metz Incident* (1988). His 1990s projects include *Narrow Margin*. He is divorced from his first wife and has three children from the marriage. Hackman loves flying and owns three planes, races cars in events like Sebring and Riverside, and is a talented painter and avid film collector.

Larry Hagman

❝ ... hssssssssss." Watch out for your toes, America, watch out for your fingers. Don't pick-up any stray ten-gallon hats, there's a snake in there and his name is J.R. Ewing, America's Lone Star viper with a honeycured tongue. "The time is right for a real bad buy and, well, I guest I'm it," says the son of Mary Martin who, as the star villain of the TV super-soap "Dallas" is watched weekly and worldwide by over 40 million viewers, endeared to them, no doubt, by *that* smile: as rapid as a rattlesnake's, as flashy as a silver bullet bucking from a pistol called sweet revenge. On the air as J.R. since 1977, Hagman is still pulling awards as "Best Villain." He won the Soap Opera Award in 1988.

Larry Hagman was born 21 September 1934 in Weatherford, Texas. He says he bases his money-making character J.R. on some of the "oil rich boys" who employed his lawyer father, the late Benjamin Hagman, in the Texas of his youth. "They had such a nice, sweet smile but when you finished meeting with them your socks were missing and you hadn't even noticed they'd taken your boots." After his parents' divorced, he moved to Los Angeles with his mother. Many schools later he turned to New York to pursue an acting career, making his stage debut in a City Center production of *The Taming of the Shrew*. He spent five years with the Air Force in Europe as the director of USO shows, then returned again to New York where he starred on the soap opera "Edge of Night." He appeared in the films *Fail Safe*, *The Group*, and *Harry and Tonto* before his five-year orbit as an amiable astronaut visited by the curvaceous Barbara Eden on TV's "I Dream of Jeannie." Married since 1954 to wife Maj (whom he met when they were both appearing in a production of *South Pacific*), they enjoy a quiet lifestyle in Malibu with their two children Heidi and Preston.

In Dallas, on location, Hagman spends his off-camera time shooting around the streets in his "Texas taxi," a white Cadillac convertible with steer-horn adorned grille, waving a can of Lone Star beer, tipping his hat to everyone, and hooting out howdy-do's, sort of a J.R. for president do-si-do on the range. And why not J.R. for president; he's got the smile and the ratings.

Arsenio Hall

The 12-year-old Arsenio Hall told his mother he wanted "to do what Johnny Carson does." At age 30, with the 3 January 1989 premiere of "The Arsenio Hall Show," that dream was fulfilled, But Hall was more than just another talking head. By the time his show (of which he is also executive producer) hit the airwaves he was already known as a talented comedian and actor. With a comedic style he has described as "'brown bread' on the edge," he has succeeded in clubs, film, and television.

Born circa 1958 Hall grew up in Cleveland, Ohio, the son of a Baptist preacher. He inherited his father's ability to work a crowd, starting at age 7 performing magic at wedding receptions while working birthday parties and local talent shows. The young magician was fascinated by "The Tonight Show," especially the Mighty Carson Art Players, and began to switch his focus from magic to comedy. A high school promotional visit by comedian Franklin Ajaye convinced Hall to try stand-up comedy after completing his education. In high school, Hall explored other areas of his talent. He was a drummer in the marching band and orchestra and had his own music group. While at Kent State University, he became involved in theatre arts and was a deejay for the campus radio station.

After graduation Hall embarked on an advertising career but began doing stand-up comedy on a dare in 1979. He quit his job, relocating to Chicago where he was discovered in a nightclub by singer Nancy Wilson. She funded his move to Los Angeles. Hall opened for dozens of top name performers including Aretha Franklin, Tom Jones, Wayne Newton, and Tina Turner. Making the transition from clubs to television in 1983, Hall co-hosted the ABC summer series "The Hour Comedy Hour." The following year he was a regular on "Thicke of the Night" and went on to co-host the music/variety series "Solid Gold". He hit his stride when he signed as an interim guest host on Fox Broadcasting's "The Late Show." The show enjoyed some of its highest ratings ever during his tenure, and he eventually hosted it for 13 weeks. Following the "Late Show" stint, Hall signed an exclusive 2-year, multi-film agreement with Paramount Pictures, leading to his acclaimed performance in the box office blockbuster *Coming to America*. Returning to television, Hall was the sole host of the 1988 "MTV Awards." While promoting *Coming to America*, Hall decided to return to the talk show circuit. Preferring the immediacy of television to film, Hall explains: "A talk show is a blessing for a stand-up. It's the perfect vehicle." Hall wrote his own monologues while hosting "The Late Show" commenting on a wide variety of subjects. His role as the executive producer of his current show fills another need. "I've worked very hard all my life to educate myself, and now I get a chance not only to show the funny side of my personality, but the businessman locked inside me as well. . . . If this show succeeds, there will nothing greater than hearing someone say, 'Arsenio Hall is a great businessman.'"

With all the success he's achieved, Hall still sets goals for himself. "I want to be an artist respected by other artist, which I don't think I've achieved yet. . . . I want a person to look at me and be affected by my work. . . . And I'm going to keep working until I do it right."

Mark Hamill

H e's recognized by his fans as anyone from Luke Skywalker, the doe-eyed goody in the 1976 superhit-flic *Star Wars* (and its sequels *The Return of the Jedi* and *The Empire Strikes Back*,) to *The Elephant Man* (where he made his Broadway debut) and Mozart (for his role as Wolfgang Amadeus in Peter Shaffer's award-winning play *Amadeus* on Broadway).

Born 25 September 1951 in Oakland, California, into the family of a U.S. Navy officer, Mark Hamill spent a peripatetic childhood moving with his parents and two brothers and six sisters to posts as far afield as Yokosuka, Japan. As a child he was mildly interested in acting, but when he accompanied his father on a visit to New York City for a

marathon of live theatre, he was bitten by the show-biz bug. "After seeing eight plays in six days," he says, "I was hooked." He majored in Theatre Arts at Los Angeles City College and began his professional career with a nine-month stint on the daytime TV soap "General Hospital." He later starred in the MTM series "The Texas Wheelers" and a number of television movies, including "Sarah T.," "Eric," "In Circumstantial Evidence," and "Delancey Street." Besides the *Star Wars* trilogy, his other films include *Britannia Hospital*, *Corvette Summer* (also known as *Dantley and Vanessa*), *The Big Red One*, *Avalon Awakening*, and *Slipstream*.

Married and the father of one son, he returned to Broadway in the ill-fated musical *Harrigan 'N Hart* in 1985 (playing the 19th-century American actor Tony Hart). In his next show, *The Nerd* (1987), Hamill played a beleaguered architect whose ordered existence turns to chaos when he begins to share his home with a man who once saved his life. The walking, talking human catastrophe known as "the Nerd" was played by Robert Joy, and the production was directed by Charles Nelson Reilly.

George Hamilton

"I f," suggested Pauline Kael in *The New Yorker* in 1981, "you could combine the screen images of Douglas Fairbanks, Sr., and Peter Sellers, the result might be pretty close to the slinky, self-mocking George Hamilton" in his on-screen guise of *Zorro, the Gay Blade*—a satire of the swashbuckler of the 1930s. A far cry from his early years as a Cary Grant lookalike emoting in a series of mostly forgettable films to generally lukewarm reviews, the erstwhile glamorboy first showed his "joyously silly" *farceur* side in the 1979 comedy, *Love at First Bite*, playing a modern-day Dracula driven from Communist Transylvania to put down new roots in New York City. To many critics (perspicacious Pauline among them), his "gleaming-eyed Zorro with his idiotic leering grin and his idiosyncratic Spanish accent" was even funnier.

The actor once nicknamed "Gorgeous George" was born George Hamilton IV (no relation to the country singer of the same name) in Memphis, Tennessee, (12 August 1939) but spent most of his boyhood bouncing around to 254 different schools while his social, much-married mom followed the sun and party circuit. It was a long-time family friend, the silent screen star Mae Murray, who first pointed him in the direction of Hollywood, and he made his debut in the quickie *Crime and Punishment, USA,* in 1958. Always suavely polite and impeccably dressed, he cut a wide Tinseltown swath with his 1939 white Rolls Royce ("The car got more publicity than I did"), which sometimes earned as much money as he did, for he often rented the car to his studio for $100 a day. He also earned publicity points as one of "Hollywood's most eligible bachelors," his most headlined romantic fling being with Lynda Bird Johnson when her dad, LBJ, was in the White House. He married Alana Collins in 1972 (one son, Ashley Steven, born 1974), divorced her in 1976 (after which she went on to marry rocker Rod Stewart), and has been back in the bachelor ranks ever since. Among Hamilton's most note-worthy screen credits during the first phase of his career were *The Light in the Piazza* (1962), as Moss Hart in *Act One* (1963), and in the title role of *Evil Knievel*, a film bio of the motorcycle stuntman which he produced for himself in 1972. He appeared on television's "Dynasty" during the 1985 season, and in 1990 he co-starred in *The Godfather, Part III.*

Linda Hamilton

It seems ironic that Linda Hamilton, the "Beauty" of CBS-TV's "Beauty and the Beast," insists "glamour is hardly my style," but her previous roles support her claim. Prior to portraying the beautiful lawyer Catherine Chandler on "Beast," Linda had played a rape victim on "Hill Street Blues," a battered wife in the CBS-TV movie "Rape and Marriage: The Rideout Case" with Mickey Rourke, and usually ended up getting killed in her action adventure films. Her image began to change with the role of heart surgeon Amy Franklin in Dino DeLaurentiis' *King Kong Lives.* She wore a designer wardrobe and got the guy. Then came "Catherine." "The show wouldn't work as well if Catherine didn't have some beauty. It is the extremes in the characters' looks that help make the story work. But I never thought Vincent wouldn't love Catherine if she weren't beautiful." She added she's always found "Vincent" attractive—"leonine and magnificently proud and with a great voice."

Linda was born 26 September 1957 in Salisbury, Maryland, along with her identical twin sister, Leslie, a registered nurse. She grew up there with her older sister and younger brother. Her father, who died when she was five years old, was a physician. Her stepfather, now retired, was the police chief of Salisbury. Hamilton began acting as a child with children's theater groups. Acting became her career choice at Washington College in Maryland, where she studied for two years and appeared in school productions of *Story Theatre*, *Prometheus Bound* and *The Adding Machine*. She then went to New York where she attended workshops at the Lee Strasberg Theatre Institute and also studied with Nicholas Ray. Student productions of *Richard III* and *A View from the Bridge* were followed by her professional debut with an appearance on the daytime drama "Search for Tomorrow." In 1979, Hamilton reluctantly moved to Hollywood. She landed movie-of-the-week appearances, including "Secrets of a Mother and Daughter," "Secret Weapons," and "Club Med." Hamilton also appeared in the pilot "Wishman" and was a series regular on "Secrets of Midland Heights" and "Kings Crossing." Her movie career blossomed as well. Starting out with low budget features *Nightflowers* and *TAG* (where she met her husband, actor Bruce Abbott), Hamilton moved on to *The Stone Boy* and *Children of the Corn*. Her co-starring role opposite Arnold Schwarzenegger in *The Terminator* gained her recognition and led to other starring roles in *Black Moon Rising* with Tommy Lee Jones and *King Kong Lives*. The role of Catherine has earned Hamilton two Golden Globe nominations for Best Actress (1988 and 1989) and a People's Choice Award nomination as Favorite Female Performer in a New Television Program in 1988.

Hamilton relaxes by reading, interior decorating, and playing Scrabble. She's a Los Angeles Dodgers fan and a lifelong lover of horses. The 5'5", 115-pound Hamilton has light brown hair and green eyes like "Catherine" but lives "a much shaggier lifestyle" than her television counterpart. She resides in Marina del Rey with husband Bruce Abbott and their 115-pound German Shephard-St. Bernard mix, Bosco. About children she says: "They're the real legacy we leave in this world—not your face on film."

Tom Hanks

With the face of a teasing little boy who just put a whoopie cushion on a chair, Tom Hanks displays playful, dry, quick-witted comic sense that has helped skyrocket him to the forefront of the new generation of comic actors. Since the premiere of the sitcom "Bosom Buddies" in 1980, Hanks has been in demand.

Although the show about two strug-gling advertising men who dress in drag to live in a low-budget women's hotel only lasted two seasons, it proved to be a showcase for his comedic talents. "I enjoyed working in television," he said. "Sure, the pace is hectic, but the work has substance as long as you keep men-tally stimulated." After the release of the TV movie "Mazes and Monsters" in 1982, Hanks made the transition to mov-ies. His first film was 1980's *He Knows You're Alone*, and his first box office smash was as a young man in love with

a mermaid in the 1984 Ron Howard film *Splash*. Howard sees Hanks as "a terrific leading man, like Jack Lemmon or James Stewart . . . funny guys who make you care." Joe Dante, director of Hanks' film *The Burbs*, also says Hanks is "definitely in the mold of Jimmy Stewart or Jack Lemmon."

Since *Splash* Hanks has appeared in *Bachelor Party* (1984), *The Man with One Red Shoe* (for which Hanks learned to play the violin; 1985), *Volunteers* (with John Candy; 1985), *The Money Pit*, a Spielberg production directed by Richard Benjamin and co-starring Shelley Long (1986), *Nothing in Common* (where Hanks had to deal with his mother divorcing his father, played by Jackie Gleason; 1986), *Every Time We Say Goodbye* (1986), and opposite Dan Aykroyd in *Dragnet* (1987). His next movie, the 1987 Penny Marshall box office hit *Big* (1988 Golden Globe Award, Best Actor), could have been written for the star. His role as a thirteen-year-old boy who makes a wish and wakes up the next morning in a man's body won Hanks widespread acclaim. After playing a stand-up comic opposite Sally Field in David Seltzer's *Punchline*, the indefatigable Hanks completed two films for 1989 release: *The 'Burbs* (a suspense-comedy directed by Joe Dante) and *Turner and Hooch* (a Disney production). "Hanks is an actor capable of acting funny, rather that funny acting," says producer Larry Brezner. "He's now proving himself as one the country's most versatile actors." His latest films are *Joe Versus the Volcano* (1990) with Meg Ryan, and *Bonfire of the Vanities* (1990), opposite Melanie Griffith.

Born 2 July 1956 in Oakland, California, Hanks started acting in high school. Even though he was bitten by the comedy bug ("I was always trying to stuff myself into lockers—crazy things like that"), Hanks was inspired to pursue serious acting after seeing a produc-tion of *The Iceman Cometh* while attending college in San Francisco. Studying acting at California State University in Sacramento, Hanks performed in *The Cherry Orchard*, directed by Vincent Dowling. As luck would have it, Dowling was also the resident director of the Great Lakes Shakespeare Festival in Cleveland and invited Hanks to intern with the classical company. In his first season, Hanks made his professional debut as Grunico in *The Taming of the Shrew*, followed the next season by *The Two Gentlemen from Verona*, which earned him The Cleveland Critics Award for Best Actor. At the end of the second season Hanks moved to New York where he appeared in *The Mandrake* at the Riverside Shakespeare Co. Following his third and final season in Cleveland, Hanks returned to New York to make his first feature film, *He Knows You're Alone*, before returning to the stage in *Taming of the Shrew* in New York and *The Dollmaker* in Los Angeles. It was during one of his stints in New York that he learned of the auditions for a new sitcom. Impressing the producers, the classically trained Hanks landed the role on "Bosom Buddies," left the stage for the little screen, and returned to his first love, comedy.

Tom has two children from previous marriages; he married Rita Wilson in 1988. They live in his native California.

Daryl Hannah

She is as versatile as she is talented. She has assumed a variety of roles ranging from a mermaid in the hit comedy *Splash*, to a lovestruck astronomer in *Roxanne* to an upwardly mobile interior decorator lacking in scruples in *Wall Street*. Her talent goes beyond the big screen. Daryl has studied extensively in theatre, and has appeared on television as well.

Daryl Hannah was born in 1960 in Chicago, Illinois, and began studying acting at the Goodman Theatre. In 1978, before she even graduated from high school, she made her film debut with a small part in *The Fury*. Upon finishing high school, Daryl moved to Los Angeles where she attended U.C.L.A., and studied under Stella Adler. Within a few short years, she was being cast in starring roles in feature films such as *The Final Terror* (1981), *Summer Lovers* (1982), *Blade Runners* (1982), *Reckless* (1984), *Splash* (1984), *The Pope of Greenwich Village* (1984), *The Clan of the Cave Bear* (1986), *Legal Eagles* (1986), *Roxanne* (1987), *Wall Street* (1988), *High Spirits* (1988), *Steel Magnolias* (1989), and *Crazy*

People (1990). Her television appearances include a role in the successful telefilm "Paper Dolls" (1982).

Tall, lean and physically fit, in her spare time Daryl enjoys dancing, swimming, and diving. Currently single, she has frequently been seen with Jackson Browne and around New York City with John F. Kennedy, Jr.

Mark Harmon

He was dubbed "The Sexiest Man Alive (1986)" by *People* Magazine and thrust into the national spotlight. After years of toiling on television and in films, Mark Harmon was suddenly a hot household name. The 6-foot, 170-lb. actor with brown hair and blue eyes adorned magazine covers along with television and movie screens. His easygoing style coupled with his "All-American" good looks sold America on him as he pitched beer-making in a series of Coors Beer commercials. Although his fame may have seemed sudden, it was not unexpected. Rather, with Harmon's background, it seemed preordained.

Mark Harmon was born 2 September 1951 in Burbank, California, the son of football player/broadcaster Tom Harmon and actress Elyse Knox. The family also includes Mark's sister, Kelly Harmon, a top spokesmodel, and Mark's niece, actress Tracy Nelson. Harmon's first brush with stardom came during his college days as an All-American quarterback at UCLA, where he graduated with a degree in communications in 1974. From 1975 through 1977, Harmon appeared in numerous guest shots on shows like "Adam-12," "Laverne & Shirley," and "Police Story." Televison has always favored Harmon, casting him as a regular on four different series: the forgettable "Sam" (1978) and "240-Robert" (1979-1980), the romantic lead Fielding Carlyle on NBC's nighttime soap "Flamingo Road" (1980-1982), and the plum role of playboy Dr. Caldwell who eventually contracts AIDS on the acclaimed NBC series "St. Elsewhere" (1983-1986). Harmon also portrayed Sam the astronaut, on part of the controversial "Moonlighting" romantic triangle during the 1986-1987 season. He starred in the TV film "Dillinger" for the 1990-91 season.

The industry recognized his potential as he earned an Emmy

nomination for his performance in the 1977 movie-of-the-week "Eleanor and Franklin: The White House Years." A variety of film and television roles were interwoven between his series commitments, including "Comes a Horseman" (1978), "Little Mo" (1978), "Beyond The Poseidon Adventure" (1979), "Goliath Awaits" (1981), "Intimate Agony" (1983), the charming lead in "The Prince of Bel Air" (1986), and the Depression-era farmer fighting for custody of his children in "After the Promise" (1987-1988). Harmon was featured in the miniseries "Centennial" (1978-1979) and "The Dream Merchants" (1980), but arguably his best role to date has been that of the executed serial killer Ted Bundy in the NBC miniseries "The Deliberate Stranger" (1986). Bundy was a definite departure from Harmon's usual good guy roles. His chilling portrayal of this real-life figure drew critical raves and excellent ratings. Its success helped Harmon secure the lead in three distinctly different feature films. He segued from the California cool teacher wooing Kirstie Alley in the comedy *Summer School* (1987), to the aging ballplayer returning home for his best friend Jodie Foster's funeral in the dramatic *Stealing Home* (1988), to the cop going up against Sean Connery in the police action adventure *The Presidio* (1988), and *Worth Winning* (1989).

Harmon married actress Pam Dawber on 21 March 1987 in Los Angeles. Their son, Sean Thomas, was born 25 April 1988. They reside in California while both pursue individual acting projects. Harmon's hobbies include carpentry; his most ambitious project was building his own home. With his devotion to family and the exciting direction that his career has been taking, it appears the Harmon won't have much time for crafting anything else.

Valerie Harper

Best known for the irrepressible character "Rhoda Morganstern," Valerie Harper has enjoyed a long and varied career in show business spanning the worlds of dance, theatre, television, and film.

Born 22 August 1940 in Suffern, New York, Harper made her professional debut in the corps de ballet at Radio City Music Hall. Musical comedy captured her interest while performing on Broadway in *Li'l Abner*, leading her to study acting with Marcy Tarcai and John Cassavetes' workshop. She continued her dancing while studying, appearing in major stage productions of *Take Me Along* with Jackie Gleason, *Wildcat* with Lucille Ball, and *Subways Are for Sleeping* with Orson Bean and Carol Lawrence. Eventually she became involved with Paul Sills' Second City Troupe and developed her skills by performing in nightclubs, summer stock, and regional theater, including the prestigious Seattle Repertory Company. Live performances included roles in Carl Reiner's *Something Different* and Paul Sills' production of Ovid's *Metamorphosis* and the Tony Award-winning *Story Theatre*.

Television has given Harper her greatest recognition as "Rhoda" and brought her popularity and awards for her efforts. The character debuted on "The Mary Tyler Moore Show" in 1970 and earned her three consecutive Emmy Awards for Outstanding Performance by an Actress in a Supporting Role (in 1970/1971, 1971/1972, 1972/1973). Supporting turned to lead as "Rhoda" premiered as an "MTM" spinoff in 1974. The hit show lasted five years, earning Harper another Emmy—this time as Best Television Actress in a Comedy or Musical (1974/1975). Harper has also been honored with a Golden Globe Award in 1975, the Golden Apple Award from the Hollywood Women's Press Club, Harvard's Hasty Pudding "Woman of the Year" Award, and the Photoplay Gold Medal Award. After "Rhoda's" departure, television continued to welcome Harper's presence. She starred in movie-of-the-weeks for all three networks, ranging from light comedy to serious drama. They included "Drop Out Mother," "Strange Voices," "The Execution," "Farrell for the People," "Don't Go to Sleep" with Ruth Gordon, "Invasion of Privacy," "When The Loving Stops," and the Paul Newman-directed "The Shadow Box." Harper also starred in the Jim Brooks-scripted "Thursday's Game" with Gene Wilder and Ellen Burstyn and the special "The Night of 100 Stars." Feature films explored Harper's comedic side with roles in *Blame It on Rio, Chapter Two, The Last Married Couple in America,* and *Freebie and the Bean*. Returning to her theatre background, Harper toured in *Agnes of God* and still occasionally returns to the Paul Sills' Co. in Los Angeles to perfect her improvisational skills.

Attuned to the needs of less fortunate people, Harper devotes much of her time to the Hunger Project, whose goal is to end world hunger in this century. She is one of the founders of LIFE (Love Is Feeding Everyone), dedicated to ending hunger in Los Angeles, and works with the End Hunger Network, Save the Children, Africare, Oxfam, and the Santa Monica Rape treatment center as well as actively supporting women's rights issues.

Harper marked her return to situation comedy in 1985 with "Valerie," a show she helped create. Her success was marred when

Lorimar Telepictures abruptly fired her. A legal battle ensued, and she eventually won a substantial monetary award in court.

Divorced from first husband Dick Schaal, the 5'6" brown-haired, green-eyed actress married Tony Cacciotti 8 April 1987. They adopted a daughter, Christine, and the three reside in California. Future plans include a comedy series pilot for MTM Productions.

Julie Harris

As a girl, Julie Harris once recalled, "I was very plain, all knobby knees." Despite her mother's intense ambition, Julie was not a glossy deb type. "I had some dates," she says, "but never the ones I wanted . . . the school heroes. . . . " And so she "escaped into acting." "The movies became almost a sickness to me," Julie has said. Sometimes she sat staring at the silver screen of Vivien Leigh and Joan Crawford "all day Saturday and all day Sunday." And at night she lived in the fantasy of becoming "a great star like Bernhardt." Years later, though she lacked the flamboyant life style of Madame Sarah, her special brand of stage magic made her one of the most versatile and widely acclaimed actresses in the American theatre, which is precisely why she was inducted into the Theatre Hall of Fame.

Julie Ann Harris was born 2 December 1925 in Grosse Pointe, Michigan, the daughter of an investment banker. She arrived on Broadway via circuitous routing, which included the finishing schools of Miss Wheeler and Miss Hewitt, as well as Yale Drama School and the Actors Studio. She made her debut in *It's a Gift*, and went on to win more than 20 awards (including two Emmys, five Tonys) for performances in such diverse stage, film, and TV vehicles as *A Member of the Wedding, I Am a Camera* (her first Tony), *The Lark* (five top awards, including a Tony), *Victoria Regina, East of Eden, Little Moon of Alban, The Power and the Glory, Forty Carats* (Tony), *And Miss Reardon Drinks a Little, The Last of Mr. Lincoln* (1973 Tony), and *The Belle of Amherst* (1976 Tony). Beginning in the 1981-1982 television season, she became a regular on the CBS primetime series "Knots Landing." Her character married (actor Red Buttons) and she departed the show in 1988, with the possibility of returning at any time. She also appeared in two telefilms "The Woman He

Loved" (1988) and "Too Good to Be True" (1988) in addition to the Sigourney Weaver film *Gorillas in the Mist* (1988).

Mount Holyoke College awarded Harris an honorary Doctor of Fine Arts degree in 1976. She had earlier received honorary degrees from Smith, LaSalle, Ithaca, and Wayne State, among other institutions. Harris was brought up an Episcopalian, but after her confirmation she did not attend formal church services. "I don't hesitate to say that I found God in the theatre," she told an interviewer for *The Christian Science Monitor* in 1975. In 1977 Julie Harris married William Carroll, a writer. She had two earlier marriages, in 1946 to Jay Julien, a lawyer and producer whom she divorced in 1954, and to stage manager Manning Gurian from 1954 to 1967 (one son, Peter Allen Gurian). Reading 19th-century American literature is one of Harris' favorite pastimes, as well as tennis and cooking.

Richard Harris

"Why should a man know exactly who he is?" asks Richard Harris. "I've no idea who I am. I'm five people, and each of them is fighting the other four." He is so aggressively professional, with the tongue (and capacity) of a Behan and the talent of a latter-day Olivier, that his offstage antics have brought him preciptiously close to being tagged as that most loathsome of Gaels, "a professional Irishman." But by sheer force of personality and staggering versatility, he manages to disarm his critics and fortify his friends.

Born 1 October 1930 in Limerick ("When I'm in trouble, I'm an Irishman. When I turn in a good performance I'm an Englishman"), he rejected a job with his family's flour mill business to pursue acting studies at London Academy (having been turned down by the August Royal Academy of Dramatic Art). While still in school he produced and acted in a production of Brendan Behan's *The Quare Fellow*, and lost every penny of his investment.

Following appearances with Joan Littlewood's Theater Workshop in *A View from the Bridge* and *Macbeth*, he turned to the screen; his first part was in *Shake Hands with the Devil*, a film starring Jimmy Cagney about the IRA, followed by *The Guns of Navarone* and *Mutiny on the Bounty*. But it wasn't until his stunning performance in 1963 as an inarticulate rugby player in *This Sporting Life* (Oscar nomination) that he reached the pinnacle as a dramatic actor. He turned to musicals in 1967 as King Arthur in *Camelot*, and that in turn led to a singing career ("no Irishman need be taught to sing"), resulting in, among others, a haunting version of "MacArthur Park." He has mixed a film career (*Cromwell, The Hero, A Man Called Horse*) with a successful concert career, combining songs and poetry. (In 1988 he appeared on stage at Carnegie Hall, performing with The Chieftains). "Poetry is bred in my loins," admits Harris. "I can't remember when I first started writing it, maybe when I was 5 or 6, but I only began writing it down recently." His book of poetry, *In the Membership of My Days* (1974), was recorded with his sons assisting in the reading. Although he continues his devotion to poetry, he received good notices from the literary reviewers for his 1982 thriller, *Honor Bound*.

Originally taking over the role of King Arthur for his ailing friend, Richard Burton, Harris' triumphant national tour in *Camelot* (climaxing in Broadway and television productions) was received with glowing notices. When Frank Rich did not feed the flame in his 1981 *New York Times* review, Harris snorted: "He doesn't deserve a job. He couldn't even get a job with the *Liverpool Legend*. Send him off to the *Cardiff Courier*." He reprised his role in *Camelot* in 1988 for another stage production.

"I want to do *Hamlet* before I'm too old, to do *Coriolanus, Macbeth, Oedipus*, Marlowe's *Edward II*. I'm going to spend the rest of my acting career basically in the theatre now," admitted Harris in a 1982 interview. "I don't know what's ahead but the night and the fog. When I was coming along in the mid-50s, I used to steal sugar lumps to live on. Remember I never quit. They haven't heard the last of Richard Harris, and neither have you." In 1989 he filmed *The Three Penny Opera* with Raul Julia.

Mary Hart

She's perky, pretty, wholesome and ambitious. Possessing an All-American, Doris Day kind of attitude, Mary confesses, "Sometimes I must seem like the world's biggest cornball, but that's who I am, and what I do." Well, corny or not, this acclaimed singer, dancer, actress and former beauty queen—with the 2 million dollar legs (insured by Lloyds of London)—has won her way into America's hearts.

Mary Hart was born in Sioux Falls, South Dakota, on 8 November 1950, the daughter of a homemaker and an executive with a farm equipment manufacturer. She developed a love for Broadway show tunes and classical music at an early age. While still a young child, Mary and her family moved to Europe, where they lived for 11 years. Upon returning, Mary attended a Lutheran college in Sioux Falls. In 1970, Mary entered and won the Miss South Dakota Beauty Pagent. A few years later, she began her career teaching high school English while teaching piano and doing community theatre on the side. Shortly afterward (while still teaching), she was approached to host a daily talk show on cable television. Her talent was quickly discovered, and she was asked to host a daily program on a network affiliate in Sioux Falls. Moving on, Mary took a position hosting

radio and TV shows in Cedar Rapids, Iowa, and later Oklahoma City, where she co-hosted as well as produced the popular daytime talk show "Danny's Day." Continuing to move up the entertainment ladder, Mary became the host of "PM Magazine" in Los Angeles, followed by the nationally televised but short-lived "Regis Philbin Show." By now, her talent was known nationally, and she was asked to join "Entertainment Tonight" as the weekend co-host in 1981. Within weeks she was moved to the daily segment of the show. Her other television credits include the miniseries "Hollywood Wives," "Circus of the Stars," and guest appearances on "Good Morning America" and "David Letterman," in addition to hosting the Tournament of Roses Parade and the Macy's Thanksgiving Day Parade, for both of which she received an Emmy nomination. Mary made her musical debut on ABC's "Dolly," and has since been heard singing the National Anthem at Dodger Stadium, and before a Lakers-Celtics game. In addition Mary has been a headliner dancer and singer, making her Vegas debut in 1988 at the Golden Nugget as well as performing at Resorts International in Atlantic City. Hart is also part owner of the Los Angeles video production company Custom's Last Stand.

Mary Hart wed Burt Sugarman on 8 April 1989. The couple reside in California.

Mariette Hartley

"I am comfortable with my life," Mariette Hartley has said. And well she should be. The Emmy Award-winning actress (for her guest starring role in "The Incredible Hulk") on stage, screen, and television has starred in everything from Shakespeare (*Measure for Measure* for the famed Joseph Papp "Shake-

speare Festival in the Park" in New York), to feature films (Peckinpah's *Ride in the Country*), to television (as Claire Morton in the series "Peyton Place"), to stage (*Chemin de Fer*, co-starring Cronyn and Tandy). The multi-dimensional Hartley extended her credits by co-hosting the 1987 "CBS Morning Program", winning three CLIO Advertising Awards in 1979 through 1981 for her Polaroid commercials with James Garner, and singing in a summer stock production of *The King and I*, which led to her autobiographical one woman show, with comedy and music, that Hartley considers to be "a work in progress." In 1987, as a tribute to her various industry contributions, Hartley's star was installed on the Hollywood Walk of Fame.

Born 21 June 1940 in New York City, Hartley was bitten early by the "creative" bug. The pull to the theatre was too irresistible for her to consider doing anything else. At fifteen, Hartley won a full tuition drama scholarship at Carnegie Tech in Pittsburgh. When she was just sixteen, Hartley left school to appear in Chicago in *Merchant of Venice*, then went to New York for *Measure for Measure*, followed by a national tour with the Stratford Shakespeare Festival, which culminated with her first appearance in Los Angeles. Now bitten by the screen bug, Hartley tried Hollywood and Peckinpah signed her for her first film *Ride the High Country* opposite Randolph Scott and Joel McCrea before MGM grabbed her and signed her a seven-year contract. Television soon followed. After her first exposure as Leslie Nielson's wife on "Peyton Place," Hartley was given her own series "The Hero," which folded after the first thirteen weeks. When she looks back, Hartley states, "It was a lovely series, but we were ten years ahead of our time." That original draw to the theatre was still pulling Hartley, so she returned to the stage in her first comedy, *Happiness Bench*, followed by the French farce *Chemin De Fer*. With her diversified talents it's not surprising that Hartley has a total of six Emmy nominations to her credit for "Rockford Files," two TV movies, and "Goodnight Beantown" plus a Golden Apple Award in 1979 from the Hollywood Woman's Press Club.

Married to French producer and director Patrick Boyriven and the mother of two, Sean (born in 1975) and Justine (born in 1978), Hartley was named in 1984 Outstanding Mother of the Year by the Mother's Day Committee. She is working on her autobiography and has formed her own production company, Maraday Productions, with her manager Arlene L. Dayton. The granddaughter of John B.

Watson, internationally renowned psychiatrist who founded the school of psychology known as behaviorism, is also an active and dedicated supporter of a variety of humanitarian organizations (M.A.D.D., SOJURN, and the Children's Museum). Always in demand, Hartley says she is "comfortable with my life."

Lisa Hartman

Her short skirts, tight pants, and lace blouses have set fashion heads turning and men's hearts fluttering. She's played the daughter of a witch, a reincarnated singer, and a district attorney posing as a hooker. The TV and film roles keep rolling in, yet this actress prefers pursuing her dream goal. Lisa Hartman wants to crack the record chart; she would like a hit record. And why not? In 1977 her first album, *Lisa Hartman*, was released on CBS/Kirshner records and *Cash Box* claimed, "Ms. Hartman displays a talent and a poise far beyond her 19 years." When her second album, *Hold On*, came out in 1979, *Billboard* chose her as a recommended pick, saying "She's a versatile, pleasing vocalist." Both albums established a select group of music fans for Lisa, but not the widespread acceptance she hoped to achieve. In the interim, Hartman struck gold in the TV medium and starred in her own series "Tabitha," her own ABC variety special, a five-hour miniseries of "Valley of the Dolls," and then landed a leading role in the CBS nighttime soap "Knots Landing" (1982) playing a rock-roll singer, Ciji Dunne. In this part, she was able to express her acting abilities alongside a record release. She says "the producers agreed to let me do the songs from my *Letterock* album, which had first been released by RCA in 1982. I loved playing Ciji, we both shared the same goal: to have a hit record." The public loved her portrayal of Ciji Dunne too; when her character was killed off in the storyline, the writers resurrected Lisa in another role on the same show. An unusual TV twist!

Lisa Hartman was born in Houston, Texas, on 1 June (circa 1956). Her father was an actor/singer and her mother a producer of television shows. She made her debut at the age of four, in her father's stage act. When she was seven, her family moved to New York City for a two-year period where Lisa was attracted to the

Broadway lights. After graduating from the High School of Performing Arts, Lisa put together a nightclub act and was eventually
spotted by producer Jeff Barry. Recent TV films include the miniseries "Roses Are for the Rich" (1986), about a woman's obsession
for revenge, and "The Sex Tapes" (1988), where Hartman played a
mini-skirted district attorney trying to find a murderer involved
with homemade sexual video tapes. In 1984 she appeared in the
motion picture re-make of *Where the Boys Are*.

Lisa remains singles and resides in California, while pursuing
her dreams as a singer. Her last album, *Til My Heart Stops* (1988),
only dented the airwaves—not enough to satisfy Hartman. As she
sang on her 1979 record, "Hold On I'm Comin'," with each release
Lisa Hartman is coming closer to her dream.

Goldie Hawn

O n "Laugh In" in 1968 she
"watched helplessly as her
lines seem to flutter out of reach. She
embodied the trusting excitement of a
baby seeing a cat for the first time. She
was a dumb blond, but she was 'learning.' She would surely get it right next
time. She was irresistible." So chants
Cathleen Schine who interviewed the
star for *Vogue* in 1984.

Born Goldie Jean Hawn in Washington, D.C., 2 November 1945, she
was named after a late great aunt whom
she still regards as a guardian angel. ("I
can remember almost all of my childhood, and all the memories are
pleasant. There was no conflict, no push, and no competition in my
family.") Studying drama at American University, she paid her
tuition by operating a dance school. When she reached New York,
she landed a job as a can-can dancer at the World's Fair. A
depressing interlude of go-go dancing in cages led to a stint as a
chorus girl in Las Vegas. ("It was the saddest time of my life. I woke
up one morning with a hunch I would do better in Los Angeles. I left
right away.") She was hired for Rowan and Martin's "Laugh-In"
after producer George Schlatter saw her in "Good Morning World,"
an ABC bomb.

She married Gus Trikonis in 1969 when she was a fledgling
dancer in New York city and he a struggling movie-director. Their
starving-in-a-garret existence was very romantic but the romance

ceased when she was hired for "Laugh-In" and sudden stardom threw the relationship out of kilter. After four years of stresses and strains, the star and the would-be director agreed to divorce. In 1975 she married Bill Hudson of the Hudson Brothers comedy group; the couple had three children, Oliver, Kate, and Garry. That marriage fell apart, and today Goldie is raising her children and living with actor Kurt Russell (one child together, Wyatt, born 10 July 1986). Among her post-*Cactus Flower* (1969; Academy Award for Best Supporting Actress) films are *Butterflies Are Free* (1971), *Shampoo* (1975), *Foul Play* (1978), *Private Benjamin* (1980), *Best Friends* (1982), *Swing Shift* (1984), *Protocol* (1984), *Wildcats* (1986), *Overboard* (1987), and *Last Wish* (1988).

Helen Hayes

Already a legend in her lifetime, with *two* Broadway theatres named after her (when the first, on 46th Street, was razed in 1984 to make way for a new hotel, the second, on 44th Street, was christened immediately to honor "the first lady of the American theatre"), she has been hailed by producer Robert Whitehead as "a great actress because she is a great woman." And with applause ever roaring in her ears, she has said, "The greatest reward of acting is that one moment of miracle when you and the audience get together." Hayes' favorite tribute came from her playwright husband, the late Charles MacArthur. "She has," he said, "a star on her forehead."

Born Helen Hayes Brown in Washington, D.C., 10 October 1900, she attended dancing school to correct pigeon-toes. After *Dear Brutus* (1919) and *Clarence* (1920), she continued playing comedy ingenue roles "until," she sighs, "I was squeezing cuteness out of my greasepaint tubes and scooping charm out of my cold cream jars. It became a compulsion to get away from all that." She then began studying acting seriously ("acting talent is an instinct for understanding the human heart"), and scored enormous successes in *What Every Woman Knows* (1926), *Coquette* (1927), *Mary of Scotland* (1933), and later, *Mrs. McThing, The Skin of Our Teeth, The Glass Menagerie, Time Remembered, A Touch of the Poet, The Front Page,* and *Harvey.* Films include *The Sin of Madelon Claudet* (1931, Oscar),

Arrowsmith, A Farewell to Arms (1932), *Anastasia* (1956), and *Airport* (1970, another Oscar). Although she won't name her favorite play ("It's like asking a mother which of her children is her favorite"), she has said of *Victoria Regina*, "It was a beautiful friendship." Her interpretation of O'Neill's *Long Day's Journey Into Night* (1971) garnered the following from *New York Times*'s critic Walter Kerr: "The standing ovation she received at the performance I saw was in order, and not simply because she has spent a lifetime being Helen Hayes. It was Eugene O'Neill she was working for, first to last."

Since her retirement from the stage in 1971 (because of an allergic reaction to stage dust), Hayes has devoted her time to television, radio, writing and public service. Some of her TV performances include the series, "The Snoop Sisters" (with Mildred Natwick), "A Family Upside Down" (with Fred Astaire), "A Caribbean Mystery," and several documentaries, among them "Miles to Go Before We Sleep" (Peabody Award) and "No Place Like Home." Her books include *A Gift of Joy* (1965), *On Reflection* (1968), *Twice Over Lightly* (1971, in collaboration with Anita Loos), *Loving Life* (1987, with Marion Gladney), and *Where the Truth Lies* (1988).

In 1929 Helen Hayes met the fun-loving Charles MacArthur (*The Front Page*) at a cocktail party. He passed her some peanuts, with the much-quoted remark, "I wish these were emeralds." Their actress daughter, Mary, died of polio in 1949; their adopted son, James, is an actor (TV's "Hawaii Five-O"). Among her many honors was Helen Hayes' salute from the Kennedy Center in Washington for an "Extraordinary Lifetime of Contribution to American Culture Through the Performing Arts." In 1984, the U.S. Mint struck a commemorative gold coin bearing her likeness and in 1987 she was saluted in a special ceremony during which she placed her footprints and signature in cement on the sidewalk outside the theatre on West 44th Street (NYC) named in her honor. In 1988 she was presented with the National Medal of Arts by President Reagan at the White House.

Florence Henderson

She is as versatile as she is talented. Her career has spanned over three decades of work in stage, screen, and television. Florence has done everything from nightclub entertainer, television hostess, country recording artist, and actress to author. The commitment and professionalism she has for her work makes her one of the most respected of today's entertainers.

She was born on 14 February 1934 in Dale, Indiana, and was the

daughter of a tobacco sharecropper. The youngest of ten, she along with her siblings helped raise tobacco in Owensboro, Kentucky, where she spent her childhood. After attending grade school at the St. Francis Academy in Owensboro, she entered New York's prestigious American Academy of Dramatic Arts at age seventeen. While still at the Academy, Florence landed her first part in the Broadway production of *Wish You Were Here* (1952), a Joshua Logan musical. Catching the eye of Rodgers and Hammerstein, she was cast to
play the lead part in *Oklahoma* (1952-1953). Following *Oklahoma* she appeared for a brief stint in *The Great Waltz* with the Civic Light Opera of Los Angeles. She then returned to Broadway to perform in the lead role in *Fanny* (1954), which ran for 19 months; *The Sound of Music* (1961); and *The Girl Who Came to Supper* (1963). Following her Broadway performances, she played the lead role in *South Pacific* at the New York State Theater in Lincoln Center (1967). Not limiting herself to stage, she made her first film, *The Song of Norway*, in 1970, and it brought her international exposure. Her television appearances began as frequent talk show guest bookings; she appeared with such hosts as Ed Sullivan, Bing Crosby, Dick Cavett, Merv Griffin and Phil Donahue. Florence was the first woman ever to host the "Tonight Show." She is best known on television, though, as Carol Brady in one of the longest-running situation comedies "The Brady Bunch" (1969-1974). Several "Brady Bunch" specials have run over the years, including "The Brady Bunch Hour" (1977) and "A Very Brady Christmas" (1988). She has also made regular appearances on such shows as "Murder, She Wrote," "The Love Boat," "Fantasy Island," and "It's Garry Shandling's Show." Florence also hosts her own program, "Country Kitchen," which has been running for four years on the Nashville Network. The response to her show has been so enthusiastic that it prompted her to write a cookbook entitled *A Little Cooking, A Little Talking and a Whole Lotta Fun*. Even with her hectic schedule, Florence still finds time to participate in charitable activities, including hosting the annual United Cerebral Palsy Telethon, working with the City of Hope, and helping the House Ear Institute.

Florence has four children from her first marriage to Ira Bernstein (married 9 January 1956): Barbara (1956), Joey (1960), Robert Norman (1963), and Elizabeth (1966). The couple later divorced. She married John Kappas on 4 August 1987.

Audrey Hepburn

She was a gracefully elfin 22 when the French novelist Colette spied her in Monte Carlo on the set of an English movie and said to herself, "There is Gigi." That afternoon she relayed the information to Gilbert Miller who subsequently offered Hepburn the part in the Broadway play. So the slender Belgian-born ballet student came to New York, charmed everyone she met and was whisked off to Hollywood to become a dainty legend. She collected an Oscar for her first American film, *Roman Holiday* (1953), and wove her "alternately regal and childlike" way through such box-office blockbusters as *Sabrina* (1954), *Funny Face* (1956), *Nun's Story* (1959) and *Breakfast at Tiffany's* (1960) before finding herself in the midst of her only big Hollywood brouhaha for being chosen over Julie Andrews to play Eliza Doolittle in the screen version of *My Fair Lady* (1963). Post-Eliza assignments have included *Two for the Road* (1966), *Wait Until Dark* (1967), *Robin and Marion* (1976), *Bloodline* (1979), and *They All Laughed* (1981).

Born Audrey Hepburn-Ruston (her mother was a Dutch Baroness) on 4 May 1929 in Brussels, she grew up in Holland during the German occupation and acted as a courier for the Dutch Resistance during World War II. "When I was a little girl," she recalled later, "my nose wasn't pretty and I was terribly thin. I was sickly too, and quite miserable about my prospects." Nevertheless, she studied ballet in Amsterdam and headed for London in 1948 in search of a stage career. In addition to her 1951 Broadway triumph in *Gigi*, she collected a Tony for her 1954 appearance in the Jean Giraudoux play *Ondine* and later married her co-star Mel Ferrer (a son, Sean, was born in 1960).

Her biography, written by Ian Woodward, was published in 1984 (St. Martins Press). Once the second-highest paid actress in films (Elizabeth Taylor being the first), she is now content with a less frenzied lifestyle and lives in Switzerland with her son Luca (born 1970) by her second husband, psychiatrist Andrea Dotti, from whom she is divorced. Named as a Special Ambassador for UNICEF, Hepburn spends her free time devoted to the charity. During the 1986-1987 television season she appeared in the ABC telefilm "Here's a Thief, There's a Thief."

Katharine Hepburn

"I 've never written a diary. . . . But there are some happenings you can't forget. There they are. A series of facts—pictures—realities. This happened to me with *The African Queen*. I remember it in minute detail—I can see every second of its making and of me at the time. . . . So here it is . . . thirty-odd years after the fact." So begins the fascinating introduction to Katharine Hepburn's memoir, *The Making of the African Queen; or How I Went to Africa with Bogart, Bacall and Huston and Almost Lost My Mind*. Charged with the adven-

ture of trekking to Africa and the character of the "crazy, psalm-singin' skinny old maid" who cleverly maneuvers the rummy river-boat skipper into action with the WWI German gunboat, Hepburn leaped at the challenge of jockeying the unique giant talents and personalities of director John Huston and actor Humphrey Bogart (both drinking buddies). Her account of daily routines, the magnificence and mystique as well as the muck and mire of Africa are recorded with total recall, and Hepburn's candor and humor (about herself as well as the area and the entourage) make it a rare and winning piece of reportage. It's a fascinating tribute to her colleagues and rip-roaring movies like "they used to be." Based on the life of John Huston, Clint Eastwood's 1990 movie *White Hunter, Black Heart* is reported to include footage evoking the filming of *The African Queen*, with Marisa Berenson as the Katharine Hepburn character.

She was born Katharine Houghton Hepburn on 8 November 1909 into a hyperactive, unconventional, upper-class Hartford family. ("My parents were much more fascinating people, than I am.") Her father was a urologist and pioneer in social hygiene who insisted that his five youngsters start out every day with a cold shower; her mother was an early women's libber battling for votes and birth control. "They gave me freedom from fear," Hepburn said in a television interview. (She dedicated her book to them.) And about her role in *On Golden Pond*: "The woman reminded me very much of my mother. She was tough, but she was infinitely kind, and brilliant. But she wasn't afraid to say: 'You're a bore.'" It was a surprise to no one when, after Bryn Mawr (and after a brief marriage to a Philadelphian named Ogden Smith), the red haired Hartford hell-raiser headed for Broadway. Her first big success, playing a leggy Amazon in *The Warrior's Husband* (1932), catapulted her west into the arms of RKO, where—starting her film career as John Barrymore's daughter in *Bill of Divorcement* (1932), and continuing it in *Little Women* (1933), *The Little Minister* (1934), *Alice Adams* (1935), *Mary of Scotland* (1936), *Stage Door* (1937), and others—she turned in often brilliant perfomances but carried on a running battle with autograph hunters and the Hollywood press corps and earned the nickname of "Katherine of Arrogance" for her highhandedness off screen. She is the first actress to receive four Academy Awards for Best Performance by an Actress.

Prior to her rebirth as a golden girl in Philip Barry's Hepburn-tailored *Philadelphia Story*, five of her six previous films were losers. Then she starred in *Woman of the Year* (1942), which clinched her comeback and, even more importantly, marked the debut of what was to develop into one of Hollywood's most remarkable associations, her relationship with Spencer Tracy. She describes Tracy as a "brilliant actor." Says Hepburn, "I discovered my hands and he discovered his soul." The two co-starred in eight films in the next twelve years, nearly all of them wonderful: among them, *Without Love* (1945), *State of the Union* (1948), *Adam's Rib* (1949), *Pat and Mike* (1952), and *Desk Set* (1957). Interspersed among these releases was her superb rendition of a proper lady missionary mixed up with Humphrey Bogart in the Congo in *The African Queen* (1951). Busy in the 1950's in Shakespeare and Shaw, (*As You Like It, The Millionairess*), she soared to greatness again in 1962 in the film version of Eugene O'Neill's anguished memoir, *Long Day's Journey into Night*, and then entered a quiescent period during which she focused most of her energies on caring for an ailing Tracy. "I have had twenty years of perfect companionship with a man among men," she told a reporter in 1963. "He's a rock and a protection. I've never regretted it." *Guess Who's Coming to Dinner* was her ninth and last film with Tracy. She did not desert the stage and has returned in several productions on Broadway: *Coco, A Matter of Gravity,* and *West Side Waltz.*

Hepburn is boundlessly energetic and seemingly indestructible. She's been called the "unchallenged first lady of American cinema." "If you survive you become a legend. I'm a legend because I've survived over a long period of time," she once said. "I'm revered rather like an old building."

Pee-wee Herman

"**I** had a little one inch harmonica that said 'Pee-wee' on it," Paul Reubens (better known as Pee-Wee Herman) says. "I just loved the way it sounded. . . . Growing up I knew a kid who was extremely obnoxious . . . and his last name was Herman. And the rest is history."

The eldest of Milton and Judy Rubenfeld's three children, Paul was born in Peekskill, New York in July 1952; the family moved to Sarasota, Florida during Paul's childhood years. While Paul entertained friends in his "theater," Milton and Judy operated a retail lamp store. A local production of Herb Gardner's *A Thousand Clowns* enticed eleven-year-old Paul to audition for a major role. By the start of high school, Paul was performing regularly in summer stock at Florida's Apollo State Theater. He attended a program for highly gifted thespians one summer where he set himself apart when his skills earned him the honor of the workshop's best actor after his lead performance in their production of *David and Lisa*. Paul was off to Boston University after graduation. Remaining for only two semesters, he decided to attend an institution of higher education that would further help him develop his talents. Transferring to the California Institute of the Arts at Valencia in 1971, Paul wowed audiences with his versatility in their production of *The Death of Jesse James*, in which he portrayed several minor characters. Convinced that southern California was the place where he could accomplish his dream, Paul remained there after his graduation from the institute in 1975. Supporting himself with odd jobs, he changed his surname to Reubens and joined a comedy improvisation troupe called the Groundlings who performed regularly at a small L.A. venue called the Groundling Theater. For his act, Paul developed off-beat characters; one such character was a junk food junkie whose form of communication was uncouth grunts. During those years he was a frequent contestant on Chuck Barris' "The Gong Show," but he never received the dubious honor of worst act. In 1979 he tried out a character that became the launching pad to stardom. Clad in bow tie and shrunken suit, Paul Reubens evolved into Pee-wee Herman. Originally designed as a five-minute skit which parodied such children's entertainers as Captain Kangaroo and Mister Rogers, Pee-wee was received so enthusiastically that Paul was encouraged to lengthen his repertoire. In 1980 Pee-wee moved to the Roxy Theater in L.A. where his "Pee-wee Herman Party" ran for a year. HBO taped the performance and ran it in 1982. Pee-wee's movie debut came in 1980 as a minor role in *The Blues*

Brothers. In 1981 Pee-wee was temporarily shelved and Paul appeared as a punked-out cocaine demon in *Cheech and Chong's Nice Dream.*

On a wider scale, Pee-wee appeared frequently on NBC's "Late Night With David Letterman" and on "The Tonight Show" when Joan Rivers would substitute for Johnny Carson. In 1983 he appeared at the Manhattan comedy club Caroline's where his act was billed as "Paul Reubens Presents Pee-wee Herman." A sold-out performance for "Pee-wee Herman's Party" at Carnegie Hall in New York was the final catylast for the fine line drawn between Paul Reubens and Pee-wee Herman. His 1985 feature film *Pee-wee's Big Adventure* surprisingly became a box office hit among adults as well as children. After that success Pee-wee became the third comic to win the Harvard Lampoon's Elmer Award. In the fall of 1986 Pee-wee created a Saturday morning children's program on CBS-TV "Pee-wee's Playhouse." The expensive venture made daytime television history by being the only show to receive over twenty Emmy nominations. In its first year it received twelve nominations and won six Emmys. Having created an environment where children are encouraged to use their creativity, Pee-wee's Playhouse also teaches them that it's okay to be different. *Pee-wee's Big Top* was his second feature film in 1988. In the works for Pee-wee is an album of pop songs featuring some of the music world's top artists and an amusement park appropriately named "Pee-weeland."

Pee-wee Herman loves to visit New York but is dedicated to his home in Los Angeles.

Werner Herzog

"**F**ilm is not the art of scholars but of illiterates," says the man often considered the leading figure in West Germany's critically acclaimed new wave of cinema. Yet ironically his deeply personal films are frequently impenetrable to viewers. Sometimes painfully slow and vague, his work has nevertheless been acclaimed on the art house and festival circuits for its originality and its visually beautiful, if disturbing, imagery. His characters are usually tortured, aimless and confused, sometimes deformed and grotesque. *Even Dwarfs Started Small* (1970) had a cast consisting totally of midgets and dwarfs. For *Heart of Glass* (1976) he had his entire cast put under hypnosis to achieve a stylized portrayal of hallucination and madness. He's a visionary who explores the essence of humanity by depicting it at its most precarious extremes in some of the world's most exotic, remote locales. His two best-known works are based on bizarre historical incidents. Set in the 16th century, the ironic *Aguirre,the Wrath of God* (1973) is about Pizarro's mutinous, power-mad lieutenant who led a small band of followers to destruction in the Amazon jungles on a futile quest for El Dorado. *The Mystery of Kasper Hauser* (aka *Every Man for Himself and God Against All;* 1974), a parable of innocence destroyed, is based on the story of the 19th-century young man of Nuremberg who became a public oddity after apparently spending his entire youth locked in a cellar. The latter film starred Bruno S., a compelling but emotionally damaged man who had been placed in an asylum for mentally retarded children by his prostitute mother at age three, although he was in no way retarded. He stayed there for ten years, and then spent the next 20 in and out of hospitals, reformatories, and prisons. Although he had never acted, "it didn't take too long for me to convince him to take the part," the director says, "because he understood right away that it was about him, too."

Born Werner H. Stipetic in Munich, Germany, 6 September 1942, he was taken a few months later by his mother to a small village about 60 miles away in the Bavarian mountains to escape the Allied bombing of Munich. "I was very much alone in my early childhood," he recalls. "I was quite silent, and wouldn't speak for days. My parents thought I was insane, or retarded. I was very dangerous, my character was peculiar; it was almost as if I had rabies." His parents divorced when he was young and at age 12 he moved back to Munich with his mother and two brothers where they lived in abject poverty sharing a single room. As a teenager he traveled widely, wrote poetry and screenplays, and decided to become a filmmaker. After graduating from school (as a mediocre student) in 1961, he went to the U.S., where he lived in Pittsburgh and supported himself by working in a steel factory, parking cars, and riding in a rodeo. Eventually two of his film shorts—admittedly shot with a stolen 35mm camera—reaped prizes at international festivals. In 1967, in Crete, he directed his first feature, *Sign of Life.* His other films include: *Stroszek* (1977), filmed mostly in Wisconsin, about a trio of born losers—one played by Bruno S.—who leave West Germany with vain hopes for a better life in the U.S.; *Nosferatu* (1979), his remake of Murnau's vampire classic; *Woszeck* (1979), from Buchner's play; *Fitzcarraldo* (1982); and *Cobra Verde* (1988). The last four starred Klaus Kinski, who had played Aguirre so memorably.

Uncompromisingly individualistic in his (generally low budget) film-making and a loner by temperament, he has sometimes been described as a nineteenth-century romantic, but he insists that he is closest in spirit and aesthetics to the late Middle Ages. In his teens he had a brief flirtation with Roman Catholism. His conversion upset his militantly atheistic father. "Since I had become so deeply involved in religion, I have become much more violently against it." He and his wife Martje (married in 1966) are the parents of a son, Rudolph Amos Achmed, whom he calls "Burro" and whom he has instructed to call him "Herzog."

Charlton Heston

Though best known for such larger-than-life roles as Moses (*Ten Commandments*, 1957), Judah (*Ben Hur*, 1959 Best Actor Oscar), and Michelangelo (*The Agony and the Ecstacy*, 1965), this Hollywood veteran of more than 50 films has starred in contemporary dramas as well as historical spectaculars. He says the epic roles taught him humility. "When you're playing Moses, you go to your hotel and try to part the water in the bathtub. When it doesn't part, you feel pretty humble." In recent years, however, with the fervor of a Moses, Heston has become a leading force in Hollywood politics, repeatedly locking horns with ex-Screen Actors Guild president Edward Asner over Asner's public political statements. SAG's board "has no right to set our position on save-the-whales or gun control or Israel," declares Heston, a former six-term guild president who now heads a conservative "watchdog" group called Actors Working for an Actors Guild. While following in the footsteps of several illustrious ex-SAG presidents who have since found a larger political stage (George Murphy, John Gavin, Ronald Reagan), Heston has disclaimed ambitions for a political career. "I've played three presidents, three saints, two geniuses. That should satisfy any man."

Born 4 October 1923 in Evanston, Ill., Chuck Heston was bitten by the acting bug at the tender age of five after appearing in a school play and can't remember ever wanting to be anything but an actor. (Charlton was his mother's maiden name; Heston was his stepfather's name.) "I had what must be a relatively unique childhood for my generation." He recalls "a one room school with 13 pupils in eight grades, three of whom were my cousins." Raised in Michigan timber country in the town of St. Helen (pop. 120), he moved to Winnetka, Ill., and prepared for the stage at Northwestern's School of Speech (classmates included Patricia Neal, Cloris Leachman). After a stint in the Air Corps, he headed for Broadway, first supporting himself as a model and attracting his first major notice as an actor in 1947 with Katharine Cornell in *Antony and Cleopatra*—an auspicious Broadway debut. During the run of the play, he appeared in a number of "live" TV dramas. "It was all set up for us," he recalls. "In the first 16 months of 'Studio One,' I did *Taming of the Shrew, Wuthering Heights, Of Human Bondage, MacBeth, Jane Eyre, Julius Caesar*. Now I submit the actor doesn't exist who can't make an impression in one of those parts." Making an impression on Hollywood, he appeared in Hal Wallis' *Dark City* (1950) and entered the big time in Cecil B. DeMille's big-top spectacular, *The Greatest Show on Earth* (1963). Other films include *El Cid, The Greatest Story Ever Told, The President's Lady, Planet of the Apes, Airport,* and *Mother Lode*, which was directed by Heston and written by his son. Returning to TV drama in the 1980s, he starred in CBS's mini-series "Chiefs" and in "Nairobi Affair" (1984). In 1985, he directed and starred in *The Caine Mutiny Court Martial* in London's West End and returned to television as Jason Colby, the patriarch of "Dynasty II: The Colbys of California." In 1978, Heston received the Jean Hersholt Humanitarian Award from the Academy of Motion Picture Arts and Sciences and that same year published *The Actor's Life—Journals, 1956-1976*. He's a frequent performer at the Ahmanson Theatre in Los Angeles. He is married to Lydia Clarke, whom he met at Northwestern (two children).

Gregory Hines

"**M**ost people don't know what tap dancing is today. They've never seen it in a contemporary light. The image of a tap dancer is still someone in a top hat and tails dancing up a shiny black lacquer staircase. We need to shake that up." Gregory Hines would like to educate the public on a form of dancing that's been put on the back burner in recent years. His 1989 film, *Tap,* was a dream come true for Hines, co-star Sammy Davis Jr., newcomer Suzanne Douglas, and a stellar line up of master hoofers from tap's "heyday."

Born on Valentine's Day 1946 in New York City, young Gregory was accessible to the artistic benefits the Big Apple offers. Along with his brother, Maurice, he began his dance instruction under the tutelage of tap teacher Henry LeTang. When Gregory turned 5 years old the two brothers teamed up as the "Hines Kids" (1949-1955) and started performing in nightclubs and theatres around the country. These appearances afforded them the opportunity of watching such dance legends as "Honi" Coles, Sandman Sims, The Nicholas Brothers, and Teddy Hale from an insider's view. As they matured, the brothers renamed themselves the "Hines Brothers" (1955-1963); when Gregory was 18 his father, Maurice, joined the act and they became known as "Hines, Hines and Dad" (1963-1973). The family trio toured the U.S. and Europe and were seen on the "Tonight Show." Eventually feeling burned out, Gregory quit the tour and headed for Venice, California, where he formed a jazz-rock band "Severance." He stayed on the West Coast for six years, then upon his return to New York he landed a part in *The Last Minstrel Show* (closed in Philadelphia), followed by the lead in *Eubie* on Broadway—a vehicle earning him a Tony nomination. With his stage acceptance certified, Gregory decided to branch out in other areas of show biz. Some movies include: *Deal of the Century* (1983), *The Cotton Club* (1985), *Running Scared* (1985), and *White Knights* (1985; co-starred with Baryshnikov). Hit Broadway shows include: *Comin' Uptown* (1980), *Sophisticated Ladies* (1981), and *I Love Liberty* (1981-1982). He has accumulated three Tony nominations (1979, 1980, 1981), a Theatre World Award, and an Emmy nomination for an appearance on the "Motown Apollo" TV special. Although he is a diversified showman, Hines insists: "I am a tapper. That's the way I think of myself." In 1988 he released his first album as a solo performer and takes his club act on the road in between new movie roles.

After his first marriage failed (two children), he married Pamela Koslow in 1981. They have one son, Zachary, and this trio happily resides together in New York City.

Judd Hirsch

As a junior engineer, he couldn't hold down a job. Eventually he turned to acting. "I'd started to look around me, to read, to go to plays, and actors fascinated me. Wow! Guys who could, through their work, have some kind of an effect on society. The instant I enrolled in acting school and stepped on a stage to do a scene in front of people, I knew I'd found a home."

Although he was received with acclaim on and off Broadway in shows such as *Barefoot in the Park; Scuba Duba; Knock, Knock* and *The Hot L Baltimore,* Hirsch claims that his big break came as a result of a television movie made in 1974 called "The Law." His performance won him an Emmy and led to further television opportunities. He appeared as a regular on the series "Delvecchio," had a part in the film *King of the Gypsies* and won a second Emmy for a one-shot appearance on "Rhoda." Neil Simon wrote *Chapter Two* for him, and his work as the star of the five-year-running series "Taxi" won

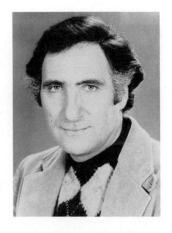

him two more Emmys and millions more fans. (That second Emmy for "Taxi" came after the show was cancelled. During Hirsch's acceptance speech he castigated the show's executives who had dropped the guillotine.) His next television series, "Dear John" (debut 1988-1989 season), also became an immediate hit. He won an Obie for his performance in Lanford Wilson's play *Talley's Folly* and a Tony Award (Best Actor in a Play, 1986) for his role in *I'm Not Rappaport.* He repeated his performance in *Rappaport* for a thirteen-week Broadway run in 1987. His films include *Ordinary People, Without a Trace, The Goodbye People,* and *Running on Empty.*

Twice married, he is the father of one son. In the early days of his career, he made hundreds of commercials—his face coined the native (born 15 March 1935) New Yorker's image. "I come from a family where self preservation was the only instinct. I was a troublesome kid, a kid who couldn't stop making jokes, a kid who got C's and D's in deportment." Hirsch regularly turns down money parts for better, although frequently less lucrative, roles. "If turning down a bad part means it is all over for me tomorrow, as far as fame, riches and all those bad reasons for being an actor goes, well you'll find me back at the Circle Rep, doing some unknown play by an unknown writer. And enjoying it. I don't care what it is, or how big it is, I just want a thing to be good."

Dustin Hoffman

D ustin Hoffman received Academy Award nominations for his performances in *The Graduate, Midnight Cowboy, Lenny, Little Big Man, All The President's Men, Papillon, Marathon Man, Tootsie,* and Oscars for *Kramer vs. Kramer* in 1979 and *Rain Man* in 1989. On his return to the stage in the 1984 Broadway revival of

Arthur Miller's *Death of a Salesman* after more than a decade's absence, Hoffman was cited by *New York Times* drama critic Mel Gussow as "one of America's finest and most popular actors. In a career spanning 17 films, playing characters of remarkable diversity, he has given unfailingly good performances—even in his lesser movies. . . . But for all the measurable successes, he remains a man obsessed by his work, craving perfection and driven by private demons in pursuit of his goal, which he considers artistic excellence." The film version of the play was a highlight of the fall 1985 television season.

"Yes, I am very difficult," he admitted to Marie Brenner in *New York* magazine. "If someone is saying to me, 'That's fine, don't worry about it,' well, for me, 'fine' ain't good enough—and tell me if I'm crazy, but it's like in *1984* when they have that kind of double-talk, 'War is Peace.' Now when I'm called a perfectionist, it's like being cursed. Well you bet I'm a pain in the ass." But the audience reaps the rewards. Memorable characters like Ratso Rizzo in *Midnight Cowboy* and Dorothy Michaels in *Tootsie* could only have been created by the performing genius of Dustin Hoffman.

He was born in Los Angeles, 8 August 1937, to a starstruck mother who named him after Dustin Farnum (the silent cowboy star), and a father who wanted to be a film director but wound up a successful designer and salesman of Danish modern furniture. As a child, Hoffman was "pint-sized," wore braces, and had the worst case of acne on the block. Originally his passion was to become a concert pianist, and he studied music at both the Los Angeles Conservatory of Music and Santa Monica City College. Then one spring when he was at his Aunt Pearl's for the Passover feast, he suddenly announced that he was going to become an actor. "You can't," said the astonished Aunt Pearl. "You're not good looking enough." In 1958, a graduate of the Pasadena Playhouse, he packed his bags and left for New York. ("I didn't go out of the house for three weeks. I slept on Gene Hackman's kitchen floor, and every morning at three the refrigerator would have a heart attack and wake me up.") He checked coats at the Longacre Theatre, washed dishes and served as clean-up man at a dance studio. According to Gussow, in one of Hoffman's most convincing acting feats while working in the toy department at Macy's, he "sold" Hackman's 18-month-old son as a life-size doll. ("I did the waiter bit too. Once the boss of a restaurant on Columbus Avenue told me I could eat as much as I wanted to, so one night I ate six steaks, and they fired me.") Remembering those days he told Gussow: "I got on stage whenever I was allowed to. . . . Acting is the only art form I'm aware of in which you cannot practice your craft and be unemployed at the same time. It's so tough to have this ego and not be able to work. A writer can write, a painter can paint, but what can an actor do? He pays the other actors to be the audience and calls it 'class!'" He made his Off Broadway debut as a hunchbacked homosexual in Ronald Ribman's black comedy *Harry, Noon and Night* during the 1964-65 season and won an Obie in 1966 in *The Journey of the Fifth Horse*. In 1968 he appeared on Broadway in Murray Schisgal's *Jimmy Shine*. Mike Nichols spotted him in Alan Arkin's film *Eh?* and flew the young actor out to Hollywood to test for the lead in *The Graduate*. At his first meeting with Joseph E. Levine, the producer mistook the young actor for the window washer. Dustin Hoffman triumphed in the film that widened the generation gap. In 1990 he was up for a Tony Award for his role as Shylock in *The Merchant of Venice* and was spotted in a cameo role disguised as Mumbles in the 1990 movie *Dick Tracy*. Divorced from first wife Ann Byrne (two daughters) he is now married to Lisa Gottsegen, a lawyer and the grandaughter of his mother's best friend (four children).

Hal Holbrook

Billowing in white hair, mustaches and cigar smoke, he has transformed himself into Mark Twain on stage *Mark Twain Tonight!* over 2000 times in this country and abroad, making his one-man show of the 19th century genius muckraker one of the most successful solo theatrical productions in history. He also played the junior maverick Senator Hays Stowe on TV's "The Bold Ones" but has a hankering to do a farce or western in the future. "You've got to grow as an actor, and change as you grow as a person" he says. "That's . . . the beauty of acting—it's a way of fighting a society that locks you into position."

Born in Cleveland, Ohio, 17 February 1925 and abandoned by his parents at two, he spent "Huck Finnish summers" with "Uncle Sabe and Aunt Ruby." ("I had a tree house with a rope ladder, took long hunting trips with a wooden gun, and I got on fine with Uncle

Sabe. He was grumpy but his eyes laughed. There's a lot of Uncle Sabe in my Mark Twain.") He conceived the idea for *Mark Twain Tonight!* as an alternative to selling hats at Macy's when he couldn't get work as an actor. He performed it in 1955 at San Francisco's Purple Onion and later in a Greenwich Village nightclub (while working daytimes in the TV soap opera "The Brighter Day"), and made a hit with it Off-Broadway in 1959, putting together the two-hour show from some nine hours of material. As an actor he has a wide range. On stage he has appeared in *The Glass Menagerie* and *Does a Tiger Wear a Necktie,* as well as various Lincoln Center Repertory productions. His film credits include *The Great White Hope, Wild in the Streets,* followed by *All the President's Men* (1976), *Julia* (1978), *Creepshow* (1981), *The Unholy* (1987), *Wall Street* (1987), and *Fletch* (1989). He appeared in the two television miniseries "North and South: Book II" (1986) and "The Fortunate Pilgrim" (1988). Divorced from Ruby Johnson (two children) and Carol Rossen (one daughter), he tied the nupital knot in spring 1984 to singer-actress Dixie Carter. He joins her on the CBS-TV hit show "Designing Women" in a recurring role.

Celeste Holm

" '**M**y God, young lady,' I replied in astonishment. 'You ask if Celeste Holm takes theatre seriously? She is a star. Do you know what that means?' " Agnes DeMille's spirited response to a thoroughly chastened FBI agent inquiring into the credentials of Celeste Holm for a post with the National Endowment for the Arts is typical of the high regard her colleagues have for the actress who became a Broadway star in 1943 as Ado Annie in *Oklahoma!* (stopping the show each night with her hilarious rendition of "I Can't Say No") and for more than four decades has continued to light up—with her talent, charm and good humor—stage, screen and television. The theatre, however, remains her first love, as attested to by her willingness to risk arrest rather than remove herself from the path of a bulldozer that was about to demolish two venerable Broadway houses to make way for yet another skyscraper. Less spotlighted is Celeste's longtime dedication to a variety of humanitarian causes, most notably UNICEF (her 50¢ an hour autograph charge has netted that organization more than $15,000) and mental health, an interest sparked by her visits to military hospitals during WWII and her experiences while researching her role in the film *The Snake Pit*.

Born 29 April 1919 in New York to an insurance executive and his portrait painter wife, Celeste's education took her from New York to Chicago to Paris, and she made her Broadway acting debut in the Theatre Guild's 1939 production of William Saroyan's Pulitzer Prize winning play, *The Time of Your Life*. Four years later came *Oklahoma!*, then *Bloomer Girl* in 1944, then Hollywood (with frequent trips back for additional Broadway appearances). She won an Oscar early on, as best supporting actress in 1947 for her blistering performance in *Gentlemen's Agreement* (which also led to a lifelong dedication to combating anti-Semitism), and received Academy Award nominations for her roles in *All About Eve* and *Come to the Stable* (for which she won the French Oscar equivalent for her portrayal of a French nun). Other notable films include *The Tender Trap*, *High Society* and as Aunt Polly in the 1973 version of *Tom Sawyer*. In 1987 she appeared in the popular movie *Three Men and a Baby*. Television has seen her as a continuing character on "Archie Bunker's Place," as the Fairy Godmother in Rodgers & Hammerstein's "Cinderella," as Mrs. Warren G. Harding (Emmy nomination) in "Backstairs at the Whitehouse," in the premiere presentation of the PBS American Playhouse series, John Cheever's "The Shady Hill Kidnapping" and as co-star in 1984 of the series, "Jessie." In 1985 she appeared in several episodes of CBS' "Falcon Crest" as neighboring vintner Anna Rossini. Recent theatrical triumphs include starring roles in the British premiere of *Lady in the Dark* and a 1983 revival of Noel Coward's *Hay Fever* at L.A.'s Ahmanson Theatre. Of Norwegian descent, Celeste was knighted in 1979 by King Olav; in 1982 she was named by President Reagan to the National Arts Council (having long since passed muster for the National Endowment), and in 1983 Governor Kean appointed her Chairman of the New Jersey Motion Picture & Television Development Commission. Although she and her husband, actor Wesley Addy (she has two sons from an earlier marriage), make New York City their principal residence, they spend weekends restoring an 18th-century New Jersey farmhouse.

Bob Hope

He is the most American of comedians, but the superstar with the ski-jump nose and the scooped chin was born in Eltham, Kent, England 29 May 1903. He came to Cleveland, Ohio, at

age 4 with the name Leslie Townes Hope. He's travelled millions of miles to entertain the troops around the world. He is a friend of Presidents and notables, and once traded ad-libs with the King of England. ("The only time I ever had a King for a straight man.") His 80th birthday in 1983 was celebrated in the Senate and NBC devoted an entire evening's prime time airwaves to a lavish tribute broadcast from the Kennedy Center in Washington. At the time an ecstatic Hope quipped, "Security is so tight in the President's box, one agent checked me for bombs and threw out half my monologue." Describing his brand of humor as "pseudosmart" he says, "I want the audience to enjoy it like I do."

One of the few performers to triumph in five major entertainment media—vaudeville, stage, radio, motion pictures, and television—he was the fifth of his stone-mason father's seven sons. In Cleveland he helped out at home by working as a delivery boy, soda fountain clerk, and shoe salesman before making his vaudeville debut dancing in a Fatty Arbuckle Revue. Known at school as "Les," he says he changed his name to Bob after schoolmates started calling him "Hopeless." Soon after his Cleveland vaudeville debut he also worked as a reporter, a dance instructor, and a prizefighter ("I was the only one they ever carried both ways") after which he soft-shoed his way to Broadway to make his debut in *Sidewalks of New York* in 1927. While working in the musical *Roberta* in1933, he met and married singer Dolores Reade, still his wife and mother to his four adopted children. A star of his own radio series starting in 1938, he continued on the NBC wireless for a total of 1,145 programs. During WW II he began his tours to entertain the troops. His recent TV Special, "Bob Hope's USO Road to the Berlin Wall and Moscow," aired in May, 1990. Hope made his film debut in *The Big Broadcast of 1938* and starred in a long parade of big-screen comedies, some of the most popular being the many "road" pictures (*Road to Singapore, Road to Rio* et al) made with his longtime buddy, the late Bing Crosby. He also starred on scores of TV specials and is the author of ten books, including *Road to Hollywood* in 1977, *Confessions of a Hooker* in 1985, and *Don't Shoot, It's Only Me* in 1990.

Hope, who lives in a 25,000 sq. ft. home in Palm Springs, California that's been compared to "Disneyland . . . made to be toured," confesses that he's "slowing down a bit. George Burns, Lawrence Welk and I, for excitement on Saturday night, all sit around and see whose leg falls asleep faster." Every night he heads for the center of Palm Springs for his constitutional walk down the main drag, window shopping and signing autographs. "I still need the laughs and the adulation." He is the recipient of more than a thousand awards and citations for humanitarian and professional efforts including the President's Medal of Freedom and 1985 Kennedy Center Honors for Lifetime Achievement in the Arts. Hope is a dedicated golfer and his annual Bob Hope Desert Classic has produced nearly $10 million dollars for charities in the Palm Springs area. He averages 15 to 20 celebrity golf benefits every year.

Anthony Hopkins

"**A**cting is a craft. It's common sense. Talent—I don't know what that is. It's knowing the alphabet of one's instrument, knowing the text, and getting on with it." Welshman Anthony Hopkins has been getting on with it on stage, television, and in films, winning in 1973 the Actor of the Year Award from Great Britain's Society of Film & Television Arts for his portrayal of Pierre in the miniseries based on *War and Peace*; in 1976, an Emmy for his impersonation of Bruno Hauptmann in the NBC docu-drama "The Lindbergh Kidnapping Case"; and in 1975 the New York Drama Desk Best Actor Award and the Outer Critics Award for his performance in Peter Shaffer's play *Equus*.

Born on New Year's Eve 1937 in Port Talbot, a small town in South Wales, Hopkins was as a youngster big for his age ("fairly brainless") and his peers hung nicknames of "ox," "ape" and "pig" on him. His father, "a man of little tolerance, was always putting me down." Although his parents "slaved all their lives in a bakery for peanuts," they sent him to an exclusive boarding school, Cowbridge, in nearby Glamorgan. "I loathed it . . . academically, I was an idiot. I wouldn't learn math . . . the only talent I had was for playing the piano and impersonating the schoolmasters. . . . It was a snob school." After a two-year stretch in the army, he studied drama at the Royal Academy of Dramatic Art in London (1961-1963), and made his London stage debut in a 1964 production of *Julius Caesar*. After his second audition for the National Theatre, Laurence Olivier snapped, "I don't think I'm going to lose any sleep tonight, but would you like to join us?" He stayed with the National from 1966-1972, earning the accolade of "most promising actor" in *Variety's* 1970-71 poll of London theatre critics. (He left twice, but returned both times. "I had a marvelous stay there. I had a bad-boy reputation. During the '60s it was fashionable to be very wild and crazy. I was very unsuccessful at it. I couldn't do it with panache. But I had a go at trying to get a bad reputation. . . . It's all forgiven now.") Hopkins was introduced to American audiences in the 1974 production of *Equus*. In 1984 he made an appearance in New York off-Broadway in Harold Pinter's *Old Times* with Jane Alexander and Marsha Mason which was highly praised. He received glowing notices in 1985 for his West End portrayal of Rupert Murdoch-like press lord in *Pravda*. He made his screen debut in 1968 in *A Lion in Winter* with Katharine Hepburn and Peter O'Toole. Other films include: *The Looking Glass War* (1970); *When Eight Bells Toll* (1971); *Young Winston* (1972); *A Doll's House* with Claire Bloom (1973); *Juggernaut* (1974); *Audrey Rose* and *A Bridge Too Far* (1977); *Magic* (1978); *The Elephant Man* and *A Change of Seasons* (1980); *The Bounty* (1984); *84 Charing Cross Road* (1986); *The Good Father* (1987); *The Old Jest* (1987); *A Chorus of Disapproval* (1988); *Three Penny Opera* (1989) and *Great Expectations* (1989). Noteworthy television appearances: "All Creatures Great and Small" (1975); "Dark Victory" (1976); "Kean"; "Mayflower: The Pilgrims' Adventure"; "The Bunker" (he portrayed Adolf Hitler); the miniseries, "QB VII"; "Hollywood Wives"; "Mussolini: The Decline and Fall of Il Duce" (1985); and the Hallmark Hall of Fame presentation "The Tenth Man" (1988).

His first marriage ended in divorce in 1972. He and his second wife, the former Jennifer Layton (a former production secretary on one of his movies, whom he married in 1973), maintain a home in Beverly Hills. He has a daughter by his first wife. His hobbies are astronomy and playing the piano. "I love the stage." says Hopkins. "That's where I obviously want to go back to. But I get the same thrill out of working in television. There's a magical thrill of having words come out of one's mouth in the right order. It's a comic way of making a living, saying lines. But in working it out, the excitement starts. . . . It's easier to work in television and movies. . . . I don't go along with suffering for the sake of art."

Lena Horne

S till almost as impossibly beautiful as when she was a 16-year old chorine in Harlem's Cotton Club, this personification of the black female entertainment experience found it ironic that she was chosen to be the pioneer that she became. "I was an ingenue, for Christ's sake, you know. I'd suddenly got thrown into this never-never land of Hollywood. . . . I didn't really have the strength to show people how I really was inside." But Lena Horne grew to find that strength, and what's more, at age 63 imparted that quality in her triumphant *Lena Horne: The Lady and Her Music* to world-wide audiences who made it the longest-running one-woman show in history. And what did she make of her rejuvenated career, with its Kennedy Center Honors, two Grammys, special Tony, and NAACP

Spingarn Award? "I'm a late bloomer," the glamorous grandmother says. "I hate that I waited so long to let my barriers down. Now you'd have to take a bullet to drive me offstage."

Born "in the better part of Brooklyn" on 30 June 1917, Lena Mary Calhoun Horne had a grandmother who was the child of a black slave woman and her white owner. Lena's numbers-running dad and travelling actress mom were divorced when she was three, so she was passed around as a youngster to the homes of various relatives down South (from whence comes her syrupy Southern inflection). After her debut at the Cotton Club, which at the time catered to whites-only audiences, she was on the move again as a singer with Charlie Barnet's band, and then became the first black woman to ever sign a long-term Hollywood contract. Featured in many films in the 1940's (*Cabin in the Sky, Stormy Weather, Ziegfeld Follies*), she often found herself photographed leaning against a pillar or in some other solo situation so her scenes could be scissored out when the films were shown in the South. But all the while, Lena recalls, "you had to be grateful, grateful, grateful." Married while still in her teens to "incredibly handsome" Louis Jones, she became the mother of two children (daughter Gail is divorced from director Sidney Lumet; son Teddy died in 1970), and was divorced in 1938. In 1947, she was wowing Europeans on her first singing tour of the Continent, she married white musician Lennie Hayton in Paris. "It was cold-blooded and deliberate. I married him because he could get me into places a black man couldn't. But I really learned to love him." When he died after 24 years of marriage, followed closely by the deaths of her father and son in the early '70s, Lena said, "I thought that I was nothing. But the pain of the loss somehow cracked me open, made me feel compassion. Now I'm kinder to myself and to other people."

Her friendship with black actor and activist Paul Robeson

clarified her people's history for her, and in Hollywood she was ready to chuck the loneliness of her singular black star status until Count Basie asked her to remain and use the chance for black advancement. She became an ardent civil rights activist early on (supporting Dr. Martin Luther King's marches, and voter registration by speaking throughout the South), as well as giving 30 benefit concerts in Israel in 1952 in support of the fledgling state. She and singer Harry Belafonte gave similar performances in the U.S. for civil rights; all fitting, since in the '40s and '50s she'd had to fight for contracts guaranteeing that blacks could attend her club performances.

In 1979, she said, "the biggest thing that ever happened" to her was Howard University's conferring upon her an honorary doctorate of humane letters. Unlike others she'd rejected, she "was ready to take" that one. The single singer, who says, "Rather than marrying again, I might go as far as hiring somebody to whom I have formed an attachment," lives in a restored olive mill in Santa Barbara, Calif., where she has planted 53 trees, and in an apartment in Washington, D.C. In 1989 she released the record album *The Men in My Life*.

Ron Howard

Only in his thirties, this actor has been a star on TV and in movies, and now he's a major film director. As a little boy he charmed a nation of viewers playing "Opie," that inquisitive little tyke with eyes of chocolate chips, on "The Andy Griffith Show." He was "Winthrop" in the film *The Music Man*, "Steve Bolander" in *American Graffiti* and "Richie" on the teen hit "Happy Days" playing the sweet foil for the randy "Fonz" (Henry Winkler). He has directed the films *Grand Theft, Night Shift, Splash, Cocoon,* and *Gung Ho*. Then, in the truest of Hollywood traditions, he must be, in private, a real creep? A monster? A sleaze? Forget it. According to all reports, Ron Howard is as good as gold, described by insiders as "homespun . . . down-to-earth .·. . modest."

Ron Howard was born 1 March 1953 in Duncan, Oklahoma, and he was raised off-camera in Burbank, California. "I always had a choice about continuing my career," he has recalled. "I remember my mom and dad saying, 'You don't have to do this. If you're not enjoying it, you just have to tell us.'" He met his wife Cheryl when they were in the 11th grade and they have been married since 1975 (they have three daughters, one son).

"I have a lot of patience. I rarely feel betrayed or disgruntled. I don't get revved up," the self-proclaimed workaholic told writer Lisa Birnbach in *Parade* magazine. "Far from reveling in his position," Birnbach writes, "Howard says he regards what he does as simply a job—not, like many of his colleagues, as a 'craft' or 'art.'" Howard confesses: "I've only felt that I was of value to people when I was working. That's the only time I've been useful and interesting." The man whose favorite album is Cat Stevens' *Teaser and the Firecat* believes you can work hard and be good to people, "and it makes me feel good when I see examples of that in life and in the movies. So I tend to want to work that into the stories. . . . I'm always interested in characters who are being told one thing, being told they can't do something—'you can't fall in love with a mermaid'—and turn that around because they don't agree with it." His recent list of movie-making ventures include *No Man's Land* (1987), *Clean and Sober* (1987), *Cowboy Way* (1988), *Willow* (1988), *Dream Team* (1988), and *Bay Window* (1988).

William Hurt

Tautly handsome and effortlessly charming with a demeanor as cool as a summer's morning in Maine, this ex-prepster, who undoubtedly read Kierkegaard before and after crew practice at Middlesex School, is, according to some critics, a maverick in a major movement in American theatre away from the darkness of stark realism toward romantic yet disciplined drama.

Born 20 March 1950 in Washington D.C., William Hurt spent his early childhood in the South Pacific where his father was director of trust territories for the State Department. When his parents divorced he moved with his mother and two brothers to Manhattan where, in 1960, his mother married Henry Luce III, the son of the founder of Time, Inc. Home became a 22-room duplex in place of a four room Upper Westside flat. Sent off to prep school, Hurt turned inward. "I'd been a street fighter, a little punk kid," he recalls, "and suddenly I was in an Eastern establishment-type school wearing Bass Weejuns, white socks, herringbone jackets and ties, the transition at the time was too great." At Tufts University he graduated magna cum laude, having majored in theology intending to become a minister, but show biz was biting him. "I found myself increasingly interested in theatre. There is a very close relationship between the theatre and theology—both are very concerned about morality and the search for personal values." Three years after intensive training at Juilliard's acting program, his marriage on the rocks, he took off on a cross-country motorcycle tour which ended up in Ashland, Oregon. Appearing there in a production of O'Neill's *Long Day's Journey Into Night*, the light was struck. "I walked onto the stage one day and realized I had some craft. It felt so good." Back in New York his performance in Corinne Jacker's *My Life* won him an Obie.

Hurt went on to win critical acclaim in Lanford Wilson's *Fifth of July*; Albert Innaurato's *Ulysses in Traction*; *The Runner Stumbles*; *Childe Byron*; and *Hamlet*, a performance drama critic Clive Barnes called "a marker stone in the career of a great actor." After a successful round of films beginning with *Altered States*, and followed by *Eye Witness*, *Body Heat*, *The Big Chill* and *Gorky Park*, he returned to off-Broadway in 1984 to star in David Rabe's *Hurlyburly*. Subsequent films include *Kiss of the Spider Woman* (1985 Cannes Film Festival Best Actor Award), *Children of a Lesser God* (1986), *A Time of Destiny* (1987), *Broadcast News* (1988-nominated Academy Award for Best Actor, 1989), *The Accidental Tourist* (1988), and *I Love You to Death* (1990). In 1988 he won the UCLA Spencer Tracy Award for screen performance and professional achievement.

Divorced from actress Mary Beth Hurt, he had a son with ballet dancer Sandra Jennings. In June 1989, Ms. Jennings took Hurt to court and, under the scrutiny of television cameras in the courtroom, the couple battled whether or not their union was to be considered a common law marriage. However, Hurt married Heidi Henderson (daughter of Skitch Henderson) on 4 March 1989. They have a son, Sam, and expected a second child in late summer, 1990.

Lauren Hutton

She is "the link between the dream and the drugstore. She's the girl next door but she moved away," said top fashion photographer Richard Avedon, whose bold and willowy shots of the gap-toothed blonde made her a supermodel. As a *Vogue* magazine covergirl, and then the glamorous representative of Ultima's line of cosmetics, she remained a whimsical fashion maverick whose throw-away sex appeal epitomized the canny, carefree nature of the contemporary woman.

Mary Laurence Hutton was born in Charleston, S.C. 17 November 1943. Tall and awkward as an adolescent, she painfully recalls bombing out in cheerleader tryouts and attending the prom with a date arranged by a teacher. After a year at a Florida university, she worked as a Playboy Bunny before landing her first fashion job in New York at age 21: a $50-a-week gig as house model with Christian Dior. Rejected by nearly every major modeling agency, she finally persuaded top agent Eileen Ford to sign her by agreeing to fix her curved nose and gap-teeth. The adjustments proved unnecessary.

Hutton's career took off with her first *Vogue* cover in 1966, but top model status eluded her until the more casual, accessible look took over fashion in the early 1970s. In 1973, her $200,000 exclusive contract with late cosmetic magnate Charles Revlon made her the highest paid model at the time and popularized the notion among advertisers that a model can be more effective if she represents only one product. During her decade with Revlon, Hutton—who made her film debut in the 1968 *Paper Lion*—appeared in *American Gigolo* and *Paternity* (both 1980), *Zorro, The Gay Blade* (1981), *Flagrant Desire*, and *Bulldance*. Released from her modeling duties, she concentrated on her theatrical skill in the gritty, physically demanding off-Broadway play *Extremities*, while continuing to travel extensively in her spare time. She also appeared in the CBS telefilm "Sins."

Jeremy Irons

Britain's Jeremy Irons is equally at home on stage (he was a Tony-winner for *The Real Thing*), in film (e.g. *The French Lieutenant's Woman, The Mission*), and on TV ("Brideshead Revisited"); he also succeeded in another medium: recording. On a London album, released in October 1987, he played the role of Henry Higgins in the Alan Jay Lerner/Frederick Loewe classic *My Fair Lady*. The show album teamed the acting star with opera's Kiri Te Kanawa as Eliza Doolittle and Sir John Gielgud as colonel Pickering, all performing under the baton of John Mauceri conducting a singing group called London Voices and the London Symphony Orchestra. Although Irons says he had a few qualms about taking on a role so closely associated with the masterful Rex Harrison, "Eventually," he says, "I took it because

if I hadn't someone else would have had all the fun."

Jeremy Irons first became a household name, both in the U.K. and U.S., after his portrayal of Charles Ryder in the TV series, "Brideshead Revisited." The stylish, 1920's set series turned out to be so popular that it's been shown on numerous occasions around the world and has become the actor's flagship role. Though he's been in considerable demand by Hollywood in the years since, Irons has opted instead for the more demanding and less financially rewarding path of re-establishing himself as a stage actor, only fitting films in between stage engagements. He was a big hit with summer visitors to England in recent seasons playing in the Royal Shakespeare Company's Stratford productions of *The Winter's Tale* and *Richard II* and on the London stage with Stephanie Beacham in *The Rover*. Films include: *Betrayal* (1983), *The Wild Duck* (1983), *A Chorus of Disapproval* (1988), *Dead Ringers* (1988; Best Actor Award from New York Film Critics) and *Danny, Champion of the World* (1989). Recent films include *Reversal of Fortune* (1990), director Barbet Schoede's film of the Klaus von Bulow trial. Irons suspects the lure of his low-key intensity may be in what he holds back, rather than what he delivers. Says Irons, "I generally don't like giving more than required. If a moment requires A, I won't give A plus 3 just so my technique will dazzle the audience. In fact, I believe that they are moved by the structure of the work, not by an actor going through hoops and dancing on high wires." Indeed, even when ablaze in a scene, the audience looks for what smoulders beneath. Irons married accomplished British stage actress, Sinead Cusack, in 1978; they have two sons: Samuel (born 1979) and Maxmilian (born 1985).

Amy Irving

What a life! She began on Broadway in 1982 playing Mozart's wife in *Amadeus*. She was the sole survivor of Sissy Spacek's bloody revenge in Brian de Palma's *Carrie* and she appeared in other films, usually playing "sweet young things. . . . I suppose it's because I look young and innocent and virginal. Little do they know." Some of her films include: *The Fury, Voices, The Competition, Mickey and Maude*. Reportedly she had affairs with her co-stars Willie Nelson (*Honeysuckle Rose*) and Ben Cross in the televison movie "The Far Pavilions." (She insists they were just friends, but has wondered: "Sometimes you think you may as well do it; you have to deal with it anyway.") She did kiss a male-garbed Barbra Streisand in *Yentl* and she had Steven Spielberg's baby (Max Samuel born June 1985). Amy married Spielberg in November 1985 and divorced him in April 1989. Irving and director Bruno Barreto have a child, Gabriel, born in May, 1990. Barreto and Irving worked together on the 1990 feature *A Show of Force,* co-starring Robert Duvall.

Ah, the modern cinema. Amy Irving, born circa 1953, is the daughter of actress Priscilla Pointer (who played her mother in both *Honeysuckle Rose* and *Carrie*) and the late Jules Irving who founded the San Francisco's Actor's Workshop and later became artistic director of New York City's Repertory Theatre of Lincoln Center. Irving who co-starred with Rex Harrison in Shaw's *Heartbreak House* on Broadway in 1983 and also appeared on Broadway in *The Road to Mecca* in 1988, rejects the money principle of Hollywood filmmaking and prefers theatre as her medium, or so she told *People* magazine writer Andrea Chambers: "You explore every facet of your instrument onstage. When you become one with a character, it's like falling in love. It's that kind of high. . . . If someone said to me, 'You can't do films anymore,' I wouldn't shed a tear." She played the lead role in the light romantic film *Crossing Delancey* (1988).

Judith Ivey

"I feel like Cinderella and I hope the ball goes on forever," says the Tony Award-winning (*Steaming,* 1982) actress who generated "beaucoup d'applause" in the 1984 smash hit *Hurlyburly* in which she appeared with William Hurt, Sigourney Weaver, and Christopher Walken and walked off with another Tony for her efforts. It's hard to imagine the magnetic blond was ready to leave the theatre for good in 1981 to become a veterinarian. "It wasn't that she'd failed to get good roles," reported the *New York Times*, "in fact she'd just won praises for her performances in *Piaf* and *Pastorale*; it was more that she was tired of being poor, tired of waiting in the unemployment lines between shows, and was impatient for success." In *Steaming,* she played many of her scenes in the buff and it didn't seem to bother her as much as she thought it would. "Once I

read the play, I realized an integral part of it—this stripping away of layers and all that philosophical stuff."

Born in El Paso, Texas., 4 September 1951, Ivey is the daughter of a college administrator who changed jobs often: her family moved some 15 times before she entered college. She originally wanted to become a painter and it was not until she turned 17 that she discovered her penchant and love for the stage via a high school production of *The Man Who Came to Dinner*. ("Making people laugh: That was the bug.")

Following graduation from Illinois State, Ivey wended her way toward Chicago where she worked at the Goodman Theatre. Five years down the road would find her in New York City, where she worked at Joe Papp's Public Theatre and received glowing notices for a one-woman show *Second Lady*. Her movies include *Compromising Positions, The Lonely Guy, Harry and Son, Brighton Beach Memoirs, Hello Again, In Country, Miles from Home* and *Love Hurts*. Recent stage performances include *Precious Sons* (1986), *Blithe Spirit* (1987), and *Mrs. Dally Has A Lover* (1988). She acted as assistant director for the play *The Palace of Amateurs* in 1988. Ivey says she doesn't have to be an actress to feel satisfied. "If someone said 'Tomorrow, actors no longer exist' I'd miss it, but I know I'd find something else that would motivate me as much as acting does." Ivey is single and lives in Manhattan.

Glenda Jackson

For someone who considers enrolling in drama school her "most irrational act," the lady hasn't done too badly. The two-time Oscar winner (*Women in Love; A Touch of Class*) made her initial impression on American audiences on Broadway in 1965 as the mad, murderous Charlotte Corday, who used her floor-length hair as a whip in Peter Brook's *Marat/Sade* with the Royal Shakespeare Company, a play she "really loathed." It's been a mutual admiration society between the former colonials and the laborer's daughter from Birkenhead, Cheshire, ever since. Like her personal heroines—"Bette Davis, Joan Crawford and Katharine Hepburn"—it's been playing forceful females that she's been most successful. On stage, she's scored in *Hamlet, The Three Sisters, Hedda Gabler*, Genet's *The Maids, Rose, Stevie, Antony and Cleopatra*, and in 1984 alone, the demanding roles of *Phaedra* and Nina Leeds in Eugene O'Neill's five-hour psychodrama, *Strange Interlude,* which she recreated on Broadway in 1985, looking like (wrote the *New York Times'* Frank Rich) "a cubist portrait of Louise Brooks . . . equally mesmerizing as a Zelda Fitzgeraldesque neurotic, a rotting and spiteful middle-aged matron and, finally, a spent, sphinx-like widow happily embracing extinction." With a career heavily weighted with the classics and historical figures, Jackson feels that "modern playwrights

don't find women interesting to write about, except as adjuncts to a male story," adding that she's "not going to hang around waiting for the old lady character parts to come along. . . . When the work isn't interesting, I won't do it," she told an interviewer for *W* in 1985.

Born 9 March 1936 in Birkenhead, the eldest of four daughters of a bricklayer (which might account for her disdain of "that English obsession with public schools and universities"), Jackson won a two-year scholarship to the Royal Academy of Dramatic Arts, from which—armed with one of its top awards—she embarked on what she calls "the traditional English round: repertory and unemployment." After a half-dozen years in rep, she made her London stage debut in *Alfie* in 1963, and was selected by Peter Brook to play a nude Christine Keeler (a principal in the sex scandal that ruined a cabinet officer) in a Theatre of Cruelty revue. She joined the RSC in 1964, and made her big splash in *Marat/Sade.* "We all felt at one point or another that we were suffering from some kind of mental illness, but by the time I left it, I didn't have to scratch for work any longer." She returned to London—and the RSC—with *Variety's* Most Promising Actress prize, and appeared in *US, The Three Sisters* and *Fanghorn* before making her film debut in 1968 in *Negatives.* A banner year was 1970 when, for her portrayal of Gudrun in Ken Russell's version of D.H. Lawrence's *Women in Love,* she walked off with the Oscar, and the New York Film Critics and National Society of Film Critics awards. Next she played the nymphomaniacal Nina Tchaikovsky in Russell's film biography of the composer, *The Music Lovers,* then the third part of a triangle in John Schlesinger's *Sunday, Bloody Sunday,* sharing the love of a bisexual young artist with a homosexual doctor. She displayed her comic side (and won another Oscar) for *A Touch of Class* in 1973. Other films include *Mary, Queen of Scots* (as Elizabeth vs. Vanessa Redgrave as the doomed Catholic queen), *The Nelson Affair, Stevie, House Calls, Hopscotch, The Return of the Soldier, Turtle*

Diary, Beyond Therapy, Defense of the Realm, The Rainbow and *Salome's Last Dance*. She starred in *Macbeth* (1988) on Broadway, and on television, she won an Emmy for her portrayal of Elizabeth I (aging from 17 to 70) in a BBC six-parter, and in 1985 on HBO as Dr. Elena Bonner to Jason Robards' "Sakharov" ("to tell them they're not alone"). In 1988 Jackson was honored by The Women's Project to receive their Exceptional Achievement Award. Her marriage (1959) to Roy Hodges, whom she met in rep and who later became an art gallery owner, ended in 1976. Resolutely mum about her private life, she will say she hopes her son Daniel (born 1969) doesn't become an actor. "It's hard enough to actually go through the process of trying find work oneself. To watch a child go through it would be torture." She also confesses a fondness for gardening and says she knows "what is meant by the saying, 'You're closest to God in a garden.'"

Michael Jackson

1987 was the *Bad* beginning of a two year hit streak. Living up to all pre-hype expectations, Michael Jackson's long-awaited album rocked the record charts and video channels with such hits as "The Way You Make Me Feel," "The Man in The Mirror," "Dirty Diana," and, of course, the title track "Bad." A piece of phenomenal vinyl, the album itself was actually an added touch to Michael's extraordinary career.

Born 29 August 1958 in Gary, Indiana, one of nine children, Michael began singing with his parents and four other brothers as The Jackson Family before the boys went out on their own as The Jackson Five. They were discovered at New York's Apollo Theatre by singer Gladys Knight and pianist Billy Taylor, whose recommendations to Motown Records kingpin Berry Gordy resulted in the group's huge success in the late 1960s and early 1970s when they charted four consecutive #1 singles, "I Want You Back," "ABC," "The Love You Save" and "I'll Be There." The Jackson Five was one of the most amazing success stories in the music biz, with the group selling over an estimated 100 million records, breaking box office records and causing general pandemonium wherever they appeared. Michael's been doing his thing alone, compiling an array of hit singles and albums, since 1971, when he was just a 12-

year-old. His fame skyrocketed to incredible heights with the wildly successful *Thriller* album (1983). Aided by the emergence of MTV's 24-hour videos, his singing and dancing in "Beat It" and "Billie Jean" during the summer of 1983 (and later "Thriller" with its narration by Vincent Price) captured the nation's attention. In 1984 Jackson made a sweep of the American Music Awards. He won a total of seven awards (including a special award for merit) which placed him in *The Guinness Book of World Records* for winning the most awards ever at that event. Next came the Grammys where he won another eight awards. The LP "Thriller" held the #1 place on top of *Billboards's* chart for over 30 weeks, and in a more subtle guise, Jackson narrated the bestselling storybook LP of Steven Spielberg's *E.T. the Extraterrestrial*.

1984 was certainly his year, but the thrills and spills of success gave him his moments. Rock singer Prince came along and took some of Jackson's more sophisticated fans away from him, those who'd had it with the hoopla of The Victory Tour and who preferred their rock more raunchy. Then Michael's hair went up in flames during the making of a Pepsi commercial, and although millions were sympathetic, many wondered what he was doing making a Pepsi ad in the first place. Then there were the endless stories about his nose job, his cheek job, his hormone shots and last, but never least, the possibility of his being gay. Against the advice of his manager a press conference was called and a statement was read, its purpose to "once and for all" deny that he was a homosexual. "It saddens me," the statement went, "that many may actually believe the present flurry of false accusations. To this end, and I do mean END!—No! I've never taken hormones to maintain my high voice. No! I've never had my cheekbones altered in any way. No! I've never had cosmetic surgery on my eyes." (The nose went unmentioned.) "YES! One day in the future I plan to get married and have a family. Any statements to the contrary are simply untrue. . . . I love children." On the upside, Michael recorded the *Victory* (1984) album with The Jacksons and a duet with Mick Jagger "State of Shock" climbed to the number three slot on the charts as the LP went double platinum. In November 1984, Michael was honored with his own star on the Hollywood Walk of Fame.

Although 1985 seemed like a relatively quiet year for Michael, he actually accomplished many musical dreams. In January of that year, he wrote "We Are The World" with Lionel Richie as a call to help fight the starvation in Africa. History was made when more than forty of his peers recorded and released the song. In August 1985, the enterprising young man purchased the ATV music catalogue (which includes the Beatles 251-song collection) and became a part of the music publishing world. 1986 saw Michael win a Grammy for Song of the Year ("We Are The World") and the long-awaited release of *Captain Eo* (a 15-minute film collaboration with George Lucas and Francis Coppola which is seen at Disneyland and Disneyworld). Then, the cycle started again. With the release of *Bad* in 1987, the album, videos and tour were all smashes.

Diana Ross, who got to know Jackson well when he appeared as the Scarecrow in 1978's *The Wiz*, singing their duet "Ease on Down the Road," became a mentor to him. "I saw so much of myself as a child in Michael. He was performing all the time. That's the way I was. He could be my son." But unlike Ross who enjoys the limelight *and* the at-home-light, Jackson prefers the isolation of his Encino, Calif., family compound. There amid his electronic toys, his menagerie of exotic animals and his collection of life-size mannequins, he dances unobserved by his adoring fans. On the rare occasion when he leaves the mansion he's likely to be elaborately disguised. Reportedly, he likes to wander about in shopping malls and Disneyland. Otherwise, he may be out on a religious mission: a Jehovah's Witness, he regularly attends prayer meetings and even does door-to-door field service on behalf of the church. He fasts on Sundays and spurns alcohol and drugs. His church frowns upon premarital sex and he is never seen racing around like some Romeo with any old Juliet on Rodeo Drive. In 1988 Michael released his autobiography *Moonwalk* and in 1989 he was the Executive Producer of the astonishing home video "Moonwalker."

Norman Jewison

Norman Frederick Jewison is one of Hollywood's most prolific producer-directors. "I derive inspiration from the nature of the material I am working on, and it is for this reason that I prefer a new subject matter on every film. As a director, I've got to know who and what I'm making a film about, so I have to spend a good deal to time researching the materials." A very ambitious and hardworking man, he has not travelled this road because of the lure of success, although his films have been both critical and box-office hits (*The Cincinnati Kid*, *In the Heat of the Night*, *The Thomas Crown Affair*, *Fiddler on the Roof*, *Rollerball*, *Moonstruck*). Mr. Jewison is a man of integrity who affirms that "the film you present should preserve your intentions for all time." He is also an outspoken director. Disgusted by the turn of events which transformed American filmmaking into a technical extravaganza, he spoke out during the filming of *Moonstruck*. "Yes, it's a romantic comedy, but it's also a literate piece. Its charm and its power come out of John Patrick Shanley's beautiful dialogue. People will walk out of this film saying, 'I know these characters.' No I know we're into an age where you're not supposed to talk very much in films, because, God forbid, you should bore someone. And as a result, there's not too many people writing, using words anymore. This all started around the time of *Star Wars*, when American films moved into a comic-book era of highly visual movies of endless reels of mindless action. They moved away from the written word. But I think we're moving back to the written word and out of this anti-intellectual period. And I think the Academy Award nominations in the past few years bear me out."

Born 21 July 1926 in Toronto, Ontario, Canada, his early academic career was colored by the study of music at the Royal Conservatory. This perhaps attuned him to the musicality of language, so important in his films. He eventually earned his bachelor's degree at Toronto's Victoria College. His early professional career was in television. After seven successful years in Canadian television, he accepted an invitation from America to direct "Your Hit Parade." He carried off three Emmy Awards. Nineteen sixty-one marked his debut in feature filmmaking, and in 1965 he took the plunge as an independent filmmaker with *The Cincinnati Kid*, creating a cult classic.

Married for thirty-six years to Margaret Ann Dixon, or "Dixie" as he calls her, he is the father of three. All of his children are involved in filmmaking (a camera assistant, an assistant editor and an actress). After having lived in the United States for nineteen years, he returned to Ontario to make his home there once again. His latest film is *The January Man* (1989), while rumors abound for a sequel to *Moonstruck*. A much-represented producer-director, he has received many accolades from members of his profession, but his greatest tribute will be his cinematic "oeuvre."

Don Johnson

C lad in pastel suits with sleeves pulled up to elbow-length and wearing tee shirts underneath, Don Johnson was the forerunner of the casual male chic look. Possessed with a sweet yet sly smile, the dimple-faced hazel green-eyed actor has become the quintessential sex symbol.

Johnson was born 15 December 1949 in Flatt Creek, Missouri. His desire to act was instigated by undesirable circumstances. During a high school business administration class Don fell asleep. Feeling somewhat insulted, his teacher expelled him from the course. This led him to take a drama course in order to fulfill his credit requirements. Discovering his niche, Johnson landed the male lead in the high school production of *West Side Story*. Upon graduation, Johnson was granted a rare full scholarship to the University of Kansas in 1966. He remained there until 1968 when he joined the American Conservatory Theatre in San Francisco. Having spent a year in the Conservatory, he auditioned for and was cast by the late Sal Mineo in the Coronet theatre production of *Fortune & Men's Eyes* (1969). Johnson made his feature film debut in *The Magic Garden of Stanley Sweetheart* (1970). To follow, were the features *Zachariah* (1971), *The Harrod Experiment* (1973), *Return to Macon County* (1975), and *A Boy and His Dog* (1976). Making the transition to television in 1977, Johnson appeared in "Big Hawaii," "Ski Lift to Death," "First You Cry," "Amateur Night at the Dixie Bar and Grill," the mini-series "The Rebels" and "From Here to Eternity—The War Years." Adding yet another mini-series to his credit he appeared in "Beulah Land" in 1980 and the TV movies "The Revenge of the Stepford Wives" and "Elvis and the Beauty Queen" in 1981. It was not until 1984 that Johnson finally received the critical acclaim his abilities deserved. His role as Detective Sonny Crockett in NBC's "Miami Vice" was his vehicle to become a household word and receive an Emmy nomination. While his work on the series certainly kept him busy for its five-season run, Johnson still made time for other projects. In 1985 he appeared in the TV movie "The Long Hot Summer." He occasionally directed episodes of "Miami Vice." He displayed his vocal abilities in 1986 with the release of his album *Heart Beat* for Epic Records and executive produced an NBC sitcom pilot "Flip Side." He teamed with Barbra Streisand in 1988 for the duet "Till I Loved You" (the love them from *Goya*). Johnson was also seen in the feature films *Sweethearts Dance* and *Dead Bang*.

While he has been labeled a ladies' man, Johnson had his share of commitment-oriented relationships. A marriage to what was reportedly a high school sweetheart ended in divorce in 1976. On the set of *The Harrod Experiment* he met his second wife, actress Melanie Griffith. That marriage also ended in divorce in 1976. A long-term relationship with actress Patti D'Arbanville produced a son, Jesse Wayne, born 7 December 1982. The union between D'Arbanville and Johnson ended in 1986. He was also teamed with Barbra Streisand. His fateful reunion with former wife Melanie Griffith led to a trip down the aisle on 6 June 1989 in Aspen, Colorado, where they share a home with Jesse and Melanie's son, Alexander. The couple were awaiting the birth of their child together in the fall of 1989. An avid skier, Johnson also enjoys songwriting, fishing, and a good relaxing game of golf.

Van Johnson

"I was the biggest movie fan you ever saw. What a kick it was to drive through those MGM gates in the smog every morning and see that big Leo the Lion looking down at me . . . and when I'd take my little tin lunch box into the dressing-room building and see those signs on the doors— Clark Gable, Spencer Tracy, Robert Taylor, Lionel Barrymore, Fred Astaire— I'd say to myself, "What are *you* doing here, you schnook?" He arrived in Tinsel Town at the height of its glitter in 1941 and his red-haired, freckle-faced

boy-next-door grin soon made him an idol of the bobby-soxers; by 1945, he was one of the industry's top ten box office draws. ("I made my living with my freckles," he once joked. "I get a dollar a freckle.") And demonstrating that the beaming high-wattage Johnson smile hadn't dimmed with the years, he celebrated his fiftieth year in showbiz in June, 1984, still working, alternating mostly between made-for-TV movies and regional theater. In 1985, he returned to Broadway in the role originated by Gene Barry in the musical hit, *La Cage Aux Folles*.

Born 25 August 1916 in Newport, R.I., the son of a plumbing contractor, Van Johnson was starstruck from the start. Heading for New York at 18, he made his debut as a song-and-dance man on stage at the Cherry Lane Theatre in Greenwich Village and later strutted his stuff as a chorus boy on Broadway in *New Faces of 1936*, and *Too Many Girls* and as an understudy to Gene Kelly in *Pal Joey*. On his first venture before the cameras (*Murder in the Big House*, 1941) he attracted little notice, but when he signed on at Metro the magic began. Among his more than 100 films: *Dr. Gillespie's New*

Assistant (an early "Dr. Kildare" offering in 1943), *A Guy Named Joe* (1943), *Thirty Seconds Over Tokyo* (his first star vehicle, in 1944), *In the Good Old Summertime* (with Judy Garland in 1949), *Battleground* (1949), *The Caine Mutiny* (1954), *Miracle in the Rain* (1956). Married to (and divorced from) the former Evie Abbott Wynn, he has one daughter, Schuyler. And for collectors of Hollywood trivia: yes, he still wears his trademark of fire-red socks, even with black-tie.

James Earl Jones

In *The Great White Hope*, James Earl Jones' powerful, Tony Award-winning portrayal of America's first black heavyweight boxing champion Jack Johnson reduced spectators to tears. Some critics called it the most exciting theatre to hit Broadway since Marlon Brando played Stanley Kowalski in *Streetcar Named Desire*. And the *Times* decided that if anyone deserved to become "a star overnight" it was Jones. Later, when he wowed Broadway audiences again in *Fences* (1985-1987; Best Actor Tony and Drama Critics Award), people realized that his success did not come overnight. Behind were years of work in the theatre doing everything from sweeping floors to performing off-Broadway (he won the Obie in 1962) and the great Shakespearean roles.

Jones was born on a farm near Arkabutla, Miss., 17 January 1931. When he was very young, his father left home to become an actor, and the boy grew up on his maternal grandparents' farm in northern Michigan ("a Huck Finn kind of life"). He won a scholarship to the state university, starting as pre-med and ending as a drama major. After a stint in the army, which he came close to making his career ("I wanted to be a Ranger, but I was in with bunch of Southern boys . . . to them a black man could not be a man"), he joined his father in New York and began the climb that led from experimental plays in the Village to *Othello* in Central Park (his Desdemona, Julienne Marie Hendricks, became the first Mrs. Jones) to Broadway. He's portrayed the first black U.S. president in the film *The Man* (1972), the singer-actor-activist in the Broadway play *Paul Robeson* (1977), and the author Alex Haley in TV's "Roots: The Second Generation" (1979). Jones' short-lived 1980 TV show, "Paris," about a non-violent detective, whetted his appetite for another series. His hourlong series, Gabriel's Fire, debuted in the 1990-91 season. His rumbling bass voice was heard on Chrysler and other commercials, and he hissed menacingly as the voice of evil Darth Vader in the *Star Wars* films. He starred in the made-for-TV film "The Atlanta Child Murders" (1985) and a variety of major motion pictures, including *Quarterman* (1985), *Soul Man* (1986), *My Little Girl* (1987), *Gardens of Stone* (1987), *Matewan* (1987), *Fugitives* (1988), *Coming to America* (1988), *Shoeless Joe* (1989), and *The Hunt for Red October* (1990). He was inducted into the Theatre Hall of Fame in 1985. Recent telefilms include "By the Dawn's Early Light," "The Last Flight Out," and "Heat Wave," about the 1965 Watts riots.

Jones lives in Pawling, N.Y., with "three dogs, three horses, three goats, chickens, and rabbits" and his second wife, the former Cecelia Hart. He voices despair over the roles most often written for black actors. "Most American black characters of my time were written around a basic conflict: the character's problems with the white world—and that frankly gets a little dull. 'Whitey' is often the least of black men's problems."

Madeline Kahn

"I 'm not always trying to make people laugh. But they laugh anyway," says the petite redhead. Madeline Kahn considers herself an actress rather than a comedienne, although she's fully aware that she "understands what's funny." Kahn is known to many as the zany and talented leading lady of director Mel Brooks's films. She gave a side-splitting performance as the sexy café singer, Lili von Shtupp, in Brooks' 1974 Western film parody, *Blazing Saddles*. Other memorable Brooks films include *Young Frankenstein*, with Kahn bursting into rapturous song during a "love" scene with the monster. Of her role as Empress Nympho in the 1981 film *The History of the World Part I*, director Brooks commented, "Who but Madeline could look so magnificent, so regal, so stunning, until she spoke and then suddenly metamorphosed into an American princess from Rego Park?"

Born in Boston, Massachusetts, 29 September 1942, Madeline won a scholarship to Hofstra University where she studied drama, music and speech therapy. Deciding against teaching, she set out on an acting career and earned her Equity card in a 1965 City Center revival of *Kiss Me Kate,* before capturing a Tony nomination for her sensitive portrayal of Chrissy in David Rabe's *Boom Boom Room,* in 1973. She made her film debut in Peter Bogdanovich's *What's Up Doc,* and as reviewer Vincent Canby noted, played the part "with picture-stealing lunacy." Next followed her Oscar-nominated role as the carnival dancer, Trixie Delight, in Bogdanovich's *Paper Moon.*

According to Kahn, "flexibility is the key." The versatile actress hops from screen to stage, wherever there's a challenging role. In 1978 she starred in the Broadway musical *On the Twentieth Century,* portraying an eccentric movie queen. Television viewers saw her in two series: "O Madeline" (1983), and "Mr. President" (1987-1988). She also appeared in the movie *Clue* (1985) and on Broadway in *Born Yesterday* (1989). Her 1990 projects include *Betsy's Wedding.* Kahn has never been married ("Men don't feel comfortable being romantic with a funny woman") but doesn't rule out that possibility for the future.

Casey Kasem

With twenty-plus years of experience behind him, he is the most recognized voice on radio today, and the youngest person ever to be inducted into the Radio Hall of Fame. This fame has also earned him a star on Hollywood Boulevard. In addition to being at the top of his radio profession, Kasem is involved in many social and humanitarian campaigns against smoking, discrimination, drunk driving, alcohol abuse and hunger; he has also cohosted the Jerry Lewis Muscular Dystrophy Telethon since 1981.

Born Kemal Amin Kasem in Detroit in 1933, the son of Lebanese Druze parents, Kasem dreamed of becoming a baseball player but ended up as a radio sports announcer in high school. He was also a member of his high school's radio club. Upon entering college (Wayne State University), he majored in Speech and English, and landed roles in shows like "The Lone Ranger" and "Sergeant Preston of the Yukon." His college years were cut short when he was called to serve in the U.S. Army in Korea (1952). During his military service, he coordinated and acted in radio drama on the Armed Forces Network. By 1954 Kasem was back in the U.S. as a civilian, and soon became a disc jockey. He landed jobs in Detroit, Cleveland, Buffalo, Oakland, San Francisco and finally Los Angeles. In 1963, when he moved to Los Angeles, Kasem added TV to his radio work and hosted "Shebang," a dance program produced by Dick Clark. He also branched into film acting and voice-overs, and has done over 2,000 episodes in series such as "Scooby Doo," "Super Friends," "Mister Magoo," and "Transformers," as well as "letters and numbers" on "Sesame Street." His acting continued through the 1970's and 1980's and include such TV series as "Charlie's Angels," "Quincy," "Fantasy Island," "Matt Houston," "Mickey Spillane's Mike Hammer," "America's Top Ten," and the American Video Awards. Kasem also created and hosted the ever-popular "American Top 40," which debuted in July, 1970. In 1989 he presented his countdown show on the Westwood One Network.

Off the air, Kasem is very much involved in philanthropic causes. He is a member of the board of directors for FAIR (Fairness & Accuracy in Reporting), he supports Operation PUSH, which encouraged young people to complete their education, has aided the Great Peace March in the U.S.A., and participated in the American-Soviet Walk To End an Arms Race Nobody Wants, which was held in the U.S.S.R. (1987). His awards include a Distinguished Alumni Award from Wayne State University and the Goodwill Ambassador Award (1987) from the Arab-American Press Guild for his contributions to the Foundation for Mideast Communication.

Kasem and his second wife, Jean (also an actress), live with their three children Kerri, Michael, and Julie, all from his previous marriage.

Elia Kazan

"I 've always been crazy for life. As a young kid I wanted to live as much as possible, and now I want to show it—the smell of it, the sound of it, the leap of it. 'Poetic realism' I call it when I'm in an egghead mood." So exults this award-winning stage and film director, novelist, Broadway actor, and co-founder of Actors Studio. Kazan, who once exerted a strong influence on the works of Tennessee Williams and Arthur Miller, can today boast of having directed five plays that won Pulitzer Prizes (two of them,

Death of a Salesman and *J.B.* won Tonys). He has become a writer himself with solid hits like *America, America* (1962), *The Arrangement* (1967) and his largely autobiographical sixth novel, *The Anatolian* (1982). His directorial credits include a string of Hollywood film classics such as *East of Eden, Baby Doll, Cat on a Hot Tin Roof, Gentlemen's Agreement* (Oscar, 1947), *On the Waterfront* (Oscar, 1954). He was once described by *Vogue* as "rugged without being tough, opinionated but not obnoxious, charged with energy, perception, and a nice fast shot of humor." Said the late Vivien Leigh, "He's the kind of man who sends a suit out to be cleaned and rumpled."

Born Elia Kazanjoglou 7 September 1909, in Istanbul, Turkey, "Gadge" Kazan first made a name for himself as an acting member of the famous 1930s Group Theatre company, appearing from 1934 to 1941 in such classics as *Waiting for Lefty, Golden Boy* and *Lilliom.* His directing career began in 1942 with *Skin of Our Teeth* for which he won a New York Drama Critics Award. He won four subsequent Drama Critics Awards, among them one for *Streetcar Named Desire* (1947). He has acted in some dozen plays and four movies, and directed more than 40 plays and films. He was co-director of the Repertory Theatre of Lincoln Center (1960-64). His autobiography, *Elia Kazan: A Life* was published in 1988.

Kazan and his first wife, Molly Day Thatcher (who died in 1963) had four children. He married actress-director Barbara Loden in 1967. Following her death in 1980, he married Frances Rudge in 1982. He was a recipient of the Kennedy Center Honors in 1983.

Stacy Keach

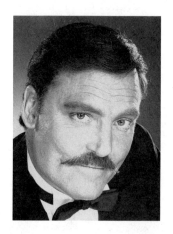

This "finest American classic actor since John Barrymore" (in the eyes of Clive Barnes) decided that a classic American hero could also be done well. "I thought that with enough time and flexibility," says Stacy Keach, "I could make [Mike] Hammer as interesting as any Shakespearean character I have ever played." By using "shtick mannerisms," and suits that he'd made to look appropriately wrinkled by throwing them into a corner, he made the Mickey Spillane-created detective interesting enough for CBS to launch a series after two TV movies. (The series went on hiatus in 1984 while Keach served a six-month plus jail sentence in Great Britain for cocaine smuggling, and upon his release in June, 1985, he went public about his cocaine addiction.) Rather than resume the continuing series, special telefilms of "The New Mike Hammer" pop up once or twice a year with Keach in the starring role. The actor previously gathered bravos, Obies, and Tonys for playing LBJ in the off-Broadway *MacBird*, Buffalo Bill in Broadway's *Indians*, Jamie in *Long Day's Journey Into Night*, and Hamlet in a Central Park production of the New York Shakespeare Festival. He stays busy directing and starring in public or commercial TV movies and in films. In 1989 he filmed *L'Amante* in Paris. His 1990 film *False Identity* was the first U.S. film to have its world premiere in the Soviet Union.

The actor, born Stacy Keach, Jr., in Savannah on 2 June 1941, arrived to actor parents painfully familiar with the hazards of a theatrical career. While his parents wanted him to become a lawyer, his early acting mentors thought he'd be handicapped by the scar left from four childhood operations for a harelip. "The harelip is me," he said, refusing further corrective surgery. Discouragements notwithstanding, he prepared himself with drama studies at the University of California, Yale Drama School, and the Royal Academy of Dramatic Art in London. In 1964 he started making the rounds in New York. In addition to plays, his film credits include *The Heart is a Lonely Hunter* and *That Championship Season*, and in addition to golfing, sailing, and polo, his athletic skills include tightrope-walking for the 1981 musical, *Barnum*. "Audiences started taking it for granted that my character was an accomplished wire walker and there was thus no suspense in my getting up there and taking the 35-foot walk. So I inserted a fake fall, saving myself by grabbing the wire with my hands. . . . Thing is, when . . . will I ever use that skill again?" Divorced from his third wife, former model Jill Donahue, Keach married actress Malgosia Tomassi in 1986.

Diane Keaton

"I wanted to be more than a nice girl. I felt I wasn't really interesting enough," she says. "I was a California girl—I mean *beach*. I think that's one of the reasons I went into acting." She first became famous playing Al Pacino's wife in Coppola's two *Godfather* films ("background music" is how she dismisses this part) and, more importantly, as the female star of a half dozen Woody Allen films. For her title performance in one of these, *Annie Hall*, she swept the '77 Best Actress honors: the Oscar, Golden Globe, N.Y. Film Critics and National Society of Film Critics Awards. Keaton (which is her mother's maiden name; the actress' own surname is Hall) proved her versatility that year in *Looking for Mr. Goodbar* by

playing the intensely dramatic role of a doomed, promiscuous schoolteacher.

Born in L.A. on 5 January 1946, Keaton sang and acted in high school and local theatre productions. After briefly attending two California colleges, she went to N.Y., at 19 to study acting with Sanford Meisner at the Neighborhood Playhouse. She also sang and danced with an obscure rock band. Appearing in the original '68 Broadway production of *Hair*, she eventually assumed the lead role, and the following year starred opposite Allen in his second play, *Play it Again, Sam,* (she repeated the role three years later in her first film with him.) Her initial film appearance was in 1970's *Lovers and Other Strangers*. Her other Allen films are: *Sleeper* ('73), *Love and Death* ('75), *Interiors* ('78, as a death-obsessed poet in his first noncomedy) and *Manhattan* ('79). Her own directorial debut came with *Heaven* (1987).

Keaton sang at N.Y.'s Reno Sweeney cabaret in 1974 before displaying her singing talent in *Annie Hall.* She is also a photographer and has published books on the subject. In analysis, she says, "In my past I've done an awful lot of apologizing. I always liked to say I'm sorry before anything happened, but I don't do that as much anymore." In the early '80s she romanced Warren Beatty. (Rumors were rife that he was willing to end his lifelong bachelorhood by proposing marriage to her but she refused). Beatty directed and co-starred with her in *Reds* (1981), which earned her a second Oscar nomination. Later movies include *Little Drummer Girl* (1984), *Mrs. Soffel* (1985), *Crimes of the Heart* (1986), *Radio Days* (1987), *Baby Boom* (1987), *The Good Mother* (1988), *The Lemon Sisters* (1990), and *The Godfather, Part III* (1990).

Michael Keaton

He is a successful and talented actor and comedian who has performed in theatre, on television, and in films, both in front of and behind the camera.

He was born and raised Michael Douglas in Pittsburgh, Pennsylvania on 9 September 1951. The youngest of seven children, Michael performed Elvis Presley imitations with Hershey bar wrappers stuck to his ears for sideburns for his family when he was a child. He later spent two years at Kent State University as a speech major, where he also began acting in plays and writing comedy material. After leaving college, he returned home and earned money by driving a taxi, and an ice cream truck. In 1972 he began working for the Pittsburgh PBS station WQED taking a job as a part of the technical crew. Three years later he moved to Los Angeles, where his first job as a singing busboy lasted only two nights. He then became a member of the comedy group Second City in Los Angeles. Soon after that he made his television debut, landing a small part

on the show "Maude." Norman Lear liked him so much that he gave him a recurring role as a joke writer on the show "All's Fair," which launched a five year television career that never really quite took off. Other TV appearances include "The Mary Tyler Moore Comedy Hour," "Working Stiffs," "Report To Murphy," and "All in the Family." His film debut was as a morgue attendant in the 1982 comedy *Night Shift*. He was starting to become a recognized actor, so he decided to change his name, since there was already a Michael Douglas. His new name was inspired by a picture of Diane Keaton which he saw in the *Los Angeles Times*. His next film, *Mr. Mom* (1983), was also a comedy. Several other films followed, including *Johnny Dangerously* (1984); *Touch and Go* (1986); *Gung Ho* (1987); *Beetlejuice* (1988); his critically acclaimed performance in *Clean & Sober* (1988) for which he won the best actor prize from the National Society of Film Critics; *The Dream Team* (1989); and the title role in *Batman* (1989), which brought him superstar status.

Michael and Caroline MacWilliams were married in 1982, separated in December of 1988, and were back together in August 1989. They have one son, Sean, who was born in 1983.

Howard Keel

W hen Clayton Farlow proposed to Miss Ellie on the top-rated TV series, *Dallas*, the entire Ewing family (with the exception of J.R., naturally) and their rich Texas friends approved. Moreover, so did millions of televison viewers. From that moment Clayton was "launched," and so was a new TV acting career for singer Howard Keel. Born Harold Keel 13 April 1919, the son of a miner in Gillespie, Ill., he was 17 when his widowed mother moved

to Los Angeles. Working as a supervisor at Douglas Aircraft during WWII, he started singing as a hobby until an agent arranged a meeting with Oscar Hammerstein. "Auditions generally were shattering, but singing for Oscar was like singing in the living room for your father." Signed to a 3-year contract, Keel made his stage debut in *Carousel* (1946) followed by *Oklahoma* that same year. "There was very little notoriety when I replaced John Raitt here in *Carousel* and followed Alfred Drake in *Oklahoma*," recalls Keel. "I was making $250 a week, and the Theatre Guild had two hits. Even in London [*Oklahoma*, 1947] our names were nowhere except in the program."

In 1948 he signed for the movie version of *Annie Get Your Gun* followed by a string of "noteworthy" Hollywood musicals—*Seven Brides for Seven Brothers* (his favorite), *Kiss Me Kate*, *Show Boat* and *Rose Marie*. His most frequent co-star in these films was Kathryn Grayson. "She was the most gorgeous girl and she'd been with MGM since she was 13. Oh, she got a little dingy once in a while," chuckles Keel. "We work well together." For several years Keel and Grayson continued their professional pairing in a successful variety act that played Vegas, Miami and Los Angeles clubs. Never staying out-of-tune with the theater during these movie years, Keel appeared in *Saratoga* (1959), *No Strings* (replacing Richard Kiley, 1963), and *The Ambassadors* (1972) on Broadway, as well as touring in many hit musicals, In 1988 he completed a successful concert tour with an entertaining nightclub act. When one of his three children (1 boy, 2 girls) once expressed interest in pursuing an acting career, Keel reflected: "I was one of God's chosen people, doing what I wanted to do in life. If you find your real thing in life, you've got life 90% made."

Ruby Keeler

"It's really amazing. I couldn't act. I had a terrible singing voice and I can see that I wasn't the greatest tap dancer in the world either," says Ruby Keeler, looking back on those zippy, cornball Hollywood extravaganzas (*Forty-Second Street; Gold-Diggers of 1933; Footlight Parade; Dames; Flirtation Walk; Shipmates Forever*) in which she magically captivated audiences during the bleak

Depression years. "I'm most impressed with how talented the kids are today. They can do anything."

But in January of 1971, at the age of 61, Keeler stepped onto the stage of New York's 46th Street Theater and broke into a sizzling tap routine. In Busby Berkeley's revival of *No, No, Nanette* she wowed audiences as might a newly-discovered star. "Everytime something opens up for me, I call a family conference," she says, so close is she to her four children and her grand-children (her late husband, to whom she was married for 27 years, was John H. Lowe, a prominent broker). Yet four years ahead lay a performance she would have no way of negotiating or planning—the struggle to conquer the damaging effects of a stroke. It was while riding in a car with her daughter and son-in-law in Montana that she suffered an abnormally severe headache, and asked to be driven to the nearest hospital. She was operated on for an aneurysm of the brain, and lay comatose for two months; doctors doubted her chances of pulling through and speculated that, if she did, it was doubtful she would ever walk again. She did emerge from the coma, and, with patience and determination, began walking with the aid of a cane. "I can't run or jump or dance," she said, "but, thank God, I'm still here." In 1981, at a gala at Lincoln Center, Ruby Keeler again stepped out on stage singing "I Want to Be Happy" and broke into dance—only a few simple steps with chorus, but enough to bring the house down in a moving finale. "Never give up. That's the worst," she advises everyone.

Born in Halifax, Nova Scotia, Canada, 25 August 1910, and brought up on New York's Lower East Side, she was dancing at Texas Guinan's at 13. When the legendary Flo Ziegfeld spotted her in a musical called *Lucky*, he signed Keeler up for *Whoopee* with Eddie Cantor, and sent her on the road. Keeler married Al Jolson in Pittsburgh, lived with him in California, but returned to Broadway to star in his *Showgirl*. Her marriage to Jolson ended in divorce. "I really prefer not talking about my life with Al. It's just that my life since then—my husband, my children—has been so full that what came before seems an entirely different life." She occasionally lectures aboard the Queen Elizabeth II about the old Busby Berkeley days and speaks about her illness. Determination, courage, and honesty are her virtues. She begins each day with a simple prayer, "Please keep me well. I fully depend on you and trust you."

Gene Kelly

"Has anybody here seen Kelly?" He was on view briefly during the TV season of 1971 as part-time host of a short-lived NBC-TV series "The Funny Side," and appeared in the movies *Forty Carats* (1973) and *Xanadu* (1980). As a director he was responsible for the Broadway musical *Flower Drum Song*, the film version of the musical *Hello Dolly* (1970), and the film comedies *A Guide For The Married Man* (1967) and *The Cheyenne Social Club* (1970). One of Hollywood's favorite song and dance men during the 40s and 50s (in such films as *Anchors Aweigh, Brigadoon, American in Paris, On the Town* and *Singin' in the Rain*), Kelly revealed his talent as a choreographer in a *Pas de Deux* for the Paris Opera for which he was made a Chevalier of the Legion of Honor by the French government. In 1982 he was accorded Kennedy Center Honors, in 1985 he was honored with the American Film Institute's Life Achievement Award and in 1988 he received the Campione d'Italia Merit of Achievement Award at the Lake Como Festival.

Born Eugene Curran Kelly on 23 August 1912 in Pittsburgh, Pennsylvania, he started dancing as a way to impress girls. "It was strictly a case of male ego," he later recalled. "I'd do a buck-and-wing and they all thought it was nifty. But I hated it at the time. No, there was no inner impulse. It was just a way to meet girls." After studying economics at Penn State and the University of Pittsburgh, he found himself stuck mid-Depression in filling-station and ditch-digging jobs, decided dancing was easier, and opened up a studio in his basement at home. Almost completely self taught, he did so well he soon had a branch studio in Johnstown, and he did equally well when he decided to pull up stakes and try his luck on Broadway in 1938. Within his first year, he'd won attention as Harry, the hoofer in William Saroyan's *The Time of Your Life*, and in 1941 he danced the lead in *Pal Joey*. After his Hollywood debut with Judy Garland in *For Me and My Gal* (1942) his dancing star status climbed. Wed first to actress Betsy Blair (on daughter, Kerry) he married former dancing assistant Jeane Coyne (now deceased) in 1960 (one son and daughter, Timothy and Bridget). He has only occasional regrets that dance fans sometimes relegate him to the ranks of museum retrospectives and whatever-happened-to? "It's only my ego that says, 'Gee, I wish they knew I do something else.'" He displayed his talents in 1986 during a Liberty Weekend special stage presentation. Kelly provided an introduction to accompany a performance of his choreography from *An American in Paris*, performed by Leslie Caron, Rudolf Nureyev and Mikhail Baryshnikov.

Joanna Kerns

She is tall, blonde, and striking, and as talented as she is versatile. This gymnast turned actress has done everything from dancing, to singing, theatre, television, and writing.

Joanna Kerns was born in San Francisco, and grew up in Santa Clara, California. At age 13, Joanna, influenced by her older sister, a two-time Gold Medal winning 1964 Olympic swimmer, decided to move to Fresno to study gymnastics. In spite of her height (5'8") she ranked 14th out of the 28 competing for the 1968 Olympic gymnastic team. A knee injury ended her gymnastic career, so she turned to dance. She later attended UCLA where she majored in dance. While a student at UCLA, she answered a call for the Broadway-bound production of *Clown Around*. She landed a part in the play, but it never got beyond San Francisco. Next, she took a job at Disneyland as a dancer. Soon following, she landed a part as a singer in Joseph Papp's highly successful *Two Gentlemen of Verona*. It was the positive experience that she had in this musical that led her to make the transition into acting. She then moved to New York and began studying under Lee Strasberg, and soon after found herself performing in the acclaimed Broadway production of *Ulysses in Nighttown*. Wanting to pursue television and film work, Joanna returned to Los Angeles, where she studied with Peggy Feury, Jeff Corey and David Craig. She appeared in numerous television shows including "Hill Street Blues," "Magnum, P.I.," "Quincy," and "Laverne and Shirley," but her first real claim to fame on the tube was as Hollywood stunt woman Pat Devon in the CBS series "The Four Seasons." Simultaneously, she appeared in 18 national commercials. More recent TV work includes "A Bunny's Tale," "The Rape of Richard Beck," and the made-for-TV movie "The Mistress," and the successful ABC-TV weekly series "Growing Pains," in which she portrays Maggie Seaver who is a mother, wife and professional journalist. Moving on to film, she has been seen in *Love Struck,* which was nominated for a 1987 Oscar for Live Action Short Film, *Street Justice,* and *Cross My Heart.* During the summer of 1989 she was filming the telefilm based on the Robert Chambers/Jennifer Levin story. In addition to acting, Joanna writes. She has co-written an episode of "Growing Pains," in addition to writing a biographical screenplay entitled *Freestyle.*

Joanna is also active in community organizations and charities. She is National Chairperson of Find the Children, National Chairperson and a member of the Board of Directors of the Institute for the Community as Extended Family in Santa Clara, California. In addition, she has participated in events to benefit such groups as the Muscular Dystrophy Association, Concern II, The Santa Monica Girls Club and The Nancy Reagan Drug Abuse Fund. She participated in June, 1990, in the Golden Eagle Awards of Nosotros, a group that promotes those of Latin American descent working in the entertainment industry.

Deborah Kerr

"Damn it, I am not the dowager empress," she says "but then, they have seen me play all those ladies-in-pearls, so that one really can't blame them." Even her Karen Holmes, the alcoholic nymphomaniac of *From Here to Eternity* didn't change her image. Before it had been *The Hucksters* and *Young Bess,* and after it, *The King and I, Separate Tables* and *The Arrangement,* in which she was, as she put it, "about as sensual as an oyster." But she is no spiritless dowager empress.

Born Deborah J. Kerr-Trimmer, 30 September 1921, in Helensburgh, Scotland, she recalls being one of "those awful English children with a good bringing up." She won a Sadler's Wells ballet scholarship but doggedly pursued a theatrical and film career. Coming to Hollywood in 1947, she was bogged down in the ladylike-serenity type-casting department ("I came over here to act, but it turned out all I had to do was to be high-minded, long suffering, white-gloved, and decorative"), finally rebelled and wangled her MGM release. She came dramatically to the surface in *"Eternity"* (1953) and scored again with her sensitive portrayal of the housemaster's wife in the Broadway production of

Tea and Sympathy (1954). Divorced from TV producer Anthony Bartley (two daughters), she married screenwriter/novelist Peter Viertel in 1960. "All the most successful people seem to be neurotic these days," she says, "Perhaps we should stop being sorry for them and start being sorry for me—for being so confounded normal." She describes herself as "really rather like a beautiful Jersey cow, I have the same pathetic droop to the corners of my eyes." Her biography (*Deborah Kerr*) was published in 1978 and she's been seen periodically on televison in such telefilms as "Witness for the Prosecution" (1982), "Reunion at Fairborough" (1985), and "A Woman of Substance" (1985). She and Viertel divide their time between homes in Switzerland and Spain.

Richard Kiley

"It's something in my nature, that I don't like groups of any kind—not political or religious groups," says the reticent veteran of such smashes as *The Incomparable Max* and *The Man of La Mancha* (for which he won the 1966 Tony Award for "most distinguished performance in a musical"). Widely known as the creator of the title role in *La Mancha*, he repeated the role with success in London and in January, 1980, concluded a record-breaking tour of the United States. An Irish Catholic schooled by priests, Kiley has earned plaudits as both a musical star and straight actor. He toured in 1983 as Father Tim Farley in *Mass Appeal*, and received awards for his role in the television mini-series "The Thorn Birds" and "A Year in the Life" (1988; Emmy and Golden Globe Award for Best Lead Actor). He also received the American Image Award from the Men's Fashion Association in 1988.

Born in Chicago, Illinois, 31 March 1922, he attended Catholic schools until he "seceded" at age 18 after "a set-to with a particularly belligerent cleric" at Loyola University. "I decided that in the process of inclusion there's also a process of exclusion, and I don't believe in that," recalled Kiley. He wasn't out of Barlum Dramatic School very long before World War II began. After serving three and a half years as a gunnery instructor in the Navy, he wangled his way into bit parts on radio shows. By 1953, he was ready for his Broadway debut in Shaw's *Misalliance*, followed quickly by *Kismet* (in which he introduced the memorable "Stranger in Paradise"), and eventually for Tony Awards for *Redhead* (1958) and *La Mancha*. He shined on Broadway again in *All My Sons* (1987). As fans began raving about his explosive actor-singer talents, Kiley remarked with amusement, "I think it's ironic that after I've spent over 20 years in the business, some people are just now finding out about me." His television credits include the roles of George Mason in "George Washington," Emperor Claudius in the TV mini-series "A.D.," and Bea Arthur's romantic partner in the telefilm "One More Time" (1988). His films include *The Blackboard Jungle*, *The Little Prince* and *Looking for Mr. Goodbar*. In 1968, he married Patricia Ferrier. (With ex-wife Mary Wood he has two sons and four daughters.)

Alan King

He's a stage and screen actor, a writer and producer as well as a stand-up comic. "We live," he grouses, "in a suburban town in Long Island. My wife convinced me we were getting our house from an ex-GI. I think it was Benedict Arnold."

Alan King was born in Brooklyn, New York, (as Irwin Kniberg), 26 December 1927 and made his professional show biz debut as a 15-year-old when he formed a four-man band and landed a summer job in the Catskills. When he discovered that comics pulled down $400 a week (he was making $10), he shifted gears, names and professions. Before long he was a headlining comic at Manhattan's famed Leon and Eddie's and by the early 1950s was hitting it big with singers Patti Page, Billy Eckstine and Lena Horne, with the really Big Break coming when he closed the first act of Judy Garland's second appearance at New York's Palace Theatre. During the 1960s he made his stage debut as Nathan Detroit in a New York City Center revival of *Guys and Dolls*. He also appeared on Broadway in *The Impossible Years*. He made his screen debut in *Bye Bye Braverman* in 1968 and in the Eighties was seen in *Just Tell Me What You Want*, *Lovesick*, *Author Author*, *Goodnight Moon*, *Memories of Me* and *Enemies: A Love Story*. His first film-producing venture was *Cattle Annie and Little Britches* (1980). As author, King's credits include *Anyone Who Owns His Own Home Deserves It* and *Help! I'm a Prisoner in a Chinese Bakery*. On balance King has fared well professionally in all his tangential pursuits. He has been married to Jeanette Spring since 1947 and they've reared two sons and a daughter. King has raised millions of dollars in charity benefits around the country but his pet project of them all is the Nassau Center for Emotionally Disturbed Children, a research and rehab complex on Long Island.

Ben Kingsley

"I knew that I was playing a star, and that I wasn't one," says Ben Kingsley of the film role that ended nearly 20 years of obscurity as a classically-trained actor on the British stage. "And the more I learned about Gandhi, the more I felt genuinely ennobled by my task." Kingsley's only previous screen appearance had been a decade earlier in a British adventure film flop, but his portrayal of the title role in Richard Attenborough's controversial, internationally popular *Gandhi* earned him a slew of awards, culminating in an Oscar (beating out no less than Dustin Hoffman, Jack Lemmon, Paul Newman, and Peter O'Toole).

Kingsley was born Krishna Bhanji 31 December 1943 in a Yorkshire village, the son of an Indian physician who emigrated from South Africa to England to study and a British fashion model/ actress. As associate artist of the Royal Shakespeare Co., Kingsley was in the original cast of *Nicholas Nickleby* and has also performed at London's National Theatre and on British television. He confirmed his versatility with his portrayal of an intense, articulate cuckold in the post-*Gandhi* film version of Harold Pinter's play *Betrayal*. Later films include *Harem* (with Natassja Kinski), *Turtle Diary* (with Glenda Jackson), *Pascali's Island* (a suspense drama based on the Barry Unsworth novel), *Secret of the Sahara*, *Without a Clue* and *Testimony*. He also starred in the 1988 HBO production "Murderers Among Us: The Simon Wiesenthal Story."

Kingsley is committed to "good modern writers who encourage a degree of thought and consciousness about society." But, he claims, "Shakespeare's my great love. If I play other parts I get withdrawal symptoms—chemical longings in my veins." Kingsley's one-man show, *Edmund Kean* (in which he evoked the 19th century tragedian's legendary Shakespearean interpretations), was a New York hit in fall of 1983. It was directed by his second wife (since

1978), Alison Sutcliffe, with whom Kingsley and their son Edmund (named for Kean) live in a rambling old house in a village eight miles from Stratford-upon-Avon. Kingsley also has two children from his former marriage to actress Angela Morant.

Nastassja Kinski

"I guess I have been the creature of the director's imagination. You see, I want to get a glimpse of his eyes searching things out inside me. I want to go to heaven and hell for him. I want to make his dreams come true," says the woman who some say is most likely to succeed as Garbo's ethereal replacement in the late 20th Century. "You live and love twice as deeply in the movies. I always fall in love when I'm working on a film. Then you slip out of it, like a snakeskin and you're cold and naked. What worries me is that when these loves die, they hardly leave a trace on me. I wonder why I don't suffer?"

Maybe no suffering, but all that living and loving did leave its trace. Nastassja, born 24 January 1961, the daughter of the German film star Klaus Kinski, was pregnant in 1984 and reluctant to name the lucky father. This sparked a lot of gossip. (The German magazine *Bunte* printed the names and photos of eight of the film star's possible baby-maker boyfriends.) A son was born July, 1984, and mummy was mum until the baby was named (Aljosha) and a father/fiance produced as well (Ibrahim Moussa, the Egyptian-born talent agent-producer). At least the international media calmed down, especially when the couple finally wed in September of 1984. The couple have another child, Sonia, born in 1986.

Discovered in a Munich rock and roll club when she was in her early teens, Kinski made her film debut in the German-made *The Right Move*. Introduced by her mother, who also doubled as best friend, to Roman Polanski, the actress and the director made *Tess* together, a painstaking evocation of 19th Century English countryside life based on a Thomas Hardy novel. After receiving the Polanski polish, she alighted tender and dewy, a true camera animal in films such as *Cat People, One From the Heart, Exposed, Hotel New Hampshire, Paris, Texas, Revolution, Torrents of Spring* and *Up to Date,* Lina Wertmuller's controversial film dealing with AIDS. Of all her films, it was *Tess* that lighted the fuse. Richard Avedon's 1981 nude photograph of Kinski melding with a sprawling python straight from Central Casting's Garden-of-Eden bin became an international sell-out poster, boosting her notoriety. It said: "Nastassja is nasty, but so very divine."

Robert Klein

H is parents wanted him to go into medicine but as he explains, "things got in the way, like chemistry and physics." Instead, Robert Klein went on to become a multimedia personality as a comedian and actor. From clubs to Broadway, records to home video, television to movie appearances, Klein has done it all successfully.

Robert Klein was born 8 February 1942 in the Bronx, New York, to Ben and Frieda Klein. The family, including Klein's sister Rhoda, filled the house with singing and laughter but no show business aspirations. The closest Klein got to it was when at the age of fourteen, he appeared with the Teen Tones, a singing group, on the "Ted Mack Amateur Hour." They lost to a one-armed piano player. The Dewitt Clinton High School graduate entered Alfred (New York) University as a pre-med student but graduated in 1962 with a B.A. in political science and history. Klein had joined the school's acting company, whose drama teachers encouraged him to enter the Yale University School of Drama. He spent a year there after graduation. Regarding his Yale experience, Klein said, "Drama coach Connie Welch . . . didn't give me a very good advice, but she did say one thing that rang in my ears. 'Klein,' she said in front of Drama 22, 'You ought to do a one-man show.'" Klein supported himself as a substitute teacher in the Mount Vernon, N.Y., school system while making his foray into stand-up comedy. He performed at Greenwich Village coffeehouses like Cafe Wha? and Bitter End. Initially a hit, Klein began to feel like a "bomb," so he auditioned for the Second City Improvisational Troupe in Chicago, which he joined in March, of 1965. "I learned everything. Discipline, improvisation, and the art of working a comedy routine. It matured me as a performer, and gave me a feeling of control." Klein returned to N.Y. in 1966 with the troupe's revue and was cast in the Broadway musical *The Apple Tree* directed by Mike Nichols. Other Broadway appearances included *New Faces of 1968* and *Morning, Noon and Night* (1968-1969). Carnegie Hall welcomed him in 1973 with "The First Annual Robert Klein Reunion." The show's successors still sell out annually. Klein's Broadway triumph came in 1979 with the musical *They're Playing Our Song*, for which he was nominated for a Tony Award as Best Actor and awarded the L. A. Drama Critics Award. Broadway led to film roles: *The Landlord* (1970), *The Owl and the Pussycat* (1970), *The Pursuit of Happiness* (1971) and *Rivals* (1972). He has also performed in *Hooper, The Bell Jar, Nobody's Perfect* and the animated *The Last Unicorn* (voice over). Television also called, with a 1968 appearance on "The Ed Sullivan Show." He hosted the 1970 CBS series "Comedy Tonight," and made countless appearances on "The Tonight Show Starring Johnny Carson" (as a guest and guest host), "Late Night With David Letterman" and as a regular on NBC's "Bloopers and Practical Jokes." He acted in the new "Twilight Zone" series as well as television movies such as "Summer Switch," "This Wife for Hire," "Poison Ivy" and "Your Place or Mine?" Cable TV has carried five of Klein's one-man shows on HBO and his special "Robert Klein at Yale" (1982) has become a permanent part of the Museum of Broadcasting collection. He also acted in HBO's "Table Settings" and Showtime's "Pajama Tops" and starred in two home videos, "Robert Klein: Child of the 50's, Man of the 80's" (1984) and "Robert Klein on Broadway" (1986). Klein hosts the USA Network show "Robert Klein Time," which debuted in October, 1986. Two of Klein's comedy albums, *Child of the Fifties* (1973) and *Mind Over Matter*, earned him Grammy nominations and from 1979 to 1981 he hosted "The Robert Klein Radio Show," a syndicated comedy/rock show.

Klein resides with his wife, opera singer Brenda Boozer, and their son, Alexander Stewart, in Manhattan. He relaxes in his spare time by traveling throughout the country appearing at colleges, universities, and theaters as well as Atlantic City.

Kevin Kline

"Acting humanizes me. When I saw a movie and was moved or allowed to feel something deeply that transcended the mundane, it was very exciting. Music for me was transcendental, it made me feel more alive. It was a peak experience. And when I was moved by acting, it was the same kind of celebratory experience. Actually, when I first did it I was attracted to it because it was impossible to do. I stank when I first started acting. I was really wretched. Very stiff, repressed, inhibited. Acting was a release for me. I'm much more expressive of emotion now than I used to be. Eventually, I found that simpering emotional wreck that I really am. I feel actors are very fortunate because they can get this stuff out. You get to explore those things in yourself. When I was moved by an acting performance, I'd think, 'I'd like to do that  for somebody. I'd like to make people feel alive.' I love sensation. . . . I'm just a cheap sensationalist, is what it comes down to."

Born 24 October 1947 in St. Louis, Missouri, to a Jewish father who owned a record store, sang opera, and played the piano, and a Catholic mother, Kline attended Catholic schools run by Benedictine monks. After discovering acting in college, he moved to New York to attend the drama division of Juilliard and was on hand when John Houseman formed The Acting Company. "It was a cushy introduction to acting profession," he explains. "I didn't have to bang on doors and try to sneak into Equity auditions. We were given our Equity cards and about 47 weeks of employment a year, along with the opportunity to play great roles in the classical repertory as well as modern. It was a great training ground."

After four years touring with the company, this "1980's Errol Flynn" (*Vanity Fair*) returned to New York's theatre scene and, as quick as you can say. "The envelope, please," he won two Tony Awards—one for *On the Twentieth Century*, a second for *Pirates of Penzance.*

In 1985, Kline appeared on Broadway in a revival of Shaw's *Arms and the Man* as well as the Off-Broadway production of *Hamlet.* He made a brilliant film debut as a schizophrenic opposite Meryl Streep in *Sophie's Choice* and went on to film fame in the cinema version of *Pirates*, then *The Big Chill, Silverado, Cry Freedom, The January Man, A Fish Called Wanda* (for which he won the Academy Award for Best Supporting Actor) and *I Love You to Death.* In 1990 he returned to the New York stage as star and director of another production of Shakespeare's *Hamlet.* Noting his "come-hither charm" and his "cavalier-cad" quality, *Vanity Fair* borrowed a line from *Sophie's Choice* and called him "utterly, fatally glamorous." The dashing actor left the single scene in 1989 when he married actress Phoebe Cates.

Kris Kristofferson

Probably the only Rhodes Scholar ever to use his Oxford educational opportunity to pen American country music, Kristofferson writes lambently literate lyrics that have become more soul-baringly autobiographical than ever. His songs haven't been recorded by more than 450 crooners without good reason, and the man Willie Nelson referred to as the most prolific contemporary songwriter ("If he could sing, he'd be a threat to me") used his disappointments as material for even more hits. Afterwards, he says, "Everybody was welcoming me back to the record business when I'd never been gone. God knows, I've been on tour every year almost, but I was the world's best-kept secret."

The tough-but-tender screen and recording star who has been able to command $1 million per role also draws down half a million a year for song royalties. Son of an Army general (now retired), Kris Kristofferson spent most of his boyhood in Brownsville, Texas (born 22 June 1936), and became a fan of late country singer Hank Snow. An aspiring songwriter at age eleven, he was the winner of four *Atlantic Monthly* fiction prizes, and as a football player and boxer at Pomona College won a Rhodes scholarship in 1958. While deep in the classics at Oxford, Kristofferson was approached by a British promoter who tried to transform him into a rock idol, but the experience almost turned him away from the music business entirely. "They renamed me Kris Carson and my friends were calling me the Golden Throated Thrush," he says. After collecting his degree he "bailed out, got married, and went into the army," and there picked up the songwriting habit again. When he was assigned to teach English at West Point, he spent all his leaves in Nashville. ("I got so excited I wrote ten songs the first week I was there.") He tended bar part-time and was a janitor in the same studios where Johnny Cash was plying his trade. His 1965 hit, "Vietnam Blues" set him up for a bigger blues smash, "Me and Bobby McGee," which made him a full-time performer-songwriter. He made his debut as an actor in 1972 in *Cisco Pike*, and has been in evidence since in *Pat Garrett and Billy the Kid* (1973), *Bring Me the Head of Alfredo Garcia* (1974), *Alice Doesn't Live Here Anymore* (1974), *The Sailor Who Fell from Grace with the Sea* (1976), the 1976 unkindly-received remake of *A*

Star Is Born, Heaven's Gate (1981), *Rollover* (1981), *Songwriter* (co-starring Willie Nelson, 1985), *Trouble in Mind* (1986), *Dead or Alive* (1988), *Helena* (1988), *Big Top Pee-Wee* (1988), *Millennium* (with Cheryl Ladd, 1989), *Welcome Home* (1989) and *Ryder* (1989). He also appeared in the CBS miniseries "Blood and Orchids" in 1985. The lithe, square-jawed, twice-divorced balladeer said after his break-up with singer Rita Coolidge (divorced, 1979), "I don't feel any anxiety about my solo condition. I ain't gonna be a hard case, but the next one will have to be carrying notes from the Pope." Neverthe-less, in 1983 he married attorney Lisa Meyers. The couple have a son John Robert (born 15 May 1987); Kristofferson has three children (Tracy, Kris, Casey) from his previous marriages. During an inter-view with the *Gavin Report* he comments on his optimistic point of view. "If I didn't have hope, I wouldn't get out of bed. I feel like a person can make a difference and that it matters to try and make a difference."

Stanley Kubrick

"The most powerful level on which a film works on the audience is on the subconscious," he says. "On this level we are all equally perceptive and equally blind. Watching a film is really like taking part in a controlled dream." Director Stan-ley Kubrick controlled the dreamy im-agery for us in his futuristic epic, *2001 A Space Odyssey* (1968), in the disturbing 1971 opus, *A Clockwork Orange,* and in *Sparatacus* (1960), *Dr. Stangelove* (1964), *Barry Lyndon* (1975) and *The Shining* (1979).

Born 26 July 1928 in New York, he started out as a photojournalist (on *Look,* among other publications), did documentary films, and crested as a much-heralded New Wave director with his stark 1958 anti-war film, *The Paths of Glory.* Explaining that he operates 'three-quarters on intuition," he con-siders the most important part of filmmaking what he calls "the C.R.P.—crucial rehearsing period." ("Shooting is the part of filmmaking I enjoy the least. I don't particularly enjoy working with a lot of people. I'm just not an extrovert.") But he is a perfectionist who has been known to call for more than 100 retakes, and who not only oversees every aspect of filming and post-production, but even promotion.

Twice married and divorced, he's now wed to painter Suzanne Christiane Harlan (three daughters), with whom he lives outside London. He owns a wardrobe consisting almost exclusively of blue blazers, gray trousers, black shoes and socks (thereby eliminating tough decisions about what to wear). The admitted safety nut won't ride in a car going faster then 30 mph unless he's behind the wheel, nor will he fly in planes. And he thinks moviegoers ought to see films more than once to absorb them. "The thing I really hate," Kubrick says, "is to explain why the film works, what I had in mind, and so forth." In 1988, Kubrick received the Luchino Visconti Award in Italy.

Swoosie Kurtz

Named after "the Swoose", a B17 bomber flown by her father Colonel Frank Kurtz (the most decorated pilot of World War II), she had her first taste of Broadway stardom playing a pill-popping heiress in *The Fifth of July* (1981), and soon thereafter walked off with a Tony, a Drama Desk Award and an Outer Critics Circle Award. "I think what made me a good actress is the fact that as an Army officer's daughter, I was always on the move. I attended seventeen different grammar schools and was constantly assaulted with traumas. I had to keep adjusting. Thank God for my wonderful parents. If it hadn't been for them, I might be deeply disturbed instead of only mildly disturbed."

Born in 1944 Swoosie (rhymes with Lucy, not woozy) Kurtz describes herself as a "late bloomer." After aspiring to be a ballerina and a writer, she instead chose acting and, following high school, attended the London Academy of Music and Dramatic Art. Arriving back in the U.S., she experienced the usual slings and arrows of an unknown actress trying to become known but when things finally started to happen, she found her two years in London hadn't been wasted: "I learned to get right on with it in rehearsal, to simply 'have a bash.' So that's what I do, with total commitment. And then I work backward to figure out why things happen." The '77-'78 theater season was a crucial one for Kurtz. She appeared in *Tartuffe* (Tony nomination) and *Uncommon Women and Others* (Obie and Drama Desk Award nominations). Nearly stealing the show for her performance in the latter production, Swoosie says that it was *Uncommon Women* that really "did it" for her. Since then she has cruised at high altitude—a 1980 role with the Yale Repertory Company as Honey in *Who's Afraid of Virgina Woolf?* was "one of the greatest experiences in my life." After trying her television wings on the shortlived "Mary Tyler Moore Variety Show," she spent two seasons on the tube (opposite Tony Randall) on NBC's "Love Sidney" and was twice nominated for an Emmy Award. Her film credits include *Slap Shot, The World According to Garp, Against All Odds, Wildcats, Vice Versa, Bright Lights, Big City, Dangerous Liasons,* and *Letters.*

Burt Lancaster

One-time acrobat, veteran of the tank-town carnival circuit, and a former floor-walker in Marshall Field's ladies lingerie department, Burt Lancaster vaulted to filmdom's center ring only after—so the Hollywood legend goes—he was discovered in an elevator by Harold Hecht. "Movies," Lancaster is supposed to have said to Hecht with whom he later formed a successful production company (1957), "I'm not interested." Clearly he changed his mind, exploding onto the screen in 1946 in *The Killers* and later appearing in such films as *Brute Force, All My Sons, Come Back Little Sheeba, From Here to Eternity, Sweet Smell of Success, Separate Tables, Elmer Gantry* (an Oscar in 1960), *Bird Man of Alcatraz* (Best Actor, Venice Film Festival), *The Train, The Swimmer, Airport, The Leopard, Atlantic City, The Goldsmith Shop, The Suspect, The Betrothed, Rocket Gilbraltar,* and *Shoeless Joe.* As New York Times' critic Vincent Canby has pointed out, Lancaster began evidencing a pattern in the late 1950s. "For each mass-market entertainment film he made, there was always one comparatively risky, 'artistic' venture." At about the same time, columnist Roberta Ashley suggested Lancaster was acting with his hair, meaning when his hair looked "leading-mannish" in stills one could bet the movie would be on the order of *I Walk Alone* or *Ten Tall Men* as opposed to his more "serious" films (*Sheeba, Judgment at Nuremburg, The Leopard*) which portrayed him wearing a bowl-shaped cut, plastering his hair down, or parting it in the middle. On

TV he acted as the host-narrator of the highly praised series on the life and music of Verdi.

Born Burton Stephen Lancaster 2 November 1913, he was the two fisted baby of a large Irish family in Manhattan's East Harlem. "If you want to know love," his mother is said to have counseled, "stay in the house with me. But if you want to know life, go out in the streets." Little Burt opted for the streets, became an accomplished scrapper, and won a scholarship to New York University, where he stayed just two years before hitting the tanbark trail in tandem with a partner improbably named Nick Cravat. "I'd always wanted to be an acrobat," he explains (and he played one in *Trapeze*). At some point amid the somersaulting, Lancaster began to itch to do some acting and so left Cravat and went on his first audition. (He "wasn't nervous. . . . I said to myself, 'What can happen to me? I can miss a line, but I can't get hurt.'" Except by the critics, of course.)

He was first married to a woman trapeze artist (it "did not work out"); his second wife was Norma Anderson, whom he met overseas during World War II and from whom he divorced more than two decades and five children later. He is known for his love of animals, for his short temper (he once walked off a Mike Wallace interview. When the "Big Temper" blows, one columnist wrote, he chews out like "an angry dockworker") and for his consistent refusal to adhere to filmtown standards. "The streak of nonconformity appeared early," a friend says. As a kid, "he was supposed to be an angel in the Christmas pageant . . . the audience roared. I looked up and there was Burt peeling the chewing gum off the sole of his shoe."

Michael Landon

"If Michael Landon bombs, I don't want anybody else to have to take the blame but Michael Landon." Few stars have managed to influence the total production of a television series with the authority he wielded over "Little House on the Prairie." As executive producer and lead, as well as frequent director and writer, he imbued the wholesome program with his ideologies about faith and family. Soon after the show's demise, he returned to the tube in 1984 with a new series, "Highway to Heaven." The show ran through 1989, with the possibility of resurrecting the cast for yearly telefilms.

He was born Eugene Maurice Orowitz 1 October 1936; his mother was the former Broadway comedienne Peggy O'Neill. Raised in Collingswood, N.J., he was one of two Jewish children at his school and painfully recalls suffering anti-Semitic taunting from his classmates. At home, his parents waged a silent cold war. "My parents never spoke much to each other and didn't even argue. We never hugged or showed any emotion. Basically, I was a loner. . . . I'm a driven man because from the time I was a kid, I wanted to show myself and others I was somebody." He found solace in athletics, earning honors in the javelin throw and winning a sports scholarship to the University of Southern California.

Picking his stage name out of the Los Angeles phone book, he pursued acting roles while working odd jobs, and was cast as little Joe Cartwright, the upstart son of a ranching patriarch on "Bonanza." During a popular 14-year run, it held the number one ratings position for seven consecutive seasons and was aired in 87 countries. While growing up before the cameras, he worked behind the scenes as a scriptwriter, and occasional director. However, his growing expertise made him critical of the show's scripts, leading to friction on the set. With "Bonanza" finished in 1973, he looked for an opportunity that would allow him to make a greater contribution and decided on NBC's answer to "The Waltons," "Little House on the Prairie," an adaption of Laura Ingalls Wilder's children's classic about an American frontier family. Again, Landon battled his associates over the direction of the storyline, favoring greater deviation from the original book series. He prevailed and provided the network with almost a decade of well-rated, noncontroversial programming. "People still say I'm arrogant. They just don't say I'm insecure anymore."

After an early marriage ended in divorce, Landon married model Lynn Noe in 1963, and they have five children. Their divorce, in 1982, which received much attention in the gossip press, was quickly followed by Landon's marriage to a young make-up artist, Cindy Clerico. They have a daughter and a son.

Jessica Lange

The daughter of a traveling salesman, she moved 18 times as a youngster. "I just know that how I survived all those family years was my ability to withdraw and live in a dream world," she says. "It's not that it was horrendous—it was my way of

removing myself." Although this one-time dreamer began her film career inauspiciously in 1976 via the Fay Wray part in a second-best remake of *King Kong*, her contrasting roles in two films released at Christmastime, 1982— *Frances* and *Tootsie* — clinched her reputation. Her performance in the latter as a romantically victimized soap opera actress earned Lange several supporting actress awards: from the New York Film Critics, National Society of Film Critics and, ultimately, the Oscar.

Born in rural Minnesota on 20 April 1949, Lange was an 'A' student in high school and won an art scholarship to the University of Minnesota. She soon dropped out, however, and, while still a teenager, married Spanish photographer Paco Grande, with whom she traveled the U.S. extensively, living in an old truck. They later divorced. After spending about two years in Paris studying mime with Marcel Marceau's teacher and dancing at the Opera Comique, Lange moved to New York, where she studied acting and worked as a waitress and model. Following her *King Kong* debut, her career languished for three years—during which she resumed acting lessons—until her friend Bob Fosse offered her a small part in his autobiographical film, *All That Jazz*. The following year, 1980, marked Lange's first professional stage appearance in summer stock in North Carolina. She was praised for her sexually-charged performance in another disappointing film remake, *The Postman Always Rings Twice* .

Making *Frances* "devastated" her, Lange told *Newsweek*. "I was really hell to be around. I took on the characteristic of Frances [Farmer, the talented but troubled actress] that was elemental in her demise—battling every little thing that came along." Kim Stanley, who played her mother in *Frances*, advised Lange: "Make a comedy as fast as you can." Hence *Tootsie*.

Keeping her single status, Lange has one daughter, Alexandra, by ballet superstar Mikhail Baryshnikov, whom she never married and two children, Hannah and Samuel, by present live-in boyfriend, playwright Sam Shepard. Lange leads a nomadic existence: apartments in New York and Los Angeles, a lakefront cabin (on 120 acres she owns) near her parents' home in Minnesota, another retreat near Taos, N.M., to which this self-described "loner" might "just retire and paint." As a young girl, Lange couldn't wait to escape from northern Minnesota; now when she's "in trouble," that's where she retreats, to "get my head clear. . . . All those midwestern traits—honesty, simplicity, lack of ambition—those virtues I used to see as dull. I now see as admirable." Her films include *Country* (1984, she also produced and co-starred with Shepard), *Sweet Dreams* (1985), *Crimes of the Heart* (1986), *Far North* (1988), *Everybody's All-American* (1988) and *Men Don't Leave* (1989). She also starred in a television remake of "Cat on a Hot Tin Roof," in which she scored as a smouldering and clawing Maggie the Cat.

Frank Langella

"I'm bred for the theatre." Frank Langella told writer Judy Klemesrud, "I'm sensory. I love to touch, feel, smell, love, kiss, hug, and that's what happens when you're in front of an audience every night." The gamut of his stage lives stretches from a sea lizard named Leslie to Count Dracula, the Prince of Homburg, Cyrano, Salieri in *Amadeus*, to the explorer of the erotic in *Passion* and one of the capricious trio in the 1984 revival of Noel Coward's *Design For Living*. That same year his portrayal of Quentin in the revival of Arthur Miller's *After the Fall* ("absorbing is Mr. Langella's driving performance in the marathon role") added another dimension to his keenly crafted career. In 1987 he mesmerized the Broadway audiences again in *Sherlock's Last Case*.

Born in Bayonne, New Jersey, New Year's Day 1940, the son of the president of the Bayonne Barrel and Drum Company was nourished as a child by a close-knit Italian-American family. He realized early that the theatre was the life for him, "the combined passions of the kitchen table and the Catholic Church" instilling in him "a great love of majesty and size, heroism and grandeur." In his early years, a "funny looking kid with glasses who competed for attention with a beautiful sister and a brilliant brother by standing upon restaurant tables and reciting poems," he imitated John Gielgud's Shakespearean recordings in a concentrated effort to get rid of his New Jersey accent. He attended Columbia High School in Maplewood, N.J., Syracuse University, and after apprenticing at the Pocono Playhouse, made his official New York debut in a revival of *The Immoralist*. Off-Broadway, Obie-award performances for three consecutive years (*The Old Glory*, *Good Day* and *The White*

Devil), were followed by Lincoln Center Repertory appearances in *Yerma* and *A Cry of Players* and a Circle in the Square production of *Iphigenia in Aulis*. He made his Tony-winning debut on Broadway in 1975 with painted face and wearing a tail in the bizarre role of a talkative sea lizard in Edward Albee's Pulitzer Prize-winning play, *Seascape*. Following the brief off-Broadway run of *The Prince of Homburg*, he opened again on Broadway in 1977 in a virtuoso portrayal of *Dracula*. Langella's movie debut was the 1970 *The Twelve Chairs* with Mel Brooks, followed by *The Diary of a Mad Housewife* for which he received the National Society of Film Critics award. Other films: *The Deadly Trap, The Wrath of God, Dracula*, a remake of *Invasion of the Body Snatchers, Sphinx, The Men's Club*, and *Masters of the Universe*. Television roles include: "Eccentricities of a Nightingale," "The Sea Gull," "The Prince of Homburg," "Sherlock Holmes," and a series based on the life of George Washington. Married in 1977 to the former Ruth Weil, he shares with her a handsome Manhattan apartment. Not content to rest on his laurels, Langella says:"I would rather have a sixty-year span as a good, fine actor than have five hot years as a superstar, become rich and then disappear. My work is my life, and I want my work to last the length of all my lifetime."

Angela Lansbury

When mystery writer Jessica Fletcher became involved in the solving of a murder in the inital episode in 1984 of the hit television series, "Murder, She Wrote," Angela Lansbury began another phase of her phenomenal career. "My sense is that Jessica Fletcher also embodies many of the qualities which are quintessentially American," she asserted in a *New York Times* interview about the series. "She's very open, resilient and brave, a woman of very strong moral character. But she's never a bore."

The London-born (16 October 1925) daughter of the respected Irish actress Moyan Macgill and Edgar Lansbury, an English lumber merchant and mayor of Poplar in the East End of London, Angela Lansbury first studied acting and singing as a teen-ager. "I had a make-believe life that I would be like the characters in the movies I saw," she recalls. "I had a whole secret life and used to sit on buses, staring out the window and looking as though I had T.B., always playing someone other than myself. I thought a lot about America, but I never thought of myself as an actress playing these roles. I was going to go to America and walk down those golden sidewalks, step into a club and meet Boston Blackie on the corner. That was my Make Believe Mountain." She was only 15 when World War II changed her whole way of life. She and her mother were evacuated from London and she went to New York to continue her theatrical studies. She first became a favorite of American movie audiences in 1944 (after a move to Hollywood) when she played the Cockney maidservant in *Gaslight* for which she was nominated for a "Best Supporting Actress" Academy Award. ("One day I was making $28 a week at Bullock's department store and the next day I was up to $500 a week at MGM.") She received a second nomination the following year for *The Picture of Dorian Gray*. Subsequently, she appeared in more than seventy films, most often in character roles of either hussies or heavies. "There's nothing like a good villainess," Lansbury confesses. "You can go to town and chew on great chunks of scenery." Her favorite film portrayal was the monstrously malevolent mother in *The Manchurian Candidate*.

Lansbury launched what she calls "Phase II" of her career in 1957, making her Broadway debut as the object of the adulturous affections of Bert Lahr in *Hotel Paradise*. Audiences on Broadway have cheered her in *A Taste of Honey;* the Stephen Sondheim musical, *Anyone Can Whistle; Mame;* her portrayal of the seventy-five-year old Madwoman of Chaillot in *Dear World;* the persona of Mama Rose in a revival of *Gypsy;* and as the fiendish piemaker, Mrs. Lovett, in Sondheim's *Sweeney Todd*. She won Tony Awards for all four of the latter shows and, in 1982, was inducted into the Theatre Hall of Fame. Her love for the theatre and her professional charm makes Angela a favorite host of the yearly Tony Awards.

Before settling into her series, which finished up in 1990, Lansbury zigzagged between movies and television. Recent films included *The Mirror Crack'd, Death on the Nile, Bedknobs and Broomsticks, and Pirates of Penzance*. On television, she's starred in: "Little Gloria . . . Happy at Last" (1982), "A Gift of Love" (1984), "A Talent for Murder" (1984), "Rage of Angels: The Story Continues" (1986), "One More Time" (1988), and *A Green Journey* (1990). On the home video scene, she released "Angela Lansbury's Positive Moves" in 1989.

In 1949, Lansbury married American Peter Shaw, who manages her career. "We decided long ago to make it a tandem operation," she says. They have a son, Anthony, a daughter, Deirdre, a stepson, David, plus grandchildren. When asked if she would ever consider giving up her career, Lansbury quickly replied, "No, I need it desperately. I need that outlet in my life. I need to perform very much or I'm just not happy. I often try to describe what it is that I want to share with the audience. I want to achieve those high, screaming moments in theatre which you can't always hit, but which, when you do, there's no experience in the world that can match it."

David Lean

"**G**ood films can be made only by a crew of dedicated maniacs," declares this "Michelangelo" of film directors whose credits include such classics as *The Bridge on the River Kwai, Lawrence of Arabia, Dr. Zhivago,* and *A Passage to India.* A man with a tremendous sense of environment, a photographer's eye for composition, a musician's feel for rhythm, Lean immerses himself completely in his work. The hardest part of filmmaking is finding a story to fall in love with says Lean, confessing that it's love stories that he's always enjoyed most of all. "I like telling stories," he says. "I want to direct films where the audiences come out discussing the characters they've just been watching. . . ." Since 1955, when he depicted an unforgettable image of Venice, as seen through the eyes of Katherine Hepburn in *Summertime,* he's shown a fascination for locations. The essence of places has continually pervaded Lean's cinema, whether barren and exotic as the desert in *Lawrence* or verdent and storm-tossed like the west coast of Ireland in *Ryan's Daughter.*

Born into a Quaker family in Croyden, England, 25 March 1908, David Lean was educated in a local Quaker school. His father wanted him to be an accountant, but David decided he wanted to work in films. A top film cutter by the 1930s, he also had a complete grounding in newsreel making. ("It's essential to learn to use the tools of the trade, then it's up to talent.") Noel Coward gave Lean his first chance to direct with *In Which We Serve* (1942). Lean formed his own company, Cineguild, the next year, and followed with such notable Coward pictures as *This Happy Breed, Blithe Spirit,* and *Brief Encounter.* ("I learned a lot from working with Noel. A lot about handling actors . . . tactful as anything, encouraging to frightened rabbits, tough when necessary.") After the Coward films, Lean made *Oliver Twist* and the unforgettable *Great Expectations.* Three of his films (*Dr. Zhivago*, 1965; *Lawrence of Arabia*, 1962; *The Bridge on the River Kwai*, 1957) collected a total of 19 Oscars and Lean won the award for best director on the latter two. *Ryan's Daughter* (1970)—which he viewed as his most realized work but was condemned by most critics as his worst—was Lean's last film until *Passage to India*, the long-awaited movie based on E.M. Forster's great 1924 novel. "*Passage* is a very special subject." says Lean. "There are six wonderful characters, which is a rare thing in a movie. . . . There are a lot of loose ends just as there are in real life. You meet people, you understand certain aspects of them, but others are hidden and you have to guess what they are. This kind of interplay intrigues me enormously." Producer Anthony Havelock-Allan once said of this master filmmaker: "David is a marvellous storyteller, not only of the main scene but of each scene in a story. In another age, he would have sat around a fire and told stores." In February, 1989, the revered and legendary film director participated in a starstudded presentation of the eagerly-awaited restoration of *Lawrence of Arabia*, and in 1990 he began production on a film of Joseph Conrad's novel *Nostromo*. Lean has been through three divorces (Kay Walsh, Ann Todd, Leila Devi), and he tied the knot with his fourth wife, Sandra Hotz, in 1985.

Norman Lear

In a quip that succinctly described this ridiculously-successful TV and film producer-director-writer's Midas touch, host Johnny Carson regreeted viewers in the 1972 Emmy Awards show with "welcome to an evening with Norman Lear." That night, Lear's "All in the Family" comedy series received seven awards, only a fraction of the total that his profitable sitcom stable of "Sanford & Son," "Maude," "Good Times," "Mary Hartman, Mary Hartman," "The Jeffersons," and "One Day at a Time" has piled up. Writer Paddy Chayefsky credited Lear with taking "television away from dopey (TV character) wives and dumb fathers, from the pimps, hookers, hustlers, private eyes, j·inkies, cowboys and rustlers that constituted television chaos and in their place he put the American people. . . . He took the audience and he put them on the set." Norman Milton Lear himself (born in New Haven on 27 July 1922),

"I want to entertain but I gravitate to subjects that matter and people worth caring about."

The WWII Air Corps radioman-turned-publicity agent-turned-salesman got his biggest breaks by collaborating with his cousin's husband on comedy routines that they sold to L.A. comedians, and, in particular, to Danny Thomas. Lear obtained access to Thomas by contacting the funnyman's agent, and, on the pretext that he was from the *New York Times,* got Thomas' personal phone number. After Danny-Boy bought the sketch for "five bills," David Susskind saw it and asked Lear and his partner to write for "The Ford Star Review," a TV series. In quick succession, Lear was spinning gags for other 1950s shows starring Dean Martin and Jerry Lewis, Matha Raye, Tennessee Ernie Ford and George Gobel. As a partner in Tandem Productions, he put on TV specials and feature films (*Come Blow Your Horn,* 1963; *The Night They Raided Minsky's,* 1968) but really struck paydirt when he decided to adapt a British TV comedy series to U.S. sensibilities. "My father and I fought all those battles,"Lear said of the bigot in the BBC show, and he borrowed his own dad's admonitions that Mrs. Lear "stifle herself" in launching "All in the Family" in pilot form in the late 1960s, ABC steered clear of the show, but in 1971 CBS went with it, "vulgarity," "irreverence" and all, and Archie Bunker became the nation's lambastador or laughing stock, depending on a viewer's values. Spin-offs proliferated at an amazing clip. Lear, criticized by fundamentalist and/or ethnic groups for making light of subjects they consider serious matters, helped found People for the American Way, a star-studded organization, to encourage freedom of expression. The award-winning creative mastermind has far too many productions under his belt to name. For the 1990-91 TV season he created the family sitcom "Sunday Dinner." He has received numerous awards and was inducted into the TV Hall of Fame in 1984. His marriage to Frances Loeb produced three children. Since their divorce in 1986, Frances struck gold by launching *Lear's* magazine and Norman remarried Lynn Davis in 1987. The couple have one son, Benjamin Davis. Lear was also the Executive Producer for the feature film *The Princess Bride* (1987).

Michele Lee

"**A** part from the notable strength, the sheer likability of Michele Lee is infectious," T.E. Kalem once said in *Time* magazine, speaking of the perky, highly energetic singer, dancer and actress who stars as Karen Fairgate Mackenzie in the hit TV series, "Knots Landing." In recognition of her talents, Michele was named "The Best Actress of the Year" (1981) by Gannett Newspapers, was nominated for an Emmy Award (1982), and won the 1988 Soap Opera Digest Awards for "Best Actress" and "Super Couple" with Kevin Dobson. Aside from the series, Michele was also seen on the small screen in three TV movies: "Dark Victory," "Bud and Lou," and the 1985 version of "A Letter to Three Wives." However, TV is not this active star's only forte. Aside from a highly successful Broadway background—two years in the hit musical, *How to Succeed in Business Without Even Trying* and *Seesaw*, earned Michele

the Drama Desk Award, the Outer Circle Award, the Outer Circle Critics Award and a Tony nomination—Michele also won acclaim for her role in the film version of *How To Succeed In Business Without Even Trying*, when she received the Motion Picture Exhibitors of US and Canada's 1967 "Fame" Award as the country's most promising new actress. The multitalented Michele showed her versatility by recording a hit album, *A Taste of the Fantastic*, a hit single, "L. David Sloane," and preparing her nightclub act.

Born Michele Dusick on 24 June 1942 in Los Angeles, California, Michele knew almost from the beginning that she wanted to be a performer. Her parents, Sylvia and Jack (a make-up artist based primarily at MGM studios, which is now Lorimar TelePictures, the studio that films "Knots Landing"), watched Michele as she sang in school assemblies in junior and senior high school. At sixteen she was a semi-professional, singing with a local society band. After graduating from high school, Michele learned of an open audition for a musical review set to play in Hollywood. Thinking that their seventeen-year-old daughter Michele would not get the part because the director would want someone more mature, her parents let her try out. She sang "You Make Me Feel So Young" and landed the part. The show, *Vintage 60* went from Los Angeles to Broadway eight months after opening. Although it closed soon after its move to the east, Michele had made it to Broadway on her first audition. Back in Los Angeles, the energetic teenager landed starring spots in two more reviews, *Parade* and *Point of View*. Hearing about an audition in New York for the ingenue lead in a new musical called *Bravo Giovanni*, Michele borrowed money from her father and flew to New York to give it a shot. The eighteen-year-old auditioned and won the role. While the musical only ran for three months, it was long enough for Michele to be seen and be signed to star opposite Robert Morse in *How to Succeed*, which ran from 1962-1964, followed by the film version in 1967. After a variety of television appearances, an album, and a dazzling nightclub act which played in both New York City and Las Vegas, the busy Michele made two motion pictures, *The Love Bug* (1969) and *The Comic* (1969), which showed her strength as a dramatic actress.

Michele is a private person who places family, close friends and principles first. She, along with second husband CBS Vice President Fred Rappoport (married 27 September 1987) and her son, David Farentino, (son of James Farentino, whom Michele divorced in April, 1981), live in West Los Angeles. She keeps over forty photo albums containing four generations of her family. Michele also finds time to serve as Vice-Chair of the Entertainment Industries Council, Inc. (for a Drug-Free Society) and Chairperson of California's Action for Youth. For her public service work, she has been honored by a number of groups, including the California Women's Council on Alcoholism and The Anit-Defamation League of New York.

Spike Lee

"**O**ne of the biggest lies going is that no matter what race, creed, or religion you are, it doesn't matter: we're all Americans. . .. I want people to feel the horror at the end of the movie. I want people to know that if we don't talk about the problems and deal with them head on, they're going to get much worse," states Spike Lee.

Spike Lee is the producer, writer, director, and star of the 40 Acres and a Mule Filmworks Production of the film *Do the Right Thing*. The purpose of this picture is to combine humor and drama to expose the absurdity of racism, and to explore social realism. In the movie, he combines music with a heavy dose of social commentary. The inspiration for this film was derived from racial incidents.

Spike was born in Atlanta, Georgia, but grew up in Brooklyn. His film career began while he was a graduate student in Film School at New York University. His thesis film *Joe's Bed-Stuy Barbershop: We Cut Heads* won the Student Academy Award from the Academy of Motion Picture Arts and Sciences. His next film was about bicycle messengers and wasn't successful. Determined to make it, he went on to write, direct, and co-star in *She's Gotta Have It*, which won the Best New Director award at the Cannes Film Festival. His second feature film, the $6 million musical *School Daze*, which he also wrote, directed, and co-starred in, was Columbia's most profitable picture in 1988. He followed the acclaimed *Do the Right Thing* in 1990 with *The Mo' Better Blues* (1990).

Jack Lemmon

"Happiness is discovering that your daughter is in love with an older man—J. Paul Getty. Happiness is having a doctor who smokes four packs a day. Happiness is working with Jack Lemmon." So says director Billy Wilder of one of Hollywood's hardest working, best liked and most "bankable" stars. For over three decades the actor with the jittery but jaunty air has been generating giggles in such screen comedies as *Mister Roberts* (for which he won an Oscar in 1955), *Some Like It Hot, The Apartment, The Fortune Cookie* and *The Odd Couple.* Nor has this engaging man failed to received critical kudos for his serious dramatic roles in such films as *Days of Wine and Roses, Save the Tiger, Missing* and *Mass Appeal* (1984). "He has that very fortunate Mr. Everyman face and it's very difficult not to believe him," says director Stuart Rosenberg.

He was born John Uhler Lemmon III, 8 February 1925 at the Newton-Wellesley Hospital in Massachusetts—in the elevator. (His mother had been playing bridge and had ignored the labor pains. "I was born two months premature, with a testicle that refused to drop and acute jaundice—and the nurse quipped, 'My, look at the yellow Lemon.' At least that's what my mother told me.") He was educated at Phillips Andover and Harvard, where in his senior year he was elected president of the Hasty Pudding Club. He had his pick of Back Bay Businesses but chose the theatre and New York. Over the next five years, Lemmon did about 500 parts on television and by 1953 had a Columbia contract and the male lead in *It Should Happen to You.* After two more films, Lemmon played Ensign Pulver to Henry Fonda's *Mr. Roberts* and became a star. Lemmon's first marriage (which ended in divorce in 1956) produced one son Chris (1954). Actress Felicia ("Farfel" as he called her) Farr became his second wife (one daughter Courtney). One of his favorite pastimes is composing and playing the piano and he always keeps one near studio sets to while away the periods between takes:

"For me, a piano can make an hour and a half seem like five minutes—it's a joy—an a terrific outlet." Seen on Broadway in 1978 in *Tribute*, in 1985 he returned to the New York stage in a revival of Eugene O'Neill's *Long Day's Journey into Night*, directed by Jonathan Miller. Other films include *The China Syndrome, That's Life,* and *Dad.* He also appeared in the NBC television miniseries "The Ballad of Mary Phagan" in 1987.

Jay Leno

"I would rather make fun of the corporation or whatever it is that dehumanizes people than make fun of the people themselves," says the stand-up comedian Jay Leno, whose forte is using a common-sense point of view to satarize America's consumer culture. Unlike some of his contemporaries, Leno refuses to tell sexist, racial or ethnic jokes stating, "I find I get more laughs working clean." With such targets as all-night gas stations or minimarts ("This way criminals don't have to drive around all night wasting gas") or gratuitous violence in horror films ("Woman opens refrigerator and gets her head split open by an axe. Now there's a common household accident, huh?"), the burly six-foot tall Leno has been called a "natural"—a genuinely funny man who does not need gimmicks to get laughs—by his fellow comedians. Since his first appearance on the "Tonight Show" in 1977, Leno's star has been rising. He began making the rounds of talk variety shows, was a warm-up act for such entertainers as Johnny Mathis, John Denver and Tom Jones and hones his act on the road, playing everything from shopping malls to Las Vegas casinos. When asked about being named as one of the two permanent guest hosts of the "Tonight Show," (1986) Leno replied, "I host most Mondays and a bunch of weeks a year, except for sweeps week or weeks without vowels in them or something." Despite his commitment to the "Tonight Show," Leno (who in 1986 also played a sold out engagement in Carnegie Hall, had his first hour-long comedy special and signed an exclusive multiyear contract with NBC) continues to spend much of his time on the road where he finds inspiration for many of his routines. "I love to travel the country and identify the absurd."

Born James Douglas Muri Leno on 28 April 1950 in New Rochelle, New York, Leno came by his quick wit naturally. His father, Angelo, an Italian-American insurance salesman, made jokes at sales meetings and served as master of ceremony at company banquets. Leno, an indifferent student in grade school, was known for his "boyish" pranks—flushing tennis balls down a toilet and hiding a dog in a locker. His fifth grade teacher unknowingly predicted the future when stating on his report card, "If Jay spent as much time studying as he does trying to be a comedian, he'd be a big star." While attending Emerson College in Boston, Leno often emceed campus talent shows. To help pay for school, Leno tried doing stand-up comedy at some of the local Boston night spots. His first agent booked Leno into the Boston Civic Center and then tried to convince the six-foot one-hundred-eighty-pounder to become a "funny wrestler." Over the next few years, he entertained at birthday parties, in nursing homes, and at bar mitzvahs and served at the opening act for local strip clubs. After graduating with a speech degree, he took a part-time job as a mechanic/auto delivery man for a shop that specialized in luxury cars (one of his future passions). When delivering cars to New York City, Leno took advantage of the opportunity and began making the rounds of comedy clubs, becoming friendly with Robert Klein and David Brenner. After landing a job writing for Jimmie Walker in the TV hit "Good Times," Leno helped another aspiring comic David Letterman by introducing him to Walker, who hired Letterman as a gag writer for the show. Although Leno went on to make numerous appearances on the "Tonight Show," he feels it was his frequent appearances on "Late Night with David Letterman" that brought him more national attention. Letterman, a long-time fan of Leno, says he's "the funniest comedian working today."

Married since 1980 to Mavis Nicholson, a scriptwriter, the couple enjoys seeing the country while living out of a suitcase. When not traveling, Leno and wife settle into their large home in Beverly Hills where he maintains his growing collection of "Kinetic Art"—more than a dozen motorcycles and a half-dozen vintage cars.

Jerry Lewis

D on't look for Jerry Lewis at the poolside of his palatial mansion. Philosopher, clown and movie tycoon, Jerry

believes that guys who sit by the pool long enough, wake up one morning to find it isn't there. A comedian who can make you laugh or cry, Lewis is "the Pied Piper of the business" according to Leo McCrary, "the heir to the mantle of Charlie Chaplin and Harold Lloyd." Born Joseph Levich, 16 March 1926 in Newark, N.J., he busted into showbiz as a teenager with a record act on the Borscht circuit and, joining singer Dean Martin in Atlantic City in 1946, was half of the hottest entertainment act in the country by the time he was 20. His ten-year stint with Martin ended with their spectacular split in 1956. Regarding his film career, Lewis not only starred in such international hits as *The Geisha Boy, The Bellhop, Cinderfella* and *The Nutty Professor*, but in many instances also served as director, producer and co-author. He later made his dramatic debut with Robert DeNiro in *The King of Comedy*.

Lewis as a child was wracked by feelings of abandonment. "I'm nobody," he complained as a lowly urchin, when his showbiz parents left him with his grandmother. Married and divorced to singer Patti Palmer, Lewis has six sons. After his second marriage to Sandee Pitnick in 1983 he moved to Paris. The couple were expecting to have a child together in 1989. Anyone bumping into him might notice that under his vicuna coat he wears a tiny red strip of ribbon on his collar. "That signifies that I have the Legion of Merit," Lewis says beaming. He was awarded the medal by President Francois Mitterrand of France where Lewis is a hero because of his films. "Look at the company I'm in. There's a guy named Pasteur and there's Albert Schweitzer, John F. Kennedy, Emile Zola, General Pershing and Alfred Hitchcock. Not bad, huh?"

He was nominated for the Nobel Peace Prize in 1978 for his work on behalf of a number of charitable causes, most notably his telethons which have raised upwards of $200 million for the Muscular Dystrophy Association. In 1990 Lewis stepped down as producer of the MDA telethons, though still serving as host, and the show's twenty-fifth anniversary telethon was headquartered in Los Angeles, moving from Las Vegas. Lewis underwent open heart surgery in 1983 and since then has been working out and watching his cholesterol. "Listen, when you have your chest opened with a Black and Decker chain saw, you begin to think. My scar runs from my throat all the way down to Hoboken."

Richard Lewis

Affectionately referred to as the comedian from hell with bad posture, Richard Lewis is regarded by his peers as a true "comic's comic." He claims that he could have marketed a signature line of bad-posture clothing had he not spent almost a quarter-million dollars to date on therapy. His neurosis, however, has become a part of our language ("I had a date from Hell") and his warped sense of humor is very much in demand. It is so in demand that he appears on *GQ's* list of the 20th Century's Most Influential Humorists.

Lewis was "born and lowered," as he refers to it, in New Jersey on 29 June. His first attempt at a career was in advertising in New Jersey. Not satisfied, he created a stand-up routine and began performing at the Improvisation in New York, which marked the beginning of his successful career as a comic. Since then, his credits include more than 40 appearances on "The David Letterman Show," featured performances on HBO's "Salute to The Improv," "Comic Relief I & III," "No Life To Live," the concert special "Richard Lewis: I'm Exhausted," the Showtime special "I'm In Pain," the cult film *Diary of a Young Comic* (which Lewis also co-wrote), a co-starring role on the ABC-TV series "Harry," and a co-starring role with Jamie Lee Curtis on ABC-TV's series "Anything But Love." In addition to television performances, he has co-headlined at Caesars Palace in Las Vegas and The Sands in Atlantic City.

Although Lewis remains single, he states: "I think by the turn of the century I will make a good husband. I just pray that I don't wind up having to marry myself in drag and sell the screen rights to De Palma. I'll call it 'Myself, My Bride.'"

Shari Lewis

Described by *Boston Globe* critic Carol Stocker as " . . . a five-foot monument to positive thinking," and as a "diminutive fireball of a performer whose talents have universal appeal" by another reviewer, Shari Lewis possesses a combination of exceptional talent, versatility and imagination. Her many talents include:

actress, dancer, musician, ventriloquist, puppeteer, author and symphony conductor.

Shari was born 17 January 1934 in New York City into a family where her father was a magician and always had magicians and ventriloquists around the house. One day Shari's father heard her sister screaming to be let out of a closet. When he opened the door, the closet was empty! To his surprise, Shari had thrown her voice into the closet and made it appear as though her sister was inside. Her father was so impressed with this that he gave her some books on ventriloquism, along with an old dummy (named Buttercup). Her father said, "If Mary has a little lamb, why shouldn't Shari have a little lamb?" The rest is history. She began studying music at a young age and attended Music and Art High School. Later she studied acting with Sanford Meisner and also worked with Lee Strasberg. Her first television appearance was on the "Captain Kangaroo Show," where Lamb Chop made her debut. They were so well received that NBC gave Shari her own Sunday morning show in New York City called "The Shari Lewis Show." A year later, the show was on six days a week, and the following year it went national. In the years that followed, Shari and Lamb Chop had a weekly TV series on the BBC in London (1969-1973) and a weekly show in Great Britain (1970). She wrote, produced and starred in the NBC special "A Picture of Us" (1971). Starting in 1977, she conducted and performed in over 100 orchestras. Shari has also given three Command Performances for the Queen of England (1970, 1973, 1978). Television appearances include hour-long specials on the Disney Channel, "The Shari Show" on the Nickelodeon Channel, and "Shari's Christmas Concert" which was aired Christmas 1988 and 1989. She has written several books, some of which include: One Minute Bedtime Stories (1986), 101 Things for Kids to Do (1987), and 101 Magic Tricks for Kids to Do (1986). Some of her videos are: One Minute Bedtime Stories, Kooky Classics, 101 Things for Kids to Do, Shari's Christmas Concert (1988), and Lamb Chop's Sing-Along, Play-Along (1988).

Among Shari's numerous awards are five Emmys, a Peabody Award, a Monte Carlo TV Award for the World's Best Variety Show (1961), the Kennedy Center Award for Excellence and Creativity in the Arts (1983), the Girl Scout Grace Award, The Video Choice Award for 101 Things for Kids to Do (1988), and the American Video Conference Award for Lamb Chop's Sing-Along, Play-Along (1988).

She was selected to *V* magazine's "Video Hall of Fame," and she was selected as one of the Ten Most Influential Women in America.

Shari and her publisher husband Jeremy Tarcher (married 15 March 1958) live in Beverly Hills. They have one daughter, Mallory.

Hal Linden

He was the inimitable Barney Miller for 170 episodes in the late 1970s until he finally closed the door of the 12th Precinct of which he was the lovable captain for eight television seasons. Before that, he was awarded the Tony for best musical actor in 1970 as Mayer in *The Rothschilds*. ("This is for you, too." he shouted to the Palace Theatre balcony. "All you veterans of the Saturday morning understudy rehearsals. I'm a sticker. Don't give up.") Up until his big splash, Linden had indeed been the King of the Stickers. He had understudied more luminaries (Keith Andes, Louis Jourdan, Arthur Hill, Sydney Chaplin) than Shubert Alley has closed doors for young hopefuls.

Born 20 March 1931 into a traditionally Jewish family, he left P.S. 98 to attend the High School of Music and Art and later Queens College. After the Korean war (where he had been a member of the U.S. Army Band and also been involved in revues) he realized he had found his metier—acting. Following his discharge, Linden enrolled at New York's American Theatre wing and for six years he worked until he got his big break in 1958 in *Bells are Ringing*. Following *Bells: On a Clear Day, Wildcat, Something More, I'm Not Rappaport, Man of LaMancha*, etc. He was also the host of "FYI," ABC's Emmy award-winning public service program. On the big screen, he starred with Ann-Margret and Alan Alda in 1987's *A New Life*.

Married to Frances Martin (four children), Hal lives with his family in Los Angeles. Of his marriage he says: "Living with anyone for 25 years is hard and I'm not being facetious. I don't think that man was *meant* to live with a woman for that many years." Despite the candid testimony, Hal is proud of the way the relationship has weathered the vicissitudes of married life compounded by the added pressures of a show business career.

Art Linkletter

"I cannot sing or dance and I was never much of an actor," says this frequently off-the-cuff link between the common man and microphones. "My art," asserts Art, "is getting other people to perform. If I had talent I'd probably be unbearable." Born Arthur Gordon Kelley, 17 July 1912 in Moose Jaw, Saskatchewan, Canada, he was deserted by his own parents as an infant and adopted by a family named Linkletter, the patriarch of which was a one-legged itinerant evangelical preacher who held side-walk meetings at which young Art clanged the triangle. Parlaying "a microphone, a natural curiosity, and a gush of words," into a radio career, starting in San Diego in 1934, he made a national name for himself on both radio and TV with such hardy audience participation perennials as "People Are Funny," "House Party" (Emmy Award-winner), and "Life with Linkletter." He has also written a number of books (*Kids Say the Darndest Things*—one of the top 15 best sellers in American publishing history, it was #1 for two straight years in the non-fiction list; his latest *Old Age Is Not for Sissies: Choice for Senior Americans*) and is involved in multitudinous business interests ranging from Peruvian copper mines to a sheep ranch in Australia, not to mention a few oil wells. "Some of them," he says modestly, "wouldn't give enough to oil my lawn mower." His chief interest today is his work in the crusade against drug abuse. He writes, speaks and broadcasts from coast to coast in the fight against drug abuse. (Daughter Diane committed suicide in 1969 after experimenting with LSD.)

He married the former Lois Foerster in 1935; his eldest son, Jack, has been following along in dad's ad-libs on various TV game shows since he was 20. He also has a son, Robert, and two daughters, Dawn and Sharon. A caustic *Time* critic once described Linkletter as "a toothy paragon of commercial insincerity," but most associates seem to feel the genial MC really believes in what he's doing, both off-screen and on. His autobiography, in any case, is entitled *Confessions of a Happy Man.*

John Lithgow

With almost twenty years of professional acting experience under his belt, John Lithgow boasts talents of great stature and diversity. He demonstrates his tremendous depth and range as an actor through such diverse roles as Roberta Muldoon in *The World According to Garp* (Academy Award nomination), his Tony Award-Winning performance in *The Changing Room*, the psychopathic murder in *Blow Out*, and a panic stricken airline passenger in a segment of "Twilight Zone."

Born in Rochester, New York, he was destined to be in theatre. His father, Arthur, was one-time head of Princeton's McCarthur Theatre. When Lithgow was an infant, the family moved to Ohio where his father began running Shakespeare Festivals throughout the state. It was in one of his father's productions that Lithgow made his stage debut. He appeared in *Henry VI, Part 3* when he was only six years old. Later, upon receiving a Fulbright scholarship, Lithgow traveled to England to study at the London Academy of Music and Dramatic Art. While in England, he interned with the Royal Shakespeare Company and The Royal Court Theatre. After finishing his internship, he returned to the U.S. and moved to New York to pursue a career on Broadway. Some of his stage performances include: *My Fat Friend, Comedians, A Memory of Two Mondays, Secret Service, Anna Christie, Once in a Lifetime, Spokesong, Division Street, Beyond Therapy, Kaufman at Large, The Front Page* and *M. Butterfly*. His performance in the latter show not only burned up the boards but brought superlative reviews. Frank Rich of the *Times* proclaimed that in *M. Butterfly* Lithgow "projects intelligence and wit, and his unflagging energy drives and helps unify the evening." Clive Barnes, in the *Post*, cites the star's exquisite sketching of his character's "tortured bafflement and wimpish determination" and concludes, "Lithgow has never been better." His Off-Broadway appearances include the New York Shakespeare Festival production of *Hamlet, Trelawny of the Wells*, and *Salt Lake City Skyline*. In addition to numerous stage credits, Lithgow has also appeared in several films. He received an Academy Award nomination for Best Supporting Actor for *Terms of Endearment* and held leading roles in *Footloose, Buckaroo Bonzai, 2001, All That Jazz, Obsession, Rich Kids,* and the critically acclaimed *The Manhattan*

Project. Although he has been devoting most of his time to theatre and films, Lithgow has found time for television. Some of his roles include: the part of John Waters in an episode of "Amazing Stories" (for which he won an Emmy), "The Oldest Living Graduate," "Big Blond," and the televison movie "The Day After" (nominated for an Emmy). He also found time for a music video, singing for "Baby Songs Presents John Lithgow's Kid-Size Concert." He pairs with James Woods for a TV movie about writing partners facing death in "The Boys," scheduled to air in 1991.

Lithgow resides in Los Angeles with his wife Mary, their daughter Phoebe, and their son Nathan George. He also has a fifteen-year-old son, Ian, from a previous marriage.

Rich Little

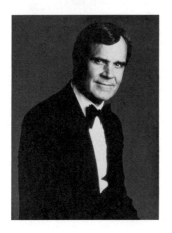

"I think the voices I do best are the people I admire the most," Rich Little, man of 1,000 voices, has said. Yet Little is perhaps best known for seeing the nation through the sticky Watergate era with his dog-faced, peace-signing harpoonery of Richard Nixon, making "one thing perfectly clear."

Richard Caruthers Little was born 26 November 1938 in Ottawa, Ontario, Canada to a wealthy family. After gaining confidence from impromptu schoolyard performances and dinner shows for local civic groups, Little developed skill for banter that landed him a disc jockey job in Ontario in 1957. His impressions became a popular nightclub act and a 1963 album, *My Fellow Canadians,* made record-sales history. That same year, Judy Garland imported him as a featured guest on her variety show, and spots on other leading programs followed. He became a regular on a short-lived 1966 series, "Love on a Rooftop," leading to frequent appearances on the "Tonight Show" and finally his own variety program, "The Rich Little Show" on NBC in 1975.

Little, whose uncannily accurate impressions are often five years in preparation, makes three-dimensional cartoons of his subjects, with vocal mimicry so exact he has dubbed dialogue for both Peter Sellers and David Niven when they became too ill to complete films. "You don't have to be letter-perfect. In fact, the best impressions depend on exaggeration," he says, admitting that the essence of some personalities he would like to imitate still eludes him. Always on alert for new material, Little manages to perform for the political scene as he sizes up his next imitatable candidate. In April, 1989, he was Master of Ceremonies at the Association of White House News Photographers annual dinner honoring the President and his wife.

Little married Jeanne Worden in 1971, and they have one daughter.

Sophia Loren

"To have perfect beauty is not so special. To have a special look, one must have irregularities, otherwise you look like everyone else," says Italian superstar and author (*In the Kitchen with Love; Sophia: Living & Loving; Women & Beauty*) Sophia Loren. The high cheekbones, generous mouth and voluptuous figure have made her into a worldwide legend. Says Sophia: "My nose is too long, my chin too short, my hips too broad. But together, all these irregularities seem to work. On second thought, I rather like the way I look." Her autobiography, *Sophia: Living & Loving* (1979), was made into a TV movie a year later—with Sophia in an unusual dual role playing her mother and herself (ages 20-40). In 1981, she teamed up with Coty Cosmetics Company and launched a new fragrance line named especially for her—"Sophia."

Born out of wedlock in a Rome charity hospital Sofia (Villani) Scicolone, 20 September 1934, she was reared by her grandparents amidst the poverty of wartime Italy in Pozzuoli, on the Bay of Naples. After winning second place in a beauty contest at the age of 15, she headed with her starstruck mother for the movie studios in Rome, seeking work as an extra under the name of Sofia Lazarro. Producer Carlo Ponti (one of the contest judges) took notice of her, changed her name to Sophia Loren, and took control of her career. "I believe in luck," she says, "but I also believe one has to know how to grab at luck, to seize the moment. Otherwise opportunities can slip through one's fingers." In 1954 with *The Gold of Naples*, she came to the world's attention. Her career now spans over 70 films (her favorites: *Yesterday, Today, and Tomorrow; Marriage, Italian Style*; and

Two Women, for which she won an Oscar in 1961 as best actress). She was reunited with frequent co-star Marcello Mastroianni in 1985 in *Saturday, Sunday, Monday*. She followed that movie with the telefilm "Mother Courage" on CBS in 1986. For her next project, Loren dropped her customary sex-symbol persona to play a gutsy Italian emigre mother in the NBC blockbuster five-hour miniseries, "Mario Puzo's The Fortunate Pilgrim" in 1988.

Choosing between Cary Grant and Carlo Ponti, she declined Cary Grants' proposal of marriage ("I would cherish forever what Cary brought into my life"), married Carlo Ponti by proxy in Mexico in 1957 (he subsequently became a French citizen to avoid a bigamy suit pending against him in Italy), and in 1966 remarried Ponti in France. After suffering four miscarriages, Sophia took to bed nine months in a Swiss clinic. Carlo, Jr. ("Cipi") was born in 1968; Edoardo ("Eli") in 1972. In July, 1980, Italy's highest appeals court ordered her to serve a 30-day jail term for failure to pay $180,000 in supplementary taxes in 1963-64. Arriving at Rome airport in May, 1982, she was taken to Giudidiario Prison in Caserta, north of Naples. She told reporters: "I am content to go and serve this sentence because I want to see my mother, sister, my friends, my country . . . my roots," and claimed that she was incorrectly advised in not declaring the income she earned outside Italy in 1963. She served 17 days in prison until a Naples court granted her leave. "My jail sentence was not in vain. It's something I will never forget. It was the ugliest experience of my life."

Rob Lowe

After completing the movie *Class* in June 1983 Rob Lowe told *Seventeen* magazine: "I like the fact that I come from the Midwest. . . . I like the people I know who come from there; it's not that the Midwest is better than anywhere else, but it's like real life. And you grow up with a good sense of values." Those *values* were tested in May, 1989, when the mother of a teenage girl sued Lowe for having sex with her daughter and recording the event on videotape. The case also brought Atlanta's district attorney into the investigation. Although the handsome actor had originally refused to speak to the press about the accusations, the media had a heyday exploiting the tale. After making a deal to perform 20 hours of community service over a period of two years, Lowe finally spoke his mind on the "Today" Show. He said, "There was never anything wrong with my ethics, there were things wrong with my judgment."

Rob Lowe does have a special screen presence—that *je ne sais quoi*. His figure looms large on the screen, magnetism radiates from the finely sculpted features and those eyes, oh those eyes. . . . With just the lift of an eyebrow, tilt of the head, hearts are sent fluttering. "People are always making such a big deal about the way I look," he says, a little wearily. Warren Beatty and Robert Redford are the actors he admires most—"for overcoming their faces."

Born 17 March 1964 in Dayton, Ohio, Lowe has been acting since he was 8, contracting the bug after seeing the musical *Oliver*. His parents divorced when he was only four years old; when his mother and stepfather relocated to Los Angeles, Rob and younger brother, Chad, received the opportunity to grow up in California. Lowe began making the rounds as an actor while still an undergraduate at Santa Monica High. He made his small screen debut on two After School Specials, "A Matter of Time" and "Schoolboy Father." He also appeared with Eileen Brennan in the ABC-TV series, "A New Kind of Family." About that time, Lowe's career hopes began to fizzle. "I was washed up at 17," he says. He was losing teenage roles to rivals who were over 18 and thus not subject to child labor laws. His agent persuaded him to ride the tide till he was "legal." And as luck would have it, it was a worthwhile hiatus. Labeled as a 1980's screen idol, he hit big in several major films—*The Outsiders* (his feature film debut), *Class*, *The Hotel New Hampshire*, *Oxford Blues*, and *St. Elmo's Fire*. Surrounding himself with his co-stars at night and at Hollywood parties, he became a member of the "brat-pack." Presently, he lives in Malibu and is adjusting to his star-status. "I hope I can still do the things I like to do. I know now that I can't go to a theatre in Westwood and stand in line," aware that he'd be immediately pursued by swarms of young girls. As for romance and girls—"I've always been in love with them," he says. He has been linked variously to actress Melissa Gilbert (those rumors ended when she married another actor) and sultry beauty Nastassja Kinski. His recent movies include: *Youngblood* (1986), *Square Dance* (1986), *About Last Night* (1986), *Illegally Yours* (1988), *Masquerade* (1988), and *Bad Influence*. Lowe seems finally to be comfortable with his leading-man status, whether it be on screen or off.

Myrna Loy

"**I** don't know how it started— the 'perfect wife' label—but I saved more marriages than you can imagine," laughs Movie Queen Myrna Loy who, playing William Powell's wife in a film that only took 21 days of shooting in 1934—*The Thin Man*— earned a lifelong tag of the "perfect wife" (meaning married but attractive; sexy but humorous; romantic but fun). "I was the perfect American wife— which I wasn't. It was so funny." (Offscreen, she was married and divorced four times; Arthur Hornblow, Jr., John Hertz, Jr., Gene Markey, and Howland Sargeant.) "All anyone seemed to care about was my marriage. I can't see what that has to do with my work. I think carrying on a life that is meant to be private in public is a breach of taste, common sense, and mental hygiene. I made my mistakes, paid for them, recovered from them, and did it all in privacy. And I'm glad."

Born Myrna Williams 2 August 1905 in Helena, Montana, she first appeared in front of a camera opposite Rudolph Valentino in a screen test for *Corba*. Typecast into portraying sinuous Oriental sirens and vamps (*Noah's Ark*, 1929; *The Squall*, 1929; *The Mask of Fu Manchu*, 1932), she found it was director W.S. Van Dyke who recognized her true potential, accomplished her metamorphosis from "homewrecker" to "homemaker" with *Penthouse* (1933), then "perfectly" cast her opposite William Powell in *The Thin Man*. Her career sky-rocketed, and to movie audiences the name Loy became linked with Powell, with whom she co-starred in *Manhattan Melodrama*, 1934, *The Great Ziefeld*, 1936, *Libeled Lady*, 1936, and the classic *Thin Man* series (six in total); and with Clark Gable, for *Night Flight*, 1933, *Manhattan Melodrama*, 1934, and *Test Pilot*, 1938. She was Franklin Roosevelt's favorite actress. John Dillinger was so enthralled with her screen images that he let himself be lured to see her in *Manhattan Melodrama*, only to be gunned down by G-men's bullets outside Chicago's Biograph Theater. And in 1937, through a national newspaper poll, Myrna Loy and Clark Gable were officially crowned "'King' and 'Queen' of the Movies," with a coronation ceremony in Hollywood. "I made so many marvelous pictures, but I suppose *The Best Years of Our Lives* is *the* one. When I see those movies now I just sit and cry." A veteran actress, Myrna Loy turned to the stage in 1962 with *There Must Be a Pony*, subsequently toured with Neil Simon's *Barefoot in the Park*, and on Broadway appeared in a revival of *The Women*. After WW II, Myrna Loy became active in the fledgling United Nations ("I'm an actress but not such a dedicated one that I'm not concerned with other things"); she has a rarely given UNESCO medal for her work. With a career spanning seven decades in movie making, Myrna Loy appeared in the first European-American co-production (the silent *Ben-Hur*); the first film with a score (*Don Juan*); the first talkie (*The Jazz Singer*); and the first filmed operetta (*The Desert Song*). In 1985 the Academy of Motion Picture Arts and Sciences paid special tribute to her at a gala evening at Carnegie Hall. She was also honored by the Kennedy Center Honors in 1988 and her autobiography *Myrna Loy: On Being and Becoming* was released in 1987.

George Lucas

G eorge Lucas's career is a dem- onstration of how far a film school graduate can go. He claims to have made his second film, 1973's beloved *American Graffiti*, for 16-year-olds, and his third, *Star Wars* (one of the all-time box-office champions), "for kids of all ages." The latter film's huge success has enabled Lucas—regrettably perhaps—to retire early (temporarily?) as a director and concentrate instead on producing other blockbusters, like Spielberg's *Raiders of the Lost Ark*, and on providing financial assistance to fledgling filmmakers just getting in to the business.

Born on 14 May 1944, in Modesto, Calif. (and raised nearby on his father's walnut ranch), Lucas "barely squeaked through high school," aspiring to be a motor car racer until, days before his graduation, a near-fatal accident in his souped-up Fiat crushed his lungs and sent him to the hospital for three months. His second career choice was art, but cinematographer Haskell Wexler encouraged his filmmaking and helped him gain admittance to the University of Southern California's film department. While there, he made a science fiction short which—with Francis Coppola's help—he expanded into his first feature, 1971's *THX-1138*. Starring Robert Duvall and set in the 25th century, the film's white-on-white visual texture belies its grim undercurrents.

By contrast, the ebullient *American Graffiti*, set during one summer night in 1962, is based on Lucas' own coming of age in Modesto (where it was filmed on a shoestring budget in 28 days). "It all happened to me, but I sort of glamorized it," the director says. Divorced from film editor (*Taxi Driver*) Marcia Griffin Lucas (whom he married in 1969), the short, slightly-built Lucas lives near San Francisco and, for fun, enjoys "flicking out" in movie theatres. His religious faith, developed while recuperating from his car accident, is based on a belief in a power roughly similar to the concept of *Star Wars'* "The Force." His continual drive has kept him busy throughout the 1980's. He was the executive producer for *The Land Before Time, Tucker: The Man and His Dream, Willow,* and *Indiana Jones and the Last Crusade.*

Susan Lucci

Susan Lucci, resident villainess on daytime's "All My Children" has millions of fans and says, "It's fun to play Erica. It's a way to express a part of my personality that's there and to give people insight into why they behave the way they do." The abominable behavior that her TV character has engaged in since Susan Lucci got the part of the rotten high school tease in 1969 has included having affairs, divorcing, aborting her baby, and breaking up marriages. Lucci's personal life is apparently quite different. Born 23 December 1950, she's the product of a strict Catholic, Garden City, Long Island family. (Dad, a building contractor, "would wait for me when I went on dates," she admits.) Bitten early by the acting bug, a flubbed Broadway tryout at 19 sent her into serious training and she was ready for the Erica part when it happened along later that year. With only a couple of TV and movie roles under her small belt (she's five-feet-two, and 95 pounds), she hints she'd like more. "Frankly, when I started they weren't making all these movies where the leads were young girls. . . . I thought . . . 'If I leave "All My Children," what will I play—someone's daughter or girlfriend?' Now I'm grown up and there are a lot of grown-up parts for me to play and I feel I'm ready." Home life is said to be sedate, unlike TV persona that brings her a half million a year, with Austrian-born restaurant impresario hubby Helmut Huber. Still living in Garden City, Lucci commutes into Manhattan every dawn to go to work. "I always thought that being on a daytime show was the only way I could combine being a full-time mother and a full-time actress," says she, the mother of Susan. In 1985 she starred in "Mafia Princess," an NBC movie for TV. Joining in on the fragrance wars, Lucci became the new Revlon Woman in 1986. She is promoting the aptly titled perfume "Scoundrel."

Sidney Lumet

A directorial dynamo who's happiest "working at white heat," Sidney Lumet first warmed the cockles of critical hearts during TV's Golden Age. Back in the 1950s when the name of the game was "live," his dramas for such shows as "Kraft Television Theatre" and "Studio One" stamped him as a promising comer; by the time he collected an Emmy for his 1960 TV production of "The Iceman Cometh," he definitely had arrived. Switching from little screen to big, he chalked up another O'Neill triumph with the darkly brooding *Long Day's Journey into Night* (1962) and subsequently attracted notice with *The Pawnbroker* (1965), *The Group* (1966), *Child's Play* (1972), *Serpico* (1974), *Murder On the Orient Express* (1974), *Prince of the City* (1981), *Deathtrap* and *The Verdict* (1982), *Daniel* (1983), *Garbo Talks* (1984), *Power* (1985), *The Morning After* (1987), *Running on Empty* (1988), *Family Business* (1989) and *Q & A* (1989).

He was born in Philadelphia 25 June 1924, moved with his family to New York when he was two, and working with his actor father, Baruch, was a greasepaint veteran of the Yiddish Art Theater by the time he was four. Then, studying at the Professional Children's School by day, he labored on Broadway at night, progressing from a tough East Side *Dead End* kid in 1935 to the young Jesus in Maxwell Anderson's *Journey to Jerusalem* in 1940. After performing as a radar man in another sort of theater (the CBI) during World War II, he began working as a director off-Broadway and joined CBS-TV in 1950, quickly establishing himself as a whirlwind of energy and talented innovator. Among the more than 200 plays he directed for TV was "Twelve Angry Men," the drama which later marked his film debut (1957). He was married first to actress Rita Gam, then to

Gloria Vanderbilt, then to Gail Jones (daughter of Lena Horne), then to Piedie Gimbel (1980). He moves through wives like he moves through movies, covering a lot of ground. "I believe in continuity. All I want to do is get better, and quantity can help me to solve problems."

Andie MacDowell

"Every time I meet someone for a reading, I'm aware they know my work, know I'm a model—it's this fact. And there's a stigma," claims Andie. She has managed to dispel the myth that models are dumb, and has overcome the obstacles that models often come up against while auditioning for a part in a film, She has made the transition from successful model to successful actress.

Andie MacDowell was born Anderson MacDowell in the small town of Gaffney, South Carolina. When she was only six years old her parents divorced. Growing up in a broken family with an alcoholic mother, she had to take on a lot of responsibility at an early age. Because she was so busy having to take care of her mother as well as herself, she never did well in school. In her second year of college, she decided to drop out to pursue a career in modeling. She started out in newspaper ads for a department store, and soon began working for the Elite Modeling Agency. Since then, she has modeled in commercials for Calvin Klein jeans and L'Oreal. Her studies in acting include training with Shakespeare and Company, as well as being a student of the Meisner technique. Andie made her film debut in 1984 playing the role of Jane in *Greystoke: The Legend of Tarzan, Lord of the Apes.* Following that she appeared in *St. Elmo's Fire.* In Europe, she played the role of Anthea in "Sahara's Secret," which was the highest rated mini-series on RAI Italian television in 1988. Her latest film, *sex, lies and videotape* (1989), in which she starred as Ann, was the winner of both the Best Film Prize and the Best Actor Award (for James Spader) at the Cannes Film Festival.

Andie is married to model Paul Qualley and is the mother of two boys, Justin and Rainey.

Shirley MacLaine

"I 've wondered for 26 years what this would feel like," the redheaded singer, actress, dancer, writer and spiritual crusader said in her 1984 Oscar acceptance speech. "Thank you so much for terminating the suspense." The award was for her portray of Aurora Greenway, "a feisty, frustrated Houston widow," in the film *Terms of Endearment*. The film shows Aurora's relationship with her defiant daughter, played by Debra Winger, over a period of thirty years. The Oscar followed four previous nominations—as best actress in *Some Came Running* (1958), *Irma La Douce* (1963), and *The Turning Point* (1977); a documentary feature which she produced, *The Other Half of the Sky: A China Memoir*, was also nominated for an Academy Award in 1975. For her forty-ninth birthday she'd retreated into the Rockies to "project," as she calls it, three wishful visualizations: that she'd win an Oscar (she did), that her book on spiritualism and reincarnation *Out On a Limb*, in which a nice WASP lady-liberal discovers her Karmic thread, would become a bestseller (did it ever; it became a 1986 TV miniseries with its author as the star), and finally that her nightclub act would score big on Broadway (and it did at the Gershwin). Proud, inspired, elegant, joyous, a globetrotting Renaissance woman—(and author of bestsellers: the autobiographical *Don't Fall Off the Mountain* (1970) and *You Can Get There From Here* (1975) in which she discussed her involvement with American politics and her reaction to the Chinese Revolution)— MacLaine is her own best emblem. "I basically think of myself as a dancer," she explains. "It's the first thing I learned to do." Her recent literary offerings include *Dancing in the Light* (1985), *It's All in the Playing* (1987), and *Going Within* (1989).

Born on 24 April 1934, Shirley MacLaine Beaty (brother Warren added the second "t" later) was raised in Arlington, Virginia, and was a whiz in ballet slippers by the time she was three. When her legs grew too long for ballet, she was heartbroken. At sixteen she shifted to musical comedy and went to New York and got a part in a regional touring production of *Oklahoma*. Two years later, having completed high school, she moved back to New York. When she was not yet twenty she got her first break when, while understudying Carol Haney in *The Pajama Game* on Broadway, Haney sprained her ankle three days after the show opened and Shirley went on for her. MacLaine was spotted by Hollywood producer Hal Wallis and within months she was signed to star in her first picture, Alfred Hitchcock's *The Trouble with Harry*. By 1969 she was one of Hollywood's highest-paid performers, getting as much as $800,000 for a film.

"My strongest personality trait is the way I keep unsettling my life when most other people are settling down." Indeed this is key in mapping her many ways, be it as wife and mother (to Steve Parker, divorced in 1982, one daughter Sachi), to running with the Hollywood Rat Pack, meditating in the Himalayas, campaigning for McGovern and keeping to the left romantically with the likes of Pete Hamill and Soviet director Andrei Mikhalkov-Konchalovsky. "I have mostly used relationships to learn, and when that process is over, so is the relationship." She remained Parker's wife for nearly thirty years, although they lived separately from the time he moved to Japan soon after they were married. One observer described her relationship with her brother Warren as the "most explosive in her life." Warren has said: "As for what goes on between Shirley and me, you can safely call it complicated." Shirley once remembered that the two had "sat for twenty years, warily watching each other grow up. . . . He knows me and I know him. . . . I think in terms of black and white . . . he's a respecter of gray."

Borrowing a line from her pal Gloria Steinem when she turned fifty MacLaine said: "This is what fifty looks like. . . . I love the idea of fifty because the best is yet to come. I am going to live to be one hundred, because I want to, and I am going to go on learning." MacLaine is working as hard as ever. Her recent movies include *Madame Sousatzka* (1988), and *Steel Magnolias* (1989), and *Postcards From the Edge*. Sharing some of her longevity secrets, she released a home video, "Shirley MacLaine's Inner Workout" in 1989.

Madonna

"**M**adonna is a video vamp, her trademark a coyly exposed navel, and her only apparent desire, to drive all the boys crazy," wrote *Newsweek* magazine. "People like her give people like us a hard way to go. She doesn't help anybody take women seriously. But you know what? I love the record," said Gina Schock in *Rolling Stone* about the popular singer who, at the age of twenty-five in 1985, emerged with the top selling LPs *Madonna* and *Like A Virgin*, a string of hit singles including "Material Girl," (which spent three weeks in the Number One slot of *Billboard's* Hot 100), and a starring role in a motion picture, *Desperately Seeking Susan*, with Rosanna Arquette. In an age of music videos broadcast twenty-four hours-a-day to record consumers, she livened up the medium with her state-of-the-art titillations and became video's Number One female artist by appearing partially clothed, wearing a belt tag that said Boy Toy. ("Spelling out the most hackneyed male erotic fantasies,'" said *Newsweek*, "she's like Veronica of the Ronettes without the tenderness, the vulnerability or the clothes.") Maintaining her popularity throughout her consecutive hair colors (brown to blonde  to brown to auburn to blonde again) and movie hits and misses, she continues to turn out the commercial stuff that expands her superstar status.

The *Time* (June 1985) covergirl and indifferent *Penthouse* and *Playboy* (both September 1985) layout girl was born Madonna Louise Ciccone in Bay City, Michigan, 16 August 1960, one of eight children. When she was six her mother (after whom she was named) died, and Madonna was raised by her father, by relatives and eventually by her step-mother ("a real disciplinarian"). "From the time that I was very young I just knew that being a girl and being charming in a feminine sort of way could get me a lot of things, and I milked it for everything I could," she recalls. She devoted herself to ballet as a teenager because her junior-high teacher "told me I had a beautiful ancient Roman face. No one had ever talked to me like that before. I latched onto him like a leech and took everything I could from him." After a year at the University of Michigan, she headed for musical Manhattan, where she learned to play the guitar and studied briefly at the Alvin Ailey Dance Theater. Boyfriends introduced her to the club world and she cultivated her look of strategically torn lace and mostly religious-themed junk jewelry. To get a deejay to play a cassette of her song "Everybody," she danced in front of the music booth and requested a lot of tunes. When the deejay finally played it the disco's patrons loved her music. So did Sire Records, which signed her in 1983. The single "Holiday" made it as one of that summer's big hits.

"I get so much bad press for being overtly sexual," says she. Her first film was an underground ditty called *A Certain Sacrifice* (1979, in which she played a dominatrix with three slaves). She described the film as "not hard-core porn—it's mostly just weird." Following her success in *Desperately Seeking Susan*, she flopped with *Shanghai Surprise* (1986) and *Who's That Girl* (1987), although she scored with the soundtrack from the latter film and LP from *Vision Quest*. Against all odds, she made her Broadway stage debut in *Speed-the Plow* (1988) which packed the house each night. Later that year she appeared in the movie *Bloodhounds of Broadway*, and she appeared as Breathless Mahoney in on-again, off-again beau Warren Beatty's screen adaptation of the comic strip *Dick Tracy*. Her recent LPs include *True Blue* (1986), *You Can Dance* (1987) and *Like A Prayer* (1989). The last album spawned the hit singles "Like A Prayer" and "Express Yourself." Although the title song was to be a promotional vehicle tied in with Pepsi, the deal was canned when the advertising people viewed her controversial video scenes. In August 1985, Madonna married temperamental actor Sean Penn and their rocky relationship became fair game for tabloid headlines. In 1989 the couple filed for divorce.

Karl Malden

It's another night in front of the TV. You haven't been anywhere outside Poughkeepsie in three years. Then he appears, watchdog-extraordinaire, in his trench coat and he says, in the last voice of authority you are likely to hear that night, "Don't leave home without them—American Express Travelers' Checks." You wake up a bit. You see the sad folks in the foreign country who've lost their everything and now they're stranded, so you dive into a sack of potato chips and decide never to leave home again, but if you do, he's right. You'll do anything Karl Malden says to stay safe in trecherous Abu Dhabi, Lyford Cay, Biarritz . . . anyplace beyond your driveway's delta.

"Work," he says, "is one of the greatest things I do, and if I'm not working, I get terribly depressed." Through the years he's kept busy on Broadway in such stage successes as *A Streetcar Named Desire*, *Desperate Hours* and *Desire Under the Elms*, and in Hollywood in film versions of the first two (he won an Oscar for *Streetcar*) plus *On the Waterfront*, *Birdman of Alcatraz*, *Nevada Smith*, *Gypsy*, *Patton*, *Billy Galvin* and *Nuts*. TV, he once said, was "too hectic" for him. "Do you want to make a violin in a week or do you want to make a Stradivarius? I always try to make a Stradivarius." He succumbed to the tube, however, with the series "The Streets of San Francisco," in

1972-77, and the short-lived "Skag." His telefilm appearances include leading roles in "Alice in Wonderland" (1985) and "My Father, My Son" (1988).

Born to Yugoslav parents in Chicago, Illinois, 22 March 1913, as Malden Sekulovich, he grew up in Gary, Indiana, where he worked in the steel mills, dug ditches, and delivered milk, but through it all, "I knew I'd be an actor. My father was an actor in Yugoslavia." In 1938, after dramatic training in Chicago, he moved to New York, began working on Broadway and, after time out for Army service in World War II, tried acting before the cameras. Married to actress Mona Graham (two daughters), whom he met in 1938 while he was appearing in a production of Tolstoy's *Redemption* at Chicago's Goodman Theater, he occasionally conducts acting seminars in colleges. As president of the Academy of Motion Picture Arts and Sciences he presides over the Oscars.

John Malkovich

"When I originally saw John in *True West*, I figured that either a psychopath was up on that stage, or he was one the great actors of our times," recalled Robert Benton, writer-director of *Places in the Heart*, the 1984 film in which the protean actor-director made his film debut. The "child-like . . . trivial . . . circus freak," who is both "funny [and] odd" (all self-described traits) from the Windy City's adventurous Steppenwolf repertory company set Off-Broadway ablaze in 1983 as the loutish and beefy slob in Sam Shepard's *True West* (for which he won an Obie while evoking memories of early Brando), travelled uptown to share the stage with Dustin Hoffman in the 1984 revival of Arthur Miller's *Death of a Salesman*, portraying Biff, the sensitive, neurotic and inspired son of Willie Loman who is trapped in the imposed role of simple-minded jock (the play was filmed for TV in the fall of 1985). Malkovich responded to Hollywood's call to play a blind man in *Places in the Heart* (Oscar nomination). For research he "went to the Dallas Lighthouse to observe blind people (he told Marjorie Rosen for a *New York Daily News* profile) . . . but I try never to do any more research than is absolutely necessary . . . I became an actor to exercise my imagination, not my research skills." His follow-up film (for which he also earned an Oscar nomination) was *The Killing Fields* (1984), and in 1985 he filmed *Eleni*, playing Nicholas Gage (a former *New York Times* reporter) in his search for the killer of his mother in the Greek Civil War.

"We weren't really trainable," Malkovich recalled for Rosen of his growing up with four siblings in Benton, Illinois, where he was born 9 December 1953, and where his grandmother founded and still runs the Benton *Evening News*. "Although my parents were bright and articulate and well-mannered, something just went awry. We had a lot of freedom, too much freedom, it was always chaos." A loner who read a lot as a child, Malkovich entered Illinois State University with the intention of becoming a conservationist like his father, but soon switched to acting. After graduation he joined the newly-formed Steppenwolf company in Chicago. It was there that he met his wife (married 2 August 1982), Glenne Headley ("She's very odd . . . a funny mix . . . a city kid") whom he directed in 1984 off-Broadway in Lanford Wilson's *Balm in Gilead* and in 1985 in a Broadway revival of Shaw's *Arms and the Man*. His next hit was the critically acclaimed Broadway play *Burn This* which opened in October, 1987. Malkovich's recent movies include *Making Mr. Right* (1986), *Empire of the Sun* (1987), *The Glass Menagerie* (1987), and *Dangerous Liasons* (1988), and he was also the co-executive producer of *The Accidental Tourist* (1988). In 1990 he appeared opposite Debra Winger in Bernardo Bertolucci's film of Paul Bowles novel *The Sheltering Sky*. When asked how he keeps so much acclaim in perspective, he replies, "Well, I count on my good friends to treat me as they always do—like dirt."

Louis Malle

"It's not that I see things others don't," said the French director living and working in America, "but I'm curious about things that, probably if I were born here, I would take for granted." He was speaking of his critically acclaimed 1980 movie *Atlantic City*. Starring Burt Lancaster, *Atlantic City* is about frantic efforts to create hope in a crumbling environment, and several reviewers noted that the director's perceptions as a foreigner added something fresh and vital to John Guare's insightful screenplay. For his next feature he picked what almost anyone else would consider a hopelessly uncinematic subject: two middle aged friends, intellectuals, conversing in a restaurant for an hour and a half. To his astonishment, *My Dinner with Andre,* shot in less than three weeks for $450,000, turned out to be the sleeper of the year 1981, breaking house records in big cities from coast to coast.

With these two solid successes Malle achieved recognition as one of the most accomplished and innovative filmmakers at work in the U.S. While his subsequent releases—e.g., *Crackers* (1984), which the *Village Voice* called "something of a fiasco and clearly a labor of love"—did not come up to the great expectations aroused by *Atlantic City* and *Andre,* his record suggested that he would soon score big again, given his audacity and versatility. ("The only quality common to the films of Louis Malle," critic Pauline Kael has written, "is the restless intelligence one senses in them.") He did succeed again in 1988 as the director and screenwriter for the film *Au Revoir, Les Enfants* which received an Academy Award nomination for best foreign language film.

Born 30 October 1932 in Thumieres, in the department of Nord, France, Malle is the seventh and youngest child of sugar heiress and her onetime naval officer husband. After a standard Catholic secondary education he was destined for a degree in political science, but switched from the Sorbonne to the Institut des Hautes Etudes Cinematographiques, then left to become an assistant to underwater explorer Jacques-Yves Cousteau, filming marine life in the Red Sea, Persian Gulf, and Indian Ocean. The feature-length documentary *Silent World* (1956) won top honors at Cannes and became a classic. In 1957 Malle was Jacques Tati's cameraman on *Mon Oncle,* and later that year completed his first feature, released here as both *Elevator to the Gallows* and *Frantic.* His most notable films include *Zazie* (1960, about an 11-year-old *gamine*), *The Fire Within* (1964, about a suicide), *Lacombe, Lucien* (1974, about a French collaborator with the Nazis) and his first American film *Pretty Baby* (1978, about a child prostitute, played by Brooke Shields). *May Fools* (1990), is a semi-autobiographical comedy about the student riots that took place in Paris in 1968.

The director has two children born out of wedlock to separate women. In 1980 he married Candice Bergen, and since then, he says, "My life has become much more important than my work." The couple have a daughter Chloe born 8 November 1985.

Dinah Manoff

"Look at me . . . the real me, the cheerleader from hell!" Riding the rave reviews of the 1989 hit TV sitcom "Empty Nest," Dinah Manoff insists she's not exactly like the character, Carol, that she portrays on the show. But she's also quick to note that it has been wonderful working with such a fine group of players, including Richard Mulligan, Kristy McNichol, Park Overall and David Leisure.

The talented Tony-winning actress was born in New York City circa 1957 to playwright Arnold Manoff and actress Lee Grant. Dinah lived in the Big Apple until she was seven, then in Malibu for awhile, then back to New York again when her Mom's career forced them to return to the east coast. She told *TV Guide* in June, 1989, "My rhythm is New York. My inside clock ticks New York. I get on the subway and feel serene. I've been in every New York neighborhood at every time of night, and I have no fear. I just blend in." Manoff attended public schools on both coasts, and she later discovered she didn't blend in; she proved her acting talents to be outstanding in her early productions. After appearing in the films *Grease* (1977), *Ordinary People,* (1979), the TV sitcom "Soap" (1977-1978), and the telefilms "High Terror" (1977), "The Possessed" (1977), and "Raid on Entebbe" (1977), she won the role of the spunky daughter in Neil Simon's Broadway play *I Ought To Be In Pictures* (1980) which earned her a Tony Award and a Theatre World Award. More roles followed, including another Broadway show, *Leader of the Pack* (1984-1985 with Patrick Cassidy), telefilms "Flight 90" (1984), "A Matter of Sex" (1984), "The Seduction of Gina" (1984), and "Classified Love" (1986), plus the NBC miniseries "Celebrity" (1984) and the movies *I Ought To Be In Pictures* (1981), *Backfire* (1987), and *Childsplay* (1988). Her latest film, *Boy's Life* (1989) was directed by her mother. Of their relationship, Dinah says, "It's hard when Mommy is directing. Very Hard. I instantly become the rebellious teenager. I want to please her, but I don't want her to tell me what to do. I know that isn't logical. When I can separate her giving me direction from her telling me to make my bed in the morning, we do very well."

Manoff's marriage to French designer Jean-Marc Joubert lasted only five years. Now living alone in a house in Laurel Canyon, California, she prefers her privacy.

E.G. Marshall

"There's a saying among actors that goes, 'who's E.G. Marshall, get me E.G. Marshall, get me an E.G. Marshall type and who's E.G. Marshall?' I used to go anywhere and people would . . . know me from my television shows," the actor says, referring to his two longtime TV hits, "The Bold Ones" and the "Defenders" for which he won two Emmys. "Now there's a group of people who have grown up and don't know me at all." But perhaps the best thing to have happened with age to this actor, whom Orson Wells once called "one of the only three actors to think while he was acting" (the other two were Garbo and Chaplin) is what Marshall calls "the era of the character actor. At one point everything was going to all the young studs, like Brando and Dean. But things go through phases and now it's turning around and the character actor is really coming into his own."

Born 18 June 1910 in the small Minnesota farming community of Owatonna, E.G. Marshall once considered becoming a Protestant minister. He settled on an acting career and started out in 1933 performing with a Shakespearean company in the South and Southwest, moved with it to Chicago for four years, and then headed for Broadway. He debuted in 1942 in *Jason* and received critical acclaim in such landmark productions as Eugene O'Neill's *The Iceman Cometh*, Thornton Wilder's *The Skin of Our Teeth* and Samuel Beckett's *Waiting for Godot*. Demonstrating his skill at comedy as well as drama, he was a standout in Neil Simon's *Plaza Suite* and replacing Hume Cronyn opposite Jessica Tandy in the Pulitzer Prize-winning *The Gin Game*. His many film roles have included *Twelve Angry Men, The Caine Mutiny, Compulsion, My Chauffeur* and *The Power*. He also played the President of the United States in the film *Superman*, and the father in Woody Allen's *Interiors*. He appeared in a 1983 revival of the Broadway hit *Mass Appeal* and the two television miniseries "At Mother's Request" (1986) and "War and Remembrance" (1988).

Garry Marshall

During the past twenty five years he has distinguished himself as a master of contemporary comedy. Not only has he created, written, directed, and produced some of the biggest hits on TV, but he has also proven his talent in feature films as well. Garry has directed five motion pictures, in addition to writing and producing over 1,000 television shows.

Garry Marshall was born 13 November 1934 in New York City. His formal education included Northwestern's Medill School of Journalism. Upon graduating, he left for the Army where he pursued his interest in jazz by playing the drums with his own jazz group. After his commitment to the Army was completed, he went on to become a reporter for the *New York Daily News*. Soon following, he began writing scripts for television shows. He entered into the world of television as a writer for Jack Paar's "Tonight Show" in 1960, and later for the "Joey Bishop Show." While in California, Garry met Jerry Belson, and together they became one of the most prolific writing teams ever. The two are responsible for such popular television sitcoms as "The Danny Thomas Show," "The Lucy Show," the "Dick Van Dyke Show" which won an Emmy, and "I Spy." They also created and wrote their first series "Hey Landlord" in 1966. In 1969, the team brought Neil Simon's "The Odd Couple" to TV, in which Garry served as the executive producer for five years. Their first experience with motion pictures came soon after when they were contracted to write and produce the comedy *How Sweet It Is*, followed by a drama entitled *The Grasshopper*. Deciding to go solo, he created and produced several successful comedy shows including "Happy Days," "Laverne and Shirley," "Mork and Mindy," and "Blansky's Beauties," as well as directing the films *Young Doctors in Love, The Flamingo Kid, Nothing In Common, Overboard*, and his most recent endeavor, the hit drama *Beaches*. Not limiting himself to writing, creating, and producing, Garry made the move to the other side of the camera performing in the films *Lost in America*, and *Jumping Jack Flash*, which was directed by his sister Penny Marshall.

Garry and his wife Barbara reside in California and have three children.

Penny Marshall

She has a special talent for making people laugh. Penny has appeared in numerous television sitcoms, made-for-TV movies, and films, as well as directing two hit movies.

Penny was born on 15 October 1944 in New York City. She spent her childhood (from age three) tap dancing at her mother's dancing school, and it was her dancing that introduced her to the world of show business. She and a group of friends competed on and won "Ted Mack's Amateur Hour" at fourteen, and then went on to perform on the "Jackie Gleason Show." After attending the University of New Mexico in Albuquerque, and spending six years there, she left for Hollywood and made her television debut in California on "The Danny Thomas Hour." Other TV appearances include: "The Odd Couple" (1972-1974), "Chico and the Man" (1975), "The Mary Tyler Moore Show" (1975), "Saturday Night Live" (1975-1977), "Happy Days" (1975), "The Tonight Show" (1976-1977), and "Laverne and Shirley" (1976-1983). She made appearances in the TV movies *More Than Friends* (1978), and *Love Thy Neighbor* (1984). She also performed in the films *How Sweet It Is* (1967), *The Grasshopper* (1970), and *1941* (1979). Proving that she is as versatile as she is funny, she has directed two hit movies, *Jumpin' Jack Flash* (1986) and *Big* (1988).

Penny has been married two times; the first time to Michael Henry, with whom she had her daughter Tracy, and the second time to Rob Reiner, married 10 April 1971 and divorced in 1979. She is currently single and resides in Los Angeles.

Dean Martin

The basic ingratiating ingredients of this card-shark-turned-actor and crooning superstar has been said to be five parts gin to one part forsooth. In any case, he wryly insists, "I drink only moderately. I've got a case of Moderately in my dressing room."

Born Dino Crocetti, 17 June 1917 in Steubenville, Ohio, into the

family of a barber, he toiled as a gas station attendant, boxer and croupier before turning to singing. "There wasn't much else for a kid to do," he remembers genially, "except a little stealing, of course. Why, even today when I go into a fancy haberdashery and spend $500, I always steal a necktie or something." When he switched to singing in Steubenville night spots, he was surprised by the low pay. ("When the guy offered $50 a week, I thought he was crazy. I was makin' more than that just palmin' silver dollars.") Eventually he warbled his way up to the $750-a-week bracket at Atlantic City's 500 club where, in 1946, he shared the bill with a gangly, long-jawed comedian named Jerry Lewis. When their scripted show brought no laughs, they turned to ad-libbing and became one of the most popular teams in show business, in clubs, and on TV. The team made a total of sixteen films together before severing the partnership with raging animosity. (Their reunion in the late 1970s on one of Lewis' annual Muscular Dystrophy telethons was an A-level tearjerker.) "It was wonderful," Martin says of his days with Lewis, "we did all the crazy things I'd always wanted to do. Hearing a whole audience laugh is just like getting drunk." He admits that the general consensus was "I'd drown without Jerry," but the singer famous for his sly winks, double entendres and boozer image made it even bigger on his own. After making a less-than-impressive solo film debut in a clinker called *10,000 Bedrooms*, he began to be taken seriously as an actor when he landed the juicy role of the draft dodger in *The Young Lions* in 1958. Since then, he's alternated between serious roles (*Rio Bravo, Airport,*) with those featuring light comedy and music (e.g. *Bells Are Ringing*). In the recording studios, Martin has made his gold and/or platinum mark with such hits as "That's Amore" and "Memories Are Made of This." He has been associated with NBC-TV since 1948 ("Actually, it's the only network I know how to get to") where, among a number of innovations (including sliding down a brass pole in his mock bachelor pad by way of making his entrance on his variety show) is his having transformed "the roast" into a fresh new entertainment art form. The thrice-married six-footer (to Betty McDonald, Jeanne Biggers and Catherine Mae Hawn) is the father of seven (he also adopted his third wife's daughter). His talented actor/singer son, Dean Paul Martin, was killed in 1987 in a crash near the Air Force Base where he served as an Air National Guard Captain.

Mary Martin

"**M**ary Martin flew like Peter Pan again last night, sprinkling magic dust over the audience" marvelled the reviewer about her October, 1984, performance benefitting the trauma center (now renamed the Mary Martin Trauma Center) at San Francisco General Hospital. "Last night she said she wanted to do 'something nice' for the hospital that saved her life after a San Francisco traffic accident in 1982" (claiming the life of her manager and seriously injuring the now-late actress, Janet Gaynor, and her husband, Paul Gregory).

She was born on 1 December 1913 in Weatherford, Tex., the town in which she made her singing debut at five at the local fireman's ball. In 1938, on Broadway, after she sang "My Heart Belongs to Daddy" in the musical *Leave It to Me,* audiences' hearts belonged to her. Because of her performance, Paramount offered her a 10-picture deal, so she "returned" to Hollywood (she had been there for two years earlier with no luck in landing a job—"I tried so hard that people in Hollywood nicknamed me 'Audition Mary'"). She made half a dozen pictures (*The Great Victor Herbert* and *Rhythm on the River* among them), but she hated the countless retakes, the lack of spontaneity ("It was all so boring, so wasteful, so enervating"). Under the guidance of Richard Halliday, a tall, dignified story editor at Paramount whom she married in 1940, she returned to Broadway and a string of musical hits including *One Touch of Venus, Lute Song,* the touring *Annie Get Your Gun, South Pacific, The Sound of Music* (Tony) and the perennial *Peter Pan* (Tony). (She says that *Peter Pan* is "absolutely" her favorite of all the shows she's performed.) Stricken with a serious illness after the long run in *I Do, I Do* (1968) she and Halliday took a four-year sabbatical at Nossa Fazenda, their ranch in Brazil. He died in 1973.

Martin first appeared on TV in 1953 when she co-starred with Ethel Merman, live, in the famed Ford 50s Anniversay Show. She then co-starred, again live, with Noel Coward, in a 90-minute dual sing-along, a program which *Time* magazine said proved that "talent has no need for production numbers." Other productions (also live) were "Annie Get Your Gun," "Peter Pan" and (after touring 3 months in 87 cities from Texas to Alaska) "Music with

Mary" *and* "Magic with Mary Martin" on the afternoon and evening of Easter Sunday, 1959. Recent television projects include her first TV movie, "Valentine" (1979) which received a Peabody award, and "Over Easy," the 1981-1983 PBS-TV series, which she co-hosted with Jim Hartz. In 1969 Martin published her first book, *Mary Martin's Needlepoint* ("I read books and did needlepoint to save my sound whenever I did a show. Since Richard's been gone, I haven't stopped.") The first edition of her autobiography, *My Heart Belongs* was published in 1976, and the second edition in 1984. For three years she was associated with Fieldcrest Mills, both as a designer and their roving ambassadress.

These days, she is in residence (but seldom indoors) in a new house in Rancho Mirage near Palm Springs. She meditates, swims, and (of course) needlepoints. Will she return to the stage? (Her last appearances were on Broadway in *So You Turn Somersaults*, 1977, and touring with Carol Channing for a year in *Legends!,* in 1986-87.) "I don't wish to do eight shows a week and go back into my cocoon," she confesses, "I'm having such a lovely life with my children, and my six grandchildren ('they're all so gorgeous') and my friends." From an early Texas marriage she is the mother of actor Larry Hagman, the infamous J.R. Ewing on television's long-running "Dallas" ("he's a *fabulous* actor," boasts his mother). Her daughter, Heller, (so named because "prenatally she kicked like mad") is the child of her second marriage to Halliday ("she's a *fabulous* mother," boasts Martin). Hagman says of his mother: "She has magic. Olivier has it. Brando has it—that 'other' thing that makes us want to look at her on stage." Although she may not return to stage, we will see her in other media. "Never stop working" she advised readers in a 1983 *New York Times* interview. "Keep active. I've been practicing what I preach. I tend to think I'm 19. I'm sort of retarded that way . . . I always have a good time. I really love living. I love every second of it. I guess it's my stubborn Texas determination to continue to the last breath." TV viewers experienced a special treat in 1989 when "Peter Pan" was rebroadcast after a long hiatus from the small screen.

Steve Martin

H is motto: "Be courteous, kind and forgiving . . . be oblong and have your knees removed. Be tasteless, rude and offensive." Irreverent, for sure. "Well, excuuuuuuse me. It's blow your brains out time." The comedian blows on, "I'm so mad at my mother. She's 102 years old and she calls up wanting to borrow ten dollars for some food. I told her, heyyy, what is this bull? I work for a living!" Described as "Jekyll and Hyde alternating between frenzy and sobriety," he offers this bit of self analysis: "I think ultimately, when I'm at my best, it's a total presentation of a human being, on-stage, being vulnerable, being afraid, being confident, fooling myself, you know lying to myself . . . the different little jokes and things are held together by an attitude of that personality."

Steve Martin was born in Waco, Texas, in either 1945 or 1946. His birthdate is his mystery. At three he became stagestruck, the result of seeing a Jerry Lewis film, and at age five he began his career as a comedian. "I'd watch the skits on the Ed Sullivan show, memorize them and then go to school and headline them during Show and Tell." When the family moved to Garden Grove, California, the ten-year-old Martin took a job selling twenty-five cent guidebooks to Disneyland just two miles down the road. Throughout his teen years he performed in those special Disneyland clean-and-safe revues, then spread his Dumbo ears and flew through Long Beach State College majoring in philosophy. He appeared in local comedy clubs and received his big break writing gags for the "Smothers Brothers Comedy Hour." Then in big demand with other comedy performers, he wrote for them for a while but stopped. "Comedy comes down to a split second and by the time it leaves the typewriter and gets to the director or the star, it's gone." Success was slow in coming. On the road for years, he vowed to quit performing until in 1975 his despair actually transformed his act. Close to the edge, he changed his routine by allowing the outrageous to blossom into his trademark shtick—self-styled absurdity. Television appearances on nationwide talk and variety shows lead to regular appearances on NBC's popular "Saturday Night Live" and his "wild and crazy guy" routine became as popular overnight as the hula hoop. Suddenly Martin was the new pop of the American funnybone. His mood swung, back to Hollywood where he appeared in films such as *The Jerk*, 1979, the musical *Pennies From Heaven*, 1981, and comedies such as *Dead Men Don't Wear Plaid*, *The Man with Two Brains*, *The Lonely Guy*, *All of Me* in 1984 (for which he received Best Actor honors from the N.Y. Film Critics), the film version of *Little Shop of Horrors* (1986), *The Three Amigos* (1986), *Planes, Trains and Automobiles* (1987), *Roxanne* (1987; won award from National Film Critics), *Dirty Rotten Scoundrels* (1989), and *My Blue Heaven* (1990). He expanded his horizons to live theatre and appeared in the Lincoln Center production of *Waiting for*

Godot in 1988. Martin is also the author of the autobiographical *Cruel Shoes*, published in 1979. Having guested more than fifty times on NBC's "Tonight Show," he has commented, "It's rumored that Johnny Carson moved to the West Coast to be closer to me." After sharing some live-in chuckles with the likes of Bernadette Peters, the comedian married actress Victoria Tennant on 20 November 1986 in Rome.

Marsha Mason

"**I** believe there's a certin amount of luck in everybody's life. Director Elia Kazan once said that an actor gets about three lucky breaks. You have to be ready for them. Everybody has some luck. It's a question of whether or not you take advantage of it." It may have been one such lucky break that brought Mason together with leading playwright Neil Simon. During their decade-long marriage (1973-1983), Simon created several films, including *The Goodbye Girl*, that showcased Mason as an appealing but emotionally tattered woman squaring off against life and men.

Mason was born in St. Louis, Mo., 3 April 1942. Star-struck as a child, Mason did not let her strict upbringing and education deter her from pursuing the Bohemian life of a struggling actress in New York. She debuted off-Broadway in *The Deer Park* and soaped some suds on "Love of Life," before making it to Broadway in 1970 in *Happy Birthday, Wanda June*, based on the Kurt Vonnegut satire. After extensive performances with the San Francisco-based American Conservatory Theater, she drew critical notice on film as a troubled prostitute in the 1973 film *Cinderella Liberty*. "If you play a down-and-out loser part, they send you down-and-out loser parts," she noted. She sidestepped typecasting roles and auditioned, instead, for *The Good Doctor*, Simon's Chekhov inspired production. She got the part, met Simon, and three weeks later, they were married. Mason's high-key performance opposite Richard Dreyfuss in *The Goodbye Girl*, which Simon rescripted for them, helped make the upbeat story of loathing-turned-to-love one of 1977's most heralded movies. In Simon's 1979 autobiographical tale, *Chapter*

Two, Mason had the rare opportunity to play a character based on herself.

She was a study of charm and vulnerability in *Only When I Laugh*, Simon's 1981 remake of his 1970 play, *The Gingerbread Lady*. Although the movie, like the play, earned lukewarm response from critics, Mason was applauded for her portrayal of an actress battling alcoholism to win a second chance with her teenage daughter. Noted one reviewer, "Mason handles her bravura moments superbly; she gives you great technique and fierce emotional honesty." Her other film credits include Simon's 1978 comedy, *The Cheap Detective*, Simon's 1983 *Max Dugan Returns*, and the non-Simon movies *Promises in the Dark* (1979), *Heartbreak Ridge* (1986) and *Stella* (1989). She starred in the CBS-TV Schoolbreak special "Little Miss Perfect" (1986) and the telefilm "Trapped in Silence" (1985) as well as appeared on stage in a New York Theatre Workshop limited run of *The Big Live* (1988) and a one-time-only performance in the A.R. Gurney play *Love Letters* in April, 1989.

Marcello Mastroianni

"**M**ethod acting is pure nonsense. All an actor must do is cultivate intelligence. For instance, if you have to play someone who's mad, there's no use going to an asylum to watch a madman. The madness you see is his, the gestures, the looks are his, not yours. To play a madman as I did in (Pirandello's) *Henry IV*, you must search within yourself, above all, invent." Ever since *La Dolce Vita* (1961) Mastroianni has been an emblem of romantic Latin fascination. ("I can't understand why this label has stuck to me. . . . In pictures I've been a homosexual, impotent, and in one I was pregnant, but never a seducer. The label is even more unreasonable now that I am sixty.") Whatever the reason, he is indeed, highly sought after: (After *Henry IV* closed in Paris in 1983, Mastroianni underwent thirty-eight interviews in seven hours in Italian, French and English.)

Born 28 September 1924 in Fontana Liri, Italy, the son of a carpenter, he moved with his family to Turin at age five, and then to Rome. After WWII he attended the University of Rome and did some collegiate theatre, meeting and acting with Federico Fellini and Giulietta Masina in the process. Hired in 1948 by Luchino Visconti, who headed Italy's leading theatrical troupe, he worked with heavyweights like Vittorio Gassman and Rina Morelli. His first major screen-role was in *Una Domenica d'Agosto* (1949); *La Notte*, *Divorce Italian Style* and *The Priest's Wife* followed. Of cinema he says, "[It's] a pure lie, and the actor is a liar, the most ancient seller of smoke who finds satisfaction in simulation. Yet some say acting is complicated, a torment. Come on. Complaining when it's enjoyable. Acting is a pleasure like making love. No, wait a minute, not always; lovemaking is often an ordeal." He harbors a penchant for beautiful blonds, be they wife (former actress Flora Carabella, one daughter) or mistress (Faye Dunaway, who ditched him in 1971 for another man), or Catherine Deneuve, (his co-star in the tearjerker *It Only Happens to Others* and mother of his second daughter). His films include: *Wifemistress* (1979), Fellini's *City of Women* (1981), *La Nuit de Varennes* (1983), a film version of *Henry IV* (1985), a reunion with frequent co-star Sophia Loren in *Saturday, Sunday, Monday* (1985), *Ginger and Fred* (1985), *Marconi* (1985), *The Two Lives of Mattia Pascal* (1985), *Miss Arizo* (1987) and *L'Intervista* (1987). He received an Academy Award nomination as best actor for his striking performance in *Dark Eyes* (1987).

Marlee Matlin

Marlee Matlin once spoke of her spiritual mentor, Henry Winkler. "I actually live with his family and they are so wonderful, so giving, so loving and so funny. I met Henry at a benefit in Chicago when I was just twelve years old. I was doing a play and just before I went on stage he tapped me on the shoulder at the curtain and said 'I love you' in sign language. Once I got on stage, I gave the audience all I had. I told Henry I wanted to be an actress and he said, 'Believe in yourself and you'll do what you want.' I can honestly say I wouldn't be here if it weren't for him. He still knows best." And this fine young actress went on to prove Mr. Winkler's words true.

In 1987, at the age of 21, she became the youngest recipient of the Best Actress Oscar for her outstanding debut film performance in *Children of a Lesser God*. Although she won this prestigious Award at a very early age, she had already been acting for fifteen years!

Marlee Beth Matlin, born in 1965 in Morton Grove, a Chicago suburb, was a normal, happy child. "I had roseola when I was 18 months old. My grandmother's best friend was babysitting and told my parents there was something wrong with my hearing." She began to act as an outlet for her immense frustration. Her mother, Libby Matlin, a powerhouse in her own right, took her to the Center for Deafness in Chicago and she immediately won the role of Dorothy in *The Wizard of Oz*. "I stayed seven or eight years. We did plays all over Illinois, Nebraska and Indiana." Eventually, she got a minor role in a stage production of *Children of a Lesser God*. She was spotted by a talent agent and the rest is history.

Marlee is determined to build on this first success and have a long and varied career. She has spoken publicly, as a presenter at the 1988 Academy Awards, and continues to improve her speech with the aid of voice coach Lillian Glass. She has become the spokeswoman for the hearing impaired who are also potential film lovers and hopes to convince movie studios and televison networks to automatically "close caption" their movies and programs. She desperately wants them to understand how frustrating it is "to be denied access to the world's most powerful communication media."

Walter Matthau

"A nybody with a bulbous nose and beady eyes looks like me," the superstar once remarked. "It's a fairly ordinary physiognomical phenomenon. In the ghetto, you develop facial muscles in order to survive, and they can serve you well as an actor." People who expect him to be like the beer-swilling Little League coach he played in the film *Bad News Bears,* or the vaudevillian of the *Sunshine Boys,* or the happy-go-nowhere slob, Oscar Madison, in the *Odd Couple,* are taken back by his elegance in speech and sartorial  manner. He sprinkles his conversation with bits of French and German, does the *New York Times* Sunday crossword in 20 minutes (using a pen) and, reportedly, on one of his very first dates with his wife, Carol, arrived with a puzzle and asked her, "What's a three-letter word for beverage?" And she, not used to the game, replied,

"7-Up." Matthau fell in love with her immediately. They'd met first when they both appeared in the play *Will Success Spoil Rock Hunter?* He married the former Carol Wellington-Smythe Marcus Saroyan (she was a debutante pal of Gloria Vanderbilt and Oona Chaplin as well as wife of the late playwright William Saroyan) in 1959. He had two children, David and Jenny from his first marriage to Grace Johnson. She had two children from her marriage to Saroyan. Together they have a son, Charles.

"Social adversity frustrates you. You need a place to express yourself. Had I grown up in a palace, I doubt I would have made much of an actor." Born 1 October 1920 on the lower East Side of New York, he was raised on potato soup and the Yiddish Theater. "I was in a religious festival play when I was four," he remembers. "I knew that I liked to get up in front of people and do things." As a teenager he locked himself in the bathroom to read Shakespeare aloud because he "liked the sound." In 1942 he enlisted in the Army Air Corps, saw action in Europe, and after his discharge studied at the New School's Dramatic Workshop on the G.I. Bill. Though constantly employed on Broadway and television, he never got his name above the title until Neil Simon picked him to play Oscar Madison in his play *The Odd Couple.* At first Matthau wanted to play the part of finicky Felix Unger because he felt it would be too easy to play Oscar. ("That part I can phone in," he told Simon.) But the playwright had his way and the *Odd Couple* ran on Broadway for two years and made Matthau a star at age 45. He once said he preferred to act on stage rather than films, but after a severe heart attack while making *The Fortune Cookie,* he settled down to a regular California life of two films a year and weekends in the desert. He's appeared in many films, such as *First Monday in October; Buddy, Buddy; Hopscotch; California Suite; House Calls; Movers and Shakers; Pirates;* and *The Couch Trip.*

At a meeting with studio executives during the filming of *Hopscotch,* Matthau walked in somberly, aware that everyone was concerned about his serious heart condition, since he had just had surgery. In one cold beat he said, "My doctor has just given me six months to live," The executives were stunned. "And when he found out I couldn't afford to pay his bill—he gave me another six months."

Paul Mazursky

"There are two kinds of movies: movies made out of passion and movies made to make money. They're both authentic, but the pictures I've loved were made out of passion," says the writer-director-actor-producer whom Pauline Kael has called "the manic poet of the middle class quirk." Mazursky's 1978 production, *An Unmarried Woman*, garnered an Oscar nomination for Best Picture and earned him a slew of critics' awards for the screenplay. But regarding passion, how closely can a man identify with a woman (Jill Clayburgh) whose husband leaves her? According to the man in question, very easily: asked where he got the material for his intimate exploration of his title character's emotional evolution, he replied, "Can't you tell I'm the Unmarried Woman?"

As Mazursky has said, he writes (and directs) "personal comedies about very serious subjects." During the 70s his best movies—*Bob & Carol & Ted & Alice*, *Blume in Love* and *An Unmarried Woman*—were, in the words of one reviewer, "bulletins from a combat zone," i.e., affluent urban America in the throes of sexual revolution, "that document the changing mores of an exasperating decade." In 1982 he tried his method on a classic, Shakespeare's *The Tempest*, but the outcome got negative reviews. Andrew Sarris called it "a disaster of sufficient magnitude to require the services less of a critic than a coroner." Subsequently, however, he won plaudits for an original comedy (co-authored by Leon Capetanos) *Moscow on the Hudson*, about a Soviet visitor to Manhattan (Robin Williams) who defects to the consumer society in—where else?—Bloomingdale's.

Born Irwin Mazursky in Brooklyn, 25 April 1930, he acted off-Broadway while at Brooklyn College, had bit parts in movies and bigger ones in television plays, and after moving to Los Angeles in 1959 was a writer on the CBS-TV "Danny Kaye Show," finally teaming up with Larry Tucker to write and produce *I Love You, Alice B. Toklas*. Their next collaboration was *Bob & Carol*. His more recent projects include *Down and Out in Beverly Hills* (1986) and *Moon Over Parador* (1988). From his more domestic collaboration with the former Betsy Purdy, whom he married in 1953, he has two daughters, Meg and Jill.

Andrew McCarthy

H e has starred in at least ten feature films since his 1983 film debut opposite Jacqueline Bisset and Rob Lowe in *Class*. In addition to films, this versatile, talented actor has performed in the

theatre, and both off and on Broadway.

Andrew McCarthy was born in 1962 in Westfield, New Jersey, where he attended Pingry School before going on to New York University where he majored in theatre. It was in high school, though, when Andrew decided to go into acting. "I decided on acting in high school when I was cut from the basketball team," he states. While attending NYU, a fellow classmate told him about the casting for the upcoming movie *Class*. Andrew auditioned and won a starring role in the film. Still attending NYU, he studied acting at Circle in the Square, and appeared in the Off-Broadway productions of *Life Under Water*, *Marion's Camera*, *Been Taken*, and *Herself as Lust*. Other stage performances include the *Festival '88* of the Arts in New York, the Ensemble Studio Theatre's production of *Neptune's Hip*, and on Broadway, he co-starred with Matt Dillon in the drama *Boys of Winter*. Returning to films, he starred in several movies after *Class*, including *Heaven Help Us*, *St. Elmo's Fire*, *Pretty in Pink*, and *Mannequin*. Although *Mannequin* turned out to be one of the biggest sleepers of 1987, it was his biggest personal box-office smash. Following that film, he took a supporting role in the American Playhouse production of *Waiting for the Moon* in France. Upon his return to the U.S., he appeared at Lincoln Center in the theatre presentation of *Bodies, Rest & Motion*, and took the lead roles in the films *Less Than Zero*, *Kansas*, *Fresh Horses*, and *Weekend at Bernies*. After filming *Weekend at Bernies*, Andrew was off to Paris again to appear in the film *Quiet Days in Clichy*.

Andrew, an avid Yankees fan and golf enthusiast, currently resides in the Greenwich Village section of New York.

Rue McClanahan

C ast in the role of Blanche, a southern belle who owns the Miami Beach home which she occupies along with three other older women, Rue McClanahan is not only winning acclaim for "The Golden Girls," she's also enjoying herself. "I'm playing a man-crazy, self-centered widow, and I'm having a lot of fun doing it," says the 1987 Emmy Award winner for best actress in a comedy series. The show has also been a reunion for some of the cast. "I'm very lucky and thrilled to be back with Bea (Arthur) and Betty

(White), two fantastic actresses I've worked with before." The five-foot-four, blue-eyed actress played Vivian Cavender Harmon in the award-winning TV series "Maude," starring Bea Arthur, which ran from 1972 through 1978. Rue starred with Betty White in NBC-TV's "Mama's Family" (1983), playing Aunt Fran.

Born on 21 February, in Headtown, Oklahoma, Rue was educated at the University of Tulsa. Moving to New York City, she studied with Uta Hagen and Harold Clurman before going on to become a veteran of theater, film, TV and commercials. Rue was seen on Broadway in "Father's Day," while her off-Broadway credits include "Who's Happy Now?," "Secret Life of Walter Mitty" and "Dark of the Moon." Traveling to California, Rue did regional and stock theater, such as "The House of Blue Leaves" in Pasadena and "Picnic" in Denver and California. With a love for the small screen, Rue has appeared as a guest star on "Trapper John, M.D.," "The Love Boat," and "The Lou Grant Show." Her TV movies include "The Day the Bubble Burst" and "The Little Match Girl." The smiling belle most recently completed three made-for-TV movies: "My Darling Daughters" (NBC), "The Man in the Brown Suit" (CBS) and "Liberace" (ABC), in which she plays the virtuoso's mother.

A resident of the San Fernando Valley, Rue, six times married, shares her home with five dogs and two cats.

Kelly McGillis

"I 've always been rebellious," she acknowledges. "I must say I grew up in a very perfect way." Although this feisty Irish beauty has been compared to Grace Kelly, Lauren Bacall, and Ingrid Bergman, she is still insecure about her talent as well as her looks. In response to how she feels being compared to these legends, she sums up her feelings by replying, "How can anybody live up to all that?"

Kelly McGillis was born in 1958 in Newport Beach, California, the eldest daughter of a housewife and a doctor. Although she grew up in a comfortable home, she had a weight problem (she weighed 210 pounds at one time) and she was a bit of a rebel. Her first ambition was to become a doctor like her father, but that all came to

an end when she went on a house call with her father. He went to the aid of a man who had torn off his thumb. The man was crying, and seeing him in pain caused Kelly to cry as well. It was then she realized that she was too sensitive to become a doctor. A few years later, when Kelly was 15 years old, she won an acting award for her role in her high school production of *The Serpent.* When she was sixteen, she became consumed with acting, and when she was seventeen, just six months before she was to graduate from high school, she dropped out to become an actress. "I was a pretty wild girl," states Kelly. "My outlets were acting. I decided not to do anything else. I didn't like anything else." Soon after, she packed her bags and headed for the Pacific Conservatory of Performing Arts in Santa Maria, where she studied for three years. She then was accepted into the Juilliard School of Drama in New York City. While she was attending Juilliard, Kelly appeared in theatre productions of *Three Sisters, Love for Love, Six Characters in Search of an Author,* and *The Winter's Tale.* While she was still attending Juilliard, she was doing summer work in Shakespeare in the Park, where she was discovered by producer Philip Epstein. He was the author of the film *Reuben, Reuben,* in which she made her debut in 1983. Other films to follow include *Witness* (1985), *Top Gun* (1985), *Made In Heaven* (1987), *Promised Land* (1987), *The House on Carroll Street* (1988), *Dreamers* (1988), *The Accused* (1988), *The Winter People* (1989), *Down with the Lions* (1989), and *Cat Chaser* (1989).

Kelly has been married three times; to writer Boyd Black, actor Barry Tubb and currently, to yacht broker Fred Tillman (married January, 1989).

Elizabeth McGovern

W hat the *New York Times* headlined as "the Swift, Magical Rise of Elizabeth McGovern" began when Robert Redford, in his film-directing debut, cast her as Timothy Hutton's high-school girlfriend in *Ordinary People.* The picture won an Oscar in 1981 (so did Redford and Hutton), and the blue-eyed nineteen-year old was off and running to her own first Oscar nomination for her subsequent portrayal of the bird-in-a-gilded cage beauty, Evelyn Nesbit, in Milos Forman's *Ragtime.* "I was shocked," she said afterward. "I mean, I was very pleased, but at the same time, I didn't think I'd got to the point where I deserved it." Which may give a clue as to why a second feature story in the *Times* about McGovern was headlined "How to Succeed by Being Talented, Ambitious and Nice." "How ambitious?" asked writer Chris Case. The star, in rapid succession, of *Lovesick* with Dudley Moore, *Once Upon a Time in America* with Robert DeNiro and *Racing with the Wind* with Sean Penn, allowed that it was probably "relative. I suppose, compared to Joan Crawford, I'm a sweet little cotton puff." More films followed, including *Native Son* (1986), *The Bedroom Window* (1986), *She's Having a Baby* (1987), *The Handmaid's Tale* (1989) and *Johnny Handsome* (1989).

A middle child of a middle-class family in the Midwest, McGovern (born in 1962) grew up in Evanston, Illinois, where her father was a law professor at Northwestern and her mother taught high school. When her dad switched classrooms to UCLA, Elizabeth transferred to a North Hollywood high school and, after toying with notions of becoming a veterinarian, a painter or a ballerina ("that died because I never could do a pirouette"), she "started to do plays, and it felt right, so I thought, maybe I'll be an actress." It was after an agent spotted her in a school production of *Lysistrata* that she auditioned for Redford and the "swift, magical rise" began. McGovern has alternated film roles with a number of stints Off-Broadway, including Lorraine Hansberry's *To Be Young, Gifted and Black,* Wallace Shawn's *The Hotel Play,* an Obie Awardwinning– production of *My Sister in This House, Painting Churches, A Map of the World, The Two Gentlemen of Verona* and the New York Shakespeare production of *A Midsummer Night's Dream.* "Acting makes me feel alive and thinking," says the versatile young woman whom Walter Kerr placed in his category of "actresses of special grace." "When I go see a play and my imagination is stimulated, it just makes the sky wider."

Maureen McGovern

The singer of the Academy Award songs "The Morning After" and "We May Never Love Like This Again" has an extraordinary four-octave range. Whether making records, performing live, or appearing on television or in a motion picture, Maureen McGovern demonstrates her unique and moving way of interpreting a song.

The daughter of James Terrence and Mary Rita (Welsh), Maureen was born in Youngstown, Ohio, on 27 July 1949. Although she was interested in music, the future singer started her career in the business world as an executive secretary for the Youngstown Cartage Company (1968-69). Finding her forte was singing folk songs, she eventually stretched her vocal ability to perform jazz and soft rock. McGovern first invaded the public consciousness via her million-seller recording of 1972's Oscar-winning "The Morning After," followed by an appearance in *The Towering Inferno*, singing another Oscar winner, "We May Never Love Like This Again" (1974). On a streak, she scored again with the theme from *Superman*, entitled "Can You Read My Mind?" (1978). That tune reached #1 on the *Billboard* chart. Spreading her wings, McGovern tried acting again and landed the role of a guitar-playing nun in the spoof *Airplane!* (1980). In the eighties, in an effort to break out of the mold of easy musical categorization, she branched out into theater, making her debut in the Pittsburgh Civic Light Opera's 1981 production of *The Sound of Music*. Joseph Papp gave the singer her first Broadway role (replacing Linda Ronstadt) in *The Pirates of Penzance*, and she followed by playing the sultry Luisa Contini in *Nine* (replacing Karen Akers). She has also appeared in touring productions of *South Pacific, Guys and Dolls,* and *I Do, I Do*. McGovern has performed at all the major clubs from coast to coast, and she made her solo Carnegie Hall debut in May, 1989. Among her many albums are *Maureen McGovern* (1979), *Another Woman in Love* (1987), *State of the Heart* (1988) and *Naughty Baby* (1989). She has won many gold records and awards, among them the Gold Leaf Award (1973), the Australian Gold Award (1975) and the Grand Prize at the Tokyo Music Festival (1975). A much-admired participant in such presentations as the Kool Jazz Festival, she has also, since making her concert debut with the Honolulu Symphony, sung with the Boston Pops, New York Pops and other concert orchestras.

Ed McMahon

"**H**-e-e-e-r-r-e-'s Johnny!" TV's reigning second banana, superpitchman, and talk-show foil booms out five times a week, heralding the start of another "Tonight" show starring Johnny Carson. Big (6'4", 225 lbs.), jovial, and quick to guffaw at

Johnny's jokes ("He's been accused of laughing too much," Carson once said, "but I think he really thinks I'm funny"), Edward Leo McMahon, born 6 March 1923 in Detroit, Michigan, was the son of a onetime minstral-show interlocutor who turned pro fund-raiser. He worked his way through Catholic University by, among other things, selling pots and pans door-to-door and hawking vegetable slicers on the Boardwalk of Atlantic City. He broke into bigtime TV in 1954 as Carson's sidekick on a daytime quiz show called "Who

Do You Trust?" and has since gone on to host "Star Search" (the popular national TV talent forum which premiered in '83) and co-host NBC-TV's runaway hit "TV Bloopers and Practical Jokes" (which also premiered in '83). Over the years, he has moved more and more into acting, with a list of credits that includes the movie *Butterfly* ('81) and the telefilm "The Golden Moment." He also appeared on Broadway in the comedy, *The Impossible Years.* For many years he has also served as co-host of Jerry Lewis's annual Muscular Dystrophy Telethon. He is one of America's top TV salesmen, as evidenced by his long association with Budweiser, Alpo, and Chris Craft Boats. Ed and his wife Victoria divorced in 1989 (one baby girl, Katherine Mary), and he has since remarried. He is the father of four by his first marriage, which ended in divorce. In 1988 McMahon was awarded an Honorary Doctorate in Communications from his Alma Mater, Catholic University of America. One of McMahon's proudest achievements was receiving the prestigious "Horatio Alger Award," an honor he shares with former Presidents Eisenhower and Ford as well as Reagan. He is also the author of two books, *The Art of Public Speaking* (1986) and *Selling* (1989).

Anne Meara
(see Stiller & Meara)

Dina Merrill

"Dina Merrill," once gushed an admirer, "is glamour— with both feet on the ground." Although she grew up in

more of a castle than a home (her bedroom was decorated to look like the Sleeping Beauty's; the door-knobs were silver squirrels, and a specially designed rug told the whole story) and could have slept through her whole life, she wasn't the type. "I always wanted to stand on my own feet and be somebody," says the granddaughter of the inventor of Postum, named Nedenia for her stockbroker father, Ned Hutton (Barbara Hutton was her cousin). "Besides," added Dina, "I come from hardworking pioneer stock and was brought up with the work ethic."

As a child (born 29 December 1925) Dina used to sit on her mother's lap and watch her make up and comb her hair. At six, she already knew she wanted to act. Although her parents, Marjorie Merriweather Post and Edward F. Hutton, were not in favor of their daughter joining the acting profession, after a year at George Washington University, Dina enrolled at the American Academy of Dramatic Arts while working as a fashion model to support herself. "It never occurred to me to ask my parents to pay for something they didn't believe in. I wouldn't, so why should they? They could have stopped me but they didn't; they were sure I'd never stay with it," After summer stock, she made her Broadway debut in *The Mermaids Are Singing*. But in 1946 she married Stanley Rumbaugh, Jr., and for the next ten years led an active Long Island North Shore social life centered around a home in Locust Valley and her three children, Nina, Stanley and David (who later died in a boating accident). In 1952 she took time out to appear on television with Dick Powell, and in 1957 made her film debut.

Her motion pictures include *Catch as Catch Can*, *Butterfield 8*, *Operation Petticoat*, Robert Altman's *A Wedding* and *Just Tell Me What You Want*. Her television performances include "The Tenth Month" (1979) co-starring Carol Burnett, "Anna to the Infinite Power," a cable-TV movie, "The Brass Ring," a series, "Hot Pursuit" (1984) and numerous guest appearances. Broadway stage appearances include *Angel Street* (1976), *Are You Now or Have You Ever Been . . .* (reading Lillian Hellman's letter to the House Un-American Activities Committee, 1979) and *On Your Toes* (1983).

After a divorce from Rumbaugh in 1964, Dina married actor Cliff Robertson in 1966 (one daughter, Heather). They separated in 1985 and their divorce was finalized in 1989.

Bette Midler

"**I** may put several thousand feet of tulle around it, but my message is that people should feel hope, overcome fear and stand on their own. Of course I'm discreet about it *in my way* . . . but I think of it as a grand thing, almost as a mission," explains this entertainer whose special blend of talent, vocal versatility, high-speed locomotion, camp sophistication and wide-eyed innocence has earned her devoted fans, gold records and several box-office breakthroughs. Her 1975 sell-out revue *Clams on the Half Shell* grossed more than $1.8 million. She's also won one Grammy—for her 1972 debut album, "The Divine Miss M," a special Tony award in 1973, an Oscar nomination for her portrayal of a self-destructive hard-rock singer in *The Rose,* and an Emmy for her 1978 TV special "Ol' Red Hair is Back."

She was appalled recently when an admiring fan asked her, "How does it feel to be an institution?" Her reply: "Don't *say* that! I'm too young to be an institution. Besides, I'd rather be a bank!" She was born 1 December 1945, named after Bette Davis (but pronounced *Bet*) and raised in Hawaii in the family of a transplanted New Jersey housepainter. She spent a year at the University of Hawaii studying drama, then dropped out to work in a pineapple cannery until she was hired to play a missionary's wife in the film *Hawaii.* (Despite dropping out of school, Midler is an avid and eclectic reader. According to *People* magazine's Andrea Chambers, "volumes of Shakespeare and Molière are lined up on a bookshelf near a pair of rhinestone platform heels, a gift from Cher," in her New York loft.)

The part in *Hawaii* paid her $350 and took her to Los Angeles for final shooting. With her life's savings she went to New York and worked as a go-go dancer, a glove saleswoman at Stern's and a typist at Columbia University, until she landed a part in the chorus of *Fiddler on the Roof,* eventually graduating to the principal role of Tzeitel, Tevye's eldest daughter, which she played for three years. About that time, she saw a production of the Theater for the Ridiculous. "There was this character, Waterfront Woman. . . . I'll never forget her. I wanted to be just like her." That, perhaps, formed the early nucleus for her "Divine Miss M" persona.

Midler's career breakthrough came in the winter of 1971, when she beguiled the sybarites at the all-male Continental Baths with her "rock and raunch blend of music and action." She became an overnight cult figure and word of mouth quickly brought her to the attention of Ahmet Ertegun, who-signed her to a recording contract at Atlantic Records. It's been "Venus de Midler" ever since, hoopla and Hollywood, mostly highs, but some lows, such as *Jinxed* (1981, a movie that most certainly was well named) and management troubles in 1979. Married in December, 1984, to business consultantmusician– Martin von Haselberg, she is the author of two books, *A View from a Broad* and *The Saga of Baby Divine*. In 1985 she released the album *Mud Will Be Flung Tonight,* and the video and single entitled "Wind Beneath My Wings," from her film *Beaches,* became a smash hit in 1989. Her other movies include *Down and Out in Beverly Hills* (1986), *Ruthless People* (1986), *Outrageous Fortune* (1986), *Big Business* (1987) and *Stella* (1989). Her collaboration with Woody Allen, *Scenes From a Mall,* was released in 1990. She also did the voice-over for the animated 1988 feature *Oliver and Company* and appeared as Mother Earth in the TV special celebrating Earth Day 1990. An ABC-TV special aired in the 1990-91 season.

Julia Migenes

"**J**ulia Migenes Johnson [she dropped the Johnson after her divorce] has the full potential to be, in her very different fashion, the greatest actress/singer since Callas," said *New York Post* drama critic Clive Barnes. That high compliment and others like it are echoed throughout the opera world today. Her highly acclaimed title-role performance in the 1984 film of Bizet's *Carmen* with Placido Domingo is a significant achievement. (She was nominated in both France and Italy as best actress in a dramatic role.) Her next two films, *Berlin Blues* (1987) and *Three Penny Opera* (1989), also displayed her extraordinary talents. In addition, her performance in *Lulu* at the Met in 1985 gained more critics' praise.

Born of Greek and Puerto RicanIrish– descent in New York City circa 1946, she made her first stage appearance at three-and-a-half in *Madame Butterfly.* When she was four, she and her older brother and sister began performing in an RCA show at Macy's, and on other stages and stores around New York. Julia attended the Moser Academy (for performing children) and at the age of six was chosen for a role in the touring company of the Rodgers and Hammerstein classic *South Pacific*. She continued her vocal and dance studies at the High School of Music and Art and during her junior year was chosen by Leonard Bernstein as a soloist for a "Young People's Concert." On Broadway, Julia appeared in the revival of *West Side Story* and in the original-cast production of *Fiddler on the Roof*. While in *Fiddler*, Migenes found time to perform with the New York City Opera. Performing around the world, the diva gained recognition in many roles at the Vienna Volksoper and in television appearances in a variety of European countries. She has been honored with numerous awards, among them the Golden Bambi (the most coveted award in the German-speaking countries) and the prestigious Golden Lion of Luxembourg for her work in television. In 1985 Migenes participated in the Grammy Award ceremonies as both performer and award winner for her vocal performance in *Carmen*. Having demonstrated superior ability to sing both the popular and operatic repertoire as well as dance and act, Migenes has remained a prominent fixture in opera, popular music and film. She was the subject of a lively "60 Minutes" segment in 1985.

Divorced from her husband, Julia lives with her two daughters on Long Island, New York.

Ann Miller

Moira Hodgson in the *New York Times* described the Technicolor tap dancer thus: "Ann Miller . . . a genuine old-fashioned movie star. At 13, with a forged birth certificate, she put poverty behind her and became a star at a top Hollywood studio. . . . Now, years, later, remembering her struggles as a child, she keeps a jar of candy and bubble gum by her bed. She also saves all her old clothes, just in case. Her bedroom in her Beverly Hills mansion has ancient Egyptian decor, right down to a Tutankhamen-style throne, because she believes in reincarnation and is convinced she lived in Egypt in an earlier life."

Born Lucy Ann Collier 12 April 1923 in Chireno, Texas, she started ballet lessons at the age of five to cure knock-knees and weak legs, the result of rickets. She did so well that her mother took her backstage one day to meet Bill (Bojangles) Robinson and show him how the kid could dance. He responded by giving Miller her first tap lesson. After her parents divorced when she was ten, she supported her mother by tapping at Rotary luncheons until she won a local "personality" contest and, soon thereafter, a seven-year contract at RKO, making her debut in *New Faces of 1937*. Her father forged her birth certificate so that the young teenager would meet the legal requirements of being eighteen. ("It was the only kind thing he ever did for me," she says.) She took small parts in *Room Service, Stage Door*, and *You Can't Take It with You*, with a brief term on Broadway in *George White's Scandals of 1939*. Ultimately she played supporting roles and second leads in over forty musical films, most notably *Easter Parade, Kissing Bandit, On the Town, Two Tickets to Broadway* and *Kiss Me Kate*. In 1979, she signed on to return to Broadway in the burlesque-inspired *Sugar Babies* with Mickey Rooney. In rehearsals for the super-hit she was about to throw in the towel when made to feel like a chorus girl, but pal Mickey threatened to leave with her. "I said, 'I am a star from MGM and the public expects glamour.' They finally gave me some showstoppers." And stop the show she did. Miller continues to please her audiences by appearing in revised *Sugar Babies* productions. Her latest opening was in London (September, 1988).

She has been married (briefly) three times: first to playboy Reese Milner, heir to Consolidated Steel; next to William Moss; and lastly to Arthur Cameron. The latter two were wealthy Texas oilmen.

"I have worked like a dog all my life, honey," she told Rex Reed in 1979. "Dancing, as Fred Astaire said, is next to ditch-digging. You sweat and you slave and the audience doesn't think you've got a brain in your head. So every time a good-looking millionaire came along chasing me with cars and jewels, I married him because he promised I'd never have to dance again." These days her two long-haired poodles, Cinderella and Jasmine, are her companions. Once a year she visits her jewels in their bank vault. "I look at all the pretty things sparkling and it makes me feel good. Yet they are nothing but pieces of earth."

Liza Minnelli

With her days at the Betty Ford Clinic behind her, Liza Minnelli has been doing what she does best—performing in concert, appearing on television and in films, plus giving her all to the entertainment industry. The recipient of three Tony awards, one Oscar, and one Emmy is happy to be on the right track. "I like my life. It feels good to be on the move and surefooted. Drugs are a banana peel—why fall down when you don't have to?" The famous singer/actress has gone through some big highs and lows in her personal and professional life. Her first two marriages (Peter Allen, Jack Haley, Jr.) failed as her career wavered between "comebacks." "Her life," one observer says, "has seemed both flight from and fulfillment of the Garland legacy."

Born 12 March 1946 in Los Angeles to Judy Garland and Vincente Minnelli, she was a student at sixteen different schools on both sides of the Atlantic before she reached the age of sixteen. Still, she claimed hers was not an "unhappy childhood, my mother wasn't always in Europe, and I didn't have a nanny. I lived at the Plaza Hotel. . . . A lot of kids lived there, and I really wasn't any different—it was like everybody poured water down the mail chute." Liza made her first public appearance at seven where her mother, who was playing at the Palace, called her onstage to dance. The eldest of Judy's three children, Liza left home before her sixteenth birthday: "Mama went on a kick every now and then where she used to kick me out of the house. Usually, I'd stand outside the door and pretty soon she'd open it and we'd fall into each other's arms, crying and carrying on. But one day she did it and I took her up on it. I went to New York; I had my plane fare and $100 and I've never taken a penny since." (Unlike her mother, who was often broke, Liza had invested astutely.) Before her money ran out she got work in summer stock and a part in an Off-Broadway revival of *Best Foot Forward* and cut her first record, "You Are For Loving," that same year (1963). The following year her mother asked her to share the bill at the London Palladium, and the year after Liza won a Tony for the title role in *Flora, the Red Menace* and also made her nightclub debut at the Shoreham Hotel in Washington, D.C. In short order she was appearing on the top TV variety shows and in the leading nightclubs in the U.S. and Europe.

Minnelli's first film was *Charlie Bubbles* followed by her Oscar-nominated portrayal of a mixed-up college student in *The Sterile Cuckoo*, and next, as the victim of a battery-acid attack, in the touching *Tell Me That You Love Me, Junie Moon*. Her fourth film, *Cabaret*, brought her the Oscar for best actress, something even Garland never accomplished. That same year (1972) she won an

Emmy for her TV special "Liza with a Z." Some of her other credits include: narrating *The Owl and the Pussycat* for the Martha Graham Dance Company at the Metropolitan Opera House; movies *New York, New York, Arthur, Rent-a-Cop,* and *Arthur on the Rocks;* the TV special "Baryshnikov on Broadway," and in 1984, on Broadway, *The Rink.* She starred in the NBC telefilm, "A Time to Live" (1985) as the mother of a terminally ill son; the role brought her a Golden Globe Award. In 1987 she appeared on stage at Carnegie Hall and released a two-album recording of the event. Also in 1987 she hosted a PBS documentary "Minnelli on Minnelli: Liza Remembers Vincente." The following year she made a unique ABC-TV special "Liza Minnelli in Sam Found Out: A Triple Play."

After her cure at the Betty Ford Clinic, she and third husband, theatrical producer Mark Gero, put their lives on the back burner so that Liza could take a year off from all activity. Finally feeling fit, she embarked on a six-month, twenty-seven-city concert tour in the summer of 1985, reportedly sounding "better than ever." With two earlier broken marriages, assuming responsibility for her mother's debts, two miscarriages, a fire in her Manhattan apartment, hospitalizations for lung infections and exhaustion—as well as heartbreaking romances with Martin Scorsese, Desi Arnaz, Jr., and Peter Sellers—the actress-singer-dancer, who once said: "I believe in grabbing at happiness . . . if you have to pay later for a decision you've made, that's all right," is off gathering new forces, recovering herself and no longer grabbing. Making her claim in the Pop field, Minnelli released a new album, *Results,* in September, 1989. Minnelli stood in for an ailing Elizabeth Taylor at the Art Against AIDS gala benefit held in May, 1990.

Robert Mitchum

H e lived for years with the image of Hollywood Bad Boy mostly because, in 1948, long before pot-smoking came into vogue, he was arrested for marijuana possession and served six months in a work camp. When asked what it was like, he reported, "Just like Palm Springs. Without the riffraff, of course." Asked in court to give his occupation, he dryly stated, "Ex-actor," figuring the negative publicity would ruin his career. Instead, he found himself bigger than ever and he's remained a "bankable" star ever since.

He was born Robert Charles Duran Mitchum 6 August 1917 in Bridgeport, Conn. As a Depression Kid he spent most of his teens traveling the country on the bum (with time out for a short stretch on a Georgia chain gang for vagrancy). Landing in California, he went to work at Lockheed Aircraft until overexposure to noisy machinery began to take its toll and a doctor suggested he change his line of work. He signed up as a film extra, brushed up on his horsemanship, and appeared in eight Hopalong Cassidy movies before becoming a big-league movie star in 1945 with *The Story of G.I. Joe.* Since then the actor with the battered, belligerent face ("I agree with the guy who wrote that I looked like a shark with a broken nose") has been a standout in such films as *Crossfire* (1947), *Night of the Hunter* (1955),

The Sundowners (1960), *Ryan's Daughter* (1970), *The Friends of Eddie Coyle* (1973), *The Big Sleep* (playing the Bogart role in a 1978 remake of the 1946 Raymond Chandler detective thriller) and *That Championship Season* (1982). More recent films include *Maria's Lovers* (1985), *The Conspiracy* (1986), *Mr. North* (1988), *Scrooged* (1988), and *Presume Dangereux* (1989). In 1983, he had a high-rated week on ABC-TV starring in Herman Wouk's novel-for-television, "Winds of War." The sequel "War and Remembrance" in 1988 did not fare as well in the ratings. He also appeared in NBC's "The Brotherhood of the Rose" (1988) and "Family Man" (1989).

Though Mitchum became the center of a cause celebre at the 1954 Cannes Film Festival when he was photographed with a bare-bosomed starlet, and has made on-screen love to some of the most glamorous females in Hollywood (Elizabeth Taylor, Rita Hayworth, Ava Gardner, Susan Hayward), he's been married since 1940 to the former Dorothy Spence, mother of his three children. Both of his sons, James and Christopher, are now film actors. Why is the laconic Robert Mitchum of the somnolent eyes so very "definitely a survivor" (as one critic called him) when so many other '40s faces have fallen by the wayside? "When I first went to work," he recalls, "I'd go into casting offices and they'd say, 'What's he do?' Or, 'Did you ever think about getting your nose fixed or changing your name?' Later, not too much later, they'd say, 'We need a Mitchum type'. . . . I turned out to be the only one, which ensured my longevity."

Matthew Modine

"It's nice to be able to slip through because that's how you get your material—in the streets," says this versatile young actor of his relative anonymity among celebrity watchers.

The only advantage of movie stardom (he opts for movie "actordom"), says Matthew Modine, is "the ability to work with people that you want to work with. . . . I don't give a hoot about the money and stuff." Unless he takes a vow of poverty and assumes a Brando/Garbo attitude, it's unlikely he'll escape for long the "money and stuff" destined to come his way as he rides the crest of the wave of youth-oriented movies that became standard cinema fare in the mid-1980s. What makes Modine different is his unwillingness to go the pin-up poster and fan-magazine cover route that might prevent "teen-idol Modine" from being cast in the offbeat roles that have brought him screen prominence, ranging from the sexually-ambivalent soldier knifed to death in the screen version of David Rabe's play, *Streamers* (1983 best actor award at the Venice Film Festival), to the title role in the film adaptation of William Wharton's cult novel, *Birdy*, in which the central character thinks he's a bird.

The youngest of seven children, Matthew Modine (born 22 March 1959) in Loma Linda, California) grew up with the movies as his baby-sitter—his father managed drive-in theatres in California and Utah. At 18, he went to New York to pursue a stage career, studying with Stella Adler, doing commercials and eventually landing a role on the TV soap opera "Texas." John Sayles tapped him for a bit part in *Baby, It's You* and that four minutes on the screen convinced Harold Becker, director of his 1985-starrer, *Vision Quest*, that "he's a natural. . . . I've always used the term for him . . . there are no rough edges on him." The sex romp *Private School*, helped his career only to the extent that it displayed his versatility when viewed in conjunction with his next film, the shattering *Streamers*, about which he recalls, "I was terrified of that part. . . . I don't think I stopped sweating that entire film." He agreed to do *Hotel New Hampshire* because "I got to play two different people—Ernst and Chipper Dove."]

In *Mrs. Soffel* he had the opportunity to work with one of his idols, Mel Gibson who played his jailbird brother. Modine also had a chance to "listen to the kind of range I didn't even know Diane [Keaton] and Mel had". His most acclaimed performance to date is *Birdy*. "I never auditioned," he says. "I didn't think I was appropriate. . . . It's hard to talk about how I became the bird. You have to be there physically, but not mentally. It sounds inane, but you just do it." More Modine movies include Stanley Kubrick's *Full Metal Jacket*

(1987), *Orphans* (1987), *Married to the Mob* (1987) and *La Partita* (1988). Naturally, this pursuer of the offbeat could not have met his wife, Carrie, in a conventional way. Instead, he engaged her on a New York City street in 1982 and offered to carry her packages, then took her to a movie, dinner, and finally Central Park, where they talked—about the importance of friendship—until 4 A.M. Offbeat.

Ricardo Montalban

He is set apart from the proto-typical Hollywood fold by virtue (and the sentence could end right there as his strong religious conviction carries over into his life) of the facts: he is not a social gadfly, has been married only once and is still married to Georgiana Young (youngest sister of Loretta Young), and believes an actor is never an actor unless he is working (this includes bad roles.) "Gene [Lockhart] once told me always take the best of three roles offered, but if only one offer came along, take it, no matter what I think of it."

Mr. Roarke, the man who made dreams come true (from 1978-84) for a price on ABC's "Fantasy Island" was born in Mexico City, 25 November 1920, the youngest of four children. After finishing grade school in Northern Mexico he was brought to the United States by an older brother and entered Fairfax High in Hollywood, soon attracting the attention of a studio scout. Shunning an MGM screen test, he wended his way toward New York to try his luck in legit theatre. His first break came when he was cast in a small part with Tallulah Bankhead in *Her Cardboard Lover* after which he appeared in several plays, returning to Mexico in 1941 to make 13 Spanish language films in four years. When he re-surfaced on Yankee turf it was to make his American feature film debut in *Fiesta*. *Neptune's Daughter, Latin Lovers, Battleground* and *Sombrero* followed. Later films include *Sweet Charity* (1968) and *Return to Planet of the Apes* (1972). Today he does his share of TV guest spots, periodically returning to the stage. (He played on tour *Don Juan in Hell* in the early 70s under the respective direction of Agnes Moorehead and John Houseman playing 138 cities to good notices). As spokesman, he has chanted the amenities of the Chrysler Cordoba, Maxwell House Coffee, and Bulova Watches but what he is especially proud of is the publication of his autobiography *Reflections: A Life in Two*

Worlds (1980). His most recent projects included *Star Trek II, The Wrath of Kahn,* a continuing role on the nighttime "Dynasty" spin-off "The Colby's" (1986-1987) and a starring role in the film *The Naked Gun* (1988). He also appeared in the *Spy* magazine send-up, "How To Be Famous" that aired in 1990. For his contributions to film and Latin culture, Montalban has been awarded many honors in Mexico City. He and Georgiana (four children) live in the Hollywood hills.

Yves Montand

Hollywood wasted him in such light romantic bromides as *Let's Make Love* (with Marilyn Monroe in 1960) and *On a Clear Day You Can See Forever* (with Barbra Streisand in 1970). Europe let him demonstrate his full dramatic mettle in Clouzot's classic, *Wages of Fear* (1955), Costa-Gavra's *Z* (Best Foreign Picture Oscar in 1970) and many more. A hit on Broadway in 1959 with his one-man show ("If Trenet has 'the sound,'" wrote a critic, "and Chevalier 'the charm,' it is Montand who has 'the soul'"), he returned in 1982 (after a triumphant "comeback" tour of Europe) to become the first popular entertainer ever to be presented on the stage of New York's Metropolitan Opera House—to an ecstatic reception. His most recent films *Jean de Florette* (1987) and *Manon of the Springs* (1987) were both critical successes and he was honored by the Film Society of Lincoln Center at their annual Spring gala.

Though viewed by many as the quintessential Frenchman, Yves Montand was actually born Ivo Livi in Monsummano, Italy, 13 October 1921, the youngest child of a peasant family. When he was two, his socialist father fled from Mussolini's fascism to France and the tough harbor district of Marseilles. Forced to leave school at 11 ("It was a time of real misery"), he found a job in a spaghetti factory and worked successively was a waiter, barman, and apprentice hairdresser before displaying his talents as a singer in the local public square, which was an incubator for fledgling entertainers. He made his first professional bow at 18 at the Alcazar in Marseilles, was "discovered" by Edith Piaf in Paris and proceeded to become one of France's favorite Music Hall *chanteurs populaires.*

Touring in 1949, he met actress Simone Signoret and married

her in 1950. (She died 30 September 1985.) The "sex symbol nonpareil" also had much publicized affairs along the way with both Piaf and Monroe. He's presently living with his young secretary, Carole Amiel, and the couple have a child Valentin Gioanni Jacques (born 31 December 1988). He also has one granddaughter, Clementine. Once considered as a candidate for the 1988 French Presidential elections, he denied the opportunity in favor of working on a movie musical about his life.

Dudley Moore

"I think my own desire to be loved is really what makes me sexually attractive. It stands out so blatantly in me," he says, expounding on his theory of how he became Hollywood's unlikely romantic hero. Short of stature and long of nose, he boasts a bawdy sense of humor and teddy-bear appeal that have made him a box-office magic in the cinematic world of tall, dark and handsome.

Dudley Stuart John Moore, born 19 April 1935, recalls a childhood in the gray town of Dagenham, Essex, England, made lonely and painfully self-conscious by stunted growth and a club foot. Humor was his only defense. "I got funny so I wouldn't get beaten up anymore."

He graduated from schoolyard performances to the English pub circuit with *Beyond the Fringe*, a satirical revue he formed with Alan Bennett, Peter Cook and Jonathan Miller in 1960. Its risqué, dark-humored flavor caught on, leading Moore to star in a weekly English series, "Not Only . . . but Also," "I have a very ribald sense of humor, which is conventionally known as obscene," he has said. American audiences found him hysterical as the midlife bumbler who lusts after Bo Derek in *10*, and the 1981 *Arthur* provided Moore with the perfect vehicle for his deadpanning and raucous laughter. He came across as the perfect lovable drunk, bringing out the maternal in women and comradeship in men. However, he didn't fare as well with the critics in the 1988 sequel *Arthur on the Rocks*. Other film credits include *Six Weeks* and *Lovesick*, both in 1983, *Unfaithfully Yours* in 1984, *Santa Claus—the Movie* in 1985, *Like Father Like Son* in 1987 and *Crazy People* in 1989. He is also an accomplished jazz pianist and composer.

Divorced twice—from British actress Suzy Kendall and actress Tuesday Weld (a son, Patrick)—Moore married his third wife, Brogan Lane, in February, 1988.

Mary Tyler Moore

"I 'm not an actress who can create a character. I play me," said she, when still a pixie comedienne, known first as the beautiful but slightly birdbrained wife on "The Dick Van Dyke Show," and then as perky Mary Richards, heroine of "The Mary Tyler Moore Show." She, and the critics, would wish to retract that assessment later in her career, when she delivered powerful performances on screen and Broadway. She said of the transition, "As a comedienne, I'm an observer of life and people. That's what enables one to do dramatic work. I didn't have to study or train for it. It was there."

Moore, born in Brooklyn, N.Y., on 29 December 1937, debuted in show business as a singing spokeswoman for Hotpoint Appliances, and sported her legs as a telephone operator in 1957 detective series "Richard Diamond." She was likeable in "The Dick Van Dyke Show," as Laura Petrie, suburban housewife who responded to strife with a quivering upper lip and heavy sigh, "Oh, Rob." But it was with the premiere of "The Mary Tyler Show" in 1970, a sitcom set in a television newsroom, that Moore reached her comedic prime. Said one reviewer, "Much, justifiably, has been made of Miss Moore's extravagant gestures, superb sense of timing, comic instinct, repertoire of tricks."

When the hit show finally went off the air in 1977, Moore tackled challenging dramatic projects, including "First You Cry," a somber TV movie on breast cancer, which won her an Emmy. *Whose Life Is It Anyway*, an emotionally grueling play about a paraplegic, earned her a Tony. Her stark, controlled performance in the 1980 film *Ordinary People*, the story of a family torn apart by the accidental death of a son, came the same year as the loss of her own son, Richard, who committed suicide. Said Moore, "I've grown to know myself better, to trust myself. I am still a person who enjoys having control. But I know there are some things over which you have no control, and you just have to accept that."

Divorced twice, the second time from NBC television chief Grant Tinker, Moore married Dr. Robert Levine in 1984, with the press playing up their age differences: she was 45 and he was 30. Her stay at the Betty Ford Clinic in 1984 was, she admitted, to rid her of a "social drinking" habit that threatened her health, already impaired by diabetes. She returned to the television world again with an HBO film, *Finnegan Begin Again* (1985), a story about two people mismatched, but in love. Her next project was the NBC miniseries "Gore Vidal's Lincoln" (1987), in which she played Mary Todd Lincoln, a role that earned her another Emmy nomination. Giving another weekly television series a shot, she developed "Annie McGuire" for CBS's 1988-1989 season, but it never clicked. Other recent projects have included the Broadway show *Street Sue* (1987), the film *Just between Friends* (1986), and the telefilm "Thanksgiving Day" (1990).

Roger Moore

The sleek British actor, who starred for seven years as "The Saint," was well experienced in playing sweatless heroes when he was picked to portray the most sweatless of them all, James Bond. Taking over the role from Sean Connery, Moore brought an aristocrat charm to Bond, shaking off danger with a vodka martini and expressing emotion with the raising of an eyebrow.

Moore was born 14 October 1927, the son of a London policeman. He left school at age 15 to become an artist but failed to demonstrate any impressive talent until he found his way to the Royal Academy of Dramatic Art. Again, Moore found himself out of place around serious students, as he was given to a lighthearted attitude and a flair for self-effacing humor. After service in the army and sporadic performances in the London theatre, Moore moved to New York and signed with MGM. A series of mostly unimpressive film performances followed, including, in 1954, *The Last Time I Saw Paris*, and in 1956, *Diane*, in which his name appeared above the title for the first time. Even so, Moore recalls that a reviewer for *Time* magazine noted that "he invariably wears the expression of a peevish raisin."

But as James Bond, Moore's lack of dramatic abilities hardly seemed to matter. Audiences alike generally agreed that the dapper

Moore, with his slim, athletic build, blue eyes, and ample light brown hair, fit the bill. Some said Moore came closer to the character as originally conceived in Ian Fleming's novel than did Connery. Moore played Bond beginning in 1973 with *Live and Let Die*, then in *The Man with the Golden Gun* (1974), *The Spy Who Loved Me* (1977), *Moonraker* (1979), *For Your Eyes Only* (1981), and *Octopussy* (1983). His last 007 role was in *A View to a Kill* (1985) as he passed the torch to Timothy Dalton as the new Bond. Early in 1989 he attempted musical theatre with Andrew Lloyd Webber's London production of *Aspects of Love*, but he withdrew from the show. Divorced twice, Moore married Italian actress Luisa Mattioli in 1968 and has three children.

Esai Morales

E sai Morales knows how to turn his ethnicity to his own advantage: "It allows more people to identify with me and puts me in a unique position to help bridge gaps in human understanding."

Brooklyn-born, he grew up as a ward of the state and a foster child. He attended the much-celebrated New York High School of Performing Arts, and at seventeen he originated the title role in *El Hermano* at New York's Ensemble Studio Theater. Joseph Papp recognized his talent and cast him along with Raul Julia in a production of William Shakespeare's *The Tempest*. But it was his electrifying performance opposite Sean Penn in *Bad Boys* (1983) that finally attracted the attention this fine young actor deserved.

His next poignant role was that of Ritchie Valens' troubled brother in *La Bamba* (1987). In this performance he made a weak and jealous brother seem both pathetic and touching and took the evil out of the villain. In 1987 he also appeared in a less successful film called *The Principal*.

His acting career has been varied, and his frequent appearances on television have added to his visibility. He participated in the Emmy Award-winning "Afterschool Special" *The Great Experiment* as well as making guest star appearances on "Miami Vice," "The Equalizer" and "Fame." He is perhaps most remembered on television for his portrayal of Rashid, the Iranian hero of the NBC miniseries "On Wings of Eagles," starring Burt Lancaster.

His brave and positive outlook on life permeates all of his work. He has received several awards for his contribution to Latin culture. He was applauded as the Most Promising Actor at the NOSOTROS Golden Eagle Awards, named Entertainer of the Year by the organization Latino Playwrights and won the New York Image Award. He has also become a spokesperson for New York City's Foster Care Program, and because of his commitment to fighting major problems facing runaways and homeless youths and his vocal support in the fight against AIDS, he is as much in demand as a speaker addressing students and community groups as he is as an up-and-coming young actor, Clearly, he has taken seriously the responsibility his fame has brought him.

Jeanne Moreau

"I act and I direct. I sing and I record and I cook and I do different things. Why not? They're complementary," says Jeanne Moreau ("La Moreau," as French audiences call her), who changes moods and emotions faster than a chameleon changes color. Witness any Moreau film (*Frantic*, 1958; *La Notte* and *Jules et Jim*, 1961; *The Bride Wore Black*, 1968; *Chimes at Midnight*, 1967; *Going Places*, 1974; *The Trout*, 1982; *Querelle*, 1982) and invariably she is of blinding intensity—dark eyes seducing an audience. "While I'm doing a role, I'm the part. I'm the person. But once I'm finished, I'm me." She has worked for Renoir, Truffaut, Buñuel, Antonioni, Fassbinder, Orson Welles, Joseph Losey, Louis Malle, Peter Brooks, Paul Mazursky. She chooses a role for its director, not for its character.

Born in Paris, 23 January 1928, her mother an English dancer and her father a Monmartre restaurateur, Moreau spent her early years in England, gained recognition as a member of France's famed Comédie Francaise in 1949, and rose to international stardom after appearing in Louis Malle's *The Lovers* in 1959. "I'm not successful by accident," she says firmly. "I've worked hard. I'm passionate and my world is cinema, acting, theatre, creativity, art, painting, books, music, sculpture, landscapes, movements of the people in the streets. Everything!"

Three times married and divorced: in 1949 to Jean-Louis Richard, one son, divorced 1951; in 1966 to Teodora Rubanis, divorced; and in 1977 to director William Friedkin (*The French Connection, The Brink's Job, The Exorcist*), whom she divorced in 1980. Moreau says: "It's very moving to be loved and hard to resist."

Having worked only with the finest directors, Moreau herself turned director in 1976 with *Lumière* (which she wrote and also starred in) and followed her directorial success with *L'Adolescente* in 1979. She recalls that some directors were shocked or resentful at the prospect of her decision to direct, except Orson Welles, "who was," she says, "the first person to whom I spoke about directing, and the only one who wasn't protective about it." Today she finds herself in the flattering position of being approached by newcomers for advice on the craft. On this she remarks: "There's room for everybody." She appeared on Broadway in the 1985 revival of Tennessee Williams' *The Night of the Iguana* and appeared on stage at the Atelier theatre in Paris in *The Servant Zerline* (1987).

Rita Moreno

S he's listed as the only performer to receive the four highest entertainment awards—the Tony, the Oscar, the Emmy, the Grammy. "My photo is in the Guinness Book of Records," Rita Moreno chuckles, "I'm right there in the book with Kermit the Frog." For years she was cast as the beautiful little Injun that could, and, after her outspoken refusal to take any more such roles, her next role was a Latin halfbreed. When in 1972 she turned up on daytime children's public TV in "The Electric Company" (her Grammy Award for Best Children's Recording in 1973) aimed at seven-to-ten-year-old children trying to improve their reading skills, she stated: "I represent all the Hispanic peoples in America . . . because I have a mother who does not read English fluently . . . I am Latin and know what it is to feel alone and ignored because you are different [they called her Pierced Ears and Gold Teeth when she was a kid]. . . . I was for six years in analysis in Hollywood. The ethnic problems galvanize some people into action. Me, they paralyzed." She continues to support her ethnic concerns, in 1990 she hosted the Golden

Eagle Awards of Nosotros, a group that boosts Hispanics working in the entertainment industry.

Born Rosita Dolores Alverio, 11 December 1931 in Humacao, Puerto Rico, she was brought to New York at the age of four (her mother had come the year before, worked as a seamstress, saved her money, and returned to bring her daughter to America). She made her nightclub debut the very next year and was singing and dancing in clubs when she was 13, "ducking the juvenile officers." At 13 she did her first Broadway show, and at 17 joined MGM's starlet stable for a string of B movies in which she was required merely to "flare my nostrils, gnash my teeth, and look spirited." But a fine job of acting in *The King and I* led to her role as Anita in the film *West Side Story* and the 1962 Oscar, firmly implanting her in the mind of Hollywood as "the Latin girl." "It's not that I mind playing Latins," said Moreno in 1981. "They have to be the real ones, not that you-stole-my-people's-gold crap. I've been lucky for five years now. Ethnic considerations don't come up any more." Later movies include *Marlowe, Popi, Carnal Knowledge, The Ritz, Happy Birthday Gemini, The Boss's Son,* and *The Four Seasons.* Her Broadway credits include *The Sign in Sidney Brustein's Window* (1964), *Gantry* (1969), *The Last of the Red Hot Lovers* (1970), *The National Health* (1974), *The Ritz,* for which she won the 1975 Tony Award, and *Wally's Cafe* (1981). Neil Simon reworked *The Odd Couple* for a female duo, and she appeared in it on Broadway in 1985 with Sally Struthers. After winning two Emmys for performances on television, she starred in the 1982 "9 to 5" TV series.

Married to New York physician Dr. Leonard I. Gordon (1965), Moreno lives in Manhattan and spends weekends at their house in upstate New York. They have a daughter, Fernanda. The lady shows no sign of tiring. Of her nightclub act she said, "I dance my butt off and sing my lungs out."

Richard Mulligan

R ichard Mulligan must have made the most hilarious corpse in cinematic history in the wonderful sleeper, *S.O.B.* Well, the funny man has come back to life, and so much so, that his new TV series "Empty Nest" was one of the 1988-1989's biggest hits. For his role, he won a Best Actor Emmy in September 1989. You may remember his quirky face from "Soap," another very successful televison series which also brought him a 1980 Emmy.

Born 13 November 1932 in New York City, he is the son of a policeman. One of five sons, he grew up in the Bronx and was a serious student at Cardinal Hayes High School, and later Maryknoll

Junior Seminary where he thought of becoming a priest. He changed his mind a year later when he discovered a certain affection for playwriting at Columbia University. After a stint in the Navy as a crash rescue man in Pensacola, Florida, Mulligan landed his first acting role. While driving to Miami, his car had a flat tire right in front of a local theatre. Hoping to sell a play, he entered the theatre, but ended up auditioning for a role in Eugene O'Neill's play *Beyond the Horizon*. With good reviews rolling in, Mulligan went back to New York and wound up performing in more plays. He appeared in productions of *All the Way Home, Never Too Late, Nobody Loves an Albatross* and *The Mating Game*. Branching out into television, he won roles on "The Defenders," "Route 66," "The Dupont Show of the Month," and the "Armstrong Circle Theater." In 1977 he cracked up TV land with his portrayal of Burt Campbell on "Soap" which made him an overnight household name. Being chosen by Blake Edwards for the films *S.O.B.*, *Trail of the Pink Panther, Micki & Maude*, and *A Fine Mess*, added to Mulligan's popularity.

Other recent performances include the CBS-TV film "Poker Alice" with Elizabeth Taylor and the theatrical release of *Babes in Toyland*. Divorced from Patricia Jones and Joan Hackett, Mulligan was separated from his third wife, Lenore Stevens in 1989.

Eddie Murphy

"H is friends call him Money. He looks like money, like $40 million, if perchance one speculates. He looks crisp, controlled. He is twenty-eight yet not terribly youthful; he fancies himself much older, more world-weary. He stares straight ahead and seems to notice no one, but he sees all and hears even more. Unless he's erupting into his deft repertoire of character voices, his presence is shy, inscrutable. Usually he is sullen, almost somber—but this creates a quiet aura of power. You feel him before you see him; first you see his men. He is insulated by bodies, a cleaving pack of old friends and relations on the payroll. These are Eddie's Boys." An apt description by Bill Zehmen in the 24 August 1989 issue of *Rolling Stone*. Labeled as a king of the box office, Eddie Murphy has secured his standing as one of the world's most popular movie, television, concert, and recording artists. However, Murphy tries to remain humble about his surroundings. He insisted to *People* magazine, "I don't have an entourage. . . . I don't have bodyguards. I don't have anybody to, like, choke you and say, 'Get away from this man!' My cousin Ray, he takes care of all my little stuff. Kenneth Frith, who we call Fruitie—he went to school with me—he's a production assistant now. And Larry [Johnson] is an assistant. They're big guys. People see them and it's like, 'Oh. Bodyguards.'"

Murphy was born 3 April 1961 in the Bushwick section of Brooklyn. His father was a New York City cop and amateur comedian who died when Murphy was eight. Murphy, his brother, and stepbrother were raised by his mother and stepfather in suburban Long Island in comfortable, middle-class surroundings. His energetic good looks and contagious, wide-brimmed smile made him stand out immediately from the pack of young comedians hired for NBC's revamped late-night comedy show, "Saturday Night Live" in 1980. He proved himself both charismatic and versatile with his characterizations of such unsavory fellows as Velvet Jones, the pimp who hard sells how-to books; Tyrone Green, the illiterate convict who becomes a celebrated poet; and Buckwheat from the old serial, "Our Gang." In that skit, Murphy, hair braided and standing on end, explained, "I have a sister named Shredded Wheat, a sister who's a prostitute named Trix, an older brother who's gay, Lucky Charms, and a mentally retarded brother, Special K." Audiences loved his uncanny impressions of Stevie Wonder, Mr. Rogers, Bill Cosby, James Brown and Richard Simmons.

Teamed with Nick Nolte in 1982 in *48 Hours*, Murphy was engaging as a smart-aleck convict. In 1983, he teamed with SNL veteran Dan Aykroyd, playing a begger who strikes it rich in *Trading Places*. Other films include *The Best Defense* (1984), *Beverly Hills Cop* (1985), *Golden Child* (1986), *Beverly Hills Cop II* (1987), *Coming to America* (1988), *Harlem Nights* (1989), and *Another 48 Hours* (1990). There have been a slew of Eddie Murphy comedy albums, two singing albums, a cable TV special that is more than a bit raunchy, and *The Unofficial Eddie Murphy Scrapbook*, published in 1984.

Still single, he says his film *Coming to America* parallels his own personal situation. He told *Ebony* magazine, "I think everybody who doesn't have somebody is looking for someone to call their own, even though they might say they want to be single. . . . When I'm talking to my friends, I say the same thing about wanting to be single, but if I met the bomb tomorrow. . . . I don't care who you are, what you have or what you did, there's always a woman out there who can bring you down to one knee. I can be brought to one knee, but the woman would have to have a helluva punch. I've been wobbled a couple of times already, but I haven't been to one knee."

Bill Murray

He is (according to David Edelstein of *The Village Voice*) "the most serenely corrupt comic actor since W.C. Fields with a "whiff of Cary Grant's unflappability." Pauline Kael of the *New Yorker* sees him as "a master of show business insincerity. . . . Part of him is always in hiding, and there's a wild strain loose inside the doughy handsomeness which saves him from predictability. He looks capable of anything, yet he isn't threatening; he'd just do something crazy." After four comic seasons on NBC's "Saturday Night Live," Bill Murray made an effortless transition to movies and, in short order, became what one reporter called "a young people's star of major proportions." That fact was verified by his 1984 box office smash, *Ghostbusters* ranking as one of the biggest movie money-makers of all time and reinforced by *Ghostbusters II* in 1989.

Born 21 September 1950 in the Chicago suburb of Wilmette, Bill Murray was one of nine spirited youngsters in the home of a lumber salesman and the family dinner table was, traditionally, "bedlam." Bill started out with the notion of perhaps becoming a doctor or pro baseball player but dropped out after only a year at tiny Jesuit-run Regis College in Denver, entered a hippie phase and became the self-described "family black sheep." After an uninspiring series of odd jobs, ranging from hauling concrete blocks to cooking pizzas in a window, Murray decided to try emulating his older brother, Brian, who was getting paid for improvising in the comedy company, Second City. (Bill still insists that Brian—who now uses the name Brian-Doyle Murray—is the more talented of the two.) First learning the ropes in Second City's workshop for novices, he was at last signed on to join such future cohorts as John Belushi, Gilda Radner and Dan Aykroyd and he followed them to New York in 1975 to perform on "The National Lampoon Radio Show" and later, in the cabaret revue *The National Lampoon Show*. (Murray credits

Belushi for his early breaks. "He was like my big brother. . . He made this whole thing possible for me.") At the time of the historic launching of the frenetic NBC comedy show, "Saturday Night Live" in 1975, Murray went with his old Second City buddies to audition but was turned down the first time at bat and the show premiered without him. It wasn't until Chevy Chase departed from the line-up of the Not Ready for Prime Time Players in January, 1977, that Murray got his chance (Brian ended up on the show too) and, after a slow start, was one of the SNL superstars by the 1978-79 season. He made his big-screen debut in the 1979 comedy *Meatballs* and subsequent films include *Caddy Shack* (1980), *Stripes* (1981), *Tootsie* (1982), *The Razor's Edge* (1984), *Scrooged* (1988) and *Quick Change* (1990), which he also directed.

Murray's feelings about stardom, fame, riches and all that jazz? When he was getting his first heavy sampling of it, he was a bit ambivalent. He told a *Rolling Stone* reporter: "No one is raised by their parents to be prepared for what happens when you become famous." But, he concluded, "It's bullshit to hear people whine and complain about their success, and I don't like to hear about it." The deadpan comic is married to Mickey Kelley and the couple have a son, Homer.

Patricia Neal

"Courage? It isn't something you are born with. It comes to you with experience. I've learned that," says actress Patricia Neal in the honey-and-sandpaper voice famous on stage and in Hollywood. Despite a brilliant career (acting credits included a Tony Award in 1946—the first year the award was given—for her Broadway debut in *Another Part of the Forest*; and Oscar in 1963 for *Hud*; accolades in such plays as *The Children's House*, 1952; *Cat on a Hot Tin Roof*, 1956; *The Miracle Worker*, 1960, Patricia Neal is probably best known for her extraordinary recovery from the damaging effects of a massive stroke suffered in 1965. Unable to speak, read, write, or walk, she underwent extensive therapy and emerged three years later to deliver a stunning performance in the film *The Subject Was Roses*, bringing her an Academy Award nomination.

Born 20 January 1926 in Packard, Kentucky, the daughter of a coal company bookkeeper, she studied at the University of Tennessee and Northwestern. "I first got the bright notion of becoming an actress when I was in the sixth grade. Have had a one-track mind ever since." With the shooting of her second film, *The Fountainhead* in 1948, a publicized romance with co-star Gary Cooper lasted four years. When Cooper would not divorce his wife, she resigned herself to leaving Hollywood for New York. There she married British writer Roald Dahl in 1953. They faced tragedy. In 1960, a Manhattan taxicab hit the pram of their 4-month-old son. The child survived after remaining in critical condition two years, having undergone five brain operations. Two years later their 7-year-old daughter died of measles. In 1965, six months pregnant, Patricia Neal was crippled with a stroke. "In everyone's life a lot of bad things happen," she remarks. "I just seemed to have had a larger dose of the bad things."

Her fortitude, coupled with her husband's devotion and dogged encouragement, was the subject of "The Patricia Neal Story," a television film aired in 1981 (script written by playwright Robert Anderson, starring roles played by Glenda Jackson and Dirk Bogarde). Ironically, in 1983, after 30 years of marriage, she found herself divorced. (Roald left her for a wardrobe woman she had befriended while filming a TV commercial for Maxim coffee.) "It's as if the worst dream I can think of has happened," she acknowledges sadly. "But my husband did a lot, I've got to give him credit. He's really the one who pushed me to get well, and he pushed me back into acting. I'm so very glad he did because now it's all I've got." A pioneer of strength, she travels extensively on lecture tours for the handicapped; a rehabilitation center was named for her in Atlanta. Her autobiography, *As I Am* was published in 1988.

Kate Nelligan

When she appeared in David Hare's *Plenty*, critics ran out of superlatives. Hers has been a career blessed with instant, deserved recognition and opportunity, beginning with her 1974 London stage debut in Hare's *Knuckle* and including star parts in John Schlesinger's London revival of Shaw's *Heartbreak House*, playing Josie in the American Rep's 1984 revival of O'Neill's *Moon for the Misbegotten*, and an exceptional performance in 1988's *Spoils of War*.

In films, she's appeared in *Without a Trace*, *Dracula*, *Eye of the Needle* and *Eleni*. On television, she starred in the 1989 miniseries "Love & Hate: The Story of Colin and Joann Thatcher."

"I'm often hired to play from the eyebrows up," she has commented. Born 16 March 1951 in London, Ontario, Canada, she says one of the keys to her success is her "tremendous self-confidence. There were six children, but my mother always made me feel that I would do something important, which stood me in good stead." At age 16, she entered the University of Toronto and discovered the theater and of her first time on stage she says, "I didn't feel elated or ecstatic—just at home. From that day forward I never thought I would do anything else. Acting satisfied something very deep in me, and I suppose it still does." At the end of her second year, she traveled south to audition at Yale University and became one of two from among hundreds of North American drama students to be selected to attend London's prestigious Central School of Speech and Drama. Once there she ran into a problem: finances. "I sat down at the typewriter and wrote to people I'd been told were interested in the theater: 'I'm poor. You are rich. Give me money.'" The money came. Her next hurdle was her Canadian accent and she decided not only to sound British but to become British in every possible sense of the word. "I did what was necessary. Once I made the decision to adopt that speech, it became mine." After graduating from the Central School, she joined the Bristol Old Vic Company. "I was in seventeen plays and in fourteen of them I was bad. In *Private Lives* I was so bad I actually cried on stage . . . it's so agonizing to be bad in public. But the Bristol experience gave me five year's experience in twelve months." She is so adored as an artist that when she ruptured a vocal cord during a performance of *Moon for the Misbegotten* (her mouth had filled up with blood; although she carried on with the show, the next day she was unable to speak), her recuperation was watched hawkishly by her fans and reported daily in the papers.

Her stage triumphs haven't yet been matched in films. Nowadays, she is very much based in America, "In retrospect, I'm not sure I should have gone to the lengths I did in becoming English," she confesses, "I gave up too much, I sacrificed relaxation, humor, kindness, classlessness, democracy." At long last love, Nelligan married arranger/pianist Robert Reale on 19 February 1989.

Willie Nelson

The bedraggled outlaw of country music reached the pinnacle of commercial success by way of backwoods bars and dance halls across Texas. He never relinquished the scraggly beard, baggy pants, and red bandanna befitting a rebel, even after his remarkably tender voice came to dominate country charts. Nelson is credited for forging a progressive movement toward a purer country sound, expanding the tastes of country and pop music fans.

Born 30 April 1933, Nelson grew up in a small Texas town hit hard by the Great Depression. While he garnered some success as a songwriter early in his career, his first recording efforts hit a sour note. The Nashville music industry was intimidated by the popularity of the British rock invasion of the 1960s, and Nelson's honky-tonk style violated the twangy, orchestrated formula considered commercially viable for Country and Western. He did score a big hit for the late Patsy Cline with "Crazy" in 1961, but it wasn't until 1973 that Nelson, having left Nashville for Austin, recorded his first hit album, *Shotgun Willie*. In the next decade, his rambler laments, such as "Mama Don't Let Your Babies Grow Up to be Cowboys," and "On the Road Again," and his ballads of love unfulfilled, such as "Always on My Mind," became country standards. His rich, sweet voice was instantly recognizable.

Nelson acted in the 1979 movie, *The Electric Horseman*, starred as a Willie-like character in the 1980 *Honeysuckle Rose*, co-starred with Kris Kristofferson in 1985's *Songwriter*, and played in the CBS-TV movie "Where the Hell's That Gold" in 1988. He also released his autobiography *Willie: An Autobiography* in 1988.

His personal life appeared to be the stuff love ballads are made of, until he separated from his third wife, Connie in 1987. All told, Nelson has five children from his three marriages.

Bob Newhart

His sober low-key comedy style is "so diffident," says one critic, "that he can bite the hand that feeds him and make it feel like a manicure." He rose to popularity almost overnight early in the 1960s with a comedy album called "The Button Down Mind of

Bob Newhart" and has been on and off the air-waves and in and out of clubs ever since. His first regular TV series (1961-62 season) won a Peabody and an Emmy, but was a casualty of the ratings war. After a decade of guest spots, he launched a new "Bob Newhart Show" in 1972 (six seasons). In 1982 CBS reinstated him, this time simply as "Newhart" lasting into 1990, with a final episode that brought back Suzanne Pleshette from the previous sitcom.

Born George Robert Newhart in Chicago on 5 September 1929, he took law courses at Loyola and began his working career as an accountant. "But I was a bum one," he said after cheerfully escaping from business life. "I always figured that if you came within six or eight bucks of it, you were going to be OK." The album that served as his showbiz passport, a satiric epic of split-second timing, aimed gentle darts at the everyday working man: bus drivers, real estate salesmen, and 50-year employees ("I had to get half gassed to get down to this crummy joint every day"), plus a Madison Avenue braintruster who, on the eve of the Gettysburg Address offers advice to Abe Lincoln on how to polish up his image. His film credits include *Catch-22* (1970), *Little Miss Marker* (1980) and *The First Family* (1980). Married to the former Virginia Quinn, he's the father of two sons and two daughters.

Paul Newman

S tar of stage, screen and supermarket, and likewise a winning auto racer, Paul Newman is, according to one writer, "almost universally a catalyst of moist and turbulent emotions. Men's eyes mist over, and women's knees go wobbly." A very private person, with "a moat and a drawbridge which he lets down occasionally," he writhes under the screenland sex symbol image and refuses to play celebrity. He avoids being the public "Paul Newman" as much as possible; even in his films, he takes pains to look

as gruesome as possible when the scene can use it. Scriptwriter William (*Harper* and *Butch Cassidy*) Goldman says that the star "could be called a victim of the Cary Grant syndrome. He makes it look so easy, and he looks so wonderful, that everybody assumes he isn't acting." A serious actor who believes "an actor should act" when the scripts are right, he "is very sensitive to writing, and is the best director of actors I know," states writer Stewart (*Rachel, Rachel*) Stern, who explains "I think there's less impediment between his talent and its expression when he's directing. That's probably because, as in racing, 'Paul Newman' doesn't have to be there."

Newman grew up in Cleveland Heights, a comfortable suburb of Cleveland, where he was born Paul Leonard Newman on 26 January 1925. The son of a prosperous Jewish businessman, Newman refers to himself as a Jew ("because it's more of a challenge"), although his mother was a Catholic of Hungarian descent. He did a lot of acting in children's groups and high school. When the brilliant blue eyes turned out to be partially color blind, he was dropped from flight training and spent World War II as a radioman in bombers in the Pacific Campaign. After acting his way through Kenyon College (graduated 1949), he spent two years doing stock and married actress Jacqueline Witte (one son, two daughters). His father's death recalled him to the family business, but 18 months later he enrolled in Yale's Drama School. "I wasn't driven to acting by any inner compulsion," he recalls, "I was running away from the sporting goods business." Within months, he was in New York, where he did television bits before opening on Broadway in *Picnic* (1953) to excellent notices. During *Picnic*, he joined the Actors Studio, landed a long-term Warners contract and met *Picnic* understudy Joanne Woodward, whom he married five years later (three daughters). His film debut was in *The Silver Chalice*, "The Worst Picture Ever Made" (a Newman family consensus). In the 1954 religious costume drama, he was garbed in a "cocktail dress," and the parts left exposed gave rise to the affectionate family sobriquet "Old Skinny Legs." He fled back to Broadway for *The Desperate Hours*, and didn't make another film for two years, returning only for *Somebody Up There Likes Me* (1956). He garnered his first Best Actor Oscar nomination for *Cat on a Hot Tin Roof* (1958) and Best Actor nominations followed for *The Hustler* (1961), *Hud* (1963) and *Cool Hand Luke* (1967), in which he created a trio of miscreant antiheroes so fallible and faulted that the American public has willed them into the national character, along with his other lovable loser, *Harper* (1966). Newman ended the sixties with his hedonistic romp through *Butch Cassidy and the Sundance Kid* ("too bad they got killed at the end, 'cause those two guys could have gone on in films forever") and *Winning*, which he later called a "pretty good story about racing." Sports car racing has since become an integral part of his life; from April to October, he does not make movies, seeking instead the anonymity of P.L. Newman, amateur sports car driver. He has twice been a national champion in his class.

In the seventies, Newman made such films as *Sometimes a Great Notion* (1971), *The Life and Times of Judge Roy Bean* (1972) and *The Sting* (1973). Of *Sting's* famous scene in which Newman and Robert Shaw cheat each other at draw poker, director George Roy Hill said "one of the best pieces of comedic acting I've ever seen. I defy any actor to play the scene better." There followed: *The Towering Inferno* (1974), *Buffalo Bill and the Indians* (1976) and *Slap Shot* (1977). Oscar nominations came for *Absence of Malice* (1981) and *The Verdict* (1982). ("It was such a relief to let it all hang out in the movie—blemishes and all.") Other 1980's films include *The Color of Money* (1986), which earned him an Oscar; *Blaze* (1989); and *Fat Man and Little Boy* (1990). Co-writer and co-producer of *Harry and Son* (1984), he also directed and starred "for the last time. Never again—you can't do both." Frequently Oscar-nominated for tasks other than acting, Newman made his directorial debut with Oscar-nomination *Rachel, Rachel* (1968), starring Woodward, and has since directed her in film versions of the plays, *The Effect of Gamma Rays on Man-in-the-Moon Marigolds* (1972), with daughter Nell, "The Shadow Box," made for ABC-TV (1980), and *The Glass Menagerie* (1987).

Up until 1986, Newman had never received an Academy Award. That year, he became the recipient of an honorary Academy Award for career achievement. However, in typical Hollywood style, Newman won the Best Actor Oscar the following year for his performance in *The Color of Money*.

A daily runner, sailor, fisherman and general cut-up, he maintains an athletic 145 pounds on his 5'10" frame, but is under family pressure to give up auto racing. A life-long liberal, he speaks out on civil rights, the nuclear freeze, gay rights and seat belts. His various charities include the Scott Newman Foundation, an anti-drug campaign in the film industry named in honor of Paul's late son who died in 1978 of an overdose of painkillers and alcohol at age 28. The Foundation and his other charities are partially funded by profits from his "Newman's Own" brand of olive oil and vinegar dressing, which forced the actor and writer-pal A.E. Hotchner (*Papa Hemmingway*) "out of the basement" and into marketing of their blend, and "Newman's Own Industrial Strength Spaghetti Sauce," also on grocers' shelves lawsuits notwithstanding. Although the Newmans maintain an apartment in Manhattan and a house in Beverly Hills, they have been happily exiled from celebrity in Westport, Connecticut, for many years.

Olivia Newton-John

"When it came time to do this album, I'd gone through some new experiences," says Olivia as she talks about *The Rumour* (1988), "I'd been raising my daughter Chloe, and had come to see things differently. I wanted the album to reflect that, and I co-wrote many of the songs myself. There's songs about ecology, AIDS, single parenting and role reversal in marriage—different kinds of subjects from what I'd done before." The sweet, pretty blonde girl has matured into a musical mainstay as well as a model mother. Her first single was a recording of Bob Dylan's "If Not for You" and next came the ballad "Let Me Be There" which established her first U.S. beachhead in 1973 and won her the best country vocalist Grammy. She donned a new, sharper-focus image when she teamed up with John Travolta to rock-and-roll in spike heels and black leather in the film version of *Grease* (1978)—the all-time highest grossing movie musical. After playing a romantic enchantress in the musical film *Xanadu* (it barely said "howdy-do" at the box office, but she met her 10-years-younger husband-to-be Matt Lattanzi—they were married in 1984), she sent music video watchers in 1981 for a spin with her sexy, sweaty hit "Let's Get Physical" and "Heart Attack" (1982). Some of her other hit titles have been: "I Honestly Love You," "Have You Never Been Mellow," and from the *Grease* score, "You're the One That I Want." From sweetheart to temptress makes a Pop Goddess grow, but to know her, one suspects, is to know a home-loving, animal-loving, easy-going woman who has been able to teach quite a few cash registers to play her tune.

Born 26 September 1948 in Cambridge, England, the daughter of a Welsh university don and a German mother, her maternal grandfather was Max Born, a Nobel laureate in physics. The family moved to Australia when she was five and it was there she launched her singing career. At 15, she won a talent contest that took her back to England, and by 1971 she'd been voted Best British Girl Singer, an honor she received two years in a row. Since winning her first Grammy (1973) for "Let Me Be There," her awards have multiplied and her total record sales are in the millions. In 1983 she teamed up with Travolta again and made the film *Two of a Kind*. The film received mixed reviews but the song "Twist of Fate" became a hit record.

Touring gives her sleepless nights and butterflies in her stomach, although she did manage to cap on SRO tour of the U.S. in the mid-seventies with a solo concert at New York's Metropolitan Opera House. "I don't have the desire I think a lot of performers feel," she told George Christy in 1983, "to get the applause. It's not life and death to me. I like to sing, and I love doing what I'm doing, but it's not a dire need."

Craving things Australian, she and her ex-singing pal Pat Farrar opened the Koala Blue boutique in West Hollywood in 1984. Going with this winning idea, there are now over fifteen stores in a chain of outlets across the US and Canada, plus plans for a Koala Blue to open in Japan. Keeping her heart in Australia, she produced a HBO special about the Aussies in 1988 to coincide with the release of *The Rumour* album. In a surprise move, Olivia left her record company of eighteen years, MCA, to go with Geffen records in 1989. Her first project will be an album for children. Olivia lives on a three-acre ranch in Malibu with what she called her "zoo," a household filled with many animals she adores (five cats, seven dogs, five horses). She said as a youngster she wanted to become a veterinarian. When she's not working, the singer likes to spend time with her handsome actor-husband Lattanzi, and their daughter Chloe Rose (born 17 January 1986).

Mike Nichols

"**H**aving fame is wonderful, if you can control its tendency 'to make you feel like a baby,'" says director Mike Nichols, who feels he can most effectively deal with actors from the other end of the spectrum; to him, the process of his craft "is in some ways like being an ideal parent." Jeremy Irons, star of *The Real Thing* (1984), which earned Nichols his sixth Tony award for directing, has said "Mike creates a very protective environment. He's like the best of lovers; he makes you feel he's only for you." Sigourney Weaver, assessing Nichols' technique with the disparate training and professional backgrounds of her fellow actors in *Hurlyburly* (1984), affirmed that he "worked with each actor and part individually," but noted that "the end result was ensemble playing." In a play, as in movies, Nichols relentlessly strives to convey what is "really going on," so that the audience will perceive "real people living their lives." According to playwright Neil Simon, Nichols' guidance enables him to "get the actor to physically express what the author gives only clues to" and thereby, achieve Nichols' event, the moment(s) of arch truth that illuminates the author's meaning in each scene. Nichols has attributed the concept of the hidden event to his years of improvisation with Elaine May. Doing improvisation, he says, "You learned to damn well pick something that would happen in the scene—an event . . . as long as something is happening, you can continue." An author's script is made to unfold within this content. Apparently, Nichols' success is in identifying each event, working mechanically within it and, most importantly, leaving it unstated.

Born Michael Igor Perschkowsky in Berlin, 6 November 1931, he is the elder son of a Russian who fled his homeland in 1917, became a physician and married a Jewish girl. His father Anglicized his patronymic, Nicholaiyevitch, when he left Germany during the rise of Hitler and requalified as a physician in the U.S. Nichols was reunited with his father in New York on 4 May 1939. A "little bald kid" from age four due to an adverse reaction to a whooping cough injection, Nichols bounded through boarding schools even after his father's death when he was 12. After studying pre-med at the University of Chicago and acting with Lee Strasberg in New York, he returned to Chicago where he connected with the Compass troupe which became the Second City company. He then teamed with Elaine May in a satiric comedy improvisation act that captivated nightclub and television audiences, made three records and spent a year on Broadway with *An Evening with Mike Nichols and Elaine May* (1960). The play *A Matter of Position*, written by May and starring Nichols, upset the teetering balance between the two and, closing the play out of town, they split personally and professionally in 1962. "When Elaine and I split up—that was a shattering year for me. . . . I was the leftover half of something." Within months, Neil Simon tapped him to direct *Barefoot in the Park* (1963) for which he won his first Tony. He has since directed three more Simon plays, *The Odd Couple* (1965), *Plaza Suite* (1968) and *The Prisoner of Second Avenue* (1971), and each has earned him a Tony. Numbers five and six were for *Luv* (1964) and *The Real Thing*. Nichol's most successful serious play was David Rabe's *Strangers* (1976); the duo teamed again in *Hurlyburly*, a tragicomedy. Nichols' approach to all plays is the same ("I don't think comedy is an escape from tragedy. The are both *life.*'') In 1986 he directed Marlo Thomas on Broadway in *Social Security.*

First married to Pat Scot, a singer, Nichols had just married Margot Callas (one daughter) when he undertook his directorial debut with *Barefoot.* He used revelation of his own experience to enhance his actor's consciousness, a tool which he continues to utilize with great success. His third marriage is to Annabel Davis-Goff, a screenwriter-turned-novelist (one son, one daughter). He married his fourth wife, "60 Minutes" anchorwoman Diane Sawyer on 29 April 1988. Hollywood has tapped his directorial dexterity for such films as: *Who's Afraid of Virginia Woolf?* (1966), *The Graduate* (1967) for which he won an Oscar; *Catch-22* (1969), *Carnal Knowledge* (1971), *Heartburn* (1986), *Biloxi Blues* (1987) and the Academy Award-nominated *Working Girl* (1988). In 1990 he was filming *Postcards From the Edge,* based on Carrie Fisher's novel.

Jack Nicholson

"What is it that makes people think you're this high-liv-ing maniac of Herculean proportions?" asked Martin Torgoff of this two-time Oscar winner (*One Flew Over the Cuckoo's Nest* and *Terms of Endearment*) whose star appeal Pauline Kael once called "a satirical approach to macho." The avuncular anti-hero responded: "I don't do anything about shaping my public image. I'm also very protective of my private life—you could come through [my] house and not find out a thing about me. Therefore, into this vacuum come  other impressions from the little bit that people do know about me from my background—plus the roles I've played, of course. . . . My friends know that I don't drink that much, and when I do get loaded—twice in my life, *I think*—I've fallen down. But more generally I don't do anything like that. Chase girls? Certainly, as all men have—[His first marriage to actress Sandra Knight (one daughter) ended in divorce; he's lived for may years with Anjelica Huston in Hollywood Hills and Aspen, Colorado]—if it's a chase, it's too long. I didn't always feel that way . . . I did believe that candid was what you should be . . . it's only misused. I can't really know that my reputation is, but I can tell you from what I hear that it's extremely distorted."

Born 28 April 1937 in Neptune, New Jersey, he's always had a sense of destiny about being involved in films. Initially, he thought about directing. He moved to California at age 17 and worked for 15 years in television ("Daytime Divorce Court," "Matinee Theater") and made nearly 20 B films for producer Roger Corman, including *Hell's Angels on Wheels* and *Back Door to Hell*. "I always sort of stunk of TV. At the time Roger was the only guy who would employ me as a professional." At age 32, he became a star by replacing Rip Torn in *Easy Rider* (1969) starring opposite Peter Fonda in the counter-culture cycle romp. Since then he has starred in such films as: *Five Easy Pieces, On a Clear Day You Can See Forever, Carnal Knowledge, King of Marvin Gardens, A Safe Place, The Last Detail*, Roman Polanski's *Chinatown*, Antonioni's *The Passenger, The Fortune, Goin' South* (which he directed), *Reds, The Shining* and *The Postman Always Rings Twice*. His latest pics are 1985's *Prizzi's Honor* (Academy Award Best Actor nomination), *Heartburn* (1986), *The Witches of Eastwick* (1987), *Ironweed* (1987, Academy Award Best Actor nomination), *Broadcast News* (1987), *Batman* (1989) and he directed as well as appeared in *The Two Jakes* (1990). Blending his talents to another medium, he recorded the album *The Elephant's Child* with Bobby McFerrin for which he received a Grammy for Best Recording for Children in 1987. He followed that success with another well received rendition of Kipling *Just So Stories*.

"I've always felt that I could come at the work from first principles. Start from zero, take by take. That's been where my enthusiasm comes from. I've never felt obligated to my talent—in other words, I don't have the impression that anyone would give a shit if I didn't make another movie . . . you can always retire. To sum it up, I like making beautiful things. That's really my desire in life."

Leonard Nimoy

E very Trekkie knows the story behind the *U.S.S. Enterprise*, its galactic mission: "to seek out new life and civilizations, to boldly go where no man has gone before." And every Trekkie knows the Vulcan's survival was based on the decision to extirpate emotionalism from their race. Logic would rule supreme. Ears are pointed. And every Trekkie worth his TV is enraptured by the famous Vulcan hybrid Mr. Spock, in whom exists a very special mixture of space age tensions. The logic and emotional suppression of the Vulcan people through his father Sarek, in conflict with the emotional and humanistic traits inherited from his human mother Amanda, a scientist.

"For three years, twelve hours a day, five days a week, approximately ten months a year," he says, "I functioned as an extraterrestrial and years later I am still affected by the character of Spock. Of course the role has changed my career. Or rather, gave me one. It made me wealthy by most standards and opened up vast opportunities. It also affected me deeply. To this day I sense Vulcan speech patterns, Vulcan social attitudes and even Vulcan patterns of logic and emotional suppression in my behavior. What started out as a welcome job to a hungry actor has become a constant and ongoing influence in my thinking and lifestyle."

Born in Boston, 26 March 1931, the intense actor was passed over by all the pretty girls in high school in favor of the more popular jocks. Nimoy vowed to get his revenge by becoming a famous actor and with $600 in his pocket, set out for California's Pasadena Playhouse. He struggled towards success for years. Endeavoring to rid himself of his Boston accent, he intentionally developed a temporary stutter. In 1954 he married actress Sandi Zober (divorced, 2 children). He worked a variety of menial jobs and wanted to quit acting but Sandi changed his mind. In the early '60s, he began to get regular work on television and in 1966, cast in the part of Mr. Spock, his star was fixed in the Hollywood firmament. After "Star Trek" Nimoy went on to appear for two years on TV's "Mission Impossible" and then to expand into other fields. As a writer he has published three volumes of poetry—*You and I* (1973), *I Think of You* (1974), and *We Are All Children Searching for Love* (1977). His autobiography, *I Am Not Spock,* was published in 1975. He lent his name to a chain of curiosity museums, Leonard Nimoy's World of the Unexplained. Nimoy has also cut several albums (*Leonard Nimoy Presents Mr. Spock's Music from Outer Space,* etc.) and has toured the country appearing in serious theatrical works, including a tremendous success on Broadway in *Equus* (1977), and in a one-man-show *Vincent* about the painter Vincent Van Gogh. Turning his talents to directing he's gone behind the camera for some of the *Star Trek* movie sequels as well as directing the popular *Three Men and A Baby* (1987) and *The Good Mother* (1988). His film parts include *Invasion of the Body Snatchers, Star Trek—The Motion Picture, Star Trek II: The Wrath of Khan, Star Trek III: The Search for Spock* (he also directed), *Star*

Trek IV: The Voyage and *Star Trek V: The Final Frontier*. In 1989, he married Susan Bay.

Nick Nolte

"**Y**ou've got to be attached to both the piece and the character, so that your commitment to them eventually transcends your critical faculties. What we're all trying to do is get to where we're totally without self-consciousness as the characters before the cameras roll." The blond-haired, brawny actor trashes the 1977 underwater thriller *The Deep*. "I wasn't attached to it, so doing it was an alienating and isolating experience." It may have alienated Nolte, but movie-goers loved it, and it established him as a box office draw.

Born in 1942 in Omaha, Nebraska, Nolte recalls a rebellious childhood that may have molded his Brando-like appeal. After portraying shady characters on television episodes of popular shows and made-for-TV movies, Nolte made that long leap to film with the 1975 release, *Return to Macon County*. It was back to the small screen in 1976 for the ABC landmark mini-series, "Rich Man, Poor Man," based on Irwin Shaw's best-selling novel. As the down-and-out brother of a wealthy businessman, Nolte raised blood pressures with shirtless scenes of passion and earned an Emmy nomination. Nolte's other film credits include *Who'll Stop the Rain* (1978), a somber effort dealing with the Vietnam war; *North Dallas Forty*, a 1979 football farce; *Cannery Row* (1982); *48 Hours* (1983) with comedian Eddie Murphy and *Teachers* (1984). In 1985, he co-starred with Katharine Hepburn in *Grace Quigley* and filmed *Down and Out in Beverly Hills* with Bette Midler and Richard Dreyfuss. His recent movies include *Weeds* (1987), *New York Stories* (1988), *Three Fugitives* (1989), *Farewell to the King* (1989), *Everybody Wins* (1989), *Q & A* (1989), and *Another 48 Hours* (1990).

Nolte is known by his peers for going to strenuous lengths to prepare for his roles. He worked out four hours a day and wore a back brace for one, and gained 40 pounds for another. Nolte is also known for his stormy personal life, including three marriages and a palimony suit by former girlfriend Karen Louise Eklund. He married Becky Linger in 1984, and they have one child.

Chuck Norris

"Do what has to be done without complaint and think only positively. Don't allow yourself to think negatively," says movie tough guy Chuck Norris, known for his action-thriller movies and his knowledge of the martial-arts. In 1987, he toured the talk shows and chatted up his autobiography hardcover, *The Secret of Inner Strength: My Story.* This paean to the power of positive thinking, co-written with Hollywood veteran Joe Hyams, gives the low-down on how the author progressed from collecting kudos for his karate skills to become a popular box office hitmaker. The biographical details are interspersed with philosophical nuggets and conclude with a two-page listing of "Chuck Norris's Code of Ethics.""A true champion can deal with his failures and losses as well as with his successes, and he learns from both."

Born, equal parts Irish and Cherokee Indian, in Ryan, Oklahoma, in 1940, the youngster christened Carlos Ray Norris dates his life's true beginning to the early 60's when he joined the Air Force and was sent to Korea. It was during this overseas stint that he became interested in the martial arts and when he obtained his Black Belt in karate; it "changed my entire outlook on life. I realized there was nothing I couldn't achieve if I just had the determination and persistence." After his discharge, Norris began to pursue karate professionally and, in 1968, became the World Middleweight Champion, a title he held until his retirement from competition in 1974. "A combination of discipline and learning leads to confidence. Remember that everyone is a beginner at some point in his life; even your teacher was once a pupil."

Operating a karate school in Los Angeles, Norris soon attracted a number of celebrity pupils (including the entire Osmond family) and it was Steve McQueen who pointed him toward an acting career. After making his movie debut with another friend, Bruce Lee, in *Return of the Dragon,* he appeared in several martial-arts action releases. The karate whiz graduated to the status of action hero in the Clint Eastwood/Charles Bronson mold in 1984, when he first portrayed the battle-scarred Vietnam vet, Colonel James Braddock, in the hit, *Missing in Action.* He later reprised the role in a "prequel" called *Missing in Action 2: The Beginning,* and other Norris-starrers have been *The Delta Force, Invasion, U.S.A., Braddock: Missing in Action III,* and *Hero and the Terror.* With his wife, Dianne, he has two children.

Carroll O'Connor

His ten-season run as the beer-drinking, bigoted Archie Bunker—beefy, middle-aged, and lower-middle-class, with about as much room for "them-not-his-own-kind"—on the TV show "All in the Family" and then, later, "Archie Bunker's Place," was the quintessence of characterization, and American archetype of all seasons. "I'm not playing him to make people hate him for his attitude," he said of Archie, "or to make them like him, either. I'm just playing his attitude as truthfully as I know how." O'Connor won an Emmy as best comedy actor in the 1971-72 season and was nominated many more times for the same award.

A veteran of nearly 30 feature films and more than 100 TV programs, this New York-born actor, 2 August 1924, was spotted in a college production at the National University of Dublin, where he was studying for his B.A., and offered a part in a play at the Gate Theater. He stayed with The Gate for three years, then went on to act in plays in London, Paris, Edinburgh and New York. Of people who now connect his name with his face, he says, "I was in a very old-fashioned department store and two elderly ladies spotted me. 'We always watch you, Mr. O'Connor,' they said. 'We don't always like you, but we always watch you.'"

When Archie went the way of worldwide re-runs à la "I Love Lucy," O'Connor, who is a licensed English teacher, went on to write and star in a 1973 television version of "The Last Hurrah," publish an autobiography in 1981, play in and direct *Brothers* on Broadway in 1983 and return to the Great White Way in 1984 in James Duff's *The War at Home.* In 1985 he starred in the CBS-TV series "Brass." Although the actor underwent heart bypass surgery at Emory University Hospital in March 1989, he continues to be active in the industry. His NBC-TV show "In the Heat of the Night" was a favorite for the 1988-89 season, and again in 1989-90. The 1990 TV movie "The Father Clements Story" co-starred O'Connor and actor Lou Gosset, Jr.

Ryan O'Neal

What can you say about a Hollywood boy with freckles? That he is built like the best of Malibu studs; that he's got the girl all America wants (Farrah Fawcett, one son, Redmond); that he makes about one film each year (included are *Paper Moon, Love Story, The Games, What's up Doc?, Barry Lyndon, Nickelodeon, A Bridge Too Far, Oliver's Story, The Main Event, Irreconcilable Differences, Fever Pitch, Tough Guys Don't Dance* and *Chances Are*) and that he has fallen arches and wears rose-colored foot supports to prove it.

Born in Los Angeles 20 April 1941, the son of playwright-novelist Charles O'Neal and actress Patricia O'Callaghan, Ryan O'Neal grew up roving with his family in Mexico, the West Indies and England, but went to high school in Los Angeles. In 1959, while the family was in Germany, the blond with a boxer's alter-ego (he competed in the Los Angeles Golden Gloves of 1956 and 1957) got a job as a stunt man on the TV series "Tales of the Vikings." When the series ended he went to Hollywood, worked for a while as a busboy, lined up an agent and began appearing on such TV shows as "Bachelor Father," "The Untouchables," and "My Three Sons." As Rodney Harrington, the good-looking bad boy on television's first prime-time soap, "Peyton Place," he became the nation's leading weekly heartthrob.

Roving photographers and assorted others must not come too close or they are likely to receive an O'Neal autograph: below-the-belt epithets or a sharp right. Ryan served 51 days in a Lincoln Heights, California, pesthouse for assault and battery on an unfriendly stranger at a 1960s New Year's Eve party. In 1964, he took out a New Orleans entertainment writer with one punch. In 1983 he removed his son Griffin's two front teeth in an altercation over some missing stereo equipment. Soon after, the son was sent off to a drug rehabilitation center in Hawaii. Griffin is his son from his first marriage to Joanna Moore. He starred with their daughter Tatum in *Paper Moon*. She got the Oscar. His second wife was the beauteous Leigh Taylor-Young; one son Patrick.

Lately he asserts a calmer facade. "Farrah pulled the rug out from under me," he says. "For the first time in my life, something took precedence over myself." O'Neal and Fawcett returned to television in a sitcom for the 1990-91 season.

Tatum O'Neal

Since her blast-off in *Paper Moon* (1975), she's no longer "Ryan's daughter." She was only 10 years old when director Peter Bogdanovich told Ryan, "If you don't let her play it (Addie Loggins in *Paper Moon*), I don't want you for the picture." Ryan had been reluctant because he didn't know if she could act or even if she wanted to be an actress; as it turned out she was overjoyed at the offer but later admitted she didn't know making a picture was hard work. "If I knew after a week on location, I wouldn't have taken the job." (She thought since you see a movie in a day, it should be finished in a day.) In her next two films, *Bad News Bears* (1976) and *Nickelodeon* (1976), she did nothing more than play herself. "A brat." *International Velvet* (sequel to the original *National Velvet* that shot 12-year-old Elizabeth Taylor to stardom) was made when Tatum was 14 and "was really Tatum's first crack at acting" according to one critic. Interviewed during the shoot she explained, "I also get to wear nice clothes. I have a boyfriend and you'll see my very first screen kiss. There is no sex or even heavy petting in 'Velvet.'" She pulled off *Velvet* and the ensuing *Little Darlings* (in which she and Kristy McNichol wager which one will be the first to lose her virginity at summer camp) and *Circle of Two* (both 1979 releases).

Born 5 November 1963, she was named after her mother's (Joanna Moore) grandmother. ("I'd rather be named Elizabeth.") Neither parent pushed her toward acting. Said Ryan, "She will not become an adult with a bankrupt childhood." In fact she never had an acting lesson. Her ambition at one time was to be a great actress or a secretary, *Time* reported, and she continued her screen appearances into the 80s (*Captured*, 1981; *Certain Fury*, 1985). She has lived with her father in the past but in 1984 set up housekeeping in Malibu with tennis ace John McEnroe. The couple married in Oyster Bay, Long Island, on 1 August 1986 and have two sons (Kevin Jack and Sean Timothy). She has a brother, Griffin, two years her junior, a stepbrother Patrick, five years her junior (from Ryan's second wife,

Leigh Taylor-Young) and another stepbrother, Redmond, whose mother is Farrah Fawcett.

Jerry Orbach

To his cueball pals from the pool hall—Brooklyn Joey, Johnny Eyebrows, and Hundred Ball Blackie—he is known as Jerry the Actor. But to New York's greasepaint set he is a player of no mean talent who bounced from pocket to pocket on and off Broadway for more than a decade before scoring a solid hit as the key-lending hero of *Promises, Promises* in 1968 (which netted him a Tony Award). "It's like 'Wow,'" Jerry Orbach crowed when the verdict was in. "'By gosh, you're a star!' It goes on and on 24 hours a day and it's a lot of fun . . . people get used to it. . . . I'm getting used to it." At times in the past things had been different. "Like when a television name who everybody knew was really terrible would get the lead in a big Broadway show that I wanted desperately. . . . A lot of things that went on in the business used to make me brook." But not enough to make him quit.

The son of a restaurant manager (who had once tried vaudeville himself and did not object when his son began to lean towards the stage), Jerry was born 20 October 1935 in the Bronx, and grew up in Waukegan, Illinois. He studied drama at Northwestern, worked in summer stock, and after graduation made straight for New York, where he and a friend shared a shabby flat. Pounding the pavement looking for jobs, he remembers, "we got by on peanut butter, beer and whatever food my friend brought back from parties." The Orbach star began to rise when Joel Grey's wife helped Jerry get a job as an understudy in *The Threepenny Opera* in 1955. He worked his way through seven parts to the starring role (in the process marrying Marta Curro, another understudy, and raising two sons). He married again in 1979 (Elaine Cancilla). After *Threepenny Opera*, Orbach went on to play in *The Fantasticks* (1960; he introduced the haunting "Try to Remember"), *Carnival, Scuba-Duba, Promises, Promises, 6 Rms Riv Vu, Chicago* (Tony nomination), and *42nd Street* (1980). He made a stunning screen debut in 1981 in *Prince of the City*, directed by Sidney Lumet. His recent movie credits include: *F/X* (1985), *I Love New York* (1986), *Someone to Watch Over Me* (1987), *Dirty*

Dancing (1987), and Woody Allen's *Crimes and Misdemeanors* (1990). He also starred in the CBS-TV series "The Law and Harry McGraw" (1987). The climb to the top "seems short" Orbach insists. "I was never forced into a job I didn't want. . . . I've had a good time on the way." He has also learned his craft. "I found out that real acting takes a great deal of energy and an attitude slightly bigger than life," he once explained. "Over the years this washed and washed over me. Do you see," he asks rather gently, "how a star is born overnight?"

Peter O'Toole

"**F**rom the age of sixteen, I couldn't put my foot wrong no matter how hard I tried. And I tried. I had a lot of bumps. I look at it now, and it's almost as if it were inevitable," says the actor. At age 40 he retreated to some family property in the west of Ireland, where he did nothing but plant trees for a year. After this sabbatical, he performed an assembly of plays at the Bristol Old Vic; refreshed, he found "the work was better than ever." In 1975, however, the life of ease collapsed when doctors discovered in his stomach "a sort of form of malignancy." Battling the illness which, "proved inconvenient to a few people, but there you go," he had other battles to confront. Although his two daughters and his mother-in-law continued to live with him, he and his wife of many years, actress Sian Phillips, divorced. And both his parents died. His luck changed when *My Favorite Year* was released in 1982. In it he played Alan Swann, an elegant, boozy, swashbuckling star. Critics began comparing O'Toole to John Barrymore.

Born Seamus O'Toole in County Galway, Ireland, 2 August 1933, the son of a roving bookie who finally settled with his family in the London slums, he was sent to St. Anne's in Leeds, where the nuns tried to beat discipline into him. ("I was just left-handed and, Lord how they whipped me just trying to get me to write with my other hand. Today I have no religion as such.") Quitting school at 13, he got a job in a warehouse wrapping cartons, then landed a job as a copy boy with the Yorkshire *Evening News*. ("It was a jump from being a poor slum kid to meeting people," he said.) In a 1982 *Rolling Stone* interview he amended his background. "The one thing I am *not* is working class." It's just that his father was the black sheep of an Irish Catholic family. His mother was from an aristocratic Protestant Irish family, and both met at the running of the 1929 Epson Derby in England. Still, Leeds was tough. "The bravest thing I ever did in my life was to walk through that district at the age of 11, when I was Little Lord Fauntleroy in a kilt." Following a two-year hitch with the Royal Navy, he won a scholarship to the Royal Academy of Dramatic Art in London. ("I thought I'd died and gone to heaven when I went into RADA.") Having spent three and half years with the Bristol Old Vic, he was appearing onstage in a London production of *The Long and the Short and the Tall*, when Katharine Hepburn, having seen his performance, recommended the young actor to movie producer Sam Spiegel. O'Toole had been named 1959's Actor of the Year in London and was invited by Spiegel to test for *Lawrence of Arabia*. O'Toole arrived on the set reeking of a grog "ordinarily used to remove rust from old car bumpers," and when a pint of scotch fell out of his hip pocket, Spiegel gasped, flung his hands into the air, and rasped, "Never!" However, at the insistence of director David Lean, O'Toole got the part. Some of O'Toole's other films include *What's New Pussycat?*, *Goodbye Mr. Chips*, *Under Milkwood*, *Man of La Mancha*, cult favorite *The Ruling Class*, which was re-released in the early 1980s, *Becket*, *The Stunt Man*, *Creator* and, with Hepburn, *Lion in Winter*. Other films include *Club Paradise* (1985), *Banshee* (1985), *The Last Emperor* (1987), *Helena* (1988), and *King Ralph I* (1990). He also appeared on Broadway in *Pygmalion* (1987).

About all those stories of his legendary carousing with Richard Harris and the late Peter Finch and Richard Burton, O'Toole, who in 1983 had a son with Karen Brown, recalls: "Our hours as actors are absurd, be it stage or cinema. It's impossible to be drunk or stoned and perform at high definition. It's impossible. So the carousers that I knew—Fincy, Bob Shaw, Richard, any of them—were practically monkish during the week. Then came what we used to call collier's night out. And we went *whoopee*. And if we weren't working, we went *whoopee, whoopee, whoopee*. Yes, we had a ball."

Al Pacino

Both a bankable movie star and serious stage actor—a rare breed—unlike others who might feel acting is somehow akin to prostitution, he honors his calling as a most noble endeavor. "What can you say," he asks, "about a profession where you can be anybody and do anything?" *New York Times* critic Mel Gussow described the Pacino cast of characters as "misfits, people out of the

mainstream, besieged by and battling society's expectations of conformity. The essential Pacino character is a loner—isolated, but with a burning intensity. Within this framework, Pacino's range is extraordinary. The characters are, by turns, extroverted and withdrawn, articulate and barely literate, assertive and acquiescent."

He made his film debut as a manipulative junkie in *The Panic in Needle Park* and soon cornered the market on deadly effective anti-heroes. Next he portrayed the implacable Mafia don, Michael Corleone, in *The Godfather* and *The Godfather II*. These were followed up by more Pacino successes such as *Serpico* and *Dog Day Afternoon* and the more notorious *Cruising* and *Scarface*. Such anti-social characters are in direct contrast to Pacino's tradition-bound upbringing in the Bronx where he was born 25 April 1940 of Sicilian descent. Lonely, bright and bored, Pacino spent much of his time at the movies and afterwards would act out for his family and friends the stories he'd seen. "Every time I came home, I fell down as if I were dead. I *always* made an entrance into my house." He quit the High School of Performing Arts after the first two years—the end of his formal education. Since then all he has studied is acting. While attending the Herbert Berghof Studio, he met Charles Laughton who volunteered to work with Pacino on his craft. Encouraged by the veteran, he auditioned for Off Off-Broadway parts. His first appearance was in William Saroyan's *Hello Out There* at the Cafe Cino. Aside from the classroom this was his first time acting in front of an audience. The experience was so unnerving he refused to perform in public for one year. He was admitted after a second try to Lee Strasberg's Actor's Studio. It was there that he received most of his training. He began auditioning again and, in time, became involved in Israel Horovitz' *The Indian Wants the Bronx* and won an Obie in 1968 for his performance as a drunken hood. His "discovery" led him to Broadway where he won a Tony for his part as a psychotic in 1969's *Does a Tiger Wear a Necktie?* He won a second Tony in 1977 for *The Basic Training of Pavol Hummel*. In 1983 he struck a critical stride in the revival of David Mamet's *American Buffalo*. Other films include *Revolution* (1986) with Nastassja Kinski, *Sea of Love* (1989), *Dick Tracy* (1990), and *The Godfather, Part III* (1990). Pacino lives in New York and guards his privacy so much that columnist Earl Wilson once dubbed the actor "the male Greta Garbo."

Alan Pakula

His particular strength as a director is handling difficult actors—or is it better to say actors in difficult parts? Under his direction, Jane Fonda (for *Klute*), Jason Robards (for *All the President's Men*), and Meryl Streep (for *Sophie's Choice*) won Academy Awards. Liza Minnelli (*The Sterile Cuckoo*), Jane Alexander (*All the President's Men*), Jill Clayburgh and Candice Bergen (*Starting Over*) and Richard Farnsworth (*Comes a Horseman*) all received Oscar nominations. "If a director has one job with actors," he explains, "it's to make

them feel safe and to try to dare. The reason I became a director was that I've always loved actors. The very first time I worked with actors on stage, while I was still at Yale, I got this very exulted feeling that I was finally a part of the universe, in the adolescent, Thomas Wolfian sense. I remember leaving the theatre that night and leaping, goat-like all the way home, full of the arrogant belief that those actors had done something they could never have done without me. Now I'm not so sure."

Born of Polish-Jewish parentage, 7 April 1928, Pakula penned plays at Pennsylvania's prep palace, The Hill School, before his ivy days as a drama major at Yale. The summer before his studies in New Haven, he responded to a want-ad and wound up the office boy to the late, great agent Leland Hayward. His job was to deliver scripts to directors, producers and actors, but instead he would take the scripts home at night, read them, and then deliver them in the morning. He gunned his way to success in Hollywood after college, first as an assistant to the head of cartoons at Warner Brothers, then at age 23 when his mentor at Hollywood's arty Circle Theatre, Don Hartman, was made head of production at Paramount Pictures, Pakula went with him. In 1955 he got the green light to produce *Fear Strikes Out* about a baseball player's struggle with mental illness, starring Anthony Perkins. Joining forces with fellow director Richard Mulligan, soon Pakula-Mulligan Productions was popping out box office hit after hit. Among them were *To Kill a Mockingbird; Love with a Proper Stranger; Baby, the Rain Must Fall; Inside Daisy Clover* and *Up the Down Staircase*.

He began directing in 1968 with *The Sterile Cuckoo*. "I was interviewing lots of directors for the job. Suddenly I realized it was something I wanted to do myself. I'd always wanted to direct, not produce." He had a major turning point with the film of William Styron's *Sophie's Choice* in 1983. Although it was his ninth film as director, it was his first as a screenwriter and he received an Oscar nomination for best screenplay adaptation. Other endeavors include *See You in the Morning* (co-produced/screenplay) and *Orphans* (produced/directed).

Once married to actress Hope Lange, in 1973 he married the former Hannah Cohn Boorstin. (Her 1985 biography about Queen Marie of Rumania—*The Last Romantic*—drew critical raves.) They reside in New York.

Joseph Papp

He is an indefatigable champion and indisputably a force behind some of the best American theatre in the past fifteen years. Almost thirty seasons since he put his first *Julius Caesar* into the East River Amphitheater, his New York Shakespeare Festival has produced over 400 works. These include: the original production of *Hair*, which, in 1967, opened the Festival's year-round home, the converted landmark Astor Library (it is actually five theatres under one roof); *No Place to Be Somebody, Two Gentlemen of Verona, Sticks and Bones, That Championship Season, Streamers, A Chorus Line, Miss Margarida's Way, For Colored Girls Who Have Considered Suicide When the Rainbow Is Enuf, I'm Getting My Act Together and Taking It on the Road, Plenty, The Pirates of Penzance, La Boheme,* starring Linda Ronstadt, and *The Normal Heart*. His summer, 1990, production of *The Taming of the Shrew* for the New York Shakespeare Festival in Central Park paired Tracey Ullman and Morgan Freeman in the starring roles. From 1973 to 1977, the NYSF served as the theatre constituent at Lincoln Center where its productions included *Threepenny Opera, The Cherry Orchard* and *Streamers*. On 29 September 1983, *A Chorus Line* became the longest running show in the history of Broadway when it gave its 3,389th performance at the Shubert Theatre. As of 1984, NYSF productions had collectively won 23 Tony awards (including three special Tonys), 76 Obies, 19 Drama Desk Awards, 6 New York Drama Critics Awards and three Pulitzer prizes. In 1962 Papp built the Delacorte Theatre in Central

Park and in 1964 developed a mobile theatre to tour city parks and playgrounds.

A list of Papp's credits is immeasurable as is the list of the many battles he has waged in the name of art. In 1990 he launched a letter-writing campaign against the National Endowment for the Arts' rule that grant recipients sign an anti-obscenity pledge; he turned down a grant by refusing to sign. He also testified at a Congressional subcommittee hearing in 1990 on a proposal to restructure the NEA. In 1988, he was honored by the Vietnam Veterans Ensemble Theatre Company at their second annual Vetty Awards.

Born Joseph Papirofsky in the Williamsburg section of Brooklyn 22 June 1921, he discoverd Shakespeare when he was 12 years old. "Shakespeare," he says, "was tied into a lot of things. . . . I learned one of Mark Antony's speeches. Then I went into Manhattan to a place on 14th Street that made recorded discs, and I recorded myself reading it with Stravinsky's 'Firebird Suite' in the background. . . . I love the sound of the English language because we spoke only Yiddish at home. To have a guy get up like Mark Antony and talk to a crowd and have him change their minds . . . that was very persuasive." Papp staged his first productions while in the Navy during WW II. After his discharge in 1946 he studied acting and directing at the Actors Lab in Los Angeles on the G.I. Bill. Back in New York in the 1950s, he worked as a stage manager at CBS. He first realized his vision of the New York Shakespeare Festival in a church on East 6th Street after he convinced the minister that the church resembled the Globe Theatre of William Shakespeare's day. Papp is both a nurturer of talent and a ruthlessly competitive businessman and fundraiser. Once after *New York Times* critic Walter Kerr gave one of his productions a bad review, Papp screamed at him the next time they met at the Public: "Keep out. I don't want you here. You are incapable of judging and evaluating new works."

These days the NYSF is rich and its masterbuilder, after four marriages (his fourth and present wife is Gail Merrifield, a longtime NYSF staffer) and five children (from the first three marriages) he is ready for even bigger shows and tougher battles. "I wouldn't mind being called upon by the government to do something of a cultural nature . . . if the U.S. government appointed me to be cultural ambassador-at-large, I would be interested."

Estelle Parsons

"I hate the theatre. That whole thing about the theatre being sacred is ridiculous," says the energetic and outspoken actress. "It's full of boring, unimaginative, third-rate people. Every

good actor I know has moved to Hollywood." She walked off with an Oscar as best supporting actress in 1967 for her portrayal of the knee-knocking gangster's moll in *Bonnie and Clyde*. Her favorite part was in the film, *I Never Sang for My Father*, in which she played "the only woman who is brighter than I am. The part lasted 14 minutes on the screen. I come in at the end, tell everybody off, and leave." Other films include *Rachel, Rachel* with Joanne Woodward, *Don't Drink the Water* ("I learned more from Jackie Gleason than any actor I've ever worked with") and *The Night the Sun Came Out* ("I play a woman who wakes up one morning and discovers her husband has turned into Godfrey Cambridge"). Commenting on her film career Parsons says, "I get scripts and my agent gets scripts, continually for film roles, but I haven't found one worth doing recently."

Born in Lynn, Massachusetts, 20 November 1927, she holds a B.A. in political science from Connecticut College for Women and attended Boston University Law School. She landed her first job as a reporter and production assistant on the old Dave Garraway "Today" show, and then made her way into the theatre, playing a small part in the 1957 Ethel Merman musical *Happy Hunting*, followed by *Skin of Our Teeth* for Arthur Penn. Other stage appearances include *Miss Margarida's Way*, for which she won a Drama Desk Award in 1977 as a wacky, authoritarian schoolteacher, and *The Pirates of Penzance*, in which she appeared as the aging nursemaid. "I always like to do something new," says the actress. In 1983 she starred in the one-woman show, *Adulto Orgasmo Escapes from the Zoo*, a series of sketches on the subjugation of women which Parsons says, "fall in the crack between cabaret and theatre. I love them more than anything I've ever done." She hit the stage again in 1989's *The Unguided Missile*.

Divorced from the late magazine writer Richard Gehman in 1953 (twin daughters), Parsons has since married Peter Zimroth, a trial lawyer. The couple adopted a baby boy in 1983—a surprise to some, but not to Estelle's 28-year-old daughter, Abbie—"There's nothing Mom would do that would stun me."

Dolly Parton

"**H**er visual trademark is not far from that of Diamond Lil: a mountainous, curlicued bleach-blonde wig, lots of make-up, and outfits that accentuate her quite astonishing hour-glass figure," was John Rockwell's *New York Times* observation when Dolly Parton opened at New York's Felt Forum in 1974 with the newly-formed Travelin' Family Band (two brothers, two sisters, an uncle and a cousin). "But Miss Parton is no artificial dumb blonde. Her thin little soprano and girlish way of talking suggest something childlike, but one quickly realizes both that it is genuine and that she is a striking talent." The leading lady of country music who became a

pop-rock superstar surfaced in Nashville as the protégée of the legendary Porter Wagoner. She struck out on her own in 1974, was chosen Best Female Singer of the Country Music Association in 1975 and 1976, blazed into pop with her rockish backup band Gypsy Fever in 1977 (her touring van was a whopper studio-and home-on-wheels with a closet for twenty gowns and four wigs, and sleeping accommodations for eleven), and by the '80s had become a multi-faceted entertainer in concert, on records, television and films.

Dolly Rebecca Parton was born 19 January 1946 in a two-room wooden shack in Locust Ridge, near Sevierville, Tennessee. As the fourth of twelve children of a struggling dirt farmer and a preacher's daughter (her mixed ancestry is Dutch, Irish, and Cherokee Indian), she helped raise her younger brothers and sisters. "We had absolutely nothin'. We wore rags. . . . For make-up we used merthiolate and mercurochrome . . . flour for powder. I was fascinated even then with make-up and stuff. Course they never allowed us to wear lipstick. My daddy would whip me . . . but the whippin' was worth it for a few days with a red mouth." She had "the best mama and daddy in the world" and she and her brothers and sisters had "fun . . . love . . . music." Parton's first love was gospel music ("my grandaddy bein' the preacher, we didn't feel ashamed to sing and play our git-tars. We believed in makin' a joyful noise unto the Lord.") At six her first musical instrument was a "busted-up mandolin"; at eight her uncle gave her a guitar and at eleven she had radio bookings in Knoxville. The day after her high school graduation in 1964 (she played the snare drum in the marching band), she took off for Nashville. In 1967 she joined Porter Wagoner's band, the Wagon Masters, and with him for the next seven years she sang at the Grand Ole Opry, wrote and recorded songs, and eventually co-founded the Owepar Publishing Company in Nashville. (She was later sued by Wagoner for $3 million in back fees and royalties; it was settled out of court.) From being a frequent guest on prime-time television shows, she went on to star in her own specials (a 1984 Christmas special with Kenny Rogers was followed by a recording with him and writing the title tune "Christmas in America" for Kenny's 1989 album), concerts, and records. She is a prolific lyric writer (many have been recorded and "thousands" fill trunks and boxes in her home). She writes, or sings, into a tape recorder, up to twenty sets of lyrics a day. "A strange feeling usually comes over me; almost like being in a trance. When you're talented I think much of the inspiration is spiritual—from God." Parton's film career leaves her with definite opinions: *9 to 5*, with Jane Fonda and Lily Tomlin, "the best experience I could have had;" *The Best Little Whorehouse in Texas,* with Burt Reynolds, "the worst"; *Rhinestone,* with Sylvester Stallone, "my favorite." (Many critics, on the other hand, put the latter on their "Ten Worst Films" list in 1984.) She also appeared in 1989's *Steel Magnolias.* Her ABC-TV special aired in the 1990-91 season.

A woman with many of her dreams fulfilled, she opened Dollywood (a theme park tourist attraction) near Pigeon Forge, Tennessee, in 1986. She runs Dolly Parton Enterprises, making her own decisions on investments and charitable contributions and has homes in Hawaii, Hollywood, New York and Nashville, all of which she shares with her husband, Carl Dean. "I enjoy the way I look, but it's a joke," chuckles Parton. "They know I'm going to come out with every spangled thing I can get on. It's a joke we share."

Mandy Patinkin

"To say that Mandy Patinkin became inhabited by the ghost of George Seurat, the 19th century artist, is hardly an exaggeration," said the *New York Times'*s Nan Robertson about his performance in Stephen Sondheim's controversial musical *Sunday in the Park with George,* "At least Mr. Patinkin thinks so, at the risk of sounding 'pretentious, corny and a fool.'" Pointing out that he was 31 and that Seurat died at the age of 31 in 1891, Patinkin added: "I even look like the guy, too. I get a little freaked about how much I looked like him." Raised in Chicago, Patinkin "grew up" with the painting that has hung in the Art Institute there for years, and before the show started workshop rehearsals (later moving to Broadway) he made several trips to Chicago and sat for a total of seven hours in front of the painting that inspired the musical—"Sunday Afternoon on the Island of La Grande Jatte."

Mandel (everybody has called him "Mandy" since babyhood) Patinkin was born 30 November 1952 in Chicago. After attending the University of Kansas he went to New York and studied at the Juilliard School. From 1975 to 1981 he appeared frequently with the New York Shakespeare Festival as well as the Hudson Guild Theatre. His Broadway appearances include *Shadow Box;* an outstanding portrayal of Che Guevara in *Evita*, for which he won a 1980 Tony Award; *George* (nominated for a 1984

Tony); and the two-day concert version of *Follies*. In 1989 he starred on Broadway in a one-man show *Mandy Patinkin in Concert: Dress Casual.* He also appeared in 1987's *The Knife*. His films include *The Big Fix, French Postcards, The Last Embrace, Night of the Juggler, Ragtime, Yentl, Daniel, Free Spirit Maxie, Heartburn, The House on Carroll Street, Alien Nation* and *Dick Tracy*.

His vocal acrobatics have won accolades from music critics, including Sondheim who calls Patinkin's voice "brilliant—a gift from God. That's in addition to his terrific stage presence and acting skill." The actor has "wide tessitura, both top and bottom," continues Sondheim, "a working two-octave range, up and down to G-sharp." Reacting to those remarks, Patinkin said: "If I knew what that meant, it would really scare me. I don't read music. I read the words. I just know when it goes up and down." He married actress Kathryn Grody in 1980 and they live in Manhattan's West Side (two sons, Isaac and Gideon).

Luciano Pavarotti

"I 'm an ordinary man," insists this extraordinary tenor who made operatic history in a production of *La Fille du Regiment*, hitting all nine high C's in the aria "Quel destin" perfectly. He's been the cause of what one critic calls "Pavarotti Pandemonium" among music lovers since his La Scala debut in 1966. Hailed by *Newsweek* as "opera's greatest turn-on," Luciano Pavarotti has drawn throngs to the world of classical music with his ebullient

manner and superb voice via "live" televised broadcasts, his appearance in the film *Yes, Giorgio* (which was panned by the critics) and the publication of his autobiography, *Pavarotti, My Own Story* (a national bestseller). In addition, his recordings have made it to the top of both classical and pop charts and he's appeared on numerous talk shows (often giving cooking demos) and on TV commercials for American Express. His latest recording was *Pavarotti at Carnegie Hall* in 1988.

Born in Modena, Italy, 12 October 1935, Pavarotti was indoctrinated into the music world by his father, a baker who sang with a local choral group. The Pavarotti phenomenon began in this country in 1965 when the tenor gave several performances of *Lucia di Lammermoor* in Miami with Joan Sutherland and exploded with full force after his Metropolitan Opera debut in *La Boheme* in November 1968. Since then his fame and popularity have spread like wildfire. Lately, however, "opera's golden tenor" has been disappointing audiences with last minute cancellations and in 1983 he was booed and whistled at in *Lucia di Lammermoor* (which once had brought him standing ovations) because of a sudden weakening of his voice. More recently, he was banned from the Lyric Opera of Chicago for backing out of a performance in 1989. This was the twenty-sixth time he had cancelled an appearance at the Lyric during this decade. More recently, he has worked as a stage director as well as singer. Pavarotti tries not to think about the day he'll have to give up singing. "We don't have time to pause and see where we are. If someone asks an old singer how he is feeling he will either say he doesn't know or lie. Because every moment of every day is a new experience to be conquered. People my age don't ask who and why and what is it like to be great—we just do, and be the best we can. I love people. I genuinely love everybody," says the equally lovable singer who never fails to bring enthusiasm and sheer delight to his performances. His hectic performing schedule keeps him on the road ten months a year and he puts in time to conduct master classes and appear in documentary films. When he does make it home— one month each year—to Rimini, Italy, he spends the time with his wife Adua and their three daughters. Pavarotti also keeps a Manhattan apartment, the scene of many late-night poker games with fellow singers and musicians.

Gregory Peck

His screen credits provide a cross-section of some of Hollywood's finest cinematic contributions, including *Twelve O'Clock High, Spellbound, The Gunfighter, Roman Holiday,* and *The Guns of Navarone.* But it was his classic portrayal of the Lincolnesque southern lawyer, Arthur Finch in the widely-hailed *To Kill a Mockingbird* that won him an Academy Award in 1962.

The legendary Peck (born Eldred Gregory Peck in La Jolla, California, 5 April 1916) was a pre-med student at the University of California at Berkeley when the compulsion to act overrode his interest in medicine. A back injury, which had previously caused him to drop out from the university rowing team, also barred him from military service in World War II. After a drama scholarship and short-run appearances on Broadway, he attained instant stardom in RKO's *Days of Glory,* followed by *The Keys to the Kingdom* (which won him one of four Oscar nominations he would receive). In due time he produced features as well, one of which, *The Trial of the Catonsville Nine* was a "labor of love," a militant, anti-war movie based on Father Dan Berrigan's play. "We made it," says Peck, who also helped underwrite the costs, "because we wanted to get it said." In making *Catonsville* (1972), Peck could not bring himself to endorse civil disobedience to the extent propounded by author Berrigan. At the same time he and his associates felt that the picture itself was their way of saying *no* to war. Peck has also produced or co-produced: *Pork Chop Hill, Cape Fear, Behold a Pale Horse, The Dove and Dodsworth* (1983). Other screen credits include *Sea Wolves* (1981), *Amazing Grace and Chuck* (1986) and *The Old Gringo* (1989).

Peck was first married to Greta Rice, from whom he was divorced in 1954 (three sons, one of whom committed suicide in 1975). In 1955 he married the French newspaper writer Veronique Passani (two children). His significant distinctions include The Medal of Freedom in 1969 and an appointment as National Chairman of the American Cancer Society in 1966. From 1967-70 he was President of the Academy of Motion Picture Arts and Sciences, and in 1968 he was reappointed for a six-year term as a member of the National Council on the Arts. He is a member of the Board of Trustees of the American Film Institute.

Sean Penn

If *Time* magazine is correct in calling them the "sons of De Niro," referring to the new breed of intense, young matinee idols, then this consummate pro is the heir-apparent, the likeliest-to-succeed of the lot. In fact, he co-starred with DeNiro in the 1989 feature film *We're No Angels,* allowing viewers to see them work side by side. Penn's realistic portrayals of a diverse group of characters in movies such as *Racing with the Moon* and *The Falcon and the Snowman* have won him plenty of praise. "I like to spend my time researching my parts, the people I play, because I feel a need and a responsibility to the people who *live* the life I'm portraying, so that they're not disappointed or feel misrepresented when they see the film. So they recognize something real," says Sean Penn about whom director Louis Malle recalls: "I'd seen him in *Fast Times at Ridgemont High* and I thought he was brilliant as the stoned surfer— to the point that I didn't think it was a characterization at all. When he came to my office to interview for *Crackers,* I nearly fell off my chair because in front of me was someone who had nothing to do with that character; this young man, lean, not very tall, good looking, very shy, very quiet. Sean has exceptional talent for absorbing all sorts of different characters." His most challenging role may have been the one he assumed in August, 1985, when he married pop singer Madonna. After continual on-again-off-again battles, they filed for divorce in January, 1989.

He was born 17 August 1960 in Santa Monica, California, the middle son of a show biz family: Pop Leo is a TV director; mom Eileen Ryan is a former New York stage actress and younger brother Chris also acts. He was just a bebopper with a surfboard when he decided to skip college to work at the Los Angeles Repertory Theatre, and his parents had reservations. "They said, 'You've got to have something solid, some solid profession to fall back on.' I said, 'I won't fall back!'" His professional debut came in the TV series "Barnaby Jones" in 1979 and he made his Broadway debut in Kevin Heeland's *Heartland,* and from there starred in the film *Taps.* He returned to Broadway in *Slab Boys* with a perfect Scottish accent and next blew into his film part in *Bad Boys* with long hair, a tattooed arm and a few weeks' experience hanging out with Chicago Street gangs. For the part of the Texan musician in *Crackers* he went down to Austin and Dallas and brought back two real-life Lone Star musicians to hang around with—authenticity is everything, you see. However, when he was about to have his near-perfect teeth filed down and capped with"grubby looking covers, maybe a few cracked ones as well," his mother, the daughter of a dentist, vetoed that idea with a firm parental no. "Ruining perfectly good teeth is definitely going too far," she told her hot-in-Hollywood son. Other movies include: *At Close Range* (1985), *Shanghai Express,* (1986), *Colors* (1987), *Judgement in Berlin* (1988), *State of Grace* (1989), and *Casualties of War* (1989).

George Peppard

Just 16 days into filming the pilot for TV's super hit soapsud, "Dynasty," he was replaced by John Forsythe in the part of Blake Carrington, Denver's multi-millionaire. Rumors were he was trying to run the show; he says he resented the notes on his acting from the producers. In any case, he worried that the rest of his dollars would have to be made on the obscure route of dinner theatres across the land. "I was about to lose the only asset I had, which was a house." he says, "and what I was saying in my prayers and to my friends was, 'I'm sure the good Lord will find work for his humble servant,' and there it was, the 'A-Team,' one of the best roles in my career." Despite raising the umbrage level of the National Coalition on Television Violence to ultra high frequency (they found a record-breaking 34 offensive acts per hour, versus seven on other prime-time offenders), the tall, handsome and now silver haired Peppard justifies the "A-Team's" huge success with its viewers this way: "What matters is what the show, as an excuse in escapism and entertainment, means in terms of service to people."

Success is no stranger to this veteran method actor whose good looks have been the madness and the method behind a variety of movies (*Breakfast at Tiffany's, How the West Was Won, The Carpetbaggers,* and the *Executioner*), television shows ("Banacek," "Doctor's Hospital," and "The Sam Sheppard Murder Trial"), and four broken marriages, the first to Helen Davies, two marriages to wildcat Elizabeth Ashley, and the third to Sherry Boucher. He gave matrimony another try in 1984 when he wed artist Alexis Adams.

Peppard was born in Detroit, Michigan, on 1 October 1928, son of a building contractor and mother who sang light opera. After studies at Purdue and Carnegie Tech, he worked at odd jobs on Wall Street and drove a taxi so he could afford to study with Lee Strasberg. He was so confident of immediate Broadway success that he demanded an unlisted telephone number, but nobody called for a long time until bit parts led to increasingly important roles in New York television dramas, such as "Little Moon of Alban" with Julie Harris. His starmaking role in films was MGM's *Home from the Hill*. Peppard's most recent film is *Silence Like Glass* (1989).

The actor is said to be moody but to have an irreverent and whimsical sense of humor. He has three children—Bradford and Julie from his first marriage, and a son Christian from his marriage to Elizabeth Ashley.

Anthony Perkins

With his blend of boyish charm and haunted intensity, he is "Hollywood's perennial pubescent" and brilliant portrayer of "psycho" personalities and inner conflict. Most widely known as the classic manic inkeeper Norman Bates in Hitchcock's 1960 gothic thriller *Psycho* and the sequels, Perkins excels in projects and roles rich in psychological complexities, injecting depth and realism to bizarre situations. (He played the mentally unstable baseball player Jim Piersall in *Fear Strikes Out*, a war-torn Army chaplain in Mike Nichols' *Catch-22*, a megalomaniacal scientist in *Winter Kills*, a tormented psychiatrist in the Broadway hit *Equus* and a sadistic minister in *Crimes of Passion*.) Perkins' insight is rooted in his own tormented childhood, growing up under a smothering widowed mother. He became an actor to escape himself. "There was nothing about *me* I wanted to be," he once recalled, "but I felt wonderfully happy about being somebody else. I made up my mind to be a great actor, greater than my father" (stage and film actor Osgood Perkins). He did just that, and also happily overcame his personal obsessions. Perkins, in *Psycho IV: The Beginning*, which aired on Showtime cable television in Fall, 1990, played Norman Bates as he relives his tormented youth through a series of flashbacks.

A veteran of three dozen movies and many Broadway productions, Anthony Perkins was born 4 April 1932 in New York City to Janet Rane and Osgood Perkins, a suave actor of proper Boston origin who died when Tony was only five. After private schooling in Cambridge, Massachusetts, and half-hearted college attempts at Rollins and Columbia, he turned to acting with quick success. Following an impressive film debut as the juvenile lead in *The Actress* with Jean Simmons and Spencer Tracy, he hit Broadway in 1954 in *Tea and Sympathy*. Returning to Hollywood to play Gary Cooper's son in *Friendly Persuasion*, he became a star. Following *Psycho* he made films in Europe, winning the Cannes International Film Festival's best actor award for his role in *Goodbye Again* opposite Ingrid Bergman. Other films include *Pretty Poison, Murder on the Orient Express, Mahogany, Destroyer,* and *Lucky Stiff.* Other Broadway appearances include *Steambath* (which he also directed) and *Look Homeward Angel* (his favorite role). On television, he starred in the movie "Les Miserables" and with Mary Tyler Moore in "First You Cry." He collaborated with Stephen Sondheim on the screenplay for the suspense film *The Last of Sheila.*

He is married to Berry Berenson, granddaughter of Elsa Schiaparelli, kid sister of actress Marisa Berenson. They have two sons, Osgood and Elvis.

Ron Perlman

"I was one of these actors who landed wonderfully artistic projects once a year and then just sat around because nobody ever thought of me as a commercial property." Ron Perlman, star of the critically acclaimed CBS series "Beauty and the Beast," has made a career of being unrecognizable in quality roles. His greatest success, portraying Vincent, the half-man/half-beast, kept him covered under layers of make-up requiring four and a half hours of application. Hesitant at first to accept the part, having previously been hidden in make-up for the film roles of Salvatore, the hunchback, in *The Name of the Rose* and a prehistoric man in *Quest for Fire*, Perlman relented because "Vincent is so romantic, it's like playing Hamlet every week. This may be the greatest role of my life."

Perlman was born 13 April 1950 in Manhattan, the son of a jazz drummer who played with Artie Shaw's band before giving up music as a profession. He began performing on stage while still in high school, first as a comedian, then as an actor. He continued to appear in theater productions as a student at the City University of New York and while earning a Master of Fine Arts degree at the University of Minnesota. On his return to New York he joined the Classic Stage Company where he performed the works of Shakespeare, Chekhov, O'Neill, Ibsen, and Pinter for almost two years. Director Tom O'Horgan then cast Perlman as the Emperor in the Off-Broadway production of *The Architect and the Emperor of Assyria*, which later toured Europe. Perlman also starred in the Broadway production *American Heroes*, *The Resistable Rise of Arturo Ui* Off-Broadway, and in the regional tour of *Pal Joey* with Joel Grey and Alexis Smith, all of which O'Horgan directed. Other stage appearances in New York and regional theater included *Tartuffe*, *Two Gentlemen of Verona*, *House of Blue Leaves* and *The Iceman Cometh*. Perlman also appeared on Broadway with F. Murray Abraham in Isaac Bashevis Singer's *Tiebele and Her Demon*. After appearing in the MGM film *Ice Pirates* with Anjelica Huston, Perlman returned to New York for Peter Brook's production of *La Tragedie de Carmen* at Lincoln Center.

"Beauty and the Beast" brought Perlman awards as well as praise. He received 1988 and 1989 Emmy nominations as Outstanding Lead Actor in a Drama Series and a People's Choice Award nomination as Favorite Male Performer in a New Television Program. In 1989, a Golden Globe Award for Best Actor followed. Perlman was voted Best Actor in a Quality Drama by the Viewers for Quality Television. He was honored by the Hollywood Women's Press Club with their 48th Annual Golden Apple Award as Male Discovery of the Year in 1988.

Since "Beauty and the Beast," Perlman has also appeared in the telefilm "A Stoning in Fulham County." He resides in Los Angeles with his wife, fashion designer Opal Stone, and their daughter Blake Amanda. After having received attention as Vincent, Perlman feels as if his career is actually beginning. "If things go the way they should, I see myself ending up as perhaps the next antihero—like Jack Nicholson. . . . That will be the ultimate experiment—to see if anyone is interested in my face."

Bernadette Peters

"I 've done it all. I'm doing it all—except circus acrobatics," says Bernadette Peters, whose childhood acting career has left no visible marks on her porcelain, doll-like beauty. She is at home on stage, screen, television, nightclubs, and recording studios, and wears all five career hats with a distinctive flair.

She was born Bernadette Lazzara in Ozone Park, Queens, in New York City, 28 February 1948; her father, a first generation Italian-American, drove a bread truck. Thanks to her mother, a stage-struck housewife, she was taking tap dancing lessons at the age of three and singing sessions soon after. ("Mom . . . always wanted to become an actress herself. When I was a kid, she fulfilled herself through me.") At five, while attending kindergarten at P.S. 58, Peters made her professional debut as a regular on TV's "Horn and Hardart Children's Hour," and won $800 on "Name That Tune." At nine she joined Actors Equity; at ten she changed her name to Peters, and at eleven appeared in the New York City Center revival of *The Most Happy Fella* (1959). Two years later she won her first major role, as Baby June in a road tour of *Gypsy* (accompanied by her mother). As a teenager she stopped performing ("The words are sticking in my mouth and all I could think about was how I looked"), and she attended Quintano's School for Young Professionals in Manhattan. "I used to get home from high school in time for the 4:30 movie, and I got to see all those great old pictures. I developed a real love for Ruby Keeler and Rita Hayworth and Mary Martin. . . . I have a photographic mind, and I remember exactly how they were sometimes when I sing." In 1967 she appeared off Broadway in *Curley McDimple*, a musical parody of Shirley Temple movies, the next year on Broadway in *George M* and later that year (1968) off-Broadway again in *Dames at Sea*. (*New York Times* critic Walter Kerr was captivated by Peters, whom he found "especially interesting in relation to her feet: she dances as if they'd stuck to her and she were frantically trying to get rid of them.") Other Broadway appearances include a musical production of *La Strada*, a revival of *On the Town*, *Mack & Mabel* (1974), *Sally and Marsha* (1982) at the Manhattan Theatre Club (*New York Post's* critic Clive Barnes rhapsodized: "Miss Peters has become a virtuoso actress with flying saucer eyes, a sincerity as tangible as her nose, and a transparent inner range for feeling made all the more poignant by her manic doll-like exterior"), and Stephen Sondheim's Pulitzer Prizewinning *Sunday in the Park with George* (1984) ("I've never worked with anyone I like working with more than Bernadette," said Sondheim in *Life*. "She tells you exactly what's on her mind.") Other professionals agree on her directness, efficiency, and competence. She returned to Broadway again in 1985 as the star of Andrew Lloyd Webber's *Song & Dance*, for which she received the Tony Award. In 1987 she played the witch in another Sondheim show, *Into the Woods*.

Her movies include *The Longest Yard* (1974), Mel Brooks' *Silent Movie* (1976), *The Jerk* (1979), the innovative *Pennies From Heaven* with Steve Martin (1981), *Tulips* (1981), *Heartbeeps* (1981), *Annie* (1982), *Slaves of New York* (1989) and *Pink Cadillac* (1989). Peters' many appearances on television were climaxed with her own series in 1976, a Norman Lear sitcom, "All's Fair" in which she co-starred with Richard Crenna. She also appeared on the 1990 Tony Awards show. She's recorded two albums, *Bernadette Peters* (1980) and *Now Playing* (1981). Peters tours with her nightclub act and in 1980 received the first annual "Best of Las Vegas" Award. "It's very good practice to sing the same songs and get just as involved in them every time; it feeds my craft".

Regis Philbin

Regis Philbin, co-star of "Live with Regis and Kathie Lee" (the ABC morning show which went national in 1988) traveled a long hard road until he finally found "his" show.

Born in New York on August 25th and raised in a strict Catholic family, he made quite a leap to turn towards show business. He caught "the bug" in 1958 during a stint as an NBC page on Steve Allen's "Tonight" program. It was this particular form of entertainment (talk show host) that appealed to him, so he packed his bags and did whatever he could (he was a stage hand, a truck driver) until he eventually landed a job in San Diego as a news broadcaster and talk show emcee. His first big break came in 1964 when he caught the eye of comedian Joey Bishop, who had his own talk show. Regis was hired and played a marvelous second fiddle to Bishop's dry and depressed sense of humor. Their relationship was grand. "Regis Philbin is like a son to me. He's one of the nicest persons I've ever met," said Joey of his announcer. The show eventually failed and in 1981, NBC gave him a shot at his own show, but this one did not succeed.

His new format with Kathie Lee Gifford, however, provides just the right chemistry. Jeff Jarvis, critic of *People* magazine, describes his unique ability to play with people and not offend them. "He may seem like a game show host with no prizes. . . . Sure he's pleasant and charming but don't hold that against him. He's also witty, if harmlessly so. He can insult guests and get away with it. He can talk about mundane frustrations in his own life . . . and not put us back to sleep." This is an art which very few can master. Accordingly, he is very popular with his fans.

Occasionally, you can see him appearing with his present wife, Joy, (he was first married to Catherine Faylen, a former TV actress, and has two children from this marriage) when Kathie Lee is on vacation. He is wonderfully irascible, describing his daily exasperations at life in the Big Apple. Everyone knows he has two more teenage daughters that drive him batty and that he doesn't own a car, but prefers to rent "clunkers." Why buy a car when these rentals provide him with such marvelous material for his show? He is a fine craftsman, for he makes his work appear effortless, the sign of a true professional.

Lou Diamond Phillips

Initially thought of as the "kid who got a lucky break," Lou Diamond Phillips has proven himself to be an actor worthy of impressive roles. Born 17 February 1962 in Arlington, Texas, Phillips developed a yearning to act in the sixth grade. Carrying his interest through his school years he studied the dramatic arts while attending the University of Texas. Displaying an insatiable appetite to learn and perfect his craft, Phillips studied film technique vigorously with Adam Rourke. Having appeared in numerous theater productions, among them *Whose Life Is It Anyway?*, *P.S. Your Cat Is Dead*, and *Hamlet*, Phillips moved into television with spots on CBS-TV's "Dallas", NBC'S "Miami Vice" and an NBC Movie of the Week "Time Bomb." Although experienced and somewhat recognized, Phillips was basically unknown until that fateful day when he was cast in the role of Richie Valens in the Columbia feature *La Bamba* (1987). The film, which Lou is deeply indebted to and proud of, propelled him into the throes of stardom. Since his "lucky break,"

Phillips has starred in the Warner Brothers feature *Stand and Deliver*. ("Miami Vice" co-star Edward James Olmos suggested the young Phillips after having been impressed with his work on "Vice") and Twentieth Century's *Young Guns* (1988) with Emilio Estevez and Kiefer Sutherland. He joined them for the sequel, *Young Guns II*, released in 1990. Although he has launched a successful and popular film career, Lou still manages to find time to engage in television production. He appeared in the ABC-TV movie "The Three Kings" (1989) in which he portrayed an insane asylum inmate whose delusions of grandeur, after being involved in a Christmas play, lead him to believe he is one of the three wisemen. With his workaholic film schedule, Lou has completed two more feature films: Universal's *Renegades* (again placing him side by side with Kiefer Sutherland) and Disney's *The Bank Job.* He plays a villain in the 1990 feature film *A Show of Force*, which also stars Amy Irving and Robert Duvall.

"Although I consider myself an actor," says Lou, "my other interests excite me too. Writing, directing, producing and teaching all help me to be a better actor." Already having guest-lectured at the prestigious American Film Institute, Phillips hopes to be able to reach more aspiring thespians by committing himself to open an extension of the Film Actors Lab in Los Angeles.

Many may embark on an acting career for money or fame, but for Lou Diamond Phillips acting is something spiritual. "It gives me the opportunity to say things about love, courage, and conviction that I feel need to be said. We in the film industry have an obligation: people should leave a movie having learned something about themselves, about others, and about life."

Lou lives in Hollywood Hills with his actress wife Julie Cypher.

Joe Piscopo

W hether he's Frank Sinatra leading a band of heavy metal rockers, or Joan Rivers sporting a five o'clock shadow, Joe Piscopo is a multifaceted entertainer who's always "on target." The talented Piscopo was born to a Passaic, New Jersey, couple on 17 June 1951. Raised in Essex County, the middle child of his family, he led a happy childhood playing little league baseball and catching the waves at Bruce Springsteen's beloved Jersey Shore. Not particularly swayed by homework, Piscopo was somewhat rebellious during his high school tenure. Caught smoking and cutting classes, he was suspended from school on at least eight occasions. However, it was during high school that Joe discovered he had a home on the stage. Performing in high school productions not only whetted his appetite for the performing arts but also earned him the honor of being a recipient of the Lincoln Center Student Arts award. Being limited in his choices of which college to attend, Piscopo made his decision based on what any young student would consider the essential factor—better surf! With surfboard under arm he headed south to Jones College in Jacksonville, Florida where he majored in broadcast management. To better prepare himself for what he does best, he chose community theater and worked at the school's four radio sta-

tions. Graduation led him back to New Jersey where he found employment at a radio station in Trenton, and continued his participation in community theater. Ripe with experience at twenty-five, he decided it was time to give acting his undivided attention. Between 1976 and 1980 he had the fortune of being cast in commercials endorsing a wide range of products from automobiles to soft drinks. During these years he also conceived a stand-up routine which he performed at some of the most notorious comedy clubs in New York. It was in 1980 when he achieved his "big break." Joining the cast of NBC's "Saturday Night Live" he remained with the program until the 1983 season.

The show was Piscopo's vehicle in evolving new characters such as the "Sports Guy," Solomon and Pudge, and spoofs on David Letterman, David Hartman and Joan Rivers. Says Piscopo as an alumnus of the late night comedy show, "it was up to me to create a lot of the original characters for the show. I'll always be indebted to 'Saturday Night Live' because it taught me so much." His departure from "Saturday Night Live" introduced him to the world of feature films. Portraying Danny Vermin in the 20th Century Fox gangster spoof *Johnny Dangerously* with Michael Keaton in 1984, he later co-starred with Danny DeVito and Captain Lou Albano in Brian DePalma's *Wise Guys* in 1985. His new-found film career did not, however, take him away from television. On 22 September 1984, Piscopo starred in an HBO cable special. The sixty-minute program was a great project for his "ultimate tribute to my hero" Frank Sinatra. May, 1986, brought another Piscopo special this time airing on ABC-TV titled the "Joe Piscopo New Jersey Special." In late 1986 the two-time ACE award recipient added to his repertoire of characters "Python Piscopo," "Bruce Piscopo" (his Springsteen spoof) and "Rappin Fats Piscopo," characters that he developed for his Miller Lite Beer endorsements. In 1987 he returned to HBO with the special "The Joe Piscopo Halloween Party" and garnered a role in the feature film *Dead Heat*. In addition to on-camera activities, Piscopo penned a book, *The Joe Piscopo Tapes* with co-author Pam Norris. Having released a single "The Honeymooner's Rap" with Eddie Murphy, plus an album on Columbia Records—*New Jersey*—Piscopo has added recording artist to his already impressive resume. Bodybuilding is also a part of his life.

Piscopo and his wife Nancy were divorced in 1988 after 15 years of marriage. He is attentive to his young son Joey; he was named Father of the Year by the National Father's Day Committee in 1983.

Suzanne Pleshette

"**I** don't sit back and wait for great parts. I love being an actress, and I'll probably be one until I'm 72, standing around the back lot doing 'Gunsmokes'." The throaty-voiced, sultry actress, credited by some as having the most riveting hazel eyes this side of Elizabeth Taylor, has enjoyed a versatile career in film, stage, and television. She is perhaps best recognized as Emily Hartley, subdued wife of mild-mannered Bob Hartley on the popular sitcom, "The Bob Newhart Show," which ran from 1972 until 1978. A followup series, 1983's "The Suzanne Pleshette Show," failed to make the grade. Neither did her most recent series, "Nightingales" (1989). When Newhart's subsequent sitcom aired its farewell show in 1990, Pleshette returned for a cameo reprise of her Emily Hartley character, in what some regard as TV's finest parting shot.

The only child of a ballerina and a theatre manager, Pleshette, born 31 January 1937 in Brooklyn, New York, was weaned on show business through exposure to her father's colorful friends in the entertainment industry. After graduating from the High School of Performing Arts and studying at the Neighborhood Playhouse, she appeared in a production of *A Streetcar Named Desire* with Peter Falk and debuted on Broadway in the drama, *Compulsion*. Jerry Lewis enticed her to Hollywood to co-star in his film, *The Geisha Boy*. Some thirty other film roles followed, including *A Rage to Live* and *If It's Tuesday This Must Be Belgium*. Audiences remember her as the love-spurned school teacher who got pecked to death in Alfred Hitchcock's 1963 thriller, *The Birds*. Recent TV appearances include CBS's

"Bridges to Cross" and "Command in Hell." In 1990 she began filming the TV movie "Queen of Mean," portraying hotel mogul Leona Helmsley.

Pleshette, who acknowledges that she is "hopelessly middle class" in her values, was divorced after an early marriage to actor Troy Donahue. She married businessman Tom Gallagher in 1968.

Amanda Plummer

"The only other actress I've ever seen make a debut this weirdly lyrical was Katharine Hepburn," wrote Pauline Kael about Amanda Plummer's performance in her first film, *Cattle Annie and Little Britches* in 1980. For her later Tony award winning performance in Broadway's *Agnes of God*, *New York Times* critic Frank Rich practically elevated her to sainthood: "as close to an angel as we're ever likely to see on Broadway." She is not the conventional ingenue, nor is she at all glamorous. Slightly built, with a long slender neck, she has large expressive eyes, short dark hair, and a thin wide mouth. Jack Kroll of *Newsweek* says: "There's an air of suspense about Plummer's acting; you sense that she's creating her character and herself at the same time." Another observer notes: "Even when she is still, she can make her immobility the most eloquent thing onstage."

She was born on Bank Street in New York City's Greenwich Village in 1957, the child of two star performers and strong personalities, Christopher Plummer ("My father—wow—I love him. I adore him. But I don't really know him . . . he's the privatest man I know in the world"), and Tammy Grimes ("It wasn't easy being her daughter, she was travelling all the time. . . . I saw very little of her. . . . When I was older I began to miss her. . . . We've talked about it. We understand"). An only child, she became a one-parent child at the age of 4 when her parents broke up (her father lived abroad for thirteen years). "I was terribly relieved," says her father, "I didn't want to have anything to do with the upbringing of a child. . . . Children are not of great interest to me until they form their own personalities in their teenage years." When Amanda was 18, having led a fantasy childhood ("I made up different characters: some were boys, some were girls, some were animals. Going into these characters freed me. I could do anything"), she told her mother she wanted to be an actress. ("She said fine. . . . It was our coming together.") After two and a half years at Middlebury College in Vermont, she studied at the Neighborhood Playhouse, and then joined the Williamstown Theater Festival's second company. In 1979, she made her New York theatre debut in *Artichoke* at the Manhattan Theater Club. In 1980, she appeared with her mother in a Roundabout production of Turgenev's *A Month in the Country* (for which she had auditioned without knowing her mother had the lead). She made her Broadway debut as Jo in the 1981 revival of *A Taste of Honey* (Tony nomination) and won the Tony for best supporting actress of 1982 for *Agnes of God*. In 1983, she was Laura Wingfield to Jessica Tandy's Amanda in the Broadway revival of Tennessee Williams' *The Glass Menagerie.* In 1985 she appeared in Sam Shepard's *A Lie of the Mind,* and in 1987 *Pygmalion.* Her other films include *The World According to Garp, Hotel New Hampshire, Daniel, Riders to the Sea* and *Drugstore Cowboy.* She also made the NBC television pilot "Truck One" in 1989. She appears in a recurring role on TV's "L.A. Law." "Life and the stage are not separate," philosophized Plummer, "Those two hours are not separate from your night and day. The people you're working with are flesh and blood, and there's always danger involved. It's exciting."

Christopher Plummer

In America he's considered an English actor, in England he is looked upon as an American actor. Born in Canada, 13 December 1927 in Toronto, he is active on both sides of the Atlantic, with a reputation for testy independence, for doing roles he enjoys rather than those that promote his career. If he is not an international movie star, it is by his choice. "My position in films is more difficult because I do both theatre and films. . . . I've chosen a much harder path, trying to keep my position in both. Perhaps I'm a renaissance man," he has said. "I'm bored with questions about acting. There's more to life than acting. Talking about acting is murder for the artist. Most actors I know are sophisticated, charming, informed people who, contrary to popular opinion, know a good deal about other things. You don't have to sweat about it."

Plummer's first important role was as D'Arcy in a high school production of *Pride and Prejudice.* He turned pro at 17 and in the following five years appeared in over 75 plays in both French and English, ranging from Shakespeare to Tennessee Williams. Hailed by critic Brooks Atkinson at age 26 as, "a Shakespearean actor of first rank," he has played the works of the Bard in London, New York and all three Stratfords: Avon, Ontario and Connecticut. He has also starred on Broadway in Archibald MacLeish's verse play, *J.B.*, Christopher Fry's *The Dark is Light Enough* (with the late Katharine Cornell), *The Lark, The Royal Hunt of the Sun, Arturo Ui,* E.L. Doctorow's *Drinks Before Dinner,* as Iago to James Earl Jones's *Othello,* and *Macbeth.* His most popular film role was that of Captain von Trapp in 1965's *The Sound of Music.* Recent films include *Dragnet 1987* (1987), *Souvenir* (1987) and *Deadly Surveillance* (1989). A winner of many prestigious theatrical awards, Plummer made another notable contribution to theatre history via his daughter from his first marriage to Tammy Grimes, Amanda Plummer. Divorced from Grimes, he is married to Elaine Taylor, with whom he resides in Connecticut.

Sidney Poitier

At 18 he saw an ad in a Negro paper saying, "Actors Wanted." "I didn't know it was any different from 'Dishwashers Wanted' or 'Porters Wanted,'" he recalled, "So I walked into this little theatre place in Harlem and I said to the man there, 'I want one of your actor jobs.' The man put me on a stool and had me read a part. I'd read about four lines in my West Indian accent when he stopped me. 'Now, look, boy,' he said, 'You can't even talk. Why don't you get a job as a porter?'"

His Bahamian patois long behind him, the actor from Cat Island has proven himself an actor many times over in such films as *The Blackboard Jungle, In the Heat of the Night, A Raisin in the Sun* (also on Broadway), *Guess Who's Coming to Dinner* and *Lilies of the Field,* which in 1963 provided him with the vehicle to become the first black actor ever awarded an Oscar. In 1972 he passed muster as a director (as well as co-starring with Harry Belefonte) in *Buck and the Preacher.* He also directed 1990's *Ghost Dad.*

Raised on his father's tomato farm in the Bahamas, Poitier was born in Miami (20 February 1924), when his parents took a trip there to sell their produce. He had only a year and a half of formal schooling during what one reporter described as "a growing-up absurd that makes the usual theatrical hard luck story sound like a blithe bedtime fable." Odd-jobbing, he returned to Miami as a teenager and, brazenly defying the color line, worked his way up to New York where, sleeping on rooftops in the summer and in public toilets in the winter, he met the casting director of the American Negro Theater. He had his first taste of success on Broadway in *Anna Lucasta* in 1948 and within a decade had become the first Black matinee idol. He has been married twice and has six daughters. He published his autobiography in 1980 and since then has continued to direct and appear in the movies: *China Blues, Traces, Shootout, Fast Forward, Hard Knox, Little Nikita* and *Shoot to Kill*. In 1989 he was honored by the American Museum of Moving Image.

Roman Polanski

Life and its capacity for paradox still stalks this haunted cinema artist who created such macabre spine-tinglers as *Knife in the Water* (1962), commercial Hollywood vehicles such as *Rosemary's Baby* (1968), and *Chinatown* (1974), as well as the romantic epic *Tess* (1979). The Polish-born director was the toast of Tinseltown before 1969 when Charles Manson directed a demented band of drug-bent disciples to break into Polanski's L.A. home where they butchered his wife, Sharon Tate, 26, and three other friends. What police found—Tate, who was nine months pregnant, had been indiscriminately slashed as she and the others fought for their lives, and an X had been cut on her stomach—so traumatized Polanski, who was in London at the time, that for five grief-stricken days he couldn't walk without assistance. Ironically, he says, both public and the press seemed to deduce that the victims and Polanski had been involved in drugs, illicit sex, and satanic rites that had brought on the murders. Later, the director's own deeds led to his own demise—residentially at least—in the U.S. After his widely publicized affair with then 15-year-old actress Nastassja Kinski in Europe, he was convicted in California in 1977 of bedding a 13-year-old girl at Jack Nicholson's pad. Having already spent a month-and-a-half in

Chino prison and facing a longer term, Polanski fled before sentencing to France where he can't be extradited. "I know in my heart of hearts," he says, "that the spirit of laughter has deserted me. It isn't just that success has left me jaded or that I've been soured by tragedy and by my own follies. (But) I seem to be toiling to no discernible purpose."

The little man (five-feet-four) whose fictionalized screen nightmares have been nothing as compared to his life, was born in Paris, 18 August 1933. Polanski is the son of a Jewish mother who died in a concentration camp, and a father who survived one. Roman became a member of the Polish Crakow theater troupe at the age of 14 ("The stage was just, for me, one way to get to films"), and later studied film directing at the world-renowned National Film Academy at Lodz in 1954. His first wife was Polish film actress Barbara Kwiatkowska, and he met and married actress Sharon Tate when he directed her in his film *The Vampire Killers* (1966). Polanski wrote *Roman*, his autobiographical tome, in 1984. In 1985 he directed *Pirates*, and in 1987 wrote the screenplay and directed *Frantic*. Rumors flew in 1990 that he contemplated a joint project with Michael Douglas.

Stefanie Powers

A sophisticated beauty with a breezy and painlessly seductive air, she was raised by Hollywood in the style to which she always seemed accustomed. Stefanie Powers, born in Hollywood on 2 November 1942, grew up with the likes of Natalie Wood and Jill St. John, taking ballet, going to the movies, and plotting her invasion of the high studio walls that loom so large throughout Los Angeles. She slipped through once at age 15 by lying about her age to snare a bit part in *West Side Story*, but she was discovered and trounced out. After graduation from Hollywood High she commanded small, and soon larger roles in television series until she was cast in her first lead with the mid-1960s adventure entry, "The Girl from U.N.C.L.E." A spinoff from the popular "The Man from U.N.C.L.E.," expectations ran high, but the show fizzled in the ratings and the "Girl" in question found herself back at casting calls. Top billing generally eluded her until old pal Robert Wagner suggested she play his wife in the 1979 romantic-action show, "Hart to Hart." The slick and entertaining vehicle about two fabulously rich and gloriously well-wed people who find love at home and murder at every cocktail party, was a ratings hit for most of its five-year run. Many feminists praised Power's character, Jennifer Hart, as a positive role model for women. Ms. Hart was equal to her husband, smart, brave, and kind *in addition* to being fabulously rich and gloriously well-wed. The show's demise has allowed its beautiful star to do more made-for-TV movies and such mini-series as Judith Krantz' "Mistral's Daughter." She starred in 1985 in the film *The Second Lady* and in the 1986 CBS-TV show "Maggie." Ultra-fit Powers shared her prowess in the 1985 book *Stefanie Powers Superlife* and her 1989 video *Stefanie Powers: Introduction to Horseback Riding and Horse Care.*

But for the actress herself, life has been a bit more trying. Her lengthy and bitter estrangement from her father, noted photographer M.B. Paul, has received considerable—and unwanted—publicity. "The reason I don't talk about growing up is that I have a lot of unresolved conflicts and anger." An early marriage to Gary Lockwood ended in divorce, and her relationship with longtime companion William Holden ended tragically with the actor's alcohol-related accidental death. Powers maintains an active involvement in wildlife preservation, which she developed during her extensive travels with Holden.

Priscilla Presley

She has successfully balanced her life as a wife, mother, business woman, and actress. She has done everything from modeling, to designing clothing, to owning a boutique that catered to celebrities, not to mention marrying one of the most infamous, loved and remembered celebrities of all time. She was born Priscilla Beaulieu, on 24 May 1945 in Brooklyn, New York, the daughter of an Air Force officer. Although born in New York, and raised in Connecticut, she traveled extensively throughout the U.S. and Europe due to the nature of her father's profession. She attended high school in Weisbaden, Germany, which is also where she had her first experience in professional modeling. Later she moved to Memphis to pursue her modeling career, which is where she met her future husband, the legendary king of rock and roll, Elvis Presley. They wed on 1 May 1967 in Las Vegas, and a year later the couple had their first, and only child together, Lisa Marie, on 1 February 1968. Five years later, in 1973, Priscilla and Elvis divorced.

Deciding to go into business, Priscilla and her personal dress designer opened up a boutique that carried their exclusive designs, and catered to such stars as Cher, Barbra Streisand, and Natalie Wood. She later sold out to her partner. From there, she went to television, making her debut in 1979 in ABC's "Those Amazing Animals." She also began appearing in prime time commercials, endorsing Wella Balsam hair products nationally. Other television credits include hosting "Good Morning America," "Night of 100 Stars II," the nighttime soap series "Dallas," and the televison special "Life with Elvis." Moving on to film, she made her debut in motion pictures with *Comeback*, followed by *The Naked Gun* (1988). In addition to being a celebrity of TV and film, Priscilla is also a writer, and wrote a novel entitled *Elvis and Me* (1984). In 1986, she moved in with Brazilian Marco Garibaldi. A year later on 1 March 1987, Priscilla gave birth to their son Navarone Anthony Garibaldi. In her spare time Priscilla enjoys practicing the ancient art of karate and overseeing the growth of Graceland as a successful tourist attraction.

Vincent Price

"I sometimes feel that I'm impersonating the dark unconscious of the whole human race," he says of his wily and villainous roles in such memorable horror films as *The Masque of the Red Death* and *House of Wax*. "I know this sounds sick but I love it." And the versatile Vincent is equally enamoured of his role as a cultural connoisseur. For Sears Roebuck's Vincent Price Collection, he personally bought over 10,000 pictures, ranging from Rembrandt to the drawings of a talented 13-year-old. ("My taste has become, over

the years, more and more catholic. I've been through so many phases and fads that I've come out at the other end liking almost everything.")

Born 27 May 1911 in St. Louis and educated at Yale (B.A. 1933) and the University of London, Price was for years mistakenly labeled an Englishman because of his cultivated diction. He did spend some time in London during his early acting days, but after appearing as Prince Albert in a West End production of *Victoria Regina*, he returned to America in 1935 to make his debut in the same role opposite Helen Hayes, followed by such hits as *Outward Bound* (1939) and the chilling *Angel Street* (1941). He made his movie debut in 1937. Formerly married to actress Edith Barrett (one son), and costume designer Mary Grant (one daughter), he is currently wed to actress Coral Browne. He started collecting art when he was 12 years old and, on a 50 cents a week allowance, bought a Rembrandt etching for $34.50 on the installment plan. Now his collection is housed in a residence that has become a mecca for Hollywood tours. His book *I Like What I Know* tells the story, as he puts it, of "what I've seen in my life, not what I've done." He has continued to do voice-over work (*I Go Pogo, The Monster Club:* 1980) but it was his V/O work on the phenomenally successful "Thriller" (1983, sung by Michael Jackson) that won due (multiple Grammys) acclaim. He has served as host for the syndicated PBS series "Mystery" and his latest list of films include *Dead Heat* (1987), *The Offspring* (1987), *Whales of August* (1987), *Backtrack* (1988) and *Blood Bath at the House of Death* (1988).

Prince

He is a gifted musician, who, by writing and arranging and playing most all the instruments himself on his albums, has been compared to Little Richard, Jimi Hendrix and mostly Stevie Wonder. He's succeeded at fusing the 69 flavors of soul, gospel, rock, funk and punk into one sweet cone, and the most popular buzz about the busy bee is his keynote position vis-à-vis the high voltage issue of androgyny among rock stars, and particularly Prince's ambisexual eroticism. In "Controversy" he sings: "Am I white or black/Am I straight or gay/Was I what you wanted me to be?" His songs, according to *New York Times* writer Michiko Kakutani, "preach a kind of sexual evangelism—redemption achieved through erotic release." He is rhapsodic when he sings about fellatio ("Head") or incest ("Sister") or masturbation or nuclear holocaust in "1999" ("If I gotta die/I'm going to listen to/My body tonight. . . . Everybody's got a bomb/We could all die any day/But before I'll let that happen/I'll dance my life away.") He appears in garb that swings from raunch to dandy-*riche*, anything from just a pair of genital-hugging silk bikini briefs and high-heeled boots to brocaded velvet "Little Boy Blue" suits (usually in purple, his favorite shade). With his ebony curls and "I-remember-Sid-Vicious-pout" he's like a cross between a shadow in an X-rated movie house and Rita Moreno in *West Side Story*, appealing to his fans as a welcome release from societally-imposed repressive attitudes towards race, gender and sexual preference.

Born 7 June 1962 to a black jazz musician father and Mediterranean mother, in Minneapolis, Minnesota, his 1984 super-hit *Purple Rain*—film and soundtrack—made mythical his own alienated childhood. His parents split up when he was seven and in his early teens, perhaps haunted by his father's failed-musician image, he turned to music as a safe escape from the pressures of his father versus his mother and step-father. He moved into a friend's basement and formed his first band, and taught himself to play over 20 instruments. "My brain was free of everything. I didn't have anything to worry about. I knew it was okay to explore whatever I wanted down there in the basement because things weren't forbidden anymore. That's when I realized that music could express what you were feeling it started coming out in my songs—loneliness and poverty and sex." After graduating from high school at 17 he went to New York to try the music scene there. Three companies offered him recording contracts, but none offered him complete control. He returned to Minneapolis and shortly thereafter was given a contract in excess of $1 million by Warner Brothers which granted him complete control in the studio. *For You*, his first album debuted in 1978, followed by *Dirty Mind, Controversy, 1999, Purple Rain, Under The Cherry Moon, Sign O' The Times* (from movie of the same name), and *Lovesexy*. His hit single from *Purple Rain*, "When the Doves Cry," rivalled Michael Jackson's top seller "Billie Jean." One reviewer has said that to their adoring masses, "Jackson was like Peter Pan and Prince was like the seductive Pied Piper." In 1989, Prince performed the uneven beated theme from the film *Batman*. He reprised his movie role as "The Kid" in *Purple Rain* for the 1990 movie *Graffiti Bridge*, which he also directed.

Richard Pryor

In 1980 while he was preparing "freebase," a highly inflammable mixture of cocaine and ether, he accidentally set himself on fire, and received third degree burns over half his body. He was not expected to survive. The "accident" did not lack a

metaphor. Richard Pryor was, before his accident, an explosive comedian, controversial and ferociously satirical. Some faulted him for mellowing after the accident, others applauded his maturity. "People call me up and say, 'You're not like you used to be.' I say to them, 'That's right but do you know what I was really like then? Do you know what kind of insanity I was into, with drugs and liquor?' I'm not going to do that again. I'm going to be nice to myself. I don't have the same desire to succeed anymore. I don't have that push, push, push I used to have. I think I had it until I burned up. After that it didn't seem to make much sense."

Born 1 December 1940 in Peoria, Illinois, Pryor says facetiously, "We were affluent—had the biggest whorehouse in the neighborhood. My grandmother, she was the madam." He grew up there and also in his grandfather's billiard parlor, a background well represented in his night club act peopled with pimps, winos, junkies and the like. All this a far cry from his debut role at the age of 12 in a Peoria community center production of *Rumpelstiltskin*. After dropping out of school at age 14, Pryor worked a slew of menial jobs and, after spending two years overseas with the Army in Germany, began his performing career in Peoria's Harold's Club. Inspired by the success of Bill Cosby, he moved to New York in 1963, and soon became a regular at all the comedy clubs. Then, via an appearance in 1966 on the "Ed Sullivan Show," he became a national celebrity and began appearing on many other televison shows and soon had his own Las Vegas show. For his sixth film part, playing the Piano Man opposite Diana Ross in the 1972 *Lady Sings the Blues,* he received an Oscar nomination. Next came the comedy classic *Blazing Saddles* which he co-wrote with Mel Brooks and which earned him an American Writers Guild Award. Other screen comedies were *Car Wash, Silver Streak,* and *California Suite.* Pryor's most popular hits were scored after recuperating from his accident when he threw himself frantically back into his film work. "I had to make certain amounts of money to pay some bills, so I went to work fast. Also, I guess, I worked so hard because I wanted to prove I was all right." These hits include *Stir Crazy, Bustin' Loose, Superman III, Some Kind of a Hero, Richard Pryor Live on the Sunset Strip, JoJo Dancer, Your Life is Calling, Critical Condition, Moving, See No Evil, Hear No Evil* and *Harlem Nights.* "Things are real good for me," he says, but adds with realistic consideration, "but if I walk out on the street to try to get a taxi in New York, they go right by me. They think I'm going to Harlem and they ain't taking me. So what's changed?"

Married and divorced five times, Pryor has several children. In 1987 he had another son with actress Geraldine Mason. He lives in Beverly Hills.

Keshia Knight Pulliam

Learning to read lines is not an easy feat for any actor, but it's even harder when you haven't yet learned to read. Cute little five-year-old Keshia not only learned her lines for her role as Rudy, the youngest child in the Huxtable family on the NBC hit sitcom "The Bill Cosby Show," she also earned a reputation on the set for rarely flubbing her lines. Now after several years on the show, Keshia's ability to learn quickly is more than evident. Her TV father, Cosby, says "We are taking the baby out of her character and asking for more maturity." Winner of the 1988 People's Choice Award for Best Young TV Performer, the adorable Keshia has become adept at trading quips with Cosby during the show's tapings. One of her favorite things to do is to steal the microphone and the limelight from her TV dad and to tell jokes to the audience.

Born 9 April 1979 in Newark, New Jersey, Keshia has been in show business almost all of her life. At eight months of age she appeared in her first print ad for baby powder followed by numerous print ads and TV commercials. In 1984, at age 5, Keshia landed the role of Rudy. Her parents, James and Denise Pulliam, took turns teaching Keshia her lines and helping her memorize them. Since then, Keshia has starred in such TV specials as "Back to Next Saturday" (NBC), "Andy Williams and NBC Kids Search for Santa," "NBC's 60th Anniversary Celebration" and in the title role in "The Little Match Girl" (1988). Keshia also appeared in "Night of 100 Stars II," "Motown Returns to the Apollo," several segments of "Sesame Street," and in the feature film *The Last Dragon*.

Although thoroughly enjoying her budding acting career, the pixie has other plans for her adult life. Wanting to be a doctor, the little heartbreaker and showstopper says, "I want to be able to help all people and make them feel good."

Dennis Quaid

H ollywood-comer Dennis Quaid, who played astronaut Gordon Cooper in *The Right Stuff*, a space pilot from Earth in Wolfgang Petersen's *Enemy Mine*, an incorrigible, hell-raising ex-navy pilot in *Innerspace*, and a law enforcer in *The Big Easy*, topped his career in 1989 by playing Jerry Lee Lewis in *Great Balls of Fire*. Commended for his high energy performance, Quaid portrays the rock 'n' roll great who sang such hits as "Whole Lotta Shakin' Goin' On," and "Breathless." The movie, which was filmed mainly in Memphis, with some filming in Arkansas, Mississippi and London as well, gave Quaid the opportunity to expand his acting capabilities and project a man whose life was filled with turmoil and tragedy.

Dennis Quaid was born on 9 April 1954 in Houston, Texas. Although he initially wanted to be a musician, he discovered acting while in high school and was inspired to perfect his craft by his older brother, Randy, now a well-established figure on movie screens and the stage. Dennis's first major break in films came a year to the day after his arrival in Hollywood, when director Jim Bridges signed him for a role in the film about the death of James Dean, *9/30/55*. Dennis first captured wide notice from both critics and fans playing a rebellious young Indianian in Peter Yates's 1979 coming-of-age picture, *Breaking Away*. In his next role, Walter Hills's saga of the James Brothers, *The Long Riders*, he co-starred not only with his own brother Randy but with two additional sets of acting brothers, David, Keith and Robert Carradine and James and Stacy Keach. Also on his list of Hollywood credits are *Crazy Mama, Our Winning Season, Gorp, Dreamscape, Suspect* (opposite Cher), *D.O.A.*, and *Everybody's All American*. His 1990 film, *Come See the Paradise*, explores the internment of Japanese-Americans during World War II. On television, viewers may remember him in NBC's Emmy-winning Movie of the Week, "Bill," co-starring Mickey Rooney. He also received glowing reviews for his strong dramatic appearances in both the Off-Broadway and L.A. Stage Company's productions of

Sam Shepard's play, *True West*. His steady date is actress Meg Ryan, whom he planned to wed in September, 1990.

Anthony Quinn

"I *am* Zorba," says this versatile actor *cum* artist whose zest for life parallels that of his favorite character. The once dark-haired, high-cheek-boned, vaguely sinister-looking Quinn—actually Irish and Mexican—declared of the second time he played Zorba on Broadway in 1984, "Before I had to paint my hair white. Now I'm just right." And while theatre audiences agree, it was not always so easy. Quinn tells of arriving in Hollywood "in the era of the golden boys" when the only parts he got was playing Indians. Since that time he has played a Mexican revolutionary in *Viva Zapata!* (for which he won an Academy Award), Paul Gauguin in *Lust for Life* (another Oscar), a Russian Pope, the *Hunchback of Notre Dame*, a prize-fighter (*Requiem for a Heavyweight*), an Arab (*Lawrence of Arabia*), an Italian strongman (*La Strada*), and a Greek in *The Guns of Navarone* and *Zorba*. "To me," he once said, "acting . . . [is] living. I love to live, so I live. I love to act, so I act. I gotta have vitality." The actor hasn't been short of his ambition. His latest films include *Stradivarius* (1988), *Revenge* (1989), *Ghosts Can't Do It* (1989), and *A Man of Passion* (1989). On the television screen, he's starred in ABC's "Richest Man in the World: Story of Onassis" (1988) and Hemingway's "The Old Man and the Sea" (1989).

Born "in a hail of bullets" 21 April 1915 in Chihuahua, the son of a Mexican mother and an Irish-American soldier of fortune fighting in the bloody revolution then in progress, he was smuggled out of the country "hidden in a wagon under a pile of coal. . . . I nearly choked to death." He went to work in Los Angeles at the age of five ("The truant officer caught me"), later toiled as a cement mixer, dress cutter, amateur boxer, and fruit picker. He did some little-theater parts, formed an acting company at 15 "solely so I could have access to the wardrobe department, because I had no clothes," made his professional stage debut in a Mae West clinker called *Clean Beds*, bummed around the country "with my Bible, pajamas and play notices," and at 21 returned to Hollywood, "It was *horrible* breaking into pictures," he recalls. "It's a miracle that any of us survive." Quinn held on long enough to screen-test for Cecil B. De Mille, who approved him as an actor but not, when he married daughter Katherine De Mille after a brief courtship, as a son-in-law. "I think," Quinn explained, "he kind of thought I was an Indian from some reservation and was always terrified that the tribe would gather around his house some night for a war dance." Quinn's tribe came to include four children by Miss De Mille (a fifth drowned in W.C. Field's pool at the age of three), from whom he was divorced after nearly three decades of marriage.

In 1966 he wed Iolanda Addolori, an Italian teacher turned wardrobe girl (on the *La Strada* set), who had borne him two sons prior to their marriage and was carrying the third at the time of their wedding. They live in a villa near Rome, where Quinn first met Iolanda while making *Barabbas*. On a health regimen, he jogs and swims, and most days he paints and sculpts, often working on several pieces at once. "I'm like a guy playing a horn," he once said. "There's a note I hear inside me but I can't play it yet. Some day I'm going to hit that note."

Robert Rafelson

Robert Rafelson is considered a skillful filmmaker who approaches his work with an intense emotional commitment both to detail and the ideas he conveys to his movie audiences. He's been the subject of some controversy in Hollywood; it is said that Rafelson was fired from *Brubaker* after throwing a chair at a Twentieth Century-Fox exec who was pleading with Rafelson for commercial concessions and an accelerated shooting pace. After exhaustive hours of research (two years of scouting dangerous locations in Panama, which resulted in the deaths of two guides assisting him) for Peter Matthiessen's *At Play in the Fields of the Lord*, the project was shelved. Recently Rafelson directed and co-wrote the screenplay for *Mountains of the Moon* (1989) which followed his *Black Widow* (1986) and the remake of James M. Cain's classic novel *The Postman Always Rings Twice* (which was generally not favored by the critics). The mood on Rafelson's sets is often emotionally charged, sometimes almost violent. Says associate producer (*Postman*) Michael Barlow, "Bob recapitulates the emotion of the scene. The mood on the set is the same as the scene. He sucks everybody into the moment. . . . He goes for the highs."

Born in New York City in 1934, Rafelson as a teenager was riding in rodeos and breaking horses (and his back) in Arizona. At 17 he shipped out on a liner to and from Europe. At 18 he played in a jazz combo in Acapulco "faking the drums and bass and hitting up rich tourists for drinks and place to sleep." In fact, he says, "One night I woke up aboard a huge schooner and wound up crewing on a mad expedition to Panama." During this period he studied philosophy at Dartmouth College where he became especially interested in existentialism. Rafelson considers Sartre to be "his guiding light." Ultimately, he found his way into television and film. His first TV work was on "Play of the Week," for which he wrote 34 adaptations. Films include *Head* (based on the Monkees), 1968; *Five Easy Pieces*, 1970; *The King of Marvin Gardens*, 1972, and *Stay Hungry*, 1976. In 1990 he directed the epic *Mountains of the Moon*. He also directed Lionel Richie's famed 1984 video "All Night Long."

Deborah Raffin

"There are a lot of nice people in this business, but there are also people who are insecure and so wrapped up in themselves that they aren't anxious to help someone who is just starting out." Raffin was lucky to have had the generous support of Liv Ullmann in the budding stages of her career (Ullmann played her mother in Raffin's first movie, *Forty Carats*) and Milton Katselas (director of same) as well. Since then she has starred in *The Dove* and *Once Is Not Enough*, taking a hiatus after the latter to do theatre exclusively, honing her craft in the process. ("I wasn't happy with the direction my career was taking. I knew I had a great deal to learn about acting, and things were happening too quickly. I was nineteen when I made *Forty Carats*.") She worked her way up to playing Ophelia in *Hamlet* with the National Theatre in England, then returned to Hollywood to star in the ABC-TV movie "Nightmare in Badham County" (1977) which won her an Emmy nomination. A slew of films followed: *Touched By Love* (which she made in China and which became quite popular there) and the made-for-TV

"Haywire," "The Last Convertible," "Running Out" and "Dance of the Dwarfs" all in the early 1980s. Other TV starrers include "Lace II" (1985), a made-for-TV movie based on the life and lucrative loves of a Mayflower Madame-type called "Dinner Date," and the NBC miniseries of James Clavell's "Noble House." She appeared with Charles Bronson in 1986's *Death Wish III*.

Born in L.A., 13 March 1954, Raffin started studying drama at 15. At 30 she felt things were finally clicking into place. ("I'm very happy to be thirty because I think the roles are more interesting.") Asked to define some of the terms by which the public defines actors and actresses she says, "Starlet' is a term which is often used, but I don't like the image it conveys. I always associate the term with some empty-headed, sort of fuzzy little girl who wants to be famous more than she wants to create excellent films. I think it's sad when people aspire to be 'stars' when they should aspire to be actors and actresses." Raffin lives with her husband, producer/manager Michael Viner, and five dogs in homes in Beverly Hills and Vermont. Together with her husband they formed Dove, Inc.—a books-on-tape concept utilizing celebrities to read books aloud to the public. In 1989, Deborah released her own book *The Presence of Christmas*.

Tony Randall

"**C**omedy's a serious business," says this rich and busy master of it. "You've got to be true and funny, and not look as though you're trying. You have to feel funny inside." In 1970, TV's "Odd Couple" premiered, with Randall doing his schtick as Felix, the ash-tray emptying, pillow-fluffing, obsessive-compulsive half of a very funny duo, but his theatrical background includes such straight characterizations as Marchbanks in Shaw's *Candida* and as the stuttering brother in *The Barretts of Wimpole Street*. It's still his dream to go back to the classics. "No one is really more suited to certain roles in Chekhov, Shaw or Shakespeare," he says modestly. "Benedick in *Much Ado*, for example."

Born on 26 February 1920 in Tulsa, young Anthony Randall left the oil capital "as soon as it was humanly possible" and was refining himself as an actor under the guidance of acting coach Sanford Meisner by the time he was 19. After the war and several Broadway flops, he was cast as Harvey Weskit on the *Mr. Peepers* TV show in 1952, and amid guffaws shot to national prominence. Randall has since made numerous movie appearances, starred in the Broadway musical *Oh Captain* and toured as the Mencken-like reporter in *Inherit the Wind*. He starred in "Love Sidney" which premiered on TV in the early 1980s. In 1988 he starred in *Two Into One* at the Paper Mill Playhouse.

Bachelor though he is in "The Odd Couple," he is happily married to Florence Gibbs (his childhood sweetheart). He collects records, antiques, and paintings. "I love classical music with the same passion with which I despise rock and roll," he declares. Reflecting his passion for opera, he has served as a regular on Texaco's "Opera Quiz" and as intermission commentator on TV's "Live From Lincoln Center." A man of many opinions, Randall says, "There's only one thing worse than a man who doesn't have strong likes and dislikes and that's a man who has strong likes and dislikes without the courage to voice them."

Sally Jessy Raphael

"I'm trying to reach one person. There isn't a crowd out there. There's just one other human being and we're trying to figure out life together," says Sally Jessy Raphael, host of her own talk show which is now rated as the Number 3 daytime syndicated TV show in the U.S. The "Sally Jessy Raphael Show" started broadcasting over KSDK in St. Louis in 1983 each weekday. However, because of the overwhelming response, the show became syndicated only six months later. Now the petite blond with the expressive eyes, partially hidden behind those big red eyeglass frames that have become her trademark, can be seen in over 130 cities in the U.S., as well as in Canada and England. This 1989 Emmy award winner for Outstanding Talk Show Host also has the distinction of being the first nationally syndicated female TV talk show host. With an approach that's been described as "like a friendly neighbor over for coffee. Homey advice for women," Raphael focuses on what interests her viewers, choosing almost 75% of the show's topics from viewer mail and phone calls. Because of her strong belief in follow-up, Raphael also offers some of her guests post-show additional guidance and return visits to the show so the guests can share their progress with the audience. Taping her TV show isn't enough to keep the energetic broadcaster busy. Raphael has also broadcast her live three-hour radio show, NBC-TALKNET, from Manhattan each weekday evening since 1982. Between her daytime TV show and her nighttime radio show, this remarkable dynamo logs 18 hours on-air time; that's more than any other broadcaster. Even with this schedule Raphael found time to write a book, *Finding Love: Practical Advice for Men and Women* (1984), and she is planning its sequel, *Keeping Love*. When asked about the success that has earned her the 1985 Bronze Medal from the International Film and Television Festival of New York, Raphael responds, "I'm a plodder, a very slow builder, who has had a chance to grow."

Born on 25 February 1943 in Easton, Pennsylvania, Sally Jessy grew up in Westchester County and in Puerto Rico where her father had a rum exporting business. It was during one her stays in Puerto Rico that Jessy started using her mother's maiden name, Raphael, since "down there everyone has three names." She attended Carnegie Mellon in Pittsburgh and the University of Puerto Rico before obtaining her BFA from Columbia in New York City. Getting into the broadcasting business early, Sally hosted "Junior High News" on WFAS radio in White Plains, New York, Her career had its ups and downs with Raphael holding numerous jobs including rock-and-roll disc jockey, TV news anchor with WPIX-TV in New York, host of a cooking show in Puerto Rico (on WAPA-TV from 1965-1967), news correspondent with the Associated Press in the Caribbean, TV anchor and host of a radio interview show in Miami (1969-1974). As sideliners, Raphael was a part-time owner of a perfume factory (1964-1968), an owner of an art gallery (1964-1969), and an owner of "The Wine Press," a wine bar in New York City (1979-1983). After being fired from 18 jobs and spending almost 20 years of her career in Mexico, Paris and Aruba, Raphael stabilized her broadcasting career in 1976 when she took the job as anchor on WMCA-radio in New York, staying until 1981. The next year, Raphael began to host NBC-radio's "Talknet." The following year, in 1983, she began hosting her own show in St. Louis. But life was hectic as Raphael commuted from her New York home, husband, children and animals to St. Louis for four years. It wasn't until June 1987 that the show's production was moved to WTNH-TV in New Haven, CT. and then to New York City in 1989, in order to make life a little easier for Raphael.

Residing in a house in the woods in upstate New York with her second husband, Karl Soderlund (who was a local station manager in Puerto Rico when Raphael met and married him in 1963), 8 children (2 from her first marriage—Allison and Andrea; 2 of Karl's;

Robby—their adopted son; and 3 foster children) and an assortment of dogs, cats, a snake and a bird, the untiring Raphael spends her spare time dabbling in her hobby—Japanese dolls—and writing another book—this time on broadcast yarns—while running a bed-and-breakfast business.

Phylicia Rashad

She is a beautiful, intelligent, versatile, multi-talented actress and singer. Phylicia Rashad has been seen on the successful weekly series "The Cosby Show," as well as on Broadway in the starring role of *Into the Woods.*

She was born Phylicia Ayers-Allen in Houston, Texas. Born into a creative and talented family, it only seems natural that she follow in their footsteps. Her sister is actress/singer/dancer, Debbie Allen; her mother, Vivian Ayers, is a poet and scholar, whose first published works *Spice of Dawns*, earned her a nomination for the Pulitzer Prize; and her brother, Tex Allen, is an accomplished jazz musician. Phylicia began her acting studies while still in elementary school. Her musical training began at age 5, when her mother taught her to read music and play the piano. While in elementary school, she performed in assemblies and in amateur operettas. In high school she joined the Merry-Go-Round Theatre, which was a training program for talented children sponsored by Houston's Alley Theatre. After graduating from high school, Phylicia attended Howard University, where she majored in theatre and graduated magna cum laude. Her professional theatre debut came while she was still at Howard, appearing in the production of *Sons and Fathers of Sons* presented by the Negro Ensemble Company. Other NEC productions include *Weep Not for Me, In an Upstate Motel*, and *Zoo Man and the Sign.* After graduating from college, she moved to New York and appeared in *To Be Young, Gifted and Black.* Even though she didn't have an agent at the time, she managed to have fairly steady work, filling the employment gaps with temporary typing jobs. Soon after moving to New York, she got her first big break by being cast in the ensemble in the Broadway production of *The Wiz.* She was with the show for three years, and played a variety of roles including a Munchkin, Fieldmouse, and an Emerald City swing dancer. Other Broadway performances include *Ain't Supposed to Die a Natural Death* and *Dreamgirls.* Phylicia made her television debut in a series of national commercials, but made her dramatic debut on the daytime soap "One Life to Live." She has also been seen on the small screen on the CBS series "Delvecchio," the PBS program "Watch Your Mouth," and on several Bob Hope specials. In 1987 she made her TV film debut in *Uncle Tom's Cabin.* But it was her role as Clair Huxtable on the "Cosby Show" that brought her real recognition and fame. She credits her real life experience as a mother rather than her acting for landing the role. "There's a certain rhythm to motherhood," states Phylicia, "an understanding that's unspoken, but it's felt; it's just there." She also explains, "I was always somebody's mother, and I couldn't understand why that kept happening. Then I realized that I was often acting out a scene on stage that I had played for real in my living room. I guess the truth of that just came through." In addition to theatre, Broadway and television, she also has a musical side to her. She has headlined in Atlantic City, the Concord Hotel, and with the Dallas Symphony. In 1988, she returned to Broadway for the first time in four years to take on the lead role of Grindl the Good Witch in the musical *Into the Woods.* She can also be seen in the 1990 TV movie "Jailbirds."

Phylicia and her husband Ahmad Rashad married in 1986, after his on-air proposal during a Thanksgiving Day football broadcast for which he was the commentator. The couple have a daughter, Condola Phylea, and Phylicia has a son William Bowles from a previous marriage, while Ahmad has three children from a previous marriage. The Rashads reside in New York.

Robert Redford

*N*ewsweek writer David Ansen concluded his 1984 profile "American Adonis" with the following anecdote the actor told about himself; it took place when he was nineteen: "It is New Year's Eve in Rome, and the young art student Redford is staying in a youth hostel and feeling lonely and in need of revelry. He makes a reservation at Bricktop's for midnight, but first stops in at the American bar next door. More and more depressed as he sits drinking alone in the back of the room, he's suddenly aware of a commotion at the door. In walks Ava Gardner with five Italian escorts. She seems the most gorgeous creature Redford has ever seen, and he builds up the drunken resolve: Come midnight, he's going to walk over and kiss her. Twelve o'clock strikes, Redford stands up and 'all courage went out of me like steam from a valve. I could hardly walk. I got all the way to her table and lost everything. Nerve, courage, memory, vocabulary. I just stood there like a dope in front of her.' The escorts looked alarmed, sensing trouble. He stands there paralyzed. And Ava Gardner looks up at the nineteen-year-old Redford and says, 'Happy New Year, soldier.' And then reaches up, grabs his hand, pulls him down and kisses the poor boy on the lips. . . . It was his fate, even then, to be *Robert Redford*."

Being the king of American dreamboats is a mixed blessing for the actor. Born in Santa Monica, California, 18 August 1937, the son of a milkman who later became a Standard Oil accountant, he attended the University of Colorado on a baseball scholarship, although in his earlier years he preferred having a sentimental education to a formal one. ("I never learned as much in the class-room as I did staring out a window and imagining things.") His mother died his freshman year, and he spent most of his time coping by drinking or skiing; his "dark side" (both parents were of Scottish-Irish descent) as he calls it, surfacing and alienating him from his peers. He dropped out and went to Europe to study painting. ("I had a sidewalk showing of my paintings in Florence. Made $200. Enough to return to New York.") Thinking first that he would become an art director, he instead found his way into classes at the American Academy of Dramatic Arts. In 1959, he got his first acting job, a small part in *Tall Story* on Broadway. Roles in major New York television dramas followed and he made his first film, the low-budgeted *War Hunt*. Redford made his name on Broadway, first in *Sunday in New York*, and then (directed by Mike Nichols) in *Barefoot in the Park*. His success in the latter sent him to Hollywood where he worked non-stop in *Inside Daisy Clover*, *The Chase* and *This Property is Condemned*. Teamed with Jane Fonda in the film version of *Barefoot in the Park* he achieved soon-to-be-a-star recognition. His films include: *Butch Cassidy and the Sundance Kid*; *Downhill Racer*; *Little Fauss, Big Halsey*; *Jeremiah Johnson* (his personal favorite); *The Way We Were*; *The Sting*; *The Great Gatsby*; *Three Days of the Condor*; *All The President's Men*; *A Bridge Too Far*, *The Natural*, *Out of Africa* and *Legal Eagles*. He won an Oscar for directing 1980's *Ordinary People*, his directorial debut. In 1986 he directed *The Milagro Beanfield War*. A political and environmental activist, he is the owner of the Sundance Resort in Utah, the founder of the prestigious Sundance Institute for independent filmmaking and the funding source of the environmental Institute Resource Management.

Describing Redford as a mature screen star, Ansen writes, "It's as if he has arrived at the face that he had intended all along: a little wary, a little haunted, a gorgeous battlefield that can be suddenly transformed by the legendary flash of pearly white—into pure sunlight. . . . He is the master of the close-up. A slight squint of the eye, a sideways movement of the jaw tells all: his features are like microchips, carrying a startling load of information." Redford says that acting requires that one "live your character. It's like skiing. You can't be thinking too much. When you get on the hill, your skis are doing the work. You'd better just hang on. Acting is a bit the same way. You've got to behave as the character. A lot of what acting is is paying attention." Separated from his wife, Lola, they have three children.

Lynn Redgrave

She's the formerly "plump duckling" of Britain's famous theatrical family of swans. But having been Oscar- and Tony-nominated, she's proven herself worthy of the Redgrave mantle. Born in London on 8 March 1943, Lynn Redgrave almost bucked three previous generations of tradition be planning to become an equestrienne or a cook. But Sir Michael, her distinguished actor dad (who died in 1985), won the day (and shaped a career) when he persuaded her to dump gourmet cooking at Polytechnic College and enter the Central School of Speech and Drama. "Being so big," Lynn recalls, "I frequently played male roles. I was a late developer, and at 18, I looked like a giant 12-year-old." But in 1966, four years after taking up the art as livelihood, she snared the klutzy title role in the hit movie, *Georgy Girl*. "Looking up at my horrible, ugly bulk on that huge screen was the turning point of my life," she says now, and she shed pounds to become a svelte five-foot-ten, 138-pound swan herself. The Academy Award-nominated performance led to Broadway, Hollywood, and TV roles, and curiously, game show appearances. Despite her almost-hallowed background, Redgrave had no compunctions against pitching her latest play amidst the inanities of "Hollywood Squares" of "The $20,000 Pyramid." The strategy helped her pack 'em in when she toured places like Tallahassee and Skowhegan, and strengthened her conviction to "not be boxed into any category of any sort." To prove her unsnobbish approach to show biz, she hosted a so-called "pseudo-serious syndicated chat show" for a couple of years, did a TV sitcom, "House Calls," for a couple more, and in 1984 was starring on "Weight Watcher's Magazine," the cable TV show of that organization. Currently, she stars in their "This is living" commercials.

Her reputation as a substantial actress, however, was earned in Shakespearean plays for the National Theatre Company of Great Britain, in Broadway plays including *California Suite,* in films, among them *Everything You Have Always Wanted to Know About Sex* (1972) and in the miniseries *Centennial* on the tube. She co-starred with sister Vanessa in a TV remake of "What Ever Happened to Baby Jane?" for the 1990-91 season. Unlike her politically active thespian siblings, Vanessa and Corin, Lynn is a confirmed capitalist. Since 1967 she's been married to British-born producer-director John Clark, who besides being the father of her brood of three—Benjamin, Kelly, and Annabel—was at one time her manager was well as her director in several stage productions. Pleased to have escaped the pitfall of constant type-casting, Michael Redgrave's daughter once observed, "It has reached the point where I am offered most interesting work—far more interesting than I ever was—simply because nobody can say, 'Oh, but she can't do that because she only does this sort of thing.' They can't label me." She co-starred on Broadway in 1985 with Claudette Colbert and Rex Harrison in *Aren't We All* and in 1987 with Mary Tyler Moore in *Sweet Sue.* Her latest films include *Midnight* (1988) and *Getting It Right* (1989) and her book *This Is Living: An Inspirational Guide To Freedom* was published in 1988. She co-starred with Jackie Mason in the TV sitcom "Chicken Soup" for the 1989-90 season.

Vanessa Redgrave

"I give myself to my parts as to a lover," she explains. "It's the only way." Italian film director Michelangelo Antonioni thought so too, and requested that she strip to the waist in 1966 for her role in the eerie *Blow-Up.* She cut an elegant, aristocratic and daring figure, and some said the cause-oriented Vanessa had practically offered to "walk stark naked down Piccadilly for Antonioni," though she denies it.

The crown princess of a transatlantic show business royal family, Vanessa is the eldest child (born 30 January 1937 in London) of a family steeped in theatrical tradition.

Younger sister Lynn is an accomplished actress (*Georgy Girl, Getting It Right* and the television series "Chicken Soup"); brother Corin is also an actor. And of course, the patriarch of this renowned,

talented pack is Sir Michael Redgrave, the late great actor known to pose for family portraits in costume and who once said of his first-born: "She'll never be an actress, so we're having her do languages. That way she can always get a job with an airline or something." Naturally, as Vanessa's reputation grew, Sir Michael accommodated: "She's mad," he said, "I mean, divinely mad . . . an inspired actress." "Mod Goddess," and American magazine trumpeted. "A rainwashed daffodil in a fire-green Sussex meadow . . . Eleanor of Aquitaine in a miniskirt."

Vanessa launched her career after graduating from the Central School of Speech and Drama in 1958, making her debut performance in London in N.C. Hunter's *A Touch of the Sun,* as the daughter of the schoolmaster played by her father. In 1959 she joined the Stratford-upon-Avon Theatre Company, working in productions directed by the illustrious likes of Tony Richardson, Sir Tyrone Guthrie and Sir Peter Hall. She continued impressively in classics at the Royal Shakespeare Company. Gracefully moving into a film career, her performances included the startling *Isadora* (Duncan), under the direction of Karel Reisz, *A Suitable Case* (for which she won the Best Actress Award at the Cannes Film Festival, 1965), *Camelot, The Trojan Women,* Ken Russell's *The Devil, Mary Queen of Scots, Yanks* and *Julia,* for which she won an Academy Award as Best Supporting Actress in 1977. She's also starred in *Second Serve, Steaming, Consuming Passions* and *Prick Up Your Ears* (received Best Supporting Actress Award from NY Film Critics in 1988), as well as appeared on television in "Playing for Time" (receiving an Emmy Award as Best Actress), in the Shelly Duvall Faerie Tale Theatre production of "Snow White and the Seven Dwarfs" (as the Wicked Queen), in 1985 in "Three Sovereigns for Sarah," a three-part dramatization of the Salem witch trials for PBS's "American Playhouse" series and in 1986 a nine-hour miniseries, "Peter the Great." She co-starred with sister Lynn in a TV remake of "What Ever Happened to Baby Jane?" for the 1990-91 season. In 1985, she appeared in the film *Wetherby* with daughter Joely and on stage in London in *The Sea Gull* with daughter Natasha. Her recent theatre productions include *A Touch of the Poet* in London and *Orpheus Descending* on Broadway.

A controversial individual in both her personal and political lives, Vanessa admits, "I have a tremendous use for passionate statement." She has supported a variety of causes including pacifism and ban-the-bomb, in addition to the Palestine Liberation Organization. This association led to a 1984 lawsuit with Vanessa filing a complaint against the Boston Symphony Orchestra for cancelling her performance as narrator of *Oedipus Rex* for what she called "political reasons" and in violation of her civil rights. (A Federal jury awarded her $100,000 in damages for breach of contract, but rejected her claim about the BSO's motives.) In the process of issuing passionate statements, Vanessa herself has been arrested four times. But in the mother country they say it has all come about because she is an incurable romantic. "It's a kinky part of my nature—to meddle," she says. Divorced from director Tony Richardson in 1967, she has daughters Joely and Natasha from that marriage. In 1969 Vanessa gave birth to Carlo Gabriel, son of Franco Nero, her Lancelot in *Camelot*. Her latest lover is the new 007, Timothy Dalton.

Rex Reed

"I have never set out to destroy anybody," he has said. "If I see somebody is basically a s.o.b., but underneath is real, then I say they're a nice s.o.b. But if some jackass picks his nose, I'm going to write it." Rex Reed is a film critic, raconteur, and sometime actor. (Films: *Myra Breckenridge, Inchon, Superman, Irreconcilable Differences;* legit: *Rope;* books: *Do You Sleep in the Nude, Conversations in the Raw, Big Screen, Little Screen, People Are Crazy Here, Valentines and Vitriol, Personal Effects.*) Many of his critics feel he is a "master of the celebrity interview." "The old broads are the ones who interest me most," admits Reed. "Nothing bores me more than these . . . girls with nothing on their minds. . . . For years people didn't know celebrities went to the bathroom. . . . The public won't settle for pap any more. . . . It wants its copy bitchy." His style of film reviewing gets a lot of flack from fellow reviewers and writers. He currently is a syndicated film critic for the *New York Post* and the star of the TV show "At the Movies."

Born in Fort Worth, Texas, 2 October 1939, the son of a Texas oil company supervisor, he spent his formative years in the South traveling from oil boom to oil boom (13 schools, straight As, a degree in journalism from LSU). As a boy Reed was awe-struck by

Hollywood. "From what I saw on the movie screen I knew that people were living a better life than we did in the South. I wanted to live like them; to eat wonderful food and go to plays and walk through Madison Avenue at midnight. I didn't want just to trudge along dusty country roads and eat fried chicken." He dabbled in acting and jazz singing before he broke into print in 1965 with a brace of unsolicited interviews (Jean Paul Belmondo, Buster Keaton) in the *New York Times* and the late Herald Tribune's *New York* magazine. In a review of one of Reed's collections, *New York Times's* Richard R. Lingeman concluded: "Mr. Reed is the rhinestone cowboy of journalism. If he's a bit world-weary now, he's still the small-town kid from Louisiana dazzled by marquees. Deep inside his subconscious there's an old radio still playing 'Grand Central Station,' 'Mr. First Nighter,' and Jimmy Fiddler. As long as there's a Rex Reed, there'll always be a Broadway—and a Hollywood."

Christopher Reeve

The Adonis-built actor brought Superman alive on the big screen for a new generation of hero seekers. With wavy brown hair, sculpted features, and hulky virility, he was cartoon-perfect for the coveted role as The Man of Steel. However, he was far from the producers' first choice. In fact, over 200 other actors were considered—including the producer's wife's dentist—before they settled on Reeve, an extraordinarily handsome but little-known actor. His humanizing, lighthearted interpretation of the role was largely credited for making the 1978 *Superman* and its 1980, 1983 and 1987 sequels huge box office hits. "I wanted to show a character who's warm, who isn't aloof, who cares, a hero secure enough to have a sense of humor," he said. *Superman: The New Movie* was scheduled for 1991 release.

Born 25 September 1952 in Manhattan, the son of a writer and an English professor who divorced when he was young, Reeve saw the theatre as a haven from turmoil and growing pains. "If you look at pictures of me when I was a kid I never cracked a smile. Really grim. Acting was a way to help me loosen up, expose myself, relax, and I think I've made some progress. But I also think it takes twenty years to make an actor. I'm halfway there." His reverence for acting as a fine craft has kept him dedicated to talent-stretching roles in sometimes risky vehicles and away from lucrative, hero type-casting parts he could command.

Reeve began his theatrical career in summer theatres and continued to study acting in college until his Cornell University education was interrupted by a two-year stint on the soap opera, "Love of Live." His Broadway stage debut in 1976 in *A Matter of Gravity*, which starred Katharine Hepburn, received mixed reviews. He fared better with the critics as the embittered paraplegic casualty of the Vietnam War in Lanford Wilson's *Fifth of July* in 1980 and on the London stage in 1984 with Wendy Hiller and Vanessa Redgrave in *The Aspern Papers*. Other films include Ira Levins' *Deathtrap* and *Monsignor* (1982), *The Bostonians* (1984), *Street Smart* and *Switching Channels* (1987). In 1985 he played Vronsky in a television version of "Anna Karenina" opposite Jacqueline Bisset and in 1988 starred in the NBC telefilm "The Great Escape." He helped present the Tony awards in 1990. A critic of the institution of marriage (stemming no doubt from early memories of marital discord between his parents) he lived with Gae Exton (two children: Matthew and Alexandra). The couple separated in 1987. He appeared on stage again in 1989 for the NY Public Theatre production of *The Winter's Tale*.

Tim Reid

Mediocrity is a state which holds no place in the world of handsome actor Tim Reid. His drive for perfection manifests itself in his versatility. Track athlete, stand-up comedian, businessman and anti-drug activist compose the essence of the masterful Reid.

While Reid has managed to accomplish much in his life, his beginnings were humble. He was born in Norfolk, Virginia, on 19 December 1944. His family was poor, the lack of money forcing them to live a somewhat nomadic life ("We did a lot of moving, especially around the time rent was due"). Tim settled down from his wandering days at the age of nine when he was sent to live with his grandmother. The move delighted Tim, but during Tim's teen years he fell prey to a normal stage of rebellion, doing poorly in school and running around with the wrong crowd. His father (living in Chesa-peake, Virginia) decided to send for his son and detour him from the path of destruction. Although meager in financial resources, Tim's life was affluent in love. The love and devotion displayed by his father placed Tim on the correct path of life. No longer under the influence of the "bad crowd" Tim did a turn-around—a star on the high school track team, vice president of the student council and an editor on the high school yearbook staff. It was these early experi-ences that led Tim to adopt the belief: "That old cliché about all a child needs is love is true." Upon graduating high school, Tim decided to join the Air Force. Enroute to the recruitment office, he stopped through ritzy Virginia Beach and placed the Air Force idea on hold while taking a job as a waiter in a swanky seasonal restaurant. The money he earned while waiting tables enabled him to enroll in the all-black Norfolk State College. Although a business marketing major, Reid also studied drama during his college tenure. He auditioned for a major role in the college's production of *Oedipus Rex*, landed the role and was bit by the acting bug.

During his years in marketing Tim hooked up with an insur-ance agent, Tom Dreesen. Similar in their anti-drug beliefs, Reid and Dreesen decided to do their part to deter drug use with an anti-drug presentation geared towards grade-school kids. Imbued with a comedic nature, they began catching on like wild fire. "Tim and Tom" began making headway—they once followed Stevie Wonder, appeared on David Frost and Merv Griffin. In 1975 "Tim and Tom" decided they had come to the end of their alliance and Reid went solo. He toured with Della Reese as her opening act. It was not long afterwards that Tim moved into television. He started with a recur-ring role on a CBS replacement series "Easy Does It" and a role on the "Richard Pryor Show." Doing the usual rounds of guest appear-ances on various sitcoms, it was not until he landed a job as a regular on "WKRP" that he became a celebrity. The Supercool DJ "Venus Flytrap" was Reid's ticket to stardom. He remained with "WKRP" for four years. Roles that followed included a CBS-TV movie "You Can't Take It With You," a regular stint on the short-lived "Teachers Only", the role of undercover police lieutenant "Downtown Brown" on "Simon & Simon" followed by his very own CBS series "Frank's Place." His acting career may keep him busy but Reid still finds time to spread the word of drug abstinence. "Stop the Madness' was a music video Tim created and produced in 1986. Reid's anti-drug activities have also taken him to Senate hearings in Washington, D.C., where he has testified before a Senate Subcommittee on Special Investigations. A talented writer, Reid has penned televi-sion scripts and, as an avid amateur photographer, he has compiled a book of his poetry (illustrated by his photographs) titled *As I Feel It*.

Probably the most important and precious role in his life is that of husband to actress Daphne Maxwell Reid whom he wed on 4 December 1982. They have three children: Tim Jr., daughter Tori (from Tim's first marriage) and Christopher (from Daphne's first marriage). The Reids live in Encino, California, where Tim can be found dabbling in his herb and vegetable garden.

Carl Reiner

"The comedian will flourish as long as the world stays complicated and cockeyed," says this actor-reconteur - writer - producer - director who's been called a veritable "conglomerate of comedy." Launching his TV career in the late 1940s as second banana to Sid Caesar and Imogene Coca on the landmark laugh series, "Your Show of Shows," he's gone on to conceive and write the long-running (1961-1966) sitcom, "The Dick Van Dyke Show," and to appear in and/or direct and/or write an impressive succession of big screen comedy offerings. The record albums he created with Mel Brooks (as the 2000-year-old man) stand as comedy classics.

Born on 20 March 1922, Reiner grew up in an Italian-Jewish section of the Bronx and was attracted to laugh-getting as a means of self-defense. "I was what I call a charming coward," he told TV columnist Kay Gardella. "It was one of those neighborhoods where if you fought back you had to be good. So to get attention I'd turn to comedy. I'm more and more convinced that *all* comedians are charming cowards." Reiner turned to performing after studies at the WPA Dramatic Workshop (the launching pad for countless fine talents during the Depression) and, during World War II, toured the South Pacific with Major Maurice Evans's Special Services Unit, which entertained servicemen. Appropriately, Reiner's first major postwar effort was in a road company production of the back-to-civvies musical, *Call Me Mister*. His nine years on "Your Show of Shows" served as what he now calls his "writing college," laying the groundwork for all his future TV and film work. Among his screen acting credits: *It's a Mad, Mad, Mad, Mad World* (1963), *The*

Russians Are Coming (1966). He made his directorial debut in 1967 with *Enter Laughing,* the movie version of his own play of that title based on his early acting experiences. Subsequent directing efforts include *The Comic* (1968), *Where's Poppa?* (1970), and three Steve Martin comedies: *The Jerk* (1979), *Dead Men Don't Wear Plaid* (the ingenious 1982 spoof of 1940s thrillers), and *All of Me* (1984). His recent works include *Summer Rental* (1985), *Summer School* and *Bert Rigby, You're A Fool* (1988).

Married in 1943 to the former Estelle (Stella) Lobost, Reiner is the father of three children, Rob, Sylvia Ann and Lucas. Rob, following in his dad's Merry Andrew footsteps, achieved TV immortality of a sort playing the indomitable Meathead on "All in the Family," and has several praiseworthy directorial film credits.

Rob Reiner

He is a multi-talented actor, writer, director, and producer. In addition to appearing on television, in films and on stage, he has written for several comics, directed numerous hit films and is part-owner of Castle Rock Entertainment.

Rob Reiner was born on 6 March 1945 in New York City, the son of actor/director Carl Reiner. He attended UCLA, and he began his showbiz career by acting with regional theatres and improv troupes. Starting out writing scripts, he wrote for such shows as "Halls of Anger" (1970), "Where's Poppa?" (1970), "Summertree" (1971), the summer series "The Super" (1972), "Fire Sale" (1977) and "The Smothers Brothers Comedy Hour." His big break came when he appeared as a guest star on a comedy show for which he was the story editor. This appearance led to his role as Michael "Meathead" Stivic on the long-running hit comedy series "All in the Family," which ran from 1971-1978 and earned Rob two Emmy Awards. Other television appearances include "Free Country" (1978), "The Beverly Hillbillies" (for which he also received an Emmy), "Thursday's Game" (1974) and "More Than Friends" (1978). Although he was successful in front of the camera, his real goal was to be behind it, directing and producing. The first film to be directed by Rob was the rockumentary *This Is Spinal Tap* (1984), which received widespread acclaim and established him as a filmmaker with a unique talent. He has directed several other films since then, such as *The Sure Thing* (1985), *Stand By Me* (1986), *The Princess Bride* (1987), and *When Harry Met Sally* (1989).

Rob and actress Penny Marshall were married in April 1971 and divorced ten years later. He is currently married to Michele Singer (married May, 1989), and the couple reside in California.

Lee Remick

"Television is making the movies that Hollywood made during the 1940s and 50s," observed Lee Remick while making the 1982 TV version of Somerset Maugham's *The Letter.* Since 1975 she has plucked and pitted some of the small-screen plums: "Jennie, Lady Randolph Churchill" (Best Actress Award by the British Society of Film and TV Arts), "Torn Between Two Lovers," "Haywire," and the miniseries, "Wheels," "Ike," "Mistral's Daughter," "The Gift of Love: A Christmas Story," "Lena: My Hundred Children," and

"Jesse." ("The pace is a lot quicker than feature films," says Remick). The sultry blonde with the begging-blue eyes knows whereof she speaks: she twirled her way onto the big movie screen in 1956 as the sexy drum majorette in Elia Kazan's *A Face in the Crowd* and has been cheered on ever since. Other taunt-and-tease movie performances of that decade include *The Long Hot Summer*, *Anatomy of a Murder*, and *Wild River*. Since 1960 she has sizzled, snapped, seduced and has been seduced in such movies as *Sanctuary*, *Experiment in Terror*, *Days of Wine and Roses*, *The Wheeler Dealers*, *No Way to Treat a Lady*, *The Detective*, *Hard Contract*, *Loot*, *Sometimes a Great Notion*, *A Delicate Balance*, *Hennessy*, *The Omen*, *Telefon*, and *The Europeans*. She "wrapped" three movies in five months in 1980—*The Women's Room*, *The Competition*, and *Tribute* (Remick admits the rigorous filming paid for a new house in Brentwood, California, after eleven years in London, but "I wouldn't recommend a schedule like that to anyone"). In 1988 she was seen in *The Vision*.

Born 14 December 1935 in Quincy, Massachusetts, (her father owns Remick's Department Store), she was taken to Manhattan by her divorced mother when she was 7. After attending Miss Hewitt's and Barnard College, Remick made her Broadway debut in *Be Your Age* in 1953 and didn't return until 1964 in Stephen Sondheim's musical *Anyone Can Whistle*. In 1966 she starred in the stage version of *Wait Until Dark*, in 1985 in the concert version of Sondheim's *Follies*, and in 1989 she performed in A.R. Gurney's *Love Letters*.

Divorced in 1969 after eleven years from TV producer-director William Colleran (two children, Kate and Matthew), Remick married English producer William ("Kip") Gowans in 1970. In addition to the Brentwood home, they have a summer place at Cape Cod where they go clamming and sail their 16-foot boat. "I think she's one of the most important actresses working in America today—no, working *anywhere*," says Gowans. "It would be nice to make films for grown-ups again," sighs Remick, "and when they decide to start filming them, I'll start acting in them."

Burt Reynolds

Given his musclebound power to shatter box-office records, it seems likely that this screen idol who hunked his way to stardom overnight in 1972 (in the screen adaptation of James Dickey's *Deliverance* and a nude, living color centerfold in *Cosmopolitan* magazine) will triumph as the hairy chest most likely to prevail in dollar-conscious Hollywood. Reynold's take from *Smokey and the Bandit Part I* was 20 per cent of a gross in excess of 100 million dollars. Add to that similar percentages for other recent flicks like *Smokey and the Bandit Part II*, *Cannonball I & II*, *Paternity*, *Sharky's Machine*, *Best Friends*, *Stick*, *The Bourne Identity*, *Rent-A-Cop*, and *Switching Channels*, and you may have to recharge your calculator.

Early in his career, Reynolds played bit parts on Broadway and in TV series such as "Gunsmoke," "Mod Squad," and "Hawk," then starred in the title role in ABC's "Dan August." He was featured in the ABC "Mystery Movie" "B.L. Stryker" in the late 80's and returned to TV in 1990 with the comedy "Arkansas." His early movies included *100 Rifles, Skullduggery, Fuzz, Shamus, The Man Who Loved Cat Dancing* and Woody Allen's *Everything You Always Wanted To Know About Sex,* in which he played the part of a sperm. With his own special combination of modesty and egocentricity, Johnny Carson wisecracked at a Friar's Club roast of Reynolds: "We are gathered here . . . for one purpose. To watch Burt Reynolds give the finest performance of his career—being humble. Generous. Warm. Loving. Charitable . . . and to become the world's number 1 box office star without possessing any of those qualities is quite an achievement." He credits his stardom to television talk shows. ("They're the best thing that ever happened to me; they changed everything overnight.") The publicity he got by dating Dinah Shore, whom he met while appearing on her daytime show, also helped.

Burt was born 11 February 1936 in Waycross, Georgia, and grew up in Palm Beach, Florida, where his father was the chief of police. He attended Florida State for a brief spell before signing up to play football with the Baltimore Colts, but an automobile accident took him off the tackle line and into acting classes at Palm Beach Junior College. ("I read two words and they gave me a lead.") During an apprenticeship at the Hyde Park Theatre in New York, he met Joanne Woodward, who was instrumental in his early career. She introduced him to her agent who got Reynolds his first stage and TV work. Deciding that he'd never make it as a "talented New York actor," he went to Hollywood. It was slow at first trying to get himself noticed. During one interview, in which he was asked to deliver a dramatic monologue, the phone rang. Reynolds, furious with the interruption, reached over and grabbed the phone, pulling it so hard the wire ripped right out of the wall. "You have to do something to get their attention," he told a friend at the time. Sure enough, the next day he got a call from one of the agents. "That was the most exciting thing I've seen all week," she told Burt.

When he's not making a film, he's supervising the Burt Reynolds Dinner Theatre which he built in Florida in 1979. Divorced from actress Judy Carne, Reynolds tried marriage again in 1988 by taking actress Loni Anderson as his wife. The couple adopted a son, Quinton Anderson, in August of that year. Reynolds' recent pictures include *Breaking In* (1989) and *All Dogs Go To Heaven* (1989, voice-over).

Debbie Reynolds

Once dubbed by Hollywood cynics "the iron butterfly," she floated high for well over a decade on her ball-of-fluff image of apple pie America. Then, proving herself unsubmergible in more ways than one, she rose from the ignominy of being the bride Eddie Fisher traded in for Elizabeth Taylor, to score personal triumphs in *The Unsinkable Molly Brown* (1964), a revival of *Irene* (1973) and *Woman of the Year* (1983) (replacing Lauren Bacall and Raquel Welch, and earning $30,000 a week.)

She was born Mary Francis Reynolds in El Paso, Texas, an April Fool's Day baby of 1932. Her longtime Girl Scout image comes naturally; she earned a total of 48 merit badges during her years in the green uniform. Reynolds' show business career began after the family moved to California, where she won the title of Miss Burbank of 1948 doing an imitation of Betty Hutton. Spotted by a Warner talent scout, she was signed for $65 a week, and her first role was in *The Daughter of Rosie O'Grady*. She then switched to MGM and played Helen Kane, the boop-boop-a-doop girl, in *Three Little Words* (1950). Going the way of the ingenue, she soared ever upward in such films as *Singin' in the Rain* (1952), *Tammy and the Bachelor* (1957) and *The Singing Nun* (1966).

She married Eddie Fisher in 1955 (2 children, Todd and Carrie; Todd is a born-again Christian minister and Carrie an actress in her own right). In 1960 she married shoe tycoon Harry Karl, who lost $15 million of her money as well as his own fortune when his shoe business failed. "I resented it very much," she says recalling that she signed anything he asked her to. When he went bankrupt, she was responsible for another $2 million of his debts. "The banks took everything—the Beverly Hills house, the beach house, all my jewelry and art," she says. Finally out of debt in the early 80s she says, "I'm starting to build my life again. If you have faith—and a sense of humor—you can survive anything." Married in 1984 to Richard Hamlett of Miami Beach, Debbie came out in 1985 with a successful home video of aerobic exercises called "Do It Debbie's Way," followed by another home exercise program "Couples (Do It Debbie's Way)" in 1988. Her tell-all autobiography *Debbie: My Life* was released in October, 1988. Always of interest to the public, Debbie supplied her readers with Hollywood scandals and stories, while providing an insightful look on how that little girl from El Paso became a movie star.

Don Rickles

What can you say about a man who comes onstage and screams, "Hello dummy"? It's funny, but don't tell Sigmund. "I'm the guy who tells off the boss at the office party and still has a job on Monday," brags this king of the show-biz putdown. He says he has a "sixth sense" that keeps him from digging too deep with his verbal jabs at the paying customers. "My style is to rib people I like. If there is anger in it, it isn't funny."

Born 8 May 1926, the only child of a Queens, New York, insurance sales-man ("He was always on the rib. . . . I learned a lot from him."), Rickles broke into show business while still in high school as an entertainment director at a resort in the Catskills. ("I played bingo with the guests . . . if it rained, I was supposed to go out and make it stop.") After Navy service in World War II ("I grew up in the Navy . . . it was better than summer camp") he put together a nightclub act and shot straight to oblivion ("I was cancelled out of a great many places, including the worst strip joint in Boston") before his gently abrasive jibes earned him a reputation as a "comic's comic." A success on the Miami-Vegas-Manhattan nightclub circuit in the late 1950s, Rickles nonetheless "frightened" TV executives, until Johnny Carson gave him his big break on the night of 7 October 1965. Rickles' free-wheeling performance was the next day's "Topic A" of the industry, and prompted nationwide reaction. His next break was the chance to do his bit weekly on the "Dean Martin Show," followed by numerous TV shows and nightclub appearances including "The Don Rickles Show" in 1971 and as a Navy petty officer in "C.P.O. Sharkey" (1976). In 1984 he was co-host of "Foul-Ups, Bleeps & Blunders'—the show that sugarcoats the slip-ups of the stars for the benefit of those who love to watch their favorites flop. Rickles is a major headliner at the Las Vegas Sahara and Riviera Hotels, Resorts International in Atlantic City and Harrah's Clubs in Reno and Lake Tahoe.

His movie appearances include *Kelly's Heroes, Enter Laughing, The Rat Race,* and *Run Silent, Run Deep.*

Rickles' wife Barbara (one daughter, one son), whom he married in 1965 (she was at one time his agent's secretary), and his mother have asked him why he insults people. "It buys you jewels," he told his wife. Insults "got you your beautiful apartment," he told his mother. "You know what they said then?" he asked rhetorically. "'You're right. Insult people.'"

Diana Rigg

She has played an amazing variety of dramatic roles over the years, ranging from James Bond's wife to King Lear's daughter, from a TV crimefighter to Lady Macbeth, from slinky sex objects to nuns. But this leggy Yorkshire beauty (she admits to five feet eight and a half) is best known to Americans as Emma Peel, the karate-chopping widow and cult heroine of TV's stylish 1965-67 spy spoof "The Avengers," which returned in the 1980s as reruns on cable television. She also starred in the 1973 shortlived TV series, "Diana," in which she played a footloose British fashion designer adrift in the garment district. Off the stage or the movie screen, some critics have called her "brutally frank." ("I should say that for the most part, 'brutally frank' is applied to me, but why they say 'brutally' I don't know. I'd say 'frank'" she concedes.) One of Rigg's highly publicized "frank" comments came in 1973 on the "Tonight" Show when she said: "American men are boring companions and bad lovers."

The daughter of a British government official, Rigg was born in Yorkshire, England, on 20 July 1938, and grew up in India. She returned home from India to train at the Royal Academy of Dramatic Art. "I used to look at myself in the mirror when I was thirteen or fourteen and know what I saw wasn't me. It was curious seeing the chrysalis, finding it insufficient and yet knowing that something inside there was going to pop out, was going to be better," she says. The next step in Rigg's career was a short stint as a model, then an apprenticeship with The Chesterfield Repertory Company in the British Midlands, where she earned $17 a week doing a variety of jobs from hunting props to acting. Finally she auditioned for The Royal Shakespeare Company and was admitted in 1959. In 1972, she joined the National Theatre where Laurence Olivier was director.

The actress over the years has appeared on Broadway as a some-times-nude Heloise in *Abelard and Heloise,* and in Molière's *The Misanthrope,* in which she played Celimente, the accommodating but sharp-tongued love of Alceste, a rigidly unaccommodating man. Her latest movies include *Evil Under the Sun* (1982), *The Great Muppet Caper* (1981), *Madame Colette* (1982), *Snow White* (1986) and *A Hazard of Hearts* (1987). Married in 1973 to the Israeli artist Manachem Gueffen (one daughter, Rachel, born in 1977; that marriage ended), she has been, since 1982, the wife of Archibald (Archie) Stirling, a former Scots Guards officer.

Molly Ringwald

This multi-talented star of tele-vision, stage, and screen, is per-haps the most publicized member of the teenage actors who became popular in the mid-1980s.

Molly Ringwald was born in Roseville, California on 18 February 1968, and grew up in a musical environ-ment. Her father, who was blind since childhood, is a pianist who leads the Great Pacific Jazz Band. Molly quickly learned the songs that the band per-formed and would sing along while her father practiced. "I was singing before I can remember, to the cats, to the swings," recalls Molly. By the time she was four, she was appearing regularly with the Great Pacific Jazz Band, singing such old-time favorites as "Oh Daddy," and "I Wanna Be Loved by You." Those songs, along with several others comprised *Molly Sings,* an album she recorded with the band in 1974. When she was five, she was enrolled in singing, dancing, and acting classes, which led to her performance with the local commu-nity theatre in the amateur production of *The Glass Harp.* She made her professional television debut in 1977, as a guest on the "New Mickey Mouse Club," and her professional stage debut in 1978 in the West Coast production of the hit musical *Annie.* A few months later, she was cast in the TV sitcom series "The Facts of Life" (1979), but after just one season, her character was written out of the script. "I was devastated. But my mom kept saying it was for the best, and she was right. I didn't work for a year, which gave me a chance to grow up a lot." One year later, she made her theatrical film debut in Shakespeare's *The Tempest,* followed by *Spacehunter: Adventures in the Forbidden Zone* (1983). It wasn't until her appearance in the very successful *Sixteen Candles* (1984) that her career really began to take off. Soon following, she landed roles in the several other hit movies including *The Breakfast Club* (1985), *Pretty In Pink* (1986), *The Pick-Up Artist* (1988), *For Keeps* (1988), *Fresh Horses* (1989), and *Betsy's Wedding* (1990). Molly has also appeared in the made-for-television movies "Surviving," "Packin' It In," and "P.K. and the Kid."

In her spare time, Molly enjoys shopping in neighborhood malls, listening to rock music, and singing with her father's band. She is single and lives with her parents in the San Fernando Valley in California.

John Ritter

"If I had grown up with just dad, I'd have become a good ol' boy and probably been a trucker. And if I'd been raised by mother, I'd be an interior designer. Between the two, I have a nice balance." John Ritter is the offspring of the white hat star of 78 Westerns and the warbler of various Country-style hits, the late "You Are My Sunshine" Tex Ritter, and Dorothy Fay, now official greeter at Nashville's Grand Ole Opry. Luck on a stick pointed the way for this former Hollywood High Student Council President and lapsed 1960s idealist to find his star as a TV actor. On "Three's Company" he played Jack Tripper, a beguiling Santa Monican who pretends to be homosexual in order to beat the heat from vexed parents and landlords when, due to limited funds, he bunked in with two lady roommates. The sexy situation never got beyond titillation, but it afforded lots of chances for the girls to "flit around in their nighties" while poor Jack struggled to keep his heterosexual plumes from shooting out and ruining the gay facade and losing the lease. The show's theme was altered in 1984. Jack came out from behind the guise and the show was renamed "Three's A Crowd." Not as successful as the original premise, the sitcom was cancelled after one season. Making a quick comeback, Ritter became the star of a new series, "Hooperman". This show propelled his receiving the People's Choice Award for Best Male Performance in a New TV Program in 1988.

Born 17 September 1948 in Burbank, California, Ritter planned on being a psychology major at the University of Southern California but switched to acting after a successful stint at the Edinburgh Festival in Scotland. At age 20 he discovered acting was better than shrinking. His 1990 movie *Problem Child* would seem to unite the two interests at last. Following his college graduation, Ritter did many summer stock productions across the country and made his television debut in a 1971 episode of "Dan August." He went on to appear in numerous TV shows including the semi-regular part of Reverend Matthew Frowick on "The Waltons." "Three's Company" debuted in 1977. His films include 1980's *Hero at Large,* and *Unnatural Causes* (1986). Behind-the-scenes he was the co-executive producer of the ABC-TV comedy "Have Faith" (1989).

Ritter married actress Nancy Morgan in 1977. They live in California with their three children.

Geraldo Rivera

"I 'm not smarter, or better looking than Phil, Oprah, Johnny or David, but am different. . . . These mid-life eyes have witnessed the full range of the human experience: from exhilaration and triumph to the pits of misery and despair. . . . This program will have action, emotion, style, old-fashioned values and contemporary ideas. I want it to be an alternative for people afflicted by game show saturation and the talk show blahs." Geraldo speaks about "Geraldo"—the nationally syndicated daily one-hour talk show (topics include: "Prostitution," "Cross-dressing," "Sexually Transmitted Diseases," "Teen Sex," "Chappaquiddick Incident") which has shot up in the ratings to become a favorite choice of viewers. Since the young journalist came to televison in 1970, more than 100 awards have been brought to him including a Peabody, national and local Emmys, plus Associated Press kudos as a "special kind of individualist in a medium which too often breeds the plastic newsman." Rivera came to daytime with years of investigative reporting under his belt. Since turning to syndicated television, he has hosted and produced "Sons of Scarface: The New Mafia," a live two-hour investigation into organized crime; "American Vice: The Doping of a Nation" about narcotics trafficking; "Innocence Lost: The Erosion of American Childhood," and the highest rated syndicated show ever: "The Mystery of Al Capone's Vaults," during which the alleged vaults of the Chicago vice lord were blasted open. The program received a 34.2 national rating.

Born in Manhattan on 4 July 1943, Rivera was raised in the Williamsburg section of Brooklyn. Coming from a Puerto Rican family, he maintains strong ties with the Puerto Rican community in New York, and was an empathetic spokesman for the Young Lords, a Spanish-speaking youth organization devoted to "revolutionary action" (some of whose members have later done quite well themselves as TV reporters). After leaving Brooklyn, he sailed as a merchant seaman and bummed around (for a while as semi-pro soccer player) before attending the University of Arizona and Brooklyn Law School. Then, just when he was learning the hard way that "it was impossible for me to change the destinies of anyone as a poverty lawyer," TV reporter Gloria Rojas told him that New York station WABC was looking for a bilingual reporter. With his shocking reports on the Willowbrook State School for the Mentally Retarded, he established a reputation as one of TV's most passionate newsmen. Having obtained a key to one of the institution's buildings, he let himself and a camera crew in one morning to film the patients without authorization. "This is what it looked like," Rivera told the TV audience. "This is what it sounded like. But how can I tell you about the way it smelled?" As a result of the exposé, Gov. Rockefeller reinstated $20 million that had been cut from Willowbrook's budget, and elsewhere some 50 other news reports were done on prison-like mental hospitals. But, he also came under industry-wide fire for what was perceived as trigger-happy, indicting reports against the suspected "Son of Sam" killer. (By way of contrast, his 1984 report on convicted Atlanta murderer Wayne Williams, after whose capture the mass child killings ceased in that southern city, left doubts in some viewers' minds as to Williams' guilt.) While covering some of his more than 2000 other stories (award winners like his reports on the new heroin epidemic, or those leading to investigations like that on organized crime's food stamp fraud), he's also reported for "Good Morning, America," and hosted segments of "Good Night, America" from 1974-78. As the senior producer-correspondent of the "20/20" prime time newsmagazine, he conceded "I make no pretense of objectivity. But I'm not in the business of making people cry. I'm in the business of change." He scored record-breaking ratings with his segment "The Elvis Cover-up," a special report on the circumstances surrounding Elvis Presley's death on "20/20." He plays a TV news reporter in *The Bonfire of the Vanities*.

Away from the camera, he's found time to write four books: *Puerto Rico: Island of Contrast; Miguel Robles: So Far; A Special Kind of*

Courage and *Willowbrook*. In 1987 he married his fourth wife, C.C. Dyer.

Joan Rivers

"**O**h grow-up!" The lady rasps, her finger wagging at the audience. And they just love having Joan Rivers explain "it" all to them. Says she: "Nancy Reagan . . . a great lady. Sure. We're very close. She never swears. She told me to go reproduce myself . . . oh sure . . . Elizabeth Taylor? Ugh, can we talk here, I feel very close to you. I think she's a pig. Oh please. She pierced her ears and gravy came out . . . oh grow-up, mosquitos see her and scream 'buffet!' She has more chins than a Chinese phonebook. Please, can we talk? Look. I'm a very sensitive person. I only go after the ones who are big enough to take it. Bo Derek, so dumb she studies for a Pap test. Oh sure. Sophia Loren, an old tramp from World War II. I threw a Hershey bar into her dressing room and she laid down. Willie Nelson, he's so dirty he wears a Roach Motel around his neck. I am telling the truth in a very angry age. I succeed by saying what everyone else is thinking. Queen Elizabeth. A dog. Oh please. I mean, if you're Queen of England, Scotland and Ireland, the least you can do is shave your legs. Don't tell me beauty doesn't count, I don't wanna hear it," says the Brooklyn-born (8 June 1933), Barnard educated doctor's daughter whose real name is Joan Molinsky. "Oh sure, beauty is power. If you don't want the diamond, send it to me. My body is sagging so fast my gynecologist wears a hardhat. Oh grow-up. On my wedding night Edgar (Edgar Rosenberg, her late husband—one daughter, Melissa. A first and much earlier marriage to department store tycoon James Sanger lasted less than a year. "If God wanted me to cook and clean, my hands would be aluminum.") said: 'Let me undo your buttons.' I was naked at the time. Oh please."

For the woman Liz Smith adulated as the "most brilliant comic mind of all, a woman for our own skeptical times, a kind of gadfly and social goad, a phenomenon of today's entertainment industry rapidly becoming a multi-millionaire superstar thanks to the things only she dares to say," recognition was a long time coming. She defied her parents and "starved" as a Greenwich Village comic and writer and blew her big chance when she appeared on "The Jack Paar Show" because he hated her act. Her agent advised her to quit just the week before, when, in 1965 (after eight previous attempts to do so) she made it onto "The Johnny Carson Show" and was an instant hit. "He was Moses. He parted the seas and took me home. Carson was the one who stood up and said 'she's funny.'" After that she hosted the "Tonight Show" more than any other personality had up till then, and, in 1983, became Carson's sole replacement— doing so one week each month. She tried her hand at hosting her own "The Late Show" in 1986-87, but the ratings didn't fly. Instead, she spread her acting wings and joined the cast of the Neil Simon play *Broadway Bound* and became a regular center square on the "New Hollywood Squares." Her other credits include the 1974 best-seller *Having A Baby Can Be A Scream*, the 1984 best-seller (about River's mythical high school nemesis) *The Life and Hard Times of Heidi Abramowitz,* 1986's *Enter Talking;* a Broadway comedy (flop), *Fun City,* co-authored with Edgar; the LP, *What Becomes a Semi-Legend Most?* and the film comedy *Rabbit Test,* which she directed and co-scripted. She also appeared in the 1987 film *Spaceballs.* Her new syndicated talk show "The Joan Rivers Show" debuted in the fall of 1989.

Jason Robards

F requently described as "cadaverous-looking," he himself thinks he looks "stepped on." Whatever the adjective, his appearance seems perfectly matched to the tragic, disturbed characters he has so often portrayed in plays such as Eugene O'Neill's *The Iceman Cometh* and *Long Day's Journey Into Night,* Lillian Hellman's *Toys in the Attic,* and Arthur Miller's *After the Fall.* "I've always played disintegrated characters," he once said. "I don't know much about acting, but I can play those kinds of characters."

The son of Jason Robards, a well-known Broadway and Hollywood actor of the 1920s, Jason, Jr., (he no longer uses the Jr. in his billing) was born on 26 July 1922 in Chicago, grew up in Hollywood, and served seven years in the Navy before moving to New York to try for an acting career. A late bloomer, it wasn't until 1956 that he garnered major critical hosannas for his playing of the salesman,

Hickey, in O'Neill's *Iceman*. ("I didn't know at the time I got Hickey what it would lead to. I just thought it was an Off-Broadway show which I hoped would have a good run, and my family and I would all eat.") Actually, the O'Neill play propelled him into being one of the steadiest workers on Broadway, (and into the Theater Hall of Fame), not to mention movies and TV. Among the more memorable Robards films: *Tender is the Night* (1962); *A Thousand Clowns* (1966 film version of his 1962 B'way comedy hit); *Isadora* (1969); *All the President's Men* (1976 Oscar-winner for Best Supporting Actor); and *Melvin and Howard* (1979). "A Day in the Life of Ivan Denisovitch" and Eugene O'Neill's "Hughie" were both blockbusters on TV, as was 1983's much-publicized "The Day After." He won an Emmy in 1988 as Lead Actor in a miniseries for his role in NBC's "Inherit the Wind." In 1983, Robards returned to Broadway in another comedy, a revival of *You Can't Take It With You*, in 1985 he reprised the role of Hickey in *The Iceman Cometh*, 29 years after his original triumph, and in 1989 he appeared in A.R. Gurney's *Love Letters*. Recent films include *Square Dance* (1986), *Bright Lights, Big City* (1987), *The Good Mother* (1988) and *Quick Change* (1990). He filmed the TV movie "The Perfect Tribute," portraying Abraham Lincoln, for the 1990-91 season.

Married first to the former Eleanor Pitman (Jason III, Sarah, Louise, David), he married for the second time, Rachel Taylor; for the third, actress Lauren Bacall (one son, Sam); for the fourth, producer Lois O'Connor. He and the present Mrs. Robards have one son, Jake, and one daughter, Shannon born in 1971 via natural childbirth, with the father's active on-the-scene participation.

Cliff Robertson

Predictions were he'd "never work again" after he blew the whistle on what columnists called "Hollywood-gate," the pressure to hush up an embezzlement scandal involving David Begelman, then powerful president of Colu!mbia Pictures. But Robertson, shocked to discover that Begelman had forged his signature on a $10,000 studio check, notified both the police and the FBI, the papers got wind of the tale (later told at length in the 1982 David McClintick bestseller, *Indecent Exposure*) and Robertson found himself *persona*

non grata in the movie capital. ("I got phone calls from powerful people who said, 'You've been very fortunate in this business—I'm sure you wouldn't want all this to come to an end.'") It took him nearly four years to get a job, but in 1984 he clicked with playing a neurosurgeon on TV's "Falcon Crest," and serving as commercial spokesman for AT&T. He also began making movies, too.

Born Clifford Parker Robertson in LaJolla, California, on 9 September 1925, he had an even more dramatic "comeback" before he ever inaugurated his acting career. At the time of Pearl Harbor he was a 16-year-old seaman aboard a merchant ship in the Pacific; when the ship was bombed, word got back to LaJolla that he was a casualty, and his house carried the town's first Gold Star—until the young tar, very much alive, returned home. After studying at Antioch College in Ohio, Robertson landed his first professional acting with a Catskills troupe for five dollars a week plus room and board. Then came Broadway (*The Wisteria Trees*, Tennessee Williams's *Orpheus Descending*) and a long apprenticeship as one of Hollywood's faceless craftsmen, "confused in name with Dale Robertson and in appearance with a dozen other actors." After many movies (e.g. *Picnic, Autumn Leaves, The Best Man*) and more than 100 dramatic shows on the tube, he won TV's Emmy for his performance in a drama called "The Game" (1965-66 season) and three years later collected an Oscar for his film portrayal of *Charly*. His latest endeavors include the film *Malone* (1987) and the Robert Halmi 40-hour miniseries "Ford: The Man and His Machine" (1987). In 1989 he received the Campione d'Italia Merit of Achievement Award in Italy.

Married first to Cynthia Stone (who was earlier married to Jack Lemmon), mother of his daughter Stephanie, he wed actress/heiress Dina Merrill in 1966 and now has a second daughter, Heather. The couple separated in 1985; their divorce was final in 1989. A flying buff since his teens, he chose a contemporary model when he flew a mercy mission to Biafra, but his particular passion is his collection of vintage biplanes. "One man, one plane," he rhapsodizes. "There was *glamour* to those birds."

Ginger Rogers

When asked in a 1984 interview for the *Christian Science Monitor* her opinion about breakdancing, Rogers replied firmly: "I think dancing is something that's graceful, charming, lyrical. But not this. You can't dance on your back, on your derrière, on your neck, on your head. It's like flying a plane on the ground. You can't do it. It's ersatz." From Charleston champ of Texas, she danced her way to screen superstardom in such a glittering garland of superhits that in 1945 she reigned as the highest paid performer in Hollywood and one of the top ten salary earners in the entire U.S. (In 1980 when she starred with the Rockettes at New York's Radio City Music Hall, she had appeared on its movie screen more than any other actress in its 48-year history—in 21 films, from *Professional Sweetheart* to *Weekend at the Waldorf*.) Among her more than 70 films (many as dancing partner to Fred Astaire) were such

gems of glamour and glide as *Flying Down to Rio* (1933), *Top Hat* (1935), *The Gay Divorcée* (1934), *Roberta* (1935), *Swing Time* (1936), *Shall We Dance?* (1937) and *The Story of Vernon and Irene Castle* (1939). (Fans remember the effortless perfection of their dancing; Rogers remembers dancing "to the farther shores of weariness"—dancing until her "feet bled.") Off the dance floor she made her mark in films like *Stage Door* (1937), *Kitty Foyle* (Academy Award, 1940), and *Lady in the Dark* (1944). And proving herself to be enduring as well as adorable, she dazzled fans on Broadway in 1965 in *Hello Dolly*.

Born Virginia Katherine McMath, on 16 July 1911 in Independence, Missouri, she acquired the nickname "Ginger" as a moppet, combined it with "Rogers" when her mother (the driving force behind her career) moved to Texas and remarried. In a 1980 *People* interview she admitted her mother was the most influential person in her life. "She was *not* a stage mother; she was a very dignified woman." Hoofing on the vaudeville circuit in 1928, Ginger met and married Edward Culpepper (stage name, Jack Pepper), has since been married to actor Lew Ayres (1933), Jack Briggs (1944), Jacques Bergerac (1953), and William Marshall (1961) and was on her own again as of 1972. When asked in a recent interview if she would consider marrying again, Rogers answered: "Certainly. It's my nature. The only civilized way is marriage; the rest is chaos. No one believes in it more than I do. Trouble is, in my profession you must have a very secure male or the relationship is doomed. That was my problem." Bringing her shapely 19-year-old gams to the Main Stem in 1930 as star of George Gershwin's *Girl Crazy* (in which she introduced the song "Embraceable You"), she made her presence felt that same year in her very first film, *Young Man of Manhattan*, with the line "Cigarette me, big boy," which soon swept the country. Untarnished by time, the golden girl of the 1930s was busy in the 1970s serving as fashion consultant for J.C. Penney.

Although Rogers has a ranch on Oregon's Rogue River and a house near Palm Springs, she spends many months a year on the road performing in nightclubs from Las Vegas to Paris. In an interview with *People* she spoke frankly about today's movies and stage musicals. The movies: "We have fallen into the trap of trying to outdo each other with graphic sex and violence." And Hollywood: "It's Sodom and Gomorrah. The drugs, the corruption drag down an industry—and a nation. They're not going to get my money to see the junk that's being made today. No way." The musical theatre: "I don't like these shows where everybody gets undressed and does a war dance. The performers are there, but where are the Gershwins, the Berlins, the Richard Rodgerses—the creative geniuses?" Rogers admits she's no nostalgia nut. "Who wants to live in the past? I don't." In 1986 she received the first George M. Cohan Memorial Award from the 42nd Street River to River Committee.

Roy Rogers

Bedecked in a ten-gallon hat and astride his beloved palomino, he was the cowboy hero of more than 90 motion pictures, a radio broadcast, and a long-running television program. Retired from the saddle, he is best known to recent generations as the smiling image behind a large chain of fast-food restaurants.

He was born Leonard Franklin Slye on 5 November 1911 in Cincinnati, Ohio. Beset with poverty during the depression, the family headed for California in search of work. "There are parts of [*The Grapes of Wrath*] that made me wonder if maybe Mr. Steinbeck wasn't looking over the shoulder of the Slye Family." He mastered guitar and singing to earn money in his travels. After recording Western songs with a band called Sons of Pioneers, he was riding high as Gene Autry's replacement in the 1938 film, *Under Western Stars*. Among his noted films for Republic Studios were *Billy the Kid Returns* in 1938, *King of the Cowboys* in 1943 (the title of which became his trademark), and the 1947 *Springtime in the Sierras*. Rogers made 35 films with Dale Evans, beginning in 1944 with *The Cowboy and the Señorita*. The popular co-stars married three years later, after the sudden death of Roy's first wife, Arlene. In 1948, they starred in

"The Roy Rogers Show," on radio, and transferred the concept to television in 1951 for a six-year run.

By his first wife, he has two children and an adopted daughter. A deeply religious man, he turned to the Billy Graham Crusade for strength when he and Evans suffered the loss of their child to Down's Syndrome in 1953, and the death of two adopted children in separate accidents. They have reared several other adopted children of different nationalities.

The more than 500 Roy Rogers Family Restaurants are owned by Marriott Corp., of which he is a stockholder. He also owns real estate, a music publishing company, and a Museum in California. He was honored in 1988 with the International Galaxy of Fame Award from the Angel Foundation for his work with children.

Mickey Rooney

"I 've been through four publics. I've been coming back like a rubber ball for years, but I never had aspirations to remain a star—that would have been rougher," admitted Rooney a few years ago. "I just want to be a professional. I couldn't live without acting." Outshining even such supergiants as Gable and Tracy, he was Hollywood's No. 1 box-office idol back in 1939, '40, and '41. Now, after 8 trips to the altar, several career slumps and one journey to bankruptcy court, the perennial Andy Hardy is balding, but unbowed, busy and back on top. Appearing on Broadway in 1979 in the smash hit *Sugar Babies* (with Ann Miller) made him a "hot ticket" once again and put him back "in the chips." Everybody's tickled pink, especially "the Mick." He likes to be seen in the present productions of *Sugar Babies* (London, 1988), as well as try other roles. In 1987 he appeared on Broadway in the Stephen Sondheim musical *A Funny Thing Happened on the Way to the Forum* and in 1988 he starred in the CBS telefilm "Bluegrass." His latest feature film is *Erik the Viking* (1989).

Born Joe Yule, Jr., on 23 September 1920 in Brooklyn, New York, a few blocks from the theatre in which his showbiz parents were appearing, he wandered out on stage for the first time in 1921 as Baby New Year. A few months later he made his "formal" debut as a midget, wearing a tuxedo and smoking a rubber cigar, and he went on to play a midget in his first movie, a silent called *Not To Be*

Trusted. A star, at six, of innumerable *Mickey (Himself) McGuire* comedy shorts, he became Mickey Rooney (not Mickey Looney, as his mother first suggested) in such golden oldies as *Boys Town, Babes in Arms,* and *Captains Courageous,* and made his first Andy Hardy picture (*A Family Affair*) in 1937. The eight marriages (producing almost as many children) started with Ava Gardner, proceeded through Betty Jane Rase, Martha Vickers, Eileen Mahnken, Barbara Ann Thomasen, Margie Dane, Carolyn Hockett, to Jan Chamberlin, the present Mrs. Rooney.

After a bunch of "typical" Rooney performances in *Breakfast at Tiffany's, It's a Mad, Mad, Mad, Mad World, How to Stuff a Wild Bikini* (movies) and a couple of short-lived TV series ("Mickey" and "One of the Boys"), his superb television portrayals in "The Comedian," "Eddie," "Somebody's Waiting," "Bill" (1982 Emmy award) "Bill: On His Own" and his acclaimed film acting in *Black Stallion* have recently exposed the in-depth dramatic talent of the mite-but-mighty Mickey. In the late '60s Rooney joined the Church of Religious Science and says he has found a deeper, richer meaning to living. "All of the muddy waters of my life cleared up when I gave myself to Christ," declares Rooney. In 1983 Rooney was given an honorary Oscar for "50 years of versatility in a variety of memorable film performances" (he received a special miniature statue in 1938 at the height of his career as a juvenile film performer). In a 1980 *Life* magazine interview, Rooney assessed his philosophy about work and his career: "Listen, you never reach an apex in life. If you think you do, then you become effete, something starts to decay very fast. See, I'm this 59-year-old guy who's going on 34. There may be a little snow on the mountain, but there's a lot of fire in the furnace. I'm still learning, and, of course, I'll never stop paying my dues. I'd be happy carrying a spear, saying: "Your horse waits without."" Rooney's autobiography *The Beginning and the Middle* was published in 1985.

Diana Ross

"I 'd like to think one of my greatest accomplishments musically is to take the music of a specific community, put my own spin in it, and take it out to the world. I'm aware of the great gift I've been given in having a voice and a style that seem to cut across boundaries of race, age and nations. To be able to turn people onto new sounds, new ideas . . . to make them move and dance and feel excitement about living," states the Diva of Pop. The Supremes's singular siren is a celebrity who has captured the sounds of the times and bridged generation gaps. Head of her own management and film production companies, she thoughtfully plans her life by writing down her priorities, thoughts for the day, and "mind-maps." The actress-singer-fashion designer has sold more No. 1 hits—from among over 50 albums—than anyone except the Beatles and Elvis Presley, and *Billboard* called her Female Entertainer of the Century. The release of her most recent album *Workin' Overtime* (1989) cemented her slot as a continual chart buster.

Born in Detroit, Michigan, 26 March 1944, she sang in the choir of a Baptist church and learned secular music from a cousin who was known as "the girl with the golden voice." After graduating from high school, Diana and her friends Florence Ballard and Mary Wilson auditioned for Detroit's Motown Records. They were soon enrolled in Berry Gordy's specially-commissioned daily "artist's development" lessons, which included how to speak, sit, shake hands properly, and climb up on a piano. After their ditty called "Where Did Our Love Go?" hit it big they were to become the most successful of all American record-sellers in the music-filled '60s. Soon they were Diana Ross and the Supremes. In 1970 Diana went solo, but with the solid backing of Motown mogul Gordy. He took the record company into movie-making and personally supervised screen vehicles for Ross. She was nominated for a Best Actress Oscar for her portrayal of Billie Holiday in *Lady Sings the Blues*, designed the clothes for her role as a model in *Mahogany* (as well as singing the Oscar-nominated theme song), and recreated Judy Garland's Dorothy in the all-black *The Wiz*. On the drawing board as her film company's first production: a bio of the chanteuse Josephine Baker.

The divorced mother of three daughters, Diana said officially in 1983, "I'm a dreamer . . . I dreamed of building a playground in the park for some time, and now that playground is going to be a reality." The free outdoor concert she put on for that end was disastrous, however; when thunder and rain doused the 350,000 who came out for the Great Lawn event, it was postponed a day. That date was marred by gangs of hoods who thought it was a thugfest instead of a songfest. Finally, after Ross and Paramount Video, co-producer and televiser of the show, handed the city the bill, there was not only nothing left for a playground, but New Yorkers were out of $650,000 in security and cleanup. All was mended, however, when the diva, who claimed she had had to cough up almost three hundred thousand in expenses, presented

Mayor Ed Koch with a check for a quarter of a million several months later, anyway. Hizzoner presented her with garb she could have used way back when: a rain slicker. Very much in love, Diana married her second husband, Arne Naess, Jr., in two ceremonies (23 October 1985 in New York; 1 February 1986 in Geneva). All told she has five children (three daughters from her previous marriage and two sons with Arne).

Ken Russell

"**I** know my films upset people. I want to upset people," says the veteran director of such R-rated but X-ceedingly erotic pictures as *Women in Love* (1969), *The Devils* (1971) and *Crimes of Passion* (1984). "People are simply not prepared. I do hit them below the belt and they react to being exposed." So do some critics, who "would rather be bored than shocked. All good art," the great upsetter asserts categorically, "all good entertainment, shocks people."

Born in Southampton, England, 3 July 1927, Russell served in Britain's merchant marine at the close of World War II, then attended an art school and finally enrolled at the International Ballet School, where "an 80-year-old Russian martinet . . . taught us to jump very high by shouting in blasphemous Russian and beating us about the legs with a stick." After performing with the Norwegian Ballet and in the chorus of an English touring company of *Annie Get Your Gun,* he switched to acting, but finding that life too insecure, took up photography and became a successful lensman. This led to an interest in motion pictures, and before long he had shot and edited three shorts—a fantasy, a drama, and a documentary—on budgets of around £150 each; one came to the attention of a highly placed BBC producer, who commissioned Russell to make what turned out to be the first of a series of documentaries.

Russell quickly became noted—and notorious—for his unconventional methods of dealing with films of this type: "My way of directing documentaries," he declared, "finally cleared the air of the word 'documentary' and all that is dreary, reverential and schoolmastery that the word entails." (One newspaper dubbed him "the wild man of the BBC and England's most accomplished and imaginative director.") He has profiled on film, among other celebrated figures,

Bela Bartok, Claude Debussy, Peter Ilyitch Tchaikovsky, Frederick Delius, Edward Elgar, Gustav Mahler, Richard Strauss and Isadora Duncan. He completed his first theatrical feature, *French Dressing*, in 1964, and his second, *Billion Dollar Brain*, in 1967, but it was his third big picture, *Women in Love*, that brought him international attention. Though controversial, his succeeding films were, on the whole, quite respectfully received until *Altered States* (1980), which Pauline Kael characterized as "probably the most aggressively silly picture since *The Exorcist.*" While awaiting his next film project he directed operas in Florence, Lyon, Charleston (S.C.) and Spoleto.

By his first wife, Shirley, whom he married in 1957, Russell has five children: Xavier, James, Alexander, Victoria and Toby; he already had another daughter, Molly, by Vivian Jolly by the time he married that lady on 10 June 1984 aboard the old *Queen Mary* in Long Beach, Calif., with actor Anthony Perkins, an ordained minister, officiating. With *Crimes of Passion* in the can he turned to directing *La Boheme* in Italy. "After so many years making movies," he says, "I find directing operas . . . a great deal more fun. They don't take too long to direct—just a month—and they're exciting." And controversial. The climax of his recent *Madame Butterfly* was the dropping of the A-bomb on Hiroshima and his *La Boheme* had Mimi experimenting with drugs of the non-prescription kind. His recent bunch of films include *Gothic* (1987), a contribution to the opera curio *Aria* (1987), *The Lair of the White Worm* (1988) *Salome's Last Dance* (1988) and *The Rainbow* (1989).

Meg Ryan

"It's hard to pin someone with Ryan's range down to a short phrase. . . . If the roles are diverse, there's one constant: Men are bowled over by her. When describing Ryan, grown journalists—men who interview glamorous starlets all the time—resort to romance-novel words like 'breezy sexuality' and make note of her 'slow, sexy smile,'" raves an article in *Mademoiselle*. Meg Ryan is hot! Although her screen cameo in *Top Gun* brought her into the Hollywood mainstream, she doesn't feel that particular film launched her career. She insists, "I guess I never felt like it did. It's not like I walk down the street and people say, 'Oh, there's the girl from *Top Gun. . . .*' I was more famous when I was on 'As the World Turns.'"

Ryan was born in 1963 in Fairfield, Connecticut. While studying journalism at New York University, she supported herself by making commercials. Those big round blue eyes and sensuous smirk landed the young actress her feature film debut as Candice Bergen's daughter in George Cukor's *Rich and Famous* (1981). Her theatrical resume blossomed when she landed the role as Betsy on the daytime soap "As the World Turns" (1983-1985), followed by her appearances in *Amityville III: The Demon, Armed and Dangerous, Top Gun, Innerspace, D.O.A.* and *The Presidio.* She also starred in a critically acclaimed independent feature *Promised Land* (executive producer, Robert Redford). Her performance as a tough drifter won her a Best Actress Award in Europe and a nomination for Best Actress from the I.F.P. However, it was her role as Sally Albright opposite Billy Crystal in the 1989 film *When Harry Met Sally* that made Meg Ryan a household name with star billing on the marquee. In the film, her character "brings contemporary relationship problems out into the open." It is Meg's interpretation of a woman having an orgasm (in front of amazed onlookers in a restaurant) that set film audiences roaring in their seats. Next Meg appeared with Tom Hanks in the 1990 movie *Joe Versus the Volcano.* Upcoming projects include *The Butcher's Wife.*

Stepping up the ladder of success, Meg has some additional goals. She observes that good scripts are hard to find and hopes to write one herself, someday. "I just love words," she offers. "I love when a writer says something that you've thought way back in your subconscious. When it becomes a conscious thought, you're like, wooooow." She makes a steady habit of seeing her actor/boyfriend Dennis Quaid, whom she planned to wed in September, 1990.

Susan Saint James

E ver since she built her acting career on six thespian lessons, and then (as legend has it) barged into a Hollywood casting office demanding to be given a reading, this offbeat former model has not only stayed in TV roles, but has garnered an Emmy and nominations for at least seven others. Born Susie Jane Miller in the City of Angels on 14 August 1946, she grew up in Rockford, Ill., where her dad was chairman of Testor Corp., a company that makes model planes. She spent one high-school year in a French exchange-student program, "came back wriggling like Brigitte Bardot," and shortly thereafter altered her parents' agenda for her education at Connecticut College for Women by splitting after a week and hightailing it for New York with the French-inspired name Susan Saint James. Soon she left for Paris, where she modeled and "goferred" in Charles Aznavour's entourage, then in 1966 she headed for Hollywood, where her spunk impressed a Universal Studios veep. One of the last of the seven-year contract actors, she played in a TV movie that became the "Name of the Game" series, co-starring Gene Barry, Tony Franciosa, and Robert Stack. After winning an Emmy in her first season, she stayed with the show for its duration,

then landed the part of Rock Hudson's wacky spouse in another NBC series, "McMillan & Wife," on the air from 1971-76. After some uninspired movies and some memorable comedic and dramatic video flicks, she returned regularly to the tube in 1984 in the smash-hit sitcom "Kate & Allie," opposite comedienne Jane Curtin.

The thrice-married, former vegetarian is now ensconced in matrimony and motherhood with erstwhile "Saturday Night Live" producer Dick Ebersol and their children, including two from Saint James's previous marriage, and three from the current union; the youngest, Edward Bright Ebersol, was born in June, 1990. She even narrated the children's story *Peter and the Wolf* at two New York Pops concerts conducted by Skitch Henderson in 1988. Once an anti-Vietnam War activist, she says, "Having kids de-radicalizes you a bit. I had a falling out with the Catholic Church in my radical days, but now I realize I can do more being active in the church. Plus it's the only way I know to pray. That gives a deeper sense to life."

Pat Sajak

He's an enigma. He is professional and witty, and can carry on a conversation with ordinary people in a manner that puts them totally at ease. Pat is seen by millions of people every night on his incredibly successful nighttime game show "Wheel of Fortune." When asked about all this fame, he simply replies, "I'm lucky." Pat has been the host of the "Wheel of Fortune" since it's debut in 1982. "I enjoy my work for 'Wheel' very much. It's been a tremendous opportunity for me in so many ways. The contestants are a lot of fun, the staff is terrific and it really is a great game show."

Pat Sajak was born in 1947 in Chicago, Illinois. He attended

Columbia College, and from there, began his show biz career as a newscaster for WEDC, a radio station in Chicago. However, in 1968 he was drafted to serve his country in the U.S. Army in Vietnam. From 1968 to 1972 Pat was a disc jockey with Armed Forces Vietnam in Saigon. Following his discharge, he moved to Nashville and made the switch to television, working for WSM-TV, where he was the weatherman as well as host of the station's public affairs program. In 1977 he moved to Los Angeles, also working as a weatherman, for KNBC-TV. Later, he was given the position of hosting "The Sunday Show," which was a public affairs program. His position as host of "The Sunday Show" gave him the exposure that caused him to be discovered and land the role of the host of "Wheel of Fortune." Pat attributes the show's phenomenal success to the fact that the viewers at home can play along. He explains, "If you're sitting at home watching, it's a challenge to try and figure out the puzzle. It gives you the feeling of satisfaction if you can get it faster or just get it right. Plus there's that vicarious thrill of winning." In addition to the "Wheel," Pat also hosted the CBS late-night talk show "The Pat Sajak Show," which debuted in 1988 but folded after two seasons, in 1990. He has been seen on several other television shows, including the "Merv Griffin Show," "The Tonight Show," "Late Night with David Letterman," "Hour Magazine," and "Gimme a Break." Extending his talents, Pat has hosted the Macy's Thanksgiving Day Parade and made his film debut in the feature film *Airplane II.*

In his spare time he likes to play tennis and racquetball, and is an avid fan of the Chicago Cubs. Pat resides in Los Angeles and is engaged to marry fashion model Lesly Brown.

Susan Sarandon

She works "from the gut. I've never learned to make this vein here pop out or to cry on cue. But, you know, in film you've only got to get it right once and you've got all day to do it. . . . Anybody can act. It's no big deal." The brandy-haired actress with the Bette Davis eyes is somewhat of an anomaly in an industry beseiged with acting schools: She is a natural. Having never taken an acting lesson, she was cast in her first major film role less than a week after arriving in New York.

She was born Susan Tomaling on 4 October 1946, the oldest of nine children in a Catholic family in Edison, N.J. She stumbled into acting quite by accident when, as a freshman in college, her husband's agent offered to sign her. She debuted in the 1970 movie *Joe*. Her marriage to actor Chris Sarandon eventually failed but the acting bug remained. She was cast as Brooke Shields's prostitute mother in *Pretty Baby*, directed by Louis Malle, with whom she became romantically involved. Her performance in Malle's 1982 *Atlantic City* drew critical acclaim. Some of her less memorable film work has included the soapy disaster *The Other Side of Midnight*, *King of the Gypsies*, and *The Great Waldo Pepper*. Picking roles for their potential to "stretch" her talents, rather than to advance her career, she has appeared in some offbeat vehicles. "One of the reasons I've done the roles that I've done is that they freighten me so much." She appeared in the cultish *Rocky Horror Picture Show*, the grim off-Broadway play about rape and revenge, *Extremities*, and the movie *The Hunger*, in which she played a graphic love scene with Catherine Deneuve. She starred in one of 1985's more popular films, *Compromising Positions*, followed by *The Witches of Eastwick* (1987), *Sweetheart's Dance* (1988), *Bull Durham* (1988), *The January Man* (1988), *A Dry White Season* (1989) and *Erik the Viking* (1989).

Off-screen, Sarandon is active in the movement for a nuclear freeze and is outspoken in her liberally oriented political views. In 1985 she gave birth to a daughter fathered by Italian screenwriter Franco Amurri, and in 1989 she had a son with actor Tim Robbins.

Telly Savalas

Though bald-headed and fleshy-faced, he engenders an appeal that was the surprise of the 1970s. Ugly was he? Only for a few weeks when his super-hit TV series "Kojak" debuted in 1973. As soon as the world came around to his gruffer-than-thou-side, the once-ugly became the decidedly sexy. "This street-smart tough egg also has a soft and thoughtful center," wrote *Time*. "'Kojak' shows New York City in all its roach and racketeering misery. The directors neatly capture the alternately plodding and explosive rhythm of policework. But ultimately the show is a one-

man operation." It was Telly Savalas's idea to suck on lollipops while trying to give up cigars, offer the suckers to the local stooges, and wear three-piece suits. "Men watch Kojak," said *Time,* "because they see a guy they'd like to be. And women see a guy who's strong but still wounded a little bit, tough but not too tough, full of compassion."

He was born Aristotle Savalas in Garden City, Long Island, New York, on 21 January in years that have been reported anywhere from 1921 to 1927; his father was, by Telly's description, "a millionaire five times and a pauper six," and his mother was a former Miss Greece. After military service in World War II, Telly got his B.A. in psychology and was trying to get into medical school when, through his brother, he got a job writing for the U.S. Department of State Information Services. He eventually was promoted to assistant director for the Near East, South Asia and Africa. In 1955 he left government service and got a job as ABC-TV's news and special events senior director. It was while he was teaching a night course that an agent asked him if he could find someone with a European accent to play an old judge in the television play "Bring Home a Baby." Savalas auditioned and got the part. He appeared on several TV series and in movies, including *Bird Man of Alcatraz,* for which he was nominated for a Best Supporting Actor Academy Award in 1962. He first shaved his head to play Pontius Pilate in 1965's *The Greatest Story Ever Told* and kept it for *The Dirty Dozen* in 1967. He also appeared in the motion picture *Kelly's Heroes.* Based on the success of a TV-movie bringing back "Kojak" in 1984, Savalas returned to playing the cop in "The Belarius File" in 1985; the "Kojak" series was resurrected in 1989 on ABC. He has been divorced three times, and married his fourth wife, Julie Hovland, in 1985. The couple added two more children (Christian and Ariana) to his four kids from previous marriages.

Roy Scheider

"There are, I think, three essential attributes every actor should have," says the actor whose parts in *The French Connection* and *Jaws* have made him a household name. "One is intelligence, but not too much; just enough to make good choices.

The audience wants to see the actor's emotions, not his intellect. Second, is a certain physical grace, regardless of character, and third, an enormous childlike belief in the 'make-believe.' To be all those different people, to live out all those different lifetimes is a little like being God. You may even choreograph your own death many times."

Born 10 November 1935, this half-Irish, half-German Protestant never thought he'd have a life on stage or in films. Between the Depression and World War II his father sold gasoline and ran a service station. Rheumatic fever attacks at age six, ten and fifteen kept him apart from children his age. An "enormously fat" teenager, he was forbidden to play sports and he daydreamed about "being somebody else . . . I started to read . . . all my life writers have been my real heroes." As soon as he could after leaving his sickbed, Scheider started to swim every day, played baseball and even entered the New Jersey Diamond Gloves as an amateur welterweight in 1951. After graduation from Pennsylvania's Franklin and Marshall College and three years in the Air Force, he began his career in regional and Off-Broadway theater in shows such as *Sergeant Musgrove's Dance* and *The Alchemist.* (In 1968 he won an Obie Award for his performance in *Stephen D.* Later, in 1980, he won the Drama League of New York award for his performance on Broadway in Harold Pinter's *Betrayal.*)

Scheider has appeared in many films, some of which have been among the highest-earning pictures in Hollywood. His screen credits include *Klute, The French Connection, Jaws I* and *Jaws II, Blue Thunder, Marathon Man, All That Jazz, Still of the Night, Tiger Town, Across the River and into the Trees, Mismatch, Night Game* and *Listen to Me.* He beat out Edward Asner and Richard Burton to play the outspoken newspaper publisher Jacobo Timerman in the television movie based on Timerman's memoir *Prisoner Without a Name, Cell without a Number* in 1983.

Although married to his wife Cynthia for more than 20 years (one daughter, Maximillia), they recently divorced, and he took up with Brenda King. Scheider is a part-owner of Joe Allen's restaurants in Paris and L.A., and he admits liking to drop in occasionally to see who's around. "That way," he quips, "I know who my friends are." Scheider also finds himself more involved politically now than he was in the early 1970s. "I don't think it's because Roy Scheider has become politically conscious. It's because Roy Scheider, like most citizens in this country, has been forced to take a look at [the] issues."

Arnold Schwarzenegger

The prize-winning bodybuilder retired from competition in 1975 to pursue a film career, but he left an imprint both on techniques for muscle development and on the public's perception of the sport of body sculpting.

Born 30 July 1947 in Graz, Austria, to a family that stressed physical discipline, Schwarzenegger discovered bodybuilding at age 15 as a means of training for other sports. "I learned up about the body, how it works, how each muscle can be worked. I felt like Leonardo da Vinci; I was a sculptor shaping the body," he has said.

After competing successfully in junior championships in Austria and Europe and completing a year of military service, Schwarzenegger won the National Bodybuilding Association's Mr. Universe professional title for the first time in 1969. He continued on as a judges' favorite, winning more than 10 major championships. In addition to his handsome, Nordic looks and sleek muscle definition, audiences took to his engaging personality. To a public that largely viewed bodybuilding as a freakish exhibition, Schwarzenegger, who was featured in the 1977 bodybuilding documentary *Pumping Iron*, was a disarmingly intelligent spokesman for the sport (or art) of body sculpting. He was known as an aggressive competitor with a penchant for chiding his rivals with a quick wit, but always recognized as a good sportsman. Satisfying a longtime desire to be an actor, he debuted in the 1976 *Stay Hungry* to favorable reviews. His performance in the 1983 *Conan the Barbarian*, a prehistoric fantasy film based on the cartoon character, delighted the cultish devotees of action sci-fi and grossed well, as did *The Terminator* and *Red Sonya*. More films followed, including *Commando* (1985), *Raw Deal* (1986), *Predator* (1986), *The Running Man* (1987), *Red Heat* (1987), *Twins* (1988) and *Total Recall* (1990). In addition he has served President George Bush's program on national fitness.

Schwarzenegger has stated a preference for women who are, "dark haired, pretty intelligent, witty, and very charming," an apt description of his wife, Maria Shriver (married 26 April 1986). They have a daughter, Katherine Eunice, born while Schwarzenegger was filming *Total Recall*.

Martin Scorsese

"My friends used to say, 'jeez Marty, do you really be- lieve all that stuff the priests tell you?' Well I did believe it, every word of it. I wouldn't touch meat on Friday and I believed I would go to hell if I missed Mass on Sunday. As a matter of fact, I went into the seminary after school, but they threw me out at the end of my first year for rough-housing during prayers. They thought I was a thug." So did the critics after his sleeper hit *Mean Streets* caught on in 1973. It was about the wild side of New York's Little Italy, shown with a violence and realism that was often painful to watch.

Born 17 November 1942, Scorsese grew up a frail and asthmatic youth who was himself a product of Little Italy. As a youngster he fantasized himself a priest but stopped attending Mass when he heard a priest endorse the Vietnam War as a holy cause. Filmmaking became his sacred intention when he was a student at NYU. "There's a great similarity in the way I look at reality and the things I saw in the musicals and the dark 'noir' films of the '40s," he said, "my reality and film reality are interchangeable. They blend." Student films won grants from foundations, and his first big mark was the documentary of the pop-musical happening of the century, *Woodstock*. Other musical films included *Elvis on Tour* and *Medicine Ball Express*, films that followed his *Knocking at My Door* and preced- ed his first major studio film, *Boxcar Bertha*, starring David Carradine and Barbara Hershey. Ellen Burstyn won an Oscar for her perform- ance in his *Alice Doesn't Live Here Anymore* in 1974. Robert de Niro starred in his shatteringly explicit and critically controversial *Taxi Driver* as well as the bittersweet romance *New York, New York*, which also starred Liza Minnelli. "My light frothy musical turned out to be my most personal film," said Scorsese. "It's about that period in your life when you're about to make it; you know you're talented, but you just don't quite make it for another four or five years. It is that period when your first marriage breaks up, when people who are crazy in love with each other can't live with each other."

Scorsese has found Robert de Niro to be his essential representative in his films. The actor won an Academy Award in *Raging Bull* and also starred in *King of Comedy*, a film the director describes as "an examination of American values, values that give us the wrong goals to go for." Recent films include *After Hours* (1985), the picketed *Last Temptation of Christ* (1988), *Good Fellas* (1990), and a film adaptation of Gabriella De Ferrari's novel *A Cloud on the Sand*. He also directed one segment of *New York Stories* (1989). He took to acting in acclaimed Japanese director Akira Kurosawa's 1990 film *Dreams*, in which Scorsese plays painter Vincent Van Gogh.

Scorsese's first three marriages have all ended up on the cutting room floor. First married to Laraine Brennan, he has a daughter Catherine. From his marriage to writer Julia Cameron, he has a daughter Domenica. His 1979 marriage to Isabella Rossellini, daughter of the late actress Ingrid Bergman and the late director Roberto Rossellini, was a very short feature. He married his fourth wife, Barbara DeFina, on 9 February 1985. His autobiography, *Scorsese on Scorsese*, was released in October, 1989.

George C. Scott

After his Oscar-winning *Patton* in 1970, and subsequent no-show at what he called the Academy's "annual orgy of self-adulation," he became one of the stage's most memorable Willie Lomans as well as director of the 1975 Broadway revival of *Death of a Salesman*. For a time hailed by critics as among the foremost contemporary actors, George C. Scott, of the no-sell-out persona, says, "Even after being successful . . . there's dozens . . . of well-known people in this business who have met less than auspicious ends. You start feeling like a survivor. But I'm only a survivor up to this point; tomorrow I may not be."

Born in Wise, Va., 18 October 1927, he attended the University of Missouri and studied journalism until he "realized acting paid much better. I became an actor to escape my own personality. Acting is the most therapeutic thing in the world. I think all the courage that I may lack personally I have as an actor. There are ruts we get into in life that we don't have the courage to shake ourselves out of." But shake himself out he did. After two unsuccessful marriages (Carolyn Hughes, Patricia Reed), many drunken brawls, and five fractured noses, he "came to" in 1957 when his *Richard III* (with the New York Shakespeare Festival) won sudden acclaim. His "stunningly venomous" performance led to a flurry of offers from Hollywood and TV, which in turn led him to comment, "I'm getting older, mellow, and lovable."

Marriage (and remarriage) to actress Colleen Dewhurst was stormy, but it produced two sons. Scott has three other children from his previous marriages. In late 1972 he married actress Trish Van Devere. Both actresses have played on-stage opposite the man whose face critic Kenneth Tynan describes as resembling "a victorious bottle opener." Scott says, "I make movies for financial reasons and this allows me the luxury of acting on Broadway . . . (where) I lose money." Thus, for the loot, he's been in *The Hustler* (1961), *Dr. Strangelove* (1964), *Hospital* (1971), *The New Centurions* (1972), *Taps* (1981), *A Fine Mess* (1986), and *The Exorcist III: Legion* (1990). Indulging his luxury, he's been in *Children of Darkness, The Merchant of Venice, Desire Under the Elms, Present Laughter* (which he also directed) and *The Boys of Autumn*. He appeared in the TV adaptation of Dickens's "A Christmas Carol" in 1984 and starred in the NBC-TV miniseries "Mussolini: The Untold Story" in 1986. He struck out with the 1987 TV series "Mr. President."

Willard Scott

I f anyone can find the sunny side of acid rain—Willard Scott can. NBC-TV's "Today Show" weatherman and pastry-bellied gadfly made broadcasting history on a hot August morning in 1983, when he appeared on the show dressed as Carmen Miranda in an effort to raise $1,000 for the U.S.O. He then performed an original musical number with two guitarists and later walked on platform shoes to the weather map, where he proceeded to deliver the morning's weather report! That's how Willard's shtick works: outrageous clowning around with a teasing tongue (he's always knocking the competition or his own producer; he flirted with former anchorwoman Jane Pauley and bursts Bryant Gumbel's you-heard-it-here-first balloon with risable regularity). And a heart as big as his weather map! He announces droughts and country fairs, blizzards and hospital fund-raisers, earthquakes and the 100th birthdays and 75th anniversaries of his senior citizen viewers.

He was born 7 March 1934 in Alexandria, Va., and began his career in 1950 at NBC's WRC Radio. A 1955 graduate of American University in Washington, where he majored in philosophy and religion (ah, that explains his happy Buddha approach to weather), he formed, with Ed Walker, one of DC's most popular broadcast teams ever, "The Joy Boys." He did weather on WRC from 1959 through 1972 and joined the "Today Show" in 1980. He was named Washingtonian of the Year by *Washingtonian* magazine in 1979, and 1984 he was voted one of *Playgirl* magazine's 10 sexiest men. Oh sure, you either love him or you hate him, and to love him is reason enough to rise in the morning. The father of two (he is married to the former Mary Dwyer) is the author of a 1980 autobiography. *The Joy of Living, Willard Scott's Down-Home Stories* (1984), *Willard Scott's All-American Cookbook* (1986) and *America Is My Neighborhood* (1987). In 1987 he played the recurring character of Peter Poole on NBC's "The Hogan Family."

George Segal

He was one of the first in a new school of film stars who, bereft of movie-idol looks and slightly frumpled in appearance, offered comic appeal and heavy doses of personality. Born in New York City on 13 February 1936, he was raised in suburban N.Y., where he began a fledgling showbiz career at age eight, entertaining at children's parties with a magic act. After graduation from Columbia University, he dabbled in a music career as a banjo player (he still plays a number of club dates each year), formed a nightclub act, and joined an improvisational revue before making his film debut in *The Young Doctors* in 1961. A string of movies followed during the early 1960s, including the 1964 *Invitation to a Gun Fighter* and the 1965 *Ship of Fools*. Segal was praised for his strong performance in *Who's Afraid of Virginia Woolf*, the 1966 screen version of Edward Albee's acclaimed play, and he appeared as Biff, son of Willy Loman, in the 1966 television production of *Death of Salesman*.

Although one of the busiest actors in Hollywood during the late 1960s, it took the 1970 hit comedy *The Owl and the Pussycat*, with

Barbra Streisand, to solidify his bankability as a romantic lead. His gentle comedic touch was perfectly matched with Glenda Jackson's prickly performance in *A Touch of Class*, a stylish comedy about an extramarital affair and one of 1973's most popular movies. Segal dallied with Jane Fonda in the satirical *Fun With Dick and Jane* in 1977, with Jacqueline Bisset in *Who is Killing the Great Chefs of Europe?* and with Natalie Wood in 1980 in *The Last Married Couple in America*. Not known for discriminating taste in movie projects, Segal made the tasteless racial satire, *Carbon Copy*, in 1981. His latest efforts include the films *Daddy's Home* (1988) and *All's Fair* (1988), plus the CBS-TV telefilm "Take Five" (1987).

Segal is divorced from former television editor Marion Sobel, whom he married in 1956 (two daughters). In 1984 he married Linda Rogoff, one-time manager of the Pointer Sisters, who presently manages his career.

Tom Selleck

M acho televison and film star Tom Selleck chalked up another "special delivery" male film portrait as Phillip Blackwood in his fifth film, *Her Alibi* in 1989. It was important to Selleck that his latest character (a successful mystery writer, whose wife had abandoned him for a literary reviewer) did not resemble any of his former roles. "Phillip Blackwood is a guy unlike Magnum or Peter Mitchell [his character in *Three Men and a Baby*]. He's a man who has created all the action in his life through his writing.

For example, he hasn't been in a fistfight since he was six years old. Now he must face reality with the new woman in his life. During the course of this movie he realizes that he must take action. At times he fails, but that gives the film its conflict."

Born 29 January 1945 in Detroit, Michigan, Tom Selleck and his three siblings were nurtured with "traditional values" by his investment executive father and his mother. The whole family had moved to Sherman Oaks some time before his 21st birthday when Tom, like the other siblings, "received a gold Rolex watch for having successfully steered clear of swearing, drinking, and smoking." He won a basketball scholarship to USC (played baseball and football) but on the advice of a drama teacher decided to try modeling. After loads of commercials and bit parts in movies, he found steady work on the soap opera "The Young and the Restless." Selleck's first big break was in the made-for-TV movie "Returning Home," (a remake of the "The Best Years of Our Lives.") Then, a role in "The Rockford Files" and "The Sacketts," a mini-series based on the Louis L'Amour stories. Under contract to Universal Studios, Selleck turned out a bunch of television pilots before being cast as "Magnum, P.I.". . . . The series was an immediate hit, and during its eight-year run, he won an Emmy and a Golden Globe Award for Best Actor. Other television credits include the movies "Divorce Wars," and "The Shadow Riders." Big Tom's appearances on the "big screen include *High Road to China,* a 1940's jewel thief coerced into espionage in *Lassiter* (1984) and the science-fiction thriller *Runaway.* His film *Three Men and a Baby* in which he co-starred with Ted Danson and Steve Guttenberg, was one of the most popular film comedies of the decade. His recent films include *Quigley Down Under* (1990) and the character drama *Hard Rain.*

Divorced from his first wife, Selleck married Jillie Mack *(Cats)* in 1987. They have a daugher together—Hannah Margaret Mack Selleck born in 1988—and he has a stepson, Kevin. A restaurateur on-the-side, he owns The Black Orchid in Hawaii with fellow actor Larry Manetti.

Jane Seymour

She was a shy, reserved child whose only concerns were sewing and dancing. Her dream was to be a prima ballerina. But little did she know at that time she would become a well-known star of stage and screen.

She was born Joyce Frankenberg in Hillingdon, Middlesex, England, on 15 February 1951. Because of her love for dance, she began taking ballet lessons at the age of two, and made her professional debut with the London Festival Ballet at thirteen in *The Nutcracker Suite.* In 1964, Jane transferred from her high school, Wimbledon High, to the Arts Educational Trust, where she trained in dance, music, and theatre. Her performance in *Cinderella* with the Kirov Ballet in 1967 turned out to be her last because of knee problems. So instead of dancing, Jane turned to acting at sixteen. She took her stage name from the most obscure of

Henry VIII's six wives, Jane Seymour. She made her film debut in 1968 in the controversial *Oh! What a Lovely War*. Following her film debut, she decided that the stage would provide the best training, and soon after was cast in everything from Shakespeare to Ibsen to Christie. At the same time she was also performing radio dramas on the BBC. Although her next film role was in *The Only Way* (1968), it was her performance in *Young Winston* (1969) that caught the eye of one of England's most powerful casting directors. Among the roles she landed as a result of her performance include the BBC-TV series "The Onedin Line," and "The Strauss Family." Jane's next film appearance was in the James Bond thriller *Live and Let Die* (1971). To keep from being typecast, she joined the English repertory theatres. Two years later, she landed a role in the film *Sinbad and the Eye of the Tiger* (1973). Three years later she moved to the U.S. to pursue her acting career, and upon the advice of Hollywood producers, she worked diligently to lose her British accent. Soon after, she appeared in *Battlestar Galactica*. Several other films followed including *Somewhere in Time* (1979), *Oh Heavenly Dog* (1979), *Lassiter* (1984), *The Tunnel* (1988), and *Keys to Freedom* (1989). She has also been seen in numerous made for TV movies and miniseries such as "Frankenstein, the True Story" (1972), "Our Mutual Friend" (1975), "Captains and Kings," for which she received an Emmy nomination (1976), "7th Avenue" (1976), "The Awakening Land" (1977), "The Four Feathers" (1977), "Jamaica Inn" (1982), "The Haunting Passion" (1983), "Sun also Rises" (1984), "Crossings" (1986), "East of Eden" for which she won a Golden Globe (1980), "Obsessed with a Married Woman" (1988), "War and Remembrance" (1988), "The Woman He Loved" (1988), "The Richest Man in the World," for which she received an Emmy for Best Supporting Actress (1988), and "Jack the Ripper" (1989). Jane appeared on Broadway for one season in the production of *Amadeus* (1980). This accomplished actress has also written a book entitled *Jane Seymour's Guide to Romantic Living* which was published in 1986.

Jane, her husband David Flynn, (married 18 July 1981) and their two children Katie and Sean, reside in Santa Barbara, California. The couple own an estate just outside of Bath, England.

Gene Shalit

"No one has accused Gene Shalit of being another pretty face," recorded a *Newsweek* reporter. "His lumpy visage is crowned by an aureole of bushy black hair and slashed with quizzical eyebrows and a 5-inch-wide mustache, conjuring up a cross between Jerry Colonna and a startled bullfrog." NBC-TV has

stated that market-research data supports the "Colonna/bullfrog" as the most popular film critic in the U.S. Shalit has been on the NBC News' "Today Show" on a permanent basis since January 1973. In addition to his off-the-cuff "Shalitisms," funny and punny, he reviews the arts daily during his "Critic's Corner" segment, and conducts interviews (chortling all the way) with a variety of guests. His movie reviews are syndicated to many stations affiliated with the NBC television network, and he has a daily feature broadcast on the NBC radio network.

Born in New York City in 1932, Shalit grew up in Morristown, N.J. (his father was a pharmacist), where he started his career as editor of his fourth-grade newspaper, *The Forlorn News*. After studying journalism at the University of Illinois, he became a partner in a public relations firm (Scrooge & Marley) specializing in irreverent promotions for magazines. That led to his column in the *Ladies' Home Journal* and, eventually, to book reviews on the "Today Show." Former NBC News president Reuven Frank, who in 1973 added Shalit to "Today's" permanent cast, recalls that network executives expressed "doubts about my sanity. But the fact that he looked different struck me as a plus." The "clown-in-critic's-clothing" knocks himself out delivering his own material and delights in his review "gimmicks" (which he claims he slips in only when he is outraged). He used a fly swatter to demonstrate what he thought about the movie *Superfly*. His review of *The Great Gatsby* consisted of shaking his head (side-to-side) as the "great" in the title was changed to "good," "fair," and "poor." When it finally reached "yecch" he nodded assent. While presumably amusing his millions of viewers, he is infuriating "industryites" who have nicknamed him "Gene Shallow." "Publicists find it difficult to get him to screenings," growled an article in the trades, "an annoyance lessened by his seemingly constitutional inability to remain still and seated at those showings he does elect to attend." When he was asked to narrate *Peter and the Wolf* with the Boston Pops at Tanglewood, *Variety* reported: "Shalit, who likes to be on the scene, also popped up visually in several other portions of the programs, topped by waving an American flag during the closing 'Stars and Stripes Forever.' Arthur Fiedler was also at the concert." The walrus-moustached king-pun of the "Today Show" has commented on his sashaying around New York City getting his ego fan-fed: "Cops in squad cars pull over to say they like me. Little old ladies get out of limousines to shake my hand and black guys in garbage trucks shout, 'Right on.'" His book *Laughing Matters: A Celebration of American Humor* was published in 1987.

William Shatner

"If I do nothing else in life, I've made a contribution. Between 'Star Trek' on TV and in films, if Captain Kirk has become part of the consciousness of a generation, that's not a bad thing to be remembered by," he said after the demise of the sci-fi series. But Shatner was beamed back to earth for more hero doings in the 1981 cop show "T.J. Hooker." His galaxy may have changed, but his swagger remained the same, demonstrating that his machismo traveled well and did not falter with age and a toupee.

William Shatner was born in Montreal, Quebec, Canada, on 22 March 1931. Intent on acting from an early age, he ignored his parent's prodding to join the family clothing business and devoted his time to regional theater and repertory companies in Canada. After relocating to New York, he appeared on Broadway and on the "Defenders" and "Studio One," among other leading TV programs. He reportedly turned down the lead on the megahit "Dr. Kildare," deeming series television work to be a trap for a "serious" actor. He changed his mind when offered the helm of the starship *Enterprise*. Intrigued by the program's ambitious concept and scripts, he relocated to Los Angeles, anxious over the fate of such creative fare in the ratings game. The drama about a futuristic exploratory space mission guided by a virile captain and his stolid Vulcan sidekick survived a three-year search for a mainstream audience, and was cancelled in 1969. But the show's youthful and fiercely loyal fans, called "Trekkies," kept the 79 episodes alive in reruns and flocked to the five movies based on the space saga, beginning with the 1979 *Star Trek*, all the way through to *Star Trek V* in 1989. Shatner married actress Marcie Lafferty in 1973. He has three children from an earlier marriage to Gloria Rand. His latest endeavor is his creation of the science-fiction book, *Tekwar* (1989).

Charlie Sheen

In only a few short years, he has been seen in an amazing 20 or so films, as well as attaining stardom status in the world of show business.

Charlie Sheen was born Carlos Estevez in Los Angeles on 3 September 1965, and grew up in a family of entertainers. His father is the multi-talented actor, Ramon Estevez, a/k/a Martin Sheen, and his brother, actor Emilio Estevez. Charlie made his television debut at age nine in the CBS feature "The Execution of Private Slovik," which starred his father. Eight years later, he made his film debut in *Grizzly II—The Predator*. He has also appeared in *Red Dawn, The Boys Next Door, Lucas, The Wraith, Ferris Buehler's Day Off, Platoon, Three for the Road, No Man's Land, Never on a Tuesday, Eight Men Out, Wall Street, Johnny Utah, Young Guns* and *Young Guns II* with his brother Emilio, *Beverly Hills Brats, Backtrack* and *Major League*. His 1990 films include *Navy Seals*. He has been seen on television in the CBS made-for-TV movie "Silence of the Heart," the ABC special "Jack London's California," and on Steven Spielberg's "Amazing Stories." In addition to acting, he is interested in writing, producing, and directing. He has already written, produced and directed a 35mm short entitled "R.P.G. II," as well as a collection of poems entitled "A Piece of My Mind," An avid sports lover, Charlie spent several of his summers at the Mickey Owen Baseball School in Springfield, Missouri. "If I weren't an actor, I would definitely be playing college baseball at this time," says Charlie. His upcoming projects include *Rookies,* co-starring Raul Julia and directed by Clint Eastwood.

In his spare time Charlie pursues hobbies that include music and filmmaking. Still single, he resides in Malibu, California.

Martin Sheen

Tabbed "an actor's actor" for his powerful and uncompromising performances on film and Broadway, Sheen gained experience during the political turmoil of the 1960s that led him to tackle portrayals of major political figures, including John Kennedy in a 1983 television production, and John Dean in the TV version of his post-Watergate biography, *Blind Ambition.*

Sheen was born Ramon Estevez in Dayton, Ohio, on 3 August 1940, the seventh child of a poor family of ten. He earned pocket money caddying at a local golf course while dreaming of becoming a pro like his childhood idol, Arnold Palmer. But Sheen was sidetracked into acting when he won first prize—a trip to New York—in a talent show. "I let my hair grow long, listened to a lot of music and was very aware of the times. There were two big influences  on me, James Dean and Elvis Presley, and no one who had that kind of effect came along until Bob Dylan." Sheen (he changed his name to avoid ethnic typecasting) first came to critics' attention in the 1964 play *The Subject Was Roses* after an apprenticeship with the Living Theater. He appeared in productions of Joseph Papp's N.Y. Shakespeare Festival, and in episodic television, before making his first feature film, *The Incident,* in 1967, playing a hood who terrorized subway riders. He played a killer in the 1973 low-budget but critically acclaimed movie *Badlands,* and appeared on TV in "The Execution of Private Slovik."

Surviving a heart attack he suffered during the grueling filming for Francis Ford Coppola's *Apocalypse Now* in 1979, Sheen, who played Robert Kennedy in the 1974 "The Missiles of October," took on the role of John Kennedy in a seven-hour dramatization, "Kennedy." Although the project was dismissed by some as a whitewash, the longtime admirer of the Kennedys said, "He was no less human than any of us, but he was far more courageous. That's really what a hero is. Courage is the first virtue." Recent films include *Wall Street* (1987), *Judgment In Berlin* (1988), *Da* (1988; he was co-executive producer/star) and *Personal Choice* (1989). He also appeared in a Turner Network Television film, "Nightbreaker" (1988). Sheen married his wife, Janet, in 1961, and they have four children. His sons, Emilio Estevez and Charlie Sheen, are popular young actors.

Sam Shepard

S am Shepard, playwright (*Cowboy Mouth,* 1971; *The Tooth of Crime,* 1972; *Curse of the Starving Class,* 1977; *Buried Child, True West* and *Fool for Love,* 1978; and *A Lie of the Mind,* 1985),

musician (the Holy Modal Rounders) and actor (*Days of Heaven*, 1978; *Resurrection*, 1980; *Frances*, 1982; *The Right Stuff*, 1983; *Country*, 1984; *The Fever*, 1985; *Crimes of the Heart*, 1986; *Baby Boom*, 1987; *Steel Magnolias*, 1988; and *Defenseless*, 1990), has made his mark on the theatre as one of its most multi-faceted artists and has gained for himself a reputation as "a genuine American original."

Sam Shepard was born in Fort Sheridan, Ill., on 5 November 1943, to Jane and Samuel Shepard. As his father was a career army man, the family moved around when Sam was young, and eventually settled in Duarte, Calif., where Sam finished high school. He started his career in the theater with a church drama group and eventually moved to New York City. While working as a waiter at the Village Gate, he met the founder of Theatre Genesis, and his career in Off-Off-Broadway was launched. Shepard worked in theatres like Cafe La MaMa, the Open Theatre, Cafe Cino and the American Place Theatre. He settled in England for a few years, where his work was well-received. After his return, he went with Bob Dylan on tour with the Rolling Thunder Revue in 1975, and wrote the *Rolling Thunder Logbook* in 1977, an account of the tour. Most of Shepard's themes deal with the displacement and stifling of the artist's creative spirit and many have western/cowboy lead characters. His writing ("his language reminds us of Pinter, his landscape of Beckett") has earned him several Obie awards and the Pulitzer Prize for Drama (*Buried Child*). Screenwriting credits include the 1984 film *Paris, Texas,* and *Far North* (1988). Described as "soft-spoken and unaffected," Shepard, who has received critical praise for his acting (especially in *Frances* and *The Right Stuff*), maintains homes in the Middle West, Marin County, and a farm in Nova Scotia. Shepard has a son, Jesse Mojo, from his marriage to actress O-Lan Johnson Dark. His current companion is his *Frances* and *Country* co-star Jessica Lange; the couple have a son and a daughter.

Nicollette Sheridan

According to *TV Guide*, she "seems to be the quintessential siren of the younger set. Drop-dead gorgeous, with movie-star eyes and legs that last for days, Nicollette recalls Grace Kelly—icy, regal, even aloof. As Paige, Sheridan blends the freshness of youth with the sensibilities of a well-heeled fashion expert; her clothes may be daring for some, but with her panache, she brings it off without a hitch. For the adventurer in all of us, she's the one to watch."

Born 21 November in Sussex, England, Nicollette relocated with her parents to Los Angeles at ten years old. In a ping-pong progression, she first attended the Isabel Buckley Elementary School in California, then she returned to England where she attended the Milford School at Somerset. Setting her sights on acting, she came back to the United States and was signed by New York's Elite Modeling Agency. On a chance meeting while auditioning for a TV commercial, Nicollette caught the eye of the famous photographer Francesco Scavullo, who was instrumental in helping her make the February, 1984, prestigious spot as cover girl for *Cosmopolitan*. Nicollette remained a model but branched her talents to television and silver screen. Her credits include the telefilm "Agatha Christie's Dead Man's Folly," the T.V. series "Paper Dolls" and the movie *The Sure Thing*. Her biggest claim to fame is playing Paige Matheson on "Knots Landing." As the glamourous daughter of the leading male (played by Kevin Dobson), Paige cuts her weekly appearances in the nighttime soap in a way that has given her a household name. The 1989 cliffhanger saw Paige running deliriously in the rain, frightened about whether her lover (played by William Devane) or a press agent was a murderer. In 1990 Sheridan's character was a bride left at the altar.

Nicollette Sheridan is not married and has homes in New York and Los Angeles. She enjoys traveling, painting, reading, and outdoor sports such as motorcycle riding, horseback riding and snow skiing. She also starred in a 1990 cable television film, "Deceptions," with love-interest Harry Hamlin.

Brooke Shields

"**H**er beauty, her smile, that's what works," says Scavullo. Another observer asks, "Yeah, but where's the tragic flaw?" Joan Rivers, known for her sixth-sense ability to find the pea in the celebrity mattress, turned to Brooke Shields one night having nearly completed her interview with the then dewy teenager on the "Tonight" Show, took her hand and said, in effect, you're a sweet

kid, don't blow it. Brooke is the apple that inspires the American pie. She's as sweet as they grow, and now Brooke Shields & Co., Inc., is as rich as she is ripe. The photogenic actress/model also has a bright head on her shoulders. She graduated from Princeton University in 1987 with a knowledge of French literature. Shields also took many psychology courses to enrich her education. During an interview on "Entertainment Tonight" in 1989, she explained how she is applying the sense of facts she learned in school to future parts. She says her goal is to do "all different roles I can sink my teeth into."

She was born 31 May 1965 in New York; her father is six-foot-seven socialite and businessman Frank Shields (whose father was Francis X. Shields, an American tennis champion of the 1930s, and mother the Princess Marina Torlonia of Rome). Brooke's mom, Teri, came from a poor, devoutly Roman Catholic family in Newark; she worked in the cosmetics field and was a part-time Seventh Avenue model. Teri was managing a Manhattan restaurant when she met Brooke's father; the marriage lasted for less than a year. Teri launched Brooke's career almost inadvertently one day when fashion photographer and friend "Scavullo called me up," she recalls. "He was sitting in a studio with 300 screaming kids and he had to shoot an Ivory Soap commercial . . . so he asked me to bring Brookie over—he knew her—and we made $35." A few months later, legend has it, Teri was wheeling Brooke down 52nd Street when they came upon Greta Garbo, who stopped to pat the child and admire her.

Brooke became Eileen Ford's very first child model. For three years she was Avedon's model for the Colgate toothpaste ads, and for nearly as long was a lustrous Breck Shampoo girl. (It was also during this time that Teri consented to let Brooke be photographed in some nude "art" photographs which proved embarassing years later when the photographer decided to publish them. A teary Brooke and Teri tried unsuccessfully to get a court order to halt publication.) Brooke made her TV debut sitting in Christopher Plummer's lap in Arthur Miller's "After the Fall" and became a national celebrity in 1977 playing a twelve-year old prostitute in Louis Malle's film *Pretty Baby*, set mostly in a New Orleans brothel. *Time* magazine observed that as Violet she was "a child model of astounding beauty . . . also a natural actress . . . a volatile mixture of both innocence and carnality . . . she makes the audience feel that anything can happen when she is around." Still, it was risqué, and the *Washington Post* wondered what the film would do to its child star: "At the end of *Pretty Baby*, you're more intrigued by what the future holds for Brooke Shields than what it held for Violet." Brooke admitted in *New York* magazine, "Sure, I knew what was going on with the sex scenes and everything in New Orleans. I just didn't say so. I very often pretend I don't know what's going on. It works better for me."

Among her many films and projects have been *The Blue Lagoon* opposite Christopher Atkins, *Endless Love, King of the Gypsies, Tilt, Wanda Nevada, Sahara, Just You and Me Kid,* and *Alice, Sweet Alice* (a/k/a *Communion*). Her latest films are *Brenda Starr* and *Backstreet Strays.* On the little screen, she has appeared in the telefilms "Wet Gold" and "The Diamond Trap." Anyone living on this planet has seen Brooke's face grace the covers of fashion magazines; *Time* deemed her the official "Face of 1980s." The public has a never-ending fascination with her, as her nearly 2,000 pieces of fan mail a week reveal. Will success spoil Miss Shields? It's a bit like asking a bird how she feels about the air. Brooke's always been a star, still she answers the question demurely: "Sometimes it's hard to take in that *Brooke Shields* who everybody seems to be talking about is me."

Dinah Shore

H er Sunday night "Dinah Shore Show" was a TV staple (and five-time Emmy winner) back in the 1950s and she was TV's reigning Southern songbird for years (earning nine gold records). She resurfaced doing more talking than singing in 1970 on "Dinah's Place," a gabfest on NBC that covered everything from cooking and child rearing to contour sheets. "Dinah" (CBS-TV, 1974), another daily talk-variety show, followed suit. In 1989 she was at it again with "A Conversation With Dinah" on the TNN cable network.

Be that as it may, for most of Frances ("Fanny") Rose Shore's years (born 1 March 1917 in Winchester, Tenn.) the music came first. "Dinah" (from the time she had her own radio show in Nashville) established her adopted name in New York teaming with another young singer, Frank Sinatra, on radio station WNEW. She cut some records with Xavier Cugat, sang out with radio's Chamber Music Society of Lower Basin Street, and found national popularity during a three-year hitch on Eddie Cantor's weekly program on NBC radio. A World War II favorite at camp shows all over the globe, she had only a so-so film career ("I bombed as a movie star") but found greater glory as the "Mumm-wah" Chevy girl on TV. In the 1960s, she bowed out of her 18-year marriage with George Montgomery, filled her time rearing their two children, appeared in an occasional TV special and engaged in a short-lived marriage to Maurice Smith, all the while playing lots of tennis. In 1971 the sweetly smiling singer-turned-talker became a writer with the book *Someone's in the Kitchen with Dinah*. (Her second book, *The Dinah Shore Cookbook*, was published by Doubleday in 1983.) In 1972 she popped up regularly in the gossip columns as the date of Burt Reynolds, famous then for posing as the first male nude centerfold in *Cosmopolitan*. Dinah has garnered ten Emmys all told and was the first woman to be awarded the Babe Zaharias Award from the Metropolitan Golf Writers Association. She was also the first woman to receive the Silver Hope Chest Award of the Multiple Sclerosis Dinner of Champions for her contributions to sports (the Dinah Shore Open is a top women's golf tournament) and to receive the Entertainer of the Year Award from the All American Collegiate Golf Foundation.

Ron Silver

This accomplished actor has graced us with his presence on the stage as well as on the screen. Although his initial interest was in the field of Chinese studies, he went on to become well known in the field of acting.

He was born Ron Zimelman on 2 July 1946 in New York City. He attended the University of Buffalo, where he received his bachelor's degree, then continued his studies, obtaining a master's in Chinese from St. John's University and the College of Chinese Culture in Taiwan. Upon his return to New York several years later he began his acting training at the Herbert Berghof Studios, the Actors Studio, Uta Hagen and Lee Strasberg. He made his stage debut in *Kaspar* and *Public Insult* in 1971. Several theatre performances followed, including *El Grande de Coca-Cola* (1972), *More Than You Deserve* (1973), *Angel City* (1977), *In the Boom Boom Room* (1979) and on Broadway in *Hurly Burly* (1984-85), *Social Security* (1986), and *Speed the Plow*, with Madonna (1988), which won him both a Tony and a Drama Desk Award. Ron made his televison debut in 1976 in the sitcom "Rhoda" as her upstairs neighbor, and remained with the show for two seasons. Other television credits include "The Mac Davis Show," "Hill Street Blues," "Betrayal," and "Billionaire Boys Club." Moving on to film, he appeared in his first film, *Semi-Tough*, in 1977, followed by *The Entity, Silkwood, Garbo Talks, Eat and Run, Oh God! You Devil*, and *Blue Steel*. His 1990 film work includes *Reversal of Fortune*, about the Sunny Von Bulow case.

Ron and his wife, Lynne Miller, have been married since 24 December 1975.

Jean Simmons

The *Great Expectations* (1946) of an 18-year-old dancer who had disliked Shakespeare in school could hardly have included playing Ophelia to Sir Laurence Olivier's *Hamlet* (1948). One reviewer commented, "She has an oblique, individual beauty and a trained dancer's continuous grace. Compared with most of the members of the cast, she is obviously just a talented beginner. But she is the only person in the picture who gives every one of her lines the bloom of poetry and the immediacy of ordinary life." She has received the highest film-acting awards from Italy, Belgium, Switzerland, and Ireland. She was voted Britain's most popular star of 1950 at the age of 21. In the fall of that year she rocketed to Hollywood to launch her American career.

Born Jean Merilyn Simmons on 31 January 1929 in London, she was 14 when she was plucked from dancing school for *Give Us the Moon* (1942). Her first Hollywood film was *Androcles and the Lion* (1952). She has also appeared in *Young Bess, The Robe, Desiree, Guys and Dolls, Spartacus* (all in the 1950s), *Elmer Gantry* (1960), *All the Way Home* (1963) and *The Happy Ending* (1969). Divorced from British-

born actor Stewart Granger (one daughter), she married film director Richard Brooks (one daughter). Although she has announced
retirement on several occasions, the hazel-eyed Ophelia seems
unlikely ever to take the plunge. In 1983 she appeared in the
televised version of "The Thorn Birds," and in 1988 she was in a
miniseries for the Disney Channel, "Great Expectations." On the
big screen she starred in the 1988 film *The Old Jest*.

Frank Sinatra

"In today's trend-crazed world
of pop music, Frank Sinatra is
not simply the ultimate survivor but
the ultimate victor," wrote *New York
Times* pop-music critic Stephen Holden. On 23 May 1985 a double victory
of sorts came to this musical legend: at a
luncheon in the White House, he was
given the nation's highest civilian hon-
or, the Medal of Freedom; and later in
the day he received an honorary engineering degree from Stevens Institute
of Technology in his hometown of
Hoboken, N.J. Remaining an active per-
former, Sinatra still packs the house as he did on "The Ultimate
Tour" (1988) with Sammy Davis, Jr., and Liza Minnelli.

Ol' Blue Eyes was born Francis Albert Sinatra on 12 December
1915, the son of a prizefighter-turned-fire captain (who once told
his son singing was "for sissies") and a dynamic mother (Dolly) who
was active in Democratic politics. After high school, Sinatra worked
for a time as a copy boy on the *Hudson Observer*—an interesting
beginning given his later well-known love/hate relationship with
the press. Then he organized a singing group, the Hoboken Four ("I
wanted to be like Bing Crosby"). He won first prize on the Major
Bowes' Radio Amateur Hour, singing "Night and Day," and was
sent on a Bowes tour. Other jobs followed, and one night while
Sinatra was acting as a singing emcee at a small club, Harry James
caught him and signed him to sing with his band at $75 a week.
During an engagement in Los Angeles, Tommy Dorsey saw him
and offered $150. With Dorsey, Sinatra sang with the Pied Pipers
and later as a soloist. In 1942 he went out on his own and began

attracting national attention with his own radio show; by 1943, he was starring on "Your Hit Parade." When teenagers began to scream and swoon, he was booked into New York's Paramount Theatre at $7500 a week, and when a girl who had stood in line for seven hours and sat through several shows fainted from hunger, the "swooning over Frankie" fad began. Headlines blazed: "5000 Girls Fight to Get View of Frank Sinatra." He was mobbed by the attention-hungry wartime teenagers (Sinatra himself was 4-F because of a punctured ear drum). Ultimately, he became a top box-office draw in films such as *Anchors Aweigh* (1945), *On The Town* (1949) and *Pal Joey* (1957).

He has been married four times; his first wife was Nancy Barbato, with whom he had three children—Nancy, Frank Jr., and Tina. His second marriage was to screen temptress Ava Gardner, then Mia Farrow and the former Barbara Marx. After his marriage to Gardner in the early 1950s crumbled, he toppled off the top of the Hollywood heap. His vocal chords hemorrhaged, and MCA, the colossal talent agency, unsympathetically dropped him. Eventually he was able to sell himself to Columbia for an insulting $8000 to play the Italian GI Maggio in *From Here to Eternity*, a role that brought him his now-legendary comeback when he won the Best Supporting Actor Academy Award. He has made other popular films, including *High Society, Guys and Dolls, The Manchurian Candidate, The Detective* and *The Man with the Golden Arm.* He won an earlier Oscar in 1945 for the documentary *The House I Live In,* a plea for an end to prejudice.

He was once the top tail in the Rat Pack, and although Marlene Dietrich dubbed him "The Mercedes Benz of Men," he hasn't always been known for his smooth drive and purring motor. His *causes célèbres* are legendary—among them: hissing, "Get your hand off the suit, creep" to Speaker of the House Sam Rayburn at the 1956 Democratic Convention when Rayburn placed his hand on Sinatra's sleeve and requested he sing "The Yellow Rose of Texas." More recently his activity has been filled with prodigious activity in recordings, concerts, awards (he was the recipient of the prestigious Kennedy Center Honors in 1983 and the Jean Hersholt Award of the Motion Picture Academy in 1971) and he has garnered a whole new group of fans—young people. Critic Holden has written that Sinatra's albums and songs are "heroic feats of self-generation, of finding more with less and gaining in the struggle a reason for going on." (Sinatra says his greatest inspiration is Billie Holiday.) *Newsweek's* Jim Miller wrote in 1982: "Age has softened his sinister aura—the petty feuds and hair-trigger temper, his association with reputed underworld figures. . . . He presents himself as a champion of charity, an apostle of the American Way." One thing is certain: he has refuted his father's contention that singing was for sissies.

Siskel & Ebert

They are America's favorite film-critic team. Between the two of them, they have received a Pulitzer, two Emmys and the IRIS Award, and have been inducted into a hall of fame.

Roger Ebert was born on 18 June 1942, in Urbana, Illinois, where he later attended the University of Illinois and was the editor of the *Daily Illini*. He began his career as a film critic in 1967 writing a column for the *Chicago Sun Times*. In 1975 he won a Pulitzer Prize for his distinguished criticism in the *Chicago Sun Times*, and to date he is the only film critic to have ever received the prestigious award. Since then, Roger has also written several books, including *A Kiss Is Still A Kiss* (1984), *Roger Ebert's Movie Home Companion* (1985), he co-authored *The Perfect London Walk* (1986) and *Two Weeks in the Midday Sun* (1989). In addition, Ebert is also film critic for *The New York Post* as well as for WLS-TV, the ABC affiliate in Chicago, and teaches at the University of Chicago in the Fine Arts Program.

Gene Siskel was born on 26 January 1946, in Chicago, Illinois. He attended Yale, and graduated with a B.A. in Philosophy. He began his career in 1967 as a film critic with Roger Ebert in "At the Movies." Two years later he became a newspaper reporter for the *Chicago Tribune* and within seven months he became the paper's film critic. In 1974, Siskel became the film critic for the CBS affiliate in Chicago, WBBM-TV, where he still reviews movies on the evening news. In 1978 Siskel won an Emmy Award for hosting "Nightwatch," which was an experimental monthly series featuring the independent film and video works.

The duo began performing together in 1967 as film critics on the show "Sneak Previews," which was the highest-rated weekly half hour program in the history of the Public Broadcasting System. In 1979, the team won an Emmy Award for their excellent reviews on "Sneak Previews." In 1982 they joined Tribune Entertainment which produced the nationally syndicated "At the Movies," and in 1986 they teamed up again for another film show simply called

"Siskel & Ebert." They were among the initial performers to be inducted into the NATPE Hall of Fame, and received the IRIS Award for successfully moving from local to national syndicated television.

Steven Soderbergh

He began making films when he was a mere 13 years old. His first experience with filmmaking was in an animation class offered by Louisiana State University. Realizing that it involved "far too much work for far too little result," says Steven, he switched from animation to live action.

Steven Soderbergh was born circa 1963 in Georgia. Shortly after he was born, his family made several moves, the last of which was to Baton Rouge, Louisiana, where Soderbergh began high school. Acquainting himself with students from Louisiana State University had made it possible for easy access to all sorts of film equipment. He spent the next four years making a series of Super 8 short films. After graduating from high school, he followed his dreams and moved to Los Angeles. He stayed there a year and a half, during which time he landed his first job as an editor for a program that was quickly cancelled. Realizing that he needed more experience in the field, Soderbergh picked up and moved back to Baton Rouge to further develop his skills as writer and director. Upon returning to Louisiana, he spent two years as a coin attendant at a video arcade, where he aggressively worked on scripts. He later worked at a local video production house where he would produce occasional commercials for friends. A friend from LSU gave him work salvaging programs for "Showtime," for which he would fly out to LA, recut the footage and return home. His break came when someone working in management for the rock group Yes called "Showtime" to see if they knew anyone who could go on the road with the band to shoot an in-house documentary, and they recommended Soderbergh. Yes was so impressed with his work that they later hired him to direct the feature-length concert movie *9012 Live*. In the spring of 1986, the film premiered on MTV, and later was nominated for a Grammy Award for Best Music Video, Long Form. Soon following this successful concert movie, he signed on with an agent, and was hired to write a TV movie and a musical. Neither of these were made. Outlaw Productions had faith in Steven and his talent, and the outcome of this was *sex, lies, and videotape,* winner of both the Best Film Prize and the Best Actor Award at the 1989 Cannes Film Festival. *sex, lies, and videotape* is the first full length feature film to be written by Soderbergh. Not only did he write the film, but he also edited and directed it. He wrote the script in eight days in 1987 on his way from Baton Rouge to Los Angeles. When describing the film, Steven states, "The film deals with people not coming out and saying exactly what they're thinking or feeling. Sex, lies and videotape are what the film is about and a lot of the country revolves around: the selling of sex, the telling of lies and the inundation of video."

Suzanne Somers

Nude photos in the December 1984 *Playboy* brought the soft-porn public back to her favor, although she denied she posed for the glossy spread because her career was sagging. "The pictures that were published in *Playboy* [before] were test shots used without my approval. I was in awful shape. I'd just had a baby and I still had baby fat. This time I had complete control and I'm in very good shape. Besides, the things I've done that were supposed to be 'good' for my career— movies with Donald Sutherland and Ian McShane—turned out to be disasters. The things that I've done that were supposed to be 'bad'—like playing Chrissie on 'Three's Company' and taking my act to Las Vegas—turned out to be the best things I've ever done. So now I just follow my instincts."

Blue-eyed, blond-haired Suzanne Somers (real name Mahoney) was born on 16 October 1947 in San Bruno, Calif., and attended schools in San Francisco. She worked as a nurse's aide giving psychological tests for a year before she became a model. While working on "Mantrap," a syndicated show in the Bay Area, she met late writer Jacqueline Susann, who encouraged her to find a publisher for her first volume of poetry, *Touch Me.* It sold well and was followed by another volume, quite naturally, *Touch Me Again.* She then wrote a self-help volume, *Some People Live More Than Others.* She married Bruce Somers, now a lawyer and psychologist, when he was 19 and she 17. (She'd been expelled from a Catholic convent school when she was caught writing detailed love letters to him.)

Quite soon afterwards she became pregnant. Everything about the marriage, especially morning neighborhood coffee klatches, scared her. "I just panicked," Suzanne recalls. "I knew I couldn't stay in that marriage." Out from it she went, determined to become an actress via modeling, but by her own description she was "the worst model in San Francisco." She had a young child to care for and times were tough, but when she met and married Alan Hamel she began to get parts in TV commercials, summer stock, and when she won the part of Chrissie on "Three's Company" (beating out 299 other blond sexpots), she became an instant overnight star in the Farrah Fawcett mode. Since leaving the show in a salary dispute in 1980, Somers has had another child, worked in Vegas (named Las Vegas Female Entertainer of the Year in 1986), and made the TV version of Jackie Collins's super-sleaze sizzler "Hollywood Wives," playing back-stabbing actress Gina Germaine. She currently stars in the television syndicated sitcom "She's the Sheriff" and has become the honorary chairperson for the National Association of Children of Alcoholics. To top it all off, her latest book, *Keeping Secrets*, was published in 1988. In her spare time, Suzanne likes to cook or stroll around the desert.

Sissy Spacek

"The only thing I can figure is that I had so many of the basics," responded Sissy Spacek when asked where she got her fearlessness. "I always had a secure life, always had such support from my family, so much love from them . . . maybe that makes it easier to focus on what you want. You can go farther out on a limb, because you know if you don't make it, it doesn't really matter. Someone will be there when you fall." Going out on limbs has paid off for Spacek, who has played a drugged orphan in *Prime Cut*, her first professional film (1972), a naive friend of a psychotic boy on an interstate crime spree in *Badlands* (1974), a weird teenager who unleashes her telekinetic powers in Brian de Palma's *Carrie* (1976), a way-out young maid who housecleans in the nude and hustles on the side in *Welcome to L.A.* (1977) and a young Texas wanderer who steals her roommate's personality in *Three Women* (1977). But it took her strong, non-kooky portrayal of Loretta Lynn in *The Coal Miner's*

Daughter to win the 1980 Academy Award ("I was Loretta's choice. She was looking through a pile of pictures, and when she came to one of me, she said, 'that's the coal miner's daughter'"). She received Oscar nominations for *Carrie, Missing, The River* and in 1987 for *Crimes of the Heart.*

Mary Elizabeth Spacek was born Christmas Day, 1949, in Quitman, Texas. Her older brothers called her "Sissy," and the name stuck. She was adored by her family and friends, twirled a baton and led cheers, and was a homecoming queen for the Quitman Bulldogs ("after my brother Robbie died of leukemia I was elected homecoming queen, probably for sympathy reasons . . . I felt really cradled by that town"). Her high school dream was to become a singer-musician (she sang with a choral group and taught guitar for fifty cents an hour); after graduation she packed her guitar and went to New York and lived for several months with her cousin, Rip Torn, and his wife, Geraldine Page ("It gave me strength being Rip's cousin"). She enrolled in Lee Strasberg's acting class, and after a few months took off for California and a film career. Other films include *Heart Beat* (1980), *Raggedy Man*, directed by her husband (1981), *Marie* (1985) and *'night, Mother* (1986). Television appearances include Tennessee Williams's "The Migrants" (1973), "Katherine" (1975), and "Verna: USO Girl" (1978).

Spacek married Jack Fisk, an art director, in 1974, in "an eensy, sweet little chapel near the beach" in Santa Monica with Fisk's Hungarian sheepdog their only witness. Between films they take off for Quitman with their children to enjoy piney woods, rolling hills and fishing. "She enjoys getting back to grass roots," says her mother. "After she finishes a movie, she can come back there, relax and remember who she really is."

James Spader

He is a young and upcoming superstar who has appeared in theatre, televison, and film. He has co-starred with everyone from brat packers Andrew McCarthy and Charlie Sheen to the distinguished and established Robert Mitchum and Diane Keaton.

James Spader was born in Boston, Massachusetts in 1961 into a family of educators. After attending the prestigious Phillips Academy, he moved to New York City to pursue a career in acting, where he trained in theatre at the Michael Chekov Studio. To support himself during his studies, Spader loaded railroad cars, drove trucks and worked as a stable boy at the Claremont Riding Academy. He made his film debut in 1981 in *Endless Love.* Since then he has appeared in *The New Kids, Tuff Turf, Pretty in Pink* in which he portrayed Andrew McCarthy's best friend, *Mannequin*, *Wall Street*, in which he played Charlie Sheen's lawyer friend, *Less Than Zero*, *Baby Boom* in which he starred as Diane Keaton's rival at work, *Jack's Back* with a critically acclaimed performance of a portrayal of twins, *sex, lies, and videotape*, in which he plays Graham, a man in search of truth and his inner self, *The Rachel Papers*, and *Bad Influence*. He made his TV debut in 1983 in *The Family Tree*. Other television credits include the ABC science fiction film "Starcrossed," "Diner," and the made-for-TV movies "A Killer in the Family," and "Cocaine: One Man's Seduction." James's theatre work includes productions of *Equus*, and *Veronica's Room*. He also appeared in Sundown Beach for the Actor's Studio in New York.

James and his wife are bi-coastal, residing in both Los Angeles and New York.

Steven Spielberg

"I never believed in anything before I believed in movies," states this extraordinary young filmmaker whom Hollywood big chief Michael Eisner called "the highest paid human being for performing a service in the history of the world," referring to such phenomenally popular and profitable box office hits as *Jaws*, *E.T.*, *Raiders of the Lost Ark*, *Poltergeist*, *Close Encounters of the Third Kind*, *Indiana Jones and the Temple of Doom*, *Gremlins*, *the Goonies*, *Back to the Future*, *An American Tail*, *The Color of Purple*, *The Land Before Time*, *The Empire of the Sun*, *Who Framed Roger Rabbit*, *Indiana Jones and The Last Crusade*, *Gremlins II*, and *Always*. For the 1990 summer-movie season he produced *Arachnophobia*. He made his TV debut in the fall of 1985 hosting an anthology series on NBC "Steven Spielberg's Amazing Stories."

Born 18 December 1947, he moved all over the country with his father, an electrical engineer, and his concert-pianist mother until his parents separated when he was a teenager. ("Divorce was the first scary word I remember hearing.") So involved was he in movies and television and filmmaking (Richard Dreyfuss, the actor, said of him: "He's a big kid who at 12 years old decided to make movies, and he's still 12 years old") that he claims not to have noticed any of the social-political upheaval of the 1960s. "*Poltergeist* reflects a lot of the fears I had at night—scary shadows that could simply be bunched up dirty clothes or a shadow like Godzilla cast by the hall light. In *E.T.* I'm reacting to a situation in my life. When my father left, I want from tormentor to protector with my family. I'd never assumed responsibility for anything except making my home movies—my sisters were constantly getting killed off in my little 8-mm extravaganzas. Suddenly here was real life knocking at my door. I had to become the man of the house. The first scary thing I learned to do was turn off the lights. But I also knew that light was something to make things beautiful. To me light is a magnet—it can veil something wondrous or, as in the flashlights in *E.T.*, something terrifying."

His high school grades weren't good enough for him to be accepted at any of the major film schools, so as an English major at California State College he regularly fibbed his way onto movie studio lots to observe directors such as Hitchcock and Franklin Schaffner in action. His 22 minutes *Amblin'*, which he describes as an "attack of crass commercialism," won awards at both the Atlanta and Venice Film Festivals and was distributed as a featured short with *Love Story* in 1970 by Universal. At age 20 the *wunderkind* was signed to a seven-year directing contract at that studio. His first assignment was directing Joan Crawford in Rod Serling's "Night Gallery" on TV. Directing episodes of TV shows such as "Marcus Welby M.D.," "Columbo," and "The Name of the Game" was his "diploma to feature films," the first being *Duel,* starring Dennis Weaver as a mild-mannered traveling salesman chased down a lonesome freeway by a driverless truck. Shot in just 16 days for $350,000, it grossed over $5 million in Europe and Japan. His next feature was the critically acclaimed *The Sugarland Express*, made in 1974, before his mega-hit *Jaws* (1975) netted millions from a toothsome, terrifying deep blue sea.

Home for this celluloid Croesus (whom in a 1985 *Time* cover story labelled "Magician of the Movies") includes an adobe mansion-office headquarters for himself and staff of 15 on Universal's Hollywood lot and top drawer satellites in Bel-Air, Malibu and high in the sky in Manhattan's Trump Tower. Friends say he's as darling as Peter Pan and not unlike the fabled ageless boy. After the birth of his son, Max, Spielberg married actress Amy Irving in 1985. They were divorced in 1989. Spielberg and actress Kate Capshaw have a child, Sasha, born in May, 1990.

Robert Stack

I t took 20 years and 30 movies for this handsome, athletic actor to hit pay dirt as Elliot Ness in TV's outrageously successful "The Untouchables." The series ran for four years, made him a superstar, won him an Emmy, made him the most popular star on French TV and led to a flood of offers from European producers who wanted him in their films. A versatile actor who began his career in the Jack Benny comedy film *To Be or Not to Be,* in recent years Stack has starred in both comedy roles (*Airplane!; 1941*) and heavy dramatics (*Uncommon Valor*). However, TV remains his favorite medium. He's one of the few actors to star in four major television series, and the only one with so many shows dealing with crime. Starting with the Prohibition-era series "The Untouchables," he went on to portray the editor of *Crime* magazine in "Name of the Game," followed by his third and fourth series, "Most Wanted" and "Strike Force," both police action shows.

Born 13 January 1919 in Los Angeles, he's a fifth-generation Californian whose ancestors were among first U.S. families to settle in the little pueblo now known as L.A. He grew up among motion picture, concert, opera and radio favorites, many of whom were guests at his home during his childhood years. (His grandmother was the renowned singer Marina Perrini; his father was the millionaire adman who dreamed up the slogan, "The Beer That Made Milwaukee Famous.") Raised for six years in Europe as a young child, he learned French and Spanish before he knew English. Returning to the states, he became a champion skeet shooter at age 16 (holding two world records) and later, at USC, "majored in polo." Turning to an acting career, he entered the Henry Duffy School of the Theatre, was soon scouted by a Universal Studios talent scout, and made his film debut giving Deanna Durbin her first kiss in *First Love*. He scored in such films as *Written on the Wind* (Oscar nomination) and *The High and the Mighty* (his favorite role), but his career was mired in largely mediocre films for years. Bob joined the navy during World War II, graduating at the top of his class from the Naval Air Base at Pensacola and serving as an aerial gunnery instructor. Among his postwar films were *A Date with Judy*, with Elizabeth Taylor and Jane Powell, and *Mr. Music*, with Bing Crosby.

Offscreen, he was known as one of Hollywood's more flamboyant playboy types until his marriage in 1956 to starlet Rosemarie Bowe (two children). "Since Rosemarie got married it's OK to say she's well stacked," he once joked. Their fragrance and fashion ventures are being managed through Rosemarie Stack Ltd., a division of the Stacks' St. Pierre production company formed in April, 1984, of which she is chairman and he is president. Stack remains very active in the business. He's starred in CBS-TV's "Falcon Crest" and remains the host of "Unsolved Mysteries." Recent films are *Glory Days*, *Blood Relations*, *Dangerous Curves* and *Caddyshack II*.

Sylvester Stallone

"The champion represents the ultimate warrior—the nearest thing to being immortal while mortal. The champion lives on forever. The championship belongs to a single person who because of the nature of what he does, has the respect of everyone on the face of the earth." Thus spoke the most famous muscle man in Hollywood ("Pacific Palisides Pecs," they call him) and, in 1985, the highest-paid actor in Hollywood.

Born on 6 July 1946 in New York's Hell's Kitchen and raised in Philadelphia after his parent's divorce, the multi-muscled talent remembers: "I was told by my teachers that my brain was dormant, and I took it to heart and channeled a tremendous amount of energy into my physical development." An appearance in a school production of *Death of a Salesman* made him determined to make it in New York's acting world. In the peculiar early 1970s, he caged up in a fleabag hotel and practiced his craft in front of the mirror between jobs working as a food demonstrator, a sweeper in the lion's cages at the Central Park Zoo and as an usher at the Baronet Movie Theatre (where he met his wife, Sasha, also an usher). It was during this time that he became determined to create heroes for the common man and, having seen the film *Easy Rider* in 1969, convinced himself that "I couldn't write any worse." He wrote two novels that were never published and made minor appearances in several films, his first important role being Stanley in *The Lords of Flatbush* (critics singled him out). Inspired by a prizefight between heavyweight champion Muhammed Ali and an obscure New Jersey fighter named Chuck Wepner who managed to go almost the full 15 rounds before being knocked out, Stallone got the idea for *Rocky*. He dictated the script to his wife in a mere 86 hours, shooting lines at her and rejoicing, "This is it, this is it!" It certainly was. The film made Stallone not just a star but a hero. His life changed. *Rocky* won a 1977 Academy Award as Best Picture and gave birth to *Rocky II, III, IV,* and *V.* He has also revived the character he played in *First Blood* and spawned a line of (machine-gun toting?) dolls with *Rambo: First Blood II* in 1985 and *Rambo III* in 1988. Besides these films, Stallone starred in *F.I.S.T.*, wrote a successful novel, *Paradise Alley* (starring in the 1978 film version), and produced, directed and coauthored the sequel to *Saturday Night Fever—Staying Alive—*which starred a waxed and shining John Travolta. Other films include *Nighthawks* (1981), *Victory* (1981), and *Rhinestone* (1984). In 1986 he starred in *Cobra* and *Over the Top,* and in 1989 he headed the prison drama *Lock Up.* He entered the 90's with *Tango & Cash,* co-starring with Kurt Russell. Upcoming projects include a sci-fi movie titled *Isobar* and a final *Rambo* movie with an environmental theme.

Success spoiled Mr. Stallone, too. His marriage faltered and for a while he went around the ring of life without his wife and two children, Sage Moonblood and Sergio. "There are no perfect people," he said, "only perfect moments. Our separation has brought us closer together." Not for long. They split permanently in 1985, and Sly took up with decidedly non-melancholy Dane Brigitte Nielson. Bad casting from the beginning, the couple had a brief marriage (1985-1988).

The tough guy also has a soft side. Always concerned for his fellow man, Stallone was the 1988 honorary chairman for the New York March of Dimes. His character on the screen reflects to his personal life: "Just the other day I got on the subway to remind myself what it was like. I took the 59th Street BMT. I only went one stop because, being recognized, there was quite a lot of shoving, with guys yelling, 'Hey my man, you're Rock, my Rock! Come over her and kiss my sister.' That's the real wealth—it's not the money but the communication."

Barbara Stanwyck

"Attention embarrasses me. I don't like to be on display," says the striking screen legend who is sometimes char-

acterized as a "loner" because she does not attend big social events ("I never did care for big parties. You don't get to talk to anybody. I prefer groups of six or eight people"). And so it was with great reluctance that she consented to be fêted by the Film Society of Lincoln Center in 1981. "It was a terrible shock. But a splendid shock," she later admitted. After this honor, Stanwyck was not as stage shy; in 1986 she was the recipient of the Cecil B. DeMille Award at the 43rd Annual Golden Globe Awards, and in 1989 she was given the American Film Institute Award.

The youngest of five children, she was born Ruby Stevens in Brooklyn, 16 July 1907. She was orphaned at four and, for a time, was brought up by an older sister, Mildred. "But we were very poor so we were all skipped off to foster homes. Growing up with nobody, I had to cope with loneliness at a very early age. Now the psychoanalysts tell you to be your own best friend. I had to master that earlier than most people." At fifteen she worked as a night-club dancer, landed a bit with Ziegfeld's *Follies* in 1922, and subsequently worked as a chorine until 1926. Under the name of Barbara Stanwyck (taking her name from an old playbill listing Jane Stanwyck as Barbara Frietchie), she bowed as a dramatic actress in Willard Mack's play *The Moose*. Her first film was *The Locked Door* (1928), but it was with Frank Capra's *Ladies of Leisure* (1930) that she became a star. She has given many unforgettable performances (her favorites: *The Lady Eve*, 1944; *Double Indemnity*, 1944; *Sorry, Wrong Number*, 1948, and four times was nominated for an Academy Award (for *Stella Dallas*, 1937; *Ball of Fire*, 1941; *Double Indemnity* and *Sorry, Wrong Number*). Not until 1982 did the Academy of Motion Picture Arts and Sciences finally bestow upon her their award—a special Oscar for a long and distinguished career. "People talk about my 'career' but 'career' is too pompous a word. It was a job, and I always have felt privileged to be paid for doing what I love doing." Among the Stanwyck traits of honesty, generosity, punctuality ("I'd rather wait for people than have them wait for me") ranks fearlessness. She has never used a double, and in a fight scene in *Clash By Night* she was accidentally shoved against a hot projection machine. Blood dripping from her arm would not deter her from finishing the scene, hiding her injury from the camera. She still has a scar. Never demanding, she was known to the crew as "Missy," an endearment that became her nickname.

Her first marriage in 1928 (one adopted son) to Broadway comedian Frank Faye ended in divorce in 1935, and in 1939 she married Robert Taylor. After a decade, that marriage ended in painful divorce and she never remarried ("Nobody ever asked me, and that's the truth"). "Bob and I didn't stay friends. We became friends again," and in 1965 they costarred in *The Night Walker*. An Emmy Award winner for her TV series "The Big Valley" (1965-68), Barbara Stanwyck emerged in 1983 to appear in the mini-series "The Thorn Birds"; her performance considered among the best of her career, she won an Emmy as Best Actress in a Dramatic Special. She returned to the series scene from 1985-1987 as the family matriarch in "The Colbys." "I have no intention of being the old lady in a purple shawl in my rocking chair looking at my old scrapbooks," she states firmly. "I'm not a yesterday's woman. I'm a tomorrow's woman."

Maureen Stapleton

"The actor has to hang out his ego on the line for everyone to see and weigh. He better hang it on a good line." The unglamorous but glowing and immensely talented Maureen Stapleton ("I'm kind of nondescript-looking"), who is just as likely to wear a hooded Army surplus jacket as a mink, has hung her ego on such lines as *The Rose Tatoo* (1950, her first Tony), *Toys in the Attic* (1960), *Plaza Suite* (1969), *The Gingerbread Lady* (1970, her second "best actress" Tony, for which she won a *Times* accolade—"As variegated and dazzling a performance as New York has ever seen"), and the 1981 Broadway revival of *The Little Foxes* (starring Elizabeth Taylor).

Born on 21 June 1925 in Troy, N.Y., she was very young when her parents separated. She grew up "nice, fat, and unhappy," and her escapes were eating and going to the movies. ("My real ambition, from the age of 6, was to be Jean Harlow—but alive of course. I always thought if I became an actress, I'd automatically look like her.") Stapleton arrived in New York at age 17 weighing 170 pounds and with $100 dollars in her purse. Her first Broadway part was in *Playboy of the Western World*. That led to Tennessee Williams's *Rose Tatoo*, after which the stage became her playing field. In 1958 Stapleton appeared in her first film, *Miss Lonelyhearts,* for which she received an Oscar nomination. After 11 years on the stage, film acting didn't come easy ("I kept telling myself, you learn three acts in plays, why can't you remember one little passage?"). Since that time she has appeared in many films, including *Bye Bye Birdie*, *Plaza Suite*, *Airport*, Woody Allen's *Interiors*, *The Fan*, *Reds* (1982, for which she won an Oscar playing the anarchist Emma Goldman), *Heartburn* (1986), *My Little Girl* (1986), *Nuts* (1987), *Sweet Lorraine* (1987), and *Cocoon: The Return* (1988). Acclaimed television performances include "Among the Paths to Eden" (1967 Emmy), "Queen of the Stardust Ballroom," "The Gathering," "Family Secrets," and "The Thorns." Recently Stapleton admitted film is her favorite medium: "It's easier. They pay you more money. And you get two days off a week, and that's nice."

Divorced from Max Allentuck (two children) and David Rayfiel, she insists: "My children are the most exciting thing that's ever happened to me. I know that sounds Pollyanna-ish, but it happens to be true." And does she have a preference in performing comedy or drama? "Sorry to sound so crass, but whatever job pays is the one I want. . . . It doesn't sound very artistic, but I have a granddaughter now, and all I'm thinking about is money for her teeth, for her school, maybe for a little house for her."

Mary Steenburgen

Although this Oscar-winning player states, "If there's one thing I loathe about what happened to the American theatre after Brando, it's these actors who show you how much they're acting," she doesn't yearn for the torn T-shirt-and-mumble days either. "If you want naturalism in acting, you go film the butcher. For me, the whole point of acting is to 'sail' a little and give a view of what's wonderful from a few feet off the ground." It would be trite, but right, to point out that hers have been more than a few feet off the ground since her rocket-rapid rise in filmdom. The press agent's-sounding story goes that she was audition-interviewing by day and waiting tables by night when, after nearly six years in Manhattan, she read for and wowed actor-director Jack Nicholson, and he slotted her as the leading lady in his 1978 flick, *Goin' South*. She's been going strong ever since, and went on to a 1980 Best

Supporting Actress performance in *Melvin and Howard*. "I try to retain my sanity. Life is too short for me to be tortured by my roles. I hope that doesn't make me less of an actress," Mary Steenburgen says. "But if it does—tough luck."

Speaking of luck, Steenburgen (pronounced steen-berjen) has employed the paying-your-dues variety. Born in 1953, the daughter of a railroad conductor based in Newport, Arkansas, she first studied drama at her home state's Hendricks College, where her professor suggested she drop out and study acting in New York. At 19, she enrolled at the Neighborhood Playhouse to study with Sanford Meisner, supporting herself during her studies mostly by waitressing. In the years before her first paid performing job in *Goin' South*, she worked with an improv comedy troupe. Following her first movie, once again over formidable competition, she was cast as time-travelling H.G. Wells' San Francisco lady-love in the offbeat romance, *Time After Time*, opposite Malcolm McDowell. (Not long after finishing the film, she and her co-star were married, and are now the New York and Hollywood-residing parents of two.) She has also been seen in *Ragtime*, Woody Allen's *A Midsummer Night's Sex Comedy*, *Romantic Comedy* (opposite Dudley Moore) and as author Marjorie Kinnan Rawling in 1983's *Cross Creek*. Her other movies include *Dead of Winter* (1987), *End of the Line* (1988), *Miss Firecracker* (1989), *Parenthood* (1989), and *Back to the Future, Part III* (1990). Mary has dropped the distinctive Arkansas accent of her youth. "Ah tawked lahk thay-ut!" Steenburgen recalls. She also starred in the TV miniseries "Tender is the Night" and "The Attic: The Hiding of Anne Frank."

Rod Steiger

In more than half-a-hundred films and TV presentations, he's played some of history's most notable personalities: Napoleon, Mussolini, W.C. Fields, Al Capone, Pontius Pilate. While doing them, Steiger has made (film) history himself, sharing in some of the screen's best efforts: *On the Waterfront*, *Oklahoma*, *The Pawnbroker*, *Dr. Zhivago* and *In the Heat of the Night* (for which he won the 1968 Best Actor Oscar). Little wonder, then, that he peers with disdain at the New Hollywood. "The motion picture business is in bad shape,"

Steiger says. "All they want to do it to . . . make sequels and . . . a lot of money. All art is lost, out the window." When reminded, however, that occasional Steiger-starring showings (such as *The Amityville Horror*) have been deemed less than artistic, he admits, "Well, it was bad, I guess, but I needed the job. I want to act." But his transgressions, unlike Pontius Pilate's, are minor and infrequent. "I think of acting as an immediate reward and an immediate death," he says. "The greater the moment on stage, the longer the mourning." Some of his other films include *Catch the Heat* (1987), *American Gothic* (1987), *The January Man* (1988), and *Tennessee Waltz* (1989).

Born Rodney Steven Steiger 14 April 1925 in Westhampton, New York, he joined the wartime Navy at the age of 16, whiled away Pacific hours by broadcasting "Shadow" stories over his ship's intercom. "Shadow!" the captain once interrupted, "this is Phantom. Get the hell off that line and pipe down!" After the war he joined a drama group at the Vet's Administration, "because that's where all the girls were." Advised to take his acting seriously, he built a solid reputation as evidenced by his winning the 1953 Sylvania Award as one of the best five TV performers of the year. The thrice-divorced Malibu resident wants to direct movies next. "I don't want to end up playing grandpa," Steiger says. "That would be hard." His ex-wives include Sally Gracie, Claire Bloom (one daughter), and Sherry Nelson.

James Stewart

"**S**ometimes," drawls Hollywood's original Mr. Aw-Shucks, "I wonder if I'm doing a Jimmy Stewart imitation myself. I'm a lazy person. By nature I would have planned a quieter life. I don't act. I react." Since his arrival in Hollywood as a blushing, bumbling beanpole of a boy back in 1935, he's "reacted" in more than 70 films, among them such American classics as *You Can't Take It With You* (1938), *Mr. Smith Goes to Washington* (1939), *The Philadelphia Story* (1940; Oscar), *Harvey* (1950; later also on Broadway and TV), *Rear Window* (1954) and *The Spirit of St. Louis* (1957). In recognition of all this he was the recipient in 1980 of the American Film Institute's Lifetime Achievement Award, in 1983 of the Kennedy Center Honors and in 1985 of the Medal of Freedom, America's highest civilian honor (which also acknowledged his military contributions). In 1989 he wowed the literary set with his book *Jimmy Stewart and His Poems*. He has recorded the book for audiotape.

Born James Maitland Stewart, 20 May 1908, in Indiana, Pennsylvania, he was the son of a Scottish hardware store owner and grew to lanky manhood with no thoughts of being a thespian. "But then at Princeton two things happened," he explains, "I was studying engineering and I flunked math. And I took part in a Triangle show." When school chum Josh Logan suggested a summer with a stock company on Cape Cod, he packed up his accordian ("People would not only talk right through my act; they would also sometimes say 'Shut up'") and emerged in the fall as an actor on Broadway. In New York he appeared in numerous flops, acquiring an unenviable reputation for occasional malaprops. On one opening night, he recalls, "I tugged so violently at a door which wouldn't open that I lifted the whole scenery wall. It came down on my head. When I finally got it fixed again, the door creaked open by itself. So I rushed over and shut it. It creaked open again and I rushed over and shut it again. Finally it creaked open a third time and a disembodied hand from backstage appeared and held it shut. We closed the second night." Later the doors opened for him when a movie scout saw him in *Yellow Jacket* (1934), and he set off for Hollywood.

Early in his picture career he played in *Wife Versus Secretary* as a gone-to-hayseed swain. "Jean Harlow had to kiss me," he later remembered nostalgically, "and it was then I knew that I'd never been kissed before. By the time we were ready to shoot the scene, my psychology was all wrinkled." But his first MGM contract enabled him to give vent to another love—flying. He bought his first real plane. "It's something that you never forget, never tire of. It's a freedom—it's true." Many planes—bigger and better—followed, but when he got to marriage, only one was for him. After a long tenure as the movie colony's most resolute bachelor, he married the once-divorced big-game huntress Gloria McLean in 1949, and often has gone with her on safaris. (He does most of his shooting with a camera, deciding "to leave the other part to Gloria.") Mrs. Stewart had two sons by a previous marriage, Michael and Ronald (who was killed in action in Vietnam); the Stewarts also have twin daughters, Judy and Kelly.

Noteworthy for many years as the highest-ranking movie star in the military, Stewart was an Air Force Reserve brigadier general before his retirement in 1968. One of the first stars to enlist in World War II, he rose from private to bomber pilot and squadron commander, participating in more than 20 missions over Bremen, Frankfurt, and Berlin. "I always prayed," says Stewart, "but I really didn't pray for my life or for the lives of other men. I prayed that I wouldn't make a mistake." He was a much-decorated colonel by war's end. Shortly after his appointment to brigadier general in 1959 (after some Congressional hassling), he ran into engine trouble while flying a tour of duty, but managed to bring his plane to a safe landing. "All I could think of was not my personal safety," he said later, "but what Senator Margaret Chase Smith (who was then Chairman of Senate Armed Services Committee) would say if I crashed such an expensive plane."

Stiller & Meara

"**W**e felt we'd made it when we saw our picture on the wall at the local dry cleaner," answered Ann Meara with a twinkle in her Irish eye when asked when she and Jerry Stiller first knew they were a success. Today the red-headed Irish Rose, "tall, bubbly, and beautiful," from Brooklyn, and the nice Jewish boy, "short, pensive, and retiring," from the lower East Side, are now the best known husband and wife comedy team in show business since Burns and Allen. They first met in an agent's office where they swear the agent chased each of them around his desk during separate interviews. Neither one got the job, but they found each other (which turned out to be a long booking).

Stiller, born 8 June, attended the lower East Side's Seward Park High (other alumni: Tony Curtis, Walter Matthau, Zero Mostel). He went on to Syracuse University, majoring in drama. After acting in various theater groups in New York City and across the country, he met Anne Meara "making the rounds." Meara, born in Brooklyn 20 September, was brought up on Long Island. After high school, she appeared in summer stock in Southhold, L.I., and Woodstock, N.Y., studied at the Herbert Berghof studio, won an Equity award for *Maedchen in Uniform*, did some television, and then met Jerry Stiller "making the rounds." Married 14 September 1954, they joined Joseph Papp's newly-formed Shakespeare-in-the-Park. "In those days we didn't have a stage in Central Park," Stiller recalls. "So, in the middle of a play you'd have a guy yelling from the grass, 'Eh Romeo! Give it to her! Give it to her!'" Meara adds: "The lines stayed the same, but our scenes got longer and longer." The actual formation of the comedy team was in the mid 1960s, as "an act of desperation." They had decided to have a baby and were forced to find another way to make some money. They played New York clubs like Phase Two, Village Gate, Village Vanguard, Bon Soir, a record-breaking 14-week engagement at The Blue Angel, the Royal Roost, and the Persian Room of the Plaza. An appearance on Merv Griffin's afternoon talent show led to the first major break with a guest shot on the Ed Sullivan show (resulting in a contract for 6 shows a year). Today they are constantly in demand for their tandem talents. (They now create and produce prize-winning radio and TV commercials for such clients as Blue Nun, Amalgamated Bank, GTE, United Van Lines and Harrah's, via their own production company.) And, while continuing as "the team" each has had phenomenal successful "turns" on their own. Anne created the role of Bunny in John Guare's award-winning *The House of Blue Leaves*. On television she appeared on "Medical Center," "The Male Menopause," was a regular on the "Corner Bar," "Archie Bunker's Place" and "Rhoda" series, and starred on her own show, "Kate McShane." Her films include *Boys from Brazil*, Neil Simon's *The Out-Of-Towners*, *Lovers and Other Strangers* and *Fame*. She received personal praise for her appearance in Harvey Fierstein's short-lived 1984 *Spookhouse* on the stage. She recently won the Writers Guild Award for "The Other Woman," a TV movie which she co-scripted with Lila Garrett (Meara co-starred with Stiller and Hal Linden).

Stiller was "indecently funny" in the 1984 blockbuster David Rabe his *Hurlyburly*. He previously starred on Broadway in *Unexpected Guest*, *The Ritz* (also the movie) and *Passione*. He created the role of Launce in Joseph Papp's production of Shakespeare's *Two Gentlemen of Verona*. Other movie appearances: *The Taking of Pelham One, Two, Three*; *Airport '75* and *Those Lips, Those Eyes*. He also was co-star of the television series "Joe and Sons." Stiller and Meara live in Manhattan (2 children, Benjamin and Amy) and are devoted to the city. For years Stiller has been an active member of his West Side block association. And with Meara he has made TV commercials promoting block associations and an "I Love a Clean New York" spot for radio.

Sting

"**W**hy does tradition locate our emotional center at the heart and not somewhere in the brain? Why is the most common image in popular music the broken heart? I don't know. . ."

"I once asked my history teacher how we were expected to learn anything useful from his subject, when it seemed to me to be nothing but a monotonous and sordid succession of robber baron scumbags devoid of any admirable human qualities. I failed History."

"A great uncle of mine who was a seafaring man once gave me the following advice 'Never board a ship unless you know where it's going.' Sometimes it's hard to tell the game shows from the TV evangelists."

The former Gordon Matthew Summer, erstwhile leader of the British rock group, The Police, has "no intention of becoming a victim of the whole rock myth." Not blending into the mainstream, his music is a combination of reggae and pop with lyrics that make you think.

Having become something of a movie sensation—in films such as *Brimstone and Treacle;* a five-minute appearance wearing a leather jockstrap in *Dune;* in *Plenty* as the working-class black marketeer whom Meryl Streep asks to father her child; in *The Bride*, starring opposite Jennifer "Flashdance" Beals; a cameo in *The Adventures of Baron Munchausen* and roles in *Julia and Julia* plus *The Side*—he speaks defiantly about his independence from the trio that made his career: "The mistake that people always make about music groups," he told John Duka in a *New York Times* interview, "is they assume that if you're successful, the group becomes a way of life. For me, the band is only a tool in which I express my ideas, not a way of life. As soon as it becomes limited in expressing my ideas, then it's over. I can transcend it and use it to accomplish other things. Why should I have to make music with the same two people the rest of my life?" (The group disbanded in 1985, the year Sting made his first solo album—*The Dream of the Blue Turtles.*) He expanded his career one step further as he headed the cast of *The 3 Penny Opera* on Broadway in 1989.

Born 2 October 1952 in Newcastle, England, the son of a milkman and a hairdresser, he was given his nickname because of a black and yellow jersey he wore with the frequency of a second skin.

By the time The Police formed in 1977 Sting was already married, a father, and the veteran of seven British television commercials, as well as having made his screen debut in the Who's film *Quadrophenia*. The almost instant success of The Police had many comparing them to the Beatles. (Their concert at Shea Stadium topped the attendance figures set a decade earlier by the long-haired foursome.) Lisa Robinson, the syndicated rock columnist, had said that Sting is "an incredibly talented songwriter. . . . But it's strange. When the Beatles came along they affected an entire generation in terms of dress and politics. Everyone grew their hair and changed clothes. Sting has not affected people that way. I hate to say this, but Sting has become enormously successful because he is safe and knows how to sell." His music is some of the most intellectually conceived, well-crafted pop music around. Speaking about The Police's 1983 superhit album "Synchronicity," Duka wrote that Sting had become "the intellectual Dark Prince of Sadness, his persona mingling menace and melancholy." Sting agreed. "I'm very melancholic, but I'm lucky in that I have a mode of expression that rewards melancholy. I express it in song. It's heard by other people and makes them sad and melancholic. And then you have a success on your hands."

With his first wife, Frances Tomelty, he had two children, Kate and Joe. He shares his house outside London in posh Hampstead with Trudie Styler, with whom he also has kids. "My children are very important to me," he says, "I see them all the time." Sting claims to prefer classical music to rock, calling rock "a sort of wonderful mongrel that takes from everywhere. That's its genius." In recognition of other artists making music, Sting formed his own label, Pangaea Records, with Miles Copeland. The label concentrates on esoteric music rather than pop.

"It is part of his anachronistic appeal that, physically, Sting is a bit of a throwback to the old time, Hollywood type of glamour: tall, blonde and handsome, a classic heartthrob, perfectly proportioned," John Duka observed, "and able to tear his shirt off during concerts with the best of them." In 1988 he was voted the best Male Pop Vocalist by NARAS, as he received the Grammy for "Bring on the Night."

Oliver Stone

Twice-wounded Vietnam veteran Oliver Stone also has a matching pair of Oscars. The decorated Purple Heart with Oak Leaf cluster director was acclaimed by the Academy for both *Midnight Express* and *Platoon*. His follow-up film, *Wall Street*, added

more praises to the already established man of the cinema. He earned another Academy Award for Best Director with 1989's *Born on the Fourth of July*.

Oliver Stone was born in New York City on 15 September 1946. He attended Yale University and New York University, and served in the U.S. infantry (1967-1968) fighting in Vietnam. Stone was only 21 when he and the rest of his 25th Infantry Division were shipped to War Zone C in the Hobo Woods not far from Vietnam's Cambodian border. Wounded during a night ambush in his first few days in the field, the filmmaker created a similar ambush for *Platoon* and the movie's final battle that took place on New Year's Day, 1968. "I wrote the script seven years after I'd come back," says the vet. "It took me that long to come to terms with the reality of what happened there." *Platoon* was Stone's fourth directorial effort. It came on the heels of the highly acclaimed (albeit controversial) *Salvador*, another exploration of grim contemporary reality, this time in Central America. He made his directorial debut as a 25-year-old with the low-budget film, *Seizure*, made from his own screenplay. For his second outing as a director, he made the thriller, *The Hand*, with a screenplay he adapted from the novel, *The Lizard's Tale*. The 1981 release starred Michael Caine.

Stone's reputation as a screenwriter hit its first peak in 1978 when *Midnight Express* (about an American jailed in Turkey) not only won the Oscar but the Writers Guild of America Award. In recent seasons, Stone co-authored the script for *Conan the Barbarian*, wrote the screenplay for *Scarface* and collaborated (with Michael Cimino) on the script for *Year of the Dragon*. His 1990 work includes a film about the rock group The Doors. In what can be viewed as the unassailable rights of a writer-director, Stone appeared in *Platoon* as a major who is blown up in his bunker at the end of the film. A far cry from the lowly rank of "grunt" over twenty years ago.

Meryl Streep

"She has an incredible piece of working life ahead of her," says Dustin Hoffman of his co-star in *Kramer Vs. Kramer*. "She's going to be the Eleanor Roosevelt of acting." By the 1980s, she was unquestionably America's premier dramatic screen actress. In addition to her Oscar as 1979's Best Supporting Actress for

Kramer, she won another Academy Award as Best Actress of '82 for her moving performance in the title role of *Sophie's Choice*. Coincidentally her '78 Emmy Award for the TV mini-series *Holocaust* was for her portrayal of a woman like Sophie: a Gentile victimized by the Nazis. But still, the radiant actress says, referring to her childhood: "I thought no one liked me. Besides that, I was ugly."

Born Mary Louise Streep (Meryl was her mother's nickname) on 22 June 1949 in Summit, New Jersey, she was raised with two younger siblings in that state's affluent suburbs. Possessing an operatic soprano voice, she studied singing with Beverly Sills' teacher. Bossy and obsessed with her looks, Streep transformed herself into "the perfect *Seventeen* magazine knockout"—a high school cheerleader, swimmer and homecoming queen. She graduated from Vassar College in 1971, and attended Yale Drama School where, prior to her 1975 graduation, she attained near-legendary status playing over 40 roles, some at the Yale Repertory Theatre. She went on to perform extensively at New York's Phoenix Theatre and Joseph Papp's N.Y. Shakespeare Festival, winning both a Tony nomination and Outer Critics Circle Award in Tennessee Williams' *27 Wagons Full of Cotton*. Other New York stage highlights: her Lincoln Center performances in *Trelawny of the "Wells"* and Andre Serban's production of *The Cherry Orchard*; demonstrating her singing talent in Brecht-Weill's *Happy End* and Elizabeth Swados' *Alice in Wonderland*. Her 1977 film debut in *Julia* led to a larger part the next year in *The Deer Hunter*; her supporting role won an Oscar nomination. Other supporting parts in 1979's *Manhattan* and *The Seduction of Joe Tynan* preceded leads in *The French Lieutenant's Woman* (1981) and *Silkwood* (1983), both of which earned her additional Oscar nominations. The busy actress went on to star with Robert DeNiro in *Falling in Love* (1984), with Charles Dance and Sting in *Plenty* (1985), with Robert Redford in *Out of Africa* (1985; Los Angeles Film Critics Award for Best Actress), and with Jack Nicholson in *Heartburn* (1985), and *Ironweed* (1987). She received another Academy Award nomination for Best Actress for her moving performance in *A Cry in The Dark* (1988) and her next films were *She-Devil* (1989), *Postcards From the Edge* (1990), and a collaboration with versatile funnyman-filmmaker Albert Brooks, titled *Defending Your Life*.

When someone urged Streep to change her last name to "Street," she defended her own as "a perfectly good Dutch name, like

Rockefeller." She nursed her cancer-ridden *Deer Hunter* co-star and lover John Cazale through his terminal illness. After his death she married sculptor Donald Gummer in 1978. With their three children (Henry, Mary Willa, Grace), they live in Connecticut. Robert Benton, *Kramer's* writer-director, who allowed Streep to write her own lines for the film's court-custody fight scene, says of her, "She's one of the most sensible, well adjusted people I've ever met."

Barbra Streisand

The Hollywood jackals in their Armani suits had their triumph when she was denied any of 1983's Oscar nominations for her 16-years-in-the-planning musical *Yentl,* based on Isaac Bashevis Singer's tale about a Jewish girl in turn-of-the-century Poland who disguises herself as a boy so she can study Talmud at a Yeshiva. So what, she has a reputation for being a bitch? What else is a female perfectionist called, a perfectionist whose standards for herself result in a record of concurrent popularity in both pop music and movies that exceed such greats as Presley, Sinatra and Crosby? But such a snob? She wrote the *Yentl* screenplay (with Jack Rosenthal) produced, headlined, directed, sang all nine songs and recorded the album. The reviews ran from a low "Barbra Streisand wears a pillbox-contoured designer yarmulke . . . technical sloppiness is evident throughout," to Steven (E.T.) Spielberg calling it "the best directing debut since *Citizen Kane."*

"That so-called designer yarmulke is an authentic one of the period," she retorted. "It's mostly the women reviewers who are attacking me. Can't they stand to see another woman succeed?' But it wasn't just the women, it was all of Hollywood. Nevertheless, the film did very good business at the box office—despite Oscar's snub, and making it proved to be a breakthrough in the emotional life of the superstar who first burst into public notice at age 19 with her big nose and "delicatessen accent" in Broadway's *I Can Get it for You Wholesale.* Born in Brooklyn, 24 April 1942, she was 15 months old when her high school English teacher father died suddenly. "Emotionally, my mother left me at the same time—she was in her own trauma. . . . I didn't have any toys to play with, all I had was a hot water bottle with a little sweater on it. That was my doll. . . .

Growing up I used to wonder—what did I have to do to get attention? When I started to sing I got attention."

When her mother discounted her as an actress because she wasn't pretty enough, and said she should skip singing because her voice was too weak—suggesting instead that she become a secretary—Barbra grew her nails so long as to render the suggestion moot. At age 18, she won an amateur talent contest at a Greenwich Village bar—her remuneration was $50 a week and free meals. She studied the great voices of pop music past and latched onto material that lent itself to emotional interpretation. She discovered comedy when at one audition she "forgot I had gum in my mouth, and I took it out and stuck it on the microphone. It got a big howl." Her manager begged her to change her name, fix her nose and sing more conventional songs. Theatrical manager Marty Erlichman sought her out when her star was rising at *Club Le Soir*—he wanted to represent her. She asked him if he thought she should change anything about her self. Erlichman answered no and became her manager.

Her stage debut was in the ill-fated Off-Broadway *Another Evening With Harry Stones* in 1961. In rehearsals for *I Can Get It for You Wholesale*, Producer David Merrick thought she was unattractive. When the show opened, the critics changed his mind. The other novice in the play was actor Elliott Gould. The two fell in love, were married and had one son, Jason. Gould and she divorced in 1971. Streisand's career includes countless gold and platinum albums, memorable TV specials and films such as *Funny Girl*, for which she won an Oscar, *Hello Dolly*, *On a Clear Day You Can See Forever*, *The Owl and the Pussycat*, *What's Up Doc?* *Up the Sandbox*, *The Way We Were*, with Robert Redford, *The Main Event* and *A Star Is Born*.

In 1986 she produced and appeared in the film *Nuts* with Richard Dreyfuss, but was snubbed again by the Oscars. To the delight of her fans, she recorded *The Broadway Album* in 1985, followed by *One Voice* in 1987. The latter LP's proceeds went to the Streisand Foundation, which supports organizations committed to the preservation of the environment. In 1988 she recorded *Till I Love You*, a thematic album about "love in a relationship, finding it, questioning it, losing it, and finding it again." Her latest album, *A Collection: Greatest Hits & More* (1989), produced the single, "We're Not Making Love Anymore."

Elaine Stritch

When Elaine Stritch returned to New York in 1981 after eleven years in London ("Now that an actor is President

it was time for me to come home"), Earl Wilson asked her if she was aware of the new doggy bag custom in the posh restaurants since she had been away. "I'm taking not only the steak, but the bottle of wine, too,"she bellowed. "My doggy doesn't even drink." A convent-bred sometime bartender who once took a delivery boy from the grocery store to a party for Princess Margaret, the breezy blonde actress has observed somewhat ruefully: "The only time I've ever gotten great publicity is when I've done something other than my work." Not quite. It is true that she has made news for occasionally slipping behind a bar in New York or London. ("Everybody says 'What's *that* all about?'") One writer described her as "a sort of Grosse Pointe Texas Guinan having a helluva time." But it is equally true that critics and public have cottoned to her brassy brand of song and dance in vehicles like *Pal Joey, Call Me Madam, Goldilocks, Sail Away, Company* and the 1985 concert version of *Follies,* and to her dramatic performances in *Bus Stop* and *Who's Afraid of Virginia Woolf?* And English audiences cheered her stage and television performances while she resided there (very nicely, thank you, at the Savoy Hotel).

Born 2 February 1926 in Detroit, Michigan, the youngest daughter of a rubber company executive (and a cousin of the late Samuel Cardinal Stritch), she decided early on a theatrical career and went to New York after high school. At her parents' insistence, she first lived at Manhattan's uptown Convent of the Sacred Heart (the same order had been her Michigan mentors), while attending a Greenwich Village actors' studio, where Marlon Brando was a classmate. "Between Mr. B and the Mother Superior," she says of her work, "I didn't miss a thing." "I know what I'm doing," she says of her work, "and I love what I'm doing . . . the theatre . . . it's Pygmalion City. You can walk down Third Avenue in a pair of blue jeans for three days . . . then come on stage in white fox. And that's what it's all about. An actress is being someone else, but taking exactly what you've got in the blue jeans into the white fox."

Since her return to the United States she lives in New York City. Her husband, Irish actor John Bay, whom she married in 1973, died in 1982. She loves cooking and entertaining her close friends. When she learned she had diabetes (she was living in London), she quipped: "Listen, I'm just looking forward to the day they catch me in the ladies' room at the Connaught Hotel 'shooting up.' Boy, am I going to have the last laugh." In 1984, she authored *Am I Blue,* an account of her coming to terms with diabetes. She had a role on the short-lived "Ellen Burstyn Show" in 1986 and appeared in Woody Allen's film *September* in 1987, followed by a role in Ron Howard's *Cocoon II: The Return* in 1988. Working again in the theatre, she performed on Broadway in A.R. Gurney's revolving cast play *Love Letters* (1989). Rarin' to go, Stritch will play the Shirley MacLaine role for the TV series based on *Steel Magnolias*.

Donald Sutherland

"I don't see myself as a Cary Grant or a Clark Gable," says the lanky, 6′6″ Canadian who's become a favorite of film directors on both sides of the Atlantic. "I see myself playing roles where you can say, 'That's perfect for him'—not as a character actor, but as an actor performing a character which is close to one's self." Among the many perfect-for-him roles since his turning point casting as the iconoclastic surgeon Hawkeye Pierce in *M*A*S*H* in 1970: the sensitive detective who saves Jane Fonda from a homicidal maniac in *Klute* (1971); the father haunted by the vision of his drowning daughter in *Don't Look Now* (1973); the conscientious health inspector in the 1978 remake of *Invasion of the Body Snatchers* and the troubled father in the Oscar-winning *Ordinary People* in 1980. His recent films are *Revolution* (1985), *Lock Up* (1989), *Lost Angels* (1989), the Canadian epic *Bethune: The Making of a Hero* (1990), and *Eminent Domain* (1990).

Born in St. John, New Brunswick, Canada, 17 July 1934, Sutherland was raised in Nova Scotia, attended the University of Toronto, and studied at London's Academy of Music and Dramatic Art. As an average obscure repertory actor who lived a hand-to-mouth existence, he once occupied a basement room for $2 a week. ("It was an excellent deal. I lived right next to the hot-water heater and was warmer than anyone else in the building.") He now works with an almost ferocious intensity in films, being featured in anywhere from three to five a year and courted by such European directorial luminaries as Federico Fellini, Bernardo Bertolucci, and Nicolaus Roeg as well as Americans such as Alan Pakula and Robert Altman. He sees the relationship between actor and director as much like a love affair. "I become a director's plaything," he says, "something he can manipulate but upon which he must bestow a certain amount of affection. I've either loved directors or hated them. There hasn't been much in between." The twice-married, twice-divorced actor has lived since 1974 with French-Canadian actress and sometime co-star Francine Racette. They are the parents of two sons, both of whom they delivered themselves. Kiefer, his look-alike son from an early marriage to Canadian actress Shirley Douglas, is also a movie actor. A self-described workaholic who often values the creative process more than the completed film, Sutherland doesn't mind that many of his fifty pictures have not been commercially successful. "I work so much because I like to," he says, "There isn't any game plan. I'm very happy being an actor."

Keifer Sutherland

In the seven years he has been acting, London-born Keifer Sutherland has made quite an impression in both film and television. He has appeared in 12 films as well as on stage and TV. When asked about his father's influence on his success, Kiefer adds, "I've worked for seven years. I've only been living in a house for two. I'm not going to say I'm famous, but any kind of public attention I've achieved, I've achieved on my own. If my father helped me to acquire that, it's one thing; if I put myself in a position to sustain it, that's different." "Be polite. Smile. Be nice," is reportedly the only advice about showbusiness Donald Sutherland has ever given to his son Keifer.

Keifer was born in London, England on 21 December 1966, the son of Canadian actress Shirley Douglas and actor Donald Sutherland. Knowing at an early age that he wanted to act, he debuted at age nine in the Los Angeles Odyssey Theatre production of *Throne of Straw*. Following his parents divorce, he was sent to a "quasi-military" Canadian boarding school, where he was a bit undisciplined, and not into studying. By the time he reached 15, he was ready to quit school, leave the family and become an actor. "The last six months before I left home, the feeling got stronger and stronger, and then I said, 'I'm going to do this,' And I left," stated Keifer. Soon after leaving, he performed with several local workshops which later led to his first acting break and film debut. He was cast in a starring role in the Canadian feature film *The Bay Boy* (1984), for which he won the Genie Award, which is the Canadian equivalent of our Academy Award. Soon after, Keifer made his television debut in the made-for-TV movie "Trapped in Silence" (1986), followed by the telefilm "Brotherhood of Silence." On stage he has been seen in *Minnesota Moon* and *America Modern*. He has given many memorable performances in such feature films as *At Close Range, Crazy Moon, Stand By Me, The Lost Boys, The Killing Time, Bright Lights, Big City, 1969, Promised Land, Young Guns, Lakota, Renegades, Young Guns* (1988) and *Young Guns II* (1990).

Keifer and actress Camelia Kath were married on 12 September 1987, and separated in September 1988. They have two daughters, Sarah, born in February of 1988, and an eleven-year-old daughter from Camelia's previous marriage. He met love-interest Julia Roberts while making the 1990 release *Flatliners*.

Patrick Swayze

As Dalton, the rough-and-tumble bouncer who's the best in the business, actor/dancer Patrick Swayze gave another memorable film portrait in *Road House* (1989). Set amidst the sex, drugs and rock 'n' roll of the Double Deuce, a rural Missouri nightclub, *Road House* is the story of Dalton's "righteous battle against a brutal town patriarch whose lust for power barely overshadows his lewd and lascivious greed." Dalton's motto is: "It's my way or the highway." The Double Deuce is "a joint featuring chicken wire surrounding the stage, passed out bodies littering the dance floor and semicoherent power drinkers pawing the weary waitresses. At closing, the blood is mopped up, the bar is wiped down, and another day is over." A bit of a different role for Swayze who had just hung up his dancing duds from his star-making part in *Dirty Dancing* (1987). The film was set in 1963, in a summer resort in the Catskills. Patrick plays the resort dance instructor, "an enigmatic amalgam of Brando and Astaire," who comes to understand his place in a changing world through his relationship with the young guest who becomes his dancing partner. The teenager is played by Jennifer Grey.

The son of a choreographer, Patsy Swayze, he made his debut

into the world on 18 August 1954 in Houston, Texas. He began his career as a dancer under his mother's tutelage. After studying with the Harkness Ballet Company and the Joffrey Ballet, he became a principal with the Eliot Feld Dance Company. He also danced on Broadway in *Good Time Charley* (opposite Jennifer's father, Joel Grey), a revival of *West Side Story*, and, for two years, the lead role in *Grease*. Swayze made his feature film debut in the comedy, *Skatetown, U.S.A.* and went on to act in such films as Francis Ford Coppola's *The Outsiders*, the action adventure *Uncommon Valor, Youngblood*, John Milius' controversial war film *Red Dawn, Tiger Warsaw* and *Steel Dawn* in which his wife, Lisa Niemi, co-starred. In 1987 Swayze was nominated for a Golden Globe award as Best Actor for his portrayal of Johnny Castle in *Dirty Dancing*. After *Road Home* he was set to star as a Chicago cop in *Next of Kin*.

In addition to his starring role in the television miniseries "North and South," Swayze has appeared in several television movies. "The Comeback Kid" with John Ritter, "Return of the Rebels" and "The New Season." He starred in "The Renegades" which ultimately became a series. Swayze received excellent reviews for his dramatic portrayal of a soldier dying of leukemia in an episode of "M*A*S*H*" and also starred in an "Amazing Stories" episode entitled "Life on Death Row." A special added note: he is the composer/performer of "She's Like The Wind," a hit song from *Dirty Dancing*.

Jessica Tandy

She's played obedient daughters, crazed nymphomaniacs and fierce matrons. She is praised across the board as one of Broadway's greats. She first sparked the public's attention as Blanche Dubois in Tennessee Williams' *A Streetcar Named Desire* in 1947 and 36 years later played the pivotal role of Amanda Wingfield in another Williams' classic, *The Glass Menagerie*. In 1988 she won the Emmy (Lead Actress in a miniseries/special) for her performance in the television version of "Foxfire." And in 1990 she won the Academy Award for best actress for her performance as a fiesty dowager in *Driving Miss Daisy*, which also took best film kudos.

Born in London, 7 June 1909, Tandy made her first stage

appearance in the West End in 1927 and on Broadway a year later. She has won Tonys for her roles in *Streetcar* (opposite Brando), *The Gin Game* (1977), and in the musical play *Foxfire* (1983). In between she has stirred audiences in such plays as *Five Finger Exercise*, Edward Albee's *A Delicate Balance*, and David Storey's *Home*. Her repertoire is to a large extent classical with a heavy helping of Shakespeare and Chekhov. She is no stranger to the screen: (*The Birds, Butley, The World According to Garp, Cocoon, The House On Sullivan Street, Batteries Not Included, Cocoon II: The Return*) but her stellar contribution to the arts lies in the realm of theatre and in 1979 Tandy was elected to the Theater Hall of Fame. In 1985 she appeared Off-Broadway in *Solonik* and in 1986 with Cronyn on Broadway in *The Petition*. She starred in the telefilm "The Story Lady" for the 1990-91 season. In April 1988 she was honored by the American Academy of Dramatic Arts.

Her marriage to Hume Cronyn has proved as glistening as their professional work together. Wed since 1942, the pair have shared the Broadway stage together 11 times and raised three children in the process. "When you know and understand each other as well as Hume and I do, then you can be critical in rehearsal and there's no threat." She adds, "I think he's a very good actor, I know that I've got to pull my socks up if I'm going to keep up."

Elizabeth Taylor

Back in the 1940s, Universal Studios in Hollywood dropped one of its child players from the payroll because the powers-that-be decided that the little girl, who'd been cast in bit parts for a year, could never be a star. She didn't have dimples like Shirley Temple. She couldn't sing like Judy Garland, nor dance like some other child stars. And, the casting director felt, her violet eyes were "too old." MGM thought other wise, and so, in 1944, 13-year-old Elizabeth Taylor was cast in the starring role of *National Velvet*. She's been a star ever since, a star whose luster has been alternately gilded and gouged by the comet-turns of her celebrity.

Born Elizabeth Frances Taylor in London, England, on 27 February 1932, as a teenager at MGM she portrayed roles that expressed a childish shyness and onscreen sweetness. Offscreen she was intrigued by glamourous stars like Lana Turner and Ava Gardner and her biggest dream was to stimulate the same kind of response. At 15, her dream came true when columnist Hedda Hopper became the first of many who have proclaimed Elizabeth "the most beautiful woman in the world." But at home she read comic books, devoured stories in fan magazines about other, older movie stars and dreamed romantic dreams. She once confided to a chum that she "practiced kissing" with a pillow every night. At 18 she married first husband, Nicky Hilton, and ever since then, as legend and newspaper headlines have it, there always seems to be someone waiting on Elizabeth's pillow. Six more marriages followed the first: Michael Wilding (two sons), Mike Todd, killed in a plane crash (one daughter), Eddie Fisher, the late Richard Burton (twice; one adopted daughter), and Senator John Warner.

Her fans are among the most devout worshippers in filmdom, fascinated by her every new role, jewel, house, fur, child, husband, lover or illness. Taylor's films include *Little Women*, *Father of the Bride*, *A Place in the Sun*, *Ivanhoe*, *Giant*, *Raintree Country*, *Cat on a Hot Tin Roof*, *Suddenly Last Summer*, *The Taming of the Shrew*, *The Blue Bird*, *Ash Wednesday* and *Cleopatra*. She has won two Oscars, for *Butterfield 8* in 1960 and *Who's Afraid of Virginia Woolf* in 1966. In 1981, she delighted her followers undertaking her first Broadway play, Lillian Hellman's *The Little Foxes*. In 1983, she teamed up with Burton on Broadway for a revival of Noel Coward's *Private Lives*. It proved to be a general embarrassment for everyone involved—in retrospect the show foretold even greater difficulties. A lifetime of illness, near deaths and overindulgence would take its toll unless Elizabeth pulled herself together. She'd become the brunt of Joan Rivers's pointed commentary. "She's so fat," the comedienne rasped on the Carson Show, "mosquitos see her and scream: 'buffet!'" When Rivers's comic routines failed to intervene in Taylor's downward course, her family took over and the star checked into the Betty Ford Rehabilitation Center near Palm Springs and re-emerged a svelte size 8. In the months that followed her rehabilitation many crises arose that challenged her sobriety, especially when Richard Burton died late in the fall of 1984. She carried on. "Elizabeth Taylor is Elizabeth Taylor again," noted one friend, adding: "Of all the contributions she's made to people, I don't think anything counts as much as this. Elizabeth is thin and pretty again and finally sober. She's saying, 'Look, if I can do something about the quality of my life, so can you Mr. and Mrs. America.' Stars have often shown us how to self-destruct. Too few show us how to prevail."

Her most recent acting credits are on television, filling superstar slots on "General Hospital," "Hotel," with Carol Burnett in the Hallmark special "Return Engagement," portraying Louella Parsons in the TV movie "Malice in Wonderland", starring in the 1986 miniseries, John Jake's "North and South," and CBS-TV's "Poker Alice" in 1987. Next up is NBC's "Sweet Bird of Youth." In 1988 she was on the big screen in the film *Young Toscanni.*

Carrying her celebrityhood one step further, she used the power of her name and attention of her friends to help raise funds to fight AIDS. In 1985 she announced the formation of The American Foundation for AIDS Research (AmFAR) and as the National Chairman she devotes her free time to fundraising. Miss Taylor also shared some of her beauty secrets in her 1988 book, *Elizabeth Takes Off—On Weight Gain, Weight Loss, Self Esteem & Self Image.* This tome on her philosophy of dieting, etc., was preceded by her entrance into the Fragrance industry. In September, 1987, she launched "Elizabeth Taylor's Passion" in conjunction with the Parfums International Division of Chesebrough-Pond's Inc. The product was so successful that in 1989 she introduced a new men's cologne, naturally titled "Elizabeth Taylor's Passion for Men." Always acknowledged for her contributions to the theatrical world, she received an extra honor in September 1985 when she traveled to Paris to be given the prestigious French title of Commander of Arts and Letters. Her fans became concerned when, in May, 1990, she was hospitalized with near-fatal viral pneumonia. She was released from the hospital the following month.

Alan Thicke

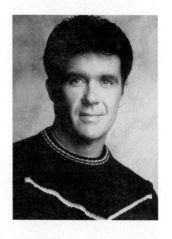

S ince the hit television situation comedy, "Growing Pains" premiered in the fall of 1985, its star has been propelled into, like his name, the thick of American popularity. However, Canadian-born Alan Thicke is no stranger to popularity and success. The multi-talented compulsive achiever has been working as a TV writer, producer, performer and host on both sides of the border for almost two decades. During the 1970's, Thicke wrote for a long list of comedy and musical series and specials in the U.S. including Flip Wilson, Sammy Davis, Jr., Sandy Duncan, Glen Campbell and Richard Pryor. In the 1980's, Thicke's writing included specials for Frank Mills and Anne Murray. His writings captured Thicke two Emmy Awards, including one for a Barry Manilow Special in 1977. As a producer/writer, Thicke's talents were not to be overlooked by his adopted homeland. The 1977 parody talk show series "Fernwood 2-Night," predecessor to the short-lived 1978 "America 2-Night," earned Thicke two Emmy nominations. Thicke, the writer, has written more than thirty compositions for TV, composed theme music for such sitcoms as "Diff'rent Strokes" and "Facts of Life," and game shows such as the hit "Wheel of Fortune," "Celebrity Sweepstakes" and "The Joker's Wild," as well as composed singles for artists Lou Rawls, David Foster and ex-wife, Gloria Loring. Changing hats again, the untiring Thicke returned to his homeland to host the TV game show "First Impressions" and the "Alan Thicke Show," a talk-variety program, which received the highest ratings of any program in the history of Canadian daytime TV. But success sometimes can be fickle. The Canadian hit was followed by the 1983 American flop "Thicke of the Night" which was cancelled at the end of its first season. While the late night variety show emphasizing music and comedy was not well received by the critics, Robert MacKenzie, writing in *TV Guide*, said, "When Thicke gets away from all this backup and wings his way through a real situation, he's charming."

The facile and funny Thicke again switched hats and recorded the show's theme song, which he composed before moving on to act in "Love Boat" episodes and in the 1985 TV movie "The Calendar Girl Murders." Pointed out to Michael Sullivan, Executive Producer, Thicke landed the role of Dr. Jason Seaver, psychiatrist and father in "Growing Pains" which, in its second season, was the tenth most popular series on the air.

Born Alan Jeffery on 1 March 1948, in a small mining town named Kirkland Lake, Ontario, Canada, Alan jokes about his hometown. ("There were two ways a guy could get out of town: play hockey or get a girl pregnant. I wasn't good at either.") His parents divorced when Alan was six and mom re-married a physician whose surname Alan and his brother, Todd (now a TV producer and director) adopted. Stepfather Thicke taught the boys a lot about drive and ambition. Alan became a good hockey player and entertained his schoolmates with imitations of the Beatles. He also developed his musical and verbal skills. "I gave sermons in the local United Church of Canada at the same time I was president of Catholic Youth Organization." To please his stepfather, Thicke took pre-med courses at the University of Western Ontario, but then auditioned with the Canadian Broadcasting Corp., (CBC) in Toronto, singing to his own guitar accompaniment and doing a comic monologue. Hired by CBC as a "gofer," Thicke began to contribute material for shows while he was chauffeuring personalities and fetching coffee. His 1960's credits include "Good Company Show,"

"Tommy Hunter Show," and "Johnny Cash Special." In 1970, at the age of twenty two, Thicke moved to Los Angeles and was introduced to show business people by some of his professional hockey friends. His first major credits on this side of the border were in 1974 as a writer for Flip Wilson's comedy specials. Since his new series, Thicke has found himself constantly in demand. He's acted in "Not Quite Human," a TV movie, "Hit and Run," a feature film with Colleen Dewhurst, and the soon to be released film *Return of the Kiwis*, in which Thicke plays a member of a rock and roll band making a comeback after twenty years. One of the most sought after hosts-for-hire in the country, Thicke has hosted the ABC Christmas Special, Disney's Easter Parade and the Olympic Kick-Off Gala. When asked about his many offers, the witty Thicke jokingly explains, "I get all the television appearances and banquet gigs that Bill Cosby can't do."

The father of two sons, Brennan and Robin, Thicke shares custody with his ex-wife, Gloria Loring (divorced in 1984), and the three men reside on Toluca Lake in the San Fernando Valley. "I still feel Canadian," Thicke told Bill Mann of the *Toronto Globe and Mail*, "and am certainly going to keep my citizenship." Named "Father of the Year" by the Father's Day Council in Los Angeles, Muscular Dystrophy, and The Juvenile Diabetes Foundation (for which he is the spokesperson), Thicke hosts ABC's educational comedy show, "Animal Crack-Ups," which is rated number one in its time slot. With his "easy, naturalistic style" (*Variety*) and wit, the good-looking, slightly built man who prefers to dress informally—but drives a Porsche—has a lot of insecurities. "I worry about things like, Am I Handsome enough? Smart enough? Witty enough?," Thicke confessed. "And that's just for a dinner date, much less putting yourself in front of a national audience."

Danny Thomas

Television's pet paterfamilias for a fantastic 11 straight seasons (1953-64), he's been "retiring" off and on since the middle 1960s. But the beak-nosed comic who persuaded the nation to "Make Room for Daddy" still turns up two or three times a year in Vegas, on commercials, and/or in the plush offices of his prosperous production complex, and there isn't much doubting that this restless, volatile Thomas will stick around in show biz for a long, long time. His latest projects include a short-lived series "One Big Family" (1986-1987) and the CBS-TV movie "Side by Side" (1988). The majority of his time is taken up with St. Jude's Children's Hospital in Memphis. At a desperate point in his career many years

ago, Thomas knelt before the statue of St. Jude (patron saint of the hopeless) and begged for a sign. Should he or should he not remain in show business? He promised to erect a shrine to St. Jude if he should succeed in the business he loved above all others—and the rest is show-biz history.

A high school dropout who caught the grease-paint virus while laboring as a candy butcher in a burlesque house, he was born Amos Muzyad Jacobs (or Jahoob), of Lebanese immigrant parents in Deerfield, Mich., on 6 January 1914. He considers his "second birthday" to be 12 August 1940, the day he stood up on stage at the 5100 Club in Chicago and, borrowing the names of two of his brothers, introduced himself for the first time as Danny Thomas. "Discovered" on radio in 1945 on the "Baby Snooks Show," he's made movies (*Call Me Mister*, *The Jazz Singer*) and has been a nightclub headliner as well as a regular on TV. "Make Room for Daddy" won 5 Emmys. Following in daddy's footsteps, daughter Marlo made a hit in another TV sitcom, "That Girl." The National Conference of Christians and Jews selected Danny "Man of the Year" and the American Medical Association presented him with its Layman's Award, the highest it can bestow on a non-medical man. Thomas was nominated for the Nobel Prize in 1981. He received a "Doctor of Humane Letters" degree from the Medical College of Toledo in 1989. Unabashedly religious, the funnyman with the epic schnozz ("If you're going to have a nose, you ought to have a real one"), is also unabashedly sentimental. "They say I'm a sentimentalist. And I am. Why, I'm so sentimental I cry at basketball games." The mother of his three children is the former Rose Marie Cassaniti, whom he married in 1936.

Marlo Thomas

S he was "That Girl" on the air waves for five years, not just any girl, mind you, but the spunky brunette who subsequently created and starred in the much lauded "Free To Be You and Me" (which won her three of her four Emmys) and who is known in the business as someone who "wants things done right."

Born in Detroit, Michigan, on 21 November 1938, the daughter of veteran entertainer Danny Thomas ("Sometimes inherited fame from a superstar father can be tough on second generation talent. It opens the doors, but you must fight to keep them from slamming shut"), she attended Beverly Hills Catholic Grammar School, Marymount High School, and the University of Southern California, where she studied for her B.A. in education. But her thespian itch would not be quashed and so she "pounded the pavement in New York and L.A. Everybody just about gave up on me." Enter Mike Nichols and Neil Simon. Offered the lead in the London production of *Barefoot in the Park* she became, as it were, an "overnight sensation." "A great new comic actress hit London last night," wrote one critic. "Hit it? She almost demolished it." After eight months of blitzing London, she returned to America to star in TV's "That Girl." Since then she has starred with Alan Alda in the feature film *Jenny* and has appeared in both the Broadway and motion picture productions of *Thieves* (1975). Her first TV special "Acts of Love and Other Comedies" (1973) was at the time the highest-rated comedy special in ABC history. Ten years later, apparently still interested in domestic tug-of-war she appeared in "Love, Sex . . . and Marriage" (ABC-TV). Her latest projects include the 1986 telefilm "Nobody's Child" (Emmy Award), a lead role in the Broadway play *Social Security* (1986) and a sequel to her *Free To Be . . .* album, called *Free To Be . . . A Family* (1988). Thomas is married to Phil Donahue and serves on the boards of the Ms. Foundation, the National Women's Political Caucus, and St. Jude's Children Research Hospital, founded by her father. In 1990 she co-hosted a fundraiser for Andrew Young in his campaign for Georgia's governorship.

Richard Thomas

"I was one of those born-in-a-trunk babies," Richard Thomas proudly reveals. "My parents were extremely happy in the theatre and saw no reason why I shouldn't be." Their positive attitude resulted in the 1973 Emmy winner's (for his portrayal of John-Boy in the television series "The Walton's") successful three-fold career on television, stage and films.

Born in New York City, 13 June 1951, the son of ballet dancers Richard Thomas III and Barbara (Fallis) Thomas (later owners and operators of the New York School of Ballet), he spent his early years

touring with his parents. "I had the discipline of having watched them work since I was young." He attended Allen-Stevenson School, McBurney School and Columbia (switching from an English major to study Chinese). His Broadway career began when he played John Roosevelt in *Sunrise at Campobello* "It was the first time I knew I was a real actor because I did it all myself. I was seven.") In 1963 he played the son in the Actor's Studio revival of Eugene O'Neill's *Strange Interlude*. Other early appearances were in *The Playroom* and Edward Albee's *Everything in the Garden*. After an absense of 15 years, Thomas returned to Broadway in the 1981 critically-acclaimed *The Fifth of July* (later televised). In 1983 he received good personal notices for the Circle Rep's production of *The Sea Gull*, proving he was one of the few actors "who had refined rather than forgotten his craft during a long career in television." That wedge of his performing pie began in the late 50s with the roles on the early live shows and soap operas ("I was always dying and I love to die, because then I knew the audience would feel sorry for me"). In 1971 he appeared in Earl Hammer's "The Homecoming" on which the 1972 Walton series was based (it ran for 5 years). His many films for television include "The Red Badge of Courage," "The Silence," "Roots: The Second Generation," "No Other Love," "All Quiet on the Western Front," "To Find My Son," "Berlin Tunnel: 21," "Barefoot in the Park," "Johnny Belinda," "The Hank Williams, Jr., Story," "Hobson's Choice," "The Master of Ballantrae" and "Go Towards the Light." He also appeared in the 1988 HBO miniseries, "Glory, Glory!" Devoting the latter part of the 80s to theatre, Thomas starred in eight plays back-to-back (beginning in 1986). These include: *The Barbarians* and *Hawthorne Country* (at Williamstown); *Two Figures in Dense Violet Light* (at Kennedy Center); *The Front Page* (Lincoln Center); *Citizen Tom Paine* (Philadelphia Company); plus *Hamlet* and *Peer Gynt* (at the Hartford Stage). He made his film debut in 1969 as Paul Newman and Joanne Woodward's son in *Winning*. Other film roles include *Last Summer*, *Red Sky at Morning*, *Cactus in the Snow*, *9/30/55*, and Roger Corman's *Battle Beyond the Stars*. Three volumes of Thomas's poetry have been published, the most recent in 1985.

Richard now lives in Los Angeles with his wife, the former Alma Gonzales, whom he married on Valentine's Day, 1975. They have a son, Richard Francisco, and in 1981 became parents of triplets —Barbara, Gwyneth and Pilar. "I get up every morning and thank

God I have three beautiful little girls and a wonderful son," beams Thomas. As a humanitarian, the actor was elected National Chairman of the Better Hearing Institute, serving in that position through 1988. Also in 1988, he spent the spring touring colleges around the country on behalf of the Kennedy Center's Education Program where he offered guidance on theatre and acting.

Grant Tinker

The former Chief Executive Officer of NBC (1981-1986) began his job by saying, "If in two or three years my efforts aren't rewarded (by increased ratings), they should let someone else try." After a five-year reign he hadn't extricated the peacock network from the bottom of the heap and said, "I was underestimating the difficulties then. If, by the end of five years, we haven't come a far piece, they should pasture me out." He lamented that "to the bulk of the audience, bad programming may not be a problem," and was so apprehensive about a turnabout that he later stated that in 15 years he'd be living in France regardless of what happened. What happened is that Tinker left NBC and formed his own company GTG Entertainment in 1987.

Before Grant A. Tinker, born in Stamford, Conn., 11 January 1926, made his return to the web headquarters at Rockefeller Center, he'd been president of MTM Enterprise for eleven years. That production company, named for his then-wife Mary Tyler Moore, crafted such highly-regarded shows as "The Mary Tyler Moore Show," "Lou Grant," "The White Shadow," "Hill Street Blues," and "WKRP in Cincinnati." With credentials unsurpassed as a producer, he was expected to elevate the level of programming tastes, but in time found himself resorting to the pragmatic choices of the television executive. "I had to watch a pilot of a new program a while ago," Tinker said. "And we made the decision: It's a little too good . . . it just didn't work." He acquired his TV savvy at NBC as a management trainee after graduation from Dartmouth in 1949. After climbing to become head of the radio network, he took off to work for Radio Free Europe. In the '50s he headed television programming departments of ad agencies McCann-Erickson and

Benton & Bowles in the days of advertiser-developed shows. For most of the '60s he was a V.P. in NBC's programming department, then was off to Hollywood to work in TV divisions of Universal and Twentieth Century-Fox before starting MTM in 1970. Tanned, white-haired and urbane, the youthfully-handsome Tinker abandons his Manhattan hotel on weekends for his L.A. home. A bachelor since his 1981 divorce from Moore, he personifies the type of creative mind he wants to recruit for NBC's shows. "I call them the 'A Group.' They have a different mind-set than the second-raters. They avoid the cheap sex joke and the easy use of violence to climax a scene. For want of a better word, you might call them literate."

Lily Tomlin

She sprang forth from "Laugh-In" with her delightful camp creations of Ernestine (the love-starved telephone operator) and Edith Ann to become a top-caliber performer in films as well as TV. Lily Tomlin has won Emmys for her comedy specials, a Grammy for an LP, a Tony for her one-woman Broadway show, and in her film debut (*Nashville* in 1975) she was nominated for a Supporting Actress Oscar. For her screen credits, which include *Moment by Moment, Nine to Five, The Incredible Shrinking Woman* and *All of Me,* she is held in high esteem by the industry that profoundly affected her as a teenager ("To say movies had a big influence on me is an epic understatement. They devoured me whole and vice versa. Like a dame in distress in a B-grade Carole Mathews swamp movie, I was caught in movieland's magical muck of fantasy quicksand.").

Born in Detroit, Michigan, 1 September 1936, she studied English at Wayne State University and subsequently became a secretary to a New York casting director, performing in a revue at the Gotham nightspot, "Upstairs at the Downstairs," and appearing off-Broadway as the lead in *Arf and the Great Airplane Snatch.* After a taste of television regularity on "The Gary Moore Show," she headed West and landed in the show, "Laugh-In," then a national craze. Now calling herself a bi-coastal person (California and New York), she owes much of her success to her ability as a people-watcher. "At school, you could almost divide girls into two groups. The squares who acted like the girls in the fun 'n surf movies and the hipper, cooler set who were like the girls in woman's prison movies. I didn't know much about feminism, but I knew it forced me to make a choice; I would rather be Ruby Gentry who wrecked a whole town, than be Sandra Dee and be wrecked by a whole bunch of surfers." Tomlin returned to Broadway in 1985 with her acclaimed solo *The Search for Signs of Intelligent Life in the Universe.* Her latest screen outing was with Bette Midler in *Big Business* (1987). She was a presenter at the 44th annual Tony Awards in 1990. Also in 1990-91 she appeared in an ABC-TV special.

John Travolta

"Man, nobody pushed me into show business. I was aching for it," Travolta says. The ache first began to pay off in the mid-70s, when he achieved his initial fame on television as Vinnie Barbarino in "Welcome Back Kotter." That character—a cocky, dimwitted but endearing punk— wasn't so unlike that of Tony Manero, which made him an instant movie star at the end of 1977 with the release of *Saturday Night Fever.* The disco music film, and particularly its star, created a sensation. He was named the year's best actor by the National Board of Review and received an Oscar nomination for his performance.

Born in Englewood, N.J. on 18 February 1954, John Travolta was the youngest of six—all involved in the performing arts. He studied acting with his late mother (who, along with one of his sisters, had a bit role in *Fever*), began his performing career at age nine in a summer stock production of *Bye Bye Birdie,* and left school at 16 for the stage. In 1974 he made his Broadway debut in *Over Here!,* the Andrews Sisters musical. At 18 he joined the original Broadway production of *Grease* in a minor part. He was acclaimed for his title role in the 1976 TV film "The Boy in the Plastic Bubble." Co-starring as his mother was Diana Hyland, who became his lover, and whose death from cancer at 41 early the next year devastated Travolta, who left the *Fever* set to be with her. A small part in *Carrie* led to *Fever,* which was soon followed by the hugely popular film version of *Grease. Urban Cowboy* (based, like *Fever,* on a true *New York* magazine story) was another hit, and the critically roasted *Two of a Kind* reunited him with his *Grease* leading lady, Olivia Newton-

John. He recreated his role of Tony in the *Fever* sequel, *Staying Alive*, directed by Sylvester Stallone. For the film, the *Rocky* star put Travolta on an intensive body-building regime. "I'm in awe of it," he says of his new body. He was named Man of the Year in 1981 by Harvard University's Hasty Pudding Club.

Mixing his pumped-up body with a dancercise score and Jamie Lee Curtis, Travolta played a reporter in the less-than-perfect film *Perfect* (1985). Seeking a successful vehicle, he was directed by Robert Altman in Harold Pinter's play "The Dumb Waiter" for ABC-TV (1987). John appeared on the big screen in *The Tender* (1988) as a father of a young daughter involved with Chicago's underworld. Other films include *Moment by Moment*, with Lily Tomlin, and *Look Who's Talking*. His latest feature, a comedy entitled *The Experts*, was filmed in Ontario for a 1989 national release.

Travolta lives on a 17-acre Santa Barbara ranch, and his hobby is flying. He pilots a $1.7 million jet. Formerly in psychotherapy, he has become a devotee of Scientology. Despite his fortune and popularity, he's a recluse who claims, "I am really a very modest man."

Kathleen Turner

The actress *Time* magazine called the "kind of treasure everyone in Hollywood should be filching the map to discover" seems a throwback to the great stars of the past—a real Hollywood leading lady—by virtue of the beauty, presence and versatility she has displayed in her films since her debut in 1981, steaming and sizzling her way through the defenses of William Hurt in *Body Heat*. Compared to Lauren Bacall in her sultry good looks, resonantly husky voice and willful spirit, and to Katharine Hepburn in her stern individualism and outspokenness, Kathleen Turner nevertheless insists that "all this is still a learning process for me. I don't know yet what I'm best at. What I want, ideally, is acting that's a jump. You can prepare as best you can, then jump—emotionally, physically or in whatever way is required." The leaps she's made thus far include murder in *Body Heat*; a satirical characterization of a nefarious screen seductress in *The Man with Two Brains* (with Steve Martin, 1983); a lonely Appalachian woman in *A Breed Apart* (1984); a repressed and frumpy writer who was scratched and bruised running through the jungle, dropped into ice-cold water, sprayed with mud and thrown down a hill in the 1984 blockbuster *Romancing the Stone* (co-star and producer Michael Douglas says, "Assuming she lives, Kathleen will come out of this a big star, and deservedly so"); a fashion designer by day and hooker by night involved in bondage and mock-rape in Ken Russell's controversial *Crimes of Passion* (1984); and in 1985 a "hit man" in John Houston's *Prizzi's Honor* (co-starring Jack Nicholson). In 1985 she filmed the sequel to *Romancing the Stone: The Jewel of the Nile*. She starred in Coppola's *Peggy Sue Got Married* in 1986, followed by *Switching Channels* (1987), *Julia and Julia* (1987), *The Accidental Tourist* (1988) and *The War of the Roses* (1989). She was also the seductive voice of "Jessica" in the animated blockbuster *Who Framed Roger Rabbit* (1988). More recently, she has appeared on Broadway as the sultry female lead Maggie in a new production of Tennessee Williams's *Cat on a Hot Tin Roof*. Offscreen, Turner is one of the few stars who are openly critical of the gladhanding and pretense that often passes for friendship and talent in the film industry.

The Missouri-born actress (19 July 1954 in Springfield) graduated from the University of Maryland's dramatic arts program in 1977 and moved to New York, where she substituted on Off-Off-Broadway parts before landing a continuing role on the NBC soaper "The Doctors." She kept her theatre credentials in order by appearing in regional theatre in roles ranging from Titania in *A Midsummer Night's Dream* at the Arena Stage in Washington, D.C., to Nina in *The Seagull* at the Manitoba Theatre Center in Winnipeg, Canada. On Broadway she appeared in *Gemini*. Although she auditioned for numerous film roles (she lost the female lead in *Oliver's Story* to Candice Bergen), she wasn't tapped for Hollywood until screenwriter and novice director Lawrence Kasdan cast her as Matty Walker in *Body Heat* against the advice of various casting directors and studio executives. When asked during a 1984 interview in *Moviegoer* magazine if she saw a danger in playing roles so varied that people "can't get a handle on Kathleen Turner," the actess replied, "Yes. But there is another sort of problem, in which you become so good as a type that people *have* to have you for a certain kind of role." In August of 1984, she relinquished her single status by marrying realtor Jay Weiss (one daughter, Rachel Ann).

Lana Turner

H ollywood's pre-eminent Sweater Girl of the 1940's joined the ranks of celebrity authors in 1982, declaring, "I refuse to leave this earth with that pile of movie-magazine trash, scandal

and slander, as my epitaph." Setting the record straight in *Lana*, she told the story of her life from her birth (as Julia Jean Mildred Frances Turner) on 8 February 1920 in the mining town of Wallace, Idaho, to her "discovery" in a Los Angeles soda fountain (*not* Schwab's) and on through her years as one of MGM's most alluring box office attractions. From her first small part in 1937's *They Won't Forget* ("I was just a 15-year-old kid with a bosom and a backside strolling across the screen"), she quickly rose to superstar status, steaming up the screen especially (with John Garfield) in *The Postman Always Rings Twice* in 1946. Her more than fifty other films include *The Bad and the Beautiful* (1952), *Peyton Place* (1957) and a remake of *Imitation of Life* (1959).

Turner made headlines with her seven marriages (to, among others, bandleader Artie Shaw, millionaire Bob Topping, movie-Tarzan Lex Barker, restaurateur Stephen Crane) and one of "the most nightmarish of all Hollywood scandals" when her daughter Cheryl Crane, then 14, murdered her lover, smalltime hood Johnny Stompanato. Later, she suffered bouts with both alcohol and depression, but, in 1980, with the help of a holistic physician, she became "very close to God" and in the 1982-83 TV season proved herself once again an audience draw in the cast of the nighttime soap "Falcon Crest." Waxing philosophical about the lights and shadows in her life, she observes in *Lana:* "I love sunshine; who doesn't feel terrific when the sun is shining and warming you? But I also love rain. Real, pouring rain, not the drizzling kind. If it's going to rain, then rain. Don't just futz around."

Tina Turner

"In ballads or rockers, she's still an indomitable singer and an indefatigable dancer . . . there's no doubt that after nearly thirty years on the road, Ms. Turner could rock for the next three decades," states John Pareles of the *New York Times*. The powerhouse singer, before breaking into her legendary song "Proud Mary" (1970), explains: "We never, ever, do nothin' nice and easy . . . So we're gonna do it nice—and *rough*." That not only sums up the musical style of the Ike and Tina Turner Revue, it also describes the demise of their nearly 16 year union. Although Tina had been the most visible asset in the duo's successful act (by 1969 it included 15 albums and 60 singles to its credit), it was Ike who directed every facet of the act. Tina's share of the earnings, it has been said, was less like a share or even a salary, but more like an allowance. "I was living a life of death; I didn't exist," she said of that period. She finally left Ike when, in Dallas, Texas, in the summer of 1976, he physically beat her shortly after arriving for a concert date. With

almost no money and just one credit card, Tina flew to L.A. to begin her new life, sans Ike. "I felt proud, I felt strong. I felt like Martin Luther King." And she had hard times with the hundreds of thousands of dollars of debt that resulted from the Turner broken concert dates. Tina did everything to pay her way, including singing at McDonalds's sales conventions. "It looked like bad times from the orthodox way of thinking, but the times without a record have been great for me." In 1984 her solo album *Private Dancer* soared to the top of the charts, and Tina Turner was rediscovered. Sexy, hot, liberated and on her own, she became part of a *McCall's* magazine ad campaign tongue-in-cheekly showing her as one of its "drab homebodies" readers, and her videos on MTV (such as "What's Love Got To Do With It") heralded the resurrection of this sultry "jungle Aphrodite." She has won multiple Grammy Awards, as well as the MTV Video Award. Her latest albums include *Break Every Rule, Tina Live in Europe,* and *Foriegn Affair.* Her biography, *I, Tina: My Life Story,* was released in 1986.

Born Annie Mae Bullock in Nutbush, Tennessee, on 25 November 1941 (some sources say 1938), she grew up in Knoxville singing in the church choir and in the cotton fields, where she and her friends "sang harmony as we worked." At 17, she joined up in St. Louis with bandleader Ike, a minister's son. One day, when he was slated to record, the scheduled girl singer failed to show up, so Tina filled in, and the resulting disc, "A Fool for Love," was a breakthrough hit in 1962, selling over a million copies and establishing the duo's popularity with all sorts of listeners, not just soul. Before long they had "ascended from the black steps of one night stands down South to the vestibules of recognition in St. Louis and finally to frontroom success in New York"—and the world. Some of their hits were "It's Gonna Work Out Fine," "River Deep, Mountain High," and "Honky Tonk Woman." Several times they were the opening act for the Rolling Stones, and Tina was the far-out and electrifying "Acid Queen" in *Tommy*, the 1975 motion-picture rock opera.

God gave Tina Turner two of the best legs in history, and she uses them to sexual-revolutionary perfection. In the words of one observer Tina pounces onstage "in midscream with both legs pumping, hips grinding, long mane whirling with her mouth wrapped around some of the sexiest sounds ever set to music." Awarded a *Ms.* magazine citation in 1984, she played "Entity," the proprietress of a post-apocalyptic Dodge City, in one of George Miller's *Mad Max* movies with Mel Gibson before she embarked on a world-wide tour in 1985. In 1989 she was signed to star in the Chrysler television commercials. She has raised four sons and now lives alone in Sherman Oaks, Calif.

Cicely Tyson

"I had to make a choice and I decided I could not afford the luxury of just being an actress. I had very definite statements to make. It was my way of picketing." A statement resounded from the roles she selected, all of which paid powerful homage to the dignity of black women, including her double-Emmy portrayal of a 110-year-old former slave in the 1974 TV movie "The Diary of Miss Jane Pittman."

She was born on 19 December circa 1933 in East Harlem, New York, the daughter of immigrants from Nevis, a small Caribbean island. Head-strong by nature, she bucked her strict upbringing—and her mother's insistence that the theatre was a "den of iniquity"—and ditched her secretarial job to pursue acting. Ejected from her home by her mother (with whom she later reconciled and enjoyed a close relationship), she debuted Off-Broadway as a prostitute in Genet's *The Blacks* in 1961-63. Her career really took off when she played a sharecropper's wife in the 1972 film *Sounder*. Her other credits include Kunte Kinta's mother in the TV blockbuster "Roots," Coretta Scott King in the mini-series "King," and Harriet Tubman in the 1978 NBC movie "A Woman Called Moses." Other telefilms include "Samaritan" (CBS, 1986) and "Women of Brewster Place" (ABC, 1989). She also starred in the 1990 TV docudrama "Heat Wave," which dramatizes events of racial violence that erupted in 1965 in the Los Angeles neighborhood known as Watts. Her Broadway performances include *The Corn Is Green*. A leading advocate in the struggle for racial equality in the arts, she is a cofounder and vice-president of the Dance Theatre of Harlem. A stunning, statuesque woman with a bold sense of style, she is largely credited with popularizing the "natural hairstyle" for American black women, and introducing into high fashion the corn row hairdo made famous by Bo Derek in *10*. She married jazz great Miles Davis in 1981, but their relationship has been rocky (filed for divorce in 1988). She is known to be reticent, even mysterious, about her personal life, yet she describes herself as an active romantic. "The only way I can give of myself emotionally is for me to have emotions, and certainly one must express one's emotions. That's what acting is all about. How can you interpret a life if you have not lived?"

Leslie Uggams

She progressed from her first flash of fame as a cheery subdeb regular on the "Sing Along with Mitch" TV series in the 1960s to become, in the 1970s and 80s, an accomplished dramatic actress and sleek cabaret star known for her "large, smooth and pliable" singing voice. In 1977, she was a standout in the cast of ABC's blockbuster TV miniseries of *Roots*, Alex Haley's saga of American blacks.

Of her own black childhood, she has said, "I never really had it that rough. Not that it was so ritzy where we used to live. I see that now, but it was all right. I don't think unhappiness is a necessity. I don't think it adds soul."

Born in Washington Heights section of New York City, 25 May 1943, she learned about the performing life from both her dad, a onetime member of the famed Hall Johnson Choir, and her mother, a veteran of the Cotton Club chorus line. Leslie made her own debut—as an actress—at the age of six, appearing as Ethel Waters's niece on the "Beulah" TV series. She began singing at 7 on local TV and her vocalizing came to full flower as a 15-year-old contestant on TV's "Name That Tune," where Columbia Records's Mitch Miller spotted her and signed her to a recording contract and for his TV show. She won a Tony her first time out on Broadway in 1967 in *Hallelujah, Baby;* went on to host her own TV series and appear in guest spots on countless specials. She and her Australian husband, Graham Pratt, have two adopted children, a daughter and a son. She spent much of 1984 and 1985 on tour in *Jerry's Girls,* a revue featuring the words and music of Jerry Herman, which opened on Broadway in the fall of 1985. In March, 1989, she replaced Patti LuPone on the hit show *Anything Goes* and in the Fall 1989 she starred in concert on Broadway.

Tracey Ullman

Tracey Ullman took America by storm in the 1980s. Her introduction to the states triggered the same impact as many of the notorious "Saturday Night Live" talents. With an uncanny ability to take an ordinary situation and expose a humorous side, she is a versatile performer who is also an accomplished dramatic actress and a trained dancer and singer.

Her father emigrated from Poland to Slough, England (near London), where he and his wife, an England native, brought Tracey into the world on 30 December 1959. When she was six years old, tragedy struck the Ullman family: her father passed away, leaving Tracey's mother with the duty of single parenthood. Even at that tender age, Tracey displayed a knack for performing, which was supported and encouraged by her mother. By the time she was twelve years old, Tracey had matured so well in her craft that she received a scholarship to stage school. Her first professional appearance was as a dancer in the Berlin production of *Gigi,* at sixteen years old. She then returned to her native England, where she further pursued a career in dance with the well-known Second Generation dance troupe. It was at this point that Tracey began appearing on television variety programs. Serving as a stepping stone, these programs ultimately led Tracey to perform in West End theater musicals. Among her West End credits: the role of a backup singer in *Elvis;* Frenchy in *Grease;* and the cult favorite *The Rocky Horror Picture Show,* in which she portrayed Dr. Frank N. Furter's rival for the perfect man's attentions, Janet. Tracey proved herself more than able in straight theater when she landed the leading role in *Talent* at the Everyman's Playhouse. The role that displayed Tracey's talents at their optimal level was her characterization of Beverly, a bizarre club singer, in the improvised play *Four in a Million.* So enthralled were they by her performance, the London Theater Critics awarded her the honored title of Most Promising New Actress of 1981. England's ingenue was now back on television variety programs with top billing in the BBC comedy series "Three of a Kind" and "A Kick up the Eighties." In 1983, she was awarded Best Light Entertainment Performance for her television portrayals by the British Academy (the equivalent of the U.S. Emmy Award for best comedienne in a sitcom). The theatre rejoiced in her return in *She Stoops to Conquer* and then in the workshop production of the musical *Starlight Express.* She took to the stage again in the summer of 1990 playing opposite Morgan Freeman in producer Joseph Papp's New York Shakespeare Festival in Central Park production of *The Taming of the Shrew.* Tracey has tried her hand at feature films, too, with her debut in Paul McCartney's *Give My Regards to Broad Street.* A second feature film placed her opposite Meryl Streep in *Plenty.* Departing from her usual endeavors, Miss Ullman has also dabbled as a recording artist—the result: four top ten singles on the British pop charts, and an album, *You Broke My Heart in Seventeen Places* (certified gold). In April, 1987, Tracey came to America with the inception of "Tracey Ullman Show," for which she won a Golden Globe Award for Best Comedic Actress. She ended the show in 1990 after starring in director Lawrence Kasdan's film *I Love You to Death.*

The "Jack-of-all-trades" lives with her British television producer/husband, Allan McKeown, and their daughter, Mable Ellen (born 2 April 1986), in homes in London and Los Angeles.

Liv Ullmann

S hortly after the filming of Ingmar Bergman's *Personna* (in which she played the role of a highly disturbed actress; 1966), the rumors began. The acclaimed Scandinavian actress Liv

(pronounced Leave) and Bergman released the news that they shared an "extraordinarily fine relationship." Soon she and her psychiatrist husband Gappe Stang divorced, and with daughter Linn (by Bergman), she moved into Bergman's posh Sheep Island retreat, the setting of his anti-war film *Shame* (1968). "As in photography, Liv is a complete commentary unto herself," said the then-spellbound Bergman. From their creative love-nest came *Hour of the Wolf* (1968), *The Passion of Anna* (1969), and *Cries and Whispers* (1972). Her non-Bergman films include *The Night Visitor* (1970), *Pope Joan* (1972), *Lost Horizon* (her first Hollywood venture, a faltering musical version of the Shangri-La story with Peter Finch), the lively and charming *Forty Carats, Zandy's Bride* with Gene Hackman, Ibsens' *The Wild Duck* co-starring Jeremy Irons, and *Bay Boy.* For NBC-TV she appeared in her first American television movie, "Prisoner Without a Name . . . Cell Without a Number" based on the Jacobo Timerman book. Playing opposite Roy Scheider, she was the personal choice of Timerman to play his wife.

Born in Tokyo, Japan, 16 December 1939, of Norwegian parents, Liv Ullmann accompanied her family to Canada during the war years and returned with her mother (her engineer father had died in the interim) to Norway. She remembers wanting all her life to become an actress and with her heart set on an acting career, dropped out of high-school and set off for Oslo to enter the National Theatre School there. Refused admission, she stubbornly turned to London, acquired intensive dramatic training, and sailed home to become a member of the prestigious National Theatre of Norway, debuting with the title role in *The Diary of Anne Frank.* While there she played, possibly in anticipation of her somber screen characterizations, "only serious roles—Shakespeare, Ibsen, Brecht." Following several Norwegian film appearances, Liv participated in her first Swedish film, *Pan,* with close pal Bibi Anderson, who soon introduced her to Bergman. Liv was the first non-Swedish actress to work in one of his films; since their break-up, they've remained close friends and have continued to make movies together: *Scenes from a Marriage, The Serpent's Egg* and the moving *Autumn Sonata,* the story of a troubled mother-daughter bond in which Liv and her co-star, Ingrid Bergman, gave stunning performances. In reference to her hunch that she ought to perform in comedies instead of the heavy dramas that have made her an international star, she says:

"Bergman has promised me a role in which I'll be neither neurotic nor suicidal. I can hardly wait." She's also won kudos for her work in *The Emigrants,* a film project about the immigration of Swedish farmers to America which featured Max von Sydow. She first captured Broadway theatre audiences in a 1975 New York Shakespeare Festival production of *A Doll's House.* Again on Broadway in O'Neill's *Anna Christie* (1977) and for the 1979 musical update of *I Remember Mama,* she has subsequently appeared as another Ibsen leading lady in *Ghosts* and starred in a highly acclaimed PBS television special of Cocteau's *The Human Voice.* Winner of several best actress awards from both the New York Film Critics and National Society of Film Critics, she has received two Acadamy Award nominations and was the first female recipient of Norway's Peer Gynt Award. Liv also wrote and directed a short film, *Parting,* in 1981.

She's a vibrant woman of substance, an actress who possesses phenomenal range and depth, so it is no surprise that her substantial and heart-warming reflections would culminate in the best-selling autobiography *Changing* (1978). *Without Makeup* came out in 1979, and a third, *Choices,* followed in 1985. Her work with the International Rescue Committee has been extensive and in 1980 she was appointed a UNICEF Ambassador of Goodwill, making a series of fact-finding visits to Latin America, Lebanon, Africa, and the Middle East. In Rome in September, 1985, Ullmann married Boston real estate man Richard Saunders. During that year she toured in Pinter's *Old Times* and filmed *Let's Hope It's a Girl.* Other films include *Gaby* (1987), *Time of Indifference* (1987), and *Girlfriend* (1988). In December, 1986, Ullmann was presented the first Great Artist Award by New York University.

Peter Ustinov

This actor, producer, director, novelist, and playwright has won two Oscars for Best Supporting Actor (*Spartacus,* 1961, and *Topkapi,* 1964), a Grammy for his inventive rendition of *Peter and the Wolf,* and the New York Critics Award for his play *The Love of Four Colonels* (1953). Regarded as one of the wittiest raconteurs in recent memory, he speaks more than a half-dozen languages and has been described as "the greatest good-party insurance." He travels widely and has a grand cosmopolitan air. "I live like an Englishman, think like a Frenchman, and write like a Russian," he once said.

Born in London, 16 April 1921, of gifted parents (his father, Iona, was a famed journalist known as "Klop," his mother, Nadia, was a painter), Peter Ustinov is part Russian, German, French, and Italian. He has relatives in many parts of the world and a number of ancestors were proficient in the arts. Educated at Mr. Cibbs Preparatory School for Boys, he was punished for writing plays instead of doing homework. He began his writing career at age 14 when he sold a satirical magazine piece about a classmate who happened to be the son of Hitler's foreign minister Joachim von Ribbentrop, nearly causing an international incident. Dropping out of school at age 16, he joined the London Theatre Studio (now part of Old Vic) and made his London stage debut at age 18, appearing in a number of his own sketches. "All old people with fascinating make-ups," he reminisces, "I always played old men in the beginning. The older I get, the younger my parts get, so I'm always in the make-up chair longer than necessary." Ustinov was a playwright by age 19 and a producer by 20. Since making his first American film (*The Egyptian*) in 1954, he's demonstrated his considerable talents on these shores on a regular basis. Among his noteworthy screen credits are Agatha Christie's *Evil Under the Sun* and *Death on the Nile* (playing the canny detective Hercule Poirot), *Billy Budd, Quo Vadis,* and his *Romanoff and Juliet.* Among his other works are a light comedy, *Beethoven's Tenth* (1984), in which he starred as a lecherous Ludwig van Beethoven, *Appointment With Death* (1987), and *King Lear* (1988). He also starred in the television miniseries "Around the World in 80 Days" (1989). How does he manage so many careers? "One relaxes me from the others," he replies. For diversion, he writes articles on the theatre, travel and political subjects.

Married twice before meeting his present wife, Helene du Lau d'Allemans, he has four children. (His two ex-wives are Isolda Denham, sister of Angela Lansbury, and French-Canadian actress Suzanne Cloutier.) Peter and Helene, married in 1972, live in a Paris apartment and have a country chalet in Switzerland. Ustinov collects rare prints and original drawings and has a collection of 6,000 classical music records. He also has time to serve as an ambassador for UNICEF and each year produces 4,000 bottles of a fine white wine from his vineyards. He admits that the only conspicuous failure in his life has been an inability to play the flute because of an unusually protuberant upper lip.

Joan Van Ark

Extending herself beyond acting, this star of stage and screen utilizes her spare time participating in philanthropic and humanitarian work. In addition to professional awards, Joan has received recognition for her personal contributions as well. She was voted Best Actress in a Leading Role on a Nighttime Soap in both 1986 and 1988 for her outstanding performance as Valene Ewing on "Knots Landing," and was also the UCLA Cancer Research Institute's Person of the Year.

Joan Van Ark was born in New York City, but her family moved to Boulder, Colorado, when she was only three. She began her theatrical studies at the Yale School of Drama. Her first acting break came when she moved back to New York to appear in *Barefoot in the Park*, where she joined the show's national theatre company and went on to perform in London. Since then, she has given excellent performances on Broadway in *The School for Wives*, which earned her a Tony nomination, and *The Rules of the Game*, for which she won a Theatre World Award. In Los Angeles, she appeared in *Cyrano de Bergerac* with Richard Chamberlain, *Ring Around the Moon* with Michael York, *Heartbreak House*, and *Chemin de Fer*. Adding to her award-winning performances, she won a Los Angeles Drama Critics Award for her "Distinguished Performance" in the Los Angeles Shakespeare Festival's production of *As You Like It*. Although she is best known for her work on the Broadway stage, Joan has made several television appearances as well. Her television debut was two appearances on the popular nighttime soap "Dallas." Audience response to her was so positive that she was cast in the successful spin-off series "Knots Landing," in which she plays the role of Valene Ewing, the sweet, innocent, author and single parent of twins. She has also appeared in numerous made-for-TV movies, including "Red Flag," "The Ultimate Game," "A Testimony of Two Men," "The Last Dinosaur," "Big Rose," "The Bionic Boy," "The Judge and Jake Wyler," "Shakedown on Sunset Strip," and "My First Love." Her guest appearances include "The Love Boat," "Quincy," "Vegas," and "The Rockford Files." In addition to acting, Joan has endorsed products from Estee Lauder, Kodak, Carnation, and Hallmark.

An accomplished marathon runner, Joan trains for such events as the Boston Marathon in her spare time. Joan and her husband, NBC newsman John Marshall, have one daughter, Vanessa.

Dick Van Dyke

Writer-producer Carl Reiner once said about this gifted comedic-actor: "He's made me the happiest bald-headed producer in Hollywood." Quite understandable. Van Dyke won five Emmy Awards for his 1960s sitcom, "The Dick Van Dyke Show," co-starring with Mary Tyler Moore, and gained wide acclaim in the Broadway musical *Bye Bye Birdie,* as well as the films *Mary Poppins, Divorce American Style, Chitty Chitty Bang Bang, The Comic, The Runner Stumbles,* and on TV's American Playhouse in "Breakfast with Les and Bes." His popular hit sitcom ran from 1961 until 1966, and went off the air after 157 episodes not because of low ratings but, in Van Dyke's words, "to quit while we're proud of it." Van Dyke tried again in 1971 with "The New Dick Van Dyke Show," but it didn't live up to the old. For a while he costarred with Carol Burnett on her prime-time variety show, and then left series-making for televison movies and commercials. He tried another "The Dick Van Dyke Show" with CBS in 1988; again it didn't last the season. He appeared in the telefilm "Ghost of a Chance" (1987) and the motion picture *Dick Tracy* (1990).

Born in West Plains, Mo., 13 December 1925, he grew up in a home in Danville, Ill., that, from all the evidence, must have been as cheerfully nourishing as his salesman father's product, Sunshine Biscuits. ("I guess you could say I had a Penrodian childhood; barefoot boy with cheek of tan and all.") Schooled in announcing on the local radio station, he did mike duty at an Oklahoma army base during World War II, and after his discharge, toured with a buddy and a trunkful of Spike Jones records as half of a pantomime lip-sync act called the Merry Mutes. He went through such a lean period professionally that in 1948, when he sent for his high school sweetheart, Marjorie Millett, to come get married, they had to do it on the radio show "Bride and Groom" in order to afford a ring and a honeymoon. It was a nomad's life until the Van Dykes settled in Manhattan in 1956. It was four more years before he got his break in the musical *Bye Bye Birdie*. He and wife Marjorie have four children. A lifelong fan of Stan Laurel, Van Dyke delivered the eulogy at the late comic's funeral. Stan Laurel's sad face was one Van Dyke could easily relate to. Everyone's clown and funny man, the times haven't always been filled with laughter. Dick is a participant in a program for recovering alcoholics, a problem he has been open about for quite some time.

Gwen Verdon

"A kaleidoscopic combination of Chaplin, Garbo, and a Picasso harlequin," this geranium-tressed hoofer with the "superior posterior" highkicked her way to Broadway stardom in 1953 in Cole Porter's *Can Can*. In 1955, *Damn Yankees* ("Whatever Lola Wants, Lola Gets") made her a superstar, and *New Girl in Town* (1957), *Redhead* (1959), and *Sweet Charity* (1966), with their multitude of Tony Awards, placed her, as one critic put it, "in that class of performers Who Can Do No Wrong."

Born in Culver City, Calif., on 13 January 1925, the daughter of a movie studio electrician and a dancing teacher, little Gwyneth Verdon says she grew up thinking that "all mothers and daughters danced and all fathers carried lunch boxes to the studio." Actually, dancing in her case was a matter of Determination over Disaster. A series of childhood illnesses threatened her with the possibility of being crippled for life and only a rigorous regimen of exercise (and steel braces on her legs) made it possible for her to follow in her mother's dancing footsteps. Half of a ballroom dancing act at 14, she "retired" at 16 to elope with James Hanaghan, a Hollywood reporter twice her age (one son, who has made her a grandma), and didn't resume her career again until the divorce five years later. Only after dancing for six more years with Jack Cole and serving as his backstage assistant on various Hollywood assignments (including coaching Marilyn Monroe to walk less sexily and Jane Russell to walk more so) did she finally, at the age of 28, become an "overnight success" on Broadway. Married in 1960 to late dancemaster/director Bob Fosse (who did the choreography for four of the five Verdon musical hits), she became a mother again in 1963 (Nicole, a dancer who can be seen in the 1986 film *A Chorus Line*). In 1982 Verdon substituted for Carol Burnett on ABC's "All My Children" and appeared in the made-for-TV movie "Legs" in 1983. She's appeared in the films *Nadine* (1987) and *Cocoon II: The Return* (1988). In 1989 she received the NYS Governor's Arts Award presented by Governor and Mrs. Cuomo. Once described as a "mobile without a conscience," she does not consider her dancing, or for that matter her personal appearance, sexually provocative; "Sex in a dance is in the eyes of the beholder. I never thought my dances sexy. I suppose that's because I see myself with my face washed, and to me I look like a rabbit."

Ben Vereen

From appearances on Broadway in *Sweet Charity*, *Hair*, and *Jesus Christ Superstar*, he channeled his highly charged talent into *Pippin* (1972) which won him both the *Tony* and the *Drama Desk Awards*. Thriving on the electricity of a live audience, his talent won him "Entertainer of the Year," "Rising Star," and "Song and Dance Star" in 1978 from the American Guild of Variety Artists. (He's the first simultaneous winner of these AGVA awards.) He gives full credit for his success to his mother: "Mom was born in Louisiana and she remembers how the entertainers would come and sing in the fields during the lunch breaks on the plantation. . . . And Mom can sing the blues too—boy, can she ever sing the blues. . . . I'll tell you the kind of woman Mom is. She's the kind of woman who finds a pregnant girl in the park, takes her home until the baby is born, and then keeps the baby."

The Miami-born (10 October 1946) super-entertainer moved as a child to Brooklyn, where his father worked in a paint factory and his mother labored as a maid. His first performance was at the age of four singing solo in the Baptist church where his father was a deacon. Discovering, after graduation from the High School of Performing Arts, no open doors in either the dance or theatre, he entered Manhattan's Pentecostal Theological Seminary, where it took him six months to find out he was not cut out to be a man of the cloth. After a few years with dance and stock companies, he landed a part in 1968 in the Los Angeles production of *Hair*, and in 1971 he joined the Broadway cast of *Jesus Christ Superstar*, eventually moving up to the Judas role. The former seminarian (divorced from his first wife and the father of her son; currenly wed to Nancy Brunner— four daughters) was reluctant at first to remove his clothes for the finale of *Hair*. When he finally did take them off he admitted, "It felt good. I took off a heavy layer, a burden." In television as well, he has made several notable contributions: Chicken George in the Emmy Award-winning mini-series "Roots" and his own network special: "Ben Vereen—His Roots" which won seven Emmy awards. In 1984 Vereen was signed as Uncle Philip on the ABC comedy series "Webster." Moviegoers saw him in *Funny Lady* and *All That Jazz*. He returned to Broadway in 1985 in *Grind* and later that year made the TV movie "Lost in London." In addition to his accomplishments as a performer, Vereen has also been honored for his humanitarian activities. In 1978, he was the recipient of Israel's Cultural Award; in 1979, Israel's Humanitarian Award, and in 1983 the Eleanor Roosevelt Humanitarian Award. He is currently planning the funding and organization for a drug rehabilitation center in his old neighborhood of Bedford-Stuyvesant in Brooklyn that will offer assistance to needy youths. It will be named in honor of his daughter Naja, who was killed in an automobile accident in 1987. Mr. Vereen presently serves as a Celebrity Spokesperson for "Big Brothers" and is the National Celebrity Spokesperson for "A Drug-Free America."

Jon Voight

"**H**is performance in *Coming Home* is closer to the truth than you'll ever see again on screen," said the film's producer, Jerome Hellman, of Jon Voight's role as a paraplegic Vietnam vet. Managing to talk himself into the part when both Jack Nicholson and Al Pacino became unavailable, Voight gave a performance (opposite Jane Fonda) that earned him honors throughout the world, including the 1979 Academy Award as Best Actor, the New York and Los Angeles Film Critics Awards and the Cannes Film Festival Award. The blond actor with the body of a college fullback prepared himself for the part by spending eleven weeks in a wheelchair living with paraplegics at Rancho Los Amigos Hospital in California. But it was the illness of his father, a Westchester golf pro who later died in an auto accident, that added the sentimental substance to his part.

"Health was the number one thing with him because he suffered so much pain. Maybe that's why I acclimated myself so easily to the role of the paraplegic in *Coming Home*. I knew the difficulties, the anger, the frustration, and the heroism too."

Despite such cinematic successes as *Coming Home*, 1972's *Deliverance* and 1974's *The Odessa File*, Voight has experienced financial difficulties and an inability to attract directors' attention for major roles on a regular basis. During the casting of the 1979 remake of *The Champ*, he was the fourth actor approached for the role of the down-and-out boxer originally played by Wallace Beery. And in *Midnight Cowboy*, the 1969 film in which he first moved into the front ranks of Hollywood's leading men, he earned a meager $17,000 (his co-star Dustin Hoffman reportedly got $700,000) for his on-screen performance as a New York hustler, which won him the New York Film Critics' Best Actor Award and an Oscar nomination. "Before I did *The Champ*," he told an interviewer, "I was flat broke, right at the bottom."

Born 29 December 1938, one of three brothers, Jon Voight seemed headed at first for the life of a pro golfer like his dad. "For a while I played in the low 70s, but I was a rebel," he recalls. "Then I played an 80-year-old man in a high-school play . . . acting was all I wanted to do after that." He has had two busted marriages, with actresses Lauri Peters and Marcheline Haven. The father of two children by Haven, Voight coproduced and starred in 1982 in *Table for Five*, the story of a divorced father trying to re-enter the lives of his kids. "In the film," he explains, "I'm trying to say something about myself." Most critics scoffed at the film's sentiment, causing Voight to make an uncharacteristically strong promotional effort to turn it around. "How do I handle a review?" he asks. "I don't handle it very well. I get hurt. That's about all. I get rejected because you've been rejected—your work is rejected." Fans are particularly fond of Voight's sensitive performance in the 1974 film *Conrack*. Recent films include *Runaway Train* (1985) and *Desert Bloom* (1986). Upcoming in 1990 is *The Eternity*.

Max von Sydow

"**M**ax von Sydow," points out the *New Yorker*, "has the longest face in movies since Stan Laurel." But unlike Laurel, "he has never played his face for laughs. Indeed, ever since . . . he appeared in Ingmar Bergman's *The Seventh Seal* as a knight returned from the Crusades, von Sydow has been film's most reliable totem of dignity, gravity and a king of lonely wisdom." His credits are truly awesome: stage classics, from Molière to Tennessee

Williams, fifty-odd numbers ranging from the Bergman collection to *The Exorcist* and *Flash Gordon*. With that long face, which mirrors every nuance of emotion, he is one of the screen's most sensitive, versatile, and powerful actors. Tall (six feet four), lean, and impressive, the talented Swede is one of the few, the very few, actors who has never been unemployed. Since high school, he's never worked at anything else.

He was born Carl Adolf von Sydow in the university town of Lund in southern Sweden on 10 July 1929; his father was a professor of Scandinavian and Irish folklore. In high school, he and a pal established their own theatre group and began to put on plays by Strindberg and Lagerkvist. Subsequently, von Sydow attended the elite Royal Dramatic Academy of Stockholm from 1948-51, and after graduation, honed his craft in provincial theatres, performing in plays like Ibsen's *Peer Gynt*, Pirandello's *Henry IV*, Moliere's *The Misanthrope* and Goethe's *Faust*. During his membership at the municipal theatre of Malmö in 1955, he met the then unknown director Ingmar Bergman and he worked with Bergman for the thirteen years, doing plays in the winter, movies in the summer. Their first film together, *The Seventh Seal* (1956), brought them both worldwide fame when von Sydow was only 27. As the famous director's pet actor, he also emoted in such classics as *Wild Strawberries, The Magician, The Virgin Spring, Hour of the Wolf, Shame, The Passion of Anna, Through a Glass Darkly* and *Winter Light*, often playing opposite Bergman's favorite leading lady, Liv Ullmann. He also starred with Ullmann in Jan Troell's *The Emigrants* (1972) and *The New Land* (1973). While 1963's *The Greatest Story Ever Told* was not a classic, von Sydow's portrayal of Jesus was considered "probably the finest we have in the long history of cinematic, biblical epics." His recent film work is a lesson in diversity: Father Merin in *The Exorcist*, 1973; *Three Days of the Condor*, 1975; the non-Nazi ship's captain in *Voyage of the Damned*, 1976; as the menacing Ming in *Flash Gordon*, 1980; *Conan the Barbarian*, 1981; *Never Say Never Again; Dune* in 1984; *Hannah and Her Sisters*, 1985; *The Second Victory*, 1986; *Duet For One*, 1986; *Wolf at the Door*, 1987; *Katinka*, 1987; *Roadside*, 1987; and *Pelle the Conqueror*, 1988.

Married for over thirty years to actress Kerstin Olin (two sons), von Sydow works hard at his craft and still performs in repertory in his native Sweden. When not involved in acting, he is at home in Rome or, in summer, an old farmhouse in Gotlan, an island in the

Baltic where he cultivates his passion for gardening and indulges his leisure interest—natural history. Of acting, he says: "There are some moments when the chemistry is absolutely right. The laws of nature cease. It is like levitation and you and the audience rise in the theatre."

Lindsay Wagner

Best known for her role as "the bionic woman" on a show bearing the same name, this diversified actress has also appeared in numerous made-for-TV movies and several films. She has a video and book out—plus the dynamic lady sings!

Lindsay Wagner was born on 22 June 1949 in Los Angeles. When she was 13 she began studying dance with Jody Best, but when that didn't pan out, she switched to acting. She took very well to acting, and performed in several plays in high school. While performing in the play *This Property Is Condemned*, she was discovered by an MGM scout who offered her a part in a series, which she turned down. Soon after that incident, she became a model for Nina Blanchard. While in her senior year in high school, she and her family moved to Portland, Oregon. It was there that she decided to make a commitment to acting as a profession. After graduating, she attended college for a brief period before she began singing with a professional rock group. In 1968, determined to pursue an acting career, Lindsay moved back to Los Angeles. She made her television debut on "Marcus Welby, M.D.," which was followed by an exclusive contract from Universal in 1971. Several television shows followed, including "The FBI," "Owen Marshall," "Night Gallery," "The Six Million Dollar Man," the Emmy Award-winning series "The Bionic Woman" (1976-78), the series "Jessie" and "The Fall Guy." Her latest series, "Peaceable Kingdom" debuted in September, 1989. In addition, she has tackled many diverse, dramatic and critically acclaimed made-for-TV movies, such as "The Two Worlds of Jeanie Logan" (1979), "The Incredible Journey of Dr. Meg Laurel" (1979), the highly successful miniseries "Scruples" (1980), "I Want To Live" (1983), "Two Kinds of Love" (1983), "Princess Daisy" (1983), "Callie and Son" (1983), "Passion" (1984), "This Child Is

Mine" (1985) "The Other Lover" (1985), "A Stranger in My Bed" (1986), "Nightmare at Bitter Creek" (1988), "The Taking of Flight 847" (1988), "Evil in Clear Water" (1988) and "Voices of the Heart" (1989). Her film credits include *Two People* (1972), *The Paper Chase* (1973), *Second Wind* (1976), *Nighthawks* (1981) and *Martin's Day* (1984). Expanding beyond TV and film, she created a video and book entitled *Lindsay Wagner's New Beauty: The Acupressure Facelift.*

Married and divorced three times, Lindsay is currently single and resides in Los Angeles with her two sons, Dorian and Alex. When not working, she likes to spend time with her sons at Salmon River near Mt. Hood, Oregon.

Robert Wagner

The deep voice quells like velvet over a storm-beaten rock. The twinkle in his eyes is sad-happy, but bright as a night in Paris. Dapper, suave, seductive as an emerald in a rich man's hand, he smiles now—and then he winks. Very subtle. He's the Cary Grant of the television medium, the armchair object of desire whether he's on "It Takes a Thief," "Switch," or "Hart to Hart"—his three superhits. He returned to the tube in the fall of 1985 with a short-lived adventure series, "Lime Street," followed by additional TV appearances in "Here's a Thief, There's a Thief" (ABC, 1986), "There Must Be a Pony" (ABC, 1986) and "Indiscreet" (CBS, 1988).

Born on 10 February 1930 in Detroit, Michigan, he grew up in California's San Fernando Valley and at 17 brazened his way into a casting office to read for a part, only to flub his lines and flee. By age 20 he was under contract to 20th Century-Fox, at Darryl F. Zanuch's urging. His one-minute appearance as a crippled soldier in *With a Song in My Heart* (tears pouring from his eyes as he listened to the singing of Susan Hayward's Jane Froman) launched him. Soon thereafter Spencer Tracy singled him out in *Beneath the Twelve Mile Reef,* and Wagner appeared in two films with Tracy: *Broken Lance* and *The Mountain.* From there it was all systems go. He has appeared in more than 30 movies. His most noteworthy casting triumph was when Laurence Olivier personally selected him to play Brick in a TV adaptation of Tennessee Williams's *Cat on a Hot Tin Roof* in the late 1970s. Maggie was played by Natalie Wood, his wife, who died tragically when she accidentally drowned near their 60-foot yacht, *Splendour*, in 1981.

Wagner married Natalie in 1957, but they divorced after she fell in love with Warren Beatty during the making of *Splendor in the Grass*. After a marriage to Marion Marshall (one daughter), he married Natalie again in 1970. (The Wood-Wagner marriage provided a nest for three daughters—hers from a marriage to Richard Gregson; his, and theirs: Courtney.) After Wood's death, Wagner and actress Jill St. John often made the columns as a duo. Said St. John about him: "I can't think of anyone who is more of a Superdad." They finally married in 1990. He still finds it hard to talk about Natalie's death. "Sometimes," he admits, "it is a struggle to make it through a day. . . . I was made a single father by a tremendous tragedy, but one thing I was very fortunate about was that Natalie was a great mother. It's just a matter of sustaining the goodness and love she put there. Thank God they had her as long as they did."

Ken Wahl

He is as talented as he is good looking. This versatile actor, who began his acting career in a feature film in 1978 with virtually no prior acting experience, is now the star of a successful weekly television series.

Ken Wahl was born in Chicago, Illinois, on 14 February 1960. He began acting in 1978, when he debuted in the role of Richie in the film *The Wanderers*. Successfully pulling the performance off without a hitch, he was cast in another feature film, entitled *Running Scared* (1979). Others to follow include *Fort Apache, the Bronx* (1980), *Race for the Yankee Zephyr* (1981), *Jinxed* (1981), *The Soldier* (1982), and *Purple Hearts* (1984). In addition to films, Ken has been seen on several popular television shows and series, such as "The Dirty Dozen: The Next Mission," "Double Dare," and "The Gladiator." He can also be seen every week on CBS in his successful television series "Wiseguy," which earned him an Emmy nomination and has been on the air since 1987. In the show he plays the role of Vinnie Terranova, an undercover agent for the Organized Crime Bureau. The show's 1990 season-end cliff-hanger left fans wondering whether Wahl would next be gracing the big screen or return to the small. When asked what he thinks is the main contributing factor to the show's success, he replies, "The television business in general is based not so much on the hope of success, but the fear of failure—and that's one fear we just don't have."

Ken and his wife Corinne have two children.

Eli Wallach

"**A**cting is the most delicious experience in life," he says. "When I'm supposed to be feeling despair on the stage, what I really feel is that I'm sitting on top of the world." One of the most eloquent advertisements for the Actors Studio (he's a charter member), he first blazed into stardom on Broadway as the Sicilian truckdriver (one of his favorite roles) in Tennessee Williams's *The Rose Tattoo* (Tony Award, 1951). He has since enhanced the playwriting fortunes not only of Williams but Eugene Ionesco and Murray Schisgal by making hit fare of *Camino Real* and *Baby Doll* (film version), *The Chairs* and *Rhinoceros*, *The Typist and the Tiger*, *Luv*, and *Twice Around the Park*.

Born 7 December 1915 in Brooklyn ("In the Red Hook section, known as little Italy . . . we were the only Jews in a sea of Italians"), Eli Wallach graduated from high school in 1932 ("one of the worst years of the Depression") and planned at first on a teaching career, although his heart belonged to the stage. Rather happy at flunking the New York City teachers' exam ("I felt free to do what I wanted to do . . . I was a little guy and I knew the odds were against me, but I was determined anyway"), he signed up for studies at the Neighborhood Playhouse and, indicative of what was to come, one of his first jobs was in an Equity Library Theater production of Tennessee Williams's *This Property Is Condemned*. There was only one other character in the play," he recalls, "a girl named Annie Jackson. We had a few arguments about how the roles should be played and settled it all by getting married." They now have three children, not to mention a long, distinguished list of co-star credits. In 1977-78 they had a real family triumph off-Broadway in *The Diary of Anne Frank*, (which also starred their two actress daughters, Roberta and Katherine Wallach). In 1984 the critics cheered their performances in Joseph Papp's N.Y. Shakespeare Festival production of *Nest of the Woodgrouse*.

Although Wallach prefers the theatre to film ("Movies, by comparison to the stage, are like calendar art next to great paintings"), he's applied his remarkable talent to, among others, *How the West Was Won; The Magnificent Seven; The Misfits; Lord Jim; The Moonspinners; The Good, the Bad, and the Ugly; The Deep; Cinderella Liberty; Movie, Movie; The Hunter, Girlfriends, Nuts* and *Funny*. He has appeared on the screen with Jackson in *How To Save a Marriage and Ruin Your Life, Zigzag,* and *The Tiger Makes Out*. He has appeared on television in the specials "I, Don Quixote," "For Whom the Bell Tolls" with Jason Robards, "Skokie" with Danny Kaye, "The Wall," Norman Mailer's "The Executioner's Song" and "Christopher Columbus." He made his series debut in 1985 in "Family Honor." His latest accomplishments at the theatre include his acclaimed performance in *Cafe Crown* and his induction into the Theatre Hall of Fame in 1988.

Wallach's passions off-stage are tennis, photography, clock collecting and architecture. However, he is still enthusiastic about his profession. "Acting is the most alive thing I can do, and the most joyous."

Sigourney Weaver

"I never went to a co-ed school, so to me it's like being put in a class with the awful boys, who spend all their time throwing spitballs and dunking your braids into the inkwell. It's a streak of masochism in me. I find it wonderful." Sigourney Weaver comments on her return as Dana Barrett in *Ghostbusters II* (1989). The dynamic actress has captured the cream-of-the-crop roles of the '80s; she played Dian Fossey in Universal's *Gorillas in the Mist* (Golden Globe Best Actress, Academy Award nomination for Best Actress) and the "beautiful, treacherous boss" in *Working Girl* (Golden Globe Best Supporting Actress, Academy Award nomination for Best Supporting Actress).

She was born Susan Weaver in 1949 in New York City, the daughter of former NBC President Sylvester Weaver and British actress Elizabeth Inglis. Early in her teen age years, she picked the name Sigourney, which was inspired from the name of a character in the F. Scott Fitzgerald classic *The Great Gatsby*. She began studying acting as an undergrad at Yale Drama School, and went on to receive her M.A. Her first acting job was as an understudy in Sir John Gielgud's production of *The Constant Wife*. Her off-Broadway debut was in *The Nature and Purpose of the Universe*, a play that was written by a friend from drama school. Sigourney also co-starred and co-wrote *Das Lusitania Songspiel* and *Naked Lunch*, as well as appearing in *Titanic* and *Beyond Therapy*. For her debut in the Broadway production of *Hurlyburly*, she received a Tony nomination. Although she made her film debut in a bit part in *Annie Hall*, it was the 1979 sci-fi thriller *Alien* that made her a star. She returned in her role of Warrent Officer Ripley in the sequel *Aliens*, for which she received an Oscar nomination. Other film credits include *Eyewitness*, *The Year of Living Dangerously*, *Half Moon Street*, *One Woman or Two*, *Deal of the Century*, and *Ghostbusters*.

In 1984, she wed Jim Simpson, a writer and director she met at the Williamstown, Mass., Playhouse. Their daughter, Charlotte, was born in April, 1990.

Raquel Welch

"**M**y body is just there," she sighs, "like Mt. Rushmore." If you have that sex-symbol image, "they try to cut you off at the knees if you want to be anything else." How delighted she was, then, when she replaced Lauren Bacall in the Broadway musical *Woman of the Year* in 1982 and met with raves and rahs from the critics. Howard Kissel, writing in *WWD*, said that she "gives the dreary musical a wonderful new energy and freshness." She said she was "shell-shocked" from all the praise. She'd come a long way from her national debut in a poster from her 1967 film *One Million Years B.C.* wearing a fur bikini, long legs spread wide, encouraging the caveman in everyman to stand up and grunt with desire. "I finally get a chance to prove in the flesh what I've said all along," she exulted, "I'm a better actress than anyone knows."

After enough shelling in such films as *The Three Musketeers* (for which she won the Golden Globe Best Actress Award), *Kansas City Bomber*, *Myra Breckenridge*, *Bedazzled*, and *The Four Musketeers*, she'd finally won some respect. The mother of two grown children (from her marriage to childhood sweetheart Jim Welch) is one of America's most popular and enduring beauties. The how-to of it all was told in her book *Raquel: The Raquel Welch Total Beauty and Fitness Program* published in 1984 with an accompanying videotape. In 1987, she made her recording debut on Columbia Records with "This Girl's Back in Town," a throbbing anthem of female survival which the glamorous one considers "a combination of strength and vulnerability—which is where I'm coming from." Her fitness video was released the same year; "A Week with Raquel" was a top videocassette seller on the *Billboard* chart. Raquel's latest telefilms include "Scandal in a Small Town" (1988) and "The Education of Leda Beth Vincent" (1988).

Born Raquel Tejada in Chicago, 5 September 1940, she studied ballet for ten years, modeled, won beauty contests and studied drama. Her studies were interrupted by the birth of her son Damon and daughter Tahnee (who made her film debut in 1985 as an exquisite space creature in *Cocoon*). When her marriage to Welch dissolved she headed for Hollywood, arriving broke and not knowing anyone. The billboard girl on TV's "Hollywood Palace," she was getting nowhere until she met Patrick Curtis, a former press agent, who became her manager. ("He is to me what the Colonel is to Elvis," she said before their four-year union dissolved in 1971.) When Twentieth Century-Fox put her under contract she became a star almost overnight, and she began making the more than 35 movies that made her known to film fans worldwide. In addition to her film and television work—which also include French-made *L'Animal*, co-starring Jean Paul Belmondo, and one of ABC's highest rated TV specials ever, "From Raquel With Love"—her nightclub act is performed to capacity audiences from Las Vegas to Rio de Janeiro, and in Paris she broke the box office record at the famed Palais des Congres.

Raquel married Andre Weinfeld on 5 July 1980, but the couple had split up in 1989.

Lina Wertmuller

Some say that *Seven Beauties* (generally considered everyone's "personally discovered masterpiece") is the best film since *Citizen Kane*; others that it is "fascist trash." The critic John Simon (uncharacteristically) called it a "milestone," adding, "A couple more films like *Seven Beauties*, and Lina Wertmuller will take her rightful place among the grand masters of cinema: the Fellinis and Bergmans, the Antonionis and Renoirs." A provocative and gifted writer-director, this Italian *auteur* is responsible for a number of heady, entertaining but challenging films like *Love and Anarchy*

(1973), *The Seduction of Mimi* (1972), and *Swept Away* (1975) which have found international success and blazed new trails in the difficult terrain between feminism and film. Wertmuller features have helped rattle and revise the myth of male supremacy in the world of celluloid. Of her American debut, *Newsweek* raved about "the most exciting woman director on the international scene and the most remarkable new talent from the Continent since Bernardo Bertolucci."

Born in Rome between 1926 and 1928 (she's mum), she is of aristocratic Swiss ancestry. Passionately Italian by nature, she refers to herself as the product of "boiling blood." Wertmuller's father was a well-to-do lawyer, but the parents had a stormy relationship and her childhood was marked by early rebellion. A prankster, she was "thrown out of fifteen schools" and counteracted her rigorous Roman Catholic upbringing and educational restrictions by sneaking off to see American films. Dramatically inclined, she took like a duck to water at the Academy of Theatre in Rome. For the next fifteen years, Wertmuller had a hodge-podge of occupations: actress, stage manager, set designer, publicist, and writer for commercial Italian radio, TV and theatre. Then she met Fellini and was recruited as his assistant on *8½*. She said of the association: "It was one of those experiences that open new dimensions of life. I was totally enlightened by his personality . . . you *can* learn . . . the freedom of art." That exposure to Fellini's effective spontaneity and imaginative juices inspired Wertmuller to become a film director on her own. A customized "bitter-sentimental/grotesque-erotic" humor came into expression. In the year following, she financed her debut film *The Lizards* (first prize at the 1963 Locarno Film Festival) and then in 1966, *Let's Talk About Men;* neither was shown commercially in U.S. Next, a young matinee idol, Giancarlo Giannini, came under her professional wing and starred in *The Seduction of Mimi* (1972) which won a Best Director Award at the 1972 Cannes Film Festival. Of its opening in New York, a *Time* critic said: "Here is the perfect summer tonic: a brainy, rowdy comedy." True fame happened in 1975 with her most far-reaching comedy, the smash hit *Swept Away*. Called "a kind of witty, slapdash Marxist comedy that owes as much to Groucho as to Karl," it captivated critics and large audiences alike. In 1978, she made *A Night Full of Rain* with Candice Bergen as the leading lady opposite that "meltable Mimi," Giancarlo, and in 1984 attracted attention with *A Joke of Destiny*. Her latest films include *Notte d'Estate* (1986), released as *Summer Night* (1987); and *Crystal or Ash* (1989). She received the First Friendship Award of National Organization of Italian-American Women in 1987.

Short and slight with signature white-rimmed eyeglasses and a barrage of jewelry, she looks (in her own words) "like a crazy gypsy." Since their marriage in 1968, sculptor and scenic designer Enrico Job has served as the art director on all of his wife's pictures. The last laugh? Of international opportunities she complains: "I learn that English has no funny dirty words."

Ruth Westheimer

"**W**hat's wrong with peanut butter or new uses for onion rings as long as there's a relationship?" asks pioneer media therapist Dr. Ruth Westheimer to a listener calling in with a question about kinky sex. Although she is not precisely the first therapist to treat her "clients" on the airwaves instead of the couch, she is certainly unique. A trained psychotherapist and former kindergarten teacher, she dispenses quickie advice in her instantly-recognizable German accent and is relentlessly upbeat about the problems that perturb her listeners. Frigidity? Premature ejaculation? "You're going to be fine, you betcha," she chirps.

Her Sunday night program over a New York radio station stirred up a hornet's nest of controversy, leading almost inevitably to even greater exposure on the "Tonight" show and to her receiving that indisputable badge of media celebrityhood: being spoofed on "Saturday Night Live." "Some critics think she is frivolous, some call her irresponsible and others say her candor is positively indecent," winked *Newsweek*. "Have good sex!" she exhorts her listeners at the close of each program, a decidedly original twist on "Have a nice day." Two years after she hung out her shingle on the Big Apple airwaves, the cable health channel "Lifetime" guided her 4 feet 7 inch frame in front of their cameras and the couchless counselor had her own TV show. Actors portray the sexually-troubled people whose problems in the sack get aired on a program titled—what else?—"Good Sex."

Born in Germany in 1928 and orphaned by the second world war, Westheimer lived in Switzerland, Israel and France (where she studied psychology at the Sorbonne) before emigrating to New York at 28. Enrolling at Columbia she earned first a master's in sociology ("Americans are the only [nationality] to worry much about armpits") and then a doctorate in family studies. But it is not her academic credentials that have made her something of a cult heroine among high school and college students, who rib her for her accent, age and stature (*Newsweek:* "She looks more like a retired jockey than an expert in psychosexual therapy") and yet tune in to her program attentively. "I don't come across as a sex symbol," she recognizes. "People trust me because I'm not a put-on." The walking talking sex lady is the author of at least five books: *Dr. Ruth's Guide to Good Sex, First Love, Dr. Ruth's Guide for Married Lovers, Sex and Morality: Who is Teaching Our Sex Standards,* and *All in a Lifetime* (her autobiography). She writes a syndicated advice column, *Ask Dr. Ruth,* and is a contributing editor to *Redbook* magazine. Another book, co-authored with Dr. Louis Lieberman, is entitled *A Guide to Sexual Self-Help and Skills.* In addition, she has marketed a board game, "Dr. Ruth's Game of Good Sex" with Victory Games, and she had a role in the Sigourney Weaver French film *One Woman Or Two.* "The All New Dr. Ruth Show" won an Ace Award in 1988.

Dr. Westheimer has two children and resides with her husband in New York City.

Betty White

All the charm, humor, sincerity and love that have captivated television audiences everywhere shines throughout Betty White's second book, *Betty White: In Person* (1987). Television's snappy Sue Anne Nivins of "The Mary Tyler Moore Show" and the endearing Rose of the current "The Golden Girls" revealed her innermost thoughts and feelings with wit and wisdom on such varied subjects as anger, jealousy, sex, superstition, love, marriage, competition, fear, and aging. She sprinkles these short pieces with anecdotes about  her colleagues and friends—Bea Arthur, Carol Burnett, Carol Channing, Fred Astaire, Rue McClanahan, Mary Tyler Moore, Grant Tinker, Connie Chung, Mel Brooks, Burt Reynolds, and, of course, her late husband, Allen Ludden. "Having been a dedicated closet writer, I have been jotting down thoughts and ideas for as along as I can remember. So that is the book I assumed I would be working on—random observations—nothing personal. What I discovered was there is no way to report about on your feelings without getting personal," says White. "As a result, there's a lot about the people who have been closest to me . . . Allen Ludden, my parents, the people I work with, my friends . . . and superfriends. You will hear about what makes me laugh . . . and what makes me cry . . . what I hate . . . what I love."

Born on 17 January 1922 in Oak Park, Illinois, Betty White moved with her parents to Los Angeles when she was two years old. After graduating from Beverly Hills High School and performing with the Bliss-Hayden Little Theatre Group, she appeared on several radio series: "Blondie," "The Great Gildersleeve," and "This is Your FBI." By the early fifties she had become the host of an L.A. television talk show. White formed a production company with producer Don Fedderson and writer George Tibbles; they produced a daytime talk-variety show and two situation comedies, including "Life With Elizabeth," which won her an Emmy in 1952. Since then she has copped more Emmy awards for "The Mary Tyler Moore Show" (as Sue Anne Nivins), one for "Just Men" as the Best Daytime Game Show Host, and for her current role (Rose) on "The Golden Girls." She pops up often on numerous game shows and TV interview programs. White has been parade hostess for the Pasadena Tournament of Roses Parade on network television for 20 years and the Macy's Thanksgiving Day Parade for 10 years. In 1976 she was awarded the Pacific Pioneers in Broadcasting "Golden Ike" for outstanding achievements in television, and in 1977 the Southern California chapter of American Women's Genii award for her extensive contributions to all facets of the industry. White's love for animals led her to create "The Pet Set" TV series and the daily radio show "Betty White on Animals." She has hosted the Patsy Awards for performing animals and their trainers since 1971. Her first book, *Betty White's Pet Love*, is now out in paperback. In 1987, she was given the AVMA Humane Award for her continual caring work with animals.

Vanna White

"**H**er first name was 'Vanya' or 'Savannah' or something like that. I mean, who ever heard of a 'Vanna'? And she was nervous; I mean nervous. Her upper lip quivered and her tiny voice trembled. She was gorgeous and seemed very sweet, but who would hire a bundle of nerves with a name no one could even remember? Merv Griffin, that's who. The rest, as someone (probably Merv) once said, is history." So writes Pat Sajak in the foreword of the letter flipper's 1987 autobiography *Vanna Speaks*. She tells her story in a frank, comfortable style, supporting the fact that there's more to her than meets the eye. She answers the ultimate question at the start: "Do I really speak? Sure. After all, I couldn't fill very many pages with just 'hi's and 'bye-bye's, could I?"

In her own words: "It was my father's twenty-eighth birthday—and Momma was just barely twenty-one—when I was born on Monday, 18 February 1957, at 2:35 P.M. There was no maternity hospital along the Grand Stand, the sixty-mile strip of beach that includes North Myrtle Beach, so I was born at the Conway Hospital, in Conway, South Carolina, about a half hour's drive away. . . . They named me Vanna Marie Rosich. The 'Marie' was after my mother's middle name, and 'Vanna' was after my grandmother's godchild . . . Momma added the second *n* just to make it different." Her mother and father split up before her first birthday; Vanna's father moved to New York, while her mother moved to Miami. In the interim, the baby was raised by her grandparents. Later that year, Vanna's Mom met her new "daddy," Herbert Stackley White, Jr., to whom she credits her upbringing and full name today, Vanna White. She attended school, but her favorite subject was studying members of the opposite sex. "I was absolutely boy crazy. . . . I was shy around boys, but that didn't stop me from having 'boyfriends' from the first grade on." Coincidentally, her other favorite subject was spelling; she was an excellent speller. "I had a photographic memory, so I didn't have to study that hard to get good grades." She credits her parents, mostly her mother, in instilling important values in her and younger brother, Chip. "Most important, they always encouraged us to go after dreams, no matter how impossible they seemed."

Vanna's teen-age years were filled with rewarding fun; she was a finalist in the Sun Fun Festival bubble gum-blowing contest. After graduating from high school, she went on to the Atlanta School of Fashion and Design, although she felt "I could have learned much of this either on my own or at a finishing school." Instead of intense study, she fell back to her favorite pastime—boys. In 1990, on Arsenio Hall's talk show, she recounted having lost her virginity on a golf course. She went out at night to clubs and eventually met a man, Gordy Watson, who was about fifteen years older. It was a relationship that lasted for over four years, while she pursued agent hunting. She signed with Atlanta Models and Talent, Inc., where the aspiring model received various assignments—a part in an industrial film, local commercials, print and catalog work, etc. By 1978, she was not just a local girl and was hired in other locales. Vanna entered the Miss Georgia Universe Beauty Pageant and came in fourth runner-up. In 1980, she moved to Los Angeles with a friend, to try and make it in Hollywood. Having the late actor Christopher George as a family acquaintance helped Vanna stay on steady ground. George's wife, Lynda Day, gave her a list of reputable agents, until she signed with a known commercial agent. She received small parts in the films *Looker, Graduation Day* and *The Burning*. Later, she landed a job on the game show "Pot of Gold." Around that same time period, she fell in love with actor/Chippendale dancer John Gibson ("The Young and the Restless"). In 1982, she discovered that Susan Stafford, the hostess of "Wheel of Fortune," was leaving the show and, with her gameshow background, she auditioned. TV land knows the rest. . . .

Vanna White remains single; her main love, John Gibson, died in a plane crash in 1986. She philosophizes that things happen sometimes faster than one can absorb them, "but you always have to just keep going and never lose sight of who you are or your dreams."

Billy Wilder

"**A**s far as I'm concerned, this ballgame is not over," vowed Billy Wilder when he was honored in 1982 by the Film Society of Lincoln Center for his work, spanning half a century. "There are still a few hits left in me." The renowned filmmaker has received six writing and/or directing Oscars (and twenty Oscar nominations) since coming to Hollywood from Europe in the 1930s. Wilder is the first filmmaker ever to win three Academy Awards in one year (Best Director, Best Story and Screenplay and Best Picture for *The Apartment* in 1960). His other three Oscars were for direction and screenplay (with Charles Brackett) for *The Lost Weekend* (1945) and for story and screenplay (with Brackett and D.H. Marshman) of

Sunset Boulevard (1950). The nominations were for *Double Indemnity* and *Some Like It Hot* (writing and directing), *A Foreign Affair* and *The Big Carnival* (writing), and *Stalag 17, Sabrina,* and *Witness for the Prosecution* (directing). In 1988 he was the proud recipient of the Irving G. Thalberg Memorial Award at the sixtieth Annual Academy Awards.

Billy Wilder was born Samuel Wilder on 22 June 1906 in the town of Sucha in Galicia, a section of Poland that was then part of the Austro-Hungarian Empire. His father ran a chain of railway cafes, imported watches, and operated a trout hatchery. His mother had spent several years in the U.S. in her youth (she died in Auschwitz during World War II) and nicknamed her younger son Billy because of her fascination with the legendary American hero Buffalo Bill. In 1926 Wilder's interests led him to a publicity job with the American bandleader Paul Whiteman in Berlin, where he also worked on newspapers and "ghosted" scenarios for silent films. In 1929 he collaborated with Fred Zinnemann and others in making *People on Sunday*. In 1933, he fled to Paris and directed his first film, *Bad Seed*, a juvenile crime thriller starring Danielle Darrieux. Summoned to Hollywood in 1934, he eventually teamed up with Brackett, and helped write such hits as *Ninotchka, Hold Back the Dawn,* and *Ball of Fire* (all of which earned Oscar nominations). His first American directorial assignment was *The Major and the Minor* (1942).

In 1936 Wilder married Judith Coppicus Iribe (divorced, 1947, one daughter). He married his second wife, starlet and singer Audrey Young, in 1949. He lives in an elegant Hollywood apartment filled with part of his modern art collection, one of the largest in private hands in the world. The master storyteller is often quoted about the liveliness of his films: "I sleep an awful lot in movie houses and I try to stop others from doing it"; on considering working for TV: "I wouldn't drink the water in television"; on meeting his second wife who lived in East Beverly Hills: "I'd worship the ground you walked on, if you lived in a better neighborhood."

Gene Wilder

His unique whimsy is the marriage of his classical acting training and his love of motion pictures, bringing to the screen a series of madcap period spoofs that filmgoers tended either to delight in or find totally inane, depending on their comedic tastes. Although he is fond of elaborate costumes and settings, his films are distinguished more for their devotion to romance and slapstick than to authenticity.

Born 11 June 1934 or 1935 in Milwaukee, Wis., Jerome Silberman, a bug-eyed and curly-topped kid, found that being funny was the best medicine for his semi-invalid mother. After studying at the Old Vic Theater School in Bristol, England, and the Lee Strasberg Studio in New York, he made his screen debut with a small but memorable role as a nervous undertaker in the 1967 winner, *Bonnie and Clyde*. Meanwhile, Mel Brooks was preparing to make *The Producers* and created a part for Wilder, this time as a nervous accountant. A series of genre spoofs followed, beginning with *Start the Revolution Without Me* in 1970, a farce on the twins-switched-at-birth theme, and marking for Wilder a break from character roles into romantic comedy leads. Wilder parodied Hollywood westerns in Brooks' *Blazing Saddles* (a 1974 loosely plotted film of questionable taste) and horror films in Brooks' *Young Frankenstein* that same year. Detective movies got the Wilder treatment in the 1975 *The Adventure of Sherlock Holmes' Smarter Brother*, which he wrote and directed. In 1977, he paid tribute to Charlie Chaplin in *The World's Greatest Lover*, adding producer to his credits. He teamed with Richard Pryor in 1980 for the hit movie *Stir Crazy* and with Gilda Radner (whom he married in 1984) for *Hanky Panky* in 1982; in 1986 the couple costarred in *Haunted Honeymoon*. His recent movies include *The Man with One Red Shoe* and *See No Evil, Hear No Evil*, for which he also cowrote the screenplay. A private person who avoids interviews like the plague, Wilder is mum about his two failed marriages, first to playwright Mary Mercier and then to Mary Joan Schutz. His third wife, Gilda Radner, died in 1989 after a long struggle with cancer.

Billy Dee Williams

O nce billed as the "black Clark Gable," he nevertheless insists he is part of an innovative force making producers project black actors in other than stereotypical roles. While saying he tires of talking about race ("It totally, absolutely bores me"), or himself, Billy Dee Williams perpetuates his sex idol status by conceding he never tires of female fan adulation. His interviews are sometimes spiced by remarks that "nothing else in the world competes with making love" for relaxation or self-expression and that he's even better in bed than his fans assume.

Williams and his twin sister, Loretta, were born in Harlem, New York City, on 6 April 1937. His father worked three jobs and his mother operated an elevator at a Broadway theatre. His artistic avocation was given early impetus by his mother (a former opera student) and his maternal grandmother who encouraged the twins in cultural pursuits. Both became adept at drawing and Bill studied fashion illustration at New York's School of Fine Arts after high school. His acting career having started with a walk-on at age seven, Billy dabbled at the craft in high school, and later while in art school, in bit parts on CBS network TV shows. He studied "method" acting from Sidney Poitier and Paul Mann, and in 1959 co-starred with Paul Muni in *The Last Angry Man.* After a well-received Broadway performance in *A Taste of Honey,* Williams couldn't land another decent part until 1963, and plummeted to emotional depths from which a former prostitute who taught him Eastern philosophy eventually helped him to emerge. His big break came with his 1971 Emmy-nominated portrayal of football star Gayle Sayers in "Brian's Song." A year later, Motown chief Berry Gordy inked him to a seven-year contract, and a major role in *Lady Sings the Blues* opposite Diana Ross. His performance as the caddish but high-voltage lady killer brought in 8,000 letters a week from adoring female fans. "A star is what everybody wants to be, even presidents," he said at the time. He co-starred in a TV series, "Double Dare," in 1985.

But from among all his roles (Martin Luther King, Jr.; composer Scott Joplin), Williams says the turning point of his career came in 1980 with his playing a space pirate in sequels to the wildly-successful *Star Wars.* The part, like he, embodied a "universal person." His latest movies include *Deadly Illusion* (1987) and *Batman* (1989). He also appeared on Broadway, replacing James Earl Jones, in *Fences* (1988).

The six-footer with the sly smile and wavy curls says he looks forward to colorless, romantic roles. Thrice-married, but a serious family man, he and Japanese-American wife, Teruko, live in Beverly Hills with her daughter Miyako, his son Corey Dee, and their daughter Hanako. A quiet man offscreen, he says his pursuit of faith led him from Buddhism to Jung. "The only way to education is to find masters in life. I feel surrounded by good, positive spirits in my private, silent moments."

Robin Williams

Brilliantly bubbling and babbling, television/club/screen pixie personality (and ad-libber par excellence), Robin Williams made his professional stage debut in the eagerly awaited Mike Nichols's production of Samuel Beckett's *Waiting for Godot* in 1988. The powerhouse cast also included Bill Irwin and Steve Martin. Taking his career another notch higher, his next film, *Dead Poet's Society* (1989), opened to critical acclaim. Not bad for the comedian who had just received an Academy Award nomination for Best Actor (*Good Morning, Vietnam*).

Born in Chicago on 21 July 1952, to an upper-middle-class family, Robin Williams displayed lovable lunacy and high school antics that got him voted "Most Humorous" and "Least Likely to Succeed" by his peers. He didn't succeed initially in impressing a producer who saw his act in a Los Angeles comedy club, but his continued clowning on comedy shows led him to an audition for the role of the famous Orkean in "Mork and Mindy" (1978). Asked to sit like an alien, Williams immediately turned on his head, and got the part. His Chaplinesque antics and ad-libbing was greatly responsible for the show being a hit. It was a "triumph of Mork over medium," quipped one critic. His other television appearances have included: "Laugh In" (the revival), "Happy Days," "Saturday Night Live," and "Seize the Day," Williams's television dramatic debut. The Williams television comedy specials include: "Robin Williams Live at the Met," "Comic Relief" (Ace Award), "Carol, Carl, Whoopi and Robin" (Emmy Award), and "A Royal Gala," (Emmy Award). He has been active in the "Comic Relief" charity specials since their inception. His film appearances include: *Popeye*, *The World According to Garp*, and *Moscow on the Hudson*. Although he did not win the Academy Award, he won the Golden Globe Award for his leading role in *Good Morning, Vietnam*. Recent films are *The Adventures of Baron Munchausen* (1989), *Cadillac Man* (1990), and *Awakenings* (1990). Upcoming is *The Fisher King*. Williams's best-selling recordings: *Reality . . . What a Concept* (Grammy Award), *Throbbing Python of Love* (Grammy nomination) and *Robin Williams: An Evening at the Met* (Grammy Award).

Williams speaks candidly about the lure of life in the fast lane,

"Cocaine is God's way of saying you're making too much money," and unabashedly advocates fits of craziness. "You're only given a little spark of madness," he has said. "You mustn't lose that madness." Williams married former dancer Valerie Velardi in 1978; they divorced ten years later (one child, Zachary Williams). He married Marsha Garces on 30 April 1989; they have a child together, Zelda (born 31 July 1989).

Treat Williams

This handsome, hairy-browed thespian with the Welch monicker stays in demand (and in roles) both on Broadway and in Hollywood. A descendant of a singer of the Declaration of Independence, Richard Treat Williams was born in 1951 in affluent Rowayton, Conn., and discovered by Broadway-connected friends of the family while in a college play. After being taken under the famous wing of the William Morris agency in 1973, within a week Williams was an understudy of John Travolta in the New York version of *Grease*. Later, he didn't use much grease and underwent a painful hair weave to play an unkempt pied piper of flower children in the film *Hair*. "I've had a taste of celebrity," Williams said after the experience. "And it left a bad taste. I got a lot of invitations (to star-studded galas) after *Hair*, but after the film flopped, the invitations stopped." After another celluloid flop he temporarily changed careers and flew planes for a living. "I felt so out of control I wasn't working with people I wanted to work with. I was very frustrated." Eventually the director Sidney Lumet called to ask him to play the lead in the true story of a New York City cop, Detective Robert Leuci, who helped the government nab 52 corrupt fellow narcotics detectives. Williams learned his role—how to treat junkies, lawyers and judges the way cops actually treat them—by spending a month hanging around a New York precinct, going on drug busts, and living with the cop who inspired his 1981 hit movie, *Prince of the City*. Since then, Williams, who sings tenor, has continued to appear in three genres: scampering around live onstage (once in the musical *Pirates of Penzance*), on TV (as Jack Dempsey in a filmed bio of the ring legend and Stanley Kowalski in *A Streetcar Named Desire*), and of course in movies (his latest: *Sweet Lies*, *Dead Heat*, *Heartbreak Hotel*;

currently filming opposite Jill Clayburgh in *Beyond the Ocean*). He assumed the James Woods role in the TV series based on the film *True Believer*, which debuted in the 1990-91 TV season. What's left for Treat to try? "I always felt it was limiting to do what you could do easily. I'm beginning to want to do some light comedy and a little more normal people. . . . I'm not avoiding playing classical leading men anymore."

Nicol Williamson

As multifaceted a Scotsman as Macbeth, he's been described as "intimidating, temperamental, bristling, and uninhibited," motivated to be chronically outspoken, he says, from "a belief in what your're doing." Because of his sinister smile and ability to create sympathetic villains, Nicol Williamson is often cast as the heavy, but feels light comedy is really his strong suit. With a reputation as an explosive actor, he's also noted for a toro-like temperament, once sloshing a glass of beer at producer David Merrick and then rapping him in the face during an out-of-town tryout of John Osborne's *Inadmissible Evidence* in 1965. "I'm a person violence just happens to," he once explained. (He's been known to chastise audiences for "rudeness," and stop a performance until latecomers were seated.) Williamson attempts to live life to its utmost, spending little time sleeping or eating and choosing only the most demanding parts because he is afraid "to waste six months of my life." Born in Hamilton, Scotland, 14 September 1938, Nicol left home against his father's wishes, to begin his acting career in 1960 with the Dundee Repertory Theatre. He soon made a name for himself as a "highly accomplished and versatile actor" at the Royal Court Theatre and with the Royal Shakespeare Company in such productions as *A Midsummer Night's Dream*, *The Lower Depths*, *The Ginger Man*, and *Waiting for Godot*. But it was not until the role of Bill Maitland in *Inadmissible Evidence* in 1964 that he won fame. London and New York critics were unanimus in weighing his performance as a theatrical event that well deserved the best actor awards on both sides of the Atlantic. His controversial production of *Hamlet*, directed by Tony Richardson (filmed, 1969), was called "the most exciting, intelligent, and straightforward *Hamlet* for a very long time."

Williamson explained that, "All I wanted was a *Hamlet* who was alive, who was real." He's since done *Plaza Suite* (1969) for New York theatregoers, and performed a rousing, fiery interpretation of the title role in *Macbeth* (which he directed for the stage and presented on television for the PBS series, "The Shakespeare Plays"). All the classical acting has prompted Williamson to comment, "When you've played *Hamlet, Macbeth,* and *Coriolanus* by your mid-thirties, you're in danger of becoming a pillar of the English theatre." Not one to be pigeon-holed, he's appeared in such films as *The Seven Per Cent Solution* (1975); *The Cheap Detective* (1978); *The Goodbye Girl* (1977); *Robin and Marion* (1977); *Venom* (1980); and *I'm Dancing as Fast as I Can* (1981). His latest films are: *Black Widow* (1986), *Apt Pupil* (1987), and *Berlin Blues* (1987). In a slightly different move, he performed in a one-man show *Nicol Williamson: An Evening With a Man and His Band* at the Hollywood Playhouse in California in August, 1986. The stage and screen equally fascinate Williamson, and he attributes his success as an actor in both mediums to his perceptiveness and a gift for communication. "I can understand people's pain, passion, fear, hurt, mirth, and I can mirror it and set it up for them to look at."

Once married to American actress Jill Townsend, Williamson enjoys quoting a favorite maxim: "Life isn't all you want, but it's all you got, so stick a geranium in your hat and be happy."

Bruce Willis

He has risen from the depths of New York City's Hell's Kitchen to the glitz and glamour of star studded Hollywood, California. Like many actors, he started out bartending. In the evening, he worked at the New York nightclub, Kamikaze, while during the day he made commercials for Levi's 501 jeans.

Walter Bruce Willis was born on 19 March 1955 in Germany. When he was only two years old, his family moved to the U.S. to New Jersey, where Bruce attended high school. After graduating, he worked briefly at a DuPont plant in a nearby town. His first entertainment work was playing the harmonica with a band called Loose Goose. Bruce attended Montclair State University where he studied acting, and made his first stage appearance in *Cat on a Hot*

Tin Roof. Soon after he made his New York stage debut in the off-Broadway production of *Heaven and Earth,* followed by the lead role in *Fool For Love* (1984). Later that year Bruce decided to take a trip to Los Angeles to watch the Olympics. While he was there, he auditioned for the role of a private eye David Addison in the television series "Moonlighting," (1984-1987) which he ultimately landed. Other television credits include appearances in the series "Hart to Hart," and "Miami Vice." In 1986 he made his movie debut in the comedy *Blind Date.* Films that followed include *Sunset* (1987), *Die Hard* (1988), *In Country* (1989), *Die Hard II* (1990), and *Bonfire of the Vanities* (1990). In addition to acting, Bruce has a knack for singing. He has recorded two albums, *The Return of Bruno* (1987), and *If It Don't Kill You, It Just Makes You Stronger* (1989).

Bruce and actress Demi Moore were married in Las Vegas on 21 November 1987, and have one son—Rumer Glenn, who was born on 16 August 1988. Bruce and Demi began filming *Mortal Thoughts* together in 1990. Although the successful, happy family resides in Hollywood, Bruce still has the lease to the apartment in Hell's Kitchen.

Oprah Winfrey

This young black woman with a megawatt smile, sparkling hazel eyes, and an unusual first name took the television world by storm in January, 1984. She began hosting a local Chicago talk show which was struggling to stay afloat opposite the "Phil Donahue Show"; within two months "AM Chicago" was beating "Donahue" in the Chicago ratings. In 1985, the show's name was changed to "The Oprah Winfrey Show" as the program hit national syndication by September, 1986. In just three years since her arrival in Chicago, Oprah had become a nationally-known personality, host of the third most popular syndicated show overall (behind "Jeopardy" and "Wheel of Fortune") and a millionaire by the age of thirty-two. Her hosting style combines "plainspoken curiosity, robust humor and, above all, empathy" (*Time*) and propelled the show, in its first year of eligibility, to capture three Daytime Emmys for Outstanding Host, Outstanding Direction, and Outstanding

Talk/Service Program. With her track record, it's not surprising that syndicator King World has extended the agreement with Oprah to host the show through 1993.

Born 29 January 1954 in Kosciusko, Mississippi, Oprah has come a long way. She was raised under her grandmother's protective wing on a Mississippi farm when her parents left her in search of separate dreams. Oprah learned to read early and made her first speech in church at age three. When she turned six, she left the sheltered farm life and went to live with her mother Vernita Lee in Milwaukee, where she was sexually abused at age nine by an older cousin and later by a family "friend." Oprah acted out her frustrations and angers by becoming a runaway at age thirteen. As a last resort before detention home, the young girl was sent to live with her father, (a barber, a businessman, and a city councilman) Vernon, in Nashville, Tennessee. Living here, Oprah's life obtained structure and security. Seeking outlets for her talents, Oprah eventually became an honor student, joined the drama club, and at sixteen won an oratorical contest, along with a $1,000 scholarship which helped her pay her tuition at Tennessee State University. While in college, in 1972, Oprah was hired by local station WVOL as a reporter, and later by CBS affiliate WTVF-TV. By 1976, the twenty-two-year-old Oprah was in Baltimore working for WJZ-TV as a feature reporter and co-anchor of the six o'clock news. Unfortunately, Oprah was dumped as co-anchorwoman. Looking back, Oprah philosophizes, "I had no business anchoring the news in a major market." What most felt to be a demotion, being moved to co-host the station's morning show proved a blessing for Oprah. She had found her niche. The show's ratings zoomed, and based upon her performance she was offered the slot for "AM Chicago." Having to wait four months to finish her contract in Nashville, Oprah started to eat . . . and eat . . . losing her beauty-queen figure (Miss Black Tennessee, 1971). This sudden gain of weight produced her debut style; overweight, sexy, and elegant, with a drop-dead wardrobe. Today, starring also in TV's "Brewster Place," Oprah is lighter while she still maintains that special winning style.

In addition to her talk show ability, Oprah has become an accomplished actress. Her portrayal of Sofia in Spielberg's film *The Color Purple* won her both Academy Award and Golden Globe nominations for Best Supporting Actress. She also appeared in the film adaptation of Richard Wright's *Native Son*. Her third acting role was in the TV miniseries "Women of Brewster Place" which was co-produced by her company Harpo Productions ("Oprah" spelled backwards). The production company also owns the movie rights to *Kaffir Boy* and Toni Morrison's Pulitzer Prize winning novel, *Beloved*. In 1988, Harpo assumed ownership and all production responsibilities for "The Oprah Winfrey Show" making Oprah the first woman in history to own and produce her own talk show. The subsequent purchase of an 88,000 square foot movie studio and TV production complex in Chicago, renamed Harpo Studios, made Oprah the first black individual and only the third woman (behind Mary Pickford and Lucille Ball) to own such a studio.

Living by herself in a three bedroom Chicago apartment with a panoramic view of Lake Michigan, Oprah carries on a long distance relationship with boyfriend, Stedman Graham, former basketball player now based in a North Carolina public relations firm. Remembering her roots, each year she endows her alma mater with ten full scholarships in her father's name, aside from her other philanthropic endeavors. "My mission is to use this position, power, and money to create opportunities for other people," she says. Renowned for her lavish gifts to friends and staff (in 1989 she hosted a television special on friendship), Oprah who reads a Bible verse every morning, believes she is guided by a higher calling. "I believe in the God-force that lives inside all of us, and once you tap into that you can do anything." Oprah is doing everything she wants to, doing it well. In 1988 she received the "Broadcaster of the Year Award" from the International Radio & TV Society, making her the youngest person and only the fifth woman to ever receive this honor in the Society's twenty-five year history. In 1989, "The Oprah Winfrey Show" won the Daytime Emmy Award as Outstanding Talk/Service Program.

Debra Winger

Pauline Kael wrote in the *New Yorker*, "Debra Winger has the vividness of those we call 'born' performers. She makes you feel that there's something humming inside her." Jack Nicholson, who costarred with her in perhaps her most important film to date, *Terms of Endearment* (1983), felt she was "a metamorphic actress, this girl. I think she's a great actress—a genius." Perhaps Winger thinks she is just lucky to be alive, let alone successful. Born Mary Debra Winger in Cleveland, Ohio, 17 May 1955 and raised in Sepulveda, Calif., she was employed at the Magic Mountain amusement park in 1973 when on New Year's Eve she was thrown from a truck and nearly died of a cerbral hemorrhage. She was left partially paralyzed and blind in one eye for several months. "Poetically, I look at my accident as a huge hunk of grace, which propelled me into doing what I wanted to do."

After high-school graduation, Winger went to Israel, where she lived and worked on a kibbutz. She applied for citizenship there and even served three months with the Israeli Army before heading back to the States. She enrolled at California State University at Northridge and planned on becoming a socio-criminologist until she realized that she was a "juvenile delinquent," at least in spirit. Then came the accident, after which she studied acting and began making television commercials, which led to parts of programs including "Police Woman" and a featured part as Drusilla the Wonder Girl, Lynda Carter's younger sister, in ABC-TV's "Wonder Woman." Her film debut was in *Thank God It's Friday* (1978), which was followed by a more noteworthy part in *French Postcards* (1979). Her real breakthrough came when she won out over 200 other hopefuls and was cast opposite John Travolta in *Urban Cowboy* (1980). She stole the show with her extraordinary ride on a bucking mechanical bronc that included eye rolling and other orgasmic notions. She was the voice of *E.T.*, won an Oscar nomination as Richard Gere's homegrown sweetheart in *An Officer and a Gentleman* (1982) and a second nomination for her portrayl of Emma in *Terms of Endearment*. As Shirley MacLaine's fictional daughter, her part spanned a period of 14 years, in which she goes from a teenager in bobby sox to become a mother herself and a young victim of cancer. All the while she "plays cello to her mother's trumpet," as described by *People* magazine, which also said that Winger "at every stage of the story is simply and translucently Emma, inhabiting her character as naturally as red inhabits a rose." Winger, who also appeared in TV's "Cannery Row" (1982) and in *Mike's Murder* (1984), said that the attention-getting film *Terms* was for "the mothers of young children, the middle-class mother . . . that's who the film was for inside of me. I've always had this deep resentment of how the middle class is treated. I mean the lower class, it's obvious what they catch, you know, life is rough. But the true crime, some of the worst psychic abuse, is on the middle-class. So here was this perfectly middle-class girl who turned into a housewife with children, and I really felt the responsibility, it was very important to me to make a hero out of this class of woman." Her most recent films have produced assorted reviews. She was acclaimed for her role as a lawyer opposite Robert Redford in *Legal Eagles* (1986) and almost ignored for her role in *Betrayed* (1988). Upcoming films include *Tea in the Desert, Everybody Wins* and Bertolucci's *The Sheltering Sky*.

Winger married actor Timothy Hutton on 16 March 1986; the couple separated in June 1988 (one son, Emmanuel Noah).

Henry Winkler

"There are a staggering number of people in the country who appear to be ready to do anything for me, women I've never met who want to mother my children, elderly ladies who stand for hours in the hope of touching my hand. It's easy to say these people are all unbalanced, or lonely beyond recall, but there are a lot of them and I have some sort of obligation to them, even if it's just to tell them to relax." His performance as a pseudo-hood with a heart of gold in the durable, wholesome comedy, "Happy Days," erupted in a rash of Fonzie fever, making Winkler one of the most popular personalities in television history.

Winkler's real-life scenario is a far cry from that of his blue-collar, motorcycle-riding TV alter-ego. Born 30 October 1945 in New York to German-Jewish refugees, he suffered through a prep-school adolescence spent in an unsuccessful quest for "cool." "I was so self-effacing it makes me sick. Every year I'd go to the really cool guys in school and say, 'Listen, this year I'm different. I've changed.' . . . I was willing to be whoever anyone wanted me to be." To his parents' dismay, he rejected the family lumber business to pursue acting at Emerson College and Yale. He performed with the Yale Repertory Theatre Company and appeared in television commercials before trying his luck in Hollywood. Within a year, he was cast as the one colorful character in the innocent comedy about a Milwaukee family during the 1950s. Featured initially as a minor character, Winkler quickly came to dominate the show as thunderous viewer response indicated the nation was hungry for a bigger role for "The Fonz." He was the big brother many kids dream about. Seeming taller than his five-foot-seven frame, he was slick, forceful, and always there in a pinch. As the show progressed (it lasted just over a decade), Fonzie grew up but never grew out of his ever-present leather jacket, or his uncanny ability to snap women to attention or start a juke box with a tap of his fist.

Despite Winkler's desire to avoid typecasting, his film attempts have failed to set hearts—or critics' pens—aflutter. His film credits include *The Lords of Flatbush*, *Heroes* and *Night Shift*, and the made-for-TV 1979 "American Christmas Carol," in which he played Scrooge. Nowadays, he spends most of his time behind the camera.

He is the producer of the popular television show "MacGyver," and he directed the Alan King film *Memories of Me* (1988). Winkler has become an advocate for children's welfare, and in 1984 he created a videocassette on the subject of child abuse entitled "Strong Kids, Safe Kids." He married the former Stacey Weitzman in 1978 and is father to her son, Jed, from a previous marriage, and their daughter Zoe and son Max.

Jonathan Winters

This orotund comic with a genius for mimicry is a veritable album of characters, small town and otherwise. You might see Jonathan Winters portraying anybody from an old grandmother to a filling-station attendant, or, as a whole new generation of fans has come to know him, the man who advertises the trash bags on television. He explains that his brand of humor holds up a mirror in which people either see themselves or their friends. Another rare talent is his way with sound effects. He can, he insists, make 5000 different sounds with his mouth.

Born 11 November 1925 in Dayton, Ohio, he planned on becoming a commercial artist, but a lost watch changed the course of his life. A local talent contest offered a watch to its top prize winner and Winters entered the contest hoping to win a new timepiece. He did win and soon was offered a job as a disc jockey by a local radio station; this gave him plenty of opportunity to perfect his monologues and voice tricks. He headed to New York and performed at a series of clubs. His big break came when he appeared on TV's "Jack Paar Show" and was selected as a regular substitute host for Paar. The comedy-obsessed workaholic had a breakdown in 1959 and was sent to a place that has always been a mainstay in his routine—a place he refers to as the "funny farm." He recovered swiftly and has spent the past 25 years appearing on televsion, including his own CBS show, "Mork and Mindy" as the son of Robin Williams and Pam Dawber, ABC's "Good Morning America," many variety shows and television movies and in films (e.g. the comedy classic *It's a Mad, Mad, Mad, Mad World*, *The Loved One* and *The Russians Are Coming*). In 1987 he released the enlightening book *Winter's Tales* (1987) and was filming *The Teddy Bear Habit* in 1989. He returned to TV sitcoms in the 1990-91 season with "The Principal."

Director Stanley Kramer once called Winters, "the only genius I know" because of the comedian's ability to create characters out of thin air. Winters, who is married and has two children, credits his talent to his school days. "I was the class clown. Other guys had more security, steady dates and all that . . . I didn't. The only thing that kept me together was my comedy. We'd all go to a tavern called O'Brien's and I would do impressions of the Indianapolis Speedway."

Shelley Winters

Her new 1989 autobiography *Shelley II: The Middle of My Century* picks up where she left off. . . . "America's most irrepressible star takes us on a wild ride through the Hollywood of the 1950s and early 1960s, with side trips to Broadway, the Actors Studio, and around the world." She freely talks about her associations with fellow celebrity friends: Marilyn Monroe, "her Hollywood roommate, who is perfect in front of the camera but helpless in the kitchen," Sean Connery, "a young Scottish actor who romances Shelley in his chilly London flat," and Tony Franciosa, of whom she states, "If there had been an Olympic sex team that year, Tony would have been the captain."

Brash and stormy ("I admit I'm not all sweetness and light, but when I speak my mind, it usually clears the air"), Shelley Winters, nee Shirley Shrift, took her first not-so-tentative steps toward an acting career when, at fourteen, she showed up at a Manhattan talent agency and announced in her best Southern (and Brooklynese) accent, "Ah'm heah to play Scarlett O'Hara." That didn't work, but she did make a significant inroad on screen stardom in 1948 complicating one of the lives of Ronald Colman in his Academy Award-winning role in *A Double Life*. She had her own first taste of an Oscar nomination after she played Montgomery Clift's inconvenient lower-class girlfriend in *A Place in the Sun* in 1951 and later won two Supporting Actress Oscars for *Diary of Anne Frank* (1959) and *A Patch of Blue* (1965). Winter's was nominated in that category again for *The Poseidon Adventure* in 1972 and later in the decade, picked up a "David," the Italian version of the Oscar, for her bravura performance playing a mute in the Italian-made film *An Average Little Man.* She has made more than a dozen films in Italy and, according to one Rome-based director, has "filled the gap left by Anna Magnani." Says Shelley about her enormous popularity in pastaland: "I think in another life I *was* Italian."

She was born into *this* life on 18 August 1922 in St. Louis, Missouri, moved to Brooklyn as a child and has made her presence felt in New York acting circles as well as Hollywood's. More secure in her craft after adopting The Method at the Actor's Studio, she has observed: "Money can be devalued or taken away from you. The only real security is talent. If you have that, you'll always have work." In recent years, she has taken to the typewriter with mixed results. After seeing her 1971 play, *One Night Stands of a Noisy Passenger,* critic Richard Watts decided that she was a "simply dreadful dramatist." But her 1980 autobiography, *Shelley, Also Known as Shirley,* was a bestseller, possibly because of her frankness in describing affairs she had with the likes of Errol Flynn, Burt Lancaster, and others, before, between and after her marriages to and/or divorces from Mack Paul Mayer, Vittorio Gassman (one daughter) and Anthony Franciosa. ("Of course, I didn't have all that many men in my life," says Shelley. "Considering today's Women's Lib attitudes, I was a piker.") How can anyone resist someone who relates: "You know, I went out with Clark Gable. When he picked me up, my mother, that most moral lady, whispered in my ear. 'Don't be careful!'"

B.D. Wong

He is a multi-talented actor, singer, dancer, and choreographer. He has appeared in the feature film *The Karate Kid* and the Broadway production of *M. Butterfly.*

Wong studied acting with Don Hotton, and in addition was a Casting Society of America Minority Committee Acting Seminar Participant. His vocal training was under Ruth Cooper, as well as Roger Love with the Seth Riggs Studio. He also studied tap under Tony Wing. His screen appearances include the feature film *The Karate Kid II* and *No Big Deal.* He has been seen on numerous television shows as well, such as "Driver's Ed," "Double Switch," "Sweet Surrender," "Shell

Game," "Hard Copy," "Blackes Magic," the weekly series "Simon and Simon," "TV's Bloopers & Practical Jokes," and the "New Love American Style." Wong has also given several outstanding theatre performances in *La Cage aux Folles, See Below Middle Sea, The Gifts of the Magi, A Salute to Sondheim, Part II, Mail* and *M. Butterfly*. In addtiion to being an accomplished actor, Wong is an excellent singer, possessing a high baritone and a superior falsetto.

In his spare time Wong enjoys designing, drawing, crafting and bowling.

Edward Woodward

Once hailed by Sir Laurence Olivier as one of the best actors in England, Edward Woodward has lived up to that statement. Woodward's thirty-five-year career span has secured his presence as a stage actor, star of feature films and television, musician, and vocalist.

Born 1 June 1930 in Croyden, Surrey England to Edward and Violet Woodward, Edward's primary career interest was in journalism. While attending Kingston College, Woodward discovered his niche after appearing in several of the college's theatrical productions and later attended England's notorious Royal Academy of Dramatic Arts. His 1954 stage debut in London's West End production of *Where There's a Will*, started a slew of successful theatrical appearances across the globe from Shakespearean tours in India, Ceylon, and Australia to New York's honored Broadway stage. The successful Broadway production *Rattle of a Simple Mind* in 1962 bestowed him with the New York Theatre Critics Award. Noel Coward's Broadway musical *High Spirits* was Woodward's vehicle to combine his acting and vocal talents. Among Woodward's theatrical credits are *Romeo & Juliet* (1985), *Hamlet* (1958), *Richard III, Cyrano de Bergerac* (1971), *The White Devil* (1971), *The Wolfe* (1973), *Male of the Species* (1975), *On Approval* (1976), *The Dark Horse Comedy* (1978), *The Beggar's Opera* in 1980 which he also directed, *Private Lives* (1980), and *The Assassin* (1982).

Successful in the transition from stage to film, Woodward has completed over a dozen feature films. Among them the starring role in 1980's *Breaker Morant*. He also appeared in *The File on the Golden Goose* (1968), *Young Winston* (1974), and *The Wicker Man* (1974). The

1980's saw Woodward in *Who Dares Wins* (1982) and *King David* (1986).

Woodward is best known to American audiences for his portrayal of Robert McCall in CBS-TV's critically acclaimed dramatic series "The Equalizer" which began in 1985. His brilliant portrayal of the mysterious benevolent avenger earned him Emmy nominations for best lead actor in a dramatic series (1986, 1989) and a Golden Globe (1987). His new series, "Over My Dead Body," began in 1990. British television audiences adored him in the successful series "Callan" and "Winston Churchill: The Wilderness Years." Telefilm credits include his performance as "Simon Legree" in the cable production of "Uncle Tom's Cabin," HBO mini-series "Code Name Kyril," CBS-TV's "Arthur the King," and "A Christmas Carol." Blessed with musical talent as well, Woodward is a renowned vocalist in England and Australia having recorded fourteen albums for which he has acquired several gold discs. During his hiatus in the Spring of 1988 he engaged in a twelve-city tour in England. With a passion for the written word, he has also recorded albums of dramatic poetry readings, prose, and Shakespeare.

A decorated officer of the Order of the British Empire, Woodward has been married twice. His first marriage in 1952 was to Venetia Mary Collet (divorced 1986; three children—Timothy, Peter, and Sarah, all pursuing acting careers). In one episode of the "Equalizer," son Timothy portrayed his dad "McCall" as a young man in a flashback sequence. Remarried in 1987 to Michelle Dotrice, herself an actress (daughter of fellow thespian Roy Dotrice), Woodward and Dotrice have found themselves working side by side in various theatrical productions and an episode of the "Equalizer." By far their proudest collaboration is daughter Emily Beth born in 1983. An avid collector of antique swords, rock and mineral specimens, plus antique and Jacobean furniture, Woodward also pursues boating, photography, and reading on such topics as American history and politics. The Woodwards have homes in New York City, upstate New York, and England.

Joanne Woodward

"Given the right parts, she is a great actress. She can find so many different facets of herself to play," explains husband Paul Newman. "That is magic." Indeed, at 27, Joanne Woodward stunned the film industry when, in her third film, she delineated the troubled *Three Faces of Eve* (1957), giving Oscar-winning depth to each characterization. Despite her range ("I've never been the same person twice on the screen"), demonstrated in

such highly regarded films as *The Sound and the Fury* (1959), *The Fugitive Kind* (1960), *From the Terrace* (1960), *The Stripper* (1963), and *A Fine Madness* (1965), she finally decided "Hollywood never really knew what to do with me." Declaring "I'm not a movie star anyway," she avoided the film capital until she found the script that was to become *Rachel, Rachel* ("I was determined I'd rather do nothing than just work for the sake of having a job"). After completion of the critically acclaimed *Rachel, Rachel* (1968), directed by Newman, she concluded she would "never do anything again unless I felt strongly about it." Newman has since directed her in three major vehicles, the films *The Effect of Gamma Rays on Man-in-the-Moon Marigolds* (1972), *The Glass Menagerie* (1987), plus "The Shadow Bow" (1980) for ABC-TV. In 1985, Woodward gave a touching performance as a victim of Alzheimer's disease in the TV movie, "Do You Remember Love?" (Her own mother is afflicted with the disease.)

Born 27 February 1930 in Thomasville, Ga., Joanne Gignilliat Woodward was raised in Greenville, S.C. and first studied acting at Louisana State University before switching to New York's Neighborhood Playhouse. While working steadily in early TV, she understudied both Kim Stanley and Janice Rule in *Picnic* (1953), playing each role about 50 times in the play's 477 performances on Broadway. She also met fellow understudy Newman, whom she married 29 January 1958, shortly after making *The Long Hot Summer* (1958), their first movie together (1984's *Harry and Son* marked their tenth). Newman had three young children (one boy, two girls) and the couple produced three more daughters. Subjugating her career to Newman's superstardom and raising the family created problems ("my tendency is to shriek and throw things, being childish myself, as most actors are"). Woodward necessarily turned down interesting offers, "and, being a total actress—I really like to act morning, noon, and night, that was another problem our girls had to suffer with, because, not always being allowed to act on stage or screen, I was giving brilliant performances at home." Home was mainly converted old buildings on rambling acres of apple tress in Westport, Conn., supplemented by "Mommie's Tree House," off-limits to those under 16. Their brownstone in New York sports a bedroom Tennessee Williams once pronounced "the finest example of Southern decadence I have ever seen" and there is the obligatory house in Brentwood, Calif. ("I've been knocking Hollywood so long it's a joke.") In addition to occasional films, she has made specials for all three television networks, including "Lady Chatterly's Lover" (1978), "See How She Runs" (1978), and "Passions" (1985). On Broadway, her appearance in the title role in *Candida* opened the 1982 season for Circle in the Square.

Her children rekindled Woodward's interest in the dance, to which she devotes time, practice, artistic energy, and financial support. In the mid-1970s, she became Chairman of the Board and chief financial backer for "Dancers," a New Yorkbased– company formed by Dennis Wayne. With the family mostly grown and more time for herself, Woodward has said "I do what I like to do now, which is to act, and that does not necessarily mean in movies. But, when I do act in movies, I do it mostly for the money, because it's very expensive supporting a ballet company."

Jane Wyman

As "Falcon Crest's" wine ty-cooness extra-ordinaire she's tougher than a plug in a bottle of cham-pagne and bitchier than sour grapes. She is reclusive, she dislikes interviews and in the words of one of her co-stars, "Falcon Crest is *her* set." From a flighty snub-nosed bit player to a mature, assured leading lady, Jane Wyman has built her career with care and shrewd-ness, using better and more challeng-ing roles to reach the top ranks of her craft.

She was born Sarah Jane Fulks, 4 January 1914 in St. Joseph, Missouri.; her father was mayor for a time and her mother entertained ambitions for little Sarah Jane to be the first Shirley Temple. At the age of 8, she made her first trip to Hollywood with her mother to break into the movie biz, but they returned to St. Joseph, daunted. After graduating from the University of Missouri she worked as a manicurist and switchboard opera-tor until, under the name "Jane Durrell," she got a job singing on the radio. A next attempt in the movies succeeded—somewhat. She was given bit parts, chorus girl roles, some publicity, and her present name. ("I posed in bathing suits with Santa Claus, the Easter Bunny, and the Thanksgiving turkey.") In 1936 she appeared in *My Man Godfrey* and following that, worked steadily as a tow-headed ingenue in comedies like *Cain and Mabel* (1936). "I was the

Joan Blondell of the B's." Married in 1937 to Myron Futterman, she divorced him in 1938, the year she starred opposite her soon-to-be second husband, Ronald Reagan, in the film *Brother Rat*. Wyman and Reagan were married from 1940 until 1948; they had one daughter Maureen and adopted a son, Michael. With *Lost Weekend* in 1945 her acting had matured and she was established as a Hollywood actress. Better and better roles followed; she became more and more the Noble Heroine and less and less the Featherbrained Flirt. In 1947 she won an Oscar nomination as the mother in *The Yearling* and in 1948 she won the award for *Johnny Belinda*, playing a deaf mute. When a second daughter, born prematurely, died, the Wyman-Reagan ticket split apart. "He's very political," she said, "and I'm not." Louella Parsons lamented that "it was the saddest break-up of Hollywood's most seemingly ideal couple since Douglas Fairbanks and Mary Pickford." Reagan thought the death of the newborn and Wyman's Oscar winning characterization had been too much of a strain and quipped at the time that the only correspondent in his ailing marriage "was Johnny Belinda."

The star of later films such as *The Glass Menagerie* (1950), *Magnificent Obsession* (1954), *Miracle in the Rain* (1956), and a successful TV series in the 1950s bears the distinction of being the only ex-wife of a United States president in history—a fact that hardly impresses her. She walks away from interviews if Ronald Reagan's name is mentioned, feeling, in the words of one observer on the "Falcon Crest" set, "that all that ended 35 years ago and has no relevance to her life now." A third and fourth marriage to Fred Karger ended in divorce. Now single she says, "I recommend marriage very highly, for everyone but me."

Michael York

He looks like a blond lightweight pugilist (his nose has been broken twice), yet his accent is very much Oxford, his style cleverly subdued. Though he received critical acclaim in such films as *Accident, Romeo and Juliet, Justine, Something for Everyone* and *Zeppelin*, it wasn't until his highly sensitive performance as a scholarly bisexual in *Cabaret* that his stock became unassailably blue chip. Recent films include: *The White Lions* (1979), *Final Assignment* (1979), *For Those I Loved* (1983), *Success is the Best Revenge* (1983), *Casablanca Express* (1989), and *The Return of the Three Musketeers* (1989). He did a season stint as the ex-boyfriend of Abbye Ewing, on the popular nighttime soap, "Knots Landing" in 1987. He also appeared in the CBS telefilm "The Lady and the Highwayman" (1988).

Born in Fulmer, England, 27 March 1942, he was admitted to

Britain's National Theatre after graduating from Oxford. ("I stayed there two years and I felt I was actually getting down to the ground roots of acting. . . . Everyone takes the same classes—movement, voice, fencing—so you suddenly find yourself doing knee bends next to Sir Laurence.") A minor role in Franco Zeffirelli's National Theatre production of *Much Ado About Nothing* proved to be the big opportunity. When Zeffirelli got around to casting his film version of *The Taming of the Shrew* in 1966, he remembered Michael, and gave him

the part of the lovestruck Lucentio. Later that year he reached a turning point in his career as the doomed blueblood in Joseph Losey's *Accident*. Broadway credits include *Bent* (1980) and the musical version of *The Little Prince* (1982).

His wife is American Patricia McCallum, a former *Glamour* magazine photographer, whom he married in 1968.

Loretta Young

Tall, slender, stylishly dressed, she swirled through a distant doorway into living rooms all across America back in the 1950s on her own "Loretta Young Show." Twenty years later, much to her chagrin, she was swirling again, via reruns, in foreign countries all over the world—tall, slender, but dressed out of style. In 1972 the actress with the "luminously virginal quality" showed her "steel butterfly" side in Los Angeles Superior Court. Suing NBC for $1,300,000 for circulating the old shows without her permission, she said, "I wanted to present myself as a well-dressed fashionable woman." The judge saw it her way.

Loretta was born 6 January 1913 in Salt Lake City. When her father abandoned his family early on, her mother packed up her pretty daughters, headed for Los Angeles, and soon had all of the girls working regularly in the movies. Polly Ann, Betty, Jane, and Georgianna eventually went on to other things (Georgianna married Ricardo Montalban) but four-year-old Gretchen, later renamed Loretta, stuck it out. She was the star of close to a hundred big screen features (she won an Oscar for *The Farmer's Daughter* in 1947, and Oscar nomination for her own favorite, *Come to the Stable*, the following year) and dramas by the score on the little screen (two Emmys as best actress in a continuing series) and won a Golden Globe Award for her role in the NBC-TV special "Christmas Eve," in 1987.

After eloping at 17 with Grant Withers (the marriage was annulled after less than a year), she married (and divorced in 1969) Thomas Lewis, father of her three children. A Catholic and unabashed Puritan, famous in her TV days for the swear box she kept on the set (anyone caught cursing had to contribute a fine to St. Ann's Home for Unwed Mothers), she believes in the merits of stern self-discipline and hard work—qualities she touts highly in her autobiography, *The Things I Had To Learn*. A believer also in the old proverb about cleanliness being next to godliness she offers a special reminder in the book's section on beauty regarding the advantages of washing one's neck.

Robert Young

"**M**etro was going through the motions of testing a producer's girlfriend. I fed her the lines. She was so terrible they kept shooting over her shoulders at me," laughs actor Robert Young, musing on the beginnings of a long and distinguished career—his first screen test with Metro in 1931. "I was signed and she wasn't." When he went home to announce the news, his mother, brothers, and sister joined hands and danced around the kitchen table. His name conjures up three careers. First he played the prototypical thirties man—smooth-faced in cable-knit sweaters and Oxford bags or changing into white tie and tails, elegantly lighting Joan Crawford's cigarettes. Second the mature forties actor played Boston Brahmin in *H. M. Pulham, Esq.*, scarred war veteran in *The Enchanted Cottage*, and David to Dorothy McGuire's classic *Claudia*. Third, Young played the all-American father figure, starring for six years on television as Jim Anderson, harrassed dad in "Father Knows Best" (which originated as a network radio show in 1949 before moving to television in 1954), and finally from 1969-1976 as the benevolent Dr. Welby in "Marcus Welby, M.D.," achieving the highest Nielsen ratings. This role sequence of dad and doctor earned Young three Emmys.

Robert Young was born 22 February 1907 in Chicago, but raised in Seattle and Los Angeles. The family barely had enough to eat and he recalls having to work from the age of eight selling newspapers. After his father's final desertion of home when he was ten, the constant struggle for survival preyed upon him. "As far back as I can remember, I was afraid—of some imagined disaster that never did eventuate. When I was a child, I used to hide in the crooks of trees, just to be alone." (His high school teacher coaxed him to act at the Pasadena Playhouse, helping him escape his harrowing shyness.) "When I became an actor I constantly felt I wasn't worthy, that I had no right to be a star. All those years at Metro, and even later, on "Father Knows Best," I hid a black terror behind a cheerful face. Naturally, I tried to find a way out. Alcoholism was the inevitable result," he confides. "It took me thirty years to realize I was poisoning myself to death. It was an immensely slow, difficult process, but after slipping back again and again, I at last made a kind of giant step and I was across the threshold to sanity and health." Coupled with the help and understanding of a sympathetic wife (married only once, he wed his high school sweetheart, Betty Henderson, in 1933 and has four daughters), Alcoholics Anonymous aided him, and he has worked on their behalf, lecturing and arranging meetings.

His indelible image—warm, wise, benevolent, understanding, and compassionate—culminated in many a television commercial for "Sanka Brand Decaffeinated Coffee," when Young was asked to play himself in a long series of commercials revolving around his presence. And in 1984 ABC brought Dr. Welby out of retirement after eight years away from his practice, with a two-hour TV-movie titled "The Return of Marcus Welby, M.D."—and Robert Young emerged, as always, dapper and dignified. In 1988 he filmed another continuation of the medical man, "Dr. Marcus Welby in Paris." Other recent television appearances include the telefilms "Mercy or Murder?" (1987) and "Conspiracy of Love" (1987).

Henny Youngman

H is "Take my wife—please!" is surely the the most famous four-word joke in the language and, as the *New Yorker* once pointed out, "it's a joke so compact it has a punch *word* instead of a punch line." That pared-to-the-bone precision is typical of the

comic Walter Winchell heralded as "The King of the One-Liners," who regularly manages to deliver an incredible 250 jokes in a single 40-minute routine. Says Henny: "For me, every joke is really a cartoon—you can see it." Another Youngman classic is a perfect example of this: "She was bowlegged, he was knock-kneed. When they stood together, they spelled 'OX.'"

Born in London, about the time of his jokes (circa 1907), Henry Youngman was brought to Brooklyn as an infant by his Russian-born parents. His opera-loving dad gave him fiddle lessons in the hope that he'd wind up in the Metropolitan Opera orchestra but instead, at 18, he formed his own band. One night, when a comedy act failed to show up, a club owner asked Henny (by now billed as Youngman) to go on and tell some of the jokes he'd been cracking during band rehearsals. He went over big and was on his way. From a two-year stint on Kate Smith's radio show, Henny progressed to night clubs and, still using his fiddle for a prop ("Would you believe it, I used to play at Carnegie Hall—till the cops chased me away"), moved into the rarefied inner circle of "comic's comics," adored as much by other joke-peddlers as audiences. (Says Milton Berle: "His *mind* has a funny bone.") The six-feet-two Henny averaged 200 shows a year and never missed a performance. And, as pointed out by Tony Hiss in Youngman's *New Yorker* profile, "he doesn't do nasty material; he never attacks people . . . and he stay away from all X-rated material; he stays clean."

Henny's wife, Sadie Cohen, whom he met when she was working in the sheet music department of Kresge's and he had a concession in the store printing business cards for actors, died in March, 1987. She had once assured everyone that she never took personally her husband's famous one-liner about her—nor any of the others which have become staples of his act. Youngman appeared in the 1987 film *Amazon Women on the Moon* and his autobiography, *Take My Life, Please* was published in 1988. In 1990 he joined Milton Berle in roasting Zsa Zsa Gabor at L.A.'s Friar's Club.

Franco Zeffirelli

"**T**o be despised by critics but loved by the audience," writes Corby Kummer in *Horizon*, is all right with Franco

Zeffirelli. The director, who has made a name for florid showmanship in theatre, opera, and film, doesn't much mind if critics accuse him of churning out trash disguised with thick coats of varnish. His audiences say his films move them deeply, and that's enough for him." His favorite entertainment medium is opera, to which "nothing else in the arts can come near," but on the other hand he has called motion pictures "a fascinating medium which gives many opportunities that the others don't give." About his own contribution to  these and other media he can be disarming with interviews: "As a director I'm so-so," he told the *New York Times* in 1983, "but as a designer I'm the best."

Born in Florence, Italy, 12 February 1923, the only child of a young couple in modest circumstances, little Franco was packed off at six to live with an aunt when his parents divorced, the latter a most unusual occurrence in prewar Italy. As a youth he studied architecture at the University of Florence and, when Italy became the scene of fighting between Germans and invading Allies, he joined up with some partisans and then with British troops. When peace came he returned to Florence and took up acting, on stage and in films, but a meeting with Luchino Visconti in 1949 led to his designing sets for several of that director's productions, including *A Streetcar Named Desire* and *The Three Sisters;* this in turn led to his designing and directing operas for La Scala of Milan. In 1959 he was invited to Covent Garden to stage a production of *Lucia di Lammermoor* starring Joan Sutherland. Thereafter, he put on numerous operas in Milan, London, New York, Paris, and Vienna. Simultaneously he has directed plays since 1960 and films and television shows since 1966.

Zeffirelli's most ambitious film is the epic *Jesus of Nazareth* (1975-76). Of *The Champ,* his 1979 remake of a 1931 tear-jerker that touched him profoundly as a child, Pauline Kael wrote that he "directed as if he had never met a human being." But the director, warned that no mass market existed for Shakespeare, also had the satisfaction of seeing his *Romeo and Juliet* gross $52 million. As a passionate opera-lover he takes special delight in recording on film live performances of great operatic works, with the world's leading singers, and he has, to date, filmed several, including *Cavalleria Rusticana, I Pagliacci,* and *La Traviata* (1983, starring Teresa Stratas and Placido Domingo). At the Metropolitan Opera he has designed and staged—with notable success—a sumptuous *La Boheme* and *Tosca*. In 1985 he turned his considerable talents to ballet, staging *Swan Lake* with two ballerinas (one as Odette, the other as Odile) instead of the traditional single ballerina essaying both roles. In 1988, he directed the film *Young Toscanini*, and in 1990 he directed a film of Shakespeare's *Hamlet*.

Stephanie Zimbalist

"I like my name. I like the rhythm. Besides, I've never had the problems that everybody assumes children of well-known people are supposed to have," says the actress-daughter of longtime TV perennial Efrem Zimbalist, Jr. ("The FBI," 1965-74) and grand-daughter of the world-famous violinist Efrem Zimbalist and opera diva Alma Gluck. As Laura Holt on TV's "Remington Steele" (1982-1987), she operated her detective agency under a fictitious male name, but Stephanie Zimbalist herself "never really seriously considered" changing her own. Zimbalist's "sexually-charged on-camera battles" with series co-star Pierce Brosnan kept viewers entranced enough for the show to last for five seasons, and then to be resurrected again in two-hour telefilms after the series was cancelled. The show established the pert, down-to-earth, frecklefaced actress as one of the hotter young performers on the prime time line-up.

Manhattan-born, 8 October circa 1958, Stephanie is not only from a famous family but of preppy Foxcroft in Virginia and, among other acting studies, she spent a year at the theatre division of Juilliard. At the end of her first term there, the powers-that-be released her with the suggestion that she'd led too sheltered a life and needed to "experience the world." "It was a devastating moment," Stephanie recalled to Michael Leahy of *TV Guide*. "I began contemplating things. Maybe I should take LSD or become a hooker." Instead, she headed for Hollywood and managed to find work on two TV movies—as a kidnap victim in "Yesterday's Child" on NBC and a high school girl in love on CBS's "Forever." Not long afterward she was asked to do the pilot for "Remington Steele" and has since appeared in films (*The Awakening; The Magic of Lassie*), assorted mini-series on TV ("Centennial"), telefilms ("Love on the Run," "The Man in the Brown Suit"), and theatre projects (e.g. *The Cherry Orchard, My One and Only,* and *Carousel*).

Photo Credits

Alan Alda: *Arlene Alda*
Loni Anderson: *Harry Langdon Photography*
Richard Dean Anderson: *Paramount Pictures Corporation*
Julie Andrews: *Zoe Dominic*
Ann-Margaret: *E. J. Camp/Paramount Pictures Corporation*
Peggy Ashcroft: *Granada TV*
Edward Asner: *Dana Gluckstein*
Dan Aykroyd: *Universal City Studios*

Roseanne Barr: *Capital Cities/ABC*
Kim Basinger: *Greg Gorman/Weintraub Entertainment Group*
Jason Bateman: *Lorimar Television*
Justine Bateman: *Paramount Pictures Corp.*
Barbara Bel Geddes: *Lorimar*
Tom Berenger: *Suzanne Tenner*
Candice Bergen: *Universal City Studios, Inc.*
Corbin Bernsen: *Timothy White/Morgan Creek Productions*
Bernardo Bertolucci: *Columbia Pictures*
Shirley Temple Black: *Curt Gunther*
Marlon Brando: *David James/Metro-Goldwyn-Mayer Pictures, Inc.*

Kirk Cameron: *Greg Gorman*
Glen Campbell: *Peter Nash/MCA Records Nashville*
John Candy: *Paramount Pictures Corporation*
John Carpenter: *Columbia Pictures*
Diahann Carroll: *Harry Langdon*
Cher: *Greg Gorman*
Jill Clayburgh: *Universal City Studios, Inc.*
Dabney Coleman: *Universal City Studios, Inc.*
Francis Ford Coppola: *Adger W. Cowans*
Bob Costas: *NBC*
Michael Crawford: *Simon Fowler/CBS Records Inc.*
Hume Cronyn: *Zoe Dominic*
Tom Cruise: *United Artists Pictures, Inc.*
Jamie Lee Curtis: *Capital Cities/ABC*

Timothy Dalton: *United Artists Pictures, Inc.*
Robert DeNiro: *Universal City Studios, Inc.*
Brian De Palma: *Columbia Pictures Industries, Inc.*
William Devane: *Lorimar Television*
Danny De Vito: *Touchstone Pictures*
Kevin Dobson: *Lorimar Television*
Michael Douglas: *Twentieth Century Fox*

Robert Downey, Jr.: *Tri-Star Pictures, Inc.*
Patrick Duffy: *Lorimar Television*
David Dukes: *ICM*

Clint Eastwood: *Warner Brothers*
Blake Edwards: *Columbia Pictures Industries, Inc.*
Emilio Estevez: *Nancy Ellison/Morgan Creek Productions, Inc.*

Harvey Fierstein: *William Garrett*
Albert Finney: *Francois Duhamel-Mega*
Carrie Fisher: *Universal City Studios*
Harrison Ford: *Twentieth Century Fox*
Milos Forman: *Los Angeles Time/Michael Edwards*
Jodie Foster: *Paramount Pictures Corporation/Rob McEwan*
David Frost: *Snowdon*

Art Garfunkel: *Caroline Greyshock/CBS Records Inc.*
Kathie Lee Gifford: *The Walt Disney Co.*
Whoopi Goldberg: *Warner Bros. Inc.*
Jeff Goldblum: *Vestron Pictures*
Jennifer Grey: *Vestron Pictures*
Tammy Grimes: *James Radiches*
Charles Grodin: *Universal City Studios, Inc.*
Alec Guinness: *Twentieth Century-Fox Film Corporation*

Gene Hackman: *David Appleby*
Larry Hagman: *Lorimar Television*
Arsenio Hall: *Bonnie Schiffman/Paramount Pictures*
George Hamilton: *Harry Langdon*
Tom Hanks: *Brian Hamill*
Daryl Hannah: *Twentieth Century Fox Film/Andy Schwartz*
Audrey Hepburn: *Roddy McDowall*
Katharine Hepburn: *John Seakwood/Cannon Films, Inc.*
Charlton Heston: *Lydia Heston*
Gregory Hines: *Tri-Star Pictures*
Dustin Hoffman: *Greg Gorman*

Amy Irving: *Patrick Demarchelier*

Michael Jackson: *Matthew Rolston/MJJ Productions*
Norman Jewison: *Columbia Pictures*
Don Johnson: *Randee St. Nicholas/CBS Records Inc.*

Diane Keaton: *United Artists Corporation*
Ruby Keeler: *Charles Caron*
Deborah Kerr: *Christy/Kerr Cutline*
Nastassja Kinski: *Twentieth Century-Fox Film Corp.*
Kevin Kline: *Metro-Goldwyn-Mayer Pictures, Inc.*
Kris Kristofferson: *Mercury/PolyGram*
Stanley Kubrick: *Warner Bros., Inc.*

David Lean: *Columbia Pictures Industries, Inc.*
Norman Lear: *Embassy Television*
Spike Lee: *Universal City Studios Inc.*
Hal Linden: *E. J. Camp/Paramount Pictures Corporation*
Rob Lowe: *Columbia Pictures Industries, Inc.*

Myrna Loy: *James Radiches*
George Lucas: *Lucasfilm Ltd.*
Sidney Lumet: *United Artists Corporation*

Andie MacDowell: *Miramax Films*
Madonna: *Herb Ritts/Sire Records Company*
John Malkovich: *Tri-Star Pictures*
Penny Marshall: *Eugene Pinkowski/Twentieth Century Fox Film Corporation*
Mary Martin: *Seawell*
Marlee Matlin: *Greg Gorman*
Paul Mazursky: *Warner Bros. Inc.*
Andrew McCarthy: *Twentieth Century Fox Film*
Kelly McGillis: *Rob McEwan/Paramount Pictures Corporation*
Elizabeth McGovern: *The Ladd Company*
Maureen McGovern: *Nancy Moran/CBS Records Inc.*
Julia Migenes: *Barbra Walz/Columbia Pictures Industries, Inc.*
Dudley Moore: *Universal City Studios, Inc.*
Richard Mulligan: *NBC*
Eddie Murphy: *Enrique Badulescu*

Willie Nelson: *Beth Gwinn/CBS Records Inc.*
Olivia Newton-John: *Herb Ritts/MCA Records*
Jack Nicholson: *Elliott Marks/Paramount Pictures Corporation*
Chuck Norris: *Cannon Films*

Ryan O'Neal: *Tri-Star Pictures, Inc.*
Peter O'Toole: *DC Comics Inc.*

Al Pacino: *Universal City Studios, Inc.*
Alan Pakula: *Universal City Studios, Inc.*
Joseph Papp: *Jean-Marie Guyaux*
Mandy Patinkin: *Peter Cunningham*
Luciano Pavarotti: *Allen Malschick*
Sean Penn: *Marc Raboy*
Anthony Perkins: *Columbia Pictures Industries, Inc.*
Regis Philbin: *The Walt Disney Company*
Amanda Plummer: *Mike Tighe*
Sidney Poitier: *Columbia Pictures Corporation*
Roman Polanski: *Long Road Productions*
Priscilla Presley: *Harry Langdon Photography*
Prince: *Jeff Katz/D. C. Comics, Inc.*

Rob Reiner: *Castle Rock Entertainment*
Debbie Reynolds: *Harry Langdon Photography*
Molly Ringwald: *Patrick Demarchelier/Twentieth Century Fox Film Corp.*
Diana Ross: *Motown/Ross Records*
Meg Ryan: *Castle Rock Entertainment*

Susan Sarandon: *MGM/UA Entertainment, Co.*
Arnold Schwarzenegger: *Harry Langdon Photography*
Willard Scott: *NBC*
Gene Shalit: *NBC*
Charlie Sheen: *Timothy White/Morgan Creek Productions*
Sam Shepard: *Paul Schumach*
Nicollette Sheridan: *Lorimar Television*
Brooke Shields: *Patrick Demarchelier*
Siskel & Ebert: *Buena Vista Television*
Steven Soderbergh: *Amy Etra/Miramax Films*

Suzanne Somers: *Stephen Hamel*
Sissy Spacek: *Greg Gorman/Universal City Studios, Inc.*
James Spader: *Miramax*
Steven Spielberg: *Lucasfilm Ltd.*
Maureen Stapleton: *International Creative Management*
Barbra Streisand: *CBS Records Inc.*
Patrick Swayze: *Vestron Pictures*

Jessica Tandy: *Zoe Dominic*
Elizabeth Taylor: *Gary Bernstein*
John Travolta: *Patrick DeMarchelier*
Tina Turner: *Henry Diltz/Capitol Records*

Leslie Uggams: *Harry Langdon Photography*

Joan Van Ark: *Dick Zimmerman*
Jon Voight: *CBS, Inc.*

Sigourney Weaver: *Twentieth Century Fox Film Corp.*
Raquel Welch: *Claude Mougin/Sygma*
Betty White: *Wayne Williams*
Billy Wilder: *Metro-Goldwyn-Mayer Film Co.*
Gene Wilder: *Columbia Pictures Industries, Inc.*
Bruce Willis: *MCA Records*
Shelley Winters: *James Haspiel*
Joanne Woodward: *Harry Langdon Photography*